$87.95

Notable Caribbeans and Caribbean Americans

A Biographical Dictionary

Serafín Méndez-Méndez
and Gail A. Cueto

GREENWOOD PRESS
Westport, Connecticut • London

Library of Congress Cataloging-in-Publication Data

Méndez-Méndez, Serafín.
  Notable Caribbeans and Caribbean Americans : a biographical dictionary / Serafín
Méndez-Méndez and Gail A. Cueto.
    p.   cm.
  Includes references and index.
  ISBN 0–313–31443–8 (alk. paper)
  1. Caribbean Area—Biography—Dictionaries.   2. Caribbean Americans—
Biography—Dictionaries.   I. Cueto, Gail.   II. Title.
CT329.M46   2003
920.0729—dc21   2001033695

British Library Cataloguing in Publication Data is available.

Library of Congress Catalog Card Number: 2001033695
ISBN: 0–313–31443–8

First published in 2003

Greenwood Press, 88 Post Road West, Westport, CT 06881
An imprint of Greenwood Publishing Group, Inc.
www.greenwood.com

Printed in the United States of America

The paper used in this book complies with the
Permanent Paper Standard issued by the National
Information Standards Organization (Z39.48–1984).

10 9 8 7 6 5 4 3 2 1

This book is dedicated to our parents

Telesforo (Forito) Méndez Deyne
and
Edith Méndez Serrano

Mi padre me enseño a pensar, mi madre que me enseño a sentir y ambos a valorar la importancia del bien en el ser y en el vivir.

My father taught me how to think, my mother taught me how to feel and both taught me how to value the importance of goodness in being and living.

Hortensia Pérez de Alejo y Romero
and
Lizardo Cueto Goizueta

Quienes no vivieron para ver este logro pero quienes lo hubieran valorado y apreciado mucho.

Who did not live to see this accomplishment, but who I know would have cherished it very much.

Contents

Contents

Contents

Acknowledgments

The Caribbean is a source of pride for us all. We have truly enjoyed the process of studying and researching the lives and legacies of the people profiled here, and appreciate the roles that they have played in defining our culture and Caribbean ethos. We would also like to acknowledge those individuals who have assisted us.

Wendi Schnaufer at Greenwood has been a true supporter of this project. Her firm but gentle guidance led us to the completion of the project. We give her countless credit for bringing this project to fruition and for standing by us. The librarians at Central Connecticut State University are some of the best! A special heartfelt acknowledgment goes to Emily Chasse from the reference desk, whose online searches were invaluable. She is a magnificent librarian. Emily spent extensive time working with us. She assisted us in identifying notable Caribbeans and tracking down original and obscure sources. We also want to thank Joan Packer and Nick Tomaiuolo for their constant availability and willingness to help. The entire staff of the circulation department, as well as interlibrary loan, must be thanked for getting books to us in a timely manner and with a smile.

Several friends provided editorial assistance to us. Attorney Richard Rochlin reviewed an early version of the manuscript and gave valuable suggestions. Josefina Ezpeleta Laplace provided us with invaluable critique and suggestions on our Cuban notables. Dr. Aino (Ayla) Kardestuncer and Julie Wright performed a labor of love in proofreading and editing the final version. Their dislike of superlatives and colloquialism and their high-quality academic and intellectual standards helped us to achieve our desired level of satisfaction and pride with the final product.

As in any reference project of this magnitude, there were many moments when we had to rely on the support of friends to keep us in check. We would like to individually thank those who emotionally nourished us.

Acknowledgments

Serafín Méndez: I owe a debt of gratitude to David L. Panciera and Emma Colón, some of my most trusted friends. We have shared pain and laughs together. They provided consistent support during the project and more wonderful meals than I can count. The cough syrup was especially useful . . . ! Prof. Luz Emilda "Mildi" Cabán for being my weekend counselor and my best friend. Carlos and Stella Lopez who opened their home and constantly reminded me of the importance of taking breaks. The pool, the gossiping and the barbecues were great! Particularly entertaining were the stories about our crow-chasing friend. . . . And yes, our theories are true. My neighbors Drs. Tarik Kardestuncer and Gita Safaian have been especially kind. Their words of encouragement and their lovely dinner invitations have meant a lot. I have been blessed by having great women friends. Dr. María Del Río, Diane Alverio, Rosaida Rosario and Marilda Gándara are much loved. They alternatively roast and smother me. I love tough women.

Dr. Cueto: A special note of thanks to Denise Shafner for her support and for allowing me to borrow her books on the Caribbean. Finally, I thank D. Lea Doran for her unfailing support and constant encouragement.

We also thank the many personalities who made themselves available for interviews and gave us photos for the book. Among them are María Celeste Arrarás, Graciela Rivera, Geoffrey Holder, Omar Pardillo for Celia Cruz, Merle Frimark for Chita Rivera, Gigi Fernández, Delisa and Jon Lucien, Euzhan Palcy, Irene Feliciano for Paquito D'Rivera, and Etsu Bradshaw-Caines for Robert L. Bradshaw.

This book culminates a two-year journey through the Caribbean. We hope that we can partially re-create that journey for those who helped us and who also know that there is far more to the Caribbean than our beautiful beaches and resorts.

Introduction

> The entire Caribbean, like all of the Americas, is the creation of that awesome process of cross-fertilization resulting from encounters that occurred on foreign soil among the civilizations of Europe, Africa, and Asia, and the ancient Amerindian civilizations that developed and flourished on American soil long before Columbus set foot here. The development of this creation has helped to shape the history of the world for over half a millennium and has resulted in distinctive cultural spheres in the Western Hemisphere, each claiming its own logic and consistency.
>
> Rex Nettleford

The Caribbean comprises a group of diverse islands distributed between the south tip of Florida to a few miles north of Venezuela. To the northwest of these islands is the Atlantic Ocean, where one finds the Bahamas and Bermuda, and to the south is the Caribbean Sea. The size of these islands ranges from Cuba, which is 42,827 square miles, to the small island of Saba, which is only 5 square miles. The islands have a combined population of almost 30 million inhabitants.

The Caribbean has great political, social, and economic significance for the Western world. Christopher Columbus' expedition to the New World in 1492, which resulted in the discovery of the Caribbean islands (and subsequently the Latin American continent), changed the existing world. It triggered a political and economic race between the western European powers of Spain, Portugal, England, France, and the Netherlands that led to the conquest and colonization of all of the islands located in the Caribbean. From the beginning, it was clear that these islands were going to play a significant role in Europe. The availability of precious metals such as silver and gold, combined with an abundance of spices and other agricultural products, represented new access to capital and wealth that was worth exploiting, mainly when the Far East became less accessible.

From the displacement and extermination of the indigenous inhabitants of the Caribbean islands—the Arawaks, the Caribs, and the Taínos—to the introduction and importation of slaves to maintain and develop the agricultural industries, the colonization of the Caribbean established a unique social, political, and economic order. This, in turn, had both a short- and long-term impact on the cultures that emerged from the Caribbean. Even though these islands share a fairly homogenous geographic landscape, their individual histories are filled with the distinct imprints of the individual government styles, historic events, and cultural traditions to which they were submitted and exposed by their respective colonial powers.

At times, throughout history, there has been a tendency to portray and depict the Caribbean islands in terms of cultural insularism. The islands have been seen as closed cultural systems with "colorful" traditions whose inhabitants are unable to transcend those systems to mix and merge with the broader cultural environments of many Western cultures. This vision of the Caribbean has been perpetuated by the tourism industry, which values the beaches, the weather, and the exotic landscapes of these islands. For many, the Caribbean is only a sunny place with friendly people. This is only a small part of the picture. During the last 500 years, the Caribbean has provided a rich and diverse mosaic of peoples and cultural legacies that have made significant contributions to the world. The legacies of individuals such as political philosopher Frantz Fanon, patriot Eugenio María de Hostos, or labor activist and politician Alexander Bustamante are representative of the diverse contributions from the Caribbean. In fact, the Caribbean will be much better understood if we accept the metaphor proposed by scholar Mark Kurlansky, who labeled the Caribbean "a continent of islands" (Kurlansky 1992).

This book presents the individual legacies of 167 notable Caribbeans and Caribbean Americans who have distinguished themselves in varied fields of endeavor. This selection includes individuals who have defined and enriched their islands through a plethora of contributions to the fields of politics and government, literature and the arts, sports and entertainment, law and labor, and education and business, among many others.

In the process of researching and writing this book the authors have been at times amazed at the richness and wealth of the cultural production process that has emerged out of the Caribbean islands and that has been disseminated to the United States, Europe, and other parts of the world. It is fascinating to see the ways in which Caribbean people have impacted other cultures and geographical landscapes. From the Little Havana section of Miami to the Barrio in New York to the West Indian neighborhoods in London, people of the Caribbean have made significant imprints around the world.

As we studied the histories of hundreds of prominent Caribbeans and Caribbean Americans, we were able to identify many underlining dynamics that have influenced their lives. Many social, political, and economic intersections have affected Caribbean people and their thoughts across languages, societies, politics, and cultures. These influences have been, to a large extent, powerful vehicles fueling their creativity and successes in their lives.

The colonial past of the islands is perhaps the leading and most important element impacting the development of Caribbean culture and thought. Whether considering the colonization and conquest of all of the islands; the first independent island (St. Domingue, now known as Haiti) in 1804; movements toward independence in the British, Dutch, and French territories during the 1950s and 1960s; the ongoing struggle for the self-determination by Puerto Rico, one of the oldest colonies in the world; or the "colonial factor" and its logic counterpart, the "struggle for freedom" is always a common denominator in the past and present of the Caribbean. Whether we are reading the works of Fanon, or the novels of Trinidadians V. S. Naipaul and Merle Hodge, reflecting on the writings of Cuban José Martí, looking at the lives of the Mirabal sisters of the Dominican Republic, or examining one of the works of art done by Wilfredo Lam, there is a tacit rejection of the colonial forces in their respective islands and a call to freedom and independence for them.

Migration is another important element affecting the cultural, political, and social dynamics in the Caribbean. There is a vibrant Caribbean Diaspora in the United States. Caribbeans comprise almost 6 million U.S. residents. The Haitian community that moved to Baltimore toward the end of the eighteenth century; the Puerto Ricans who migrated to the northeastern states of the United States during the 1950s; the waves of Jamaicans and other groups that relocated during the 1960s; the Cubans who fled to Florida after the Castro revolution; the most recent migration of Dominicans during the 1970s, 1980s, and 1990s—all have contributed to the influx of Caribbeans throughout history.

Colonialism was largely responsible for the first waves of migration by individuals who sought to escape the oppressive regimes and the stagnant social and cultural environments that permeated some of the Caribbean islands. Poverty has also been an important factor in explaining the migration from the Caribbean. A Caribbean scholar explains: "To many Caribbeans, going abroad was not a question of emigrating but simply a matter of survival, getting somewhere to get food or money for their family" (Kurlansky 1992). Political repression, as experienced by Cubans and Haitians, has also explained why individuals come to experience the perceived freedoms of the United States. No less important is the fact that many Caribbeans have traditionally sought to enhance their opportunities to succeed, personally and professionally, in a land where economic, educational, and artistic opportunities are thought to be greater, audiences for their talents broader, and opportunities for diversifying their knowledge and interest more abundant.

As will be seen throughout this book, we view the migration of individuals such as Calypso singers Lord Kitchener (Aldwyn Roberts) and "Calypso Rose" (McCartha Lewis) and educator Stuart Hall to Great Britain, or filmmaker Euzhan Palcy to France and the United States, as crucial to the process of cultural development. Caribbeans have settled in the United States and elsewhere in the world and have enriched societies with their great achievements. These individuals are embodied in the work of first-generation Americans such as painter Jean-Michel Basquiat, journalist Geraldo Rivera, or politician and presidential candidate Shirley Chisholm. The phenomenon of migration has been instrumental in spreading Caribbean images and voices throughout the world. This text especially highlights the legacies of Caribbean Americans such as Audre Lorde, C.L.R. James, and Tito Puente, who devoted their lives to exploring, enhancing, and showcasing their Caribbean roots and cultures even though they were born or raised in the United States.

Readers will also learn about individuals from the Caribbean who have built formidable institutions and organizations that have assured the passing of their cultures from one generation to the next. These institutions showcase the Caribbean islands not only to their people but also to the rest of the world. Examples are Alicia Alonso and the National Ballet Theater of Cuba, Nicolás Guillén's Union of Writers and Artists, and Rex Nettleford and the National Dance Theater Company of Jamaica.

Selecting a representative sample of distinguished Caribbean islanders and Caribbean Americans is a daunting task. There is a wealth of talented people from which to choose. In our selection process we have employed a historical canon. We have tried to select individuals whose contributions to Caribbean or American life, society, and culture have been, or will be, long-lasting and will stand the test of time. Because many prominent Caribbeans have made a mark in Canada and Great Britain, we have included some of them as well. We have chosen figures whose contributions represent a Caribbean ethos or style. In addition, we have tried to highlight those whose who have been instrumental in changing, bringing attention to, or making original contributions to their fields of endeavor. Examples are individuals such as Derek Walcott and Arthur Lewis, the first Nobel laureates from the Caribbean; José Ferrer, the first major Caribbean presence in Hollywood; Bob Marley, one of the leading creators of the genre of reggae and a man who revolutionized the world with his music; Edna Manley, considered to be the mother of Caribbean modern art; and Nita Barrow, an ambassador to the United Nations and described by many as a "Citizen of the World." Moreover, we profile Caribbeans, Caribbean Americans, and a few others of Caribbean heritage who have had an international presence. Harry Belafonte, who has struggled on behalf of human rights and the end of Apartheid in South Africa; Carlos Finlay, who found the cause of yellow fever and led to its cure; and Minerva Bernardino, who had a pivotal role in the enactment of the Universal Declaration of Human Rights. These people have transcended the Caribbean and have become Citizens of the World.

In taking this approach, we have tried to stay away from transient icons of popular culture or politics whose presence on the world stage is ephemeral. Finally, we have tried to present a balanced representation of individuals from Caribbean history and the Caribbean of today.

As the reader will eventually discover, there were many Caribbeans and Caribbean Americans who were excluded from this book. People such as Secretary of State Colin Powell, civil rights activist Malcolm X or economist Alexander Hamilton were not included. Our first priority was to highlight individuals whose lives and works have not been heavily researched. Exclusion from this work is not a reflection on their individual merits or achievements.

Because this reference work is aimed at high school students, undergraduates, and interested readers seeking a starting point in a quest for knowledge about the individuals profiled in this text, we used a conventional biographic style that provides the reader with biographical data as well as a chronologically organized profile that outlines the lives and accomplishments of these individuals and highlights events and milestones that have underscored their lives. We also provide additional bibliographic sources for each entry, as a resource for readers who wish to obtain additional information.

Writing this book has been a fascinating experience. As Caribbean scholars raised in the Caribbean but educated in the United States, we are proud to share our heritage with so many accomplished individuals who have been not only mentors and role models, but also key sources of influence in defining what we do and who we are.

REFERENCES

Kurlansky, Mark. *A Continent of Islands: Searching for the Caribbean Destiny*. Cambridge, MA: Perseus Books, 1992.

Nettleford, Rex. In Samella Lewis and Mary Jane Hewitt, eds., *Caribbean Visions: Contemporary Paintings and Sculpture*. Alexandria, VA: Art Services International, 1995.

GRANTLEY ADAMS
(1898–1971)
Lawyer and Political Leader

Sir Grantley Herbert Adams, considered the father of democracy in Barbados, was also the first premier of the West Indies Federation from 1958 to 1962. Adams also established the Barbados Labour Party and implemented one of the most significant constitutional reforms in Barbados—the 1950 Representation of People Act—which granted all adult citizens on the island the right to vote. His political success is attributed in part to his ability to satisfy the British colonial government while winning rights for the Barbadian people. A conservative thinker and a political moderate, Adams gradually became a more liberal reformer who believed that workers' grievances were born of economic inequality, and that making legislative concessions to workers would be in the long-term interest of the merchants, plantation owners, and workers themselves.

The third child of seven, Grantley Adams was born at Colliston, Government Hill, St. Michael, on April 28, 1898, to Fitzherbert Adams, head teacher at St. Giles Elementary School in Barbados, and Rose Frances Neeturney. Fitzherbert was an amateur musician who instilled in his children his love for music. From his father Adams acquired a zeal for books and cricket; as an avid cricket player, he was one of the founding members of the Barbados Cricket Association and the Barbados Cricket League.

Adams attended his father's school, St. Giles, and afterwards Harrison College in Barbados. In 1918 he was awarded the Barbados Scholarship to Oxford University where he studied law. He returned to Barbados in 1925 to practice law and begin a lifelong career in politics.

As a conservative political activist, Adams' support came from the plantation owners and merchant elite. He was editor of the leading planter journal, *Agricultural Reporter.* His views were in stark contrast to activist and writer **Marcus Garvey**'s pro-worker black nationalism. However, Adams increasingly espoused measures that were designed to assist the working class, such as compulsory education for black children, abolition of child labor laws, and workers' right to form unions. In 1934, at the age of 36, Adams was elected member of the House of

Assembly representing the area of St. Joseph. He quickly established a reputation as a masterful debater and continued his move from conservative thinker to social reformer. He was re-elected to this position in the 1935 and 1936 general elections.

A violent workers' revolt in 1937 was set off by the arrest, trial, and deportation of popular union leader Clement Payne. Even though Adams was not an advocate of Payne's radical worker views, he nevertheless served as Payne's counsel in the appeal trial and was able to overturn the conviction, although not before the British government expelled his client from Barbados. This led to more riots and political instability on the island. Adams was instrumental in the development of events that followed this violent period. He believed that the riots were a result of worsening social and economic conditions among the workers, and his view that liberal reforms could remedy social relations strengthened his leadership role. He went to England to meet with the colonial secretary and won further support for his positions. It is believed that this was an important point in his career, as he had the confidence and support of the highest ranking colonial officials, who thought he would be the right person to help reform colonial politics and help stave off the black nationalist followers of Marcus Garvey.

Adams served mainly as the primary spokesman for conservative blacks, but was also aware of the importance of middle- and working-class opinion. Shortly after his return to Barbados, he launched the Barbados Labour Party to "provide political expression for the island's law-abiding inhabitants" (Beckles 1990, 170). In 1940, the Labour Party—now called the Barbados Progressive League—won five seats in the House of Assembly, and in 1941 Adams became president of the newly formed Barbados Workers' Union, a post he held until 1954. During the 1940s there were a number of meaningful labor reforms attributed to his party leadership. Among them were the legalization of unions and the establishment of the Barbados Workmen's Compensation Act, as well as the landmark 1943 Representation of the People Bill that assured voting rights to all adults, including women. The 1951 elections secured Adams' leadership. His Barbados Labour Party won 60 percent of the vote and 16 seats in the House, while enjoying a high degree of autonomy from the British.

As Barbados made progress toward complete autonomy, Adams, as president of the Caribbean Labour Congress, succeeded in establishing a ten-nation West Indies Federation, where he served as its first and only premier. This federation was a colonial government ruled by the governor general and the British government—a fact that did not please Adams, whose real goal was to establish a more autonomous nation within the British Commonwealth. In addition to infighting among the membership, a number of federation members were more interested in gaining independence from Britain than in continuing as colonies. As a result, in 1958 the Federal Government of the West Indies was instituted and Adams' role as premier ended.

Throughout these years, Barbados had experienced great social and political changes, but not independence from colonial rule. After the formal dissolution of the West Indies Federation in 1962, Adams returned to local politics and was re-elected to the House of Assembly in 1966, the year of Barbados' independence. Considered the first leader of the opposition in newly independent Barbados, he served in the House until his retirement in 1970. He died on November 28, 1971. Barbados' international airport is named after him, and his picture is engraved on the island's $100 notes.—G.C.

References and Suggested Readings

Beckles, Hilary. *A History of Barbados: From Amerindian Settlement to Nation-State.* New York: Cambridge University Press, 1990.

Boyce, Hayden. *Hats Off to Our Heroes.* St. Michael, Barbados: Nation Publishers, 1998.

"Everybody's Person of the 20th Century: Barbados; Sir Grantley Adams." *Everybody's: The Caribbean-American Magazine* 23.11 (December 31, 1999): 20.

Howe, Glenford D. and Don D. Marshall, eds. *The Empowering Impulse: The Nationalist Tradition of Barbados.* Kingston, Jamaica: Canoe Press, 2001.

Hoyos, F.A. *Grantley Adams and the Social Revolution: The Story of the Movement That Changed the Pattern of West Indian Society.* London: Macmillan, 1988.

PEDRO ALBIZU CAMPOS
(1891–1965)

Puerto Rican Lawyer, Political Prisoner, Patriot, and Nationalist

Pedro Albizu Campos is an important figure in the Puerto Rican Nationalist movement. He was considered one of the most gifted and articulate political ideologists advocating the independence of Puerto Rico from the United States. A Harvard-trained attorney who reached the rank of first lieutenant in the U.S. Army during World War I, Albizu disregarded the potential comfort and social prestige afforded to Puerto Rican attorneys at the time, and instead spent most of his adult life as a political prisoner in both American and Puerto Rican jails. He led an ardent crusade and his political legacy and philosophy have achieved recognition in Puerto Rico, where he is regarded as the father of Puerto Rican independence.

Albizu was born in the Tenerias suburb of Ponce on September 12, 1891, to Alejandro Albizu Romero and Juliana Campos. His father came from a family of farmers and landowners but worked during his adult life as a customs official in Ponce's naval port. His mother was the daughter of slaves. As a child, he experienced hardship and poverty because his father did not support him or his family. Albizu was 19 and ready to go to college before his father legally recognized him as his son.

Albizu attended local schools in Ponce and excelled in his studies; in 1912 he graduated with honors from Ponce High School. He was able to secure a scholarship from a Freemason lodge in Ponce allowing him to attend the University of Vermont; he transferred to Harvard University in 1913.

Pedro Albizu Campos.
Courtesy of Raúl Medina Collection.

As an undergraduate, he majored in both chemistry and literature and became a member of several of the most prestigious students societies such as the Polity Club, the Cosmopolitan Club, the Speaker's Club, and the Catholic Club. He also wrote for the *Harvard Crimson* and for the *Christian Science Monitor*. There is no evidence that Albizu harbored any anti-American feelings during his years as an undergraduate or that he was subjected to any type of racial or ethnic discrimination by virtue of being a black Puerto Rican. In fact, upon graduation from Harvard in 1916, he decided to study law at the very prestigious Harvard Law School.

Scholar Carmelo Delgado Cintrón has done one of the most thorough analyses of Albizu's philosophical influences while at Harvard (Delgado Cintrón 1993). According to Delgado Cintrón, the climate of political and social liberalism shaped Albizu's political thought during the early stages of his law studies. He was exposed to the values of liberalism and progressive social change of his professors Zechariah Chaffe and Felix Franfurter, who later became a U.S. Supreme Court justice. Albizu interrupted his law studies in 1917 and enlisted in the U.S. armed forces during World War I. After joining the 375th regiment, he organized and taught at a school for non-commissioned officers in his native Ponce. Puerto Rican historian Isabel Gutiérrez del Arroyo, an expert on Albizu, has explained Albizu's participation in the U.S. armed forces as a means of acquiring military discipline, not necessarily as an expression of loyalty to the United States (Gutiérrez del Arroyo 2000). He resumed his law studies in 1919 and graduated in 1921.

Albizu returned to Puerto Rico immediately after finishing his studies at Harvard and established a law practice in his native Ponce. Instead of a career path in law, Albizu became involved in Puerto Rican politics, joining the Puerto Rican Unionist Party. Initially founded in 1904, the centrist Unionist Party advocated for more autonomic powers and self-government for the island (Silvestrini and Luque 1992). Although his initial stance in the party was extremely moderate, Albizu grew disenchanted with the Unionist Party when they moved away from Puerto Rican independence. He joined the Nationalist Party in 1924, immediately becoming its vice-president. He was the most ardent spokesman on behalf of Puerto Rican independence. In 1927, he thought that the people of Latin America needed to become aware of the plea for Puerto Rican independence and undertook a three-year trip through Latin America to argue for Puerto Rican independence. When he returned to Puerto Rico in 1930, he had become a substantially more forceful speaker and developed a more hostile and combative tone against the United States.

The 1930s constitutes a significant period in Albizu's development as a major Puerto Rican political leader. On his return from Latin America he found an island in turmoil. Puerto Rican leaders and intellectuals were struggling to achieve a final definition of the island's political status. In addition, the social and economic system of Puerto Rico had started to deteriorate as a result of decades of economic oppression and exploitation from owners of the sugarcane plantations and sugarcane processing plants in the island. Sugarcane workers, who had organized into labor unions, had rebelled against the economic establishment and launched a major strike to protest meager wages and the inhuman labor conditions.

On May 11, 1930, Albizu became president of the Puerto Rican Nationalist Party. This moment marked his transformation from a vocal political activist into a revolutionary. Albizu and the Nationalist Party adopted a separatist agenda that advocated for independence of Puerto Rico through all possible means, including violence and aggression. His political platform was:

> In summary, nationalist leaders underscored the following points: 1) the need for well distributed wealth; 2) despair over the elimination of small landowners; 3) the need to limit individual land ownership to 300 acres; 4) a proposal to create the largest possible number of small landowners and a bank to assist small scale farmers; 5) the need to turn into the hands of the government all public services (railroads, street trolleys, ports, power and lighting, and phone); 6) concerns over the situation of those people who operate public cars, small gas companies and their struggle against foreign companies; 7) the definition that all of those who can not establish independent households are slaves. (Taller de Formación Política 1982, 109)

Albizu launched a vigorous campaign for this political platform and traveled around the island making speeches and mobilizing Puerto Ricans of diverse beliefs. By 1935, the Nationalist Party had become a revolutionary organization. Puerto Rican journalist and historian Antonio Quiñones Calderón underscores the agenda of the Nationalist Party as ratified in a general assembly held in the city of Caguas on December 8, 1935:

> 1) declared that his party will not participate on colonial elections and would boycott them; 2) demanded that the government of the United States should leave Puerto Rico immediately in a peaceful way, or they will take on an arm struggle; 3) that military services should become obligatory for all of the members of his party; and 4) to raise money in Puerto Rico and abroad to defray the expenses of the armed struggle. (Quiñones Calderón 1990, 344)

By 1936, Albizu's fierce and violent rhetoric gained the attention of the FBI, and J. Edgar Hoover dispatched agents to Puerto Rico to investigate him.

On February 23, 1936, two members of the Nationalist Party participated in an armed confrontation in which Elisha Francis Riggs, head of the Puerto Rican police was killed. Since Albizu had made a call to arms previous to the attack and had encouraged the assassination, he was arrested on March 4, 1936, and charged in three counts of seditious conspiracy to overthrow the government of the United States, to recruit soldiers, and to incite rebellion against the United States. He was convicted of all charges on July 1936 and sentenced to serve ten years of prison at a federal penitentiary in Atlanta. Despite a vigorous effort by several Puerto Rican political leaders and members of the American Civil Liberties Union to gain his liberation, he served six years of his sentence in Atlanta. While in Atlanta he was thought to have suffered a debilitating stroke that impaired his health. He was released on probation on 1943 and was forced to serve the remaining four years of his sentence in New York, where he was hospitalized at Colombia Hospital between 1943 and 1945. He was then forced to remain in the city until 1947 while he finished serving the remaining four years of his sentence. He was finally able to return to the island in December 1947.

Although the political realities of Puerto Rico had somewhat changed during the years that he had spent in prison, Albizu returned to the island with an unbending will against the colonial forces that still ruled the island. Between January 1948 and December 1950, Albizu engaged in a forceful public campaign to denounce and criticize political, social, and economic conditions affecting Puerto Rico and its people. He continued to call Puerto Ricans to arms to overthrow the government of the United States.

By the end of 1950, Albizu had managed to mobilize members of his party in a series of campaigns to bring attention to the plea of the Nationalist Party. The first event was the Nationalist insurrection of October 30, 1950. Various members of the Nationalist Party, following Albizu's orders, launched an island-wide quasi-military campaign to overthrow the island's government and attacked the official residence of Governor **Luis Muñoz Marín**. On November 1, 1950, a group of Puerto Rican Nationalists attacked Blair House, where President Truman was temporarily residing. As a result of these events, Albizu was once again arrested on November 2, 1950, and charged with violating the Gag Law (*Ley de la Mordaza*). This repressive law, which had been approved by Puerto Rican lawmakers in 1948, prohibited any speech aimed at destabilizing or overthrowing the government of Puerto Rico. Despite the fact that the law was in flagrant violation of the First Amendment to the U.S. Constitution, Albizu was indicted on 12 violations of the law and sentenced to serve 80 years in a Puerto Rican prison. Because Albizu's health further deteriorated in jail, and because of the general consensus that he had been convicted of violating an unconstitutional law, Albizu was granted an executive pardon in 1953 by Muñoz Marín against Albizu's will. One of the conditions of the pardon was that Albizu not engage in political activities against the government of Puerto Rico. When Albizu praised a group of Nationalists for attacking the U.S. Congress in March 1954, he was once again imprisoned. After suffering a heart attack in prison in 1956, he was transferred to Presbyterian Hospital where he remained until 1964—when governor Muñoz Marín once again granted a pardon shortly before his death on April 21, 1965.

Albizu's staunch crusade on behalf of Puerto Rican independence and social equality for Puerto Ricans has made him a martyr of the Puerto Rican independence movement. In recent years, scholars have uncovered ample evidence of the ways in which Albizu was followed, oppressed, and persecuted by the Puerto Rican police and the FBI (Aponte 2000). One of the most interesting claims—which first surfaced during the 1950s, and which was brought forth by Albizu's widow, Laura Meneces, after his death in 1965—is that Albizu was subjected to experimental radiation treatments or attacks during his multiple stays in prison. Although the charges remain unsubstantiated and unproven, they have given more weight to the vision of Albizu as a martyr of the Puerto Rican independence movement.—S.M.M.

References and Suggested Readings

Acosta, Ivonne. *La palabra como delito:Los discursos por los que condenaron a Pedro Albizu Campos 1948–1950*, 3rd Edition. San Juan, PR: Editorial Cultural, 2000.

Aponte Vázquez, Pedro. *Albizu y su persecusión por el FBI*. San Juan, PR: Publicaciones Rene, 2000.

Aponte Vázquez, Pedro. "Enigma de un misterio." In Aline Frambes-Buxeda, ed., *Huracán del Caribe: Vida y obra del insigne puertorriqueño Don Pedro Albizu Campos*. San Juan, PR: Homines, 1993. 92–93.

Bayrón Toro, Fernando. *Elecciones y Partidos Políticos de Puerto Rico: 1809–2000*. Mayaguez, PR: Editorial Isla, 2000.

Delgado Cintrón, Carmelo. "El Derecho en Pedro Albizu Campos: La formación jurídical y la propuesta de Convención Constituyente." In Aline Frambes-Buxeda, ed., *Huracán del Caribe: Vida y obra del insigne puertorriqueño Don Pedro Albizu Campos*. San Juan, PR: Homines, 1993. 57–80.

Fernàndez, Ronald, Serafin Méndez-Méndez, and Gail Cueto. *Puerto Rico Past and Present: An Encyclopedia*. Westport, CT: Greenwood Press, 1998.

Frambes-Buxeda, Aline, ed. *Huracán del Caribe: Vida y obra del insigne puertorriqueño Don Pedro Albizu Campos*. San Juan, PR: Homines, 1993.

Gutiérrez del Arroyo, Isabel. *Pedro Albizu Campos o la agonía moral: El mensaje ético de Pedro Albizu Campos*. San Juan, PR: Editora Causa Común, 2000.

Medina, Raúl. "Tenerías: Cuna de Albizu Campos." In Aline Frambes-Buxeda, ed., *Huracán del Caribe: Vida y obra del insigne puertorriqueño Don Pedro Albizu Campos*. San Juan, PR: Homines, 1993.

Quiñones Calderón, Antonio. *50 Décadas de Historia Puertorriqueña*. San Juan, PR: Gobierno Municipal de San Juan, 1990.

Rosario Natal, Carmelo, ed. *Albizu Campos: Preso en Atlanta: historia del reo #51298-A (correspondencia)*. San Juan, PR: Producciones Históricas, 2001.

Silvestrini, Blanca and María Dolores Luque de Sánchez. *Historia de Puerto Rico: Trayectoria de un pueblo*. San Juan, PR: Editorial Cultural, 1992.

Taller de Formación Política. *La cuestión nacional: El Partido Nacionalista y el movimiento obrero Ppuertorriqueño (aspectos de las luchas económicas y políticas de la década de 1930–40)*. Río Piedras, PR: Editorial Huracán, 1982.

THE ALOMAR FAMILY

Puerto Rican Baseball Players

Sandy Alomar Sr. and his two sons, Sandy Alomar Jr. and Roberto Alomar, belong to one of the most popular Puerto Rican baseball families. For the past 40 years, the Alomars have been immersed in baseball culture. Alomar Sr. began his professional baseball career in 1961 as an infielder. He has appeared in 1,481 major league games over 15 seasons with the Milwaukee/Atlanta Braves (1964–1966), the New York Mets (1967), the Chicago White Sox (1967–1969), the California Angels (1969–1974), the New York Yankees (1974–1976) and the Texas Rangers (1977–1978). He was a .245 batter and stole 227 bases during his career. His sons Sandy Jr. and Robbie grew up among major league players and made their big league debuts with the San Diego Padres while Alomar Sr. was on the club's coaching staff. In 1990 the brothers, as starting players, became the sixth brother combination to play in the same All-Star Game and the first since the Perry brothers (Gaylord and Jim) in 1970. In addition, when Alomar Sr., who was a member of the National League's coaching staff for the game, took a bow with his two sons, it was the second time in the history of the All-Star Game that three family members participated in the game (Dom, Vince, and Joe DiMaggio were the others). By 1997, the Alomar brothers had made a combined 13 All-Star appearances—the third highest total for brothers in baseball.

SANDY ALOMAR SR.
(1943–)

Santos Conde Alomar was born in the southern fishing town of Salinas, Puerto Rico, on October 19, 1943. Even though he grew up to become an accomplished and well-known baseball player, very little has been documented about his early years. It is known that he was reared and went to school in the town of Salinas, where baseball was a family affair. Three of his brothers—Rafael, Demetrio, and Antonio—also played professional baseball in Puerto Rico's winter league.

Although baseball can be played year round on the island, winter—November to February—is considered the best season because winter is when local-hero baseball players come from the U.S. major leagues to play before island crowds. Alomar Sr. was an idol in Puerto Rico. He is one of the few players who reached 1,000 hits in his winter league career, and he was batting champion in 1970–1971. Throughout his career Alomar Sr. played every position but pitcher and catcher, and undoubtedly, was his sons' first baseball role model. He was known as a very disciplined player who took pride in his job.

Alomar Sr. is remembered mostly as an infielder, but his ability and control as a switch-hitter were instrumental in his becoming a regular player with the White Sox in 1968. During his five years as a second baseman with the California Angels, he played 648 consecutive games from 1969 to 1973, after having led the league with 689 at-bats. In 1971 he set a big league record by going to the plate 739 times (689 at-bats) without getting hit by a pitch. He was sold to New York in 1974; while playing for the New York Yankees, he led the American League in fielding at second base during the 1975 season. He stole 20 or more bases in seven seasons—227 during his career.

In 1978, to the disappointment of his sons, Alomar Sr. retired to his off-season home in Salinas, Puerto Rico, after his last season with the Texas Rangers. While living in Salinas he played in the winter league.

Following his retirement as a major league player, he coached the Puerto Rican national team from 1979 to 1984. He joined the San Diego Padres as a minor league coach in 1985 and was a coach on the major league staff from 1986 to 1990. He has managed teams in Puerto Rico, most recently as the off-season general manager of the winter league San Juan club. He earned Manager of the Year honors with Santurce in 1986 and with Ponce in 1993. He has served as the Chicago Cubs Latin coordinator (1991–1994) and the manager of the Cubs' short-season Fort Myers (Rookie) club (1995–1996). His face is painted on the outside wall of the Manuel González Baseball Stadium in Salinas, the park where all three of the Alomars played as amateurs. During the regular season, he is also a coach with the Padres, the team that initially signed his sons **Roberto**, an infielder, and **Sandy Jr.**, a catcher. Their baseball careers have clearly benefited from their genetic lineage and a childhood spent in professional baseball parks. Alomar Sr. is currently the bullpen coach for the Chicago Cubs.

SANDY ALOMAR JR.
(1966–)

Santos Alomar Velázquez Jr. was born on June 18, 1966, in Salinas, Puerto Rico. He was raised in his father's hometown and began to play baseball, with his father as coach, at age six. Known by the nickname "Sandino," he played Little League baseball while he attended elementary school and was a member of the Luis Muñoz Rivera High School baseball team.

He signed with the San Diego Padres in 1984 and went through the minors for seven years until he joined their major league team in 1988. After going over to the Cleveland Indians in 1990 he was named the American League's Rookie of the Year unanimously by *The Sporting News, Baseball America, USA Today, Sports Illustrated*, and CNN. That same year he became the first rookie catcher ever to start the All-Star Game and won a Rawlings Gold Glove. His second season with the Cleveland Indians was plagued with injuries; however, he managed to put together his first career four-hit game and threw out 30 percent of base runners trying to steal base. In 1992 he started in his third consecutive All-Star Game and was the first Cleveland Indian to start three straight midsummer classics since 1946.

By 1994 he improved his record of tossing out base runners attempting to steal to 35 percent. However, he had another season marked by numerous injuries and underwent arthroscopic surgery on his knee. Although the recovery was slow at times, in 1995 he enjoyed two two-homer games in Texas and Minnesota. The year 1997 was one of his most solid seasons with the Indians. He appeared in 127 games, the most since his rookie year, and for the first time he did not spend any time on the disabled list. He hit a career-best 17 straight games between April 11 and May 4.

Until 1997, Alomar Jr. seemed to walk in his younger brother's shadow when it came to field statistics, as it took him a year longer than his younger brother **Roberto** to make it to the big leagues. But 1997 was his best season ever. For the first time he caught in 100 games back-to-back and had the highest hitting average in his career: .324 (37 doubles, 21 homers, and 83 RBIs). He became the first Cleveland Indian to ever win the MVP (most valuable player) of an All-Star Game and the first player to win the MVP in his home park. The Indians were in the World Series that year and Alomar Jr. became the fifth player ever in World Series history to have 10 or more RBIs (runs batted in) in a single series. He also became the first player in major league baseball to homer in his home park in the World Series and in the All-Star Game. His success that year earned him a spot on the Wheaties Cereal box. He has been plagued with injuries since 1998 and once again underwent knee surgery in May 1999. Until 1999 he had the fourth-highest number of career grand slams, at 855.

During the 2000 season, Alomar Jr. had a 30-game hitting streak, the second longest ever by a catcher, and by the end of that season, he was a lifetime .276 hitter with 93 home runs and 459 RBIs. After eleven seasons with the Indians and unsuccessful off-season contract negotiations with Cleveland, Alomar Jr. signed with the Chicago White Sox in April 2001. He currently plays for the Colorado Rockies.

ROBERTO ALOMAR
(1968–)

Roberto Alomar Velázquez was born in the southern city of Ponce, Puerto Rico, on February 5, 1968. He attended elementary and high school in Salinas. Like his brother **Sandy Jr.**, he signed with the San Diego Padres in 1984, and by 1988, he was playing in the big leagues. His first major league at-bat resulted in a hit against one of the most well-known pitchers of all time, Nolan Ryan. He followed in his father's footsteps, even playing the same position—second base—and is considered one of the best players in baseball.

The year 1989 was his first full season in the major leagues, and he was the youngest player in the National League. He led the league with 17 sacrifice hits, tied for second with 42 stolen bases, and was third with his 184 hits. By the 1990 season he was selected to the All-Star Team and was second in the National League with 311 outs. During the 1991 season, he won the Gold Glove for the first time, an award also won by his brother Sandy Jr. As a member of the Toronto Blue Jays, he became the 55th player in history to homer from both sides of the plate in the same game. In 1992 he won another Gold Glove and posted 17 consecutive stolen bases until his brother Sandy, who was playing for Cleveland, threw him out. He acquired his first championship ring when Toronto won the World Series that year.

In 1993 he hit his first career inside-the-park home run, won his third Gold Glove, and made an appearance at the World Series against the Philadelphia Phillies, where he hit .480, the second best on his team, and helped Toronto win its second straight world championship. In 1994, with his fourth Gold Glove, he hit his 400th RBI and committed just one error in 66 games (and none in the final 45 games). His statistics continued to improve and in 1996 he became a free agent and signed with the Baltimore Orioles. But 1996 was also his most controversial year. During a game between the Orioles and the Red Sox, when the game was tied in the ninth inning, umpire John Hirschbeck made a call that Alomar did not agree with. An argument ensued and Alomar was ejected from the game. He reacted by spitting in the umpire's face and was universally criticized. Although he apologized, he was constantly ringed by reporters and booed by fans during games. Over time, however, prowess on the field, along with a written and verbal apology, has helped to heal some of the wounds.

In 1998, after a series of injuries, he joined his brother Sandy Jr. as a member of the Cleveland Indians. He was awarded his seventh Gold Glove, played in his ninth All-Star Game, and became the American League's all-time fielding percentage leader at second base. With the Cleveland Indians he has again made baseball history. In 1999 he became the first player in the 99-year history of the Indians franchise to hit 20 home runs, score 100 runs, steal 30 bases, and drive in 100 or more runs all in the same season. Even though the 2000 season saw Alomar go through a series of injuries, he ended the season hitting .323 with 24 home runs and 120 RBIs while providing sparkling defense that earned him his eighth Gold Glove. On December 2001, the New York Mets announced they had acquired "Hall of Fame–caliber" Roberto Alomar as a member of their team.

Having grown up in Puerto Rico, where their father was an idol, the Alomar brothers dreamed of following in their father's baseball footsteps. They now have surpassed their father's major league achievements to become two of the top stars in the game.—G.C.

References and Suggested Readings

Ahrens, Frank. "Roberto Alomar, Keeping His Eye on the Ball." *The Washington Post*, October 7, 1996, A1.

Bloom, Barry. "Alomar, As in All-Star." *Sport* 82 (March 1991): 46–48.

———. "Favorite Son." *Sport* 89 (May 1998): 40–42.

———. *Major League Handbook 2002*. Morton Grove, IL: Stats Publishing, 2002.

———. "Roberto Alomar." *Sport* 88 (January 1997): 12.

Curry, Jack. "Alomar Is Crown Jewel of Mets Infield." *The New York Times*, December 12, 2001, S1.

Kurkjian, Tim. "Public Enemy No.1." *Sports Illustrated*, October 14, 1996, 228.

Macht, Norman L. *Roberto Alomar: An Authorized Biography*. Childs, MD: Mitchell Lane Publishers, 1999.

Paré, Michael A. *Sports Stars*. Detroit: UXL, 1994.

Pietrusza, David, Matthew Silverman, and Michael Gershman, eds. "Sandy Alomar Sr.," "Sandy Alomar Jr.," and "Roberto Alomar." *Baseball: The Biographical Encyclopedia*. Kingston, NY: Sports Illustrated. 18–20.

Schonsberg, Dan. *The Baseball Almanac*. Chicago: Triumph Books, 2002.

Shatzkin, Mike. *The Ballplayers: Baseball's Ultimate Biographical Reference*. New York: William Morrow, 1990.

Verducci, Tom. "Tribal Warfare." *Sports Illustrated*, October 20, 1997, 46–49.

ALICIA ALONSO
(1921–)

Cuban Dancer, Choreographer, and Founder of the National Ballet of Cuba

A Cuban cultural icon, Alicia Alonso is considered one of the most important figures in contemporary dance. As founder and general director of the Ballet Nacional de Cuba she has been a guide and inspiration to generations of Cuban dancers and has carved out for the company a unique position in international ballet. Critics have acclaimed Alonso as one of the greatest ballerinas of all times and she has received numerous distinctions and awards worldwide. Despite the hardships currently suffered by the Cuban people, she has been referred to as "the woman who uses ballet to feed the Cuban spirit" (Myers 1996, 82).

Born in Havana on December 21, 1921, Alicia Ernestina de la Caridad del Cobre Martínez Hoyo, the youngest of four children, first started dancing informally as a child. As she describes it, "I'd move around whenever I heard music, maybe like Isadora Duncan, because I didn't know what dancing was" (Boccadoro 1998). When she was eight years old she traveled to Spain with her father. At the suggestion of her grandfather, she began to study Spanish dance, including the castanets. On returning to Cuba the following year she joined a private ballet school, the Escuela de Ballet de la Sociedad Pro-Arte Musical, and in her own words, "From the moment I put my hand on the barre, I was enthralled" (Boccadoro 1998). (The school now houses the company she founded, Ballet Nacional de Cuba.) Among her classmates was Fernando Alonso,

Alicia Alonso. Photograph by Thomas Yee. Courtesy of Photofest.

whose mother was a major contributor and president of Pro-Arte. They fell in love, and Alonso (known then as Unga Martínez), followed Fernando to the United States where he was auditioning—a feat remarkable for a sixteen-year-old at that time. While in the United States she became pregnant and married Fernando. They had a daughter and made New York their home. In New York Alonso continued to study and dance with such well-known teachers as Enrico Zanfreta and Alexandra Fedorova.

Her professional dancing career began in 1938 on Broadway where she appeared in the musical comedies *Great Lady* and *Stars in Your Eyes.* In 1940 she became a member of the Ballet Theatre of New York, the precursor to the American Ballet Theatre. It was here that she began the most successful part of her career and was acclaimed by the critics for her work in the great masterpieces of classical and romantic ballet. She worked with some of the best choreographers of that era—Bronislava Nijinska, Anthony Tudor, Jerome Robbins—and danced lead roles in the world premieres of such seminal ballets as *Undertow* and created the ballerina role in George Balanchine's *Themes and Variations.* Alonso also created roles for contemporary ballets, including that of accused murderer Lizzie Borden in *Fall River Legend* (1948), which was choreographed by American dancer and choreographer Agnes de Mille. Although detached retinas in both eyes left her virtually blind in her early twenties, she retrained herself to dance without vision, relying on her partners or on strategically placed lights for guidance.

From 1938 to 1948 Alonso was at the prime of her career as a dancer. She traveled the world as prima ballerina with the then-fledging American Ballet Theatre.

While all her performances were consistently and widely acclaimed, her interpretations of *Giselle*—her most famous role—and *Carmen* have been heralded as particularly noteworthy. It is said that Alonso's style of dancing was characterized by her ability to stay perfectly on pointe and balance until signaled out of pose by her partners.

Throughout her years dancing in the United States, she felt restless about the lack of a professional school of dance in Cuba. In a country that had no classical dance tradition, the Alonsos built a dance company in 1948—the Ballet Alicia Alonso. During layoff periods and vacation from the American Ballet Theatre, Alonso returned to Cuba to teach, choreograph, and dance with her new company. Her husband, as dancer and teacher, and her brother-in-law Alberto Alonso, ballet master and choreographer, were essential colleagues in this endeavor. The prestige of Alonso's name brought much support in the form of imported professional colleagues from the Ballet Theatre to help train new dancers and reinforced her ideal of the highest teaching standards. Knowing that a training regime is crucial to the development of a cadre of dancers, she established a ballet academy where Cuban boys and girls could be trained in classical dancing from an early age.

Alonso's career continued to prosper; she performed annually with the Ballet Russe de Monte Carlo and became the first Western ballerina ever to be invited to dance in the Soviet Union. She achieved a milestone in 1957 and 1958 as the first dancer from the North American continent to perform as guest artist with the Bolshoi Ballet in Moscow and the Kirov Ballet in Leningrad. During these years she shared her international activities with those of her own troupe in Cuba, which received little, if any, official support until 1959, when **Fidel Castro** offered her assistance and the company changed its name to the Ballet Nacional de Cuba. Since that time it has prospered, becoming one of the world's best-known and admired national ballet companies.

Starting in 1960, and with support from the Cuban government, the Ballet Nacional de Cuba toured Russia, the People's Republic of China, and a number of cities in Western Europe. The company's success went beyond performances to include numerous medals and awards at international ballet competitions for its individual dancers. In terms of its repertory, the company included a creative works program where the great traditional ballets such as *Giselle* and *Swan Lake* were augmented with new works that incorporated Latin American themes of the indigenous, African, and Hispanic heritages. Alonso herself had impressed audiences with her characteristically passionate and dazzling interpretations of classical ballet roles; in her role as general director, she sought out choreographers whose dances reflected their Latino and Caribbean roots. One of the better-known dances that has come out of the company is *The River and the Forest*, a rhythmic, almost vibratory dance that incorporates rituals to the Changó deity from the Afro-Cuban religion of Santería.

Alonso's tenure with the Ballet Nacional de Cuba, which not too long ago celebrated its 50th anniversary, has not been without political controversy. Some of the best dancers in the company have defected or spent long periods of time performing out of the country. Her close relationship with Fidel Castro, whose picture adorns the walls of the company, has been a point of contention for some of the dancers who attribute the low morale within the company to what they perceive as the repressive and retaliatory measures that are used against those who do not follow the Communist Party's political line.

Nevertheless, Alonso is highly respected and recognized both inside and outside Cuba. Throughout her lifetime she has received numerous honorary doctoral degrees and other awards worldwide. In 1998 she received the Gold Medal of the Círculo de Bellas Artes de Madrid (Fine Arts Circle of Madrid); France honored her with the Order of Arts and Letters in the Degree of Knight Commander; and the Council of State of Cuba honored her as the National Hero of Labor of the Republic of Cuba. Recognizing her extraordinary contribution to dance, she was awarded the Pablo Picasso Medal by UNESCO (United Nations Educational, Scientific and Cultural Organization) in 1999. Among the Cuban Revolution's most applauded cultural accomplishments has been Alonso's artistic vision and her creation of the world-acclaimed Ballet Nacional de Cuba. Her choreographic versions of the greatest classics are internationally celebrated and staged by important companies.—G.C.

References and Suggested Readings

Arnold, Sandra Martin. *Alicia Alonso: First Lady of the Ballet.* New York: Arnold Walker & Co. Library, 1993.

Boccadoro, Patricia. "National Ballet of Cuba" (Interview with Alicia Alonso). *Culture Kiosque*, October 26, 1998. *http://www.culturekiosque.com/dance/features/rhecuba.htm.*

Durbin, Patricia. "Alicia Alonso: Habanera Assoluta." In Marjorie Agosín, ed., *A Woman's Gaze: Latin American Women Artists.* New York: White Pine Press, 1998.

Kisselgoff, Anna. "Saluting a Star With a Galaxy of Her Own Making." *The New York Times,* November 10, 2001, 13.

Levine, Jordan. "Revolutionary Moves." *Los Angeles Times,* January 11, 1998, 6.

Lewis, Jean Battey. "American Flash, Cuban Soul." *Dance Magazine* 75.2 (February 2001): 58–61.

Myers, Leslie. "Career-Building Opportunities to See and Be Seen: Alicia Alonso International Dance Competition." *Dance Magazine* 70.9 (September 1996): 82–83.

Walter, Terry. *Alicia and Her Ballet Nacional de Cuba.* Garden City, NY: Anchor Books, 1981.

JULIA ÁLVAREZ
(1950–)

Dominican-American Novelist, Short-Story Writer, and Educator

Dominican American writer Julia Álvarez first came to the attention of the reading public in 1991 with *How the García Girls Lost Their Accents,* a collection of stories

Julia Álvarez. © Copyright 2000 by Bill Eichner. Reprinted by permission of Susan Bergholz Literary Services. New York. All rights reserved.

that tell about a family's emigration to New York City from the Dominican Republic to escape the horrors of a dictatorship. A distinguished poet and novelist, her work can be viewed as semi- autobiographical, bridging the cultural realms of Caribbean and North American culture, and as a testimonial to a variety human experience that is found among all people. Her writing is characterized by her skill in creating convincing characters. In a relatively short time, Álvarez has won a large and devoted audience who enjoy her talent for lyrical description, metaphor, and anecdotes that depict the immigrant experience and her own bicultural identity.

She was born on March 27, 1950, in New York City, the oldest of four sisters, and moved with her family to the Dominican Republic shortly after her birth. When she was ten, her family left for the United States. Her mother Julia and her father Eduardo Álvarez Perello, a physician, were forced to flee from the Dominican Republic after his involvement in a plot to overthrow the dictator Rafael Trujillo. She is part of a generation of Latino writers whose cultural consciousness reflects both her early years in the United States and a recollection of her parents' nostalgia for their island home.

Álvarez remembers her early years growing up in the United States and her struggle to feel comfortable in the new culture—one where, as a child, her family's language and appearance caused her some degree of embarrassment.

She received her early education in boarding schools, where through the encouragement of one teacher she acquired the habit of and love for reading and writing. While attending high school at the Phillips Academy in Andover, Massachusetts, she began to consider a career in writing. After high school she entered Connecticut College and transferred two years later to Middlebury College in Vermont, earning her Bachelor of Arts degree summa cum laude in 1971. In 1975 she received a Master's of Fine Arts degree from Syracuse University.

Although more widely known for her prose, Julia Álvarez began her literary career as a poet. From 1975 to 1978 she served as Poet-in-the-Schools in Kentucky, Delaware, and North Carolina. She was a professor of creative writing and English at her alma mater, Phillips Andover Academy (1979–81), at the University of Vermont (1981–83), and at the University of Illinois (1985–88). In addition, she was visiting writer and the Jenny McKean Moore Fellow at George Washington University in 1984, where she wrote and published her first book of poems, *The Housekeeping Book.* Her various teaching jobs finally led to a tenure-track position in 1988 when Middlebury College appointed her associate professor.

Her book *How the García Girls Lost Their Accents* was followed by another literary success in 1994, *In the Time of Butterflies,* the fictionalized history of the **Mirabal** sisters whose underground name was "butterflies." These Dominican heroes and political martyrs were murdered after visiting their husbands, who were jailed by the Trujillo regime for their part in a plot to overthrow the government. The novel does not have a strong plot or dominant character, but is composed of a series of linked stories. This work has been praised not only for its lyrical quality but also for its depiction of Latina women not as passive and powerless, but with courage, strength, and humanity. It won Alvarez the PEN Oakland/Josephine Miles Award and remains her best-known work.

Yolanda, the protagonist of her third novel, *Yo!* (1996), appeared in Álvarez's first novel as one of the sisters in *How the García Girls Lost Their Accents.* Narrated by Yo's family members, the story also weaves biographical aspects of Álvarez's life into the plot. Yo is portrayed as a successful Latina novelist who bases much of her fiction on her own life experiences. In this work we see a continuation of Álvarez's concerns with class, gender, and racial divisions.

Her first non-fiction work, *Something to Declare* (1998), opens a broader window into Álvarez's life, particularly her family and her development as a writer. This collection of essays is a close-up view of her early years in the United States and her struggle to feel comfortable in this new cultural and linguistic setting. The reader is introduced to her large extended family: her dapper grandfather (who reinforced her delight for poetry), the eccentric collection of aunts and uncles who danced flamenco on the tables during family gatherings. This family, however, is not only lively but also politically active. The themes of persecution and exile continue to permeate her work. We also get to see the long-term impact of the political oppression they experienced before emigrating from the Dominican Republic: "Long after we had left, my parents were still living in the dictatorship inside their heads. They didn't speak out or disagree with authorities; the First Amendment right to free speech meant nothing to them. Silence about anything 'political' was the rule in our house" (Berrios 1998, E14).

Although uncomfortable being cast as a spokesperson for the Latino community, Álvarez is aware of her ethnic and cultural diversity. She feels that she belongs to a minority group as well as to the dominant society. As such, she speaks out on issues of diversity, racism, bilingualism/biculturalism, and similar topics. An outspoken opponent of the English-only movement, Álvarez believes that biculturalism enriches our lives. Her books are included in many secondary-level English curricula, and she spends time visiting schools and sharing with students her experiences of immigration, her career, and her writings. She also encourages Latinos to stay connected to their language and heritage.

Among her most recent work is *In the Name of Salome* (2000), which celebrates one of the heroes of the Dominican Republic—**Salomé Ureña de Henríquez**, a well-known poet and political activist, who we get to know through her daughter **Camila Henríquez Ureña**. Her latest book, *Before We Were Free,* written for young adults, is about an adolescent girl living in the Dominican Republic during the dictatorial Trujillo regime. As in her other works, Álvarez brings to American shores another account of Caribbean revolutionary idealism and courage. —G.C.

References and Suggested Readings

Álvarez, Julia. "A Brief Account of My Writing Life." Department of English, Middlebury College: Faculty Profiles. *http://www.middlebury.edu/~english/facpub/Alv-autobio.html.* Accessed December 2000.

———. *How the García Girls Lost Their Accents.* Chapel Hill, NC: Algonquin Books, 1991.

———. *In the Time of Butterflies.* Chapel Hill, NC: Algonquin Books, 1994.

———. *Yo!* Chapel Hill, NC: Algonquin Books, 1996.

Arana-Ward, María. "Julia Álvarez." *The Washington Post,* May 14, 1995.

Berrios, Jerry. "Immigrant Finds Her Voice in Gap Between Cultures." *The Arizona Republic.* November 1, 1998, E14.

Gale Research. "Julia Álvarez." *Contemporary Authors: A Biographical Guide to Current Writers in Fiction, General Nonfiction, Poetry, Journalism, Drama, Motion Pictures, Television and Other Fields,* Vol. 101. Detroit: Gale Group, Thompson Learning, 2002. 22–25.

Requa, M. "The Politics of Fiction." *The Nation* (November 7, 1994). 552–556. *http://www.fronteramag.com/issue5/Alvarez.*

JEAN-BERTRAND ARISTIDE
(1953–)

Haitian President and Catholic Priest

Jean-Bertrand Aristide was one of the most visible and prominent political leaders in the Caribbean during the 1990s. His work as a Catholic priest and as a social reformer in the impoverished Republic of Haiti led him to a political career that culminated in his election to the presidency of Haiti on December 16, 1990. Aristide led his nation from February 7, 1991, until September 30, 1991, when a violent coup d'état removed him from office after just seven months in power. After spending almost three years in exile in Venezuela and the United States, where he brought national attention to Haiti's social, economic, and political ills, Aristide returned as president of Haiti in 1994. This amazing comeback was achieved after the United States, with the support of other Western nations, put pressure on the military regime led by General Raoul Cedrás to relinquish power and allow for Aristide's return. U.S. military troops were stationed in Haiti for more than a year in to stabilize the volatile political and social climate of the country. Through a remarkable story of compassion, political savvy, compromise, and sacrifice, Aristide managed to reinstate democracy in a country where military tyrannies and dictatorships ruled for most of the nineteenth century.

To understand Aristide's complex personality, it is important to understand his roots. He was born on July 15, 1953, in Port-Salut, a rural community located in the southwestern part of Haiti. His father died soon after his birth. Aristide and his only sister were raised by their mother, who moved to the capital of Port-au-Prince and supported her children by working as a trader and merchant. In his memoirs, he recalls living in many different houses, which were always filled with extended family and relatives.

Aristide's family was not wealthy. His maternal family belonged to a class of land-owning peasants who were able to subsist by farming their land to provide for their needs. As a child, Aristide was positively influenced by the generous deeds of his paternal grandfather, who shared his land with other people so that they could cultivate what they needed to eat. His

Jean-Bertrand Aristide. Courtesy of Photofest.

grandfather was seen as a community leader who often arbitrated the quarrels and disputes of less fortunate neighbors. Whenever young Aristide came to visit from the capital, his grandfather made sure that he interacted with people from the community. From early on, his grandfather cultivated values of equality, sharing, and social justice in his grandson.

Aristide received a traditional Catholic education from the Salecian monks of Port-au-Prince. While they instilled in him solid moral and religious values, they forced him to accept French cultural traditions and to disregard Haitian ones. Like **Frantz Fanon** from Martinique, Aristide was forced to speak French and to completely avoid his native Creole, which was disdained by both the priests and the members of the upper classes. He had a natural gift for language and eventually learned French, Latin, Greek, Italian, Hebrew, Spanish, English, German, and Portuguese. He also became a leader in sports, scouting, and music.

During his early school years, Aristide excelled in all of his classes and worked hard to escape the political and social oppression of his country. From an early age, he was attracted to the spiritual alternatives provided by the Salecians and eventually became enchanted with the priesthood. He said: "In my very deepest memories I can find nothing but a natural bent, a need, and a certainty that grew stronger and stronger" (Aristide and Wargny 1993, 36).

Following this spiritual vocation toward the priesthood, Aristide joined the Salecian seminary in Cap Haïtien in 1966, where he cultivated both his spiritual and academic life. He immersed himself in theological studies as a means of understanding the political oppression and poverty that surrounded Haiti during the dictator François Duvalier's regime. He focused on language as a way to understand other people and cultures because for him communion meant "communication" (Aristide and Wargny 1993, 41). His seminary experience focused on the doctrines of John Bosco, the founder of the Salecian order, whose doctrines centered on helping the poor.

Aristide finished his seminary training at the age of 21 and completed his novitiate in the Dominican Republic. He received an undergraduate psychology degree in 1979 in Haiti, and that same year was sent by his order to Israel, where he pursued advanced training in biblical studies. When he returned to Haiti in 1982, he was ordained as a priest and appointed to the parish of Saint Joseph in Port-au-Prince. However, his view that the church should be a catalyst for social and political change represented a risk for the Catholic Church, which, at the time, acted as a silent accomplice of the Duvalier regime. Therefore, that same year he was sent to Canada to a seminary that specialized in changing the views of priests who had controversial attitudes. The leaders of the Canadian seminar saw no need to change his views and sent him instead to the University of Montreal, where he completed a master's degree in biblical theology. He also finished the coursework for a doctorate in psychology in 1985, but never finished his doctoral dissertation.

After completing this sojourn in Canada, Aristide returned to Haiti in 1985 where he was shocked by the social and economic despair of Haitian society. Although the Duvalier regime had ended, it had been replaced by the military rule of General Henry Namphy, who still used the repressive power of the Tonton Macoutes, an informal army of private citizens that for decades had protected tyranny and engaged in murder and repression against anyone who disagreed with the regime. Unemployment, social inequities, lack of health services, and AIDS were a few of the maladies affecting Haiti. Aristide was given an assignment as priest in the church of St. Jean Bosco and was appointed to be Master of Studies at the National School of Arts and Crafts in Port-au-Prince. However, his pastorate quickly focused on the tenets of liberation theology, a popular religious movement in the Third World that advocates using the church as an instrument to bring social and political equality to oppressed people.

While at St. Jean Bosco, Aristide founded a ministry known as "Family Selavi" to promote the well-being of Haitian children who were victims of poverty and political repression. At the same time, he used his pulpit to preach a message of liberation to the Haitian people. His confrontational views advocating social and political change quickly put him at odds with the Catholic hierarchy and with the military regime. Aristide was the victim of three assassination attempts. Because of his controversial political beliefs he was expelled from the Salecian order in 1988.

Despite his expulsion, Aristide continued his liberation work. In 1990, after another military coup, a transitional government was appointed, and Aristide decided to run for the presidency on the Lavalas Family Party. After a violent campaign plagued by bombings and assassinations, Aristide won the presidency in December 1990, with more than 60 percent of the vote. At the beginning of his presidency, he tried to implement a progressive agenda of social change to impact on the health, education, and economy of Haiti. One of his key principles was agrarian reform.

In his first months in office, Aristide was perceived as an apt and moral leader, but some Lavalas followers engaged in violent acts against the members and supporters of the old regime and Aristide was blamed for these acts. The Catholic Church quickly denounced Aristide and began a campaign to discredit him. In addition, the members of Haiti's rich and powerful ruling class were enraged by his agenda of social and economic change—in particular, the notion of agrarian reform. The negative climate and hostility eventually resulted in a coup d'état orchestrated by Raoul Cedrás, his chief military officer.

During three years of exile in Venezuela and the United States, he was a vocal advocate for the reinstatement of democracy to Haiti. Eventually international pressure forced Cedrás to step down, and Aristide was restored to office on October 15, 1994. He was allowed to complete the term, although he was banned from running for a consecutive second term. In 1995, Rene G. Preval, one of his closest associates and former Prime Minister under his mandate, was elected to replace Aristide.

Despite Aristide's humanitarian views and stands, his first term as president was marked by a substantial bloodshed and claims of corruption that almost equaled those of his predecessors. The international community has questioned Aristide's means of instituting change during his first term in office. He has been accused of advocating violence against his political opponents and of being mentally ill; some people have labeled his government as corrupt as previous ones.

In November 26, 2000, he was elected to a second term as president of Haiti under the powerful Lavalas Family Party. He won with 92 percent of the popular vote, but other major political parties refused to participate in the election. Aristide began his second term as president on February 7, 2001. There were serious protests among members of the international community and Haiti's business sector who refused to recognize the legitimacy of his mandate. Although the Haitian masses and the lower classes trusted Aristide and his previous platform of economic and social reform, there was a substantial level of mistrust among members of the business sector, who have seen Aristide as having an anti-capitalist bias. Aware of these perceptions, Aristide has taken a guarded approach to making serious changes. Haiti continues to need new policies that will bring economic growth and prosperity. Both the people of Haiti and the members of the international community are waiting to see if Aristide can bring change to Haiti and is able to translate his moral and humanitarian beliefs into positive action.—S.M.M.

References and Suggested Readings

Abramowitz, Morton. "Too Juicy to Keep Secret." *Newsweek*, December 6, 1993, 33.
Aristide, Jean-Bertrand, with Cristophe Wargny. *Aristide: An Autobiography*. New York: Orbis Books, 1993.
Caldwell, Christopher. "Aristide Development." *The American Spectator* (July 1994): n.p.
Goldberg, J.J. "Exile's Elegant Appeal." *The Jerusalem Report*, June 18, 1992, 7.
Kirschten, Dick. "Haitian Roulette." *National Journal*, November 9, 1995, 30–34.

JOAN ARMATRADING
(1950–)

St. Kitts Singer and Songwriter

A St. Kitts native who grew up in England, Joan Armatrading has been writing and performing her music since the late 1960s. A guest of honor at her St. Kitts Independence Celebrations in 1983, she is acknowledged as the island's first woman to achieve worldwide critical and commercial success as a musician. Her unique and accomplished acoustic guitar playing and vocal interpretations of her own musical compositions that include, and at times combine, folk, jazz, soul, reggae, pop, and rhythm and blues have entertained audiences around the world for over 25 years. So far she has released 14 albums of her own compositions, and her recordings have included 10 platinum and 18 gold hit records as well as two Grammy nominations. A music critic explained that her durability and appeal were due to the fact that she "has been coming up with music that people haven't heard before for the better part of three decades, during which time she has established a fervent if cult-sized following" (Rogovoy 1999). Even though she is characterized as a cult figure in the United States, she is a major figure who enjoys star status in Europe. Known for her shyness and for notoriously guarding her privacy, for many years she has also been an activist in humanitarian causes, advocating for Amnesty International.

Armatrading, the third of six children, was born on December 9, 1950, in Basseterre, the capital of St. Kitts. When she was three years old her parents, Amos Ezekiel and Beryl Agatha Armatrading, moved with their two oldest boys to the industrial city of Birmingham, England, leaving Joan behind in the care of her grandmother on the nearby island of Antigua. Four years later she was reunited with a family she no longer remembered and who lived in an all-white Birmingham neighborhood, an experience that brought about a sense of "isolation" described by a biographer as "something which would later suffuse her songs . . . which finds an echo in so many hearts" (Mayes 1990, 2). Even though her father played guitar, the instrument was off-limits to her. However, watching her father's occasional strumming and singing whetted her musical appetite.

She received her first guitar as a gift from her mother, who purchased it from a pawnshop. A self-taught musician, Armatrading's only music teacher died one week after her first lesson. Her interest in writing and playing music was further sparked by the piano her mother purchased to decorate the front room of their house. As she described in a 1999 interview, "And it was there, so I just started to play it, and write my own songs. I never learned anybody else's songs" (Rogovoy). Although interested in music, Armatrading says she did not grow up listening to rock and roll and did not buy her first music album until she was 19 years old.

In an effort to relieve the family's difficult financial situation, she abandoned her secretarial studies in 1966 and began to work in an office. After performing (as a favor to her brother) in a concert at Birmingham University, she formed a duo with a school friend and played bass and rhythm guitar in local clubs. The turning point in her musical career came in 1968 when she got a part in the national touring company of the musical *Hair.* Aside from being part of the chorus, or "The Tribe" (Mayes 1990, 8), she also had a solo musical number—"What a Piece of Work Man Is." During her years in *Hair,* she met Pam Nestor, a singer and lyricist with whom she would write over 100 songs and collaborate on her first recordings. By 1972 Armatrading had moved to London to pursue a music career. That same year, in collaboration with Nestor, she

Joan Armatrading. AP Photo/Dave Thomson.

wrote and released her first album, *Whatever's for Us,* and made her professional debut in London's Fairfield Hall, which was followed by an invitation to join singer José Feliciano's 1973 European tour. In 1976 her third album, *Joan Armatrading,* considered her breakthrough work, made her a celebrity and the song "Love and Affection" an international hit.

By 1980, following a major record contract and various U.S. tours, she had received two Grammy nominations for best female vocalist, and 18 gold records and 10 platinum records in seven countries. She has performed to worldwide critical acclaim and has produced such music classics as *Love and Affection* (1976), *Down to Zero* (1976), *Me Myself and I* (1980), and *The Messenger* (2000). Deemed one of the best lyricists in pop music, her songs are considered revelatory in content; her performances, usually sold out, are hailed as masterful. Music critic Jim Sullivan, in reviewing one of her concerts, commented on the reasons why her fans have followed her for so many years: "Armatrading's deep expressive voice is soulful, her music is relatively complex and highly syncopated and [referring to her lyrics] her love still knows no boundaries" (Sullivan 1996, 59). Since 1986 Armatrading has been sole producer of her music albums, recording them at her home studio in Britain.

When interviewed about the evolution of their careers, successful singer/songwriters such as Tracy Chapman, Melissa Etheridge, and the Indigo Girls have credited Armatrading as being one of their female role models in the music business. During the past ten years Armatrading has produced a number of new albums and compilations, although none have reached the popularity of her earlier work. Today, almost three decades after her first recordings, she continues to receive critical acclaim for her music as well as for her philanthropic work and social activism.

The beginning of the new millennium marked additional achievements for this singer/songwriter. In 1999, she sang in and produced *Lullabies with a Difference*, a collection of bedtime songs that included contributions by Tina Turner, Melissa Etheridge, and others. The album's proceeds benefit PACE, a parent-run organization for children with cerebral palsy.

In the 1970s and 1980s, Armatrading was active in the movement to free jailed political activist Nelson Mandela. During the latter part of 1999, she was asked to write a song in tribute to Mandela's accomplishments over the years to mark his retirement from the presidency of South Africa. On April 6, 2000, at Wembley Stadium in London, Joan Armatrading, backed by the Kingdom Choir, performed the song "The Messenger" for him before a crowd of over 70,000 people. Mandela, in a demonstration of his approval, smiled and danced onstage throughout the entire song.

In addition to her Grammy nominations, she has been the recipient of much recognition throughout her career. In 1996 she received the Ivor Novello Award for Outstanding Contemporary Song Collection. In addition, in 1998 she received a platinum CD from the BBC (marking sales of 1 million) for her collaboration with other artists in the Lou Reed song and fundraising album *Perfect Day*, and she was made an Honorary Fellow of the John Moores University of Liverpool. She also appeared in VH1's 1999 television production as one of the 100 most influential women in rock. In June 2001, Armatrading received a bachelor of arts degree with honors from Open University.

In December 2002, the University of Birmingham—located in the city where she grew up—honored her with a doctorate in music in recognition of her contribution to the field. Her latest album, *Lover's Speak*, released after an eight-year recording hiatus, was written, arranged, and produced by Armatrading. Except for horns and drums, she plays every instrument in this recording—truly demonstrating her remarkable musical skills.—G.C.

References and Suggested Readings

Joan Armatrading Official Homepage: *www.joanarmatrading.com.*

Lindsey, Craig D. "Union Joan." *Houston Press,* July 13, 2000.

Mayes, Sean. *Joan Armatrading: A Biography.* London: Weidenfeld and Nicolson, 1990.

Morse, Steve. "Unplugged, Armatrading Charges the Soul." *The Boston Globe,* November 6, 1995, 34.

Rogovoy, Seth. "Joan Armatrading." *Berkshire Eagle,* July 25, 1999, n.p. *http://www.berkshireweb.com/rogovoy/interviews/arm.html.*

Roos, John. "Pop Music Reviews; Armatradings's Range and Masterful Poise Combine Triumph." *Los Angeles Times,* December 4, 1995, 2.

Sullivan, Jim. "The Timeless Soul of Joan Armatrading." *The Boston Globe,* June 29, 1996, 59.

MARÍA CELESTE ARRARÁS
(1960–)

Puerto Rican Broadcast Journalist, Anchorwoman, Writer, and Television Personality

As a newswoman, writer, and television personality, María Celeste Arrarás has established herself as one of the most visible and credible broadcast journalists in the Latino television market. Endowed with intelligence, journalistic integrity, relentless motivation, and great humanity, she has managed to gain the attention and trust of the millions of viewers who watch her Latino network news and who have consistently voted her one of the most admired personalities in broadcast journalism.

Arrarás was born on September 27, 1961, in Mayagüez, a college city on the west coast of Puerto Rico. Her father, José Enrique Arrarás, is a lawyer and was chancellor of the University of Puerto Rico at Mayagüez. For many years, he occupied a central role in Puerto Rican politics as a senator and as a prominent politician. Her mother is Astrid Mangual. Raised both in Mayagüez and San Juan, Arrarás studied at parochial schools in these two cities and graduated from high school at the elite Colegio Puertorriqueño de Niñas in San Juan.

Arrarás describes herself as an extroverted girl who always liked to say what she felt. As she grew up, she felt that she wanted to communicate not only through the spoken and written word but also through video. With this in mind, she pursued studies in communications at Loyola University in New Orleans, where she graduated with honors with a bachelor's degree in communications in 1982.

She started her journalistic career in 1986 as a reporter with WSJN-TV, Channel 13, in San Juan, Puerto Rico. During her three years at this 24-hour news station, Arrarás quickly demonstrated her talents by focusing on special events and on international news not commonly covered by other mainstream Puerto Rican television stations. Although she quickly became the prime anchor at the station and gained prominence in the fertile Puerto Rican television market, her interests in the international news market led her to accept a position as an anchorwoman with Channel 41, the local affiliate of Univision, the Spanish television network in New York.

Shortly after arriving in New York, Arrarás was asked to become the Los Angeles bureau chief and weekend substitute anchor for Univision News Network, based in Los Angeles. Recognizing the value of being a reporter at the national network level, she quickly accepted and continued to impress her audiences with her quality work. She covered news of North America, the Caribbean, Asia, Europe, and throughout the world. In 1991, she became the national weekend anchor for Univision Network News and a correspondent and substitute anchor for

María Celeste Arrarás.

Portada, a newsmagazine with a format similar to *60 Minutes.* Of the work during this time she has said: "The public got to know me doing important work such as wars, and coup d'états. I carry the news in my bloodstream. I had a rifle in my head during a coup d'etat in Haiti and was abducted by drug lords in Mexico. These are like the stars worn by a general. We are proud of them" (Arrarás 2000). She has coordinated and hosted the first live satellite transmissions "spacebridge" between the former Soviet Union and the Caribbean, and has covered live national presidential conventions, the Olympics, and state elections in California, Florida, and New York. She has had one-on-one interviews with U.S. presidential candidates, Latin American presidents, and movie stars. She has been on special assignment to the former Soviet Union, Korea, Latin America, the Philippines, Europe, and Hawaii (Arrarás 2000).

In 1993, Arrarás became a national news anchor for Univision Network's *Primer Impacto.* This infotainment magazine is seen from coast to coast in the United States, in 15 Latin American countries, and in Europe. The program follows a soft/hard news format, similar to that of American TV's *Hard Copy,* and focuses on absurd and sometimes the bizarre human stories. At the same time, she continues to be active within the news department and anchors the daytime newsbreaks for the network. Based at Univision's headquarters in Miami, Arrarás has become very successful. A special edition of *Primer Impacto* hosted by Arrarás gained a 30.6 national rating becoming the second-highest-rated show in the history of the Nielsen Hispanic Index.

The assassination of Tex-Mex singer Selena in March 1995 put Arrarás in the forefront of Latino news. Assigned by Univision to cover the assassination, she flew to Texas and followed the case closely from the day of the killing to the eventual trial of Yolanda Saldivar, Selena's killer, to a groundbreaking post-trial interview with Saldivar. This interview became one of the highest-rated shows ever broadcast on Spanish television according to Nielsen. In 1997, Arrarás published *El Secreto de Selena* (Selena's Secret), which became one of the year's best-sellers in Latino markets. The book, filled with respect and compassion for the dead singer, unraveled the turbulent last days of Selena's life.

Arrarás' career can be best summarized by her view of success. She says that success is determined by vision, luck, and motivation. It is also determined by the quality work that she has produced in less than two decades in Latino broadcasting, which is attested to by the many awards and recognitions she has received.

She has been on the cover of several magazines and featured in newspaper articles internationally, including *People, Time, USA Today,* and *The New York Times.* She is the only Hispanic journalist to have received the prestigious GENESIS award, given by the National Ark Trust Fund, and a Grammy. She was chosen by *People* magazine as one of "The 10 Most Intriguing People of the Year 2000." In 2001 she won the Humanitarian Award, the highest recognition given by the organization People for the Ethical Treatment of Animals (PETA).

Arrarás left Univisión in 2002 and joined the Telemundo Network, where she hosts *Al Rojo Vivo*, a newsmagazine focusing on controversial and entertainment stories. She is very active in many charitable endeavors, including being the Latina spokesperson for the organization People for the Ethical Treatment of Animals (PETA), for environmental protection, and the rights of the elderly.—S.M.M.

References and Suggested Readings

Arrarás, María Celeste. Personal communication. March 3, 2000.
———. *El Secreto de Selena.* New York: Simon and Schuster. 1997.
Frank. Jocelyn. "María Celeste Arrarás." *People en Español* (March 1999): 69.
Lima, Mabel. "María Celeste Arrarás: Diva puertorriqueña." *El Ritmo de la Noche* (April 1998): 26.
Vargas, Patricia. "Aquí María Celeste." *El Nuevo Día* (San Juan, Puerto Rico), December 5, 2001, n.p.
Vargas, Patricia. "En suspenso María Celeste." *El Nuevo Día* (San Juan, Puerto Rico), December 28, 2001, n.p.
Vargas, Patricia. "La más popular en Estados Unidos." *El Nuevo Día* (San Juan, Puerto Rico), January 6, 2000, 77.

HERMAN BADILLO
(1929–)

Puerto Rican American Politician, Lawyer, and Public Servant

Herman Badillo has been one of the most enduring figures on the political landscape of New York City. A self-made man who has challenged commonly held stereotypes of what it means to be a Puerto Rican in New York, he has been able to effectively establish professional and political careers that span over 40 years. In 1970 he became the first Puerto Rican to be elected to the U.S. Congress. Despite his somewhat controversial views on many issues, such as bilingual education and welfare programs, and his somewhat aloof political persona, Badillo is still perceived as the Puerto Rican elder statesman of New York City politics.

Badillo was born in Caguas, a suburban city that is considered part of the metropolitan area surrounding San Juan, Puerto Rico, on August 21, 1929. His father,

Herman Badillo. Courtesy of Photofest.

Francisco, and his mother, Carmen, died of tuberculosis when he was a small child. When his grandmother, who cared for him, also died from the disease, Badillo was brought over to the United States by one of his aunts. After arriving in the United States at the age of 12, he lived with several relatives in Chicago and California before arriving in New York at age 14.

When Badillo arrived in the United States, he didn't know English—but that didn't deter him from finding odd jobs to support himself. In his early years in the city, he worked as a cook, a dishwasher, and a pin boy at a bowling alley. He attended Haaren High School, where he graduated at the top of his class, and went on to study accounting at Baruch College of the City University of New York while working full-time for an accounting firm. He graduated magna cum laude and enrolled at the Brooklyn Law School, where was selected as the class valedictorian and graduated cum laude in 1954. He was admitted to the New York bar in 1955 and passed his certification to become a certified public accountant in 1956. He established his own legal firm in the late 1950s.

Badillo has been a maverick politician and a reformer on the very complex and competitive political stage of New York City. His involvement in politics started during the 1960 elections when he was the chairman of the East Harlem committee that was working in support of the John F. Kennedy candidacy. In 1961, Badillo ran for district leader in East Harlem but lost by 75 votes. After the defeat, the mayor of New York, Robert Wagner, noticed Badillo's leadership and appointed him deputy real estate commissioner in 1961. The next year Badillo was appointed by the Democratic machine to become commissioner of the newly created Department of Relocation, which oversaw housing renewal and planning. His tough stances on renovating areas on Manhattan's West Side and his proposals to remove many buildings inhabited primarily by his fellow Puerto Ricans brought him many political enemies. He was accused of gentrifying parts of the city by getting rid of settlements inhabited by poor immigrants. These events have fueled allegations by other Puerto Rican leaders that he is not Puerto Rican enough. These allegations, in turn, have followed him throughout most of his political life and have hindered his relationship with Latinos, minorities, and several of his obvious allies (Ojito June 8, 2001, B1).

After moving from East Harlem to the Bronx, Badillo was elected Bronx borough president in 1965, where his administrative and accounting skills served him well. He planned and submitted strategic initiatives to City Hall that brought millions of dollars in innovative construction projects to his district. His capacity to negotiate and to deal with the political establishment and city government helped him to become the most influential Puerto Rican politician at the time. His political visibility made him well-positioned to run for the office of the mayor in 1969, but he lost in the Democratic primaries. When a redistricting initiative in the city created a new congressional district, Badillo positioned himself to run for the U.S. Congress. He ran a strong campaign and won the seat for the 21st congressional district, becoming the first Puerto Rican American ever elected to Congress in November of 1970. He joined the 92nd Congress on January of 1971. After some political maneuvering, he was also appointed to serve on the powerful Education and Labor Committee of the House of Representatives. He served in Congress until 1978, when he resigned before his term was over to serve as deputy mayor of New York under the leadership of Mayor Edward Koch. He lasted only a year in the post and resigned due to constant clashes with the mayor.

After his resignation, Badillo temporarily left politics and became a partner in the powerful law firm of Fischbein, Badillo, Wagner and Harding, one of the top lobbying firms in New York City. In the 1990s, he was appointed chairman of the board of regents for the City University of New York (CUNY), where he served until June of 2001. When he arrived at CUNY, he called the institution a "swamp of mediocrity" (Traub 1999, 96). He took an extremely proactive role in raising academic standards at the institution and in eliminating special opportunity programs for students who did not have strong academic credentials. He also succeeded in eliminating open admission policies to the institution, thereby removing any unqualified applicants from the college. His blatant criticism of the educational and intellectual ability of Mexican and other Central American immigrants caused an enormous uproar among sectors of the city that accused him of being bigoted and biased.

While Badillo broke ground through his election to the U.S. Congress, he has always had his eye on the position of mayor of New York City. He entered the Democratic primaries in 1969, 1973, 1977, 1985, and 1993. Frustrated with the Democratic machinery that controls the party in New York, Badillo switched party affiliation in 1998 and became a Republican. On June 8, 2001, he announced his candidacy for mayor of New York on the Republican Party platform. He ran as an education candidate but was defeated by New York businessman and multimillionaire Michael R. Bloomberg, who spent millions of dollars of his own money in the campaign.

Herman Badillo is a skillful political leader who doesn't hesitate to voice controversial positions that do not always endear him to either the liberal establishment or to his Latino and Puerto Rican constituents. He continues to be as involved in New York City politics as he was 40 years ago.—S.M.M.

References and Suggested Readings

Blumiller, Elizabeth. "Running for Mayor in Perpetuity: Hernan Badillo Is Hoping That the Timing Is Right." *The New York Times*, May 9, 2001, B1.

Moritz, Charles, ed. "Herman Badillo." *Current Biography Yearbook.* New York: H. W. Wilson, Co., 1971. 17–19.

Ojito, Mirta. "Badillo Opens Another Run for Mayor." *The New York Times,* June 8, 2001, B1.

———. "Badillo Shares His Own Story on Bout With Prostate Cancer." *The New York Times,* June 15, 2001, B4.

Traub, James. "A Minority of One." *The New York Times Sunday Magazine,* October 31, 1999, 96.

MYRNA BÁEZ
(1931–)

Puerto Rican Painter, Graphic Engraver, and Sculptor

Walking through a retrospective exhibit of the work of Puerto Rican artist Myrna Báez, one finds it difficult to characterize the works of this accomplished painter. They are colorful, precise, and filled with familiar imagery; at the same time they are mysterious, abstract, and removed.

Báez has produced an extensive body of work that is highly representative of Puerto Rican visual arts during the second part of the twentieth century. Although she has produced many paintings and drawings in the traditional media of oils, acrylic, and paper, her most important works have been her engravings in the media of xylography, serigraphy, intaglio, and etching, which she pioneered on the island. Her artistic style is unique and filled with an intensity and passion seldom found in other artists of her generation. Despite her understated style, her works are used to make subtle but powerful personal and social commentaries in which gender struggles often occupy a central role. Her many paintings and graphic engravings denote the influence of impressionism, surrealism, and naturalistic painting. Báez has been a central figure in the support of Puerto Rican arts and graphic artists. She has taught many Puerto Rican artists through her work as an art professor and educator.

Myrna Báez was born on August 18, 1931, in Santurce, Puerto Rico, to an upper-middle-class family. She is one of five children of Enrique Báez, a civil engineer, and América González, a teacher. Biographers and critics have noted the influence of her mother, a strong, self-confident, and independent woman, on the development of her character and personality. An intelligent and gifted child, Báez attended several public and private schools in the Santurce and Hato Rey, graduating from the Colegio Puertorriqueño de Niñas in 1947.

Báez attended the University of Puerto Rico in Río Piedras, where she majored in the sciences. During her years at the university, she had the chance to participate in the intellectual ferment that permeated the institution during the 1940s and

1950s. She was exposed to many of the cultural and artistic opportunities available there and discovered the social and political realities affecting Puerto Rico and its people. She came to believe that Puerto Rico should become an independent nation.

After graduating from the university in 1951, she traveled to Madrid, Spain, where she intended to study medicine and become a doctor. That was not to be the case. She became disenchanted with her medical studies and instead studied art at the Royal Academy of San Fernando, one of the elite art institutions of Europe. The academy not only gave her a high-quality traditional arts education but also exposed her to many prominent artists of the time. She graduated from the academy with a degree in painting in 1957 and decided to go back to Puerto Rico.

Báez returned to Puerto Rico at a time when there was an artistic boom on the island. Puerto Rican artists such as **Rafael Tufiño**, **Antonio Martorell**, José Antonio Torres Martinó, Isabel Bernal, and **Lorenzo Homar** were pioneering the artistic movement that later became known as the "Generation of the 50s." Báez, who initially worked in odd jobs and taught drawing and painting at her home, joined the newly established Graphic Arts Workshop at the Institute of Puerto Rican Culture. She worked under the tutelage of Lorenzo Homar between 1957 and 1962 and mastered the media of art engraving.

In 1957 she entered her painting "Church" in the Christmas Festival sponsored by the Puerto Rican Athenaeum. The following year she participated in an exhibit of engravings held at the Institute of Puerto Rican Culture, and by 1959 she had sent one of her paintings to an exhibit of Puerto Rican artists being held in Switzerland. By 1959 she had become the vice-president of the visual arts section at the Puerto Rican Athenaeum. One of her engravings depicting a rooster was bought by the Institute of Puerto Rican Culture and used to illustrate the cover of a recording of Puerto Rican music released by the institute. That same year, her work was exhibited in New York as part of a collection of Puerto Rican engravings. The Metropolitan Museum of Art bought one of those engravings, "Yunque 1," in 1959.

Most of Báez's early works are traditional images of Puerto Rico, portraits, and naturalistic scenes. One of her works of the period is the oil "Barriada Tokio" depicting a slum in Puerto Rico. The Ponce Museum of Art bought this painting in 1964 for its permanent exhibit. In the 1960s, Báez moved toward the use of engravings and printing techniques and went to Spain to study lithography and intaglio with Dimitri Papagiourgi. She also studied printed engraving at the Pratt Graphics Center in New York. Her newly found interest in these techniques moved her art toward impressionism and incorporated some surreal elements as well as abstractions. She developed an interest in lithography, serigraphs, and xylography. It was, however, her command of the technique of collotype, developed after training in 1969 with Clare Romano at the Pratt Graphics Center in New York, which became her most favored technique during the 1970s. Her award-winning collotypes "Juez" and "Juego de Cartas" came to represent her work in that medium and toured the world as part of many exhibits. During the

1980s, she studied intaglio with David Finkbeiner at the Pratt Graphic Center and worked in etching.

Scholar Margarita Fernández Zavala, Báez's biographer and one of the foremost experts on her work, has identified Báez's uses of the portraits and landscapes, her expressions of solitude, and the presence of gender discourse about identity as defining aspects of Báez's art. She has said that in Báez's portraits: "The work acquires a broader dimension beyond the mere projection of a specific resemblance. The portrait itself becomes a subject, an element in its own right within the work of art" (Fernández Zavala 2001, 98). She further states that in the artist's exploration of the urban landscape "Báez has immortalized the daily life of the rising Puerto Rican bourgeoisie whose history coincides with her own life" (99). This critic stresses the importance of the class struggles in Puerto Rico as part of the themes in Báez's landscapes. Conversely, she notes that the artist's own identity is extremely important to the understanding of her nudes which appear as remote, amorphous, and lacking sexual connotations.

In addition to her career as a painter and graphic artist, Báez has had a prolific career as an educator. In 1962 she taught at the Luchetti School in Río Piedras. The next year she moved to the University of the Sacred Heart in Santurce, where she worked between 1963 and 1985. She has been an artist-in-residence at the university since 1988, as well as lecturer at several other Puerto Rican universities.

She has received several awards for her work. Among them are: First Prize in Painting by the Puerto Rican Athenaeum (1966); First Prize in the Annual Art Competition at the Pratt Graphic Center (1970); Graphic Award from the Puerto Rican Athenaeum (1974); and First Prize in Painting from the literary journal *Revista Sin Nombre* (1977). In 1997, she received the National Culture Medal from the Institute of Puerto Rican Culture, the highest decoration a Puerto Rican artist can receive. In the fall of 2001, she opened a major exhibit of 172 works at the Museum of Puerto Rico. Puerto Rican writer **Rosario Ferré** labeled the exhibit as "splendid" (Ferré 2002). Báez has summarized her relationship with her art as follows: "When I paint, I show what I am, what I think, what I know, and what I don't. For me, painting is neither catharsis nor exorcism, but the result of a mental process of my sensibility and the exercise of acquire skills that collect a mental archive of visual and living experiences" (Barrios 2001, 76).—S.M.M.

References and Suggested Readings

Báez, Myrna, and José A. Torrés Martinó. *Puerto Rico: arte e identidad.* San Juan: Editorial de la Universidad de Puerto Rico, 1998

Barrios, Mario Alegre. "El arte de provocar." *El Nuevo Día,* "Revista Por Dentro," October 28, 2001, 76.

Fernández Zavala, Margarita, ed. *Myrna Báez: An Artist and Her Mirror.* Santurce: Universidad del Sagrado Corazón, 2001.

Ferré, Rosario. "Myrna Báez y la mirada." *El Nuevo Día,* February 2, 2002. *http://www.adendi.com/noticia.asp?nid=486691&keyword=Myrna%20Báez.*

JOAQUÍN BALAGUER
(1907–2002)
Dominican Politician and Writer

Joaquín Balaguer was one of the most enduring political leaders in the Dominican Republic for most of the twentieth century. As a central figure in the Caribbean, his involvement in Dominican politics defined a significant period of the island's contemporary political history.

Balaguer was born on September 1, 1907, in Navarrete, a farming town in the Dominican Republic, the only boy in a family that included six sisters. His father, Joaquín Balaguer Lespier, was an agricultural merchant, originally from Puerto Rico, and his mother was Carmen Celia Ricardo. Balaguer completed elementary school in his hometown and went to high school in the neighboring town of Santiago de los Caballeros. From there, he moved on to the Autonomous University of Santo Domingo, where he obtained a law degree in 1929. He was awarded a doctorate in law and political science from the University of Paris in 1932.

During his early years in public life, Balaguer was a career diplomat with General Rafael Leonidas Trujillo's Foreign Service. He obtained his first assignment to Spain in 1932, and eventually held ambassadorial positions in Colombia, Ecuador, and Mexico. He also worked as a university professor. Balaguer gained local government experience by working as a lawyer for the agrarian courts, as undersecretary of public education and fine arts, and an undersecretary of state for foreign relations. He first entered national politics when he was appointed secretary to the presidency in 1956 during the regime of General Trujillo. In 1957, he was elected vice president as the running mate of Hector Trujillo (brother to General Trujillo). When Hector Trujillo resigned in 1960 amidst political controversy, Balaguer became president. He was president when General Trujillo was assassinated in 1961.

During the first term of his presidency, Balaguer moved to dismantle the existing dictatorship by allowing once-exiled political dissidents to return to the island. But his initiatives were difficult to implement as the vestiges of Trujillo's dictatorial regime remained a formidable force on the island, particularly in the military.

After a military coup in 1962, Balaguer left the Dominican Republic and sought asylum in New York. He spent four years in political exile in New York, returning to the Dominican Republic in 1966 at the end of the civil war. He sought the presidency again, this time on the Reform Party ticket, and was elected to the position in 1966. He was reelected in 1970 and 1974. Balaguer's leadership during this period has been characterized as an economic dictatorship marked by manipulation of the central bank and centralization of the economic resources into

Joaquín Balaguer. AP Photo/John Riley.

the office of the president (Moya Pons 1998). After a brief retirement in the late 1970s and 1980s, he was elected president again in 1986 and served until 1996.

Balaguer had a long tenure in Dominican politics. Although his regime was associated with some levels of repression and violence, Balaguer tried to distance himself from the bloody deeds that characterized the Trujillo years and acknowledged that there may have been "excesses" during his own tenure as president (Treaster 1986). Many Dominicans have labeled Balaguer as a tyrant. During his term in office, he did not hesitate to use political repression—and some allege murder—to keep political control of the island. Many have attributed the phrase "Los muertos no hablán" (Dead people do not talk) to him. However, many have also noted that he kept the poor on his island happy to maintain control of the government and to solidify his presidency. Through the years, he obtained support from diverse groups that included conservative followers in the countryside, farmers, business and industrial leaders, and poor laborers.

Balaguer was able to stay in power by building a large system of political cronyism that handed out low-paying government jobs and spent money freely in huge public works such as the national monument to Christopher Columbus and a large cross-shaped lighthouse built to commemorate the 500 years of Spanish colonization of the Dominican Republic. While president, he maintained personal control and discretionary authority over more than 50 percent of the national budget. He has been criticized for allowing his political cronies to benefit from the funds of the national treasury, but he saw this as an effective means of consolidating political power. One journalist described the power behind his ability to govern by labeling him "a collector of favors and a master of intrigue and manipulation who never makes his intentions clear or agrees to a binding commitment, leaving his opponents off balance and guessing what he will do next" (Rother 1996, 3).

Even as a disabled elder statesman who has suffered from longtime blindness, Balaguer still wielded substantial amount of political power and influence in the Dominican Republic; as recently as the 2000 elections, he broadcasted speeches from his bed. His role during the hours before and after the assassination of Trujillo has been reexamined in the publication of *La fiesta del chivo* (The Goat's Feast), a fictionalized account of the assassination of Trujillo by the noted Peruvian writer Mario Vargas Llosa (2000).

Balaguer also had a notable career as a writer. Starting in 1920, he wrote more than 30 books in the genres of critical and historical essays and poetry. Among them are *Ensayo del escritor Federico García Godoy* (Essay about the Writer Federico García Godoy; 1927); *Próceres Escritore* (Notable Writers; 1947); *Temas históricos y literarios* (Historic and Literary Themes; 1974); *Memorias de un cortesano en la era de Trujillo* (Memories of a Courtesan during the Trujillo Era; 1988); *Salmos paganos* (Pagan Psalms; 1920); and *Verdad transparente* (Transparent Truth; 1947).

Balaguer died on July 14, 2002, at the age of 94. His passing constituted the end of a unique period in the Dominican Republic's history. Thousands of people visited his home to pay their respect to the man who played a central role in their lives for over 50 years. He asked to be given a "traditional" Dominican wake, which entailed exhibiting his fully dressed body resting on his deathbed. Despite Balaguer's controversial legacy and the many historic and political interpretations of his work, there is general agreement that he helped the poor of his island.
—S.M.M.

References and Suggested Readings

Alexander, Robert J., ed. "Joaquín Balaguer." *Biographical Dictionary of Latin American and Caribbean Political Leaders.* Westport, CT: Greenwood Press, 1988. 32–33.

Farah, Douglas. "Dominican, 89, and Blind, Seeks Path to Power in Stepping Down." *The Washington Post,* June 30, 1996, A19.

Jense, Holger. "Joaquín Balaguer." *Rocky Mountain News,* September 25, 1994, 94A.

Moya Pons, Frank. *The Dominican Republic: A National History.* Princeton, NJ: Markus Wiener Publishers, 1998.

Rother, Larry. "A Dominican Institution Exiting." *The New York Times,* May 19, 1996, 11.

———. "Lawyer Raised in New York to Lead Dominican Republic." *The New York Times,* July 2, 1996, 3.

Treaster, Joseph B. "Man in the News: Joaquin Balaguer again at the Dominican Helm." *The New York Times,* August 17, 1986, 14.

Vargas Llosa, Mario. *La fiesta del chivo.* Madrid, Spain: Editorial Santillana, 2000.

THE BARROW FAMILY

Barbadian Politicians and Social Reformers

The Barrow family of Trinidad was central to the political and cultural life of Barbados during the twentieth century. Errol Walton Barrow and Nita Barrow became two of the most prestigious Barbadian citizens, with long and fruitful professional careers that benefited both Barbados and the Caribbean.

Their father, Reginald Barrow, trained at Codrington College in Barbados as a theologian and became a notable religious leader in St. Croix and Barbados. He was ordained as an Anglican priest and traveled throughout the Caribbean in several religious appointments. A man of socialist views, he often criticized both the church and wealthy plantation owners for what he perceived were unfair practices. His views about social justice were considered so controversial that he was deported from St. Croix in 1922. He eventually separated from the Anglican Church and went on to become a founder of the African Methodist Episcopal Church in the Caribbean and a founder of the St. Thomas Benevolent Society.

He and his wife, Ruth Alberta O'Neal, had five children. She came from a prosperous family who instilled in her a deep belief in education. An independent and resilient woman, Ruth traveled with her husband through the Caribbean as he was appointed to different religious positions. She used the economic resources that she had inherited from her family to provide for her children and make sure they acquired the best possible education. Her brother, Charles Duncan O'Neal, was an eminent Barbadian surgeon who was involved in politics and founded the Democratic League of Barbados.

Errol Walton Barrow
(1920–1987)

Attorney, Barbadian Prime Minister, and Politician

Errol Walton Barrow was among the most influential Caribbean political leaders of the twentieth century. Known fondly as the "Skipper," he guided the small Caribbean nation of Barbados toward independence from Great Britain and was instrumental in transforming the social, economic, and political landscape of the island by implementing a number of innovative and compassionate policies.

Barrow was born on January 21, 1920, in the parish of St. Lucy. Because of his father's job as an Anglican minister, the family traveled constantly throughout the Caribbean. Barrow began his elementary education at the Primary Danish School in St. Croix. On the family's return to Barbados, he attended the island's elite boys' schools. He graduated from Harrison College in 1939. After graduation he taught for a year in Barbados before volunteering for the war efforts and joining the British Royal Air Force in 1940.

Barrow had a distinguished military record in the Royal during World War II. He received communications training in Canada and served as a military navigator for the commander in chief of the British army in Germany. He eventually became a flying officer and flew 53 missions during the war. After his discharge from the Royal Air Force in 1947, Barrow enrolled at the London School of Economics, where he pursued a dual degree in economics and political science. Like his Jamaican counterpart, **Norman Manley**, he was influenced by the economic theories of Professor Harold Laski, which he used later during his political career. While pursuing his undergraduate education he also studied law. In 1949, he graduated from the London School of Economics and passed his legal examination to join the bar at Lincoln's Inn.

Barrow returned to Barbados in 1950. He developed a highly successful legal practice in the area of labor law and traveled the Caribbean representing labor unions in their disputes against their employers. Although he had considerable success as a lawyer, he became attracted to politics and sought the political process as a way to address the social and economic inequities in the island. Barrow joined the Barbadian Labour Party (BLP), founded by Sir **Grantley Adams**, and was elected to the Barbadian House Assembly in 1951. As a member of the assembly Barrow became frustrated by the regressive and ill-conceived political, social, and economic policies of the BLP. In 1955 he helped to organize the Democratic Labour Party (DLP), which had a more liberal agenda and advocated for major reforms in the government of Barbados. His party lost the parliamentary elections of 1956 and Barrow was unable to return to Parliament. Nevertheless, Barrow stayed active and vocal in Barbadian politics by creating alliances with other dissenting voices within Parliament. He returned to Parliament in 1958 and created alliances with the labor movement and the sugar unions. By 1961, he had become the leader of the DLP and won the 1961 elections with a solid majority of the vote. As a result, he became the premier of Barbados and started a vocal campaign to gain the independence from Great Britain. When Great Britain awarded independence to Barbados on November 30, 1966, Barrow became its prime minister.

Barrow's tenure as prime minister was characterized by vigorous reforms that changed Barbados' social and economic infrastructure and contributed to a substantial development of this Caribbean island. He built strong partnerships with private businesses and sought foreign investors who generated large number of jobs for Barbadians. Barrow teamed up with the industrial sector and developed initiatives to diversify the Barbadian economy. For instance, he supported the creation of the Central Bank of Barbados in 1973 as a way to facilitate the offering of incentives to businesses and industry. Although he believed that Barbados could not exclusively rely on the tourism industry, as many other Caribbean nations do, he set mechanisms in place to bolster tourism. He is credited with strengthening the Barbadian educational system and making education accessible to all. He also developed a social welfare system that cared for the Barbadian poor and disenfranchised.

As prime minister of Barbados, Barrow also worked hard to make the island a political leader within the West Indies. He worked closely with the governments of other Caribbean islands while maintaining excellent relations with Great Britain and the United States, who he considered his strongest allies. Under his leadership, Barbados joined the Organization of American States (OAS) and the United Nations. Barrow thought that Barbados could play an essential role in the economic development of other Caribbean nations and also believed that it could transcend the Caribbean and play a role in the international arena. This belief was proven correct many years later when his sister **Nita** became a high-profile diplomat representing Barbados in the United Nations. Errol Barrow was one of the early proponents of the creation of the Caribbean Community (CARICOM) organization. CARICOM has worked to bring the West Indian islands into a common economic market since 1968.

Barrow stayed in power as prime minister until 1976, when he was challenged by Tom Adams, the son of Sir Grantley Adams. The elections were highly contested because Adams accused Barrow of being responsible for the economic crisis Barbados was currently facing. Even after leaving the prime ministership, he remained involved in the political affairs of Barbados. For instance, he was a vocal critic of the invasion of Grenada by the United States in 1983 and believed that the invasion had profound political implications for the sovereignty and autonomy of other Caribbean countries. Barrow re-entered politics in 1986 and was again elected prime minister. Unfortunately, he died on June 1, 1987, before he was able to accomplish any substantial reforms during his second term in office.

NITA BARROW
(1916–1995)

Nurse, Public Health Specialist, Diplomat, and Governor General of Barbados

Few Caribbean leaders have accumulated as much affection, respect, and admiration as the former governor general of Barbados Nita Barrow. She was a woman of vision and sensitivity, courage and determination. Her long and prolific career in the fields of nursing, public health, and diplomacy enabled her to assume positions of leadership in organizations such as the United Council of Churches, the YMCA, the International Council of Adult Education, and the United Nations. As a member of the Eminent Persons Group to South Africa, Barrow became a staunch opponent of the apartheid regime and brought immense credibility to the efforts to bring down racial segregation and exploitation in South Africa. Barrow was referred to by many as a "Citizen of the World"; however, her Caribbean vision and values led Jamaican scholar **Rex Nettleford** to aptly say, "She is the Caribbean" (Nettleford 1988).

Barrow was born in Fairmount, a town that belonged to St. Lucy's parish, in northern Barbados, on November 15, 1916. She was the second of five children.

Although the educational system of Barbados discouraged the schooling of women, her mother Ruth made sure her daughters received the best possible education available to young girls in Barbados. She was educated in Barbados and became a teacher.

After teaching secondary school for two years, Barrow trained as a nurse at the Barbados General Hospital. Her mother and other relatives tried to dissuade her from studying nursing because of the grueling nature of the training and the racist and oppressive conditions faced by black nursing trainees in Barbados. When she trained at the Barbados General Hospital, nurses learned by watching and doing; very little direct instruction was offered. British nurses ran the facilities with a strong hand. Trainees lived in the hospital and endured long shifts, dating restrictions, curfews, menial pay, and bad treatment. Barrow protested the treatment the nurses received but was a dedicated student with a great sense of duty and responsibility. In 1940, after completing her five years of training, she went Trinidad for more specialized instruction in midwifery.

She was accepted as a fellow in post-basic nursing education at Toronto University in Canada. At the time, the university had a novel program intended to prepare nurses in a broad range of areas such as public health and epidemiology. Her sense of commitment and responsibility impressed her professors so much that they extended her fellowship for a second year and paid for a special rotation in infectious diseases at a Jamaican hospital.

Barrow finished her Canadian training in 1945. She immediately accepted a position as an assistant nursing instructor at the newly founded West Indian School of Public Health in Jamaica. When she arrived in Jamaica, she learned that the head nurse had left her position; Barrow quickly became the sole person in charge of the nursing staff at the institution. At the same time, she became the head nursing instructor for the teaching program at the hospital. One of her major contributions at the time was to refocus the training of nurses from care-giving to prevention and public health. In 1951 Barrow traveled to Edinburgh, Scotland, to pursue an additional year of training in public health. On that trip, she visited other medical facilities throughout Europe and studied their models of health care and prevention. Barrow, who had started to work with the YMCA in Jamaica, took advantage of the trip to Europe to represent Jamaica at the YMCA's 1951 world convention in Beirut, Lebanon. The trip was significant because it marked a lifelong association with the YMCA, an organization she presided over many years later.

Barrow's advanced training in the field of public health allowed her to pursue other career opportunities. On her return to Jamaica, she was appointed to the position of sister tutor at the Kingston Public Hospital. She was in charge of providing nursing training to the staff and developed such a good program that in 1954 she was offered the position of matron at the University College Hospital of the West Indies. The position of matron went beyond training responsibilities: she was the chief nursing official at the hospital in charge of a large staff. One of her challenges was to work with a large number of British doctors who thought that a black West Indian was not qualified to undertake such a huge job. In a few months she came to be regarded as a formidable administrator who ran the nursing program with a competent but kind hand.

Barrow's work at the University Hospital was so successful that when the position of principal nursing officer in Jamaica became available in 1956 she was offered the job. Despite her initial reservations about the position, she accepted and was in charge of the system of nursing training and health care for the whole island of Jamaica. The Jamaican health care system had faced many deficiencies, as the population relied on several hospitals scattered throughout the island and there was little uniformity or integration of their health care system. Barrow took a very aggressive approach toward health care and tried to integrate the hospitals within one system. She stressed the importance of community health care and established more than 100 community health care centers throughout the island. Isolated communities were provided with community health centers so that people did not have to travel more than eight miles to receive adequate care. Simultaneously, Barrow tried to improve the standards of care for patients: she persuaded the government of Jamaica to increase the health care budget more than ten times.

Barrow left her position in 1962 to go to New York and finish her college degree at Columbia University. Many of her colleagues worried that although she had achieved her nursing certification, her lack of a formal degree would curtail her ability to pursue other positions and would eventually affect her credibility as a public health official. She finished her bachelor's degree and in 1964 was selected to direct a major research project sponsored by the Pan-American Health Organization (PAHO) and the World Health Organization (WHO) to assess nursing training throughout the Caribbean.

Through her work with PAHO and WHO, Barrow became more involved with other international organizations. During the 1970s she worked closely with the World Council of Churches (WCC) and expanded her involvement with the YMCA. After attending a 1967 WCC meeting in Germany, Barrow was invited to become a commissioner for the Christian Medical Commission (CMC), the health care branch of the WCC. The CMC developed and implemented health care initiatives conducted by Christian groups throughout the world. Her work as a commissioner eventually led to her appointment as an associate director of the commission in 1970 and to the position of director in 1976. As a leader of the CMC, Barrow worked hard to develop programs focusing on community health and local medicine. Although she was based in Geneva, Switzerland, Barrow traveled throughout the world promoting different health care initiatives and gaining support for community medicine. She also became a passionate advocate of the need for more adult education programs worldwide and in 1982 became the president of the International Council on Adult Education.

In 1983 Barrow retired from her position with the WCC and completed her second term as president of the international YMCA, an organization that she had presided over since 1975. Although she intended to retire and go back to Barbados, she was offered a position as coordinator of the Non Government Organization Forum '85, a conference focusing on women's rights held in Nairobi, Kenya in 1985. By 1986, Barrow was so well recognized in international circles that the government of Barbados appointed her as Barbados' permanent ambassador to the United Nations. While at the United Nations, Barrow became the spokesperson for the U.N. Commission on the Status of Women and was a staunch defender of human rights and a critic of the apartheid regime in South Africa. She tried to bring cohesiveness to the members of the Caribbean delegation to the United Nations and to unify their work on behalf of Caribbean nations. Despite a failed bid for the presidency of the General Assembly in 1988, Barrow gained a reputation as a diplomat and came to occupy a great degree of visibility within the United Nations. She also developed a reputation as a defender of women's rights throughout the world. Because of this work, she was selected in 1986 to be the only female member of Eminent Persons Group that looked into the apartheid problem in South Africa.

Her years of hard work in so many positions of responsibility uniquely positioned Barrow to assist her island. After years of serving the world in a number of capacities, Nita Barrow was sworn in as governor general of Barbados on June 7, 1990. She was the first female governor of this Caribbean nation and worked relentlessly to improve the lives of her fellow Barbadians. Although she faced a major economic crisis during her mandate, she worked hard to bring consensus among all members of the government and recognized the importance of community organizations in helping to improve the lives of her people.

During her lifetime, Barrow received countless awards and recognitions. She had twelve honorary degrees and Queen Elizabeth made her a dame in the Barbados Order of Saint Andrews in 1980. Dame Nita, as she was affectionately called, died on December 19, 1995.—S.M.M.

References and Suggested Readings

Associated Press. "Prime Minister of Barbados, Errol W. Barrow, Dies at 67." *The New York Times,* June 2, 1987, 23.

Blackman, Francis. *Dame Nita: Caribbean Woman, World Citizen.* Kingston, Jamaica: Ian Randle Publishers, 1995.

Chamberlain, Greg. "Outspoken Barbados PM Dies." *The Guardian* (London), June 3, 1987, n.p.

Hintzen, Percy, and W. Marvin Will. "Barrow, Errol Walton." In Robert J. Alexander, ed., *Biographical Dictionary of Latin American and Caribbean Political Leaders.* Westport, CT: Greenwood Press, 1988. 44–46.

Moritz, Charles, ed. *Current Biography.* New York: The H.W. Wilson, Co., 1968. 51–53.

Nettleford, Rex. "Ideas." *Money Index,* March 1, 1988, n.p.

Southey, Caroline. "Barbados: Federalist but a Realist." *Financial Times* (London), November 30, 1987, 37.

JEAN-MICHEL BASQUIAT
(1960–1988)

Haitian and Puerto Rican American Painter, Poet, and Musician

The graffiti art of Jean-Michel Basquiat came to characterize an artistic period in New York City during the late 1970s and early 1980s. Signing his pseudo-philosophical statements and verses with the notation SAMO, Basquiat, in collaboration with his Puerto Rican friend Al Díaz, developed hundreds of graffiti murals throughout the city that brought him considerable fame and recognition. His graffiti eventually catapulted him into the highest echelons of the art establishment of New York, the United States and Europe. Because of its profound simplicity, primitive qualities, and angry tone, Basquiat's art became a powerful source of political and social commentary and made him one of the most significant black artists of his generation.

Basquiat, the oldest of three children, was born on December 22, 1960, in the Park Slope suburb of Brooklyn, New York, to Haitian Gerard Basquiat, an accountant, and Puerto Rican Matilde Andrades. He demonstrated his artistic inclinations at three when he drew pictures inspired by TV cartoons. His mother, who also had artistic abilities, nurtured his talents by drawing and painting with him and taking him to art museums. When Basquiat was seven, he was hit by a car and suffered injuries that required the removal of his spleen. During his convalescence at the hospital, his mother brought him a copy of *Gray's Anatomy* so that he could look at the drawings of the human body—images that later appeared in his art.

Basquiat's parents separated when he was seven and his father retained custody. Basquiat charged that his father was a stern disciplinarian. This created anger in his son, who turned to a pattern of rebelliousness, truancy, drug use, and mischief during his adolescent years.

As a child, Basquiat attended St. Ann's, a Catholic school in Brooklyn, where the teachers remembered him for his artistic inclinations. After the fourth grade, Basquiat was transferred to P.S. 101 in Brooklyn where he impressed his teachers by drawing elaborate cartoon comics, and by his overall interests in drawing and in art. When Basquiat was 12 years old, his father accepted a job in Puerto Rico and took his family to live on the island with him. After two difficult years in Puerto Rico, his family returned to Brooklyn in 1976. Basquiat enrolled at the Edward R. Murrow High School but was unable to complete any course.

Basquiat soon ran away from home and took shelter in Washington Square Park, where he experimented with drugs like LSD and heroin—even prostituting himself so that he could eat. He shaved his head as a disguise to avoid his father and the police. After eight months on his own, Basquiat's father tracked him down and persuaded him to return home.

Because of Basquiat's difficulties conforming to traditional schools, he was enrolled in City-As-School in Brooklyn Heights in the eleventh grade. The school helped Basquiat by nurturing his artistic talent. He developed an interest in religion, philosophy, and politics. While there, he was asked to draw for the school's yearbook and collaborated on the student newspaper, where he provided artistic illustrations and wrote poetry. He was quickly recognized as someone who was somewhat odd but who had an extraordinary talent.

During his year at the school, Basquiat forged a friendship with fellow student Al Díaz. Between 1976 and 1977 they launched the SAMO Project, a systematic effort to draw graffiti, poetry, and social commentary along the D subway line. Their drawings consisted of elaborate black letters drawn in magic markers with verses revealing their disregard for the establishment and organized religion. The graffiti expressed their frustration and anger at an oppressive social and economic system.

Basquiat spent only one year at City-As-School. He ran away from home for the last time in the summer of 1978 and earned an income by painting T-shirts and postcards. Shortly thereafter he also organized a band named Gray, in which he played the synthesizer and the clarinet.

Although Basquiat broke his artistic partnership with Díaz in 1979 because Díaz was concerned with Basquiat's use of drugs, he continued painting along the subway lines. SAMO's identity was kept from the public, but Basquiat started to draw his graffiti close to art galleries and public places where established artists could see it. The press then started to write about the artist, and in 1980 he and Díaz revealed SAMO's true identity in an interview with the *Village Voice*.

Basquiat used this exposure to change from graffiti art to mainstream painting, where he could develop his artistic concerns in a more formal way. He forged a friendship with Henry Geldzahler, curator of contemporary twentieth-century art for the Metropolitan Museum of Art. Geldzahler was influential in connecting him with artists, art dealers, and patrons who helped him develop his talent.

In 1980 Basquiat participated in the "Times Square Show," a group exhibition where he sold his first painting for $100.00. During 1981 he participated in several group exhibitions in New York and was asked to do his first solo exhibit at Galleria d'Arte Emilio Mazzoli in Modena, Italy, where his art was critically acclaimed. In 1982 he had his first individual exhibit at the Annina Mosei Gallery in New York. Mosei became an early mentor for the artist, was his first art dealer, and provided Basquiat with studio space in the basement of his gallery. This was a period of prolific production when Basquiat's art commanded high prices and when he worked and exhibited regularly.

Basquiat rejected the African and Haitian influences that were often attributed to his work. He claimed that his art was really influenced by his exposure to New York City's environment. His art was uniquely urban and incorporated many elements of city life. In the money-hungry society of the 1980s, he satirized the rich with a profound anger and with sardonic words and texts that were integrated into his canvases. Critics have said that the issue of racism in America was a defining theme in Basquiat's work. The artist often complained that despite his success and popularity he had incredible difficulty finding a taxi in New York.

In 1982, Basquiat met famous American pop artist Andy Warhol and started a long and fruitful collaboration with him. Both artists shared a passion for elements of popular culture. They developed several joint exhibits that expanded Basquiat's artistic horizons. In 1983 Basquiat became one of the youngest artists ever asked to participate at the Biennial Exhibition at the Whitney Museum of American Art. His association with Bruno Bischofberger, Warhol's dealer, led to a series of art exhibits in Europe and Japan that brought him more attention. The demand for Basquiat's art grew so large that some art dealers sold his unfinished work.

The growth in his popularity and fame created pressures that led him to increase his drug use. He became paranoid about the people around him. His drug use eventually affected his artistic production, and while he retained his popularity as an artist, his work started to get mixed reviews. He continued painting but was devastated when Warhol suddenly died in 1987.

Basquiat died of a drug overdose on August 12, 1988. Painter and film director Julian Schnabel made a film about his life in 2000. One art critic has said that "Jean-Michael Basquiat is the only black American painter to have made a substantial mark on the history of art" (Marenzi 1999, 41).—S.M.M.

References and Suggested Readings

Clemente, Francesco. "For Jean-Michel." In Museo Revoltella, *Jean-Michel Basquiat: Catalogue to an Art Exhibit*. Milano, Italy: Edizioni Charta, 1999. 50.

Geldzahler, Henry. "Interview." In Museo Revoltella, *Jean-Michel Basquiat: Catalogue to an Art Exhibit*. Milano, Italy: Edizioni Charta, 1999. 57–59.

Hays, Constance. "Jean Basquiat, 27, An Artist of Words and Singular Images." *The New York Times*, August 15, 1988, D11.

Hoban, Phoebe. *Basquiat: A Quick Killing in Art*. New York: Viking, 1999.

Marenzi, Luca. "Pay for Soup/Build a Fort/Set That on Fire." In Museo Revoltella, *Jean-Michel Basquiat: Catalogue to an Art Exhibit*. Milano, Italy: Edizioni Charta, 1999. 41–43.

Wilson, William. "The Meaning of Jean Michel Basquiat's Life." *The Los Angeles Times*, September 4, 1988, 5, 79.

HARRY BELAFONTE
(1927–)

Jamaican American Singer, Actor, Producer, and Civil and Human Rights Activist

Harry Belafonte has become one of the most widely recognized and respected personalities in the American entertainment industry. A man with great talent and charm, Belafonte has succeeded in every area of the entertainment industry he has attempted. He was one of the first Caribbean American men to win a Tony on Broadway, and his 1956 album *Calypso* was the first pop recording by a single Caribbean artist to sell more than a million records. His early participation in American films constituted one of Hollywood's first attempts to explore issues of race and become more inclusive. His production company broke ground both in television and film. More important, he has consistently lent his voice as a powerful advocate for civil and human rights in the United States and around the world.

Belafonte was born in Harlem, New York, on March 1, 1927, the older of the two sons of Harold and Melvine Belafonte. His father worked from time to time as a chef with the merchant marine. His mother worked as a housekeeper for wealthy people. Belafonte was raised in Harlem, where he acknowledges that he was influenced by the vibrant and lively cultural presence that existed in the African American community during the Harlem Renaissance. During his early years, his mother was forced to leave him under the care of relatives so that she could work to support the family. Some of these relatives had a shady past and were involved in the profitable underground business of numbers running. His mother grew concerned about the environment that surrounded him in Harlem and sent young Harry to Jamaica to be taken care of by other relatives.

Belafonte lived in Jamaica from the age of 5 until he was 12. These years strongly influenced his artistic career and his political orientations, as he witnessed the social and economic malaise created by British colonial exploitation. Many of his poor relatives worked long hours in the sugarcane and banana plantations under terrible conditions for meager wages. Most of the British owners, who lived outside of Jamaica, were not concerned with the working conditions of their employees. While witnessing the poverty and exploitation of Jamaica was a source of pain for Belafonte and helped to develop his social conscience, these experiences were also a source of artistic inspiration. The tunes sung by the Jamaican workers and their working conditions inspired many of his songs, such as "Day-O (The Banana Boat Song)."

In 1939 Belafonte returned to Harlem but found his family's living conditions intolerable. His father was an alcoholic who abused his mother. She, on the other hand, worked relentlessly to support the family. To escape his family, he left home without finishing high school and joined the navy in 1944 at age 17.

After his stint in the navy, he worked such odd jobs as assistant janitor and carpenter. In an interview with *American Visions*, he told interviewer Sharon Fitzgerald about the path that led to his entrance into show business. One day, after doing a favor for actress Clarice Taylor, one of the tenants in his building, she gave him tickets to watch a theatrical production of the American Negro Theater. He found the play to be an almost mystical experience. The silence of the audience and the power of the actors left him spellbound. After the performance, he went backstage to thank Ms. Taylor but found himself helping the crew to dismantle the props. Although he forgot to thank her, he found himself a job as a carpenter. However, he realized that if he wanted to work in theater, he needed to gain some training. He used his G.I. benefits to enroll in the newly formed

Dramatic Workshop at the New School of Social Research in New York (Fitzgerald 1996).

At the New School, Belafonte found himself surrounded by the likes of Marlon Brando, Tony Curtis, Walter Matthau, Bea Arthur, Tony Franciosa, and Rod Steiger (Silverman and Arias 1996). His classmates, as well as the bystanders, were impressed by his voice and encouraged him to sing. He sang as an intermission singer in jazz clubs such as the Royal Roost; his repertoire at the time was comprised of many of the West Indian folk songs that he had learned as a child growing up in Jamaica. Eventually he caught the eye of a nightclub owner who hired him and booked him on many national tours.

During the 1950s Belafonte's career skyrocketed and he established an artistic presence on Broadway, in television, and on film. In 1953, for instance, Belafonte debuted in John Murray Anderson's *Almanac* on Broadway and won a Tony Award for his performance. He also worked for the American Negro Theater. His successes on Broadway led to Hollywood's recognition of his talent. He started to work on film and appeared in the movies *Bright Road* (1953), *Carmen Jones* (1954), and *Island in the Sun* (1957). While his acting was first-rate, there was a great deal of controversy over using a black actor and the interracial theme of many of these films.

Belafonte continued his singing career simultaneously with his work on Broadway and in Hollywood. In 1955 he signed a recording contract with RCA Victor that led to the release of the album *Calypso* (1956), a compilation of Jamaican folk songs. This album became the first pop album by a single artist to sell more than one million copies.

The racial politics of Hollywood caused Belafonte to become disillusioned with the film industry. He perceived filmmakers as unwilling to address socially relevant themes and to hire African American actors. In 1959 he created Harbel, a production company, which initially focused on television production. One of Harbel's first works, a television show about the artist titled *Tonight with Harry Belafonte* won an Emmy that same year. Eventually the company won many other Emmy nominations for their productions. They also partnered with United Artists and worked on the films *The Flesh and the Devil* (1959), *Odds against Tomorrow* (1959), and *The Angel Levine* (1970). Although he has continued his association with Hollywood, he has nevertheless been highly critical of the film industry. He sees Hollywood as a powerful industry that basically maintains the status quo by not advocating social change through providing diverse views of race and social relations. He believes that Hollywood has blocked independent producers from providing alternative texts and views.

During the 1960s, Belafonte's career took a dramatic turn when President John F. Kennedy appointed him as a cultural adviser to the U.S. Peace Corps. At about the same time, he met Martin Luther King Jr. and became an avid supporter of the civil rights movement. He used his visibility and his contacts in Hollywood to gain support for the movement, and coordinated and organized Hollywood's support of the March to Washington in 1963.

Although Belafonte stayed active in the recording industry, television, and film during the 1960s, 1970s, and 1980s, it is his role as a social and human rights activist that has dominated most of his work. During the 1980s he was a vocal opponent of the apartheid regime in South Africa. One of his most important accomplishments was his production of the 1985 song "We are the World." The recording generated millions of dollars that were used to assist children affected by the devastating famine in Ethiopia. Belafonte was appointed as a goodwill ambassador to the United Nations Children's Fund (UNICEF) in 1987, which brought the plight of the poor and sick children of developing nations to the forefront of the public mind. In 1990 he served as the host of the World Summit for Children held at the United Nations in New York.

Belafonte has said that he learned the values of social justice from his mother, who shared with him the abuses that she endured from her rich employers, who took advantage of her because she was poor and black. As a result of that early social consciousness, he has used his fame and fortune to underscore the needs of poor and oppressed people throughout his professional career (Fitzgerald 1996).

Belafonte underwent surgery for prostate cancer in 1995. He recovered and has since become a spokesperson in the African American community to raise awareness about this disease. He has continued to work in television and film. In recent years, he has appeared in *White Man's Burden* (1995) and Robert Altman's *Kansas City* (1996). In 2001 he released *The Long Road to Freedom*, an anthology of African American music. The following year he released the epic album *Island in the Sun* (2002), a five-CD compilation that included most of earliest hits, which featured a whole array of music from the Caribbean.

In 2001 Belafonte released a collection of black music titled *The Long Road to Freedom: Anthology of Black Music in 2001*. He used an ethnographic approach to collect authentic music indigenous to American blacks. The collection was very well received. In fall 2002 Belafonte found himself in the middle of a national controversy. While being interviewed in a radio program, he made a statement suggesting that U.S. Secretary of State Colin Powell was the equivalent to a "house slave"—slaves that owners kept in the house because they behaved like white people and did as the owners asked. Powell declared publicly his disappointment with Belafonte and his remarks. While Belafonte minimized the importance of the controversy, he never apologized for the remark. He still criticizes Powell and the Bush administration for what he perceives as oppressive social, political, and racial politics.

Belafonte has received countless recognitions and awards, such as a Tony Award (1956), the Albert Einstein Award from Yeshiva University (1981), Kennedy Center Honor for Excellence in the Performing Arts (1989), the Nelson Mandela Courage Award (1994), and UNICEF's Danny Kaye Award (1997). In 1996, the University of the West Indies awarded him an honorary doctorate for his humanitarian endeavors. He has received honorary degrees from many other American universities, such as Morehouse College in Atlanta, Park University in Missouri, and the new School of Social Research in New York.—S.M.M.

References and Suggested Readings

Fitzgerald, Sharon. "Belafonte: The Lionhearted." *American Visions* (August/September 1996): 12–18.

Leland, John. "The Way We Live Now: 8–26–01: Questions for Harry Belafonte; Sing Out Strong." *New York Times*, August 16, 2001, 17.

Mitchell, Gail. "Belafonte Revives Black Music Anthology Set on Buddha." *Billboard*, April 14, 2001, n.p.

Silverman, Stephen, and Ron Arias. "Day-O Reckoning." *People Magazine*, August 26, 1996, 61–63.

MINERVA BERNARDINO
(1907–1998)

Dominican Feminist, Diplomat, and Signer of the U.N. Charter

Dominican native Minerva Bernardino was one of only four women to sign the U.N. Charter in 1945, and most of her life's work took place within that body. In 1948 she was also one of the signers of the U.N.'s Universal Declaration of Human Rights, one of the most influential and impressive documents of our times. The 30 articles of the Universal Declaration of Human Rights delineated the inalienable rights of all human beings and set the direction for all further work in the area. A leading figure behind the founding of the U.N.'s Commission on the Status of Women and a pioneer among Latin American feminists, she questioned the proposed terminology "free men" of the Universal Declaration of Human Rights and was responsible for changing the wording to "free human beings."

Born on May 7, 1907, in the town of El Seibo in the Dominican Republic, Bernardino was one of seven children. She grew up in a home that believed strongly in women's rights, and her parents encouraged her to be independent: "My mother was very progressive and I was reared in an atmosphere that was most unusual in my country" (Crossette 1998, A20).

Her parent's liberal views on women's self-sufficiency were well engrained when she was orphaned at the age of 15. By then she was studying for a bachelor's degree in science and had decided to seek a career in government. By 1929 she was a leader of Acción Feminista Dominicana (Dominican Feminist League), whose efforts led to the broadening of rights and a more inclusive 1942 Dominican constitution.

On June 26, 1945, at the U.N. Conference on International Organization in San Francisco, the delegates of 50 governments adopted and signed the U.N. Charter, a document that established and set forth the aims of the United Nations.

By then Bernardino worked for the Dominican government, and as its representative in San Francisco, was one of four women to sign the U.N. Charter. At the time, she was vice chairman (and later chairman) of the Inter-American Commission on Women, the first regional body set up to advance the rights of women. In 1946, Bernardino joined Eleanor Roosevelt and the two other women delegates to the first U.N. Assembly, and together they wrote an "Open Letter to the Women of the World," urging women to become active participants in politics and government.

At the end of World War II, as a result of the atrocities committed by the Nazis and the extensive number of political prisoners and exiles worldwide, the issue of human rights was a major international issue. Bernardino was unswerving in her vision for human rights, and due to this dedication the 1948 Universal Declaration of Human Rights included the phrase "to ensure the respect for human rights and fundamental freedoms without discrimination against race, sex, condition or creed." Throughout her life she shared with other women the account of the three-month struggle it took for her and the only other three women to convince the mostly male delegation to include the term "sex" in the document.

In 1950 Bernardino became the U.N. representative from the Dominican Republic. She fought for the formation of the Commission on the Status of Women and was elected its chairperson from 1953 to 1955. Under her leadership, one of the commission's first accomplishments was to formalize women's political rights. The outcome of this would pay off 20 years later, under the U.N.'s Decade for Women (1975–1985). Bernardino also played an active role in the United Nations Children's Fund (UNICEF) and was the first woman vice president of the U.N. Economic and Social Council.

The political dictator of the Dominican Republic, Rafael Leonidas Trujillo, clashed with her strong beliefs in freedom and human rights. To demonstrate her opposition, she lived in the United States in a self-imposed exile during his regime. She has been honored and recognized as an advocate for women and children's rights. In 1995 she received the Hispanic Heritage Award for excellence in education. On the 50th anniversary of the U.N. Commission on the Status of Women, Secretary General Kofi Annan paid tribute to her contributions to the commission and characterized its existence as "to an important extent her creation" (Crosette 1998, A20). She died on August 29, 1998, at the age of 91 in her native Dominican Republic.—G.C.

References and Suggested Readings

Crossette, Barbara. "Minerva Bernardino, 91, Dominican Feminist." *New York Times,* September 4, 1998, A20.

Inter-American Commission of Women: A Summary of the Activities of the Inter-American Commission of Women, 1928–1947, Minerva Bernardino, Chairman, Amalia de Castillo, Vice Chairman. Washington, DC: Pan American Union, 1947. Minerva Bernardino Foundation: *http:/ www.mbernardinofoundation.org*.

RAMÓN EMETERIO BETANCES
(1827–1898)

Puerto Rican Patriot, Political Leader, and Writer

Ramón Emeterio Betances was Puerto Rico's first revolutionary leader and is credited with the 1873 abolition of slavery on the island. As a political leader and writer he dedicated his life to the cause of freedom and democracy not only in Puerto Rico but throughout the Antilles. In 1868 he organized an armed pro-independence insurrection against the Spanish colonists in Lares, Puerto Rico. For his involvement in the liberation struggles of Puerto Rico, Cuba, the Dominican Republic and Haiti he was known as "The Antillean," a pseudonym he used in some of his writings.

Ramón Emeterio Betances y Alacán was born into a wealthy family of landowners in Cabo Rojo, Puerto Rico, on April 8, 1827, the youngest of six children of María del Carmen Alacán and Felipe Betances Ponce. Even though they were financially well off, they were considered mulattos in a slave-owning society under Spain's rule. Defeating this system of racial inequity, particularly slavery, became young Betances' life mission, and the main avenue toward his goal was Puerto Rican independence.

Betances grew up on the 200-acre Hacienda Carmen, his parents' sugarcane plantation, which included a small number of slaves. In 1837, when Betances was only ten years old, his mother died and he was sent to the Real College in Toulouse, France, where he competed his secondary education and where he obtained a Bachelor of Science degree in 1848. In addition to receiving an academic education, he experienced life as a man of color in France without slavery.

After a brief visit to Puerto Rico in 1848 he returned to France to pursue medical studies. While in France he began his political work through meetings with Caribbean compatriots. In addition, he published political and literary writings in Spanish, French and English. His translation of Wendell Phillips' essay commemorating **Toussaint L'Ouverture**, *Los dos indios* (The Two Indians), was published in 1852, and the socio-historical treatise *Las cortesanas en París* (The Courtesans of Paris) in 1853. In 1855 he completed his medical degree and returned to Puerto Rico.

On his return to Puerto Rico he settled in the western city of Mayagüez, where he established the San Antonio Hospital, which was open to all but particularly to the poor and blacks who were disproportionately affected by the cholera epidemic that had broken out in that area. Equally important to Betances was his commitment to autonomy for the island; along with other supporters he founded a secret society committed to liberating slaves and fomenting violent revolution against the colonists. In 1867, the Spanish government charged him and his accomplices of sedition and they were exiled. He spent time in New York City, the Dominican Republic, and Paris practicing medicine and meeting with other Puerto Rican and Caribbean political leaders in search of a plan that would free the islands from colonial domination.

During that time he also worked with other revolutionaries in planning an armed pro-independence insurrection that was to take place in the town of Lares, Puerto Rico. From New York City and through his clandestine group "Society for the Independence of Cuba and Puerto Rico" Betances organized cells throughout Puerto Rico that would be involved in the revolt. On September 23, 1868, hundreds of insurgents invaded the city of Lares on foot and horseback, and African slaves staged an uprising that weakened the Spanish military garrison. They raised the flag of the newly proclaimed Republic of Puerto Rico, but the insurrection was short-lived and was brought to an

Ramón Emeterio Betances.
Courtesy of Raúl Medina Collection.

end by a very bloody suppression from the Spanish military, which had discovered the plot beforehand. Even though the uprising failed, one of Betances' goals was eventually achieved in 1873 when the Spanish abolished slavery in Puerto Rico. The period between 1858 and 1869 was one of great political activity for Betances and resulted in his exile from Puerto Rico on three occasions.

Betances continued the struggle for Puerto Rican and Cuban autonomy by publishing numerous articles for newspapers and organizing meetings with other revolutionaries. By 1871 he had returned to Paris where he continued correspondence with Cuban patriot **José Martí**, who had solicited his help in Cuba's struggle for independence. During that time he served as a delegate to the Revolutionary Cuban Party, where he engaged in various diplomatic efforts with other European countries trying to establish solidarity for the Cuban independence movement. Throughout this period he continued his medical practice and research. In 1887 the French government, in recognition of his leadership, honored him with the prestigious Legion of Honor award, the first Puerto Rican to hold this distinction.

Betances spent the last years of his life actively engaged in political work in Paris. Between 1895 and 1898 his apartment on Chateaudun Street in Paris was a principal meeting place for many visiting Caribbean intellectuals and journalists who sought information about the independence movements of Cuba, Puerto Rico, Haiti, and other Caribbean islands. Betances was known for using the foreign press as a vehicle to promote the cause of independence. His revolutionary activism continued until September 16, 1898, when he died in Neuilly. In 1920, his remains were returned to Puerto Rico and buried in his native town of Cabo Rojo, where they are now interred at the Plaza Ramón Emeterio Betances. His legacy of activism and political righteousness is kept alive by many contemporary followers. Political activists dedicated to the issue of Puerto Rican independence and advocating the end of the U.S. Navy's use of Vieques Island to conduct military practices publish their writings in a popular electronic site named after him known as the Red Betances (Betances Network).—G.C.

References and Suggested Readings

Estrade, Paul, and Félix Ojeda Reyes. *Ramón Emeterio Betances: el anciano maravilloso.* Río Piedras, PR: Instituto de Estudios del Caribe-Comité del Centenario de 1898, Universidad de Puerto Rico, 1995.

Fernández, Ronald, Serafín Méndez-Méndez, and Gail Cueto. "Ramón Emetrio Betances." *Puerto Rico Past and Present: An Encyclopedia.* Westport, CT: Greenwood Press, 1998. 46–47.

Godínez Sosa, Emilio. *Cuba en Betances.* Havana, Cuba: Editorial de Ciencias Sociales, 1985.

Hernández Aquino, Luis. *Betances poeta.* Bayamón, PR: Ediciones Sarobei, 1986.

Ojeda Reyes, Félix. *El Desterrado de París: Biografía del Doctor Ramón Emeterio Betances (1827–1898).* San Juan, PR: Ediciones Puerto, 2001.

———. *Peregrinos de la libertad.* Río Piedras, PR: Editorial Universidad de Puerto Rico, 1994.

Red Betances: Información sobre Puerto Rico y sus luchas (Information on Puerto Rico and Its Struggles). *www.redbetances.com.*

MAURICE BISHOP
(1944–1983)

Attorney and Former Prime Minister of Grenada

On the morning of March 13, 1979, Maurice Bishop, a young attorney and member of the Grenadine parliament, took control of the airwaves and informed the people of Grenada that the People's Revolutionary Army had overthrown the government of Prime Minister Eric Gairy. The emotional speech, titled "A Bright New Dawn," marked the beginning of one of the most intense and tumultuous periods faced by Grenada since its independence from Great Britain in 1974. These events culminated with the assassination of Maurice Bishop in 1983 at the hands of members of his own political party and with the U.S. invasion of Grenada on October 25, 1983.

Maurice Rupert Bishop was born on May 29, 1944, on the Caribbean island of Aruba, the youngest of three children of Rupert Bishop and Alimenta Le Grenade. His parents had relocated from Grenada to Aruba during his childhood. In 1950, the family returned to Grenada and his father launched a series of successful businesses that provided a comfortable upper-middle-class life.

As a child, Bishop attended local private schools on the island and enrolled at Preservation College, an elite Catholic secondary school where Bishop was a good student. At 19, Bishop left Grenada and went to London where he studied law at Gray's Inn and was accepted into the legal profession in 1969.

Like many other Caribbean leaders who studied in London, Bishop became involved with the West Indian Student Union and the Standing Conference of West Indian Organizations, both of which advocated the independence of British colonies in the Caribbean and were a source of political activism for West Indian students living in England during the 1950s and 1960s. Bishop was also influenced by the civil rights struggles taking place in the United States, the emergence of the radical Black Power movement, and the works of Karl Marx, **Frantz Fanon**, Che Guevara, Malcolm X and **Fidel Castro** (Heine 1991; Hintzen and Will 1988; Lewis 1991). He joined the Campaign Against Racial Discrimination during his London years.

When Bishop returned to Grenada in 1970 he had become a thoughtful individual with established political views about social justice and ways to improve his native land. He developed a successful law practice on the island and became interested in its politics. Like many other Grenadians, he was concerned with the dysfunctional and repressive government of Sir Eric Matthew Gairy. Gairy and his Grenada United Labor Party (GULP) had dominated Grenada's politics for almost three decades. Gairy had become the island's first premier after the island was declared an associate state by Great Britain in 1967.

Bishop became involved in the founding of several groups interested in the political and social realities of Grenada. These groups worked to develop better living conditions for the people of Grenada. One of these groups was the Movement for Assemblies of the People (MAP), which tried to empower poor people in their fight for social justice. By 1973, MAP had evolved into the New JEWEL (Joint Endeavor for Welfare Education and Liberation) Movement (NJM). This movement was organized very much like a formal political party and challenged Gairy's policies.

By the end of 1973, when Great Britain was considering granting Grenada independence, Bishop became a vocal leader who favored holding elections for the position of prime minister. Instead, Gairy, who wished to become prime minister without free elections, launched a powerful campaign to silence the opposition and allowed a group of supporters to launch a militia known as the Mongoose Gang to intimidate and kill his detractors. After holding a highly successful rally to protest the lack of free elections in November 1973, opposition leaders including Rupert Bishop, Bishop's father, were killed by the Mongoose Gang. Bishop was jailed, and when Grenada received its independence on February 7, 1974, Gairy became the prime minister.

By 1976 Bishop was out of jail and had grown extremely disenchanted with the state of affairs in Grenada. He saw no choice but to build a coalition between the

Grenada National Party and his NJM. Although his party did not win control of the government, Bishop became the opposition leader in the Grenadian parliament. Bishop was also appointed minister for information and culture and minister for foreign and home affairs by his party's leadership. His new positions gave him a sense of frustration about the political system in the island; the party in power was corrupt and they had not fostered the level of social change that Grenada needed and that he expected. He grew disenchanted with the political system and realized that it was going to be impossible to make any meaningful changes from within the system. As a result, he broke off the alliance with the National Party and started a more aggressive and militant approach within the NJM, which led to the creation of a People's Army. On March 13, 1979, when Gairy was out of the country, Bishop and 43 other members seized power in a fairly quiet military coup that gave him firm control of the government and had substantial support from the people.

The nature of Bishop's regime as prime minister of Grenada has been the object of many distortions and misrepresentations. The People's Revolutionary Government, which Bishop set up after the revolution, was organized along a socialist ideology. While Bishop believed that the people of Grenada would be best served by a socialist government, his political ideologies were extremely moderate and he did not engage in major redistributions of income. In fact, he built partnerships with the private sector and did not take control of their private holdings. The People's Revolutionary Government only took control of land deeds from people who owned more than 100 acres of land and were not using it for agricultural purposes. During the first months after the revolution, Bishop asked for the assistance of the U.S. government in securing funding for many of his development initiatives. After they refused to support him, Bishop felt forced to turn to socialist governments such as Cuba, the U.S.S.R., and Nicaragua.

His association with socialist countries, his refusal to hold elections, and the passing of restrictions on freedom of the press generated much criticism of Bishop's government. He defended himself by saying that such restrictions were temporary "dislocations" needed by any new revolution (Kinshasa 1984). The United States publicly criticized Grenada for its leftist government. When Bishop sought funding to build a modern international airport for the island with the assistance of Cuba, the U.S. government became concerned that the airport was going to be used by Soviet and Cuba armed transports. While the United States saw Bishop as a dangerous socialist, members of his cabinet disagreed with him because they thought that he was not radical enough. By September 1983, Bernard Coard, his deputy prime minister and a close childhood friend, and other members of the central committee of the People's Revolutionary Government disagreed with Bishop about the direction he was taking the revolution (Thomas 1983). The economy had deteriorated and his colleagues thought that Bishop had lost his ability to lead and had failed to implement a "firmer" form of Leninism (Desmond 1984). They decided that Bishop had to share power with Coard in order to make the revolution move ahead with its economic goals.

Bishop grew suspicious of his colleagues and spread a rumor that they were planning to kill him. In response to what they perceived as insubordination, his colleagues placed Bishop under house arrest on October 13. Six days later, on October 19, two members of his cabinet and two business leaders organized a crowd who went to the prime minister's home and freed him. Bishop led the crowd to Fort Rupert where they intended to gain control over the armed forces. He fired on the military but they shot and killed him and ten members of his cabinet. Coard and 14 other members of the government were accused of Bishop's assassination and sentenced to death. The sentence was later commuted to life in prison without parole.

On October 25, 1983, Ronald Reagan ordered the U.S. military to invade Grenada. He justified the invasion by saying that the United States needed to protect American medical students studying in Grenada whose well-being had been endangered by the turmoil following Bishop's assassination. The United States assisted in the dissolution of the People's Revolutionary Government and in the restoration of Gairy as prime minister. Despite considerable criticism by the international community, the United States justified the invasion by saying the Bishop government was a threat to the Caribbean.

A careful examination of Bishop's legacy in Grenada does indeed reveal a substantial collection of social and economic reforms that improved the quality of life for the people of Grenada during his brief regime. In the introduction to a collection of Bishop's speeches published after his death, Steve Clark, a scholar who has studied the Bishop administration, points to many of Bishop's achievements: the recognition of labor unions and the increase in unionized workers; the work toward establishing a new constitution; a 14 percent increase in the gross national product since the revolution; the development of a new international airport that facilitated inter-Caribbean and international trade with Grenada; major overhaul of agricultural incentives such as the creation of farm cooperatives; lending of agricultural equipment and loans to farmers; improvements in the transportation infrastructure such as the creation of new roads; the acquisition of new modes of public transportation; assistance to the island's tourism industry; the reformation of the island health care system to provide free medical and dental care to all people; free educational access to Grenadian children; the development of adult education programs that lowered the island's illiteracy rate to 2 percent; assistance with house improvements for the population; the creation of a social insurance plan to provide for the welfare of all people; and the passing of legislation to protect and empower Grenadian women such as compulsory maternity leaves for workers (Clark 1983).

Despite the controversial nature of his government, the people of Grenada still remember Bishop as a charismatic and humane leader.—S.M.M.

References and Suggested Readings

Bishop, Maurice. "A Bright New Dawn." In Chris Searle, ed., *Nobody's Backyard: Maurice Bishop's Speeches, 1979–1983*. London: Zed Books, 1984. 7–8.

Clark, Steve, ed. *Maurice Bishop Speaks: The Grenada Revolution, 1979–1983.* New York: Pathfinder Press, 1983.

Desmond, Edward W. "From Out of the Rubble." *National Review,* December 14, 1984, 35, 52–53.

Fineman, Mark. "Grenada Looks for Closure in a Gravedigger's Discovery." *Los Angeles Times,* January 14, 2000, A5.

Heine, Jorge. "The Hero and the Apparatchick: Charismatic Leadership, Political Management, and Crisis in Revolutionary Grenada." In Jorge Heine, ed., *A Revolution Aborted: The Lessons of Grenada.* Pittsburgh: The University of Pittsburgh Press, 1991, 217–255.

Hintzen, Percy C., and W. Marvin Will. "Maurice Rupert Bishop." In Robert J. Alexander, ed., *Biographical Dictionary of Latin American and Caribbean Political Leaders.* Westport, CT: Greenwood, 1988. 59–61.

Kinshasa, Kwando M. "Prime Minister Maurice Bishop: Before the Storm." *The Black Scholar* (January/February 1984): 41–59.

Lewis, James E. "Maurice Rupert Bishop." In Phil Gunson and Gregg Chamberlain, eds., *The Dictionary of Contemporary Politics of Central America and the Caribbean.* New York: Simon and Schuster, 1991. 50–51.

Lorde, Audre. "Grenada Revisited: An Interim Report." *The Black Scholar* (January/February 1984): 21–29.

Thomas, Jo. "From a Grenadian Diplomat: How Party Wrangle Led to Premier's Death." *New York Times,* October 30, 1983, 20.

EDWARD WILMOT BLYDEN
(1832–1912)

St. Thomas Minister, Scholar, Diplomat, and Politician

Edward Wilmot Blyden was one of the early proponents of the philosophy of Pan-Africanism, a social movement that instilled pride in African cultural forms and in their legacy. Leaders who proposed this ideas tried to persuade American and European blacks to go back to Africa. **Marcus Garvey** and Malcolm X were Africanists. His early scholarly and political work proposed that Egypt, not Greece or Rome, was the birthplace of Western civilization. Blyden suggested that blacks look to Africa to recover their culture and civilization and overcome the results of oppression and slavery. Blyden was a native of the Caribbean island of St. Thomas who began his life as a Christian missionary and became one of the leading Africanists of his time. The work of this educator, philosopher, and scholar provided a theoretical basis and a source of inspiration for many black activists and writers such as Garvey, **Stokeley Carmichael**, and **C.L.R. James**.

Blyden was born to Romeo Blyden, a tailor, and Judith Blyden, a schoolteacher, on August 3, 1832, in Charlotte Amalie, capital of the Caribbean island of St. Thomas. At the time, St. Thomas, like St. Croix and St. John, were Dutch colonies later sold to the United States.

There is a lack of reliable information about Blyden's early educational process. However, biographers tend to highlight the fact that Blyden lived in Venezuela between 1842 and 1844, where he learned Spanish. This marked the beginning of a lifelong passion for languages. Religious beliefs were an important part of life in the Blyden household. John P. Knox, pastor of the Dutch Reform Church, which the Blyden family attended, played a key role in Blyden's early education. He recognized Blyden's motivation and intellect, mentored him, and influenced his decision to serve God through a career as an evangelist.

Blyden traveled to New York in 1950 to try to gain admission to a theological seminary. Since seminars were segregated institutions, Blyden was unable to secure admission or a scholarship. He learned instead that there were some opportunities for study in Liberia, an African country founded by Americans in 1822 with the settlement of 5,000 American blacks. It was one of only two independent black countries in Africa. After Liberia obtained its independence in 1847, American missionary societies began to work closely with the government to establish educational institutions. The American Colonization Society, a group affiliated with the Presbyterian Church, had one of the largest evangelization initiatives in Liberia.

Blyden was persuaded to travel to Liberia where he could study at Alexander High School and help in the evangelization process.

Blyden went to Liberia in 1851. He liked the country and immediately developed an active professional and religious life. He became a protégé of the Rev. D.A. Wilson, the school principal, and became exposed to a wealth of newly found knowledge and information about classic Western works and African history and culture. Blyden graduated in 1853 and became a non-ordained minister. His educational progress was great and he worked at the school part-time tutoring and helping with administration. By 1855, Blyden was editor of the newspaper *Liberia Journal*. He believed that newspapers were one of the most important vehicles for spreading the African plea for development. When Rev. Wilson left his position in 1858, Blyden was appointed to replace him and was ordained as a Presbyterian minister that same year.

Although Blyden had only a high school education, he devoted his spare time to learning and in a relatively short period of time became a self-taught scholar who studied African history, religion, and culture, eventually developing significant expertise in these areas. Biographer Hollis R. Lynch noted that Blyden spoke all romance languages fluently, as well as Hebrew and Arabic. He had a solid grasp of mathematic and the sciences as well as the classics (Lynch 1971).

Blyden's erudition led him to take a leadership role in the organization of Liberia College. The institution was the first English-speaking non-religious university in Africa. Blyden started a long association with the college and taught classics there between 1862 and 1871. He was appointed to the presidency of the college in 1880. Because of his expertise in the area of higher education, Blyden also helped to establish the Lagos Training College in Nigeria.

As Blyden's intellectual pursuits progressed, he came to believe that the constituent elements of Western civilization had started in Egypt and Africa. He identified many more commonalities between Egyptian and African cultures than between Egyptian culture and Western ones. He marveled at the sophistication and richness of Africa and its people and thought that classical scholars and anthropologists had overlooked and ignored them. He realized that the ideas evangelists and missionaries brought to Africa from the West were misguided and that it was more important to bring Africa to the West than the West to Africa. He argued that the Muslim religion was the only uniquely African religion. For him, Islam had more relevance and utility than the Christian religions that were promulgated in Africa. The evolution in his thinking led him to abandon his religious work and resign his Presbyterian ordination. He was very sympathetic to Muslims and eventually gained enough fluency in the Arabic language to begin teaching it to his college students.

Blyden traveled frequently to North America and Europe to raise money for Liberia and to speak about his religious and political philosophies. During many of these visits, Blyden called on American blacks to look to Africa in search of their roots. He condemned slavery and believed that if American slaves and blacks were to develop and gain independence, they needed to learn their history and create institutions similar to those institutions that existed during the early days of African civilization. He believed that racial equality needed to be preceded by social, political, and economic equality. Blyden thought that it was going to be easier for blacks to develop these institutions in Africa. He also thought that if blacks throughout the world were to reach equality, they needed to have their own businesses and representation in government. His provocative arguments provided the philosophical underpinnings for people like Marcus Garvey, who in the beginning of 20th century asked blacks to become self-reliant and to resettle in Africa. These beliefs came to be the essential assumptions of the movement known as Pan-Africanism.

Blyden's educational and philosophical work gave him a great deal of credibility and respectability in Liberia and in other African countries. He was appointed Liberian educational commissioner in 1861, a position that he held simultaneously with his teaching and administrative responsibilities at Liberia College.

Blyden also served Liberia in many other positions. He became Liberia's secretary of state in 1864 and served in the position for two years. He acted as a mediator of the conflicts between Liberia and Sierra Leone, believing that the two countries needed to work together for the benefit of the black race. Between 1880 and 1882 he was the minister of the interior. Blyden also became one of Liberia's first diplomats. He represented Liberia in missions to the United States, France, Great Britain, and Nigeria. He was appointed ambassador to Great Britain on three separate occasions, and in 1885 ran unsuccessfully for the presidency of Liberia.

After losing the presidential bid, Blyden became unwelcome in Liberia. He had developed antagonism with some of Liberian leaders who by virtue of having a lighter skin tone could not relate to the combativeness of Blyden's ideas and his interest in seceding from Western societies and cultures. Blyden moved to Sierra Leone in 1885, where his expertise in Islam allowed him to become a director of Muslim education. He gained the respect and admiration of the people of Sierra Leone who treated him as an erudite scholar and as an elder statesman. Although he returned to Liberia in 1900 and took over the directorship of Alexander High School, he had to leave again when his teachings favoring polygamy created problems.

Blyden returned to Sierra Leone, where he died on February 12, 1912. The people of Sierra Leone gave him a hero's funeral. His philosophical postulates are still seen as some of the foundations of the black power movement that emerged during the 1970s. Blyden's thoughts were presented in the books *A Voice from Bleeding Africa* (1856), *A Vindication of the African Race* (1857), and *Christianity, Islam, and the Negro Race* (1887). These books are thought to contain the early ideas defining Pan-Africanism and are considered classics in the field.—S.M.M.

References and Suggested Readings

Carney Smith, Jessie, and Joseph M. Palmisano, eds., "Edward Wilmot Blyden." In *The African American Almanac*. Detroit, MI: Gale Group, 2000. 384–385.

Livingston, Thomas W. *Education and Race: A Biography of Edward Wilmot Blyden*. San Francisco: Glendessary Press, 1975.

Logan, Rayford W., and Michael R. Winston, eds. "Edward Wilmot Blyden." In *Dictionary of American Negro Biography*. New York: W.W. Norton and Company, 1982. 49–50.

Lynch, Hollis, R., ed. *Black Spokesman: Selected Published Writings of Edward Wilmot Blyden*. New York: Humanities Press, 1971.

———. *Selected Letters of Edward Wilmot Blyden*. Millwood, NY: KTO Press, 1978.

Welch, Kimberly. "Edward Wilmot Blyden." In John A. Garraty and Mark C. Carnes, eds., *American National Biography*. New York: Oxford University Press, 1999. 79–80.

JUAN BOSCH
(1909–1996)

Dominican Writer and Politician

Juan Bosch was a defining figure in the literary and political scenes of the Dominican Republic throughout most of the twentieth century. As a writer, he was considered to be one of the most important short story writers and novelists of his island. As a politician, Bosch led a lifelong struggle to free his country and his people from dictatorships and tyrannical governments in a number of roles: as a political dissident, as a refugee, as president of the Dominican Republic, and as an opposition figure. Although his political life tended to overshadow his literary career, it is his great literary legacy that has immortalized Bosch's contribution to his country, to the Caribbean, and to Latin America as a whole.

Bosch was born on June 30, 1909, in the small town of La Vega, which is part of the Northern Cibao region of the Dominican Republic. His father, José Bosch, was a Catalonian immigrant who went to the Dominican Republic to work as a master mason. His mother, Angela Gaviño, was born in Puerto Rico but emigrated to La Vega with her family at an early age. A child with an inquisitive mind, Bosch later identified his music teacher as the most important early intellectual influence (Fernández Olmos 1994). He was a precocious child who wrote at a young age. His biographers have said that he delivered a speech at the grave of a town teacher before he was 9 years old; he himself acknowledged producing his first newspaper with a friend when he was 14.

He moved to the capital of Santo Domingo at the age of 15 and worked in a series of sales jobs. By 1925, the mostly self-taught intellectual was actively writing and publishing poetry under the pseudonym Rigoberto de Fresni. In 1929, his family sent him to Barcelona, Spain, where he worked as a salesperson and founded an artistic variety group that he took to Venezuela. After his group failed to attract audiences in Caracas, he took a job with a traveling circus and traveled throughout the Caribbean. In 1931, he finally returned to the Dominican Republic and launched his literary career.

Throughout the 1930s, Bosch developed an active presence in Dominican literary circles. In 1929 he joined a literary group known as *La Cueva* (The Cave) and in 1933 he published his short story "La Mujer" (The Woman). The story, which has been translated into many languages and is considered one of his masterpieces, tells of a woman abused by her husband and describes the dynamics of oppression and gender roles. This story was initially published as part of an anthology of his short stories entitled *Camino Real* (Royal Trail), the first of dozens of books that he wrote during his lifetime. He also directed the literary section of *Listín Diario*, the leading newspaper of the Dominican Republic. Because he was raised in agricultural town, his literary work is filled with the images of the feudal relationships he was exposed to as a child.

His early political involvement and criticisms of the Trujillo regime led to a brief arrest and imprisonment in 1934. Facing an unwanted government appointment as part of the dictatorship of Rafael Leonidas Trujillo, Bosch decided to leave the country and seek refuge in Puerto Rico. Two years later, in 1936, he published his first novel, *La Mañosa* (The Tricky Woman), considered a classic of Dominican literature.

While in Puerto Rico, Bosch quickly found a job collecting the works of Puerto Rican patriot **Eugenio María de Hostos** for a commission that was compiling Hostos' complete works to commemorate the 100th anniversary of his birth. At the same time, Bosch's work also appeared in *Puerto Rico Ilustrado* and *Alma Latina*, two of the most important Puerto Rican publications of the time. Eventually, he became an expert on Hostos, on whom he gave many lectures. This expertise led to the 1939 publication of *Hostos, el Sembrador*, his biography of the patriot. He was also one of the early organizers of the Dominican Revolutionary Party, which challenged Trujillo's regime.

Bosch moved from Puerto Rico to Cuba during the early 1940s. While he held several jobs in Cuba, his most important activity during the period was the organizational work he did on behalf of the Dominican Revolutionary Party. He traveled throughout Latin America raising awareness about his country's political situation. Clashes with the Batista regime in Cuba, favorable to Trujillo, and his participation in an armed insurrection to bring down Trujillo eventually forced Bosch to move first to Venezuela, then Costa Rica in 1950. He spent most of the 1950s traveling through Latin America.

In 1961, after Trujillo's assassination—and after 24 years of political exile—Bosch returned to the Dominican Republic. In 1962 he became the first democratically elected president of the Dominican Republic on behalf of the Dominican Revolutionary Party. His government platform, opposed strongly by Jesuit segments of the Roman Catholic Church in Santo Domingo, proposed agrarian reforms, human rights, and civil liberties. For a nation that had been under the yoke of the Trujillo tyranny for so many decades, Bosch's government was perceived as too leftist and he was accused of being a communist (*Gran enciclopedia Dominicana* 1997). On September 25, 1963, just seven months after his inauguration, he was deposed in a military coup partially sponsored by the U.S. government.

After his ouster he was forced once again to seek political asylum in Puerto Rico. His removal threw the Dominican Republic into chaos because some factions wanted Bosch to be reinstated as president while other groups preferred new elections. The U.S. Army intervened to restore order and Bosch returned to the island in 1965, only to see **Joaquín Balaguer** elected as president in 1966. After Balaguer was elected, Bosch left the Dominican Republic for Europe, where he lived for many years.

Throughout the years, Bosch remained a prolific writer of short stories, poetry, biography, and novels. He worked with the themes of liberty, freedom, economic underdevelopment, exploitation, domination, and dependence. The collapse of his political career, however, forced a shift in his literary production, and he started publishing social and political expository works that occupied the remainder of his literary life. He stated that although he had fiction in his heart, these later genres were better suited to express his political ideologies (Fernández Olmos 1992). Bosch continued publishing, traveling, and lecturing throughout the world during the 1970s, 1980s, and 1990s. In 1974 he organized the Dominican Liberation Party and ran for the presidency several more times but was always defeated.

Bosch died on November 1, 2001 at the age of 92. His death was mourned by thousands of Dominicans who saw him as the ultimate advocate for freedom in the Dominican Republic. He was a major literary and political figure in the Dominican Republic for most of the twentieth century, having published more than 45 books, as well as dozens of short stories, articles, and essays. His literary work has been widely recognized throughout the Spanish-speaking world and has earned him numerous awards and recognitions. In 1975 he was given the National Prize for Novel in the Dominican Republic. In 1987, **Fidel Castro** awarded him the Martí Memorial Order Medal, the highest civil award given by Cuba.—S.M.M.

References and Suggested Readings

Fernández Olmos, Margarita. "Juan Bosch." In Angel Flores, ed., *Spanish American Authors: The Twentieth Century*. New York: H.W. Wilson, 1992. 122–123.

———. "Juan Bosch." In William Luis and Ann González eds., *Modern Latin-American Fiction Writers, Second Series*. Detroit: Gale Research, 1994. 66–72.

Gerón, Cándido. *Juan Bosch: la traición a un símbolo: matices de una conjura electoral*. Santo Domingo, DR: C. Gerón, 1999.

Gran enciclopedia Dominicana. "Juan Bosch." Santo Domingo, DR: Enciclopedia Dominicana, S.A., 1997. 273–277.

Jiménez, Felucho. *¿Cómo fue el gobierno de Juan Bosch?* Santo Domingo, DR: República Dominicana: Editora Alfa & Omega, 1998.

Lewis, Paul. "Juan Bosch, 92, Freely Elected Dominican President, Dies." *The New York Times*, November 2, 2001, D9.

Salas, Susan, ed. "Juan Bosch." *Hispanic Literature Criticism Supplement*. Detroit: Gale Group, 1999. 241–254.

DAVID BOXER
(1946–)

Jamaican Artist, Curator, and Art Historian

David Boxer is one of the most provocative Jamaican painters of our day. As a painter and assemblage artist, he has generated eclectic and controversial paintings, assemblages, and collages. His work, although clearly Jamaican and Caribbean, is heavily influenced by the work of other Western artists. As an art historian, he has played a leading role in the development of Jamaican arts from his position as the national director and curator of the National Gallery in Kingston, Jamaica.

Boxer was born in St. Andrew, Jamaica on March 17, 1946, and obtained a bachelor's degree in the history of art at Cornell University in 1969 in Ithaca, New York. From there, he went to the Johns Hopkins University in Baltimore, where he finished a master's and a doctorate in art. His doctoral dissertation studied the work of English painter Francis Bacon. The eclecticism of his art is in many ways related to his divergent career experiences. Boxer was a medical technician for the Ministry of Health in Jamaica, which helps explain his extensive use of medical illustration and medical paraphernalia in his work, and also worked as a film editor and as a producer for the Jamaica Broadcasting Corporation. He has incorporated his technical knowledge of video and television in his assemblages and collages—a new and radical art of expression for Caribbean artists. He was a director and curator at the National Gallery in Jamaica from 1975 to 1990. In 1990, he became its director curator emeritus and chief curator.

Although he received limited artistic training from American painter Fred Mitchell, Boxer is mostly a self-taught artist. His academic training is in the field of art history and not in plastic arts per se. However, his knowledge and familiarity with the forms of art that he has studied have influenced his work: "My preparation as an artist has been limited almost exclusively to the study of the history of art and a great deal of looking at art, and it is this, a quite intense involvement with the art of Europe, of Africa, and of the New World, which has been a key element in the development of my work" (Lewis 1995, 150).

Veerle Poupeye, who has collaborated with him in his scholarly and critical work, is the foremost expert on Boxer's art. According to Poupeye, Boxer has gone through several stages in his process of artistic production (Poupeye 1997, 1999). During the early- to mid-1960s his work was mostly autobiographical and soft and abstract. In the late 1960s, he started to produce politically charged paintings that explored conflict. An example of this, according to Poupeye, was his "Viet Madonna" (1967), inspired by the pain and carnage created by the use of Napalm in Vietnam. Then, during the 1970s, he made a sharp transition to neo-figurative art, which included the strong and often shocking use of violent and macabre elements within his paintings. The influence of British painter Francis Bacon, who used some of the same techniques and introduced suffering into his work, is evident in Boxer's work of this period. His paintings were motivated by many of the harsh social and political realities of the Caribbean. A recurrent trend in his paintings is the use of self-portraiture and surrealism. He blends himself into his realities and allows himself to suffer, albeit vicariously, those realities that he graphically depicts (Poupeye 1997, 1998).

Poupeye often uses the word "appropriation" to describe the work of this Jamaican artist. For instance, she identifies African and Renaissance art as major influences on his work. Boxer's compositions also show deep concerns for the social, economic, and political dynamics that permeate Jamaica and other Caribbean societies. He is genuinely concerned with issues of race, identity, oppression, genocide, cultural annihilation, colonization, imperialism, and poverty that so often affect the lives of people in that region and throughout the developing world (Poupeye 1997). An example of this is his collage "Fourth of July over Baghdad" (1981), based on what he felt was biased coverage by CNN of the Gulf War. His work is extremely symbolic, although there are always concrete signifiers that lead the viewer to his intended referent. His paintings and collages often borrow from other classic art works that the viewer may recognize.

Boxer has had a large number of individual exhibitions. His work has been shown at the Artist Studio in Kingston, the Museum of Modern Art of Latin America in Washington, D.C., and at the Just Above Midtown Gallery in New York. He has also participated in group exhibits at the Smithsonian Museum, the First Johannesburg Biennale, the First Biennial of Caribbean and Central American Painting, the Wilfredo Lam Biennale in Havana, and at the Bienal Internacional de São Paulo, among others. He has received numerous prizes awards for his work such as the Centennial Medal of the Institute of Jamaica and the Gold Musgrave

Medal from the Institute of Jamaica in 1995. In addition to being a renowned painter, he is also considered to be one of the foremost scholarly authorities in the work of Jamaican sculptor **Edna Manley**.—S.M.M.

References and Suggested Readings

Boxer, David. *Edna Manley, Sculptor*. Kingston: National Gallery of Jamaica and Edna Manley Foundation, 1990.

Boxer, David, and Veerle Poupeye. *Modern Jamaican Art:* Kingston, Jamaica: Ian Randle Publishers, 1998.

Lewis, Samella. *Caribbean Visions: Contemporary Painting and Sculpture*. Alexandria, VA: Art Services International, 1995. 50.

Poupeye, Veerle. *Caribbean Art*. New York: Thames and Hudson, 1998.

———. "David Boxer." In Thomas Riggs, ed., *St. James Press Guide to Black Artists*. Detroit: St. James Press, 1997. 67–68.

———. "David Boxer." In Jane Turner, ed., *Encyclopedia of Latin American and Caribbean Art*. New York: Grove's Dictionaries, 1999. 101–102.

ROBERT L. BRADSHAW
(1916–1978)

St. Kitts–Nevis Political Leader

Robert Llewellyn Bradshaw was considered one of the Caribbean's most skillful and forceful leaders. For about 40 years Bradshaw was a dominant political figure in St. Kitts, Nevis, and Anguilla. He found the British political control over the islands objectionable and the plantation system that promoted racism inhumane and unjust. He dedicated his life as a politician to challenging its morality and legitimacy while establishing the political foundation that would lead to independence.

Bradshaw was born in St. Paul's Village, St. Kitts, on September 16, 1916, to Mary Jane Francis and William Bradshaw. His parents were among the few in the community who did not work in the sugar industry. Mary Jane was a skilled cook who was much in demand and his father was a blacksmith who abandoned his family nine months after his son's birth. Bradshaw grew up within a close-knit family that included his grandmother, aunts, and uncles, who had high expectations for him and provided support. While still in St. Paul's Anglican primary school, he distinguished himself for his academic and leadership skills. Even though he was mostly self-taught after completing his primary education at 16, he served as a pupil teacher in St. Paul's Village before moving to the capital city of Basseterre.

Very early in his life, through his travels around St. Kitts, Bradshaw became aware of the unequal conditions in his society: every aspect of the plantation economy was controlled by whites; young black children and old people worked the sugarcane fields regardless of the conditions. These were the scenes that provided the drive Bradshaw needed for his political work. His religious principles also contradicted the social order. He understood that to change the social order, he had to understand and work with the establishment. In dress, speech, and behavior he was able to navigate between both societies. He was as a factory worker and union organizer and served as vice president of the St. Kitts Workers League from 1932 to 1940. When Bradshaw was 18, one of the most important uprisings since the 1838 abolition of slavery occurred. In January 1935, a revolt by sugar estate workers over conditions turned violent at Buckley's Estate and three workers were killed. The Buckley's Revolt, and the massacre of workers that ensued, reinforced Bradshaw's commit-

Robert L. Bradshaw.

ment to lead the struggle for the black working class. By the time he was 24 years old he had become an authority on workers' issues and through his skilled oratory was beginning to establish himself as a political leader in St. Kitts.

During this time he began college correspondence courses from England, where his performance was described as outstanding. An admirer of black nationalist **Marcus Garvey**, Bradshaw learned to value his Africanness and was guided by the fundamental principle that blacks should be equal participants in society. In 1940, after leading a week-long sugar worker strike, Bradshaw lost his position at the factory and was elected to the executive committee of the newly formed St. Kitts-Nevis Trades and Labour Union. In this role, he exhorted the masses through Labor Day marches and praised the values of education and social mobility. He was elected president of the union in 1944, continuing as vice president of the St. Kitts Workers League, which in 1945 became the St. Kitts-Nevis-Anguilla Labour Party.

That same year, Bradshaw became assistant secretary of the Caribbean Labour Congress, whose purpose was to support labor activities and trade unionism in the Caribbean. At the 1949 inaugural conference of the International Confederation of Free Trade Unions, Bradshaw became the first West Indian to serve on the confederation's executive board. By the late 1940s Bradshaw had strengthened the union movement in St. Kitts. His greatest difficulty was trying to export union activism to the islands of Nevis and Anguilla, where most people were self-employed. Throughout political career Bradshaw encountered great resistance from these islands, who thought he focused almost exclusively on the needs of his native St. Kitts, and not enough on the other two islands.

With the advent of universal suffrage in the islands in 1951 and 1952, the working class increasingly rejected the politics of the plantation economy. The victory at the polls of the Labour Party under Bradshaw led to his appointment as minister of trade and production in 1956, and the establishment of St. Kitts, Nevis, and Anguilla into one federated colony, the West Indies Federation. At the inauguration of the newly federated colony in 1958, Bradshaw was appointed minister of finance in the government of Grantley Herbert Adams. He held this post until 1962, when the federation collapsed and he was elected to the local legislative council.

In 1966 the Labour Party won the general election and Bradshaw became chief minister of the three-island colony. In the 1967 the cabinet system of government was established in the colony, and its political system was now known as Statehood in Association with Britain. Bradshaw became the first premier of St. Kitts, Nevis, and Anguilla. Except for defense and external relations, there was some degree of political autonomy for the islands. Bradshaw's ultimate goal was total independence from Britain. As premier he focused on reshaping the economy for the long-term needs that an independent country would need. To him that meant ensuring control over the sugar industry, the mainstay of the St. Kitts–Nevis economy. However, the political stability of the three islands was always uncertain, and two months after the establishment of the Associated Statehood there was a revolt in Anguilla. In 1969 Anguilla seceded from the union and achieved a higher degree of autonomy but did not totally sever its ties with Britain. A new activism and militarism emerged in the years between 1967 and 1978. Bradshaw's leadership encouraged and facilitated the movement of blacks from work on the plantations to positions of responsibility and power in the police force, schools, banks, and government. He laid the foundation for independence by actions such as the nationalization of the sugar industry, and by improving the islands' infrastructure that resulted in progressions in the quality of life for their citizens. He created the Sugar Industry Rescue Operation in 1973 and the National Agricultural Corporation in 1975, acts that took control over the sugarcane industry.

Bradshaw did not live to see the independence of St. Kitts and Nevis. The British granted the two islands independence in 1983, five years after Bradshaw's death.—G.C.

References and Suggested Readings

Alexander, Robert J. "Robert L. Bradshaw." *Biographical Dictionary of Latin American and Caribbean Political Leaders.* Westport, CT: Greenwood Press, 1988. 71–72.

———. *Political Parties of the Americas.* Vol. 2. Westport, CT: Greenwood Press, 1983.

Browne, Whitman T. *From Commoner to King.* New York: University Press of America, 1992.

Jones-Hendrickson, Simon B. "Strategies for Progress in the Post-Independence Caribbean: A Bradshawian Synthesis." Presidential address at IX Annual Meeting of Caribbean Studies Association, Basseterre, St. Kitts, May 30–June 2, 1984.

Karl Broodhagen
(1909–)

Barbadian Sculptor, Graphic Artist, and Painter

Karl Broodhagen is an important figure in Caribbean sculpture and painting. As a sculptor, Karl Broodhagen has been most successful in portraying and capturing the essence of the African character in the Caribbean.

Broodhagen was born in Georgetown, Guyana, on July 4, 1909. When he was around 15 years old, his mother, who was moving to the United States, stopped in Barbados and placed young Karl in an extended apprenticeship with a Barbadian tailor. He became a proficient tailor and when his mother died in 1933 he decided to settle in Barbados for good (Crozier 1998).

Broodhagen started experimenting with oil paintings during the 1930s. By the 1940s, he began working with clay and produced several impressive pieces, one of which was a bust of the young Barbadian novelist **George Lamming**, which he completed in 1945. In 1947, Broodhagen left his job as a tailor and was asked to start an art department at the prestigious Combermere School in Barbados. His work as both a teacher and an artist led him to participate in an exhibition at the British Council in 1948, where he was awarded a scholarship toward formal art education in Great Britain. From 1952 to 1954 Broodhagen attended Goldsmith's College in London, where he received advanced art training and education. While he was in London, he was exposed for the first time to non-Western art. Critics have asserted that this experience led to a process of rediscovery that articulated "a new ethos in his work" (Cummins 1997).

On his return to Barbados, he continued to teach and direct the art department at Combermere, with which he was associated for almost 50 years. More importantly, he undertook an even more fruitful career as an artist and as a sculptor. The interest generated by his pieces has been credited with reintroducing the field of sculpture to Barbadian arts. Among his more important works are *Neferdine* (1961), *Benin's Head* (1971), and the *Emancipatation Statue* (1985), also known as *Bussa*, after the slave who started the revolt that brought freedom to Barbadian slaves. He has also painted several significant pictures such as "The Portrait of Ann Marie Assing" (1957). His wood, clay, and terra cotta work is produced out of his home-based studio in Barbados.

There are many critics who have tried to successfully characterize and explain Broodhagen's work. Broodhagen summarizes it succinctly by saying that he is just "interested in people" (Lewis 1995). It is generally agreed that his work expresses a naturalistic view that is consistent with the artist's simple way of life. He specializes in busts and portraits. His works are a quest to find the essential character, nature, and simplicity of the African element of the Caribbean. He has tried to find the essence, or product, that has come out of centuries of oppression and subjugation. Christopher Crozier, for instance, has called for critics to rethink their analyses of Broodhagen's work to account for a political thematic and social relevance that he thinks has been missing from their earlier assessments (Crozier 1998). He even suggests that his work has more political and social depth than the work of **Edna Manley**, generally seen as the mother of Caribbean modernism in the field of sculpture. Broodhagen's work tends to be strong but at the same time understated. It has a simplicity that reveals the true character of his subjects without pretension.

Broodhagen lives simply in his adopted Barbados. He is a generous artist who has not been overly concerned with the financial potential of his sculptures, and still owns a significant number of his completed works. Broodhagen's paintings and sculptures have been exhibited in Barbados and throughout the Caribbean; most recently, his sculpture *Benin Head* traveled throughout the United States with the exhibit Caribbean Visions (1995). His work is part of the collections of the United Nations Educational, Scientific, and Cultural Organization (UNESCO) in Paris; the University Chapel at the University of the West Indies, Mona Campus; and Drexel University in Philadelphia. Throughout his career he has received many significant awards. Among them are the Queen's Jubilee Medal of Barbados (1977) and the Gold Crown of Merit (1982).—S.M.M.

References and Suggested Readings

Crozier, Christopher. "Hands of Clay." *Caribbean Beat* (Barbados) 34 (November/December 1998): 32–39.

Cummins, Alissandra. "Karl Broodhagen." In Thomas Riggs, ed., *St. James Press Guide to Black Artists*. Detroit: St. James Press, 1997. 73–74.

Lewis, Samella. *Caribbean Visions: Contemporary Painting and Sculpture*. Alexandria, VA: Art Services International, 1995.

ALEXANDER BUSTAMANTE
(1884–1977)

Jamaican Labor Leader and Politician

On August 6, 1962, Jamaica achieved its independence from Great Britain and Sir Alexander Bustamante became the first Jamaican prime minister. This event represented the ultimate political achievement for a nation and for a leader who lived through some of the most tumultuous and intense times in Jamaican history. Bustamante's ascension to power came late in his life. He started his career as a labor activist when he was 49 years old. Despite his late start, he worked hard to safeguard the well being of Jamaican workers and to assure the protection of their human rights. The people of Jamaica regard him as one of their true democrats and a national hero.

William Alexander Clarke was born on February 24, 1884, in the Jamaican city of Blenheim, one of 13 children of a poor family who worked in agriculture. His father, William Alexander Clarke, had emigrated from Ireland to Jamaica during his youth and married a Jamaican woman. When Clarke was 15 he was adopted by Arnulfo Bustamante, a visiting Spanish colonel who took him to Spain. It was not unusual for Caribbean people of the time to give their children up for adoption to someone who could provide a better future for them. Clarke thus became known as Alexander Bustamante. While in Spain, Bustamante received private tutoring and took business and language courses at the Royal Academy of Spain. After enlisting in the Spanish army and serving in Morocco, he left Spain and returned to America.

Bustamante worked in several odd jobs throughout Latin America after his time in Spain. He was a man of eclectic interests and abilities, and worked as a traffic coordinator for a trolley company in Panama and as a police inspector in Havana. By 1923, he had settled in New York, where he worked as a dietician in a hospital, a position that he held until 1932. A savvy businessman, Bustamante invested his small savings immediately following the stock market crash of 1929. As the market started to recover, his stock holdings gained value. He redeemed the profits and used them to establish a moneylending business that made him an affluent man.

Bustamante returned to Jamaica in 1932 when he was almost middle-aged. Although he was financially independent and had brought with him considerable savings, he was distressed by the social and economic conditions of his fellow Jamaicans. The island was underdeveloped and Jamaican workers suffered abuses and exploitation at the hands of rich landowners. Bustamante wrote eloquent letters criticizing labor abuses and the indifference of Her Majesty's government to newspapers in both Jamaica and Great Britain. He met with labor leaders and spoke at protest rallies.

By 1938 the political climate of Jamaica and many other Caribbean islands was defined by an uproar of labor protests. Workers had grown tired of their treatment and began generalized strikes. They protested the lack of employment and unfair labor practices and were angered by the importation of cheap foreign labor from poor African and Asian countries, which devalued them and submitted these foreigners to awful working conditions. Jamaican workers also demanded that Great Britain give them universal adult suffrage. After participating in a protest in which he called the colonial governor a "misfit," Bustamante was arrested and accused of sedition by the British colonial authorities in Jamaica. Fortunately, his cousin **Norman Washington Manley**, one of the best Jamaican attorneys, was able to obtain his release through mediation with colonial authorities.

When Bustamante was freed from jail he saw a need for the creation of a unified labor movement and of a cohesive voice to fight for it. He created the Bustamante Industrial Trade Union in 1938 and assisted Norman W. Manley in the creation of the People's National Party (PNP). The union agreed to become the labor branch of the party. The government consented to study the labor problems, and the violence subsided to some extent.

In September 1940, Bustamante was arrested for participating in a protest at Kingston's Up Park Camp. The colonial government had developed stringent wartime regulations and alleged that Bustamante's activities threatened the national security of Jamaica and the British motherland. He spent 17 months in a Jamaican prison and was finally freed in 1942, after which he broke political ties to the PNP. An ideological rift had developed between Bustamante and his cousin during his stay in jail. While Manley focused more on Jamaican nationalism and saw the labor movement as a means to gain power and independence, Bustamante was genuinely concerned with the well being of laborers, not necessarily independence from Great Britain. As a result, Bustamante created the Jamaican Labour Party (JLP) in 1943.

Great Britain granted Jamaicans universal adult suffrage in 1944. A new constitution provided for the creation of a House of Representatives and gave Jamaica more autonomy. It also provided for a general election that same year. Bustamante ran as a candidate of the JLP, opposing his cousin Manley from the PNP. While Manley advocated a substantial reorganization of the economic system in Jamaica following socialist principles, Bustamante focused on labor reforms. His political agenda was more conservative than Manley's and he wanted to maintain association with the government of Great Britain. Because Bustamante was perceived as less of a threat to their economic interest than Manley, the middle class supported him in the general elections and his party gained control of the House of Representatives. Manley was elected as a member of the executive council and was appointed minister of communication and works.

Contrary to expectations, Bustamante took a guarded approach to government. He developed some general labor reforms but did little to change the major economic, political, and social orders of Jamaica. The constitution was amended in 1949 to provide for a ministerial form of government. Bustamante ran again and was elected chief minister of Jamaica. He continued his conservative approach to government, as well as his solidarity with Britain. Manley, a savvy politician, redefined himself as a less-threatening socialist and defeated Bustamante in the general elections of 1955.

One of the defining issues of the Manley administration was his desire to have Jamaica join the West Indian Federation. Jamaica became a member of the federation in 1958. The plan, which had been sponsored by Great Britain since 1947, created a federation of West Indian islands. Bustamante had originally supported the idea, but when he saw Jamaica lose power to other Caribbean islands he criticized the Manley government and asked for Jamaica's withdrawal from the federation. He launched such a strong opposition that he forced Manley to hold a referendum on the issue in 1961. The people voted to separate, which constituted a huge political loss for Manley, who had made the federation a pillar of his political program and government.

Bustamante and Manley both petitioned Great Britain for Jamaica's independence. When Great Britain agreed, Bustamante and Manley worked together to craft the new constitution and shape the new government. They agreed to hold a new general election in the spring of 1962 to select the new government. Bustamante ran in the elections and won. He became the first prime minister of the island when it received independence in August 1962. His last term in government was characterized by a substantial transformation of Jamaica's economic infrastructure. Bustamante worked to modernize education, health, transportation, and the communication systems. In his last term he turned 80 years old. His health deteriorated and he partially withdrew from public appearances. When the 1967 elections were announced, he decided not to run and retired from government.

Bustamante received multiple honors during his political career. The queen of England knighted him in 1955. He died on August 6, 1977. Upon his death, the people of Jamaica recognized him as one of their national heroes.—S.M.M.

References and Suggested Readings

Eaton, G.E. *Alexander Bustamante and Modern Jamaica*. Kingston, Jamaica: Kingston Publishers, 1965.

Hintzen, Percy C., and W. Marvin Hill. "Norman Washington Manley." In Robert Alexander, ed., *Biographic Dictionary of Latin American and Caribbean Political Leaders*. Westport, CT: Greenwood Press, 1988. 80–82.

Morris, Charles, ed. "Alexander Bustamante." *Current Biography*. New York: The H.W. Wilson Company, 1965. 64–67.

Rogozinski, Jan. *A Brief History of the Caribbean: From the Arawak and Carib to the Present*. New York: Facts on File, 1999.

Whitehead, Lenox. *Two Great Heroes: Norman Manley and Alexander Bustamante of Jamaica*. Toronto, ON: Front Line Publications, 1985.

GUILLERMO CABRERA INFANTE
(1929–)

Cuban Writer

Cuban writer Guillermo Cabrera Infante is considered one of the most important contemporary writers. A British citizen who has been living in exile for over 30 years, Cabrera Infante's work—particularly his novels *Tres tristes tigres* (1967), *Vista del amanecer en el trópico* (1974), and *La Habana para un infante difunto* (1979)—are considered an important part of Spanish literature. Although he has lived most of his adult life outside his homeland, most of his stories take place in the Havana of his youth before and after **Fidel Castro**'s regime. Cabrera Infante is an accomplished essayist, and has also been recognized for his short stories and film scripts written in both English and Spanish. He has won major literary awards, including the most prestigious and remunerative award given in the field of Spanish literature: the Miguel de Cervantes Prize.

The older of two brothers, Guillermo Cabrera Infante was born in the northern city of Gibara on April 22, 1929. By age four, he was enrolled in Los Amigos, a private Quaker school. He was a fan of the cartoons that appeared in the Sunday paper and he used them to teach himself to read. His parents, Guillermo Cabrera López and Zoila Infante Castro, were political activists who, along with other individuals, organized the local Communist Party in Gibara in 1933. One of the most traumatic events in Cabrera Infante's childhood in Gibara was in 1936, when he witnessed local military police violently invade his home, and arrest, and subsequently incarcerate, his mother for her political activities. His father, captured later that day, was also incarcerated. After their release six months later, no one would hire Guillermo Sr., who had been a reporter; the family scraped by on Zoila Infante's income as a seamstress. By 1941, the family moved to Havana, where six of them lived in a squalid one-room tenement, sharing a bathroom with other families. Cabrera Infante described his living conditions to his biographer, Raymond Souza: "I was genuinely ashamed of living in that place" (Souza 1996, 16). Many of the descriptions of Havana in *La Habana para un infante difunto* are drawn from his experiences at this time.

From 1942 to 1946, with the encouragement and support of his father, Cabrera Infante attended night school and learned English. These early years in Havana also stirred his interest in Cuban and American popular cultural activities; he was an avid aficionado of Cuban music and American jazz.

Cabrera Infante's development as writer was a result of various experiences during the 1940s. His first serious interest in literature had its inception in 1946 with discovery of the Greek classics *The Iliad* and *the Odyssey*. That same year he received certification to teach English, and for a while he also translated articles from the American socialist press for the Cuban Communist Party's newspaper *Hoy*, whose literal translation means "today." Through his tenure with *Hoy*, Cabrera Infante met contemporary Cuban writers such as **Nicolás Guillén**. In addition, his association with journalist Carlos Franqui, who later became his close friend, exposed him to such U.S. writers as William Faulkner, Erskine Caldwell, Ernest Hemingway, and John Steinbeck. In 1947, on a dare from Franqui, Cabrera Infante wrote his first story and presented it to the editor of the magazine *Bohemia*, who to his surprise published the parody titled "Aguas del recuerdo" (Waters of Memory) and paid him what amounted to $50. This was followed by another published story and an offer from *Bohemia*'s editor, Antonio Ortega, of a job as his personal secretary. Ortega opened Spanish and world literature to Cabrera Infante and in many ways mentored his development as a writer. His work with *Bohemia* included reviewing manuscripts and writing literary notices. He also served as a proofreader for other newspapers and was one of the founding members of the periodicals *Nuestro Tiempo* (Our Time) and *Nueva Generación* (New Generation), where he published his first movie reviews. In 1949 he completed studies in cinematography and two years later established with **Tomás Guitiérrez Alea**, Germán Puíg, Ricardo Vignón, and Nestor Almendros the film library Cinemateca de Cuba (Cuban Cinemateca).

In 1950 he began to pursue a degree at Cuba's national School of Journalism. His journalism studies were cut short in 1952 after the government was overthrown by a military uprising. Cabrera Infante's short story "A Ballad of Bullets and Bull's Eyes," which contained English profanities, was published in *Bohemia* that year. This story led to his arrest and incarceration by the Castro regime, which also prohibited him from publishing under his own name. He began writing under the pseudonyms Caín, Jonás Castro, and S. del Pastora Niño.

In 1954 Cabrera Infante was appointed feature writer for films of *Carteles*, a weekly magazine similar to *Bohemia*. One of his most memorable pieces was "The Beauty of the Bomb," written under the pseudonym Jonás Castro. It included 12 dramatic pictures of atomic explosions described as "vivid images of beauty and destruction whose symmetrical or twisted forms have haunted the human imagination since they first appeared" (Souza 1996, 28). By 1954 he was writing a regular movie column under the name Caín that became renowned in Cuba and throughout the Caribbean. At the same time, Cabrera Infante had begun writing for, and later took charge of, the anti-government paper *Revolución*, which became the revolutionary movement's official organ.

By 1956 he had received his journalism degree and was considered the most important film critic in Havana. After the 1959 Cuban revolution, Cabrera Infante—a supporter of the revolution—became a member of the Castro regime's entourage and traveled abroad with the revolutionary leader, an experience that gave him intimate exposure to Castro's personality. One of his most important posts during that era was his appointment as the editor of *Lunes de Revolución*, a weekly cultural supplement to the daily paper *Revolución* that was considered among the best magazines ever published in Cuba. *Lunes* covered the arts, politics, and philosophy, and included contributions from such well-known authors as Simone de Beauvoir, Jean-Paul Sartre, Le Roi Jones, and Wright Mills. The Castro regime, finding the magazine's articles outside the party line, eventually closed down *Lunes*; Cabrera Infante's discontent with the revolution increased as his days as an editor came to close in 1961. Perhaps to keep him far away from Havana, the government appointed him cultural attaché in Cuba's Brussels Embassy in 1962. In 1964, a manuscript titled *T.T.T.*, a predecessor to his seminal novel *Tres tristes tigres,* won the prestigious Spanish Biblioteca Breve Prize.

His first book, *Asi en la paz como en la Guerra: cuentos* (published in English as *Writes of Passage* in 1993), was nominated for the French Prix International de Literature in 1963. In 1965 he published *Vista del amanecer en el trópico* (published in English as *A View of Dawn in the Tropics* in 1978).

Cabrera Infante visited Cuba for the last time in 1965 to attend his mother's funeral. Once there, he was not allowed to leave the country until four months later when, under the pretext of meeting with his editors in Barcelona, Spain, he defected. His life in exile began to pay off in 1966 when he began working on

British film scripts, and through the publication what is perhaps his most well-known novel, *Tres tristes tigres* (1967; published in English as *Three Trapped Tigers*, 1971), a narration of nightlife in pre-revolutionary Havana that reflects his disillusionment with the Castro regime. In 1979 he produced *La Habana para un infante difunto* (translated in 1984 as *Infante's Inferno*), a fictional autobiography that takes place in the Havana of the 1940s and 1950s. Many of his novels have been translated in to English, including *A Twentieth Century Job* (1991). *Mea Cuba* (1994) is a collection of essays that depict post-revolutionary Cuba. In addition, he has written many articles and short stories, as well as numerous essays and film scripts. In 1997 he became the third Cuban writer to receive the most prestigious literary award in the Spanish literary world, the Miguel de Cervantes Prize.

References and Suggested Readings

Cabrera Infante, Guillermo. *Infante's Inferno*. New York: Harper, 1984.
———.*Three Trapped Tigers*. New York: Harper, 1971.
———. *Writes of Passage*. Boston: Faber and Faber, 1993.
Gazarian Gautier, Marie-Lise. "Guillermo Cabrera Infante." *Interviews with Latin American Writers*. Elmwood Park, IL: Dalkey Archive Press, 1989. 27–54.
Hijuelos, Oscar. "Guillermo Cabrera Infante." *Bomb* 70 (Winter 2000): 52–57.
Levine, Suzanne Jill. *The Subversive Scribe, Translating Latin American Fiction*. St. Paul, MN: Graywolf Press, 1991.
———. "Wit and Wile with Guillermo Cabrera Infante." *Américas* 47 (July/August 1995): 24–29.
Souza, Raymond D. *Guillermo Cabrera Infante: Two Islands Many Worlds*. Austin: University of Texas Press, 1996.

CACHAO (ISRAEL CACHAO LÓPEZ)
(1918–)

Cuban Musician, Composer, Songwriter, and Arranger

Cuban instrumentalist, composer, and bandleader Israel Cachao López is considered one of the most influential musicians in the world and was among the most important Cuban musical innovators of the twentieth century. Cachao and his brother Orestes are credited as the creators of the "mambo," a dance craze popularized by Cuban band leader **Dámaso Pérez Prado** that took the world by storm in the 1940s. His musical innovations transformed Cuba's European-influenced dance music, such as the *danzón*, into the African-derived mambo, a music that more accurately reflects of the racial mixture of the island.

The youngest of three children, Israel Cachao López was born in Havana, Cuba, on September 14, 1918, at 102 Paula Street—in the same house as Cuban patriot

José Martí—which is now a national monument. From the 1930s through the 1950s, more than 50 of Cachao's relatives were musicians in Cuba. The López family members were classically trained musicians who rehearsed on a daily basis, attracting an audience of neighbors outside their home. Considered a child prodigy, Cachao, who trained in Havana's Conservatory of Music, began playing bass at the age of five; by the age of 13 he had become a member of the Havana Philharmonic Orchestra—at first standing on a box so he could reach and play his bass. Cachao played with the Philharmonic for over 25 years, while at the same time playing with popular music and radio studio bands. It was during this time his surname Cachao became his artistic name.

Throughout the 1930s Cachao and his brother Orestes composed more than 3,000 *danzones* before creating their mambo compositions in 1938. They were members of the Arcaño y sus maravillas Orchestra, whose repertoire was largely made up of Orestes and Cachao's compositions. It was with this orchestra that Cachao composed his first hit song, "Resa del melton."

One of his most important musical innovations consisted of spicing up the *danzón*, transforming it into what eventually became the mambo. In fact, one of his first compositions in this new genre was titled "Mambo" (1938). This innovative song and its accompanying rhythm, which allowed drums and drumming to dominate, began a dance craze in the United States. His innovations were popularized when musicians such as Pérez Prado and Benny Moré incorporated this new form into their musical repertoires.

Cachao's music is based on traditional Cuban music, the *danzón*, which he transforms with the addition of mambo and cha chá rhythms. He was instrumental in reworking and fusing different music styles into what, during the 1950s, became known as *descargas*, which consisted of small groups of musicians playing Afro-Cuban music with the improvisational zest of North American jazz. He recorded his rehearsal sessions and popularized them. His 1957 recording *Cuban Jam Session in Miniature Descargas* sold over a million copies and became a Latin music milestone. *Descargas* were considered very innovative and were the precursor to the musical forms known today as salsa and Latin jazz.

In 1962 Cachao left Cuba and settled in New York, where he played, wrote, and recorded with such artists as **Tito Puente**, Charlie Palmieri, Rolando Valdez, and Tito Rodríguez. He also spent two years performing with fellow citizen, musician, and bandleader Mario Bauzá. Cachao, by nature an extremely modest man, always kept a low profile and for many years was not well known outside Cuban music circles. Despite his significance and contributions as a musician, Cachao's Afro-Cuban-style music seemed not to be appreciated by the Cuban exile community—particularly in Miami, where he has made his home for many years. Cachao believes they are indifferent to his Afro-Cuban music style because "they said it presented a false image of the Cuban population" (Lopetegui 1993, 7).

During the latter part of the 1970s and 1980s, Cachao survived financially by playing private parties and restaurant lounges. In the early 1990s Cuban American actor and producer Andy García "rediscovered" this musician with his filmed account of Cachao's 1992 rehearsal and all-star historic concert in Miami, "Cachao: Mambo y Descarga." The film, *Cachao: Como su ritmo no hay dos* (Cachao: Like His Rhythm There Is No Equal), is both a tribute to and a documentary of the artist and was released to critical acclaim in 1993. Since the release of the film Cachao's popularity and recognition have risen. He is seen as a world-class musician; his style of play is described as reminiscent of jazz musician Charles Mingus in both its improvisational quality and in his constant energizing of his players with shouts and gestures. Recent reviews of his shows describe concerts that begin with turn-of-the-century classical Cuban *danzónes* played with traditional flutes and strings, gradually being complemented by trumpets, trombones, and saxophones as well as with intense and extroverted drums and other percussion instruments that create sensuous and euphoric rhythmic beats engulfing the audience, who clap and rock in musical syncopation (Harrington, 1999).

In 1995 Cachao received a Grammy for his recording *Master Sessions Vol. I*, an impressive reconstruction of twentieth-century Cuban music. *Master Sessions* includes compositions by **Ernesto Lecuona**, compositions Cachao wrote with his brother Orestes, and some of his most popular *descargas*, such as "Descarga de la A" and "A gozar con mi combo." On that same occasion, at the age of 75, he was given Billboard's New Artist of the Year Award, ironic for one who helped create a new musical form that spurred a dance craze in 1939. "Those albums have become a kind of Bible for anybody who wants to study music, especially for drummers," wrote Andy García, who together with Emilio Estefan has co-produced Cachao's award-winning CDs (1999, 48).

His legacy was immortalized in 1994 in a series of interviews on his life and musical career that is now preserved by the Smithsonian Jazz Oral History Program; tapes and transcripts are available to the public at the National Museum of American History in Washington, D.C. In addition to his numerous awards, Cachao was inducted into the International Latin Music Hall of Fame (1999), and has been honored with a Hispanic Heritage Award and a grant from the National Endowment for the Arts. In June 2000, Cachao and another Latin Music Hall of Famer and Cuban great, **"Chico" O'Farrill**, were presented with the International Latin Music Hall of Fame's Lifetime Achievement Award; their presence together on stage made music history.

Cachao has played venues such as Lincoln Center and Radio City Music Hall to wide acclaim. In 1999 he participated in a star-studded concert at Washington's Kennedy Center celebrating the diversity of Latino culture, which was featured on PBS. He was among such mainstream artists as José Feliciano and **Gloria Estefan** for the grand finale "Descarga Cachao," a trademark mambo jam session.

Cachao's fusion of African rhythms with Cuban classical music created a new music form that has influenced the world and impacted the music of such masters as Copland, Stravinsky, and Gershwin. His influence can also be heard in the rhythms of rock legend Carlos Santana, who performed with him in 1989.

His March 2000 recording, *Cuba Linda,* was nominated for a Grammy Award, as was 2002's *El Arte Del Sabor,* recorded with the Bebo Valdés Trio and Carlos "Patato" Valdes. In September of that year Cachao premiered his new composition, "Mambo Mass," at St. Vincent de Paul Church in Los Angeles, California. His musicianship has also been hailed, and he is considered one of the most influential twentieth-century bass players for having "pioneered several acoustic-bass techniques, including percussive bass-body playing and masterful danzón-style bowing" (Goldsby 2000, 28). In June 2000, together with Chico O'Farrill, Cachao was presented with the International Latin Music Hall of Fame Lifetime Achievement Award. Cachao can be seen in Spanish director Fernando Trueba's jazz documentary feature film *Calle 54,* released in 2001. In 2003 Cachao's achievements earned him a star on the Hollywood Walk of Fame.—G.C.

References and Suggested Readings

Cobo, Leila. "Blue Note Soundtrack 'Calle 54' Ups the Ante for Latin Jazz." *Billboard* 113:13 (March 31, 2001): 11.

Cota, J.C. "Cachao." *Down Beat* 58 (January 1991): 14.

Fernandez, Raul, and Anthony Brown. "Interview with Cachao January 24–25, 1994 in Miami Florida." *Jazz Oral History Program.* Washington, DC: Smithsonian Institute, 1994.

García, Andy. "I Adore Cuban Music." *ULISSE 2000* (March 1999): 48.

García, Andy, director. *Cachao: Like His Rhythm There Is No Equal* (documentary). Prod. Andy García and Fausto Sánchez. Cineson Presentation, 1993.

Goldsby, John. "100 and Counting: The Players Who Shaped 20th Century Bass." *Bass Player* (January 2000): 28.

Harrington, Richard. "Latin Beat Forced into Double Time; Americanos Concert Jammed in Too Much." *Washington Post,* July 17, 1999, C01.

Lopetegui, Enrique. "Los Angeles Festival." *Los Angeles Times,* September 13, 1993, 7.

Thomas, Kevin. "An Infectious, Graceful Concert Film." *Los Angeles Times,* September 15, 1993, 4.

Watrous, Peter. "Pop and Jazz in Review." *The New York Times,* January 21, 1993, 16.

———. "Review/Pop; A Bassist and His Band: Genteel, but Not Always." *The New York Times,* December 23, 1991, 13.

Sila María Calderón
(1942–)

First Woman Governor of Puerto Rico, Politician, and Businesswoman

On November 7, 2000, in one of the closest major elections in the island's political history, Sila María Calderón became the first woman to be elected governor of Puerto Rico. Not only did she win the governorship, but also on her coattails other candidates from her pro-commonwealth Popular Democratic Party (PPD) swept a majority of the island's city halls and gained control of its House and Senate. A successful businesswoman who served as chief of staff and secretary of state under former Governor Rafael Hernández Colón in the late 1980s, Calderón rose up the political ladder when she won the PPD San Juan mayoral primary with more than 90 percent of the vote—her first run for elected office. In 1996 she became only the second woman to hold the position of mayor of San Juan. Historically, the San Juan mayoralty is considered a stepping-stone for the governor's seat. She pledged to fight widespread political corruption and promised to deal with the controversial U.S. Navy presence on the island of Vieques.

Sila María Calderón Serra was born in San Juan, Puerto Rico, on September 23, 1942, to Sila Serra and César Augusto Calderón, a mechanical engineer whose strong partisan views towards commonwealth status is said to have encouraged Sila Calderón's interest in politics. Other members of her family were also business owners, a field that would serve as her stepping-stone into the political arena. She graduated with honors from the Catholic Colegio Sagrado Corazón in Santurce in 1960. At 18, she left the island for Purchase, New York, where she received her undergraduate degree in political science from Manhattanville College in 1964. On her return to the island, she attended the University of Puerto Rico's Graduate School of Public Administration from 1970 to 1972.

Her education and her experience working for a major bank and as president of an investment firm on the island prepared her well for her tenure in government. She has served in leadership positions in both the public and private sectors of Puerto Rico for most of her professional life. Her political career began in 1973 when she was appointed executive assistant to the labor secretary and special assistant to the governor. From 1973 to 1976, under the leadership of then-governor Hernández Colón, Calderón served as special assistant to the governor in charge of economic development. She returned to the private sector after the 1976 defeat of the PPD to the pro-statehood New Progressive Party (PNP), which remained in power until the 1984 elections.

In 1984 re-elected governor Hernández Colón once more called on Calderón, this time appointing her chief of staff of his administration, the first woman to serve in that capacity in Puerto Rico. In 1986, the position of chief of staff was modified by the legislature and attained cabinet ranking. The governor named Calderón secretary of state in 1988, a position that was the constitutional successor to the governor; again she was the first woman to hold this position. She held both posts simultaneously until 1989.

In 1989, in addition to serving as member of the board of directors for Banco de Ponce and Banco Popular, she returned to her family's businesses. At the same time she worked as a volunteer toward the recovery of the Cantera Peninsula, one of the poorest neighborhoods in metropolitan San Juan, which had been devastated by Hurricane Hugo. Under her leadership, the Corporation for the Development of Cantera was created with the purpose of pursuing the social and economic development of that area. Through her administrative skills and political connections, she was able to accelerate the reconstruction of this underdeveloped neighborhood.

In 1994 she organized her campaign for mayor of San Juan, and in January 1995 she announced her candidacy. Among the first to announce their support for her was the newly formed Mujeres con Sila (Women for Sila), an assemblage of women from diverse professional sectors of the metropolitan area. With the support of women and many of the residents of Cantera and the metropolitan area, Calderón captured 91 percent of the primary vote, the highest ever in Puerto Rican politics. One of the reviews of the primaries described Calderón's candidacy for mayor in relation to her party's candidate for the governorship: "Sila is running for San Juan, but she is better qualified for the governorship of the country than even Acevedo" (Dávila Colón 1995, 69). Criticizing the political and legal scandals that had rocked the island, she ran on a platform that had as an objective reforming government, advocating that "[i]t is necessary to re-establish with great clarity, government's moral purpose and legal responsibility" (Dávila Colón 1995, 69). In 1996, after winning the election with 51 percent of the vote, Calderón became mayor of San Juan.

As mayor, she reinstated biweekly meetings with the people, similar to the practice that had been started by San Juan's first woman mayor, Felisa Rincón de Gautier. In addition, she increased taxes moderately to finance large infrastructure projects that included the restoration of public buildings, beautification and renovation of San Juan's public squares or "plazas," and augmentation of public services such as police and garbage collection. Her tenure for mayor was not without controversy. Throughout her years as mayor, particularly when she began to campaign for the governorship, her opponents accused her of using public money to foster her political image in the press and media. In addition, because of her family's immense wealth, and more markedly when she has run for public office, Calderón has found herself fighting off her "woman of privilege" stigma while emphasizing above all else that she is a public servant.

The centerpiece of her platform in her gubernatorial bid was the pledge to clean up the corruption that had plagued previous governor Pedro Rosello's administration. In addition, Calderón also ran a patriotic campaign calling for a quick exit of the U.S. Navy from Vieques. As governor she called for an immediate referendum on Vieques in which residents would choose between requiring the navy to leave by May 2003 or allowing it to stay indefinitely in return for $50 million in economic aid. Preempting the June 2001 referendum, the administration of President George W. Bush announced that the navy would permanently leave Vieques in the year 2003.

Governor Calderón has also announced her intention of addressing a historically and politically sensitive issue, one that the former governor enacted as law during his administration: recognizing English as an official language in Puerto Rico. Her administration's new policy recognizes both Spanish and English as official languages. This pro-commonwealth administration differs from the pro-statehood administration that was defeated after eight years in power. For months before the elections, Calderón had been trailing in the polls. Political pundits declared that the key to her victory would be pledging to root out political corruption, rather than concentrating on whether Puerto Rico should become the 51st state. There seemed to be consensus among Puerto Rican political analysts that the electorate's indignation with the political dishonesty associated with the previous administration was instrumental to her successful campaign. Calderón not only won the election, but her party won majority in both houses. As governor, her administration has drafted various bills intended to curb corruption. The administration has also called for a referendum in which the Puerto Rican people can decide what the final status of the island should be.

Her first two years in office saw an effort to increase the political power of Puerto Ricans and other Latinos in the United States. Calderón's visible involvement with mainland politics in 2002 was widely criticized. However, many credited her savvy political instincts in courting both Republicans and Democrats during such an important election year as a way of securing the island's legislative agenda, regardless of who won control of the Congress. In the end, the Republicans won enough seats to control both houses of Congress and her strategy paid off. Also in 2002, through her government's Federal Affairs Administration offices, Calderón embarked on a non-partisan campaign to register hundreds of thousands in the ten largest mainland cities with Latino populations, thus to increasing the political muscle and influence of this growing population. During her career Calderón has been the recipient of a number of distinctions including the Distinguished Woman of the Year conferred by the Puerto Rico Products Association in 1986, Leader of the Year Award from the Puerto Rico Chapter of the American Association of Public Works, and the Order of Queen Elizabeth by the Spanish government in 1987. In 1997 she received an honorary doctorate in Humane Letters from her alma mater Manhattanville College.—G.C.

References and Suggested Readings

"Biografía de Sila M. Calderón." Located at La Fortaleza's Official Web Page. Electronically Published by the Commonwealth of Puerto Rico. *http://www.fortaleza.gobierno.pr/ bio_sila.htm.*

Calderón, Sila. "Transparencia, servicio y propósito moral." *El Nuevo Día,* April 1, 1995, 69.

Dávila Colón, Luis. "La belleza, la bondad y virtud." *El Nuevo Día,* April 5, 1995, 69.

Figueroa, Juan A. "Getting Out the Latino Vote." *The Hartford Courant,* October 25, 2002, A15.

Magruder, Laura. "A New Governor Ushers in a New Era in Puerto Rico." *The New York Times,* January 6, 2001, A8.

Marino, John. "Puerto Rico's New Governor Makes Break With the Past." *The Hartford Courant,* November 12, 2000, A16.

New York City Mayor's Office. "Mayor Giulliani Salutes 100 Hispanic Women" (May 16, 1997). Press Release #274–97 New York.

CALYPSO ROSE (MCCARTHA LEWIS)
(1940–)

Trinidadian Singer and Songwriter

Calypso Rose, considered the "mother of calypso," was the first woman to become a calypso star and is credited with changing the sexist tone of calypso lyrics. This Trinidadian artist's songs speak strongly about social and political issues and follow the calypso musical tradition that she described as being a "domestical, spiritual, economical and political" commentary (Canby 1991, C13).

During the eighteenth century, plantation slaves were forbidden to talk to each other, so instead they chanted about political matters, jokes, and sexual innuendos in their melodic patois, a blend of British English and the regional dialect. This tradition developed further into contemporary calypso music, which became popular in Trinidad's Carnival celebrations and is now endemic to the entire Caribbean region. A melding of upbeat African and Latin American rhythms with social and political lyrics, these melodies oftentimes are full of satire and double entendre. Considered the "first lady of calypso" and a pioneer in her field, she "challenged generations of prejudice against women in the tents" by achieving parity with her counterpart calypsonian males and using lyrics that bring women's issues to the forefront (Mason 1998, 39).

Calypso Rose was born in the village of Bethel on the island of Tobago on April 27, 1940. Some sources state her given name as McCartha Lewis, and others McCartha Sandy. What is known is that she was named in honor of World War II American General Douglas McArthur. Her father was a Baptist minister and the head of a very traditional family that was opposed to her competing in carnival tents, clubs, or sites where groups of musicians perform sponsored by a particular merchant or company. Nevertheless, she began singing as an amateur at the age of 15 in Bethel and turned professional in 1964. Her composition "Fire in Me Wire," recorded in eight languages worldwide, is considered calypso's unofficial anthem and placed her on the Caribbean calypso music map in 1966. Since that time, as a woman in a male-dominated arena, she has successfully challenged and contributed to the world of music by writing and producing many hit songs.

Considered a national treasure, she has been bestowed with every honor the Caribbean can confer on its living artists. Among her awards is the title of Trinidad's national Calypso Queen, which she won from 1972 to 1976. In 1977, with her song "Gimme More Tempo" she won Trinidad Carnival's Road March competition, and the following year won the same award for her "Soca Jam." For 21 years Calypso Rose held the honor of being the only woman to win the Road March competition. Her 1978 compositions "Trinidad I Thank Thee" and "Her Majesty" were the most widely played songs during Carnival and bestowed on her the distinction of being the first woman to win the highest and most coveted carnival award, the Calypso Monarch crown (previously known as Calypso King).

Some of her songs recognized as important political commentary include "The Balance Wheel" and "Respect the Balisier." Compositions that have raised awareness of current social problems include "Gun Play on the Parkway" and "Help." A vibrant and exciting performer, she has also written unforgettable, contagiously rhythmic party songs that when combined in her live appearances with drums and whistles keep audiences dancing. Throughout her career she has performed with other well-known artists of other musical genres such as Miriam Makeba, **Harry Belafonte**, Michael Jackson, and most recently, Roberta Flack.

In 1991 she was one of the figures featured in the film *One Hand Don't Clap*, a documentary about the history of calypso and soca. Her remark acknowledging the support she received from calypso great **Lord Kitchener** during the early years of her career provided the title for the film.

She lives in New York City, frequently performs before huge audiences in other American cities, and is a recurrent featured artist on Carnival Cruise Line ships. Having effectively triumphed in the calypso world, she has branched out to combine other forms of music in her songs. "Soca" (modern Trinidadian pop music, a combination of soul and calypso) has been embraced by her fans both in Trinidad and Tobago and throughout the world. In 1994 she wrote and produced the very successful CD *Soca Diva*, which was showcased in a worldwide tour and garnered her another musical honor. In 1995 she won Best Female Soca Artist at the 1995 Reggae Soca Awards in Miami, Florida. Her *Ringband Queen* CD (2000) explores the more current and upbeat tempo of soca's offshoot, "ringband" music.

Calypso Rose has traveled all over the world with her music and has won awards during every year of her professional life. The Trinidad and Tobago government, by order of Her Majesty Queen Elizabeth of England, bestowed on her the Medal of Merit in 1975. In 1983 she was named Top Female Calypsonian by the Smithsonian Institute in Washington, D.C. She was recognized as the Most Outstanding Woman in Trinidad and Tobago by the National Women's Action Committee in 1991 and was inducted into the Tobago Walk of Fame as a charter member in 1993. In 1999 the Tobago House Assembly decreed that its new hospital would be named the McCartha Lewis Memorial Hospital, in her honor. That same year she received the International Caribbean Music Award's Lifetime Achievement Award.

Considered a trailblazer, Calypso Rose has been tearing down the door of a male-dominated field for a long time, consistently producing hit after hit, and even taking on the innovative rhythms of soca very successfully. Feeling very strongly about the social importance of her music and lyrics, and considering herself very spiritual, Rose has recently turned her attention to yet another genre—gospel music—and recently released a CD titled *Jesus Is My Rock.*—G.C.

References and Suggested Readings

Broome, Roderick. "Jesus Is My Rock: The Gospel (CD) According to Calypso Rose." *New York Beacon* 7.14 (April 12, 2000): 4.

Canby, Vincent. "Calypso, Past and Present, As Two Veterans See It." *New York Times,* August 28, 1991, C13.

Dutta, Kavery, director. *One Hand Don't Clap*. Rhapsody Films Presentation, Riverfilms Production, 1991.

Mason, Peter. *Bacchanal! The Carnival Culture of Trinidad*. Philadelphia, PA: Temple University Press, 1998.

Roberts, Paul. "The Legendary Heart and Soul of the Caribbean." *Caribbean Today* 5.5 (April 30, 1994): 15.

Thompson, Clifford, ed. "McCartha Lewis." *World Musicians*. New York: The H.W. Wilson Company, 1999. 131–132.

Waters, Christina. "Day-Oh Saving Time." *Metro Santa Cruz* (Santa Cruz California), May 23–29, 1996, n.p.

http://www.metroactive.com/papers/cruz/05.23.96/calypso-621.html.

MICHEL CAMILO
(1954–)

Dominican Jazz Musician and Composer

Dominican musician Michel Camilo is known for his energetic piano technique and extraordinary rhythm as well as for his infusion of Latin tempo into his compositions and jazz performances. Since his arrival in the United States in 1979, he has appeared in the most important music halls and jazz festivals in the world. In 2001 he was awarded a Grammy for Best Latin Jazz Album. He has also received numerous international awards and has been invited to lecture and perform at numerous universities and music conservatories worldwide. Considered one of the best jazz pianists in the industry, he has been described as representing "a synthesis of jazz and blues harmonies, funk grooves, classical influences, and Latin American and Iberian rhythms" (Tamargo 1997, 24).

Camilo was born on April 4, 1954, in Santo Domingo. He and his four siblings grew up surrounded by nine uncles who were musicians. Family gatherings were musical events. He started playing the accordion at age four, and by five he had composed his first song. In 1963 he enrolled as a piano student in the island's National Conservatory, where he received the degree of Professorship in Music, and at 16 became the youngest member of the Dominican Republic's National Symphony Orchestra. Camilo grew up listening mostly to classical music, but when he joined the symphony he heard a recording by jazz musician Art Tatum and his musical life took a new direction: "I fell in love with the extended possibilities it offered to express my feelings" (Grogan 1989, 91). By the time he was 25, he left the symphony to explore and expand his musical horizons abroad.

On his arrival in New York City in 1979 he continued his studies at Mannes College and the Julliard School of Music. Influenced by his musical family and the Caribbean style music played by his uncles, as well as his exposure to other Latin musicians in New York, he began to include Latin rhythms in his jazz.

One of his earliest compositions, "Why Not!," was recorded by Manhattan Transfer and won them a 1983 Grammy. In 1985 Camilo made his debut in Carnegie Hall with his trio, and the following year his was the lead group in a number of European jazz festivals, where he has become a well-known figure. In 1987 he briefly returned to his classical roots and debuted as classical conductor with the National Symphony Orchestra of the Dominican Republic, where his Emmy-winning composition "The Goodwill Games Theme" was included in the program. From 1987 to 1992 Camilo was the music director of the Heineken Jazz Festival, which was held in the Dominican Republic.

His debut on a major record label with the album *Suntan/Michel Camilo* (1988) was the number-one jazz album for eight weeks. That was followed by *On Fire* (1989), which was voted one of the top three jazz albums of that year. *On the Other Hand* (1990), his third album, was also among the top ten jazz albums. By 1991 Camilo had made his third appearance at Carnegie Hall and his second at the Newport Jazz Festival, and had embarked on his third tour of Japan. Other artists such as **Paquito D'Rivera** and Dizzy Gillespie began to record his compositions. Pianists Katia and Marielle Labèque performed the world premiere of his "Rhapsody for Two Pianos and Orchestra" (1992) with the Philarmonia Orchestra of London. In addition, he wrote and performed the musical score for the award-winning European film *Amo tu cama rica* (Master Your Rich Bed) in 1991.

Camilo's success continued throughout the 1990s. In 1993 his album *Rendezvous* was selected among the top jazz albums of the year by *Gavin Report* and by *Billboard*. He was also part of the All-Star Gala of jazz musicians that performed in Washington, D.C., at the White House in celebration of the 40th Anniversary of the Newport Jazz Festival, which was later shown on television by PBS as part of "In Performance at the White House." In 1994 he composed the musical score for another feature film *Los peores años de nuestra vida* (The Worst Years of Our Lives), and released the album *One More Once.* By 1995 Camilo had formed a 17-piece band that performed on National Public Radio's "A Jazz Piano Christmas" hosted by Tony Bennett and he continued composing feature film scores such as *Two Much*, directed by Fernando Trueba. He has continued his work with classical music and in 1997 performed as a soloist with the Copenhagen Philharmonic and the Queens Symphony Orchestra. In 1998 he was co–artistic director of the first Latin-Caribbean Music Festival held at the Kennedy Center for the Performing Arts, where he performed the premiere of his "Piano Concerto" with the National Symphony Orchestra. He also performed in concert with Flamenco guitarist Tomatico, with whom he recorded the album *Spain,* which won a Grammy Award for Best Latin Jazz Album in 2000.

Camilo has lectured and performed at numerous universities such as New York University, Berkelee School of Music in Boston, the Massachusetts Institute of Technology, Puerto Rico's Conservatory of Music and other educational and musical institutions in Denmark, Spain, and Switzerland.

He has also been the recipient of numerous international awards. In 1992, his alma mater, Universidad Autónoma de Santo Domingo, named him professor emeritus and the Dominican government presented him with one of its most prestigious awards, Knight of the Heraldic Order of Christopher Columbus. In 1993 he was the recipient of the International Jazz Award given by the Clearwater Jazz Holiday and was invited to serve as judge at the renowned Great American Jazz Piano Competition in Jacksonville, Florida. He became the youngest person ever to receive an honorary doctorate from the Universidad Tecnológica de Santiago in 1994, and in 1997 the Duke Ellington School of the Arts in Washington, D.C. created the Michel Camilo Piano Scholarship, to be presented to the best piano student in the school. Camilo was featured in Fernando Trueba's film *Calle 54* (54th Street). In 2002 Camilo released the long-awaited *Triangulo*, an album that was five years in the making.—G.C.

References and Suggested Readings

Birnbaum, Larry. "Michel Camilo: Caribbean Jazz Classic." *Down Beat* (March 1990): 24–25.

Cobo, Leila. "Blue Note Soundtrack 'Calle 54' Ups the Ante for Latin Jazz." *Billboard* 113.13 (March 31, 2001): 11.

Franckling, Ken. "The Jazz Condition–UPI Arts & Entertainment." *United Press International* (August 7, 2001).

Grogan, David. "Michel Camilo, Who Returned to His Latin-flavored Jazz Roots When He Left Santo Domingo." *People Weekly* 3.22 (June 5, 1989): 91.

Heckman, Don. "Fiery Jazz Pianist Camilo Takes Note of His Critics." *Los Angeles Times,* September 15, 1990, 2.

Mandel, Howard. "The Hustlers: Paquito D'Rivera & Michel Camilo Bring the Afro-Caribbean Tradition Within Earshot." *Down Beat* 62.1 (January 1995): 26.

Michel Camilo Home Page: *http://www.ejn.it/camilo.*

Tamargo, Luis. "The Rhythmic Intensity of Michel Camilo." *Latin Beat Magazine* 7.3 (April 1997): 24.

STOKELEY CARMICHAEL (KWAME TURE)
(1941–1998)
Trinidadian American Civil Rights Activist and Black Militant

---

Stokeley Carmichael was a visible leader of the U.S. civil rights movement during the 1960s and 1970s. He experienced racial and political oppression as a young boy in his native Trinidad and dedicated his life to the struggle for racial equality among American blacks. From his position as a student activist, a civil rights organizer, and as one of the founders of the Black Power movement in the United States, Carmichael became an advocate for black separatism and militancy.

Stokeley Carmichael was born on June 29, 1947, in Port-of-Spain, Trinidad, to Adolphus and Mabel Carmichael. His father worked as a carpenter in his native Trinidad and eventually as a taxi driver in New York City. His parents left Trinidad when Carmichael was two years old, but left him in charge of his grandmother and aunts who helped to raise him.

As a young boy Carmichael attended Tranquility Boys School. His education followed a British model that tried to instill in him a love for British social mores and cultural traditions, which he deeply resented later in his life. The British newspaper *The Independent* noted:

> Long afterwards he raged against the British education he received in one of His Majesty's colonies. "At school we were made to memorize Kipling's 'White Man's Burden,' and told we didn't exist till a white man called Sir Walter Raleigh discovered us," he declared in 1967. "We went to the movies and yelled for Tarzan to beat the hell out of Africa." (Cornwell 1998, n.p.)

Carmichael's parents brought him to the United States when he was 11 years old and he was admitted to the Bronx High School of Science. A bright but restless student, Carmichael found that he had little in common with most of his fellow students, who came from affluent, white backgrounds. He became of a part of a gang known as the Morris Park Dukes and engaged in many illegal activities during his adolescence. After his graduation from high school, Carmichael went to Howard University in Washington, D.C., where he graduated with a degree in philosophy in 1964.

Carmichael's years at Howard coincided with the emergence of the civil rights movement in the United States and with Martin Luther King Jr.'s vigorous crusade to liberate American blacks from racial oppression. During his years at Howard he joined the Student Non-Violent Coordinating Committee (SNCC) and traveled through the American South participating in students' protests aimed at integrating the south. He taught blacks how to write, enabling them to use their voting rights. Because of his activism as a student, Carmichael was arrested, imprisoned, and beaten by Southern segregationists more than 32 times.

After his graduation from Howard, Carmichael joined the SNCC as a full-time organizer. He worked in Lowndes County, Alabama, where he launched a vigorous campaign to register black voters. His efforts were so successful that he was able to register 53 percent of the black electorate by teaching them how to read and write. At the same time, he advocated self-sufficiency of the black community asking them to develop their own economic institutions so that they that were independent of the white community. By the age of 25, in 1966, Carmichael became the national chairman of the SNCC.

His experience working in Alabama led Carmichael to believe that Martin Luther King Jr.'s strategy of non-violence in his quest for racial equality was flawed because the extent of white economic and social oppression was so great that the use of arms and violence was warranted. Shortly after assuming leadership of the SNCC, he condemned his organization for what he thought was a too passive approach to the civil rights struggle. He also thought that King's efforts to create alliances with white and Jewish groups to gain equality were wrong as they perpetuated the reliance of black people on white people and their institutions.

After the assassination of Martin Luther King Jr. in 1968, Carmichael no longer saw any future in the "mainstream" civil right organizations. In response to King's assassination, for instance, he made a call to arms among African Americans. His disillusionment with the civil rights movement was so great that he abandoned SNCC and became a member of the Black Panther Party. The party had been founded by Bobby Seale and Huey Newton in the belief that blacks needed to separate from the mainstream white establishment if they were to gain power or equality in the United States. Following the motto of "Black Power," the party advocated equality using all necessary means. In *Black Power*, a book he co-authored with Charles V. Hamilton, he said:

> The concept of Black power . . . is a call for black people in this country to unite, to recognize their heritage, to build a sense of community. It is a call for black people to begin to define their own goals to lead their own organizations and to support their own organizations. It is a call to reject racist institutions and values of this society. (Carmichael and Hamilton 1967, 44)

Carmichael developed an ardent crusade with members of the party to raise awareness among black Americans about the need for Black Power. Using the symbol of a black panther and a raised fist, they advocated for racial equality by all necessary means.

Because of the fiery nature of his rhetoric and his explicit call for arms and violence in the struggle towards racial equality, Carmichael came to be seen as a radical and dissident voice within the American civil rights movement. Throughout the rest of his life he denounced persecution by the FBI and blamed American intelligence organizations for his having to leave the United States.

In 1969, after disagreeing with other party members, whom he perceived as being too conservative, Carmichael decided to abandon the party and relocate to New Guinea in Africa where he continued his call for black self-sufficiency and independence. Adopting the African name of Kwame Ture, Carmichael founded the All African Revolutionary Party, which called for all Africans throughout the world to unite and lead a revolution to gain equality. Carmichael spent the rest of his life traveling around the world and spreading a pan-African message. He told blacks that if they wanted to be independent, they had to go back to their land and take control of their governments and institutions. His rhetoric was so fierce that he was eventually banned from entering England and his native Trinidad.

Carmichael's radical stand in his quest for the worldwide liberation of blacks made him a pariah among most black civil right leaders and civil rights organizations. His attempt to disengage blacks from whites and their institutions led to the perception that he was too radical and extremist. He believed that blacks needed to work independently if they wanted to be independent. For him, compromising meant "selling out."

Carmichael died on November 16, 1998, after a long fight with prostate cancer.

References and Suggested Readings

Branch, Taylor. *Parting the Waters: America in the King Years, 1954–63*. New York: Simon & Schuster, 1988.

——. *Pillar of Fire: America in the King Years: 1963–65*. New York: Simon & Schuster, 1998.

Carmichael, Stokeley, and Charles V. Hamilton. *Black Power: The Politics of Liberation in America*. New York: Random House, 1967.

Cornwell, Rupert. "Obituary: Stokeley Carmichael." *The Independent* (London). November 17, 1998, n.p.

Kaufman, Michael. "Stokely Carmichael, Rights Leader Who Coined 'Black Power' Dies at 57." *The New York Times*, November 16, 1998, B10.

ALEJO CARPENTIER
(1904–1980)

Cuban Novelist and Scholar

Critically acclaimed Cuban writer Alejo Carpentier's pioneering use of magical realism—incorporating fantastic or mythical elements into realistic fiction, sometimes blurring the distinction between fantasy and reality—has inspired many writers. Considered an intellectual as well as a writer, his characteristically complex work contains references to music, history, politics, science, art, and mythology. The roots of magical realism lie in the Negritude movement (rejects the aesthetic, cultural, and ideological values of the Western world and encourages a return to the original values of native African cultures and civilization) seen in the works of other Caribbean natives such as **Nicolás Guillén** and **Aimé Césaire**, who to some degree influenced Carpentier's writing.

However, Carpentier's association with French surrealism is also powerful. It can be seen in his *El reino de este mundo* (The Kingdom of This World; 1949), written as a result of his experiences in Haiti—Carpentier discovered that what French surrealists invented in their dreams was everyday reality in Haiti. It was after his Haitian visit in 1943 that he coined the term "lo real maravilloso" (marvelous reality), where the unbelievable is no longer something from the unknown but is incorporated into the real.

Carpentier's writing examines historical and political concerns relating to life and culture in Spanish-speaking America. Biographer Roberto González Echevarría characterizes this important writer's work: "Carpentier searches for the marvelous buried beneath the surface of Latin American consciousness, where African drums still beat and Indian amulets rule; in depths where Europe is only a vague memory of a future still to come" (González Echevarría 1977, 123). He is widely regarded as one of the greatest modern Latin American writers—an important theorist of Latin American literature, as well as a historian of its music.

Alejo Carpentier Valmont was born on December 26, 1904, in Havana, Cuba, to affluent immigrant parents. His father, Georges Carpentier, a French architect and designer of many of Havana's buildings, had emigrated to Havana with his wife, Lina Valmont, a Russian pianist, in 1902, the year of Cuba's independence. Even when living in Havana, French was spoken at home; however, Carpentier spoke Spanish with his friends, many of whom were black and from vastly dissimilar backgrounds. Throughout his life he would struggle with his privileged home culture and the more vivid and marvelous everyday world outside.

Both parents contributed in different ways to the formation of Carpentier as a writer. From his mother and music teacher Carpentier acquired his talent and affinity for music. The Carpentier's home in El Cotorro, on the outskirts of Havana, was a sprawling mansion where Carpentier had access to a vast collection of literature in his father's library. He attended Colegio Mimó and began to learn English at the Candler College, a North American school for only the most affluent families. While a student at both institutions, he studied music.

Throughout his life, Carpentier spent periods living in France. During his adolescence he traveled with his family to Russia to claim an inheritance, and later went to France, where he attended the Lyceé Jeanson de Sailly in Paris. Following his father's footsteps, in 1921 he began architectural studies at the University of Havana, but the following year, he abandoned his studies when his father deserted the family. He began to work as a journalist for the avant-garde magazine *Carteles*, and within two years he was its editor-in-chief.

The early 1920s marked a period of political upheaval and demonstrations against the dictatorship of Gerardo Machado. Carpentier was involved in this movement both as a writer and as a member of the student movement to oust the government. His political activities earned him a few months of imprisonment when he openly condemned the Machado dictatorship. On his release in 1929 he fled to France with a false passport. During the following 12 years in France, he studied the history and culture of the Americas in-depth and began the realization of his future as a writer. While exiled in France, he continued to write for Cuban publications. During 11 of his 12 years in France, he was employed as the director and producer of spoken-arts programs and recordings for the French company Foniric Studios in Paris. In 1933 he published his first novel, *Ecué-yamba-O!*, which literally means "Praised Be the Lord." This work, which he had begun to write while imprisoned in Cuba, is a compassionate account of life and culture for blacks in Cuba and a condemnation of the Machado dictatorship. In 1936, after 12 years of self-exile—during which he became acquainted with surrealism and other avant-garde movements, experienced the Spanish Civil War, and accumulated an impressive work resume—he was ready to return to Cuba, where he spent the most prolific years of his career.

On his return to Cuba, Carpentier became editor of the journal *Tiempo Nuevo*. In addition, his broadcasting experience landed him a job as director of the radio station CMX in Havana. His vast musical knowledge and experience allowed him to become professor of musicology in Cuba's National Conservatory of Music in 1941. That same year, after two relatively short marriages, he married Cuban Lilia Esteban Hierro. Every book from then on was dedicated to her and their marriage lasted until his death.

After traveling all over Haiti in a Jeep with Lilia in 1943, he began working on a novel, *El reino de este mundo* (1949), published in English as *The Kingdom of This World* in 1957. The book was inspired by the stories he had learned in Haiti and the landscapes he had toured. It revolves around the story of the early-nineteenth-century Haitian tyrant Henri Christophe, and is considered historic or realistic fiction grounded in what became his trademark magical realism. He continued to travel widely, living in Venezuela from 1945 to 1959. Through his work in newspapers, radio, and novels, he began to achieve recognition and economic stability. He was a contributor to the literary magazine *Orígenes*, a major Cuban cultural journal, and *La Gaceta del Caribe* (Caribbean Gazette), one with a more political leftist bent. In 1946 he published *La música en Cuba* (Music in Cuba), the first comprehensive published history of Cuban music. In 1956, *Los pasos perdidos*, considered his masterpiece, was translated into English as *The Lost Steps*.

A supporter of **Fidel Castro**'s revolution, Carpentier returned to Cuba from his self-imposed exile in 1959 with the manuscript for *El siglo de las luces* (1962) (published in English as *Explosion in a Cathedral*, 1963), which depicts the French Revolution from a Caribbean perspective. In the mid-1960s Carpentier became director of a weekly radio broadcast series on Cuban culture. In 1970 he was appointed cultural attaché to the Cuban embassy in Paris, a post he held for the rest of his life. During those years he continued to write and publish.

While he is considered one of the greatest Latin American writers of the twentieth century, his life was not without controversy. His close relationship with the Castro regime was controversial, particularly among other Latin American writers. One of their points of contention was that while Cuban nationals could not publish or receive foreign payment for their publications, he was allowed royalty privileges and was able to travel with a diplomatic passport all over the world.

Some of the literary awards he received during his lifetime include France's Prix du Meilleur Livre Etranger in 1956 for *The Lost Steps*, the Cino del Duca Prize in 1975, and the Prix Medici in 1979. In 1977 he became the first Cuban writer to receive the most prestigious and remunerative award given for Spanish literature, the Miguel de Cervantes Prize. Only two other Cuban writers have received this award—his colleague and friend **Dulce María Loynaz**, and **Guillermo Cabrera Infante** in 1997. In 1979, aware that he was dying of cancer, he published his last novel, *El arpa y la sombra* (The Harp and the Shadow). He died in Paris on April 24, 1980, and was buried in Cuba at the Necropolis de Colón. Posthumously, Venezuela presented him with its highest honor, the Orden Libertador de Primera Clase, honoring the 14 years he lived in that country and his literary contribution to the world.—G.C.

References and Suggested Readings

Arias, Salvador, ed. *Recopilación de textos sobre Alejo Carpentier.* Havana, Cuba: Casa de las Américas, 1977.

Benítez Rojo, Antonio. "Alejo Carpentier: Between Here and Over There." *Caribbean Studies* 27.3–4 (July–December 1994): 183–196.

González-Echevarría, Roberto. "Alejo Carpentier." In William Luis, ed., *Dictionary of Literary Biography.* Vol. 113, *Modern Latin-American Fiction Writers.* Detroit: Gale, 1992. 96–109.

———. *Alejo Carpentier: The Pilgrim at Home.* Ithaca, NY: Cornell University Press, 1977.

Tardiff, Joseph C., L'Mpho Mabunda, and Rudolfo A. Anaya, eds. "Alejo Carpentier." *Dictionary of Hispanic Biography.* Detroit: Gale, 1995. 177–180.

Webb, Barbara J. *Myth and History in Caribbean Fiction: Alejo Carpentier, Wilson Harris, and Edouardo Glissant.* Amherst: University of Massachusetts Press, 1992.

FIDEL CASTRO
(1926–)

Cuban Lawyer, Revolutionary, and President

In power in Cuba for over 40 years, longer than any other contemporary leader, Fidel Castro is considered one of the twentieth century's most charismatic and controversial political world figures. His family background, his childhood, and his education at an elite Jesuit Catholic school influenced his involvement in politics at an early age. Since leading armed attacks against the dictatorship of Fulgencio Batista in 1959, Castro has been the sole political leader of Cuba. Until 1976 he held the title of premier; his current title is president of the Council of State and the Council of Ministers. While his record of the last 40 years shows great achievements in education and health, failures in regard to individual freedom, agriculture, and the economy are also clear.

Fidel Alejandro Castro Ruz was born on August 13, 1926, in Birán, Oriente province, on his family's sugar plantation. His father, Angel Castro y Argiz, was an immigrant from Galicia, Spain, who was sent to Cuba as a soldier to fight in the

Fidel Castro. Courtesy of Photofest.

War of Independence. After the war, he returned to Cuba to settle as a farmer and eventually became a well-to-do landowner of a 23,000-acre plantation and a man of considerable influence in local politics. Cuban native Lina Ruz González was Angel Castro's second wife, with whom he had seven children. Fidel, the second of three boys and four girls, grew up in a remote rural part of Oriente province and began displaying his political feelings when as a boy working in the family's sugarcane fields he tried to rally the other workers in order to demand better working conditions. It was also during this time that he developed a lifelong interest in hunting and gained experience in the use of firearms. This familiarity with arms would prove useful as he became politically active in the university, and later in the 1950s when he waged guerrilla warfare against Cuban dictator Fulgencio Batista.

At age six he convinced his parents to send him to the La Salle School. He later attended Colegio Dolores, a prestigious upper-class prep school in Santiago de Cuba. His secondary education was completed at the Jesuit-run Colegio Belén in Havana (now the Technical Military Institute José Martí), where he was voted the school's best athlete in 1944. Though he was an undistinguished scholar, his political activism at the University of Havana as a member of the Cuban People's Party (also called the Orthodox Party) provided formative experiences important to his later revolutionary and political career. As leader of the left wing during his law school years, Castro traveled throughout Latin America as an international student organizer. He had a leadership role in an unsuccessful armed expedition to the Dominican Republic against the Rafael Leonidas Trujillo dictatorship and became an activist for Puerto Rican independence after having established contact with **Pedro Albizu Campos** and other Puerto Rican leaders. He completed his law degree in 1950 and went into private law practice with two partners, concentrating his legal practice on helping the poor.

On July 26, 1953, at age 26, he gave up his law practice to focus on politics. He led a group of 165 armed men on an attack of the Moncada army barracks in Santiago de Cuba in an attempt to ignite a popular uprising against Fulgencio Batista, who had seized power in a military coup a year earlier. The attack was a failure. More than half of his men died, and the surviving rebels, including Castro, were imprisoned. It was during this period of incarceration that he prepared his defense—in essence his blueprint for revolutionary change in Cuba—which he presented in his courtroom appearance; the published manifesto was titled "History Will Absolve Me." The trial resulted in a 15-year prison sentence, and after two years Castro, his brother Raúl, and others were released from prison in a general amnesty granted by Batista in 1955.

Castro left for Mexico and organized other Cuban exiles into a fighting force called the 26th of July Revolutionary Movement. In Mexico he met physician Ernesto Guevara, whom the Cubans nicknamed "Che," and after talking with him for an entire night, recruited Guevara as the troop doctor for his guerrilla expedition. The two men shared very similar ideological identities and developed a relationship that would last a lifetime.

In December 1956, Castro and 81 other fighters returned to Cuba aboard the *Granma*, a leaky cabin cruiser he had purchased from an American in Mexico. For the next two years, Castro directed the operations of the rebel army from the Sierra Maestra mountains in what was then the province of Oriente. A few weeks after landing in Cuba, Castro staged a notorious and clever publicity stunt when he smuggled a *New York Times* reporter into the mountains. During his interview with the reporter, his brother Raúl kept marching the same men back and forth in front of the reporter, who later wrote about the "large" army Castro commanded.

Politically, if not economically, Castro has proved more successful than Cuba's previous dictators. From the beginning, he sought to incorporate the Cuban masses, particularly the poor and the blacks, who strongly supported the revolution. His revolution dismantled Cuba's own Jim Crow system and fostered a strong black middle class that now has significant representation in the professions and in the military, though few are in the upper echelons of government. His long speeches are legendary. After his triumphal January 8, 1959, entry into Havana, he gave a televised speech that lasted over seven hours. Unyielding in his distrust of and animosity toward the U.S. government, Castro allied with the Soviet Union and actively tried to export revolution to the rest of Latin America as well as to Africa. In addition, his government seized without compensation all property owned by civilians and military officials who sought exile. The nation's farms, factories, and retail stores were also expropriated and nationalized. In fact, his own family's extensive landholdings were nationalized during the 1959 agrarian reform.

Much criticism has been directed at Castro and his regime. It is believed that a combination of factors led to Castro's embracing the former Soviet Union in 1960. Although he was greatly influenced by Marxist writings and his participation in the support of Cuba's Popular Socialist Party (PSP), it is believed that his confrontations with the United States over American business and covert political activity in Cuba played an important role in his choosing the Soviet Union as Cuba's main ally.

Because Castro adopted of a communist form of government, as many as 250,000 middle- and upper-middle-class professionals fled the island between 1959 and 1962 alone. This mass departure crippled Cuba's economic system and resulted in the exodus of a large percentage of those opposed to Castro—diminishing the possibility of an internal challenge to his new government. Many of the Cubans who fled established themselves in Miami, Florida, where a large, well-funded, and active anti-Castro community now thrives. In contrast to Cubans on the island, the exile community in Miami and its political organizations are overwhelmingly white—which inspires mistrust among many black Cubans on the island, who fear that their return would mean the re-creation of white supremacy on the island.

Over the years there has been harsh criticism of Castro's revolution, particularly in the area of human rights, due to his administration's brutal stifling of civil liberties and dissent at home. In addition, decrease in the production of food and the economic blockade imposed on Cuba by the United States in 1960 have established rationing as a permanent feature of Cuban life. However, it has also been recognized that Cubans under Castro have become better educated and healthier than any other Latin Americans; that education and health services are provided free of charge in Cuba; and that every citizen is guaranteed employment. However, the Soviet Union's 1990 collapse brought a new economic hardship to Cuba.

Unlike most world leaders, Castro's private life has been very guarded. It is known that he has fathered seven sons and a daughter from four different wives and mistresses. His daughter Alina Fernández, who lives in Europe, wrote a telltale book *Castro's Daughter: An Exile's Memoir of Cuba* (1998). Two controversial film documentaries about Castro have been released recently: *Fidel* (2002), directed by Estela Bravo, and *Comandante* (2003), directed by Oliver Stone.

There have been numerous alleged assassination plots reported against Castro and rumors about his declining health abound. Against all odds and nearly all predictions, Castro continues to survive. The failures of communist regimes around the world have isolated him, and exiles in Miami predict his imminent downfall. However, he still remains one of the world's most fascinating and controversial statesmen.—G.C.

References and Suggested Readings

Anderson, Jon Lee. "The Old Man and the Boy." *The New Yorker,* February 21, 2000, 224–237.

Castro, Fidel. *My Early Years.* Deborah Shnookal and Pedro Álvarez Tabío, eds. New York: Ocean Press, 1998.

"Castro, Fidel." *Encyclopædia Britannica.* Encyclopædia Britannica Online. *http://0-search.eb.com.csulib.ctstateu.edu:80/eb/article?eu=21067.* Accessed February 16, 2003.

Fernández, Alina. *Castro's Daughter: An Exile's Memoir of Cuba.* New York: St. Martin's Press, 1998.

Gimbel, Wendy. *Havana Dreams: A Story of Cuba.* New York: Alfred A. Knopf, 1998.

Larmer, Brook. "Candid Castro." *Newsweek,* February 1, 1999, 36–39.

Quirk, Robert E. *Fidel Castro.* New York: W.W. Norton & Company, 1995.

Szulc, Tad. *Fidel: A Critical Portrait*. New York: William Morrow, 1985.
Tamayo, Juan O. "Castro's Family." *Miami Herald*, October 8, 2000, 45.

ORLANDO "PERUCHÍN" CEPEDA
(1937–)

Puerto Rican Baseball Player

When Orlando "Peruchín" Cepeda was finally inducted into the National Baseball Hall of Fame on July 25, 1999, his induction marked the culmination of a long voyage in the world of professional baseball. "Baby Bull," as he was known to many of his Americans fans, was considered to be one of the best batters and first basemen of the 1960s. After his retirement from the major leagues in 1974, Cepeda was convicted of smuggling drugs into Puerto Rico. After serving time in a Florida prison, Cepeda worked hard at redeeming himself before the legions of fans that who adored him. Working today in community relations for the San Francisco Giants, Cepeda is an ardent spokesperson against the use of drugs by adolescents and has been able to regain his admired position in the world of baseball.

Orlando Cepeda was born September 17, 1937, in Ponce, Puerto Rico, to Pedro Anibal Cepeda and his wife Carmen Pennes. His father, known by the names of "Perucho" and the "Bull," was one of the best professional baseball players in Puerto Rico during the 1940s and 1950s. The family relied on his father's income to make ends meet. However, his father had a gambling problem and quite often gambled away his baseball earnings, leaving family without any money. Thus, Cepeda's mother had to find odd jobs to support her family. During his youth, Cepeda's family lived in many places, accompanying the father wherever he needed to go to play baseball. In his most recent memoir Cepeda writes: "I have never revealed the full extent of our poverty, nor the shackles of the Puerto Rican slums where I grew up and hung out. The best of times were tough. . . . Our living conditions were never good" (Cepeda and Fagen 1998, 5). His father retired from baseball in his forties after contracting malaria while working in his day job as a water inspector. The family was then forced to move to San Juan and lived in three of its poorest and most dangerous neighborhoods. Cepeda has said that all of these hardships contributed to a build-up of anger that he fought throughout his life.

Cepeda grew up following baseball. Because his father was a professional player, he was able to meet most of the famous Puerto Rican professional players of the time. When he was 11, he decided that he also wanted to become a professional baseball player and started playing on minor league teams. After a brief disappointment with baseball, he briefly tried to become a basketball player but

Orlando Cepeda. AP Photo.

eventually switched back to baseball. After knee surgery at the age of 15, Cepeda's body and talents developed and he felt that he had what was needed to play professional baseball. At 16 he joined one of the best amateur teams in Puerto Rico and had the opportunity to go to the Dominican Republic to play in an All-Star Game. While Cepeda was in the Dominican Republic, the owner of one of the best professional teams in Puerto Rico, the Cangrejeros from Santurce (Santurce Crabbers), watched him play and asked him to come and work as a batboy. While working with the team, Cepeda came in contact with some of the most prestigious American players, who went to Puerto Rico to work during the winter season. He met players such as Rubén Gómez, **Roberto Clemente**, and Willie Mays, who were powerful mentors and teachers for him.

Pedro Zorrila, the owner of the Santurce team, had a close relationship with Horace Stoneham, owner of the Giants, then based in New York. In 1955, Zorrila persuaded Cepeda's family to allow him to go to a tryout at the Giants' spring camp in Melbourne, Florida. In Florida, Cepeda immediately felt a tremendous amount of isolation due to his meager knowledge of English the blatant racism prevalent in the South. He could not stay in the hotels available to the white players, and he could not go to restaurants where white people were served. He was not selected by the Giants, but was able to sign a contract with a minor league team in Salem, North Carolina, which later released him from his contract for below-average playing. Cepeda toured through several minor and semi-professional teams before reaching the majors.

Cepeda was eventually signed by the Kokomo Club, in the Mississippi–Ohio Valley League, where he finished his first season in the United States with an impressive 21 home runs, .397 batting average, and 91 RBIs (runs batted in). At the end of the season, in 1956, Cepeda was sold back to the Giants, which sent him to their class-C team in St. Cloud, Minnesota, where he had a great year, achieving 26 home runs, a .355 batting average, and 12 RBIs. He ended up winning the Northern League Triple Crown. His performance was so outstanding that he was transferred to the Minneapolis Millers, one of the best teams in the league, where he hit .309, 108 RBIs, and 25 home runs.

The Giants, by then based in San Francisco, signed Cepeda in time to start playing during the 1958 baseball season. After arriving in San Francisco, the right-handed Cepeda had a stellar year with a batting average of .312, 96 RBIs, and 25 home runs. He led the National League with 38 doubles and was selected as Rookie of the Year. A review of his career performance statistics reveals Cepeda's incredible power as a player. During his first seven years with the Giants, he had a batting average of .309, 32 home runs, and 106 RBIs. After two weak seasons in 1965 and early 1966, the Giants traded Cepeda to the St. Louis Cardinals. In the 1967 season, he batted a .325 average, scored 25 home runs, and led the league with 111 RBIs. His participation was crucial to the Cardinals' pennant win in 1967.

Due to recurrent problems with his knee, Cepeda was traded to the Atlanta Braves in 1968, where he had an average season but excelled during the 1969 season. Cepeda was traded to the Oakland Athletics in 1972 and played with them for one season, then was traded to Boston in 1973 and to the Kansas City Royals in 1974, where he retired after appearing in only 33 games.

During his major-league career, Cepeda had a batting average of .297, 2,351 hits, 457 doubles, 27 triples, and 379 home runs. He scored 1,131 runs and had 1,365 RBIs (Pietruzsa 2000, 187). Cepeda participated in seven All-Star Games, won the Comeback Player of the Year in 1966, and the Designated Hitter of the Year Award in 1973. He was unanimously selected as the National League's Most Valuable Player in 1967 (National Baseball Hall of Fame).

After his retirement from professional baseball, Cepeda returned to Puerto Rico, where he became involved in a series of businesses related to baseball. He also played the drums with the Apollo Sound, a popular salsa orchestra of the time. In 1975, after returning from a business trip to Colombia, Cepeda was arrested at the Isla Verde Airport after trying to claim several boxes he had mailed from Colombia that were found to contain marijuana. In 1978 he was sentenced to pay a $10,000 fine and serve a five-year jail term. He was eligible for parole after 20 months, but only served 10 months of his sentence.

After his release from prison, Cepeda had a very difficult time trying to put his career back together. However, after his discovery of the Buddhism in 1982, he was able to re-evaluate his life and come to terms with the anger generated by his childhood poverty and by the discrimination he experienced in the United States, both of which he blamed for many of his problems.

Cepeda was thrilled to be inducted into the Baseball Hall of Fame in 1999. In his induction speech he said:

> Believe me. I have a wonderful life. I am a very lucky person to be born with the skills to play baseball. Through baseball I escaped from Puerto Rico, I escaped poverty. Through baseball I built a name for myself. Through baseball I opened the gates for more Puerto Ricans, black Puerto Ricans, to come to this country and play ball for a living. (National Baseball Hall of Fame)

Today, Cepeda has a new outlook on life. He finds his work with the San Francisco Giants as a community relations officer rewarding and continues to be involved in his beloved baseball.—S.M.M.

References and Suggested Readings

Cepeda, Orlando, and Charles Einstein. *My Ups and Downs in Baseball.* New York: Putnam, 1968.

Cepeda, Orlando, and Herb Fagen. *Baby Bull: From Hardball to Hard Time and Back.* Dallas: Taylor Publishing Company, 1998.

National Baseball Hall of Fame. *http//baseballhalloffame.org/hoofers_and_honorees/hofer_bios/cepeda_Orlando.htm.*

Pietruzsa, David, ed. "Orlando Cepeda." *Baseball: The Biographical Encyclopedia.* New York: Total Sport Illustrated, 2000, 187.

AIMÉ CÉSAIRE
(1913–)

Martinican Writer and Politician

Aimé Césaire is considered one of the most important French-language twentieth-century poets. As the intellectual father of the literary and political movement known as Negritude, Césaire has served as a source of ideological inspiration for many other Caribbean and African American thinkers and writers. His involvement in the politics of Martinique has helped to define the political climate of the island and its current political status.

Césaire was born on June 25, 1913, in Basse Pointe, Martinique, a community located on the northern part of the island. His father, Fernand, was an accountant working with the Department of Revenue; his mother, Marie, was a seamstress and homemaker. He has described his childhood as one of extreme poverty and hunger, living in a wooden house infested with rats and bad odors (Frutkin 1973). He studied in Martinique and graduated from the Lycée Schoelcher. At the age of 18, he obtained a scholarship and left for France, where he spent the next eight years. On his arrival in Paris he studied at the Lycée Louis-le-Grand. He eventually went to the École Normale Supérieure and the Sorbonne, where he obtained the equivalent of a master's degree in literature.

While Césaire was in Paris, he co-founded a student publication entitled *L'etudiant noire* (The Black Student) along with Leopold Sedar Senghor, former president of Senegal, and Leon-Goutran Damas. It was from his position as editor of this publication that he helped to launch Negritude, one of the most significant literary movements within black African and Caribbean literature. Césaire has defined Negritude as "a point of departure. It is the affirmation that one is black and proud of it" (Frutkin 1973, 15). As a cultural and intellectual movement, Negritude is similar to the concept of Afrocentrism, as defined and understood in the United States. It rejects the aesthetic, cultural, and ideological values of the Western world and encourages a return to the original values of native African cultures and civilization. The Negritude movement, also influenced by modernism, adopted the values that Césaire had outlined in the poem "Return to My Native Land" (1939), where he rejected Western values and traditions and embraced African ones.

Césaire's style has a distinct and unique character. His verses and prose are characterized by an abundance of words. For him, poetry is "the reconquest of the self by the self" (Melsan 1997, 4). Words and imagery, rather than arms or insurrection, are the essential instruments for achieving that conquest. He uses metaphors extensively, and his selection of words is heavily influenced by the surreal and the fantastic. It is important to note that one of his first books contained illustrations by Pablo Picasso and that he has readily accepted the influence of surrealism in his literary work, often drawing on the irrational and fantastic. His work is filled with powerful messages and meanings that through irony and sarcasm undermine the mainstream ideology of the establishment in favor of indigenous African values.

When Césaire returned to Martinique, he found a job teaching at the Lycée of Fort-the-France from 1940 to 1945. It was at the Lycée that he taught the noted political philosopher **Frantz Fanon**, who was strongly influenced by Césaire's ideas.

An individual of deeply rooted political beliefs and convictions, Césaire entered the political arena of Martinique in 1945 and served his island in several capacities throughout most of this century. First, he was a delegate to two French Constitutional Assemblies (1945–1946), mayor of Fort-the-France (1945–1993); and deputy for Martinique in the French National Assembly (1946–1993). During his initial years in politics, he was a member of the French Communist Party. However, in 1956 he became disillusioned with the politics of the party and resigned; two years later he was one of the founders of the Progressive Party of Martinique.

Critic Thomas Wiloch points to a clear contradiction in Césaire's legacy. Although the politics of his poetry and literary work were radical, the pragmatic side of Césaire was far more moderate. Despite the nationalist themes in his poetry and his tacit rejection of the colonial forces of the dominant culture of France, he opposed the independence of Martinique and instead advocated that the island become an overseas French department under the protectorate of France. The mechanics of overseas department status are, in fact, colonial in nature. Even when his literary work spoke loudly of embracing black cultural forces, he always wrote in French rather than in his native Creole (Wiloch 1988).

During the 1950s and 1960s, Césaire also started to write plays. Among them are: *The Tragedy of King Cristophe, A Season in the Congo,* and *Une Tempete,* a Caribbean adaptation of Shakespeare's *Tempest.* As with so much of his work, his plays were influenced by the theme of Negritude and had deeply rooted political implications.

Césaire is regarded as one of the most significant writers of the French language. His political ideology encompasses some of the most important thinking both in the Negritude movement and in the field of colonial studies. His ideology and writings were a source of inspiration for the Pan-African movement that emerged in the United States during the 1960s and 1970s. In 1997, filmmaker **Euzhan Palcy** directed the film *Aimé Césaire: A Voice for History.* In this film she provides a thorough profile of the life and contributions of this notable author whose artistic mastery has been deeply applauded by literary critics of French literature and language. He is one of those unique individuals whose writings transcend the Caribbean landscape and reach universal themes. He currently lives in Martinique.—S.M.M.

References and Suggested Readings

Frutkin, Susan. *Aimé Césaire: Black Between Worlds.* Miami, FL: Center for Advanced International Studies, University of Miam, 1973.

Melsan, Annick Thebia. "The Liberating Power of Words." *UNESCO Courier* (May 1997): 4–8.

Palcy, Euzhan. *Aimé Césaire: A Voice for History.* South Burlington, VT: California Newsreel Company, 1997.

Wiloch, Thomas. "Biographic Sketch on Aimé Césaire." *Contemporary Authors.* Kansas City, MO: Gale, 1988. 114–117.

MARY EUGENIA CHARLES
(1919–)

Lawyer and Politician from Dominica and First Female Head of State in the Caribbean

Dominica's "Caribbean Iron Lady" Mary Eugenia Charles is a woman with a large number of political and professional firsts. She was the first female head of state in the Caribbean and in the American continent. "Until the media hit on it, it never dawned on me I was different," was Charles's reaction to the commotion generated after the general elections of July 21, 1980, made her prime minister of Dominica (Thomas 1980, 16). In many interviews she has stated that she did not initally seek out a political career but became interested in politics when the government, through legislation, sought to stifle dissenting views. As a result, she co-founded the Dominica Freedom Party and spent 12 years as leader of the opposition until her election as prime minister.

Charles, granddaughter of former slaves and the youngest of four children, was born in the southern district of Pointe Michel on May 15, 1919, into the well-to-do family of John Baptiste Charles and Josephine Delauney. A political activist and self-made man who believed education was everything, John Baptiste was a mason who became a farmer, land developer, and the founder of the Penny Bank in Dominica. Her father's strong belief in the importance of education was also obvious in her own schooling, which began in Catholic primary and secondary schools in Dominica and Grenada. In 1946, she received a B.A. in law from the University of Toronto. From there she went to Britain and attended the Inner

Temple, Inns of Court, where she completed her law studies in 1947 and continued studies at the London School of Economics.

In 1949, she returned to Dominica as the first female lawyer on the island. However, she lived and practiced law in London for many years before permanently returning to Dominica in the 1960s. She was almost a fixture in the letters to the editor section of the local press—so much so that in 1968 the government tried to amend the Seditious and Undesirable Publications Act with a proposal that would have limited dissenting views. Charles became active in politics and organized the opposing Dominica Freedom Party (DFP), which began its political involvement in the 1970 elections. Charles was not elected in her run for office that year, but she accepted an appointed seat to the legislature.

In 1975 she was the leader of the DFP and was elected to the House of Assembly, where she became the leader of the opposition—another first by a woman in Dominica. In 1977 she was among the leaders chosen to travel to Britain to discuss independence, which was finally granted in 1978. Two years later, after the devastation left by Hurricane David, Charles' DPF won the 1980 elections by a landslide and she became prime minister. A strong advocate of free enterprise, Charles' government initially focused on eliminating government corruption and on the development of economic reform measures. In addition, she survived two attempted coups during the first years of her rule.

Deeply anticommunist, she called on U.S. President Ronald Reagan in 1983 to help prevent Cuban infiltration of Grenada, which resulted in the U.S. incursion of Grenada. As a result, she was able to obtain millions of dollars from the United States for improving the island's roads and other infrastructure. Her government oversaw the construction of Roseau Waterfront, a protective sea wall that has become a popular promenade, as well as the construction of bridges and water and telephone systems. Her decision to call Reagan, coupled with her commanding presence, earned her the nickname "Iron Lady of the Caribbean."

In 1985, Charles was re-elected to a second five-year term and also became minister of foreign affairs, finance, economic affairs, and defense. Even though her primary concern was to improve the economy and quality of life for Dominicans, she was adamant about allowing open development of tourist resorts, but her approach focused on preserving the island's ecology and national identity. To that extent, Dominica has no casinos, nightclubs, or duty-free shops. Her vision has led Dominica to become a model eco-tourism destination in the Caribbean. Notwithstanding the progress Dominica has experienced under her leadership, her critics claimed that she ran the country too much like a business, at the expense of the people.

During her tenure in politics she had to absorb comments and insults from men unaccustomed to women in leadership roles. She was also attacked because she had never married. Despite all this, Charles was elected to a third term in 1990. Described by many as a decisive leader, her administration left a legacy of economic reform and set in place mechanisms to end government corruption. Charles was asked what advice she would give young women. She replied that women must have a good understanding of themselves and their goals as well as a plan—"And not let *anybody* interfere with it" (Listwood 1996, 121). In February 2003 she received the Order of the Caribbean Community, the region's highest award, in recognition of her work for Caribbean people.—G.C.

References and Suggested Readings

Fontaine, Kelvin. "Iron Lady Throws in Towel: Kelvin Fontaine Looks at Dame Eugenia Charles, Dominica's Flamboyant Leader Who Is Giving Up Power After 14 Years at the Helm." *Weekly Journal* 125 (September 22, 1994): 10.

Jackson, Guida M. "Maria Eugenia Charles." *Women Who Ruled: A Biographical Encyclopedia.* New York: Barnes and Noble Books, 1998. 46–47.

Liswood, Laura A. *Women World Leaders: Fifteen Great Politicians Tell Their Stories.* New York: HarperCollins, 1996.

Thomas, Bert. "Everybody's Person of the 20th Century: Dominica; Dame Mary Eugenia Charles." *Everybody's: The Caribbean-American Magazine* 23.11 (December 31, 1999): 26.

Thomas, Jo. "Quietly, She Makes History as Caribbean Leader." *The New York Times,* December 1, 1980, 16.

EDWARD CHEUNG
(1963–)

Electrical Engineer and Scientist from Aruba

Edward Bing Cheung, a native of Aruba, has been one of the scientists working to optimize the performance of the Hubble Space Telescope. The equipment designed by him and his team has been taken into space in four different missions of the Space Shuttle. The launching of the Hubble Space Telescope was a formidable achievement for the National Aeronautics and Space Administration (NASA) and for the scores of scientists and collaborating nations that worked on the project. Since its launching in 1990, the Hubble has sent back to earth spectacular images of the universe. These images have forced scientists to rethink many of the commonly held assumptions about our solar system and neighboring galaxies. The Hubble is an incredibly complex machine that requires constant monitoring, upgrading, and maintenance.

Cheung was born on February 6, 1963, in the town of San Nicolas in Aruba. He was one of three children of Kong Ming Cheung, a supermarket owner from Hong Kong, and Yok Fun Cheung, a homemaker born in Singapore. Like many other immigrants to the Caribbean island of Aruba, his father arrived in the island when he was 23 years old, following the footsteps of his father who had been a cook in an oil tanker servicing a gas refinery in Aruba. When his tanker became stranded at the island, he got off the ship and decided to begin a new life on this Caribbean island.

Cheung received his elementary education at Paulus School in his native town of San Nicolas and graduated from high school from the Colegio Arubano in Oranjestad in 1980. He migrated to the United States and enrolled at the Worcester Polytechnic Institute, graduating in 1985. He went on to earn a doctorate in electrical engineering from Yale University, where he specialized in robotics. His doctoral dissertation, "Real-Time Motion Planning for Whole-Sensitive Robot Art Manipulators (Sensitive Skin Proximity Sensor)" (1990), studied the problems faced by motion sensors installed in robots. While presenting a paper at a conference, his research attracted the attention of a NASA scientist, who recruited him to work for the space agency.

Edward Cheung.

Cheung's interests in science and electronics go back to his childhood. When he was a small boy, his father gave him a small transistor radio. He decided to dismantle the radio and became fascinated by the circuits and transistors that made it work. His father recognized the talents of his young son and nurtured his interest in science. Cheung recalls that when his father went on business trips, he would come back with electronic kits and books for him to experiment with. By the age of seven, Cheung had figured out how to build an electrical system to remotely operate his television set, his stereo equipment, and the lights in his room.

During his years as an undergraduate student at the Worcester Polytechnic Institute, Cheung became involved in many scientific and research projects. As part of the Major Qualifying Project, a graduation requirement, he built a fiber optic rotation sensor to be flown on the Space Shuttle as a student research project. While the explosion of the Space Shuttle *Challenger* derailed his research project, he didn't lose his motivation and interest in science.

At Yale he worked in the emerging field of robotics and did work on the barriers faced by motion sensors, which were used to allow the mobility of space robots. On purchasing his first home in 1991, Cheung designed a complete home automation system that allowed him to control almost every function of the house automatically, such as the phones, the doors, the alarm systems, stereo equipment, and the like. His novel work on the house was profiled in the magazine *Home Automator* in 1999.

Cheung joined NASA in 1991. In 1996 he became one of the scientists designing equipment to support the Hubble Telescope as part of the Solid State Recorder (SRR) Team. Despite the fact that the Hubble is a formidable machine, it requires a great deal of maintenance and upkeep. Some of its systems break down and others become obsolete. As a result, NASA has a team of engineers who provide support to the telescope by designing new and corrective equipment that is taken to space by astronauts in carefully structured missions designed to maintain the Hubble and to prolong its useful life.

Cheung has participated in the design of many important components for the Hubble. He built and tested an electronic digital recorder that stores the images collected by the Hubble before their transmission to earth. It was installed in the telescope in 1997 and its success caused a second copy to be installed in 1999. He also designed a computer named the HOST Controller that controls several functions of a cooling device for an infrared camera that scans the universe. He recently designed the A.R.U.B.A. (ASCS/NCS Relay Unit Breaker Assembly), which disconnects power to the instruments in case of a electrical problem and prevents a generalized instrument failure. The relay box was installed by astronauts in 2002 and is located outside the Hubble spacecraft. Cheung decided to name the device after the Caribbean island in order to build enthusiasm for space exploration among children in his homeland.

Edward Cheung has become a principal engineer for the Hubble Space Telescope Servicing Project. He works out of the Goddard Space Flight Center in Maryland. Although he is still young, he has already made significant contributions to the space program and aerospace sciences. In 1999, Worcester Polytechnic Institute awarded him the Ichabod Washburn Young Alumni Award for his professional achievements in science. He keeps in touch with his native Aruba, which he visits often. Electronics continue to be his lifelong passion.—S.M.M.

References and Suggested Readings

Cheung, Edward. "Edward Cheung's Automated Home." *Home Automator* (January/February 1999): 12–14.

———. "Real-Time Motion Planning for Whole-Sensitive Robot Arm Manipulators (Sensitive Skin Proximity Sensor)." Doctoral dissertation. Ann Arbor, MI: Dissertation Abstracts. 1990.

Méndez-Méndez, Serafín. Personal communication with Dr. Edward Cheung. February 1, 2002.

SHIRLEY CHISHOLM
(1924–)

Barbadian American Politician and Educator and First Woman to Run for U.S. President

A woman of many firsts, Shirley Chisholm rose to national prominence in 1964 by becoming the first black woman elected to the New York Legislature, and again in 1969, when she was elected to the U.S. Congress. She is considered a pioneer who skillfully battled sexism and racism and whose accomplishments as a politician led the way to increased visibility and participation of blacks and women in the political arena. Outspoken and unafraid of controversy, her lifelong motto "unbought and unbossed" became her campaign maxim when in 1972 she became the first woman in history to run for president. She often tapped her Barbadian background and regarded her experiences there as an important personal resource instrumental to her success.

Her political career was characterized by her struggle to bring equality in pay and education to the disenfranchised. Among the landmark legislation sponsored by Chisholm was expanding the minimum wage to include domestic workers and the establishment of Title I of the Education Act, which provides federal grants to

Shirley Chisholm. Courtesy of Photofest.

school districts for the purpose of helping low-achieving students succeed in school. Her views created critics as well as loyalists, but she never deviated from her opinions. Described by former House Speaker Tip O'Neill in 1972 as one of "the most eloquent woman orators we have had," Chisholm attributes her success to the example set by her family and her Quaker faith (Trescott 1982, H1).

Shirley Anita St. Hill was born November 20, 1924, in Brooklyn, New York. She was the oldest of four sisters and daughter of Charles and Ruby St. Hill. Described as a "proud black man" who was a voracious reader, Charles St. Hill worked as a baker's helper and eventually secured a job in a factory. He became a staunch union man and a follower of the black independence principles of **Marcus Garvey**, instilling in his daughters a strong work ethic and pride in their race. Her mother, Ruby Seale, when not at her sewing machine, would assist neighborhood women—many first-generation Jews from central and eastern Europe."[B]ecause she was English-speaking and could give advice about bills and other legal pitfalls of city life, she became a kind of neighborhood oracle and leader" (Chisholm 1970, 12). A believer in the importance of self-reliance and education Chisholm's mother found it very difficult to raise a family and make a living. In 1928, she went back to Barbados, taking Shirley, Odessa, and Muriel in tow with the intention of leaving them in the care of her mother until finances improved. For the next seven years Chisholm and her sisters lived with grandmother Emmeline Seale, "a tall, gaunt, erect, Indian-looking woman with her hair knotted on her neck"—a strict disciplinarian and "one of the few persons whose authority I would never dare to defy, or even question" (Chisholm 1973, 5). By the time Chisholm was four years old, her grandmother had enrolled her in the village school, where the discipline was just as strict as it was at home. She was expected to study hard and complete her chores on the farm every day after school.

At the end of 1933, now the mother of a forth daughter, whom she named Selma, and unsuccessful in regaining a financial foothold on the family's life, Ruby returned to Barbados to pick up her daughters and reunite the family in the Brownsville section of Brooklyn, New York. Nine-year-old Chisholm was not only shocked by the cold weather and the unfamiliarity of urban living, but she was placed below her appropriate grade level because she was unacquainted with American history and geography even though her reading and writing ability were above grade level. In no time, Chisholm achieved the required knowledge and completed her elementary and secondary education in New York City public schools. In 1942, after having held the office of vice president of the honor society and with scholarship offers to Vassar and Oberlin Colleges, Chisholm graduated from the prestigious Girls' High School in the Bedford-Stuyvesant section of Brooklyn, where the family had moved to in 1936. However, unable to afford out-of-state room and board, in the fall of 1942 she enrolled in Brooklyn College of the City University of New York. The racism of the time excluded blacks from entering social work professions, medicine, science, and law, so Chisholm decided on a career as an early childhood teacher majoring in sociology and Spanish. She graduated cum laude in 1946. A fluent bilingual, she speaks and writes Spanish.

She began her career as a teacher of the Mt. Calvary Child Care Center in Harlem, where her experiences with underprivileged children reinforced her commitment to fight against ignorance and poverty and led to her becoming an activist in local Democratic politics, the League of Women Voters, and the National Association for the Advancement of Colored People (NAACP). Throughout this period she also attended graduate school at Columbia University, where she completed a master's degree in early childhood education. It was during graduate school that she met and married another graduate student, Conrad Chisholm. As her interest and participation in Brooklyn politics continued to grow, so did her realization that blacks, particularly women, were treated like second-class citizens. This led her to help form the Unity Democratic Club, whose membership included black men and women interested in politics, and where she realized that sexism was just as prevalent as it was among the white male establishment.

By 1959 she began to work for the New York City Division of Day Care, supervising ten centers while serving in the executive committee of the Unity Democratic Club. By 1964, after the Unity Club ousted the white Democratic establishment from Bedford-Stuyvesant—and with the reluctance of some male members—Chisholm was endorsed as candidate for the New York State Assembly. She beat her two male opponents by more than 17,000 votes. Her most important accomplishments as a New York assemblywoman include the bill that created the SEEK program, making college a possibility to students who come from disadvantaged backgrounds. She was also responsible for the bill that set up New York's first unemployment insurance coverage for domestic employees. In addition, she sponsored a bill that allowed schoolteachers who were on maternity leave the right to return without losing their tenured status.

The redistricting efforts of the late 1960s created the Twelfth Congressional District of Brooklyn—the community where she grew up—where in 1968 "Fighting Shirley Chisholm—Unbought and Unbossed" (Chisholm 1970, 69) was elected the first black congresswoman in American history. She immediately challenged—on the floor of the house—her assignment to the Agriculture Committee, which in her view seemed inappropriate for someone who represented an urban district in one of the largest cities in the nation. Her strategy was successful, resulting in an assignment to the Veteran's Committee. In a move that was different from anything seen in Washington politics, she assembled a staff of mostly educated and outstanding women and became an outspoken opponent of the war in Vietnam and a supporter of the Equal Rights Amendment. She also made history by sponsoring a bill to pay for a memorial to Mary McLeod, the first time federal funds were used to honor an African American. Even though she was at the forefront in her support of women's rights, she was also quick to point out the racial issues and the lack of black women in the mostly white feminist movement. Eventually she was appointed to the Education and Labor Committee, became the senior Democratic woman in the House of Representatives, and the first black to sit on the House Rules Committee. Her rise to power was documented in her 1970 autobiography *Unbought and Unbossed,* where she reflected on her political life.

Chisholm's coalition-building skills played an important role when she ran for president. In 1972 she encouraged record numbers of blacks to register and vote, many for the first time in their lives. As a result she entered 11 primaries and received strong support from the south and southwest part of the country. Even though she lost the race, she received 151 votes in the Democratic convention and demonstrated that others, in addition to white males, could aspire the presidency of the United States. She documented this historical event in her 1972 book *The Good Fight.*

By the early 1980s Chisholm had been re-elected by large majorities and her seat in Congress was considered secure. She had led the fight for federal support of women's athletic programs and ended the control of white males in the House Democratic Caucus when she became its secretary. On many occasions she was at odds with her black colleagues' personal goals and publics stands. She was a supporter of black colleges, junior colleges, and community colleges, making sure they received a fair share of federal funding during the reorganization of the Higher Education Act in 1980. However, the election of Ronald Reagan in 1980 brought with it an increasingly conservative political climate and she retired at the end of 1982 in order to spend more time with her second husband, Arthur Chadwick Jr.—the first black elected to the New York state Legislature—who had been seriously hurt in a car accident that year.

Her activism led her to found two important organizations in the early 1980s, the Mid-Brooklyn Civic Association and the National Congress of Black Women, where she served as chairperson until 1992, when she received its annual award. She has spent most of her post-congressional years writing, teaching, lecturing, and traveling. Her role in public service has been recognized around the country, and she has received honorary doctorates from 31 institutions. After being nominated as ambassador to Jamaica by President Clinton in 1993, Chisholm discovered that health problems would prevent her from being able to accept the appointment. In 1993 she was inducted into the National Women's Hall of Fame and in 2000 she was awarded the Tower of Power Award from Turner Broadcasting Systems for her public service. On July 2, 2001, the House of Representatives unanimously passed a resolution that recognized Chisholm's contributions as the country's first black congresswoman. Now retired from politics, Chisholm travels and speaks throughout the country.—G.C.

References and Suggested Readings

Chisholm, Shirley. *The Good Fight.* New York: Harper & Row, 1973.
———. *Unbought and Unbossed.* Boston: Houghton Mifflin, 1970.
Hughes, Arthur J., and Frank P. Le Veness. "Shirley Chisholm: Woman of Complexity, Conscience, and Compassion." In Frank P. Le Veness and Jane P. Sweeney, eds., *Women Leaders in Contemporary U.S. Politics.* Boulder, CO: Lynne Rienner, 1987. 9–20.
Morin, Isobel V. "Shirley Chisholm: A Political Maverick." *Women of the U.S. Congress.* Minneapolis: The Oliver Press, 1994. 67–90.
Peterman, Peggy. "Shirley Chisholm Speaks With Her Mind and Her Heart." *St. Petersburg Times,* February 13, 1990, 3D.
Pinkney, Andrea Davis. "Shirley Chisholm." *Let It Shine: Stories of Black Women Freedom Fighters.* New York: Gulliver Books/Harcourt, 2000. 95–104.
Trescott, Jacqueline. "Shirley Chisholm in Her Season of Transition; The Feisty Congresswoman Wrestles With Her Leave-Taking." *Washington Post,* June 6, 1982, H1.

Austin C. Clarke
(1934–)

Barbadian Writer

Austin Ardinel Chesterfield Clarke is a Barbadian writer who now resides in Canada. He has produced a wide array of novels, short stories, and newspaper columns that explore the cultural and racial conflicts faced by native Barbadians as a result of colonial exploitation by Great Britain as well as the dilemmas faced by Barbadian immigrants in Canada.

Clarke was born in St. James, Barbados, on July 26, 1934. His father, Kenneth Trotman, was an artist, and his mother, Gladys Clarke, worked as a maid at the Marine Hotel in Barbados. He was illegitimate because his mother was not permitted to marry his father due to class differences (Cumber Dance 1986). His mother later married Fitzherbert Luke, a Barbadian policeman, who helped to raise Clarke and became his father figure.

Clarke spent his formative years in the village of St. Matthias in Barbados. Stella Algoo-Baksh, one of Clarke's most comprehensive biographers, has suggested that the poverty that surrounded Clarke and his family and the oppressive class separations between blacks and whites in St. Matthias and Barbados left deep imprints and scars on this author's psyche. These early life experiences provided Clarke with a strong sense of ambition that motivated and helped him to succeed. More importantly, they inspired many of the literary works that he produced later in life (Algoo-Baksh 1994).

Since Clarke has often used his educational process as the background for his literary work, it is important to understand his educational experience. From the beginning, his mother passed on to her son her belief in the importance of education. In the Barbadian society of the time, education was the only way to achieve a more comfortable life. However, few poor Barbadian children were able to afford a quality education beyond the elementary grades. Even when they were extremely poor, Clarke's mother didn't hesitate to take on extra work and sacrifice in order to provide him with the best possible education.

As a young boy, he attended the St. Matthias Boys' Elementary School. The school, affiliated with the Church of England, drew a mixed enrollment of white and black students from his village. Even though during school hours there was a great degree of socialization across class and color boundaries between the students, once the students left classes they moved back into fairly segregated lifestyles that hindered their ability to socialize or play.

By the sixth grade, when Clarke was ten, he moved on to attend the very prestigious Combermere School, a secondary school. His family was able to afford this elite school with the assistance of one of his aunts and with the extra work picked up his mother. Even though there were other blacks at the school, it was an elitist institution that placed great emphasis on British educational, social, and political customs and values. At Combermere, Clarke was mentored by teacher **Frank Collymore**, who was also responsible for mentoring Barbadian writer **George Lamming**. Clarke developed a fondness for English and spent countless hours reading at the library. He started publishing some of his early work in the student newspapers *The Daily Poop* and *The Combemerian*. While at the school, Clarke became a member of the Cadet Corp, the student chapter of the Barbados militia. He also became active in sports, participating in races and establishing himself as a well-known student athlete in Barbados.

After graduation from Combermere, Clarke attended Harrison College, an elite school run by a British headmaster and modeled after British preparatory schools. Clarke graduated from Harrison College in 1950 and obtained the Oxford and Cambridge High School Certificates. But it was at Harrison, more than anywhere else, that he felt completely isolated. He continued confronting the issues of race and class typical of Barbados at the time. Most of his classmates and teachers were white middle-class and upper-class Barbadians who could not relate to his living conditions and poor background. To make matters worse, Clarke had achieved a level of education that isolated from him from former friends and neighbors, who were unable to relate to the intellectual interests and opportunities available to him (Boxill 1986). Throughout his writing career, Clarke has been extremely critical of the elitist education that he received at Harrison College, where he felt different by virtue of being poor and black. Algoo-Baksh underscores the fact that "Harison College left Clarke filled with 'aggression' and 'ambition'" (Algoo-Baksh 1994, 27).

After graduating from high school, Clarke worked as a schoolteacher at the Coleridge-Parry Primary School in Barbados. Although he was accepted to both Oxford University and the London School of Economics, he was unable to attend either for lack of money. Like many other West Indian writers such as **Stuart Hall** and George Lamming, he decided to leave Barbados in search of better intellectual and cultural opportunities. Clarke immigrated to Canada in 1955 and enrolled at the University of Toronto's Trinity College, where he studied English literature, economics, and political science. By 1957, however, he left the university to pursue his interests in literature and writing.

During the late 1950s and early 1960s Clarke held many different odd jobs including working as a surveyor, a laborer in factories, an editor for the Canadian Broadcasting Corporation, and a janitor. His most significant work experience of the time was as a journalist for the *Toronto Globe Mail*, the *Daily Press* of Timmins, and the *Northern Daily News* in Kirkland Lake. He also worked as an editor for a number of industrial publications

Clarke started writing poetry when he was eight years old. His first poem was titled "The Ballad of Bandy Legged James." After he left the university in 1957, he started to write poems, short stories, and novels that were to serve as the basis for his later publications. During this time, Clarke was desperately trying to find his niche as a writer.

Clarke's successful entrance into the Canadian literary scene didn't occur until 1964 with the publication of his book *Survivors of the Crossing*. This novel explores the issue of colonial exploitation of sugarcane workers in Barbados. It was representative of the first major period in his literary production, which began during the early 1960s and centered on the complex social dynamics of Barbados. This work, which has been praised for its poignant commentaries on Barbadian life, presents some of the major problems that have affected his native Caribbean island. He depicts racism, British elitism, economic exploitation, underdevelopment, racial and class divides, and cultural isolation. His book *Amongst Thistles and Thorns* (1965), considered autobiographical in nature, further explores the issue of the Barbadian racial divide, and is also representative of this period.

Between the mid-1960s and the 1970s, Clarke's literary production shifted its focus to explore the issues arising from the process of Barbadian migration to Toronto, an important social phenomenon in Canada at the time. His novels from this period, *The Meeting Point* (1967), *Storm of Fortune* (1973), and *The Bigger Light*

(1975)—known as the Toronto Trilogy—constitute his second literary period. The novels explore the lives of sacrifice, resilience, and racism faced by Toronto's Barbadian immigrants. With these narratives he developed the themes of the preponderant influence of migration, black pride, lack of identity, economic exploitation, social alienation, and assimilation that come as the result of emigration to a foreign land.

Clarke is praised for his uncanny ability to look into the psyche of his characters and portray their feelings and emotions as they deal with the world around them. Critics also commend him for his portrayals of and insights into the lifestyles and work of immigrants (Ramraj 1993). Clarke has a gift for unraveling the soul of his characters to reveal not only their views of the world but also the way in which they are affected by the social paradigms that tragically define who they are and the ways in which they exist. In terms of style, critics have acknowledged his ability to capture, reconstruct, and present the linguistic accents, patterns, and dialects of the West Indian groups he writes about. Like **Nicolás Guillén** from Cuba and **Luis Palés Matos** from Puerto Rico, Clarke has been able to ingeniously recreate the ways in which his fellow West Indians talk (Boxill 1986; Algoo Baksh 1994).

Among his most important works has been *Growing-Up Stupid Under the Union Jack* (1980), a novel that won him the 1980 Casa de las Americas Prize for Literature. During the 1990s, Clarke published two collections of short stories, *This City* (1992) and *There are No Elders* (1993). *The Origins of the Waves* (1997) earned the honor of being the inaugural recipient of the Rogers Communications Writers' Trust Fiction Prize in 1998. His most recent novel, *The Polished Hoe* (2002), won him Canada's prestigious Giller Prize.

In addition to his writings, Clarke has explored many other fields of endeavor. He has worked occasionally in broadcasting since his arrival in Canada. Because of his interest in broadcasting and his familiarity with Barbados, he served as a cultural and press attaché for the Barbados embassy in Washington, D.C., from 1974 to 1975. The Barbadian government recruited him as general manager of the Caribbean Broadcasting Group in 1975 but he was fired shortly afterwards for not following the government's political line. In 1977 he ran as a candidate for the Progressive Conservative Party in Ontario.

Clarke has also had a prolific career as a college professor and lecturer. He has taught writing classes at a number of prestigious universities such as Yale, Duke, Williams College, the University of Southern California, and the University of Texas at Austin. He also served on the Immigration and Refugee Board of Canada between 1988 and 1993.—S.M.M.

References and Suggested Readings

Algoo-Baksh, Stella. *Austin C. Clarke: A Biography.* Toronto: ECW Press, 1994.
Boxill, Anthony. "Austin C. Clarke." In *Dictionary of Literary Biography,* Vol. 53. Detroit: Gale, 1986. 124–129.

Clarke, Austin C. *Growing Up Stupid Under the Union Jack: A Memoir.* Toronto: McClelland and Steward, 1980.
——. *The Survivors of the Crossing.* Toronto: McClelland and Steward, 1964.
Cumber Dance, Daryl. "Austin C. Clarke." *Fifty Caribbean Writers.* Westport, CT: Greenwood Press, 1986. 115–121.
Ramraj, Victor J. "Austin C. Clarke." In Lindfors Bernth, and Reinhard Sander, eds., *Dictionary of Literary Biography: Twentieth-Century Caribbean and Black African Writers,* Vol. 125. Detroit: Gale, 1993. 29–34.

LeRoy Clarke
(1938–)

Trinidadian Painter

LeRoy Clarke is one of the best-known Trinidadian painters of today and one of the leading graphic artists of the Caribbean. Through his art he has worked meticulously to reclaim the African legacy of his beloved Trinidad and Caribbean. He has said: "For the past thirty-five years I have been attempting to make sense of a vision of humanity that dwells in me. 'Eye' have come to understand, after the musings of much labor, only the task of recharting the ruins, particularly of an African soul splayed across a hostile world" (Sandberg 1999). His artistic creations are important because they provide his audiences with a collective set of symbols that allow them to understand the essential role that the African roots play in Caribbean life and culture.

Clarke was born in 1938 in the community of Gonzales, a suburb close to the capital of Port of Spain. He is a self-taught artist. He worked as a teacher in the town of John John, a suburb of Port of Spain. He held his first exhibition in 1962, where he sold his first painting for $15. His exhibit *Labour of Love,* held in 1966, marked Clarke's recognition as one of Trinidad's most talented painters.

Clarke left Trinidad in 1968 for New York City. His departure marks the beginning of a period of incredible artistic production. He was welcomed at the Studio Museum in Harlem, where he became a program coordinator and an artist-in-residence, and where he stayed until 1974.

LeRoy Clarke considers himself an artist/poet. He thinks of his art as constantly evolving in an intense attempt to reclaim the African roots of the Caribbean and his native Trinidad. His most significant works are a series of paintings that try to produce a figurative graphic history of Afro-Caribbeans in the West Indies. He began this ongoing epic, known as *The Poet,* in the early 1970s, adding new murals every few years. The series has eight major murals so far. They are: *Fragments of a Spiritual* (1971), *Douens* (1979), *In the Maze There Is a Single Line to My Soul* (1988), *The Eye Am* (1989), *El Tucuche* (1989), *Utterance* (1991), *Pantheon* (1992), and

Revelations (1994). The evolution of these works moves the Trinidadian viewer toward reclaiming his African ancestry—the "natural" identity that Clarke expects his people to have.

Clarke's work is characterized by abstraction and symbolism, and he underscores his work with the use of mythical symbols. In an interview with the *Trinidad Sunday Express*, he sheds light on the symbolic properties of his paintings:

> If you look at a garden, seeing flowers and so on, you are seeing it as it is, with your eye of actuality. But, if you stand there long enough, focusing on the one rose that stands out, you begin to interpret the presence of the rose differently. The rose is not a rose any longer. We are now moving from the realm of actuality to the realm of the abstract. What I do, is dissolve the images as much as possible, and dwell in their aura, seeing the various colors that jump out, I put these colours to canvas. This is how people are able to paint things like sounds and feelings. (Hosten 2000, 5)

The paintings of LeRoy Clarke resemble many of the naturalistic and primitive paintings that typify much Caribbean art production. Critics have said that his early work was heavily influenced by the work of Cuban painter **Wilfredo Lam** (Curnen 1997). In fact, his painting *Pantheon* resembles closely the work of Haitian primitivist painter **Hector Hyppolite**. Each element within his pictorial composition conveys a signifier that alludes to the African legacy, whether it refers to slavery, religious practices, or the like. Caribbean art critic Veerle Poupeye has characterized Clarke's work as one mostly concerned with "race and post colonial identity." She emphasizes that "he has developed a complex iconographical programme on the black experience in the New World, from oppression to transcendence" (Poupeye 1998, 138).

Clarke's pictography represents one of the most serious and comprehensive attempts of any contemporary Caribbean painter to articulate the notion that Caribbean people need to come to terms, once and for all, with those constitutive elements that define and give meaning to their reason for being; their identity. His works of art command high prices, and he recently sold his mural *The Seers* for $220,000 to the United Trust Corporation in Trinidad. His work has been exhibited in Port of Spain, Venezuela, and the United States. Clarke currently lives at the base of El Tucuche, a mountain in Trinidad featured in his paintings, where he continues to actively paint and compose.—S.M.M.

References and Suggested Readings

Curnen, Monique G. "LeRoy Clarke." In Thomas Riggs, ed., *St. James Press Guide to Black Artists*. Detroit: St. James Press, 1997. 115–116.

Hosten, Colin. "Understanding LeRoy Clarke." *Sunday Express* (Trinidad), April 30, 2000, 5.

Lewis, Samella. *Caribbean Visions: Contemporary Painting and Sculpture.* Alexandria, VA: Art Services International, 1995.

Poupeye, Veerle. *Caribbean Art.* London: Thames and Hudson, 1998.

Sandberg, Curtis, curator. *Sing Me a Rainbow: An Artistic Medley from Trinidad and Tobago* (exhibition catalogue). Washington, DC: Meridian International Center, 1999. (Also available at *http://latino.si.edu/rainbow/pages/clarke.html*.)

ROBERTO CLEMENTE
(1934–1972)

Puerto Rican Baseball Player and Philanthropist

Every nation has its famous sports figures. Only rarely, however, do these men become national figures. Baseball player Roberto Clemente became one of the national heroes of Puerto Rico. While his extraordinary prowess as a baseball player contributed to his rise to fame and popularity during his lifetime, his humbleness and charitable spirit were responsible for making him a hero even before his tragic death in a plane crash at the age of 38. A man of unique sports talent, as his induction into the Baseball Hall of Fame demonstrates, he was an even greater champion of humanitarian causes in Puerto Rico and Latin America. His love for children, the poor, and the less fortunate showed him as an enlightened spirit who not only delighted the baseball fans but also to gave his time and voice to those who needed a lift in life.

Clemente was born on August 18, 1934, in the San Antón suburb of Carolina, in the northeastern section of Puerto Rico. San Antón is a legendary community because it was one of the major enclaves where people of black ancestry and descendants of slaves settled. Clemente's father was Melchor, a sugarcane worker on a nearby plantation. His mother, Luisa Walker, ran a small family-owned grocery store that sold food to the employees of the plantation. Clemente was the youngest of seven children in a family of six brothers and one sister.

Clemente, known to his family as Momen, started experimenting with sports as a youngster. He practiced baseball using rubber balls and batted with a broomstick. He used some of the money he made delivering milk to a neighbor to buy balls. He was fascinated by baseball, but his family could not explain his obsession for the sport and scolded him for being so tired from practice that he could not to eat.

While Roberto is now remembered for his accomplishments in baseball, he actually began his career playing softball. As a high school student, he was selected by a scouting agent to be part of the softball team of the Sello Rojo (Red Seal) rice brand in Puerto Rico. Many people credit his powerful throw to the early use of heavier softballs.

During his adolescence, Clemente was active playing baseball with several amateur teams throughout the metropolitan area; at 16, he played with the Junco Amateur team in the metropolitan area. On graduation from Julio Vizcarrondo High School in 1949, he was given a three-year contract with the Santurce Cangrejeros (Crabbers), one of the most popular professional ball clubs on the island. Although earning only $400.00 per season, it was during his time with the Crabbers that Clemente was first exposed to some of the great American baseball players of the time, such as Willie Mays. At the time, many American ball players played seasonally in Puerto Rico, as the island's season runs during the American off-season. Mays, the great baseball player, spotted Clemente's talent and mentored him during his stay in Santurce.

Roberto Clemente. © MLB Photos.

Al Campanisi, a talent scout working for the Brooklyn Dodgers, discovered Clemente while he was playing for the Cangrejeros in 1954 and signed him with the Dodgers. He was given a signing bonus of $10,000 and was paid $5,000 per year. The management of the Dodgers, recognizing Clemente's potential, sent Clemente to Canada to play with the Montreal Royals, the Dodgers' International League farm team and their AAA league club abroad. This was a common tactic at the time—many clubs followed this method to prevent players being drafted by another team for the same or greater amount of money (Pietrusza 2000). The management of the Dodgers ordered the Royals to play Clemente as little as possible to minimize the chances of his being discovered and drafted by another team. Whenever Clemente played for the Royals, he generally performed in a stellar fashion. To his disappointment, after a successful performance, he was benched to protect him from scouts (Walker 1988). However, this strategy was not successful, as Clyde Sukeforth, a talent scout working for the Pittsburgh Pirates, discovered Clemente and drafted him for just $4,000—the same amount he had been paid at the time of his recruitment but with a commitment from the Pirates to send him directly to the major leagues.

During his first few seasons with the Pirates, Clemente performed well but far short of his potential. Problems adapting to the United States, the death of one of his brothers, and a car accident are often cited as explanations for his poor performance. According to several sources, one of the obstacles Clemente faced was a propensity toward injury and illness. During his first seasons in professional baseball in the United States he was often sick or injured. His ability to play was questioned. A review of these early years suggests an inability to adapt to the social and political environment of the United States, where racism was prevalent at the time, and shows that Clemente, as a black Puerto Rican, suffered directly and indirectly from discrimination.

Nevertheless, throughout his sports career Clemente built an impressive record in baseball. During the 18 seasons that he played with the Pittsburgh Pirates (1955–1972), he played in 9,454 games, batted for 2,433 games, scored 1,416 runs, and had 3,000 hits. In fact, he is the 11th of only 12 players to have achieved this feat. He also scored 250 home runs. He won the Golden Glove award 12 times for his fielding, a record he tied with his early mentor Willie Mays (Pietrusza 2000). His capacity for fielding and his gymnastic contortions are still revered today.

During his off-season stays in Puerto Rico, he was actively involved in civic and charitable undertakings. He also traveled frequently to Latin America and donated the proceeds of his sponsorship of commercial products to charities for the needy.

In December 1972 the city of Managua, Nicaragua, suffered the devastation of a powerful earthquake. Clemente, who had just visited Nicaragua weeks before, mobilized and collected relief supplies to send to Nicaragua along with $150,000 in aid. After learning that Nicaraguan soldiers working under the Somoza regime were pilfering and stealing the supplies being sent by international organizations, Clemente decided to fly along with the supplies that he had collected to ensure their proper distribution. He chartered an old surplus DC-7 that had recently been involved in an accident. On New Year's Eve in 1972, he boarded the overloaded plane flown by two pilots who were unqualified to fly that type of aircraft. Although the plane made several attempts to depart Isla Verde, it could not develop enough speed or thrust, forcing it to return to the ramp for more repairs (Ruiz 1998). On its final attempt, the plane took off only to crash over the Atlantic one mile from the Isla Verde airport. Clemente's remains were never recovered. Clemente left behind his wife, Vera Zavala, whom he had married in 1965, and three children. His family maintains a series of charitable endeavors such as camps and scholarships to remember his legacy and contributions.

After his death, Clemente was almost immediately inducted into the Baseball Hall of Fame, a rare exception to the five-year waiting requirement. Puerto Rico's immense love and pride for this national hero has not diminished, even 30 years after his untimely death.—S.M.M.

References and Suggested Readings

Meir, Monserrate, Conchita Franco Serri, and Richard García. "Roberto Clemente." *Notable Latino Americans*. Westport, CT: Greenwood, 1997. 91–94.

Moritz, Charles, ed. "Roberto Clemente." *Current Biography Yearbook*. New York: H. W. Wilson, 1992.

Pietrusza, David. "Roberto Clemente." *Baseball: The Biographical Encyclopedia*. New York: Total Sport Illustrated, 2000. 209–212.

Ruiz, Yuyo. *Las Últimas Horas de Roberto Clemente* (The Last Hours of Roberto Clemente). San Juan: Published by the Author, 1998.

Walker, Paul Robert. *Pride of Puerto Rico: The Life of Roberto Clemente.* San Diego, CA: Harcourt, Brace and Company, 1988.

MICHELLE CLIFF
(1946–)

Jamaican Novelist, Poet, Short Story Writer, and Essayist

Jamaican-born Michelle Cliff's work includes poetry, prose, novels, short stories, and essays. Her skillful use of language and treatment of culture and colonialism have been hailed as exemplifying post-colonial literature. Outstanding in these writings are significant elements of British colonialism, particularly racial and sexual discrimination and white European cultural domination. Her semi-auto-biographical fiction's focal points address issues related to race, gender, and class, particularly the interracial prejudices present in Jamaica and the Caribbean. Cliff's writing has been described as "a body of resistance literature that describes and formally enacts the struggle for cultural decolonization" (Schwartz 1993, 595).

Cliff was born to an upper-middle-class family in Kingston, Jamaica, on November 2, 1946. In 1949 her family immigrated to New York City but traveled frequently to Jamaica. Cliff attended public schools and, according to her own reports, did not associate much with Americans but lived mostly in a West Indies environment. Cliff has recounted how while in high school she contemplated being a writer and began to keep a journal after reading *The Diary of Anne Frank:* "She gave me permission to write and to use writing as a way of survival" (Raiskin, 1993, 68). However, her family did not consider it appropriate for a girl to keep a diary, and after searching for and finding the diary, her parents proceeded to read it aloud on the porch to the rest of the family. She stopped writing and did not write again until graduate school, when she wrote her thesis.

In 1969 she graduated from Wagner College in New York with a degree in European history and got her first job working for the publisher W.W. Norton, where she worked until 1971. She spent the following three years completing graduate studies in London's Warburg Institute, concentrating on languages and comparative historical studies of the Italian Renaissance. On her return to New York in 1974, she continued to pursue a career in publishing. She rejoined Norton, where she worked for the next four years, first as a copyeditor and later as a production editor. When she left Norton in 1979, she began concentrating on forging a career as a writer. At the same time, from 1981 to 1983, she collaborated with the feminist poet Adrienne Rich on the editing and publishing of *Sinister Wisdom,* a feminist journal.

Her work has been concerned with social issues and the way people's lives are affected by politics, particularly by the subjugation of colonialism, sexism, and racism. Her first book, a compilation of prose poems titled *Claiming an Identity They Taught Me to Despise* (1980), explores the issue of interracial discrimination and delves into the mind-set of its Jamaican protagonist and her feelings of perplexity and bewilderment over the preferential treatment accorded light-skinned Creoles such as herself, in stark contrast to the treatment of her darker family members and friends. Her first novel, the critically acclaimed *Abeng* (1984), a coming-of-age story about a biracial adolescent girl in Jamaica who must face questions of race, class, sexuality, dominant ideology, and identity, is to some extent autobiographical. In this novel, *abeng* is a significant term that is tied to Jamaican history and the struggle for the self-determination of its slaves. Literally, *abeng* is a conch shell; figuratively, the *abeng* was the symbol of black resistance against the British during the War of the Maroons, led by Jamaican national hero **Nanny of the Maroons**—accounts that Cliff relates in the novel. *No Telephone to Heaven* (1987), also autobiographical fiction, continues the themes presented in *Abeng*.

Cliff identifies herself as a Creole Jamaican whose writing has been greatly influenced by the colonial experience and by the works of novelists James Baldwin, Bessie Head, Virginia Woolf, and most important, Toni Morrison. Her work is often cited for the linguistic skills it exhibits. Cliff's ability to move from standard English to Jamaican Creole has been noted by one critic, who commented that even though the purpose of this code-switching is to draw attention to class and race differences in the stories' characters, it also "makes manifest the double consciousness of the postcolonial, bilingual, and bicultural writer who lives and writes across the margins of different traditions and universes" (Lionnet 1992, 324).

Among Cliff's other works are *Bodies of Water* (1990) and *Free Enterprise* (1994). Her most recent book of short stories, *The Story of a Million Items* (1998), narrates a childhood spent on two islands—Jamaica and Manhattan. Cliff explores the gaps between cultures, genders, and generations while comparing the prosperity and racism of America during the 1950s and 1960s with life in Jamaica during the same period.

Twice a recipient of a National Endowment for the Arts award (1982, 1989), she was a Massachusetts Artists Foundation Fellow in 1984, an Eli Kantor Fellow in 1984, and traveled to New Zealand on a Fulbright Fellowship in 1988. Cliff has also been visiting professor at major universities, most recently as the Allan K. Smith Professor of English Language and Literature at Trinity College in Hartford, Connecticut, and at the University of Mainz in Germany. She also speaks at workshops and symposia in the United States and abroad.—G.C.

References and Suggested Readings

Agosto, Noraida. *Michelle Cliff's Novels: Piecing the Tapestry of Memory and History*. New York: Peter Lang Publishing, 2000.

Brice-Finch, Jacqueline. "Michelle Cliff." In Daryl Cumber Dance, ed., *Fifty Caribbean Writers*. Westport, CT: Greenwood Press, 1996. 49–58.

Cliff, Michelle. *Abeng*. New York: Crossing Press, 1984.

Jones, Daniel, and John D. Jorgeson, eds. "Michelle Cliff." *Contemporary Authors* Farmington Hills, MI: Gale, 2000. 199, 209–212.

Lionnet, Françoise. "Of Mangoes and Maroons: Language, History and the Multicultural Subject of Michelle Cliff's *Abeng*." In Sidonie Smith, ed., *De/Colonizing the Subject: The Politics of Gender in Women's Autobiography*. Minneapolis: University of Minnesota Press, 1992. 321–345.

Raiskin, Judith. "The Art of History: An Interview with Michelle Cliff." *Kenyon Review* 15.1 (Winter 1993): 57–72.

Schwartz, Meryl F. "An Interview with Michelle Cliff." *Contemporary Literature* 34.4 (Winter 1993): 594–620.

FRANK COLLYMORE
(1893–1980)

Barbadian Teacher, Writer, Artist, and Actor

Frank Collymore was a central figure in Barbadian arts and literature for most of the twentieth century. Although he was a talented writer and artist in its own merit, his major professional accomplishments were as an English teacher and associate headmaster at the prestigious Combermere School and as an editor of *BIM*, a literary journal. As a teacher and mentor he was an early influence on some of the most important West Indian writers of the twentieth century.

Frank Appleton Collymore was born on January 7, 1893, in St. Michael, Barbados, to Wilhemina Clarke and Joseph Appleton Collymore, a customs official. Collymore was an only child raised by doting parents and relatives. He developed an interest in the arts as a young child, although his formal education was limited to attending Combermere between 1903 and 1910. After graduation he was asked to work as French and English teacher at the school. He later became its associate headmaster. Collymore taught at the school until he retired in 1963. He is considered an early source of inspiration to Caribbean writers such as Sam Selvon, **George Lamming**, **Austin C. Clarke**, and Nobel Laureate **Derek Walcott**.

Collymore, known as "Colly" to his fellow Barbadians, was considered an extraordinary teacher who instilled a love for English literature in his students. He had a large library at his house and made it available to his students to read and amplify their literary knowledge. Barbadian author George Lamming recalls:

> The importance of him for me was discovering the meaning of books. He really introduced me to the world of books and to the possibilities of discovering oneself through books. He had an extensive library; I used to go to his house on Saturday morning to make use of his library, I would say that he was essentially the most critical influence in the

shaping of my direction in what was called literature and in any ambitions I had about becoming a writer. He was solely responsible for that. (qtd. in Walters 1990, n.p.)

He had a similar effect on many others among his students.

One of Collymore's more important contributions to Caribbean and West Indian literature was his work as editor of the literary magazine *BIM*. The publication was started in 1942 by Tony Crozier, a Barbadian journalist, who invited Collymore to become its editor. Collymore held the position of editor from 1942 to 1975. *BIM* collected and published the works of aspiring writers such as Lamming and Walcott. It has been credited by many as the most important outlet for the early work of West Indian writers and is noted for its dissemination throughout the Caribbean. It was also one of the earliest literary publications to emerge from the area.

Collymore also played an indirect but important role in giving widespread recognition to Caribbean writers through the world in the now-legendary BBC program *Caribbean Voices*, which presented West Indian literature to Great Britain and the rest of the English-speaking world. It was aired between 1943 and 1958. Because of his friendship with Henry Swanzy, editor and producer of the program, Collymore suggested to many of his students and *BIM* writers that they submit their works to be broadcast. If the works were chosen, they were read and criticized on the air. In fact, when many of these writers relocated from the West Indies to Great Britain to study or work, they found work with Swanzy as readers and critics.

Collymore was also an accomplished artist and writer. Between 1942 and 1948 he published romantic poetry. His poetry explored the Caribbean landscape and his West Indian heritage in relationship to Great Britain. He also wrote short stories that mostly appeared in *BIM*. According to Edward Baugh, one of his most important critics and biographers, Colllymore's stories "deal with solitaries, eccentric, psychotics, and involve some of the morbid" (Baugh 1986, 12). One of Collymore's lesser-known talents was his ability as a visual artist. Many of his poems were initially accompanied by individual drawings. His drawings also appeared on covers and pages of *BIM*. He was also an accomplishd actor, who played a central role in Combermere's dramatic activities and belonged to several theatrical groups, appearing in more than 41 theatrical presentations.

The issues of *BIM* edited by Collymore are thought to contain a treasury of West Indian original literature. He published three books of poetry during his lifetime: *Thirty Poems* (1944), *Beneath the Casuarinas* (1945) and *Flotsam: Poems 1942–1948* (1945). He also published *Notes for a Glossary of Words and Phrases of Barbadian Dialect* (1955). This work is considered to be one of the first attempts to capture the richness and uniqueness of West Indian language within a scholarly work.

Collymore received many awards during his lifetime. In 1968 the University of the West Indies at Mona bestowed on him an honorary masters in art in recognition of his literary career. The Central Bank of Barbados established The Frank Collymore Literary Endowment in 1998 to celebrate the memory of this notable teacher and writer and to foster the development of Barbadian writers. The Frank Collymore Hall, a multi-purpose building, is one of the premier cultural centers in Barbados' capital of Bridgetown.

Although Collymore's literary and educational legacy is virtually unknown outside of the West Indies, he is credited as an early source of inspiration among many West Indian writers and as a teacher he made a huge difference to his students.—S.M.M.

References and Suggested Readings

Baugh, Edward, "Frank Collymore." In Daryl Cumber Dance, ed., *Fifty Caribbean Writers.* Westport: Greenwood Press, 1986. 122–133.

BIM: A 50th Anniversary Issue: 1942–1992. 19.74 (December 1992).

Griffith, Glyne. "Deconstructing Nationalisms: Henry Swanzy, Caribbean Voices and the Development of West Indian Literature." *Small Axe* 10 (September 2001): 1.

Walters, Erika J. "Music of Language: An Interview with George Lamming." *The Caribbean Writer* 13 (1990): 190–201. *http://www.thecaribbeanwriter.com/toc/tocvolume13.html.*

MIRIAM COLÓN
(1945?–)

Puerto Rican Actress

With a stellar career that spans more than four decades, Miriam Colón is a consummate stage performer who has interpreted a wide range of stage, film, and television roles with remarkable intensity and talent. She is the founder of the Puerto Rican Traveling Theater, the leading Latino theatrical organization in New York City.

She was born in Ponce, Puerto Rico. Although most of her biographers give 1945 as her year of birth, a review of her artistic development makes that date unlikely. Her father was a dry goods merchant who divorced her mother when Colón was a young child. After her parents' divorce, her mother moved with her children to the Las Casas public housing project in the Barrio Obrero, a Santurce neighborhood. Colón attended local schools in Santurce and was introduced to theater while she was a junior high school student at the Román Baldorioty de Castro School in San Juan. Her talent was so evident that her theater instructor arranged for Colón to take theatrical training at the drama department of the University of Puerto Rico in Río Piedras. After a stellar performance in the play *La Azotea* (The Rooftop) with the University Players Ensemble, Colón was given a special scholarship to the Erwin Piscator Dramatic Workshop and Technical Institute in New

York. Her mother traveled with her and worked as a seamstress to support her daughter. Colón flourished as a theater student and was the first Puerto Rican and Latina actress to be accepted to the prestigious Actor's Studio.

Colón began her professional dramatic career in the film *Los Peloteros* (The Baseball Players) with Puerto Rican actor Ramón Ortiz del Rivero, known as "Diplo." Produced by the Community Education Division of the Department of Education (DIVEDCO) in 1952, this film is considered a classic in Puerto Rico. In 1952 Colón debuted on Broadway in the play *In the Summer House*. She also had a role in the play *The Innkeepers* (1956), and appeared in the movies *One-Eyed Jacks* (1961) and *Appaloosa* (1966) with Marlon Brando. She did not pursue a Hollywood career because she found life in Hollywood "boring." Like many other Latino actors and actresses, she discovered that the entertainment industry was not ready for a Latino actress and was often relegated to minor roles. After returning to Puerto Rico and doing local theater there with the traveling theater of the University of Puerto Rico, Colón returned to New York and undertook her most significant theatrical achievement.

While participating in a staging of the famous Puerto Rican play *The Oxcart* at the Greenwich Mews Theater in 1967, Colón wanted to bring the play to poor New Yorkers who did not have had the chance to experience the theater. She solicited funds from her closest friends and found a truck that she used as a stage to bring the play to poor neighborhoods. Her efforts evolved into an organization known as the Puerto Rican Traveling Theater (PRTT), which has become the most important Latino theatrical company in the United States. The goals of the PRTT have been to establish "a professional, bilingual theater that emphasizes the contribution Puerto Ricans and other Hispanic writers have made to the canons of dramatic literature, while highlighting new plays by Hispanic playwrights living in the United States, and to make these plays accessible to the widest possible range of people" (Colón 1989, 47). Since its foundation 30 years ago, the PRTT has staged dozens of plays and has fulfilled Colón's goal of bringing theater to people who would otherwise not have access to it.

Colón has developed the PRTT into a full-fledged educational organization with a unit for training and developing Latino playwrights, an educational unit where young adolescents and children are instructed in theater, a traveling theater that continues to take drama to city neighborhoods, and a stage house on Broadway.

In 1974 Colón spotted an old firehouse at 304 West 47th Street on Broadway that had been closed. After intense government lobbying, she was able to obtain the facility for the PRTT and raised $1.6 million to refurbish it into a theater. Today, the 196-seat facility offers three to four plays each theatrical season and is recognized for its quality presentation of Latino plays.

Colón is a determined theatrical entrepreneur who works relentlessly to secure funding for her organization. When the federal and state governments cut the funding of arts of organization during the 1980s and 1990s, she worked hard to obtain funding from private business. Described by many as a savvy and ruthless administrator, she has been able to guide her organization into becoming one of the premier Latino theatrical companies in the United States. In addition to her work as founder and executive director of the PRTT, she has maintained her visibility as an actress and continues to appear in theater, television, and film. She regularly acts with her company and has made more than 250 television appearances. Among her film credits are: *One-Eyed Jacks* (1961), *Harbor Lights* (1963), *Thunder Island* (1963), *The Appaloosa* (1966), *The Possession of Joes Delaney* (1973), *Isabel la Negra* (1979), *Back Roads* (1981), *Scarface* (1983), *A Life of Sin* (1990), and *Lone Star* (1996). In 2001, Colón and the PRTT produced the musical *La Lupe*, based on the life of Cuban singer Lupe Yoli, to superb reviews. Colón's most recent films are *All the Pretty Horses* (2001), *For Love or Country: The Arturo Sandoval Story* (2000), and *Almost a Woman* (2001). She is making a substantial contribution to American theater not only through her dramatic talents but also through her commitment to bring art to the people. Viewers who may not have seen her stage work, may recognize Colón from the long-running soap opera *Guiding Light.* —S.M.M.

References and Suggested Readings

Carrero, Angel Dario. "Miriam Colón: el arte de la compassion." *El Nuevo Día* (San Juan), January 20, 2002, n.p.

Colón, Miriam. "Puerto Rican Traveling Theater." *Melus* 16.3 (Fall 1989): 47–49.

Honan, William. "After State Cutbacks, What One Theater Is Doing to Survive." *The New York Times,* July 14, 1992, C11.

Mirabella, Alan. "A Shortage of Silver." *Newsday,* April 20, 1992, 47.

Prida, Dolores. "La gran dama del teatro." *Latina* (June 1998): 84.

Rodríguez, María. "Miriam Colón." In Alice Robinson, Vera Mowry Roberts, and Milly S. Barranger, eds., *Notable Women in the American Theater.* Westport, CT: Greenwood Press, 1989. 153–155.

Shepard, Richard F. "For Street Troupe, at 20, Life Is Both Buena y Good." *The New York Times,* April 18, 1987, 9.

WILLIE COLÓN
(1950–)

Puerto Rican Composer, Trombonist, and Singer

Willie Colón has been instrumental in the development of salsa music in the United States and Latin America. A man of many musical talents, his contributions to the development of salsa have spanned more than 35 years. A central pillar of the New York and Latin American musical scene, Colón has led the revolution of salsa and has generated many compositions and recordings. Music historian John Storm Roberts has said: "Colón has always been extraordinary in his ability to stitch together disparate influences into a coherent and entirely personal whole" (1999, 227).

Willie Colón.

William Anthony Colón Román was born in New York City on April 28, 1950. His mother Aracelis was only 16 years old when Colón was born. He was raised by his mother and his maternal grandparents, Antonia Román Pintor and Feliciano Román, in the Bronx, New York. Both his mother and his grandmother worked as laborers in New York factories. His experience witnessing their hardships as workers was influential in the development of his social conscience, which would later be reflected both in his political activism and in his songs.

During his youth, his grandmother bought him a trumpet and paid for his first music lessons. By the time he was 13 years old he was a member of the New York City Youth Symphony Orchestra and also had his own small band that played at small social events. Around that time, he was exposed to the music of Mon Rivera, a prominent Puerto Rican orchestra leader, and was fascinated by the effects of multiple trombones in his band. As a result, he switched to the trombone. His music talents were so great that by the time he was 14 he already had a full-fledged band with 14 musicians under him.

Colón's adolescence coincided with a significant historical period for New York Puerto Ricans. As the Puerto Rican Diaspora in New York developed, there was a need for musical forms and styles that not only represented their musical needs and tastes but also reflected their social realities. As interpreters moved away from the traditional Latin mambo and shifted more into Latin jazz, a new musical genre that reflected their musical evolution and growth emerged, which is how the now-famous rhythm of salsa music was born. Salsa is a unique cultural manifestation of the many Latino cultures interacting in the Barrio area of New York.

In 1967, Colón, a 17-year-old high school dropout, cut his first record with fellow Puerto Rican musician Hector Lavoe. The album, *El Malo* (The Bad One), was recorded under the Fania label and sold more than 300,000 records, making Colón an instant hit. It also left Colón with the nickname of "El Malo." With his new use of the trombone and his powerful new partnership, he and Lavoe were among the early interpreters of the new music genre that later became salsa. In 1969 he recorded "Che che cole," a song that gave a new identity to the rhythms of bomba and son. Two years later, he recorded the holiday album *Asalto Navideño*, which blended new music styles and forms with the salsa rhythm. He demonstrated to audiences and music followers that he was a serious and talented musician who was breaking new ground within the Latin American music world.

One significant aspect of Colón's music is that it captures the realities and preoccupations of people from the Barrio as no other interpreter had done before. The themes of violence, desperation in the social climate of the late 1960s and early 1970s, longing for the home island, and the isolation of urban areas such as the Barrio are staples of his music.

His initial partnership with Lavoe lasted seven years, and his association with Fania Records defined the early period of salsa music encompassing the late 1960s and early the 1970s. In 1973 Colón broke his association with Lavoe and dissolved his band. He became involved with several other performers such as Yomo Toro, Ruben Blades, Ernie Agosto, and **Celia Cruz** and produced many records with them that also became hits. He also temporarily took a job as the music director of New York's Public Broadcasting Service System, where he had a chance to compose and record the music for the first-ever salsa ballet, *Mass for Little Black Angels* (1977). Colón continued playing a broad spectrum within salsa music and scored many hits, but it was his association with Rubén Blades, a Panamanian composer and vocalist, that defined a significant period of salsa music in Colón's career.

The association of Colón and Blades started initially in 1975 when they recorded the album *The Good, the Bad and the Ugly.* In that album, Colón debuted as a solo singer but still played the trombone. Their partnership did not fully develop until 1977, when they collaborated on many unique musical productions. In 1978 their album *Siembra* broke all records in Latino markets in the United States and Latin America. Laden with messages of social and political conscience, the album has become a salsa classic. Their classic song "Pedro Navaja," a musical variation of "Mack the Knife," became one of the biggest hits of the 1970s. The song tells the sad story of a prostitute who falls victim to Pedro, the neighborhood pimp, and inspired a musical of the same name that was successfully produced in Puerto Rico and New York. Toward the end of the 1970s, Colón made his real debut as a solo performer with his album *Solo* and continued into the 1980s scoring successes as a soloist while remaining loyal to the themes of social conscience and responsibilities. His song "El Gran Varón" (The Great Male), part of the album *Altos Secretos* (High Secrets; 1989), was the first recording in Latin American music to publicly tackle the controversial issue of AIDS. The lyrics present the story of a father who rejected his gay son because he had AIDS and then regretted this rejection when the son dies.

Colón is one of the foremost Puerto Rican musicians to represent the talents and concerns of Puerto Rican musicians in New York. He was elected to the board of directors of the American Society of Composers, Authors and Publishers (ASCAP) in 1995. ASCAP is the leading organization representing American recording artists. He has acted in films, on television, and in television commercials, both in the United States and in Latin America. He has received many gold and platinum records and has been nominated for a Grammy.

Colón continues performing for sold-out audiences but also has the opportunity to realize a life-long dream of involvement in politics. In 1993 he challenged U.S. Representative Eliot L. Engel in a Democratic primary for the 17th District of New York, which comprised Westchester County and the Bronx. Although a procedural glitch with the ballots prevented Colón from facing the final contest, he was able to muster huge support not only from his Latino supporters but also from African American and Jewish voters in New York. In 1999 and in 2000 he seriously considered challenging First Lady Hillary Clinton in the New York primary. In 2002 he ran for the elected position of Public Advocate for New York City and finished third. Because of the racial politics that permeated the 2001 Democratic primaries for mayor in New York City, Colón shifted political alliances to the Republican Party and supported Michael Bloomburg, the Republican candidate, who went on to win the elections and became the mayor of New York.

His exemplary career has been honored through a number of recognitions and awards such as an honorary doctorate from Trinity College (1999) and a CHUBB Fellowship from Yale University (1991). He is a consummate humanitarian who lends his voice and artistic personae to many different charitable causes.—S.M.M.

References and Suggested Readings

Campbell, Mary. "He Began Playing the Spicy Music at 15; Willie Colón Plays Salsa Music and Molds It." *Los Angeles Times*, December 23, 1988, 20.

Clarke, Donald, ed. "Willie Colón." *The Penguin Encyclopedia of Popular Music*. New York: Viking, 1989. 266.

Collazo, Roberto G. "The Colón Connection." *The Village Voice*, April 11, 2000, 28.

Roberts, John Storm. *The Latin Tinge: The Impact of Latin American Music on the United States*. New York: Oxford University Press, 1999.

Torres-Torres, Jaime. "¡Inmenso!" *El Nuevo Día*, October 14, 1997, 55.

MARYSE CONDÉ
(1937–)
Guadeloupean Novelist, Critic, and Educator

Guadeloupe native Maryse Condé is considered among the most successful and important contemporary Caribbean writers. Influenced by **Aimé Césaire** and other black Caribbean French-speaking poets and writers whose work celebrates black aesthetics and consciousness within the colonial context of racial injustice and discrimination, her prose also seeks to recover and identify the richness of black cultural values. Her critically acclaimed novels and plays are characterized by their carefully researched historical content and by the examination of stereotypes of women. She has also authored a number of children's books, critical essays on the work of Aimé Césaire, Antillean fiction, and numerous articles on Caribbean literature and cultural studies. Condé has spent long periods of her life living in Europe and Africa, and since 1978 has taught in a number of American universities.

Maryse Boucolon was born in Pointe-à-Pitre, Guadeloupe, on February 11, 1937, to Auguste and Jeanne Quidal. She was raised in a middle-class family and was the youngest sibling (by over ten years) of four sisters and four brothers. The age gap between her closest siblings led to feelings of loneliness and boredom. An academically outstanding student, her interest in writing began at age seven with a one-act play she wrote for her mother's birthday—her spirits undampened by her mother's less-than-enthusiastic response to the play's authoritarian characterization of her. Condé was fascinated with what she perceived was the power of the written word to stir people's emotions "I think that's when I wanted to become a writer, to have such power over people. A seven-year-old who can bring her mother to the brink of rage, even tears, feels very, very powerful" (Thomas 1996, 20). Included in her childhood recollections was

Maryse Condé. © Henry Roy.

the insularity of her well-to-do middle-class parents, who prohibited socialization with anyone who was dissimilar to her, such as poor blacks, whites, and people of mixed racial background, referred to as mulattoes.

After completing her secondary studies in 1953 at age 16, she was sent to the Lycée Fénélon and to the Sorbonne in Paris, where she studied English literature and experienced racial discrimination first-hand. During her time as a student in Paris, she became politically active and joined the Communist Youth. She also met Mamadou Condé, an actor she married in August 1959 and with whom she left Paris for Guinea in Africa. This was an important period in her life, where she became deeply involved with Marxism while immersed in what was for her a new and different culture. In addition, she witnessed Guinea's political upheaval and repression under the regime of Sekou Toure. Her personal life, too, was changed by the clash of cultural values she experienced while living with her mother-in-law. She escaped this situation by fleeing to neighboring Ghana in 1964 with her four children. She divorced Mamadou Condé in 1981.

Condé's years in Africa were hectic yet fruitful to her development as a writer. She was befriended by renowned African activists Kwame Nkrumah and Amilcar Cabral and attended gatherings that included Malcolm X and Ernesto "Ché" Guevara as speakers. She worked at the Ghana Institute of Language in Accra until 1968, when she was arrested for her political activities and later deported. During the early 1970s Condé moved to London to escape political persecution. In London she worked for the BBC, then served as a translator in Senegal, was an editor for *Presence Africaine* (African Presence) in Paris, and taught at the Université de Paris IV. In addition, she married Richard Philcox, an Englishman who has also translated most of her works.

Condé began her writing career as a critic and playwright, and later became a novelist while living in Paris from 1970 to 1986. The year 1976 was notable for major accomplishments: she earned a doctorate and was appointed lecturer at the Sorbonne and also published her first novel *Hérémakhonon*. *Une Saison à Rihata* (One Season in Rihata), her second novel, was published in 1981. Between 1984 and 1985 Condé published a two-part historical novel titled *Segu*, and *The Children of Segue*, both of which became bestsellers establishing her international reputation as a novelist. After living abroad for more than 30 years, Condé returned to Guadeloupe in 1986, making the island her official home while she held professorial appointments abroad. Her 1986 novel *Moi, Tutuba, sorciére noire de Salem* (I, Tituba, Black Witch of Salem), a fictionalized biography of the forgotten witch of Salem, was awarded the Gran Prix Littéraire de la Femme. In 1992 she published *Les derniers rois mages* (The Last Magi), an account of the spirit of an African king who returns to visit his descendants in South Carolina. More recent publications include the novel *La colonie du nouveau monde* (The Colony of the New World, 1993); a play, *The Tropical Breeze Hotel* (1994); and *Windward Heights* (1999), an interpretation of Emily Brontë's classic work *Wuthering Heights* as seen through the eyes of a black cast of characters. Her latest works, *Célanire cou-coupe* (1999) and *La Belle Créole* (The Beautiful Creole, 2001), have yet to be translated into English.

Her writing has received literary acclaim. Critics write that "one gains a comprehension of what a revolution is like, what new African nations are like" and conclude that "The wise reader will go home," as the protagonist of *Hérémakhonon* does, "to continue more calmly to reflect, and observe" (Bruner and Bruner 1985, 13). Condé believes that women writers have played an important role in the evolution of West Indian literature. She states that women have done this by breaking the "canon" and writing about topics that male writers do not mention, such as the interracial discrimination of "men who preferred women with fair skin and blue eyes, or long hair. So a newer generation of women has spoken out against this" (Thomas 1996, 21). Her volume of works totals six plays, over a dozen novels, and several anthologies of Francophone Caribbean and African literature. Her most recent publication, *Tales From the Heart: True Stories From My Childhood* (2001), is her first non-fiction work, an autobiographical memoir that won the 2001 Prix Yourcenar.

In 1996 Condé was made an honorary member of the prestigious l'Académie des Lettres du Québec and in 2001 she was awarded the Commandeur de l'Ordre des Arts et des Lettres, France's highest award for artists. She is currently a tenured professor and director of the Center for French and Francophone Studies at Columbia University in New York City.—G.C.

References and Suggested Readings

Bruner, Charlotte, and David Bruner. "Buchi Emecheta and Maryse Condé: Contemporary Writing from Africa and the Caribbean." *World Literature Today* 59.1 (Winter 1985): 9–13.

Clark, Phyllis. "Conversations with Maryse Condé." *Journal of Gender Studies* 7.2 (July 1998): 241–242.

Condé, Maryse. *Segu.* Translation by Barbara Bray. New York: Peguin, 1998.

———. *Tales From the Heart: True Stories From My Childhood.* New York: Soho Press, 2001.

Condé, Maryse, and Franciose Pfaff. *Conversations With Maryse Conde.* Lincoln: University of Nebraska Press, 1997.

French Guadeloupe Writer Maryse Condé Reading from Her Work in the Recording Laboratory, Sept. 24, 1999 (sound recording). Washington, DC: Archive of Hispanic Literature on Tape, Library of Congress, 1999.

Goslinga, Marian. "Memory and Identity." *Hemisphere: A Magazine of the Americas* 9.3 (Winter 2001): 42–44.

Hewitt, Leah Dianne. "Condé's Critical Seesaw." *Callaloo* 18.3 (Summer 1995): 641–651.

Lewis, Barbara. "NO SILENCE: An Interview with Maryse Condé." *Callaloo* 18:3 (Summer 1995): 543–550.

Nunez, Elizabeth. "Talking to . . . Maryse Condé: Grand Dame of Caribbean Literature." *UNESCO Courier* (November 2000): 46–51.

Perret, Delphine, and Marie-Denise Shelton, eds. "Special Issue: Maryse Condé." *Callaloo* 18.3 (Summer 1995).

Thomas, Viola. "Maryse Conde." *Belles Lettres* 11.1 (January 1996): 20–22.

GILBERTO CROES (BETICO)
(1938–1986)

Aruban Educator and Politician

Gilberto Croes was the leading advocate for Aruba's push to gain the status of a self-governing country within the Kingdom of the Netherlands. Betico, as he was known to the people of Aruba, was a martyr to the Aruban independence movement and "the liberator" of this former Caribbean Dutch colony. During the 1970s, he led a strong political movement seeking "status aparte" (separate status) from the Netherlands. Despite political repression and violence at the hands of his opposition, Croes continued a relentless campaign for independence. His dreams were partially fulfilled on January 1, 1986, when Aruba obtained self-government from the Netherlands.

Gilberto François Croes was born on January 25, 1938, to Francisco and Maria Louisa Croes. He went to primary and secondary schools in Aruba and then traveled to the Netherlands, where he obtained an undergraduate degree from Hilversum University. He returned to Aruba and worked as a schoolteacher for many years.

Croes' political involvement began in 1967 when was elected to the island council and was appointed minister of education. In 1954 the Netherlands had granted autonomy to the islands of Curaçao, Aruba, Bonaire, St. Maarten, and Saba. As part of this power, the islands united in a federation with a central administration based in Curaçao. Although this constituted a step toward self-government, the people of Aruba resented Curaçao's having control over the federation through its large majority in the Federation Council—Curaçao had eight votes in the council and Aruba only had five, a major source of political tension between the two Caribbean islands. Although Croes initially was a member of the Arubaanse Volkspartij (Aruban People's Party), which had a Christian democratic orientation, he became disenchanted with the conservative stand of his party on the issue of self-rule and independence.

Croes founded the Movimiento Electoral di Pueblo (People's Electoral Movement) in 1971. The party, a member of the Socialist International, followed a social democratic ideology advocating the rights of the people and was identified with the working class. One of the defining issues of the party was its desire to attain full independence from the Netherlands. Like **Norman** and **Michael Manley** of Jamaica, Croes exploited Aruban nationalism and gained support from his people by appealing to Aruban culture, its Papiamento language, and its national symbols. The party proposed to seek "status aparte" from the Netherlands. This political concept was meant to eliminate Aruba's problematic membership in the Netherlands Federation and to gain full independence from the Dutch colonial government. With Croes at the helm, the party won the 1975 elections and gained control of the Aruban parliament. It also led Aruba's representation in the Netherlands Federation. The party was to win the majority of the local elections six times during Croes' lifetime.

Croes' vocal activism in favor of Aruba's independence brought him political persecution by members of opposing parties. In 1977 his parents were harassed by people associated with the opposition party and their house was ransacked. While participating in a political demonstration in 1983, he was shot by a local policeman who claimed that his party did not have the proper permits to hold the demonstration. Doctors performed surgery in Aruba and transported him to Miami, where he had another operation. Despite the fact that the government appointed a commission to investigate the incident, no formal charges were brought against the police.

During the late 1970s, Croes built alliances with Latin American countries and the United States to bring independence to his homeland. He told London's *Financial Times*: "Colonialism doesn't fit our time. We are Latin Americans ruled by a European country. We have a certain amount of autonomy but not in vital matters" ("Profile: Betico Croes" 1982, 5). Croes' political and diplomatic relationships with Cuba concerned and angered the government of the Netherlands. He organized a referendum in 1977 in which the people of Aruba voted to become independent. By the early 1980s, Croes had gained enough political momentum to force the Netherlands to negotiate with him. In 1983 the Netherlands finally agreed to grant "self-governing" status to Aruba. This status allowed them to separate from the other islands. The initial agreement allowed for Aruba's full internal government and stipulated that Aruba would become fully independent by 1996.

During the mid 1980s, Croes lost political support in the country as the economy of the island went into a recession when Lagos, a major oil refinery processing Venezuela's oil, closed. The refinery was the most important source of employment for the island and was affected by the new refineries built by Venezuela. The economy also suffered from a significant drop in the tourism industry, another leading source of revenue. When elections were held in November of 1985, Croes lost the majority of the parliament to Henny Eman. On January 1, 1986, Aruba became a self-governing island within the Kingdom of the Netherlands, and Eman became the prime minister.

On December 31, 1985, the eve of one the most important milestones in Aruba's political history, Croes was badly wounded in a traffic accident. The injuries left him in a coma for 11 months. He died on November 28, 1986.

Since Croes' death, Aruba has decided to remain a colony of the Netherlands. When the time for independence came in 1996, they maintained their affiliation to the Kingdom of the Netherlands. Many of the local politicians feared that separation would seriously affect the aid level that the island receives from the Dutch government, which had made no secret of its plan to eliminate foreign assistance to Aruba once it became independent. The move was criticized by Croes' followers, who hope that one day his memory will be fully vindicated when they attain total independence.—S.M.M.

References and Suggested Readings

Alexander, Robert, ed. "Gilbert François (Betico) Croes." *Biographic Dictionary of Latin American and Caribbean Political Leaders.* Westport, CT: Greenwood Press, 1988. 129–130.

Croes, Robertico, and Lucita Moenir Alam. "Decolonization of Aruba within the Netherlands Antilles." In Betty Sedoc-Dahlberg, ed., *The Dutch Caribbean: Prospects for Democracy.* New York: Gordon and Breach, 1990. 81–102.

Gunson, Phil, and Greg Chamberlain. "Betico Croes." *The Dictionary of Contemporary Politics of Central America and the Caribbean.* New York: Simon & Schuster, 1991. 97.

James, Canute. "Aruba Takes Uncertain Step towards Independence." *The Financial Times* (London), January 7, 1986, 4.

"Profile: Betico Croes." *The Financial Times* (London), November 24, 1982, 5.

CELIA CRUZ
(1924–)

Cuban Singer and Entertainer

Celia Cruz is acclaimed as a singer, dancer, and entertainer, throughout the world. The "Queen of Salsa," as fans and fellow musicians have proclaimed her, has brought international recognition and legitimization to the rhythm of salsa music

Celia Cruz.

and to other Caribbean and Cuban musical forms. A singer with a strong professional work ethic, she continues entertaining fans from around the world through dozens of concerts every year.

Cruz was born in Cuba on October 21, 1924, and raised in a humble household located in the Santos Suarez neighborhood of Havana. Her father, Simon Cruz, was a railroad stoker, and her mother, Celia Alfonso, was a homemaker. Although Cruz's parents only had four children, they provided housing for as many as 14 relatives.

Celia displayed her musical talents and abilities early in life. While helping her mother put younger siblings to sleep, she sang to them, capturing the attention of neighbors and relatives who often congregated to listen to her beautiful voice and music. However, being a musical performer in those days was perceived as an unbecoming career for a young woman and her parents insisted that she pursue a traditional education. She graduated from the República de Mexico High School in Havana and enrolled at the Escuela Normal de Maestros to become a literature teacher. In 1947, one of her cousins entered her in a musical contest sponsored by the Radio Cadena Suaritos; she won the first prize for her rendition of the tango "Nostalgia." After her mother persuaded her father to allow Celia to sing, Cruz went on to the Havana Conservatory, where she studied voice and music theory for three years. In the meantime, she continued singing on Cuban radio at Radio Cadena, Radio Progreso, and Radio Unión. During her musical beginnings, Celia specialized in native musical forms such as *guarachas* and the *pregón*. (*Guarachas* are a lively dancing rhythm native to Cuba and the *pregón* is a type of song that emulates the chants of vendors in the streets.) She also became a partner in Las Mulatas del Fuego (The Fiery Mulattoes), an all-women singing group.

In 1950, Cruz got her big break in show business when she was recruited to become the lead singer for La Sonora Matancera, the most popular Cuban band of the time. After overcoming some initial resistance from the public, who adored her predecessor, she eventually became a hit with the orchestra. Some of the hits of the time were "Burundanga," "Yerbero," and "Mata Siraguaya"—songs that she later adapted into the popular salsa rhythm. She recorded her first songs with La Sonora and was featured in several movies. Her act with La Sonora became one of the most popular attractions at the Casino Tropicana, the Havana's principal nightclub during the 1950s. She toured extensively with the band both in Cuba and throughout Latin America.

Taking advantage of a scheduled musical tour to Mexico, Cruz and La Sonora left Cuba permanently in 1960. Like many other Cuban artists, she decided to escape **Fidel Castro**'s regime after the revolution. She spent a year and a half in Mexico and in 1961 moved to the United States, where a long-term contract with a Los Angeles nightclub made it possible for her to qualify for American residency. In 1962 she married Pedro Knight, a trumpet player with La Sonora who gave up his own career to become her full-time business manager and music director.

The early 1960s were a slow period for Cruz because Latino performers were not in high demand in the United States. Things started to change in 1965 after she sang with the **Tito Puente** Orchestra. Concertgoers were impressed by her voice, and songs such as "Quimbara Quibara" and "Bembá Colorá" were hits with her audience. She also released several recordings with the Tico label, led by Puente.

During the 1970s, salsa music became popular in the United States and gave an incredible boost to Cruz's career. A rhythm that is uniquely Caribbean in nature, salsa combines the elements of Afro-Cuban, Dominican, and Puerto Rican music. It blends themes from popular culture and combines them with strong rhythmic variations, powerful percussion, and sonorous voices. Salsa became extremely popular among Latino populations in the northeast, Chicago, and Los Angeles. The salsa phenomenon created the ideal circumstances for Cruz; an established performer, she knew the basic elements and the musical traditions that constitute salsa music. Starting with a landmark appearance in Larry Harlow's Latin opera *Hommy* at Carnegie Hall in 1973, performing with leading salsa interpreters such as **Johnny Pacheco**, Bobby Valentín, Andy Montañez, **Willie Colón**, Ray Barreto, Papo Lucca, Pete "El Conde" Rodríguez, and eventually recording with the most important group of the time, the Fania All Stars, Cruz was at the center of the salsa revolution and soon became one of the top interpreters of salsa in Latin America, the Caribbean, and the United States. Hits such as "Usted Abusó" (You Abused Me), "El Guabà" (Scorpion), and "Yerbero Moderno" (Modern Folk Healer) as uniquely interpreted by Cruz and her accomplished partners, have become salsa classics.

Almost 30 years after the emergence of salsa, Celia Cruz has retained the title of Queen of Salsa Reign. Her unique sonorous and metallic voice and vigorous dancing that would exhaust performers half her age, coupled with a powerful stage presence characterized by her long, sequined gowns and hats, colorful wigs, and high heels guarantee sold-out concerts. She has also appeared on Mexican television soap operas and in Hollywood movies. In 1991, she appeared in *The Mambo Kings Play Songs of Love*, her first English-speaking role in film.

Cruz's departure from Cuba was motivated by her fears of Castro's communist ideology. Until recently, she refrained from criticizing his political regime openly. During the 1990s she started to vocalize her resentment toward Castro's human rights policies. This was partly motivated by the fact that Castro has never granted her a visa to visit her relatives in Cuba. Her condemnation of Puerto Rican musician Andy Montañez, who went to perform in Cuba, led to a huge controversy in Puerto Rico and Miami. Although she denied that she ever criticized Montañez for appearing together with Castro, the dispute led to a boycott of her music in Puerto Rican radio stations and to the cancellation of one of her concerts on the island.

2001 was a prolific year for Cruz. Her Web site chronicles that she was honored with a star at the entrance to the Jackie Gleason Theater for the Performing Arts in Miami Beach. She made several important television appearances, and her magnificent musical talents and career were profiled in a VH1 program honoring Aretha Franklin. She also sang in Italy alongside noted tenor Luciano Pavarotti. Cruz continued her chain of successful performances in 2002 and released *La Negra tiene tumbao*, one of her most successful recordings in recent years.

The year 2002 also brought Cruz serious illnesses. Like her mother, who died from cancer, she confronted breast cancer in August and September 2002. As the year came to an end, however, her fans and followers learned that Cruz faced even a more threatening condition that forced her to undergo a serious operation to extirpate a cancerous tumor in her brain. Despite her weakened physical condition, and the grim health prospects faced by this formidable artist, she attended the 45th Annual Grammy Ceremony at the Madison Square Garden in February 2003, where the Academy of Recording Arts and Sciences awarded her a Grammy for "Best Salsa Album" for *La negra tiene tumbao*. She also received a Latin Grammy for this recording. Cruz was also recognized with four "Lo Nuestro" awards given annually by Spanish television network Univisión. Despite her serious health problems, she has promised to fight cancer with the same strength and endurance that have characterized her musical career. Latin American artists are planning to host a tribute to the artist in March 2003.

No matter what the future may hold, Cruz has had a successful and impressive musical career and has received numerous awards and distinctions. She was awarded an honorary doctorate from Yale in 1993. She won a Grammy, received a medal from the National Endowment for the Arts, had a street in Miami named after her, and has a star on the Hollywood Walk of fame. With her trademark call of "Azucar!" (sugar), her amazing talents, and her humble personality, Cruz has earned the respect, admiration, and love of her audiences everywhere.
—S.M.M.

References and Suggested Readings

Celia Cruz Online: *www.celiacruzonline.com*.

Larkin, Colin, ed. "Celia Cruz." *The Encyclopedia of Popular Music*. London: Muze UK, 1998. 1319–1320.

Ojito, Mirta. "America's Queen of Salsa: Singer's Popularity Rides Waves of Immigration." *The New York Times*, June 27, 1998, 1.

Orovio, Helio. *Diccionario de la música Cubana: Biográfico y técnico*. Havana: Editorial Letras Cubanas, 1998.

Telgen, Diane, and Jim Kamp, eds. "Celia Cruz." *Notable Hispanic American Women.* Detroit: Gale, 1993. 115–118.

Thomson, Clifford, ed. *World Musicians.* New York: H.W. Wilson, 1999.

EDWIDGE DANTICAT
(1969–)

Haitian American Writer

Since the publication of her first novel, *Breath, Eyes, Memory,* in 1994, Edwidge Danticat has garnered much recognition and is now known as one of today's most acclaimed young writers. A year later, at age 26, she published *Krik? Krak!* and became the youngest writer ever nominated for the prestigious U.S. National Book Award. Most of her writing takes place in her native Haiti and portrays many aspects of both Haitian life and the Haitian Diaspora—or as she refers to it, "dyaspora."

Edwidge Danticat, the oldest of four siblings and the only girl, was born in Port-au-Prince, the capital of Haiti, on January 19, 1969, to André and Rose Danticat. André Danticat, a cab driver, emigrated to New York City in 1971 in search of a better life for his family. Rose, a textile worker, decided to join him two years later, leaving four-year-old Danticat under the care of her aunt and uncle, a Baptist minister. Creole was the language spoken at home, but she was educated in French, the official language of Port-au-Prince's public schools. In 1981, at age 12, she rejoined her family in Brooklyn. She attended public schools in the city and remembers the hardships she endured as an immigrant, being taunted by classmates with, "Frenchy, go back to the banana boat" (Pierre-Pierre 1995, C1). She also described how Haitian students protected themselves by disavowing their ethnicity: "They would say anything but Haitian" (C1). An article she wrote and published while in high school about her emigration to the United States, which later developed into her master's thesis, eventually became her first novel *Breath, Eyes, Memory* (1994). The novel was selected in 1998 by Oprah Winfrey's Book Club, making Danticat's book an instant best-seller. Among the awards she received after that publication were the 1994 Fiction Award from *The Caribbean Writer* and a GRANTA Award in 1996 for Best of American Novelists; a similar recognition was also given to her in 1999 by *The New Yorker.*

Danticat, who excelled in English and French, completed her undergraduate education at Barnard College in 1990 and went on to receive an M.F.A. from Brown University in 1993. While at Brown, she wrote two plays—*The Creation of Adam,* produced in Providence, Rhode Island, at the Rites and Reasons Theater in 1992; and *Dreams Like Me,* produced at the university's New Play Festival in 1993.

Following the publication of her very successful novel, Danticat compiled a collection of short stories that she had begun writing as an undergraduate about tortured victims of Haiti's repressive secret police. Danticat described the book's purpose in an interview with National Public Radio: "I wanted to raise the voice of a lot of the people that I knew growing up . . . mostly poor people who had extraordinary dreams but also very amazing obstacles" (Wertheimer 2002). The resulting *Krik? Krak!* garnered her a National Book Award and the Pushcart Prize for short fiction in 1995.

In 1998 Danticat published a historical novel, *The Farming of Bones,* about the 1937 massacre of Haitian farm workers by the Dominican Republic military. Literary critic Barbara Mujica hailed it as "a gripping novel that exposes an aspect of Dominican-Haitian history rarely represented in Latin American fiction" (Mujica 2000, 62). The book received the American Book Award in 1999 and both the International Flaiano Prize for Literature and the Super Flaiano Prize.

Danticat returns to Haiti often. One of her interests is carnival, an activity that she had been discouraged from participating in as a child. In 2002 she published *After the Dance: A Walk Through Carnival in Jacmel, Haiti,* a travelogue that documents both the history and the carnival in the coastal town of Jacmel.

In addition to her novels and short stories, Danticat has edited a compilation of stories, poems, and essays by Haitian writers living in the United States and Europe: *The Butterfly's Way: From the Haitian Dyaspora in the United States* (2001). In her relatively short literary career, she has received acclaim and many awards for her fiction from magazines such as *Essence* and *Seventeen*. In the early days of her career it was obvious to many that she would succeed—in 1998 *Harper's Bazaar* named her one of the 20 people in their twenties who would make a difference and *Jane* magazine named her one of the "15 Gutsiest Women of the Year." Her work has been translated into Korean, Italian, German, French, Spanish, and Swedish. A resident of New York City, she is a distinguished visiting faculty member at New York University's creative writing program.

References and Suggested Readings

Casey, Ethan. "Remembering Haiti." *Callaloo: A Journal of African American and African Arts and Letters* 18.2 (Spring 1995): 524–26.

Danticat, Edwidge. *Breath, Eyes, Memory*. New York: Soho Press, 1994.

———. *Krik? Krak!* New York: Soho Press, 1995.

———. *The Farming of Bones*. New York: Soho Press, 1998.

Mujica, Barbara. "Review of 'The Farming of Bones.'" *Americas* (English Edition) (January 2000): 62.

Pierre-Pierre, Garry. "Haitian Tales, Flatbush Scenes." *The New York Times*, January 26, 1995, C1, C8.

Shea, Renee H. "The Dangerous Job of Edwidge Danticat: An Interview." *Callaloo: A Journal of African American and African Arts and Letters* 19.2 (Spring 1996): 382–89.

Wertheimer, Linda. "Haitian-American Author Writes Stories of Homeland." *All Things Considered* (National Public Radio), July, 12, 1995.

OSCAR DE LA RENTA
(1932–)

Dominican American Fashion Designer and Entrepreneur

Dominican Oscar de la Renta is an internationally known fashion designer whose designs for the last 30 years have had a trend-setting influence and have received international recognition. He is considered one of the most distinguished citizens of his native Dominican Republic, where he is also a philanthropist.

De la Renta was born on July 22, 1932, in Santo Domingo, to Fiallo and Oscar de la Renta. The only son of seven children, it is believed that this experience, along with his success, may have contributed to his understanding of women's fashion. In 1951, pursuing a career as a painter and wanting to prove he could survive without his family's money, de La Renta left for Madrid to study painting at the San Fernando Art School. As an art student he also made fashion sketches. The wife of the American ambassador to Spain saw his sketches and asked him to design the gown for her debutante daughter. In a stroke of luck that would determine his lifelong career, a picture of the debutante in her gown appeared on the cover of *Life* magazine. He left art school for an apprenticeship with one of Spain's top designers, Cristobal Balenciaga. From 1961 to 1963 he worked in Paris as an assistant to Antonio Castillo at the house of Lavin-Castillo.

He moved to the United States in 1963 to design for Elizabeth Arden, and in 1965 became a partner in the Jane Derby Company. During the mid-1960s, Ms. Derby retired, de la Renta became owner of the company, and he added to his collections a more straightforward, traditional ready-to-wear clothing line that had a custom-made look. The success of this line led him to include more affordable versions of the high-fashion designs that he sold to private clients. Over time, his designs have been characterized by their elegance and sophistication as well as their timelessness.

Even though he sold his company in the late 1960s, de la Renta remained as chief executive officer of Oscar de la Renta Couture. Beginning in the 1970s, de la Renta expanded his designing to include costume jewelry, furs, handbags, and many other accessories. In 1977 he launched the first of a series of perfumes for women, and in 1980 his Pour Lui cologne for men made its debut. The success of his perfume lines earned him the 1991 Fragrance Foundation Perennial Success award, as well as the 1995 Living Legend award from the American Society of Perfumes.

By the 1980s, his designs were being shown in the nation's most elaborate and well-attended fashion shows, and his designs were being purchased by such famous people as Barbara Walters and Nancy Kissinger. De la Renta frequently acknowledges his first wife, Françoise du lan Glade, former editor of *French Vogue,*

Oscar de la Renta. Courtesy of Photofest.

as the most influential woman in his life and one who was very instrumental in supporting his rise to the top of the fashion world. In 1983, after 18 years of marriage, she died of cancer.

In 1991, Balmain, one of the most prestigious French couture houses recruited de la Renta. With his spring 1993 collection for Balmain, de la Renta became the first American to design for a French fashion design house. His designs for Balmain have been heralded as tasteful, affordable, and simplified for the professional woman. One of the professional women who praised his designs was First Lady Hillary Rodham Clinton. She wore de la Renta's clothes to such events as the Kennedy Center Honors, a French state dinner, and the Democratic National Convention, and also asked him to create her wardrobe for Inauguration Day in January 1997. In 2002 de la Renta ended his partnership with Balmain and returned to his businesses in New York City, where that same year he successfully launched a new perfume "Intrusion."

Throughout his career, de la Renta has been a leader and the recipient of numerous awards. He is a two-time winner of the Coty American Fashion Critics Award, and was inducted into the Coty Hall of Fame in 1973. From 1973 to 1976, and again from 1986 to 1988, de la Renta served as president of the Council of Fashion Designers of America (CFDA), and in 1990 was awarded its Lifetime Achievement Award. In 2000 CFDA recognized him as the Designer of the Year. Other recent awards include the Legion d'Honneur as a Commander from the French government and a Hispanic Heritage Lifetime Achievement Award. In the Dominican Republic, former President **Joaquín Balaguer** presented him with the Order of Juan Pablo Duarte, and he was given the Tiberio de Oro by the Italian government. De la Renta, who frequently travels to his home on the island has helped build a much-needed school and day-care center for 350 children in the Domincan Republic. One of the children attending the school is his adopted son Moses. For his support of Dominican children he received one of the most prestigious recognitions given by his country, Knight of the Heraldic Order of Christopher Columbus.—G.C.

References and Suggested Readings

Meier, Matt S. "Oscar de la Renta." *Notable Latino Americans: A Biographical Dictionary.* Westport, CT: Greenwood Press, 1997. 112–114.

Moukheiber, Zina. "The Face Behind the Perfume." *Forbes* 152:7 (September 27, 1993): 68.

Mower, Sarah, and Anna Wintour. *Oscar: The Style Inspiration and Life of Oscar de la Renta.* New York: Assouline, 2002.

Unterburger, Amy, ed. *Who's Who among Hispanic Americans, 1994–1995.* Detroit: Gale, 1994.

BENICIO DEL TORO
(1967–)

Puerto Rican Actor

Benicio Del Toro has become one of Hollywood's most talented actors, with an ability to play complex roles that demand discipline and theatrical prowess. He has built an impressive career since he started appearing in movies during the late 1980s. His powerful interpretation of Javier Rodriguez in the movie *Traffic* (2000) brought him an Oscar in 2001. Del Toro has been compared to performers such as Robert De Niro, Humphrey Bogart, and Robert Mitchum. Although he belongs to a generation of actors that favors Hollywood's fame and glitter rather than acting as a craft, he follows a structured acting method and has worked hard to build his dramatic skills. Del Toro has stayed in touch with his Puerto Rican and Latino roots and has helped to develop programs to help Puerto Rican children acquire a love for the arts.

Benicio Del Toro, known to his family as Beno, was born on February 19, 1967, in San German, Puerto Rico. He was one of two children of attorneys Gustavo Del Toro and Fausta Sánchez. The Del Toro and the Sánchez families are well known in Puerto Rican legal circles.

Del Toro was raised in the Santurce suburb of San Juan, where he attended the Colegio del Perpetuo Socorro (Our Lady of Sorrow Academy), an elite Catholic school. His mother developed hepatitis and died when he was nine and some of his dramatic inclinations have been traced to the bedside performances he staged to entertain her during her long illness. His childhood and adolescence were seriously affected by the death of his mother. He often misbehaved at school and was given the nicknamed Bribón (Rascal) by the strict priests and nuns that ran the school. The family moved to southern Pennsylvania when he was 13 after his father remarried. Del Toro had problems adjusting to living with his stepmother and his father decided to send him to Mercersburg Academy, a boarding school. While at Mercersburg, Del Toro did not excel in academics but passed and played basketball. By his senior year, he was co-captain of the basketball team.

On graduation from high school, Del Toro went to the University of California at San Diego, where he initially planned to study business and go on to law school. While an undergraduate at UCSD, Del Toro enrolled in a theater class to lighten his course load. He liked it so much that he took two more theater classes and switched his major to acting. He then left school to pursue an acting career.

He went to New York and attended the Circle in the Square Acting School. He has said that he remembers the times when he had only change to make ends meet. His godmother kept encouraging him and at times provided him with financial support. He was able to secure a scholarship to attend the Stella Adler Acting School in New York. Del Toro also participated in drama festivals at New York

Benicio Del Toro. AP Photo/Reed Saxon.

City's Lafayette Theater. He later returned to California, where he studied with Arthur Mendoza at the Actor's Circle Theater in Los Angeles.

One of Del Toro's first theatrical productions after arriving in Los Angeles was in the play *Orphans* in 1997. That same year he also made small appearances in television series such as *Miami Vice* and *O'Hara*. His first movie appearance was in the role of Duke in the comedy *Big Top Pee Wee*.

Throughout the late 1980s and early 1990s, Del Toro found many roles in movies such as *License to Kill* (1989), *The Indian Runner* (1991), *Huevos de Oro* (Golden Eggs, 1992), *Fearless* (1993), *Money for Nothing* (1993), *China Moon* (1994), *Swimming with Sharks* (1995), *Submission* (1995), and *The Fan* (1996) He also appeared in television, in movies and miniseries such as NBC's *Drug Wars: The Story of Kiki Camarena* (1990), *Christopher Columbus: The Discovery* (1992), and *Tales from the Crypt* (1994). Although many of the roles that he played were small, directors and casting agents liked working with him for the sense of dedication, realism, and seriousness that he imparted to every character.

Most critics identify Del Toro's role in the movie *The Usual Suspects* as the first major role of his career. The movie, released in 1995, was directed and produced by Brian Singer, one of his best friends. Since the movie had a low budget, he agreed to appear in the film for free as a favor to his friend. Del Toro's acting gave a great deal of credibility to the movie, in which he played Freddie Fenster, a petty criminal. He was awarded the Independent Spirit Award, the first major award of his career, for his performance in this film. The film itself won an Oscar for the best original screenplay of the year. Del Toro followed this performance with a role in Julian Schnabel's film *Basquiat*, released in 1996. The film re-creates the life of **Jean-Michel Basquiat**, an avant-garde graffiti artist and painter who lived in New York's Soho district during the 1980s. Del Toro played the character of Benny, one of Basquiat's Puerto Rican friends. Once again, Del Toro received the Independent Spirit Award for his performance. Toward the late 1990s, Del Toro continued making appearances in Hollywood productions such as *Excess Baggage* (1998), and *Fear and Loathing in Las Vegas* (1998). His roles, mostly criminals and bad guys, were consistently praised by movie critics as being sinister, intense, well developed, and real.

In 2000 he appeared in *Snatch* and *The Pledge*. However, his most important role of the year was Steven Soderbergh's *Traffic*. His interpretation of Mexican narcotics policeman Javier Rodríguez earned him a New York Film Critics Circle Award, a Golden Globe, and an Oscar as best supporting actor. In order to prepare for the role, Del Toro traveled to Mexico, where he interviewed Mexican policemen and acquired information that would allow him to give a realistic performance. His character in *Traffic* portrays the realities faced by narcotic police in Mexico who have to work in a system plagued with corruption, temptations, and ambiguities.

Del Toro is a sensitive man who has sought ways to help fellow Puerto Ricans interested in film. In 1996, the government of Puerto Rico dedicated the Puerto Rico International Film Festival to him. During the summer of 2001 he traveled to Puerto Rico to assist in a government-sponsored initiative to teach film appreciation to school children. He is also an advocate for more Latinos in Hollywood film and television industries. In addition to his dramatic career, Del Toro is also an amateur painter.—S.M.M.

References and Suggested Readings

Benecio Del Toro Zone: *www.beneciodeltoro.com.*

Cotayo, Charles. "Benicio Del Toro, el reto de actuar en español." *El Nuevo Herald* (Miami, FL), January 5, 2001, 1C.

De Curtis, Anthony. "Hot Actor of the Moment Can Also Play It Cool." *The New York Times,* January 21, 2001, 15.

Hobson, Louis B. "Del Toro Charges Fame: Actor Has a Full Plate of Work with *Traffic, Snatch,* and *The Pledge.*" *Toronto Sun,* January 19, 2001, 56.

Kirkland, Bruce "Torrid Time for Del Toro: Personable Actor Is One of the Fastest Rising Stars in the Movies." *Toronto Sun,* March 25, 2001, S9.

Millán Pabón, Carmen. "Visita su tierra Benicio Del Toro." *El Nuevo Día* (San Juan, PR), July 18, 2001, n.p.

Miller Samantha. "Traffic Stopper." *People,* April 16, 2001, 69.

Musto, Michael. "La dolce Musto." *Village Voice,* January 30, 2001, 10.

DES'REE (DESIREE WEEKS)
(1968–)

Barbadian British Singer and Songwriter

Des'ree's best-selling music blends soft rock and Caribbean rhythms. This London native who spent some of her childhood years in her father's homeland of Barbados has quickly risen to stardom, and in less than a decade has assembled a catalogue of almost 50 songs. Her 1992 debut album *Mind Adventures* took 12 weeks from the moment it landed on an executive's desk to its commercial release—a record in the music business. The 1990s were an extraordinary decade for Des'ree as she became one of the best selling British artists in the world. Her four R&B-flavored pop music CDs, influenced by her Caribbean musical roots, have brought her much international fame and success. As the writer and singer of all of her songs, she seems to have a glowing and positive outlook on life. She is best known for the 1994 worldwide smash hit "You Gotta Be," which capitulated her to platinum status and has remained one of the most enduring hit singles of the 1990s. After its release, the feel-good song has become an anthem for young women.

Desiree Weeks was born on November 30, 1968, in London, England. Her first exposure to music came from listening to her parents play the recordings of Duke Ellington, Stevie Wonder, **Joan Armatrading**, and **Bob Marley**. She was surrounded by the Caribbean island sounds of jazz, reggae, calypso, and socca brought from Barbados to London by her parents. As a girl she entertained family and friends with her singing, imagining herself as singer Gladys Knight on stage. For many years, she sang in church gospel choirs, which gave her the spiritual quality one identifies in her compositions. Her primary schooling was in a private London school. Two influences during those years also had an impact on who she is today: ballet and poetry. Certainly a result of her six years studying ballet are the "rare skill and refinement" noted by critics when referring to her graceful movement on stage. In a 1998 interview she described the allure of poetry: "It seemed to disobey any rules. . . . I used to relate poetry to jazz together. Jazz was like musical poetry" (Johnson 1998).

When she was ten years old, her parents moved the family back to Barbados. She felt the time she spent in Barbados greatly influenced her both personally and in the form her music has taken, as it gave her a more ample and realistic exposure to the music of the Caribbean. The family returned to London when she was 14, and she had no doubt that she wanted her future to revolve around music. Increasingly, she found herself recapitulating everything she learned and experienced about her culture and history into poetry and setting this to music.

At 17, after having recorded some songs a cappella, a major London recording company became interested and signed her on. In 1992 her first CD *Mind Adventures* was released. While songs like "Feel So High" and others from that recording shot up the British and European music charts, they failed to engage listeners in the United States. She continued to write and prepare for her next release while touring with her good friend Seal as the opening performer for his concerts.

In 1994 Des'ree made her breakthrough on the U.S. charts. Her second CD *I Ain't Movin'* included the hit single "You Gotta Be," which went platinum in the United States, selling more than a million copies and reached gold status in Australia and Brazil, selling millions more around the world. "You Gotta Be" became the most played video ever on television's VH-1, and received an IAAAM Award (International Association of African-American Music), as well as a prestigious BMI Award. This song has also been included in BMI's "Million Air" list, for being among the most performed songs on radio and television, a distinction that only 1,500 titles out of over 3 millions works, have ever achieved. This album also included "Love Is Here," the first song she ever wrote.

Des'ree, who had a personal audience with Pope John Paul II, was one of the featured performers at the first secular concert at the Vatican in Rome, Italy, in

1995. In addition, her songs began to make their way into major feature films. Her song "Silent Hero" was included in Spike Lee's film *Clockers*, and in 1996 her composition "Kissing You," was used as the love theme in Baz Luhrman's *Romeo + Juliet*, starring Leonardo Di Caprio.

Critics note that Des'ree's music continues to evolve album after album, with her 1998 *Supernatural*, being the most challenging to date. This production, which includes the song "I'm Kissing You" has sold over 16 million copies worldwide. The album also includes "Proud to Be a Dread," her tribute to reggae superstar Bob Marley, which in general terms examines the hardships of life and speaks of the misrepresentations of Rastafarian culture in the mainstream. One critics notes that she is able to blend her soprano range into reggae, rap, R&B and other rhythms, "wrapping her luscious vocals around heart-wrenching lyrics" (Guerra 1998, 6). He attributes *Supernatural*'s success to Des'ree's "sublime vocal work" (6).

Des'ree has picked up numerous international awards. In 1999 she was hailed as the best selling British artist in the world. That year's World Music Awards recognized her as the Best British solo star. Her most memorable song, "You Gotta Be," is now regularly heard in Ford Company car commercials and was included on the 1999 tribute album for Diana, Princess of Wales. *Endangered Species,* a compilation album of earlier hits, and new songs has been well received, particularly in Japan, where she is extremely popular. She is currently writing and preparing music for her next musical recordings.—G.C.

References and Suggested Readings

Des'ree Official Web Page: *http://www.desree.co.uk/.*
Guerra, Joey. "Wonders Never Cease; Pop Singers Avoid Curse of Single Hit with Latest Albums." *The Houston Chronicle*, August 23, 1998, 6.
Hoskyns, Barney. "Des'ree." *Musician* 198 (May 1995): 22.
Johnson, Billy, Jr. "Des'ree: Cooler, Bolder, Wiser." *Launch,* March 17, 1999. *http://launch.yahoo.com/read/feature.asp?contentID=157386.*

JUSTINO DÍAZ
(1940–)

Puerto Rican Opera Singer

Justino Díaz has been Puerto Rico's musical ambassador to the world of professional opera for more than 40 years. He has toured the world's most important musical scenes such as La Scala in Milan, Convent Garden in London, and Teatro Colón in Argentina. His powerful voice has a range that allows him to play both bass and baritone roles. Thus, he has been able to play a wide selection of roles during a career that spans more than 45 years. Despite his travels, he has always kept in touch with his Puerto Rican roots by returning to the island almost every year to play with the Casals Festival and the Puerto Rico Symphony Orchestra. Although Díaz is semi-retired from professional opera, he has a new career as music professor in Puerto Rico.

Justino Díaz Villarini was born on January 29, 1940, in San Juan, Puerto Rico, to Carmen Vilarini and Justino Díaz. His father was a university professor of economics in Puerto Rico who often traveled to teach and study. As a result, Díaz spent substantial periods of his childhood in the United States and studied both in the United States and Puerto Rico. While attending the University High School in Río Piedras, Puerto Rico, his father enrolled him in private music classes with noted Puerto Rican soprano Maria Esther Robles and with Alicia Morales. In 1957, he had the first leading role with Robles in the city of San Germán in the role of Ben in Gian Carlo Menotti's *The Telephone*.

Díaz graduated from high school in 1958 and entered the University of Puerto Rico, where he joined the university choir, directed by Arturo Rodríguez. A gifted teacher, Rodríguez had built the choir into one of the best music ensembles in Puerto Rico and the Caribbean. He recognized Díaz's musical gifts and made him the choir's soloist. To pursue his dream of becoming an opera singer, Díaz transferred to the New England Music Conservatory in Boston, where he became a protégé and student of Boris Godovski and Fredreick Jagel. While at the New England Conservatory, he competed in the Metropolitan Opera House's "Auditions of the Air" and finished third for the New England region in 1960. He also debuted with the New England Opera Theater in 1961.

He moved to New York, where Hans J. Hoffman, a well-known music agent, became his promoter. Hoffman found him work at the American Opera Society. Due to Hoffman's influence, Díaz was able to perform with groups such as the Boston Symphony. Hoffman also encouraged Díaz to compete again for the Metropolitan Opera House "Auditions of the Air," this time representing the New York region. In 1963 Díaz won the competition. As part of the award, he received a one-year contract to perform at the Metropolitan Opera House. He debuted at the Met in 1963 with the role of Monterone in Verdi's *Rigoletto*. The contract also allowed him to travel back to Puerto Rico and perform in many different operatic productions staged by the Met at the theater of the University of Puerto Rico.

Díaz established a lifelong association with the Met as a result of winning the 1963 competition, singing more than 400 times and 29 roles there throughout his career. In 1966 he sang at the opening of the Met's new facilities at the Lincoln Center in New York with American singer Leontyne Price in the role of Anthony in the world premiere of Samuel Barber's *Anthony and Cleopatra*. In 1971, he had the honor of performing at opening night of the Kennedy Center Opera House, where he performed in Ginastera's *Beatrix Cenci*.

In his long career Díaz has performed with some of the most talented opera singers of his time. He has performed with Luciano Pavarotti, Placido Domingo, Joan Sutherland, Beverly Sills, Teresa Berganza, Nicosia Gredan, and Katia Ricciarelli. For most of his career he has sung as a bass, but he is also able to sing as a baritone. He is considered one of the best interpreters of Baron Scarpia in Puccini's *Tosca* and has also excelled playing Verdi's *Rigoletto,* and Barber's *Anthony,* a role that he pioneered. Díaz has appeared at the Salzburg Opera Festival, at the Spoleto Festival, and participated in the opening of the **Luis A. Ferré** Arts Center in Puerto Rico in 1975. In addition to his work in theaters throughout the world, Díaz has worked in opera films such as Herbert von Karajan's *Carmen,* and Franco Zefirelli's *Otello.*

In 2001, Díaz announced that he was going to start a semi-retirement process and was going to change his priorities from performing to teaching. In fall 2001, he accepted the position of visiting scholar at the Puerto Rico Music Conservatory, where he occupies the Guillermo Martínez Chair. He is in charge of nurturing young talent and is very enthusiastic about his new role. In an interview with a Puerto Rican newspaper, he said: "I consider myself a discoverer. My students are the basic material. I can help them develop a good vocal technique, eventually a stage technique, and a histrionic technique but I cannot invent the talent. I should recognize that you are born with it, and you have to work a lot to make it grow" (Vázquez Zapata, 2001, n.p.). Díaz has also been appointed as one of the trustees to the Musical Arts Corporation in Puerto Rico. He is working to build fiscal endowments that will support art organizations such as the Puerto Rico Philharmonic Orchestra and the Puerto Rico Music Conservatory.

Throughout his career, Díaz has received many multiple honors, such as the Handel Medal, an honorary doctorate in music from the New England Conservatory, and an honorary degree from the University of Puerto Rico at Mayagüez. He also received the Grand Prize in music from the Puerto Rico Arts and Sciences Academy and National Culture Prize from the Institute of Puerto Rican Culture.—S.M.M.

References and Suggested Readings

Fernández, Ronald, Serafín Méndez-Médez, and Gail Cueto. "Justino Díaz." *Puerto Rico Past and Present: An Encyclopedia.* Westport, CT: Greenwood, 1998. 102–103.
Vázquez Zapata, Larissa. "Justino Díaz: puertorriqueño universal." *El Nuevo Día* (San Juan, PR), "Revista Por Dentro," November 11, 2001, n.p.

Paquito D'Rivera
(1948–)

Cuban Jazz Musician

Cuban musician Paquito D'Rivera is one of today's best Latin jazz artists. A virtuoso of the saxophone and clarinet, he began his career with the Cuban National Symphony, and throughout his years in Cuba helped found various musical

Paquito D'Rivera. Courtesy of Lane Pederson.

groups including the Orquesta Cubana de Música Moderna (Cuban Modern Music Orchestra) and Irakere. Since his arrival to the United States in 1981, he has enjoyed a successful career that has included jazz and classical performances in the most prestigious halls and festivals in the world. His performances and compositions range from bebop to classical rhythms. He has won several Grammy awards, and made over 24 solo album recordings and numerous singles that have been at the top of the jazz charts.

Paquito D'Rivera was born in Havana on June 4, 1948, into a musical family. His Father Francisco "Tito" D'Rivera, his first teacher, was well known as a classical musician and conductor as well as a saxophone player. Paquito began his musical studies at five and by the time he was six was considered a child prodigy. By seven he signed with a saxophone manufacturer and became the youngest artist ever to endorse a musical instrument for the company. In 1958 he was performing to rave reviews at the National Theater in Havana. His musical training continued at the Havana Conservatory of Music when he was 12.

His early professional experience included performing with and conducting the Orquesta Cubana de Música Moderna, which he co-founded with Cuban musician Chucho Valdés in 1965. In the early 1970s, Valdés invited D'Rivera to co-direct the Cuban band Irakere, whose fusion of jazz, rock and Afro-Cuban rhythms made them hugely popular in Cuba. Their 1978 performances in the Newport, New York, and Montreaux jazz festivals put them on the jazz' world map, and the performances were recorded on two double LP sets titled *Havana Jam* and *Havana Jam II*, both released in 1979. This historical recording made Irakere the first post-**Castro** Cuban group to record for an American label and win a Grammy.

By 1980, D'Rivera felt constrained by Cuba's political system. During a 1981 concert tour in Spain he went to the American Embassy and sought political asylum. Among the very first people who helped him re-start his musical career were Dizzy Gillespie and Mario Bauzá who opened the doors to jazz in the United States, particularly in New York City jazz clubs.

Among his early U.S. recordings were the very successful *Paquito Blowin* (1981) and *Mariel* (1982). By 1984 his work had been featured on public television, the CBS television program *Sunday Morning*, and *Time* magazine, as well as being the cover feature story for the trade publication *Jazz Times*. With his group Havana/New York, he has performed all over the world. In 1988, D'Rivera and Dizzy Gillespie co-founded the United Nations Orchestra, with which he has performed as both conductor and as soloist. That same year, he appeared as soloist with the National Symphony Orchestra and with the Brooklyn Philharmonic Orchestra.

Since 1979 he has received three additional Grammy awards. In 1997 he received a Grammy for his recording *Portraits of Cuba* and in 2000 he received one each for the song "Tropicana Nights" and the album *Live at the Blue Note.* Also known as a composer of classical music, he has received commissions to write for a number of symphony and chamber music orchestras. In 1989 his composition "New York Suite" was commissioned and recorded by the Gerald Danovich Saxophone Quartet. He was also commissioned to write for the Aspen Wind Quintet, which premiered his suite "Aires Tropicales" in 1994 at the Frick Collection in New York City, and his 1998 "Rivers" suite premiered at the 25th anniversary concert of the New Jersey Chamber Music Society. In 1999 the German Chamber Orchestra Weneck presented a series titled *Paquito D'Rivera Meets Mozart,* which featured his chamber compositions along with music by Mozart. One of the outstanding compositions from this series was "Adagio." "Gran Danzón," the Bel Air Concerto commissioned by the National Symphony Orchestra, is considered among his best classical compositions and premiered at the Kennedy Center in 2002.

Since 1995, D'Rivera has been artistic director of Uruguay's international jazz festival, Festival Internacional de Jazz en el Tambo. In 2000, D'Rivera was commissioned by Jazz at Lincoln Center and wrote "Pan American Suite" for their *As of Now* series. In 1999, he played at the White House and at the Kennedy Center as guest artist in the "Americanos Concert." In 2000, D'Rivera published his autobiography *Mi vida saxual* (My Saxual Life), whose prologue was written by Cuban author **Guillermo Cabrera Infante.** He is also a talented writer, whose first novel *En tus brazos morenos,* will be published shortly. His 2000 recordings include *Music From Two Worlds* and *Habanera*; *Brazilian Dreams* was released in 2002.

D'Rivera performs and records as a soloist, but he has three main groups with which he also works: Triangulo, his chamber music ensemble; the Paquito D'Rivera Big Band; and the Paquito D'Rivera Quintet. D'Rivera is artistic director of jazz programming for the New Jersey Chamber Music Society, and he was one of the featured soloists in director Fernando Trueba's 2001 film *Calle 54* (54th Street).

In 2003 the prestigious Berklee School of Music in Boston honored D'Rivera's contribution to the field of music by granting him with an honorary doctorate. —G.C.

References and Suggested Readings

Cobol, Leila. "Blue Note Soundtrack 'Calle 54' Ups the Ante for Latin Jazz." *Billboard* 113.13 (March 31, 2001): 11.

D'Rivera, Paquito. *Mi vida saxual.* Barcelona: Seix Barral, Colección los tres mundos, 2000.

Mandel, Howard. "The Hustlers: Paquito D'Rivera & Michel Camilo Bring the Afro-Caribbean Tradition Within Earshot." *Down Beat* 62.1 (January 1995): 26.

Paquito D'Rivera Official Web Site: *www.paquitodrivera.com.*

JUAN PABLO DUARTE
(1813–1876)
Dominican Patriot and Political Leader

Juan Pablo Duarte is considered one of the founding fathers of the Dominican Republic. In 1831, his establishment of the secret society La Trinitaria began a 13-year campaign that ended February 27, 1844, when the Dominican Republic was declared independent from Haiti.

One of six children, Juan Pablo Duarte y Diez was born in Santo Domingo on January 26, 1813, to Manuela Diez y Jiménez and Spanish businessman Juan José Duarte Rodríguez. Duarte was eight years old when the armies of Jean-Pierre Boyer occupied the eastern Spanish-speaking part of Hispaniola and made it part of Haiti, imposing French as the country's official language. The two periods of Haitian domination in Santo Domingo created an enduring animosity between the two neighboring peoples. Haitian rule in Santo Domingo was characterized by the degree to which it tried to eliminate Spanish culture: universities were closed and communication between the Roman Catholic Church and Europe was forbidden.

Duarte completed his primary education in 1828 at age 16, and his parents decided to send him abroad to study given the political instability that reigned at home. This trip to Europe broadened his perspective and taught him a number of languages. He also gained an understanding of the underpinnings of American and European governments, and wanted the liberties that citizens of those countries enjoyed. He studied law in Barcelona, where he perfected his nationalistic political ideas.

He returned home in 1833 focused on obtaining independence for Santo Domingo and began by establishing the secret society La Trinitaria. Initially, the membership for this organization was recruited from the urban middle class. He was an excellent political orator and organizer, and his secret organization attracted hundreds of members, including Ramón Maías Mella and Francisco del Rosario Sánchez, who with Duarte, are considered the founding fathers of the Dominican Republic. As Duarte's followers increased, so did the level of oppression coming from the Haitian government. On August 2, 1843, Duarte and a number of his followers learned that they were being persecuted by the Haitian government and fled to St. Thomas. Eventually, the members of La Trinitaria were successful in bringing down the Haitian rule. Although that did not immediately bring independence to Santo Domingo, pro-independence forces were able to consolidate their power and formed a provisional government on February 27, 1844, that served as the foundation for the creation of the Dominican Republic.

After obtaining their independence, the leadership called for Duarte's return from exile in St. Thomas. He returned to a rousing welcome and was appointed general of the army. This period of victory ended in 1861, and once again Duarte went into exile when government leader Pedro Santana returned the Dominican Republic to its former colonial rulers. In 1864 Duarte returned to fight against the pro-colonial annexationists.

Duarte's comrades encouraged him to go to South American countries to gain support for the struggle. He was successful in this charge but became ill and was never able to return to the Dominican Republic. He died in Caracas, Venezuela, on July 15, 1876.—G.C.

References and Suggested Readings

Alexander, Robert Johnson. "Juan Pablo Duarte." *Biographical Dictionary of Latin American and Caribbean Political Leaders.* Westport, CT: Greenwood Press, 1988. 139–140.

Duarte personaje de la historia. Santo Domingo, DR: Worldmages: Personajes de la Historia, 2000.

"Juan Pablo Duarte." *Encyclopedia Britannica,* Vol. 4. Chicago: Encyclopedia Britannica, 2002. 246.

Patín Veloz, Enrique. *Duarte y la historia.* Santo Domingo, DR: Instituto Duartiano, 1998.

Wilson, James Grant, and John Fiske, eds. "Juan Pablo Duarte." *Appleton's Cyclopaedia of American Biography.* New York: D. Appleton & Co., 1968. 236–237.

TIM DUNCAN
(1976–)

St. Croix Basketball Player

One of the first sights seen by tourists traveling to the American territory of St. Croix after the 1999 NBA season was a huge billboard with the face of basketball player Tim Duncan stating: "Welcome to St. Croix, Home of Tim Duncan." Since coming to the United States in 1993 to attend Wake Forest University, Duncan has won the hearts and admiration of basketball fans for his superb athletic talents. *The Boston Globe* has called Duncan the "New Poster Boy of the NBA" (May 1999, D6).

Timothy Theodore Duncan was born on April 25, 1976, in St. Croix, one of four children of William Duncan, a construction worker, and Iona Duncan, a midwife. His parents instilled in him a love of both sports and education; he excelled in academics at the local school.

As youngsters, the Duncan children were encouraged to compete in swimming. Duncan's youngest sister, Tricia, represented the U.S. Virgin Islands in the 1988 Olympic Games in Seoul. By the time Duncan was an adolescent, he was rated among the top freestyle 400-meter swimmers in the United States. Unfortunately,

Tim Duncan. AP Photo/David J. Phillip.

when hurricane Hugo devastated St. Croix in 1989, it destroyed the only Olympic-size pool available for Duncan's practice. Because his dreams of becoming an Olympic swimmer were thwarted, he played football and finally basketball. Duncan had difficulty changing from the solitary sport of swimming to basketball, a sport that necessitated team effort. He didn't play with a team until he reached the ninth grade. He developed an analytic approach that focused on outsmarting and confusing the competition.

When Duncan reached St. Dunstan Episcopal High School in St. Croix, he played under the guidance of coach Cuthbert George and became a formidable player leading the St. Dunstan's team to win the local championship in 1992. The victory was attributed to Duncan single-handedly because in 1991 the team had lost every single game they had played.

Duncan graduated from St. Dunstan High School in 1993 as one of the top five students in his class. His skill at basketball had made him an ideal prospect for American college coaches visiting St. Croix in search of new talent and he accepted a sports scholarship at Wake Forest University in North Carolina, where he majored in psychology.

At Salem-Winston, Duncan played with the Demon Deacons and became one of the best and most disciplined students both in basketball and in his major. Many sports commentators have said that his study of psychology while at Wake Forest was instrumental in the development of his basketball strategy and technique. By the time Duncan reached the end of his sophomore year, he had become one of the team's star players. During his senior year he was named NCAA Player of the Year.

Despite the constant pressures to accept tempting offers from professional basketball teams, Duncan decided to complete his degree. Before his mother died of breast cancer, he had promised her that he was going to pursue an education. By staying and getting the degree he honored this promise. When he graduated in 1997, he had scored 1,500 baskets (2,117 points), caught 1,000 rebounds, blocked 400 shots, and helped with 200 assists (Kernan 2000). He had also received both the Naismith and Wooden awards. He was seen as a strategic and psychological player who often outsmarted his opponents in the court. With such a record it was no surprise that Duncan became the number-one pick for the 1997 NBA's basketball draft. He was selected by the San Antonio Spurs in Texas with a three-year contract worth almost $10 million.

Since his arrival at San Antonio's "Alamodome" in 1997, Duncan has been a major asset to the team. He understood the concept of teamwork and used his skills to complement other members of his team. He was always open to the suggestions of head coach Gregg Popovich and developed a good reputation for observing his teammates and listening to advice. He joined forces with the legendary player David Robinson to integrate their playing strategies and skills. The duo of seven-foot players became known as the "Texas Towers" because of the force and strength they brought to the game. Duncan, playing center, perfected his bank shot and led the Spurs to 56 victories during the first season. He averaged 21.1 points, 11.9 rebounds, 2.7 assists and 2.51 blocks per game (Kernan 2000). For his performance, he was named the NBA's Rookie of the Year.

The 1998–1999 season provided Duncan with unique opportunities and challenges. Because of a strike in the NBA, the season was shortened and the team had to play 50 games in a period of 91 days. They reached the playoffs with a 31–5 win-lose record and positioned themselves for the finals. Their last five games against the New York Knicks kept basketball fans transfixed while watching some of the best basketball in history. Duncan, by then nicknamed "Slam Duncan," proved that his methodical approach to the game and his successful teaming with Robinson was the key to the team's victory. After winning the first two games at their home stadium, the Spurs moved to the Knicks' playing grounds at Madison Square Garden. The Knicks recognized that if they wanted to win the series, they needed to be able to block Duncan. The strategy to keep Duncan from scoring seemed effective as the Knicks won the third game against the Spurs. Fortunately, the Spurs recognized this strategy and teamed Robinson and Duncan to win the fourth and fifth games, thus winning their team's first NBA championship in 26 years. For his accomplishments during the 1998–1999 series Duncan was named Most Valuable Player of the NBA

During the 1999–2000 season, Duncan suffered a knee injury that sidelined him for most games. Despite receiving substantially larger offers to play with the Orlando Magic, he renewed a three-year contract with the Spurs and will be paid $32.6 million during the length of the contract.

Duncan has been seen as an atypical basketball player. He dislikes the media attention and prefers video games to partying. He has not engaged in major media campaigns or sponsorships. His focus is in playing the best game possible. Meanwhile, his games are closely watched in his native St. Croix, where he is revered and was awarded the Medal of Honor, the highest award that the island bestows. Still in his twenties, he is considered a very young player with many more victories and championships ahead of him.—S.M.M.

References and Suggested Readings

Araton, Harvey. "Sports of the Times: For Ewing the Toughest Act of All." *The New York Times,* June 19, 1999, D1.

Hall, Michael. "Tim Duncan: A Sports Star Who Stands Tall." *Texas Monthly* (September 1999): 145.

"Hurricane Turned Duncan to Basketball: Fate Played Role in Spurs' Development." *Houston Chronicle,* June 17, 1999, 4.

Kernan, Kevin. *Tim Duncan: Slam Duncan.* Champaign, IL: Sports Publishing, 2000.

MacMullan, Jackie. "Silent But Deadly." *Sports Illustrated,* February 21, 2000, 70.

May, Peter. "League Has Itself a New Poster Boy: Duncan Is All the NBA Could Want and More." *The Boston Globe,* June 20, 1999, D6.

"San Antonio's Tim Duncan Keeps Promise, Re-Signs with Spurs: Inks $32.6 Million Pact." *Jet,* August 21, 2000, 47.

Starr, Mark and Nadine Joseph. "A Superstar Makes Way for the NBA's Next Great Talent." *Newsweek,* May 17, 1999, 75.

"Wake Forest's Tim Duncan Tops NBA Draft Picks." *Jet,* July 14, 1997, 46.

Edouard Duval-Carrié
(1954–)

Haitian Painter

Painter Eduoard Duval-Carrié is one of a significant group of new artists coming out of Haiti. Although he is based in Miami and considers himself an immigrant, his work has been influenced by the legacy of many older and traditional Haitian artists. His paintings have a refined style that incorporates many elements of conventional Haitian art. It also includes political, religious, and ideological connotations within its depictions.

Duval-Carrié, who comes from a large and affluent family, was born in Haiti but left the island with his family during his childhood. He has since lived in Puerto Rico, New York, France, Canada, and Miami. As a child he studied at the Union School of Port-au-Prince, but he has had a broad range of educational experiences. He has an undergraduate degree from the École Nationale Supériure des Beaux Arts in Paris, and has also studied at Loyola and McGill University in Montreal. When **Jean-Bertrand Aristide** was elected president of Haiti, Duval-Carrié intended to return to the country and become a contributor to the new Haitian society, but he stayed in Miami after Aristide was deposed (Pincus 1994).

Duval-Carrié did not receive formal artistic training and only began painting when he was a college undergraduate, yet his art reveals a high degree of refinement and sophistication. Although his work contains some of the primitivism that characterizes Haitian art, it also exhibits a certain iconic complexity. The experience of exile has helped shape the somewhat complex vision of Haiti that exists in Duval-Carrié's work. His images have mostly Haitian referents, but they also incorporate a larger vision, such as his references to the Africa that come through especially in his sculptures.

Religious influence is notable in his paintings. He has incorporated themes of the Haitian Voodoo religion and has contextualized them using modern imagery. His art, somewhat intricate and baroque, brings forth a series of mythological figures that interact with today's world. His work has been influenced by traditional primitive and naturalist Haitian art. The work of Duval-Carrié shifts constantly between the real Haiti and its images and the surreal, those myths and icons of his imagination that he brings to the canvas in the shape of religious imagery and Voodoo. He has said, "We are relatively free of roots and traditions, fundamental elements that we daily try to recreate ourselves through a constant recreation of our myths, values, and aspirations" (Lewis 1995, 140). One art critic has written that "his often fantastic forms or realism possess a liberating force that is a result of a magical universe inspired by the observation of Voodoo" (LeFalle-Collins 1997, 165).

Duval-Carrié's paintings tend to the surreal. They also seem to represent, in many ways, the magical realism movement that has influenced literature and film during the latter part of the twentieth century. His work characterizes a movement in Haitian painting beyond modernism, pointing to the postmodern. He portrays those immensurable social and political realities that are so powerful they can only be depicted through a set of magical symbols.

The work of this artist makes powerful political commentaries through his images. Art critics have asserted that his work marks the beginning of a new type of Haitian visual arts, where the painter moves away from the exotic and exaggerated naturalistic representations of their Haitian landscape and becomes adversely critical (Poupeye 1998). He has been branded by the experience of exile and expresses a point of view about the pain, tragedy, exploitation, and political degradation that have permeated his native land. Examples of this are his clownish depictions of Haitian politicians and his disenchantment with authority figures within the Haitian state.

Duval-Carrié had his first major exhibition at Le Centre d' Art in Haiti in 1979. Since then, his art has been exhibited throughout the world. Some of his recent exhibits have taken place at Contemporary Museum of Art in Monterrey, Mexico (1992); Musée du College Saint Pierre in Haiti (1996); and the Nexus Contemporary Art Center in Atlanta, Georgia (1996).—S.M.M.

References and Suggested Readings

LeFalle-Collins, Lizetta. "Edouard Duval-Carrié." In Thomas Riggs, ed., *St. James Press Guide to Black Artists.* Detroit: St. James Press, 1997. 163–164.

Lewis, Samella. *Caribbean Visions: Contemporary Painting and Sculpture.* Alexandria, VA: Art Services International, 1995.

Marger, Mary Ann. "Leaving Us with New Ideas." *St. Petersburg Times,* April 10, 1998, 18.

Pincus, Robert. "Haiti's Hellish Landscape: Artist Rich Imagery Portrays Nation's Pain." *The San Diego Union-Tribune,* August 25, 1994, 45.

Poupeye, Veerle. *Caribbean Art.* London: Thames and Hudson, 1998.

Mervyn M. Dymally
(1926–)

Trinidadian American Politician, Scholar, and Public Official

Mervyn M. Dymally has been an influential and powerful figure within the African American political establishment in the United States. An immigrant from Trinidad, Dymally became a U.S. citizen in 1957 and climbed through the ranks of the Democratic Party in California to become the first black lieutenant governor and a representative to the U.S. Congress for six consecutives terms. Throughout his long career he used his elective positions to empower the poor and to be a staunch supporter for the plea of human rights and economic equality for the people of Africa and the Caribbean. When Dymally retired from Congress in 1992, *Jet* magazine summarized the public perception of Dymally when it wrote: "Few Black elected officials were more aggressive, uncompromising and daring than Rep. Mervyn Dymally" ("Dymally to Retire from House" 1992, 10).

Dymally was born in Cedros, Trinidad, on May 12, 1926, to Hamid Dymally and Andreid Richardson. He attended Cedros Government School, the local elementary school, and studied at St. Benedict and the Naparima Schools in San Fernando. After graduation from high school at the age of 19, Dymally went to the United States in search of educational opportunities. He arrived Jefferson City, Missouri, in 1946 and briefly enrolled at Lincoln University; he later dropped out and held several odd jobs. He then moved to Los Angeles, where he attended California State University in Los Angeles and received a bachelor's degree in education in 1954. He received a master's degree in government from California State University in Sacramento in 1969, and a Ph.D. in human behavior from the U.S. International University in San Diego in 1978.

He started his professional career as a teacher for gifted and exceptional children in Los Angeles between 1955 and 1961. Moved by the grave racial, social, and economic inequities that afflicted the black people of Los Angeles, Dymally got involved in city politics and was elected to the California State Assembly in 1962.

Dymally built coalitions among the African American community; according to civil rights historian Taylor Branch, Dymally's golden opportunity surfaced when he was able to bridge the schism that existed between the Christian and Muslim communities in Los Angeles following a bloody racial incident that had occurred at Muhammad's Temple No. 27 located in South Central Los Angeles on April 27, 1962. After being denied access to an assembly held by local leaders to discuss the aftermath of the incident and the progressive deterioration of relations between African Americans, Muslims, and the police in the city, Dymally was able to get an opportunity to speak and shared the podium with Muslim leader Malcolm X:

"Then he introduced Dymally, whose first words to the crowd—the traditional Muslim greeting in Arabic, 'As-Salaamu—Alaikum' ('Peace be upon you')—produced a sharp breath of surprise and thunderous applause on the swelling inclusion of outcasts" (Branch 1998, 12–13). Dymally, an Episcopalian, gained immediate popularity with the large Muslim community. Because of the visibility that he gained at this event, he was able to attract more attention for his political campaign and eventually won in 1962. Throughout his political career he has been commended for his ability to build coalitions within the African American community.

He joined the California State Assembly in 1963. His election to public office marked the first time that a black man born in a foreign country was elected to political office in California. His election not only marked one of many first he attained during his political career, but it also started a long and successful career in California politics. He held his position at the assembly for two terms between 1963 and 1967. In 1967, he ran for the State Senate and won. Once again he was the first black person to become a senator in the state. His major political challenge came when he won the position of lieutenant governor in 1974. His most significant responsibilities during his term as lieutenant governor were chairing the Commission for Economic Development and serving on the Board of Regents of the University of California. Dymally held the position of lieutenant governor until 1979, when he lost the re-election bid. In 1980 he ran for the U.S. Congress, representing the 31st Congressional District of Compton, California. He won and once again started a long career as a legislator in Washington.

During his six terms in the U.S. Congress, Dymally developed a successful legislative platform on behalf of human rights, the balancing of trade inequities between the United States and Africa and the Caribbean, and the improvement of educational opportunities for children of color. He became known as one of the most powerful black members of congress and served as Chairman of the Congressional Black Caucus between 1987 and 1989. He also served as a member of the District of Columbia Committee and the Post Office and Civil Service Committees. His most important appointment, however, was as a member of the House Foreign Affairs Committee, where he chaired the Africa Subcommittee. He used this position for an extensive campaign to create awareness about the many social, political, and economic illnesses affecting African nations as a result of often-misguided American policies. He also supported more humanitarian aid for Africa. Dymally was instrumental in creating awareness in Congress about the Apartheid regime in South Africa.

Despite his many accomplishments in Congress, his tenure was at times controversial. During the 1980s and early 1990s Dymally was investigated several times on charges of taking improper contributions from political constituencies. None of the allegations was ever proven (Griego 1992). He retired in 1992.

In retirement, Dymally has stayed active in American politics. He launched the Dymally International Group, a lobbying firm representing mostly African nations in Washington. Although he has been sharply criticized for the making substantial amounts of income representing governments such as Mauritius and Sudan, Dymally has successfully defended himself by saying that African countries need a substantial level of access to the political establishment in Washington (Mann 1998).

Throughout his public career, Dymally has taught at many colleges and universities in California, such as the University of California at Irvine, Pomona College, and Golden Gate University. In August of 2000, the speaker of the California State Assembly appointed Dymally as the liaison between the Assembly and the state's community colleges. Throughout his political life he has been credited with helping many African Americans to pursue and gain elective political office.—S.M.M.

References and Suggested Readings

Branch, Taylor. *Pillar of Fire: America in the King Years, 1963–65.* New York: Touchstone Books, 1998.

Dymally, Mervyn. "Choice Is Peace or Violence for Pakistan's Leaders." *Financial Times* (London), July 28, 2000, 14.

"Dymally Leads Drive for Liberian Relief." *Jet,* August 24, 1992, 15.

"Dymally to Retire from House: Served Six Terms." *Jet,* March 2, 1992, 10.

Elliot, Jeffrey M. "Mervyn M. Dymally: Science and the New Orthodoxy." *Black Voices in American Politics.* San Diego: Harcourt Brace Jovanovich, 1986. 77–95

Griego, Tina. "Dymally to Retire: Blazed Path for Blacks in Politics." *Los Angeles Times,* February 11, 1992, B1.

Mann, Jim. "When Sudan Needs a Friend on the Hill, It Turns to Dymally: Lobbying Deal with Ex-Law Maker Show How Even Impoverished Nations Will Pay for Help in Navigating Washington." *Los Angeles Times,* December 1, 1998, A5.

Ragsdale, Bruce A., and Joel D. Treese, eds. "Mervyn Dymally." *Black Americans in Congress, 1870–1989.* Washington, DC: U.S. Government Printing Office, 1990. 43–44.

GUS EDWARDS
(1939–)

Antiguan American Dramatist and Playwright

Gus Edwards is an Afro-Caribbean writer and dramatist. His plays and writings have been showcased by the very prominent Negro Ensemble Company of New York and by other companies throughout the United States. An intense author who explores unconventional topics in his plays, he has been a central figure in the African American theatrical world and has received praise and acclaim from critics and audiences alike.

Edwards was born in Antigua on March 8, 1939, to Charles and Muriel Edwards. He was raised on the island of St. Thomas in the U.S. Virgin Islands. His early days in acting go back to his work in repertory theater in St. Thomas and the Caribbean. While he was acting there, he had the chance to meet actor Sidney Poitier, who suggested that he move to the United States to expand his theatrical opportunities. Edwards moved to New York in 1959, where he received dramatic training in theater from Stella Adler and William Hickey at the Herbert Berghof Studio in New York. He eventually became one of Adler's protégés. He also studied film at the New York Institute of Photography. However, as a dramatic writer, Edwards is mostly self-taught. He has acknowledged that he rejected formal academic education in the field of theater for fear of having his creativity restricted by theatrical writing rules and the dominant canon taught at schools (Gearhart and Ross 1983).

Edwards arrived in the United States at a time when dramatic opportunities for black actors were limited. For most of his early career in the United States he worked as a bartender, store manager, and waiter in order to make ends meet. Despite the fact that Edwards appeared in two minor film roles during the 1960s (*The Pawnbroker*, 1965 and *Stiletto*, 1969) and worked as an actor in many plays, he found that his West Indian accent narrowed his opportunities to play more mainstream and readily available roles. The lack of access to acting roles was in part what motivated Edwards to start writing plays.

It was while working as a waiter that he met a minister who volunteered to read his plays. Impressed by Edwards' writings, the minister put him in contact with Douglas Turner Ward at the Negro Ensemble Company. Ward read a manuscript for Edwards' play *The Offering* and committed to producing it. Yet even though his work was accepted for production, he had to wait five years until the play was staged. When the play finally opened in 1977, it received excellent reviews.

Edwards has written more than 12 plays, most of which have been initially produced by the Negro Ensemble Company. Among his most important works are: *The Offering* (1977), *Black Body Blues* (1978), *Old Phantoms* (1979), *These Fallen Angels* (1980), *Weep Not for Me* (1981), *Tenement* (1983), *Manhattan Made Me* (1983), *Ramona* (1986), and *Louie and Ophelia* (1986). He has also written several works for television including *Aftermath* (1979) and the TV adaptation for James Baldwin novel *Go Tell It on the Mountain* (1985). Considered one of the foremost historians of the Negro Ensemble Company, he wrote the narration for a documentary on its history for PBS.

Critics have described Edwards' dramas as both complex and intense. Many of his plays are set in the slums and ghettoes of New York. His dramatic productions are daring, as he has pushed non-traditional issues such as violence, promiscuity, racial tensions, drug addiction, complex romantic relationships, and adultery. He does not hesitate to venture into controversial areas, as his characters often exist outside of the boundaries of what is thought to be appropriate behavior in society. Nevertheless, he highlights the virtues of all kinds of people regardless of their background. As a playwright, he has a literary technique that uses description rather than judgment. His characters struggle to survive in a non-perfect society (Marowski and Matuz 1987). Edith Oliver, drama critic for the *New Yorker*, has consistently praised Edwards' work for its good humor, well-developed characters, and refined literary style (Oliver 1977).

Edwards still identifies heavily with his West Indian roots. Theater critic Kyle Lawson recently said after interviewing him: "Riding the interview train with Gus Edwards, every stop is the West Indies, the Virgin Islands to be specific, St. Thomas to be exact" ("Troupe's Director" 2000, E1). The themes and perspectives developed in his plays still reflect his experiences and environment as a black Caribbean immigrant to the United States who experienced his fair share of duress. Nevertheless, he has effectively developed strong bonds with African Americans, part of whose identity he seems to take. He has vehemently criticized traditional depictions of blacks in traditional American theater and television and has made a commitment to challenge them:

> Historically, in film and on stage, African Americans have been virtually invisible. Even the big roles African American actors obtained were so stereotypical that we didn't recognize ourselves, and, subsequently, became ashamed of ourselves. The force that impelled not just myself but many African Americans to stick it out was a determination to change those stereotypes, to give ourselves dimension by writing worthwhile roles that portrayed African Americans honestly. (Lawson "Valley Black Artists" 2000, E3)

For instance, he has become a fervent advocate for the technique of color-blind casting, which selects actors on the basis of their ability to play a given role and eliminates race as a factor in the casting decision.

In addition to his substantive work as a playwright, Edwards has built a respectable career as a drama scholar. He has taught theatrical writing at Lehman College of the City University of New York, Iona College, Bloomfield College and the North Carolina School of the Arts. He is currently an associate professor of theater at Arizona State University in Tempe, where he directs the very successful Multi-Ethnic Theatre and teaches in the film studies program. In 2000, he was appointed as the artistic director to the Scottsdale's Ensemble Theatre in Scottsdale, Arizona, an appointment he said marks the "third act of my life" (Lawson "Troupe's Director" 2000, E1).

He has published *Classic Plays of the Negro Ensemble Company* (1995), *Monologues on Black Life* (1997), and *More Monologues on Black Life* (2000). Several of his plays have also been published. Edwards is very active in many theatrical organizations, literary boards and committees such as The New Dramatists, New York State Council of the Arts, the National Endowment for the Arts, and the Arizona Commission on the Arts. He has received grants and awards from many of these organizations as well as from the Rockefeller Foundation. Gus Edwards is one of the first Caribbean writers to contribute to American theater.—S.M.M.

References and Suggested Readings

Bennetts, Leslie. "Negro Ensemble Company Celebrates 20 Years." *The New York Times*, October 28, 1986, C3.

Gearhart, Nancy, and Jane W. Ross. "Gus Edwards." In Hal May, ed., *Contemporary Authors*. Detroit: Gale, 1983. 136–140.

Lawson, Kyle. "Troupe's Director Plays Tried, True." *The Arizona Republic*, November 19, 2000, E1.

———. "Valley Black Artists Share Their Views: Black Artists on Struggles, Strides, Hopes." *The Arizona Republic*, February 6, 2000, E3.

Mapp, Edward. "Gus Edwards." *Directory of Blacks in the Performing Arts*. Metuchen, NJ: Scarecrow Press, 1990. 148–149.

Marowski, Daniel, and Roger Matuz, eds. "Gus Edwards." *Contemporary Literary Criticism*. Detroit: Gale, 1987. 137–142.

Oliver, Edith. "Three Grand Men." *New Yorker*, December 12, 1977, 92.

Peterson, Bernard. "Gus Edwards." *Contemporary Black American Playwrights and Their Plays: A Biographical Directory and Dramatic Index*. Westport, CT: Greenwood Press, 1988. 158–161.

TOMÁS ESSON
(1963–)

Cuban Painter and Sculptor

Tomás Esson's paintings constitute the main example of what has been called the "Generation of the 80s," and "New Cuban art." Esson incorporates sexual and erotic elements into his paintings to make poignant social, political, and religious statements and commentaries. He explains: "I have made a conscious decision to work with sex aggressively, a topic that is the most complex in the world. I want to provoke a reaction from the viewer. I want the spectator to examine the hypocritical mentality about sex" (Clary 1993, 72). Many of his pictures revolve around the sexual and excretory activities of Talisman, a devil-like mythological symbol whose acts he superimposes with elements from the social and political environment experienced by the artist. Themes of mutilation, machismo, repression, political hypocrisy, and violence are pervasive in Esson's work. His sexual and explosive art has created a great deal of controversy both in Cuba and in the United States.

Esson was born on February 8, 1963, in Marianao, a suburb of Havana. His parents, a brickmason and a seamstress, are first-generation Cubans. His grandparents were from Jamaica. Early in his childhood, his teachers identified his natural talents in the field of drawing and painting. Using the opportunities that the Cuban government made available to educate children with special artistic skills, they sent Esson to elite art schools. He received artistic training at the Academia de Artes Plásticas San Alejandro (1982) and at the Instituto Superior de Arte in Havana, where he finished in 1987.

During the early 1980s, Esson was considered a bona fide member of the Cuban arts elite establishment. He had been a member of the Union of Communist Youth since age 14 and had been privileged to receive the best arts education Cuba had to offer. However, Esson became disillusioned with what he perceived were the double standards of living in the **Castro** regime. He saw that the exquisite meals served at official receptions were beyond the dreams of most Cubans. He has said, "[T]he double standard of life makes you a sick person. Play the game or defect are your two choices. I felt I couldn't move, like I was in jail" (Kapitanoff 1993, 85). His art began to take a critical stance and he began to use sexual and scatological symbols to make "subversive" commentaries.

In 1987 he was invited to present his work at Havana's Art Center, one of the best art galleries in the island. When his exposition opened, it exhibited a picture titled *Mi homenaje al Che* (My Homage to Che). The picture, extremely grotesque and perverse, depicts animal-like monsters engaging in sexual activity against an image of a black Ché Guevara, one of the fathers of the Cuban Revolution, looking puzzled in the background. When Cuban Minister of Culture Armand Hart saw the painting, he gave Esson a long, stern speech on respect for the national symbols of the revolution. When Esson refused to remove the picture, the exhibit was closed immediately (Clary 1993, 72). The point of no return for this artist occurred in 1990, when the government censored his picture *33 microfonos* (33 Microphones). The painting satirized Fidel Castro by depicting him as a monster-like figure, speaking in front of a battery of 33 microphones that were phallic-shaped. While on an artistic tour in Boston in November 1990, Esson decided to stay in the United States and defected. His family is still in Cuba.

After arriving in the United States, Esson lived in Miami for three years. Although the product of censorship and repression in Cuba, he has rejected the anti-Castro political rhetoric and environment of Miami. He fits with neither the anti-Castro conservatives nor the liberal establishment and refuses to exhibit his work at the Cuban Museum of Arts and Culture. Since his arrival in the United States, Esson has seemingly gone through an identity crisis. He has noted, "The fact that I was born in Cuba and that I have Jamaican roots doesn't identify me automatically with Caribbean issues. I am more concerned with concepts involving the highest levels of art" (Lewis 1995, 114). One art critic has claimed that political statements are starting to disappear from his work (Poupeye 1997, 1998). Esson has now moved to New York, where he expects to better penetrate the mainstream art market. He has created commercial art for the Absolut Vodka advertising campaign and continues a prolific artistic production. His artwork sells for significant sums of money and is exhibited in many reputable galleries and museums in the United States, Latin America, and Europe.—S.M.M.

References and Suggested Readings

Clary, Mike. "Castro, No! Sex Si!: Exiled in Florida, Cuban Artist Tomas Esson Remains Uncompromising in Exploring Aggressive, Brazen Sexuality in His Work." *Los Angeles Times*, January 31, 1993, 72.

Kapitanoff, Nancy. "Cuban Expatriate Artists Paint Another View of Castro Revolution." *Los Angeles Times*, February 14, 1993, 85.

Lewis, Samella. *Caribbean Visions: Contemporary Painting and Sculpture.* Alexandria, VA: Art Services International, 1995.

Plagens, Peter, Peter Katel, and Tim Padgett. "The Next Wave from Havana." *Newsweek*, November 30, 1992, 76.

Poupeye, Veerle. *Caribbean Art.* London: Thames and Hudson, 1998.

———. "Tomás Esson." In Thomas Riggs, ed., *St. James Press Guide to Black Artists.* Detroit: St. James Press, 1997. 180–181.

GLORIA ESTEFAN
(1957–)

Cuban American Singer and Entertainer

In the past two decades, Gloria Estefan has become one of the leading female Latino singers in the United States. As a crossover performer who can sing in both English and Spanish, Estefan has been able to capture and transmit the essence of Caribbean and Latino musical rhythms to mainstream American audiences. Simultaneously, she has been able to adapt traditional Cuban and Latino musical forms and bring them to a mass of avid Latino followers who appreciate her talent and value her capacity to renew those tunes and bring them up to date with new musical arrangements and instrumentation.

Gloria María Fajardo was born in Havana, Cuba, on September 1, 1957. Her family moved to the United States in 1959 to escape the **Castro** regime. Her father, José Manuel Fajardo, had been an intelligence and military officer working for Cuban dictator José Fulgencio Batista. Since he had intelligence information about Cuba, he was recruited by the CIA to be part of the 2506 Brigade that launched the unsuccessful Bay of Pigs invasion in 1961. After the invasion failed, he spent almost two years in a Cuban prison as a political prisoner. When he was released from prison, he returned to the United States and joined the U.S. Army, fought in the Vietnam War, and eventually attained the rank of captain. Shortly after returning to the United States, he was diagnosed with multiple sclerosis.

The debilitating nature of her father's illness had severe implications for the family. Estefan's mother, who had been a teacher in Cuba, was forced to find a job and go to school at night. As a result, Estefan was left in charge and took care of her sick father and her youngest sister Emily. She found solace in this depressing situation in reading and writing poetry, practicing her guitar, and singing.

Gloria Estefan. Courtesy of Photofest.

Estefan attended Lourdes Academy, a Catholic parochial school in Miami, where she graduated from high school in 1975. She then entered the University of Miami, where she had obtained a partial scholarship to study psychology. That same year, she met Emilio Estefan, a young sales manager for Bacardí in Miami who had a local pop music quartet known as the Miami Latin Boys. After hearing her sing at a wedding where they were playing, they invited her to join the group as their lead vocalist.

In 1978 she graduated from the University of Miami with a degree in psychology and married Emilio. Their band, which had been well accepted in the Miami area, changed their name to the Miami Sound Machine.

The Miami Sound Machine was a rhythmic band that played fast-tempo Latino music with features that combined American pop and rock with Spanish rhythms. In 1980 they signed a recording contract with Discos CBS International, the Latino affiliate of CBS records, and between 1981 and 1983 released the records *Renacer* (Rebirth), *Otra vez* (Again), and *A toda máquina* (Full Speed). Their recordings and the high-energy concerts and performances they staged throughout Latin America brought considerable recognition to the band in the Latino market. Anyone who saw Estefan's performances at the time easily recognized her talent and ability. Having accumulated many hits within the Latin market, it was clear to the Estefans that their next step should be a transition into the American market, a risky strategy that had been successfully accomplished by only a few Latino performers. In 1984, the band released the English tune "Dr. Beat," a song recorded in English, on the backside of one of their albums in Spanish. Unexpectedly, the song became one of the top-ten hits on the U.S. dance charts, boosting their belief that they could be successful in the English-speaking American market.

The success of "Dr. Beat" prompted CBS records to transfer the band to Epic Records, their international rock-music division. With Epic, they released the album *Eyes of Innocence* in 1984. The album sold well but it was the following album, *Primitive Love* (1985), that brought her to the top of the charts. "Conga," one of the singles on that album, broke all records by hitting Billboard's pop, black, dance, and Latin charts at the same time, demonstrating Estefan's crossover potential. This song, rich in percussion and suitable for dance, became a favorite of discotheques and concert-goers alike. Along with the songs "Bad Boy" and "Words Get in the Way," which also became hits, the Miami Sound Machine secured two American Music Awards in 1986.

Estefan's superb stage presence, along with her vocal prowess, made it clear to the public and to entertainment figures alike that she was the primary source of talent behind the Miami Sound Machine, renamed Gloria Estefan and the Miami Sound Machine in 1987. Band members became unhappy with the fact that she was receiving all of the attention and credit, prompting her decision to leave the band and become a solo performer. In 1989 she released *Cuts Both Ways*, her first solo album containing hits such as "Don't Wanna Lose You" and "Here We Are."

In 1990, while en route to a concert, her touring bus was involved in a serious accident. She suffered a spinal injury that required emergency surgery and a lengthy recovery time. After countless hours of therapy, Estefan recovered and has made a successful comeback.

During the 1990s, Estefan reached the pinnacle of her career and released several more successful albums. Her *Greatest Hits* album went platinum in 1992. To mark her return to health, she performed in a world tour of 29 countries. She has received two Grammys, an honorary doctorate in music from her alma mater, the University of Miami, and a star on the Hollywood Walk of Fame. She received her first Grammy Award for her album *Mi Tierra* (My Land) in 1994. In 2000 she was awarded the International Women's Forum "Hall of Fame" Award and a Latin Grammy for her video "No me dejes de querer" (Don't Stop Loving Me).

Her performance of the song "Reach," official anthem of the 1996 Olympic Games in Atlanta, was viewed by billions of people worldwide. In 1999 she made her movie debut in the film *Music of the Heart* with Meryl Streep.

Estefan resides in Miami and is a spokesperson there for the Cuban American community. In recent years she has become increasingly involved with political groups in Miami that protest Castro's continued presence in Cuba.—S.M.M.

References and Suggested Readings

"Ahora creo en la reencarnación." *Hola* (Spain), August 23, 2000, 7.

"La Gloria de una Cuba libre." *Semana* (Spain), August 25, 2000, 25.

Little Joe, José María. "Gloria Estefan afina el violin." *People en español* (May 1999): 20.

Meir, Matt S. "Gloria Estefan." *Notable Latino Americans.* Westport, CT: Greenwood Press, 1997. 128–132

Telgen, Diane, and Jim Kamp. "Gloria Estefan." *Notable Hispanic American Women.* Detroit: Gale, 1993. 148–151.

PATRICK EWING
(1962–)

Jamaican Basketball Player

Patrick Ewing, a native of Jamaica, has been heralded as one of the 50 greatest players of the National Basketball Association (NBA). Ewing's strength and athletic skill made him one of the most dominant players in the history of the sport, where he was named NBA All-Star 11 times, including 10 consecutive seasons from 1988 to 1997. He was named Rookie of the Year in 1985, when he began his career with the New York Knickerbockers. He was president of the National Basketball Players Association from 1997 to 2001. In addition to his numerous athletic awards, Ewing was twice an Olympic gold medallist, leading the 1984 and 1992 U.S. Basketball Olympic teams. He also holds various basketball records as a former member of the Georgetown University Hoyas basketball team. Ewing has also co-authored a book on children's art, *In the Paint*, published in 1999.

Patrick Aloysius Ewing was born in Kingston, Jamaica, on August 5, 1962, the fifth of seven children. His parents Dorothy and Carl lived in one of the poorest sections of Jamaica's capital. However, his parents wanted to make sure their children received an education. With the help of family members who already lived in the United States, Dorothy Ewing left for the United States in 1971 and quickly found a job in the cafeteria of Massachusetts General Hospital in Boston's West End. During the next few years the family joined her in the United States. Six-foot-tall Patrick, who was already a very skilled soccer player, arrived in January of 1975.

Ewing discovered basketball at the age of 12, watching kids play in Hoyt Park and other schoolyards around his Cambridge home. Impressed by his size, they invited him to join their game, and by the time he was in the seventh grade, he had made his first "slam dunk." The following year he was 6'6" tall and ready to embark on the sport that would change his life.

When he began his studies at Rindge and Latin High School, he became the starting center of the school's basketball team, where he distinguished himself. The following year, recognized as High School Player of the Year at Cambridge Rindge and Latin, and considered one of the best high school players in the United States, coaches from all over the country tried to recruit him during the finals for the state title, where his team was playing Boston Latin High School. Among the coaches present was John Thompson, the coach of the Georgetown University Hoyas. Ewing graduated from high school in 1981 and left for Georgetown University in Washington, D.C., to begin his university studies in fine arts with a basketball scholarship.

Until Ewing arrived at the Georgetown campus, the Hoyas were not an outstanding team. When Ewing joined the team as center forward they were ranked among the top teams in the country. His aggressive style on the court and his refusal to concede interviews to journalists meant that he got "bad press." Over the years, Ewing has been consistently wary of the press and is notorious for guarding his privacy. Sports journalists from all over the nation were present during his first season at Georgetown University, when he led the Hoyas to the finals of the National Collegiate Athletics Association (NCAA) Tournament. Even though his team lost the tournament, his leadership and skill in the game began to make a difference to his team. During his years as a Hoya, Ewing and his team appeared in 3 consecutive NCAA Championship games. In 1984 the Hoyas won the NCAA title and Ewing was named the tournament's Most Valuable Player, Big East Player of the Year, and for the second straight season was named as an All-American. At this point million-dollar offers were pouring in, enticing Ewing to end his university studies and join the NBA. However, in honor of his mother Dorothy, who had died of a heart attack that year and to whom he had promised to complete his education, Ewing remained at Georgetown.

A few months after the 1984 NCAA Championship, Ewing successfully tried out for the U.S. Olympic basketball team, and was a starting player in five of the six games played in Los Angeles, where the team won the gold medal. On his return for his last year at Georgetown, Ewing led the Hoyas to another NCAA Championship game, which they eventually lost to Villanova. However, even after the season was over Ewing, whose physique and skills had earned him the nickname "The Warrior," won the prestigious Naismith Award for the best in college basketball, as well as the Eastman Kodak Award. He was also awarded the Adolph Rupp Trophy, which recognizes College Basketball's Player of the Year as selected by the Associated Press. By the time he left Georgetown, Ewing had become a well-known figure in college basketball, becoming the all-time leading shot blocker and rebounder and second highest scorer in Hoyas basketball history.

Later that year Ewing made history when the NBA developed a new way to select players—the seven teams with the worst records would take part in a lottery where the team whose name was drawn would get first pick. On national television, the New York Knicks made Ewing their number-one choice, giving him the distinction of being the first lottery pick ever in NBA history. In addition, he signed one of the highest paying contracts—$31 million over a ten-year period—which made him the highest paid rookie in NBA history. Ewing made his professional basketball debut before a sellout crowd in Madison Square Garden on October 26, 1985, and during the season averaged 36.4 minutes and 19.2 points. He was named to the All-Star game, an honor not usually bestowed on a rookie. Even though Ewing had undergone arthroscopic surgery for an injured knee that year, he played in 50 of 82 Knick games and was named Rookie of the Year.

Ewing spent 15 years with the New York Knicks and accumulated a significant number of records in the sport. Overall, he is the all-time Knick leader in number of games played (1,039), points scored (3,665), minutes played (37,586), field goals made (9,260), and free throws attempted (6,904). He also holds the lead in rebounds (10,759), steals (1,061), and blocks (2,758). More than any other Knick player, Ewing scored 40 or more points in 30 games. In 1997 he was elected president of the NBA Players Association after having served as vice president on the union's executive committee for the previous three years. As president he is remembered for his efforts to maintain a united front during grueling negotiations that resulted in a two month "lock out" of the players and the successful rejection by the players of an effort to decertify the union. In 1996 he was inducted into Madison Square Garden's Walk of Fame. Considered the best shooting center in NBA history, Ewing's 2000 trade to the Seattle SuperSonics and his departure from New York was bittersweet. He left the team without having achieved his lifelong dream of winning a professional basketball championship.

In 2000, his only season with Seattle, Ewing averaged 26 minutes and his scoring and rebounding was at an all-time career low. Considered the best player ever in New York basketball, when his new team played the New York Knicks on February 28, 2001, the fans gave him an unprecedented three-minute standing ovation. By the end of that season his contract was not renewed and he went to play for the Orlando Magic in Florida, where he played a backup role with limited playing time.

This extraordinary career has also included many injuries and surgeries. Past his prime at 39 years of age, and recently described as "a future Hall of Famer who cannot play the way he used to" (Wise 2001, 6), Ewing played for two more seasons, hoping to win a championship before he retired. However, he stepped down at the end of the 2002 season without achieving his dream of a championship ring. Later that year he joined the Washington Wizards as an assistant coach; it is believed he will someday become head coach of an NBA team.—G.C.

References and Suggested Readings

Allen, Woody. "There's at Least One Fan Down Front Who Will Miss the Big Fella." *The New York Times,* October 8, 2000, Sec. 8, p. 13.

Jacobs, Jeff. "Expectations Unfulfilled." *The Hartford Courant,* September 18, 2002, C1–C2.

Kavanagh, Jack. *Sports Great Patrick Ewing.* Hillside, NJ: Enslow Publishers, 1992.

Newman, Matthew. *Patrick Ewing.* Mankato, MN: Crestwood House, 1986.

Reilly, Rick. "The Unknown Player." *Sports Illustrated* 80.2 (January 17, 1994): 52.

Thompson, John. "I Believe." *Sports Illustrated CNN.* November 2, 2000. *http://sportsillustrated.cnn.com/turnersports/nba/news/2000/11/01/ewing_q_a/index.html.*

Wise, Mike. "Still the Big Fella, No Longer the Man." *The New York Times,* November 7, 2001, Sec. S, p. 6.

Young, Jeff C. *Top 10 Basketball Shot-Blockers.* Springfield, NJ: Enslow Publishers, 2000.

FRANTZ FANON
(1925–1961)

Martinican Political Philosopher and Psychiatrist

The theories of Frantz Fanon, a political philosopher from Martinique, have become classics in the field of colonial studies and race relations. Although highly controversial, his explanations of the role of colonial and political oppression in the development of the individual and the social psyche are key texts in understanding many of the ideological processes that have historically defined colonial oppression in the Third World.

Fanon was born in the city of Fort-de-France in Martinique to an upper-middle-class family on July 20, 1925. He was one of eight children of Casimir Fanon, a customs official, and Eléonore Médélice, a French-born immigrant who operated a small clothing boutique out of her home. He attended the Lycée Schoelcher in Fort-de-France, where he became a student of the legendary Martinican writer **Aimé Césaire**, then a literature teacher. Césaire was a strong influence on both Fanon's political thinking and his eventual writings.

In 1943, while Fanon was in high school, he came in contact with the Caribbean Free French Movement, which was working to liberate Martinique from the Vichy Army that had invaded the island. Tired of abuse at the hands of the invading army, Fanon joined the movement and went on to Dominique to receive military training. After the eventual liberation of Martinique, Fanon volunteered to go to Europe, and served with the Free French Forces in North Africa and France. He was wounded during the war and received the Croix de Guerre.

After the war ended, he returned to the Lycée in Martinique, where he graduated in 1946. That same year, he and his brother Joby worked on the election campaign of Aimé Césaire, who was running as the Communist Party candidate for the French Parliament. In 1947 his father died and Fanon obtained a scholarship to study in France. He decided to study dentistry and went to Paris with three of his friends. Just a month after enrolling in dental school he left his studies, discouraged by the mediocrity of his classmates. He transferred to the University of Lyon, where he underwent a year of pre-medical courses and pursued his medical studies, but also became involved with several left-wing student organizations that were active at the university. At the same time, he also developed an interest in psychology and social psychiatry.

In 1952 Fanon graduated from the Faculty of Medicine and Pharmacy and presented an impressive thesis on social psychiatry. He returned briefly to Martinique, where he established a small medical practice in the town of Vauclin. His early work in Martinique reaffirmed his beliefs that most medical illnesses have a social basis. In his view physical illnesses in his small island were often caused by malnutrition, which in turn was triggered by poverty and by the French colonial oppression of the people of Martinique. Frustrated and angry with Martinique's social and political climate, Fanon returned to France during the summer of 1952. When he arrived in France, he married Marie Josephe Dublé, a journalist from Lyon. Together they had a son named Olivier.

In Lyon he enrolled in a medical residency program at the Hospital of Saint Alban under the supervision of François Tosquelles. Tosquelles, his teacher and mentor, was a prominent physician who specialized in the field of social psychiatry and believed in the concept of communal psychiatry. At the time, most psychiatric patients were isolated within the hospital and were treated as terminal cases with no hope for recovery. Tosquelles believed that the integration of the patients into a community-like structure led to the normalization and improvement of their mental illnesses.

Fanon also published his first book, *Black Skins White Masks*, in 1952. The ideas set forth in the book were heavily influenced by the existentialist philosophy of Fanon's friend Jean-Paul Sartre and the ideas of Marx and Freud. The importance of this book lies in the novel nature of the arguments and theses developed by Fanon who claimed that the process of colonization has a substantial emotional, psychological, and psychosocial impact on the indigenous population. As the metaphorical title of the book suggests, Fanon states that people who are subjected to colonial and imperial nations are forced to take on a "false" white identity and disregard their own black ones. There are two ways in which this process occurs. First, the people are provided with a series of dominant—and false—ideologies that force them to identify with the history, mores, and traditions of the empire, while at the same time they are taught to devalue and disregard their own customs and values because these are seen as worthless or inferior. Second, Fanon noted that the ruling classes and their power elites require native inhabitants to give up their language. In the process, he hypothesized, they give up their very selves. The sum of these two processes leads to the development of a series of mental illnesses and pathologies that affect the way in which black people function in those colonial societies, creating fear, insecurity, instability, and psychosocial chaos. The nature of these arguments had powerful political and sociological implications for the many Caribbean societies that were subjected to French and British colonial forces. The roots of Fanon's observation came not only from his training as a physician but from his own experience under French rule in Martinique, where he was forced to speak French and disregard his native Creole and where the schools stressed French standards over island values.

After finishing his psychiatric training and passing the rigorous medical examinations required by the French government, Fanon became a licensed psychiatrist. He eventually accepted a position at a psychiatric hospital in Blida, Algeria, where he moved with his family. His stay in Algeria is significant because it marked the serious development of his political thought and the beginning of his practical work in politics. During the three years he stayed at the hospital (1953–1956), he undertook major changes in the management of psychiatric patients. He structured the units following the concepts that he had learned from Tosquelles but stressed the importance of imparting a sense of egalitarianism to medical treatment. He mixed the native patients with patients of French origin and stressed the importance of giving the same quality of treatment to all regardless of race, religion, or economic status. He also broke down some of the boundaries that existed between the doctors and nurses because he perceived that hierarchical orders hindered the quality of care. He opened the halls and allowed patients with good behavior to move freely throughout the hospital. Fanon preferred the use of medical sedation and tried to abolish the much-used straightjackets and chains.

There is considerable debate over the reasons behind Fanon's entrance into the revolutionary politics of Algeria. Many of his friends say that he went to Africa to become a revolutionary. Others claim that he became enamored with the revolutionary movement that broke out in Algeria during his time there in 1954 . The important point is that eventually Fanon became a member of Algeria Front de Libération Nationale and resigned his position at the hospital in 1956 to join them. As a result, the government of Algeria expelled him and he settled in Tunisia, where he found another job in a psychiatric hospital in Monouba. From Tunisia, Fanon worked restlessly on behalf of the Algerian revolutionaries. He helped them to structure a support route through the southern part of the country, participated in many international conferences where he used his political ideas to defend the Algerian cause, and was an ambassador of the Algerian Front to Ghana.

In 1960, Fanon was diagnosed with leukemia. He went to the Soviet Union and received treatments with the drug Myleran, which forced the disease into remission and allowed him to finish writing his book *The Wretched of the Earth*. In this book, he saw armed revolution and violence by poor people as the only effective way to end class oppression and class discrimination. He became ill again in 1961 and went to Washington, D.C., where he was eventually admitted to the National Institutes of Health (NIH) in Bethesda, Maryland. He was given experimental treatments at the NIH but died on December 6, 1961, shortly after his arrival. His work in the field of colonial political philosophy is still regarded as one of the most influential to emerge from the Caribbean during the twentieth century. He influenced scores of other Caribbean intellectuals such as **Stuart Hall** and **George Lamming** with his provocative ideas.—S.M.M.

References and Suggested Readings

Ehlen, Patrick. *Frantz Fanon: A Spiritual Biography.* New York: The Crossroad Publishing Company, 2000.

Fanon, Frantz. *The Wretched of the Earth.* Constance Farrington, trans. New York: Grove Press, 1963.

Geismar, Peter. *Fanon: The Revolutionary as a Prophet.* New York: Grove Press, 1971.

Prinbam, B. Marie. *Holy Violence: The Revolutionary Thought of Frantz Fanon.* Boulder, CO: A Three Continents Book, 1982.

GIGI FERNÁNDEZ
(1964–)

Puerto Rican Professional Tennis Player

Puerto Rican native Gigi Fernández is considered the island's first professional woman athlete and one of the greatest tennis doubles players of all-time. In a 15-year professional tennis career, Fernández accumulated 69 doubles titles including 17 Grand Slams, 5 U.S. Opens, and 4 Wimbledons. In 1992 she became the first Puerto Rican ever to win an Olympic gold medal, a feat repeated in the 1996 Olympics—on both occasions paired with Dominican native **Mary Joe Fernández**. Celebrated for her versatile serve and volley game, she was also known to demonstrate finesse and artistry at the net. After retiring in 1997, and in celebration

Gigi Fernández.

of her distinguished career in tennis, she was voted Puerto Rico's Athlete of the Century.

Beatríz Fernández was born on February 22, 1964, in San Juan, Puerto Rico. She is the eldest daughter of physician Tuto Fernández and his wife Beatríz. She grew up with four younger siblings in a well-to-do family, with boundless access to her parents' attention and affluence. She attended the best private schools in San Juan. Her parents, who were recreational tennis players, gave her a racquet and tennis lessons for her eighth birthday. Four years later, she won the women's open doubles title in Puerto Rico and was well on her way to leaving her mark on the sport. On the island, her journey to success included wide media coverage of her extravagances—her speedy black sports car and shopping sprees abroad—as well as her tournaments. By the time she was 17, she had been offered many scholarships to study in the United States and settled for Clemson University in South Carolina. By the end of her freshman year, she made the National Collegiate Athletic Association (NCAA) finals and in 1983 left her studies to pursue a professional career in tennis. The following year she was selected as a member of the Puerto Rican Olympic team.

During the mid-1980s, she became undisciplined and was prone to outbursts on the courts resulting in the loss of many matches and payment of fines. Although her family and her talent were instrumental at the beginning of her career, Fernández acknowledges that there were others who have influenced and mentored her career. Among them is tennis star Martina Navratilova, whom she credits with guiding her career with positive advice and, later, an opportunity to play doubles.

In 1988 her career began to look up when she teamed with fellow tennis player Robin White; together they took the U.S. Open Doubles Championship. In Puerto Rico she was named Puerto Rican Female Athlete of the Year. Two years later, she teamed with Navratilova and repeated the U.S. doubles victory. By 1991 she was ranked number one in the world in doubles. She and Mary Joe Fernández (no relation) captured the gold medal in women's doubles during the 1992 Olympics, beating Spanish favorites Conchita Martínez and Arantxa Sánchez. In 1994, the U.S. Tennis Association and the U.S. Olympic Committee named her Female Athlete of the Year after her 1993 performances at the Australian Open, French Open, and Wimbledon.

In 1992 she began to play with Natasha Zvereva, her third and final doubles partner, with whom she won the most championships. In two years (1992–93) they won six grand slams, the second longest streak in the history of the sport. By the time Fernández retired in 1997, she had won at least one doubles grand slam title every year since 1988 (except 1989). In 1995 she won her fifth consecutive Roland Garros doubles title, the U.S. Open doubles title, and was a finalist in the Australian Open and Wimbledon doubles and mixed doubles as well as the U.S. Open mixed doubles.

Her success, however, has not been without controversy. She played on the U.S. Federation Cup team eight times (1988, 1990–1992, 1994–1996) and won a second gold medal in the 1996 Olympics as a member of the U.S. team. Her decision to play for the United States as part of the Federation Cup team and her decision to play for the U.S. Olympic team were very controversial in Puerto Rico. Fernández herself characterized these choices as among the most difficult in her professional life.

Fernández's success and earnings led her to establishing the Gigi Fernández Charitable Foundation in 1992, which hosts the annual Gigi Fernández Invitational Cup and raises money for various Puerto Rican charities.

In addition to continuing to play tennis at the master's level in senior doubles, she has also recently turned to playing golf and occasionally plays in celebrity tours and for charitable causes, following her long-held belief in using her talents to help those who are less privileged.

Fernández has moved on from professional player to professional instructor of the game. Since 1999, Fernández has coached the Puerto Rican national tennis team, and in July 2002 she was appointed head coach of women's tennis at the University of South Florida. She has also established Gigi Fernández Tennis Camps, which run every summer for boys and girls between the ages of 6 and 18, as her way of mentoring new talent and "giving back my knowledge of the game and helping others" (Gigi Fernández February 2003).—G.C.

References and Suggested Readings

Fernández, Ronald, Serafín Méndez-Méndez, and Gail Cueto. "Gigi Fernández." *Puerto Rico Past and Present: An Encyclopedia.* Westport, CT: Greenwood Press, 1998. 127.
Gigi Fernandez Tennis Camp Homepage: *www.gigifernandez.com.*
Jenkins, Sally. "Terrible Two." *Sports Illustrated,* February 20, 1995, 156–159.
Meier, Matt S. "Gigi Fernández." *Notable Latino Americans: A Biographical Dictionary.* Westport CT: Greenwood Press, 1997. 139–142.
Telgen, Diane, and Jim Kamp, eds. "Gigi Fernández." *Notable Hispanic Women.* Detroit: Gale, 1993. 155–156.

MARY JOE FERNÁNDEZ
(1971–)

Dominican American Professional Tennis Player

Dominican-American Mary Joe Fernández won her first tennis match at the age of ten and has since accumulated seven singles and eighteen doubles titles,

Mary Joe Fernandez. AP Photo/Roberto Borea.

including two Grand Slams, in that category. She has won more Olympic medals than any other tennis player in the world. Fernández captured the gold medal in doubles and the bronze in singles in the 1992 Barcelona Olympics and the 1996 Atlanta Olympics with doubles partner **Gigi Fernández** (no relation).

Her father, José Fernández, a Spaniard, and her Cuban mother, Sylvia Fernández, settled in the Dominican Republic after marrying. The younger of two sisters, María José, who would later use the professional name of Mary Joe, was born on August 19, 1971. While still an infant, her parents moved to Florida, where she first discovered tennis. José, a recreational tennis player, would often take both his daughters to the tennis court. While he played tennis with the older sibling Sylvia, three-year-old Mary Joe would stay out of trouble by hitting tennis balls against the wall with her own tennis racquet. By the age of five, her father had enrolled her for tennis lessons with a local pro. The following year she started playing in tournaments, winning her first when she was ten years old. By the time she was a teenager she was a promising tennis player and her future seemed pretty clear-cut. Despite the advice of numerous tennis professionals and coaches, she decided she would not turn professional until she completed her high school. In 1984, at the age of 13, she was invited to play in a field that included tennis great Martina Navratilova. She stepped into center court and beat her opponent, Pam Teeguarden, in two sets, becoming the youngest player to appear in a professional tournament.

As an adolescent she juggled academics and tennis, managing to maintain excellent grades while earning a Top 10 Women's Tennis Association (WTA) ranking. In 1985, at age 14, Fernández became the youngest player to win a match at the U.S. Open when she defeated Sara Gomer 6–1, 6–4 in the first round, thus establishing herself as a professional while still a student. In 1989 she graduated from Carrolton High School of the Sacred Heart in Coconut Grove, Florida, with an A average.

Immediately after high school graduation—which she missed because she was making the semifinals of the French Open—she began her professional tennis career. In January 1990, her first full year as a professional, she reached her first Grand Slam final at the Australian Open; she won her first professional titles at the Tokyo Indoor Tournament and at the Porsche Tennis Grand Prix at Filderstadt, Germany; and she reached the semifinals of the U.S. Open—all of which added up to her being ranked fourth in the world of women's tennis that year. Her successes on the court were won despite the numerous injuries that sidelined her most of the year. The pace of professional tennis touring, poor nutrition, and the lack of a conditioning and fitness program were to blame for her injuries. After making the necessary adjustments she began to improve and was able to consistently defeat many of the top ten players in women's tennis. She began to vary her trademark baseline game and practiced and improved her game by successfully rushing the net more frequently.

In 1991 she won the Lipton Doubles Championship with partner Zina Garrison and in 1992 reached the finals in the Australian Open. In both 1990 and 1992 she came close to winning the Australian Open Singles title, only losing in the final rounds. Among the important highlights of her career were the medals she won at the 1992 Olympic Games in Barcelona. With partner Gigi Fernández she was able to capture the gold medal, and won the bronze for herself in singles. In addition to winning titles, she was also making over a million dollars a year in prize money and endorsements.

In 1993, when she believed she was playing the best tennis of her life and was fast closing in on the dream of winning a Grand Slam Championship, she reached but lost the French Open finals and was sidelined for medical reasons. Her recovery was slow and affected her ability to win a significant number of matches or titles. Even though her tennis was yet not on par with her past achievements, in 1996 she partnered again with Gigi Fernández, and together they won their second gold medal in tennis women's doubles at the Atlanta Olympic Games.

Since then, she has continued to be plagued with injuries, but made it to the semifinals of the 1997 Australian Open and the quarterfinals of the French Open. She also reached the winner's circle at the German Open, her first tour title in two years. She retired from tennis in 2000 and occasionally appears as an announcer at a few professional women's tournaments.—G.C.

References and Suggested Readings

Cole, Meie. *Mary Joe Fernández*. Elkton, MD: Mitchell Lane Publishers, 1998.

Danziger, Lucy. "Tennis Someone—America's Mary Joe Fernández." *Interview* 30 (June 1994): 86–87.

Goldaper, Sam. "13-Year-Old Plays Tennis Like a Pro." *The New York Times*, September 21, 1984, 21.

Martínez, Al. "Mary Joe Fernández." In *Rising Voices: Profiles in Leadership*. Glendale, CA: Nestle USA, 1993. 30–31.

"Mary Joe Fernández." *Latino Americans*. New York: Macmillan Library Reference, 1999. 125–127.

Meir, Matt S. "Mary Joe Fernández." *Notable Latino Americans*. Westport, CT: Greenwood Press, 1997. 142–145.

Telgen, Diane, and Jim Kamp, eds. "Mary Joe Fernández." *Notable Hispanic American Women*. Detroit: Gale, 1993. 157–158.

THE FERRÉ FAMILY

Puerto Rican Cultural and Political Leaders

The Ferré family of Puerto Rico has been at the center of the island's public life for most of the twentieth century and continues its prominence to the present day. Several of its members have had an extraordinary commitment to the well being of Puerto Rico and have served the island and its people through their careers in industry, public service, politics, philanthropy and humanitarianism, journalism, the arts, and literature. Although wealthy and socially privileged, they have put themselves in the limelight in order to serve their island and their fellow Puerto Ricans. The Ferré family is large; however, three of its members have been key players in the social, cultural, political, and economic life of the island: Luis A. Ferré, Sor Isolina Ferré, and Rosario Ferré.

LUIS A. FERRÉ
(1904–)

Industrialist, Politician, and Philanthropist

Luis A. Ferré, considered the patriarch of the Ferré family of Puerto Rico, was born to Don Antonio Ferré Bacallao and Mary Aguayo Casals on February 17, 1904, in Ponce, Puerto Rico, the second largest city on the island. His father was a prosperous industrialist who established the Puerto Rico Iron Works at the beginning of the century. Ferré studied in Ponce during his childhood. He traveled to Pennsylvania during his adolescence and received his high school education from Mercersburg Academy. After graduation, he moved to Boston where he obtained a bachelor's. In 1924 he received a master's degree in mechanical engineering from the Massachusetts Institute of Technology and studied piano simultaneously at Boston's New England Conservatory.

On his return to Puerto Rico in 1925 he worked in his father's iron works business and was instrumental in the design and development of the Puerto Rico Cement Company. This company eventually became the largest producer and distributor of cement in Puerto Rico and the Caribbean and played a key role in Puerto Rican housing developments during the 1960s.

A man with a profound admiration for the United States, Ferré has been involved in local politics for most of his adult life. His lifelong goal has been for

Puerto Rico to become the 51st state. As the voice of the Republican Party, he and his brother-in-law, Miguel Angel García Méndez, represented the pro-statehood agenda in Puerto Rico between the 1930s and 1950s. From 1937 to 1953 Ferré was a pro-statehood member of the House of Delegates. He was also one of the signing members of the Puerto Rico Constitutional Convention, which wrote the island's constitution after it became a commonwealth in 1952.

After years of dissatisfaction with both the Republican Party and the state of local politics, Ferré decided to organize the New Progressive Party in 1967. Campaigning under the slogan of "Esto tiene que cambiar" (This has to change), he was elected governor in November 1968. To this day, the party advocates statehood for Puerto Rico and assumes a pro-business and pro–private sector approach in the design of its public policies. During his tenure as governor, he undertook a series of major governmental reforms and tried to improve the overall economic and administrative infrastructure of the island. For instance, he increased the salaries of government employees, gave them Christmas bonuses, and undertook major improvements in the construction of roads, schools, and government facilities. Despite his progressive approach to government, he was defeated in the general elections of 1972 by Rafael Hernández Colón.

Although he lost the governorship, Ferré has remained active in Puerto Rican political affairs and has served his New Progressive Party dutifully. He was president of the senate from 1977 to 1981 and has been actively involved in the U.S. Republican Party—for instance, he was the head of the Puerto Rico delegation to the National Republican Party Convention in the year 2000.

Ferré's detractors believe that he has been willing to shortchange Puerto Rican values, customs, and culture in order to annex the island to the United States. Some have also accused him of using his political positions to increase his wealth and further the economic well being of the Ferré family businesses.

A lover of the arts, he is an accomplished pianist and has given professional concerts in Puerto Rico and the United States. In addition to politics and the arts, Ferré has always been involved in a series of humanitarian and philanthropic endeavors. In 1959 he used his family's money to establish a foundation that created the Ponce Museum of Art, which has a modern facility that holds more than 2,000 works of art from Puerto Rico and the rest of the world. Thanks to Ferré's generosity, the museum has become one of the premier art facilities in the Caribbean.

Despite his advanced age, Don Luis, as he is fondly known in Puerto Rico, is still an active figure in Puerto Rican politics and culture. He is considered a moral force and an elder statesman in the political affairs of the island. He has been awarded numerous distinctions, honorary degrees, and awards. On November 18, 1991, former president George H. W. Bush honored him with the Presidential Medal of Freedom.

SOR ISOLINA FERRÉ
(1914–2000)

Catholic Nun and Humanitarian

There is no doubt that of all the members of the Ferré family, Sor Isolina is the one that holds the dearest place in the hearts of the thousands of Puerto Ricans she has helped.

Isolina Ferré was born on September 5, 1914 in Ponce, the youngest child of Antonio Ferré and Mary Aguayo Casals. Although she lost her mother when she was still young, Ferré was profoundly influenced by her mother's lifetime of charity work; for example, her mother insisted that Ferré donate one of her best Christmas gifts to needy children who were without toys. After her mother died, she was raised by her father, her elder brothers and a sister, and the household staff. In her memoirs she tells the story of how the family driver, Pellín, used to take her to Ponce's poorest neighborhoods. where she had first-hand contact with the social malaise and ailments that affected the poor (Ferré 1991).

Ferré received the call to the Catholic apostolate when she was still an adolescent. The family was adamantly opposed to her becoming a nun. She recalled that her brother **Luis** tried to persuade her to become a social worker and help the poorer employees of the Puerto Rico Iron Works. Convinced that her call was genuine, she rejected her family's advice and remained determined to join a religious order. At the age of 21 she entered the order of the Missionary Servants of the Holy Trinity in Philadelphia, where she went through the novitiate and was ordained as a nun in 1937.

During her first years as a nun she worked with a wide array of needy groups in the United States. She helped coal miners in West Virginia, conducted a census of Catholic families in Brooklyn, and assisted Portuguese immigrants in Cape Cod. Starting in 1946, her order relocated her to the town of Cabo Rojo, Puerto Rico, a coastal city in the southwest west corner of the island, where she was asked to help the poor. Ten years later, and somewhat burned out by the complexity of her work, she was once again transferred to New York, where she had the opportunity to attend Saint Joseph College and eventually finished a master's degree in sociology at Fordham University.

Her college education, in addition to the solid experience that she had acquired working with the poor, placed Ferré in a key position to work with the growing problems facing Latinos in New York during the 1960s. She served as a director of the Dr. White Stellman Center, an institution that aided Puerto Rican and Latino immigrants as well as other disenfranchised minorities, and became a member of the War on Poverty Committee, which dealt with the many issues and struggles raised during the civil rights movement. She also worked with gangs in New York.

In 1968, after more than three decades of arduous work with the poor, her order sent her back to Puerto Rico to work with the needy in her native Ponce. She later said that she always believed her order assumed that she was going to be in semi-retirement. After arriving in the area of La Playa de Ponce, a poor neighborhood along the coastline of the Ponce beach, Ferré was shocked at the social and economic conditions faced by the neighborhood's inhabitants. The area was an over-populated slum full of people who lacked basic skills to work in the area's many flourishing industries.

Using the knowledge she had acquired during her studies and her years of experience performing missionary work, Ferré launched what was to become her most challenging assignment. She implemented a community development project where she trained residents of this community in a wide array of trades. With the assistance of her brother Luis and several area businesses she built a series of technical and vocational shops that offered the residents skills that they lacked. In a few years, her facility, known as Centros Sor Isolina Ferré, became the most successful economic development project on the island and one of the most emulated models of community development in the Caribbean and Latin America. The center not only provided the residents with vocational education and career opportunities, but also offered them basic social assistance and health care. The project was replicated successfully in another poor metropolitan community in the Caimitos sector of Río Piedras. Ferré's work was recognized with multiple awards. Like her brother Luis, she received the Presidential Medal of Freedom on August 11, 1999. There is no doubt that she felt her biggest honor was to serve poor and needy people.

When Ferré died, on August 3, 2000, thousands of Puerto Ricans of all creeds mourned the departure of the woman that they called "El Angel de la Playa" (The Angel of the Beach). Her work touched the lives of thousands of Puerto Ricans and she served as a role model for generations of people to come.

Rosario Ferré
(1938–)
Writer, Literary Critic, and Educator

Rosario Ferré was born in Ponce, Puerto Rico, in 1938, the daughter of **Luis A. Ferré** and the late Lorencita Ramírez de Arellano. She belongs to the second generation of the prestigious Ferré family. She was educated in elite private schools in Puerto Rico and is a graduate of Wellesley College in Massachusetts. Shortly after finishing college, she married the son of a wealthy Puerto Rican businessman and appeared to be destined for a traditional family life. This was not to be the case.

After the death of her mother she received a considerable inheritance, which she feels gave her the necessary independence to seek a life and a career of her own. She decided to return to college and pursued a career in writing. During the early 1970s she began to publish her literary work and in 1972 became the editor of the literary magazine *Zona de Carga y Descarge* (Loading and Downloading Zone), one of the most important literary venues for new writers in Puerto Rico. Her writing was quickly praised in Puerto Rican literary circles, and she became skillful in the short story genre. Some of her most important works of the time are *Papeles de Pandora* (Pandora's Papers; 1976), *La muñeca menor* (The Youngest Doll; 1976), *Fábulas de la garza desangrada* (Fables of the Bleeding Heron; 1982), and *Los cuentos de Juan Bobo* (Juan Bobo's Tales; 1981). She has recently published three major novels in English: *The House on the Lagoon* (1995), and *Eccentric Neighborhoods* (1998), and *Flight of the Swan* (2001). These novels have been widely acclaimed in American literary circles.

The work of this accomplished writer relies on the use of parody as a literary technique to bring attention to the "isms" and social, political, and economic inequities that affect Puerto Rican society (Lara-Velázquez 1996). Her writing is strongly influenced by the theoretical and philosophical underpinnings of the American feminist movement. She creates poignant constructions of the evils of capitalism, racism, classism, and sexism in Puerto Rican society.

For many years, Rosario was generally perceived to be the intellectual dissident of the Ferré family. She disagreed openly with her father's conservative views and suggested that independence is the best status for the island. She used her privileged status as a member of one of Puerto Rico's wealthiest families to put down the values and way of life of the power elite. In recent years, however, she has started to move away from her radical political stances and has started to assume a more mainstream ideology. She favored statehood in the 1998 plebiscite to decide the political status of Puerto Rico. She wrote a highly controversial opinion piece in *The New York Times,* where she said: "As a Puerto Rican writer, I constantly face the problem of identity. When I travel to the United States I feel as Latina as Chita Rivera. But in Latin America, I feel more American than John Wayne" (Ferré 1998, A21). This change of heart and her recent ideological closeness with her father have brought her criticism from the intellectual left, who feel betrayed by the perceived change in her beliefs.

Rosario Ferré holds a doctorate in literature from the University of Maryland. She is a professor of literature at the University of Puerto Rico in Río Piedras and a frequent speaker in literary circles. She has started to work closely with her father in his many charitable and philanthropic endeavors.—S.M.M.

References and Suggested Readings

Baralt, Guillermo. *Desde el Mirador de Próspero: La Vida de Luis A. Ferré: 1904–1968.* San Juan, PR: Fundación El Nuevo Día, 1996.

———. *La razón del equilibrio: Vida de Don Luis A. Ferré, 1968–1998.* San Juan, PR: Fundación El Nuevo Día, 2000.

Ferré, Rosario. "Puerto Rico, U.S.A." *The New York Times*, March 19, 1998, A21.

Ferré, Sor Isolina. *Isolina*. Río Piedras, PR: Editorial Cultural, 1991.

Lara-Velázquez, Socorro. "La parodia como poder subversivo." Dissertation, University of New Mexico. Ann Arbor, MI: University Microfilms International, 1996.

JOSÉ FERRER
(1912–1992)

Puerto Rican American Actor, Director, and Producer

Those who have traveled to Puerto Rico are generally impressed by the island's beautiful landscape as seen from any airliner flying over El Morro, turning left toward El Condado and San Juan, on their final approach to the Isla Verde's **Luis Muñoz Marín** airport. It is not uncommon for Puerto Ricans who fly to the island to get tears in their eyes when the plane descends over San Juan. For those who took this trip during the mid-1970s, this very emotional experience was often underscored and exacerbated by the deep baritone voice of José Ferrer, then a spokesperson for one of the airlines traveling to Puerto Rico, coming over the loudspeakers and saying: "This is José Ferrer and I welcome you to my beautiful Puerto Rico." Even though he spent his professional career in the United States, his love for the island was unlimited. In an age when Puerto Ricans and Latinos in the United States were lacking major role models in the world of arts and entertainment, this accomplished actor, director, and producer was one of the most visible Puerto Ricans on Broadway and in Hollywood.

José Vicente Ferrer Otero y Cintrón was born on January 8, 1912, in Santurce, Puerto Rico. He belonged to a notable and affluent Puerto Rican family known for its involvement in the island's cultural and literary landscape. His father, Rafael Ferrer, was a well-known lawyer. His mother was Providencia Cintrón. Ferrer attended elementary school at the San Agustin College in Río Piedras. When he was a young boy, his family moved to New York in search of help for Ferrer, who had been born with a cleft palate (Meier 1997). On their arrival in New York, his father continued working as an attorney and Ferrer attended La Salle College, where he graduated from high school at the age of 14.

Although Ferrer gained immediate admission to Princeton University, he went first to Switzerland, where he attended a boarding school. In Switzerland, Ferrer received advanced musical training and excelled as a pianist. He used his musical talents throughout his career. On his return to the United States, Ferrer enrolled in Princeton, where he studied architecture and graduated in 1933. While at Princeton, he formed a band called José Ferrer and His Pied Pipers. Assisted by

José Ferrer. Courtesy of Photofest.

his fellow Princetonian Jimmy Stewart, the 14-member band was a hit on campus and toured Europe during the summer of 1930 with considerable success. He had multiple roles as the band's director, singer, piano player, saxophonist, and clarinetist. In addition to his musical interests, he participated in school theatrical productions at the Triangle Club. His first incursion into theater was as a director of the musical *Fol-de-Rol.*

After his graduation from Princeton in 1933, Ferrer tried his luck as a musical performer on a Long Island showboat, where he debuted in the melodrama *The Periwinkle.* However, he moved on to Columbia University, where he did graduate work in literature and romance languages. In 1935, after a year at Columbia, Ferrer decided to try acting again and joined a Broadway production company where Joshua Logan, a member of his former band, worked. He was given a job as a stagehand and worked sporadically in several walk-on parts. One of his fellow actors spotted the the actor's potential talent and persuaded the producers to give him a one-line role as a policeman in the production of *A Slight Case of Murder* (1935). The next year he landed a more important role as one of a trio of Virginia Military Institute cadets in the comedy *Brother Rat.* In 1936 he played the leading role in Phillip Barry's *Spring Dance* at the Empire Theater. He continued reading for several different parts and asking for more prominent and demanding acting opportunities.

Ferrer's first notable theatrical role was Iago in Shakespeare's *Othello* in 1943. The critically acclaimed play was groundbreaking in many ways: it was an adaptation done by Paul Robeson, an African-American, and the producers cast the first Puerto Rican in the lead role on Broadway. One of the most important roles of his lifetime was as Cyrano de Bergerac, which he played on Broadway in 1946. This performance won him a Tony in 1947.

In 1948, while still working in theater, Ferrer began a film career. His first movie was *Joan of Arc* (1948) alongside Ingrid Bergman. Although he was nominated for an Oscar, it was a mediocre film. His Broadway success *Cyrano de Bergerac* was adapted for film in 1950 and his role won him an Oscar as best actor the same year, making Ferrer the first Puerto Rican to win both a Tony and an Oscar. Fellow Puerto Rican **Rita Moreno** later replicated this achievement.

In the early 1950s he was caught up in the general hysteria of the McCarthy era but was not blacklisted thanks in part to a successful public relations campaign launched under the advice of former Supreme Court Justice Abe Fortas. His current wife, actress Uta Hagen, was blacklisted and had considerable problems finding acting jobs for the rest of her career.

During the 1950s, which were considered by many critics as the height of his career, Ferrer appeared in many films such as *Whirlpool* (1950), *Moulin Rouge* (1952), *The Caine Mutiny* (1954), *The Great Man* (1956), and *I Accuse!* (1958), the last two of which he also directed. The final important period of Ferrer's career in Hollywood was in the 1960s, when he appeared in *Lawrence of Arabia* (1962), *The Greatest Story Ever Told* (1965), and *Ship of Fools* (1965). He appeared in more than 40 movies from the 1970s to the 1990s and entertainment critics consider him one of the best character actors of the twentieth century.

A constant element in Ferrer's life was his love for his native Puerto Rico. In 1970, when he was playing in *Man of La Mancha* on Broadway, he took the production of the island so that his fellow Puerto Ricans would have the chance to see the musical. In a newspaper column published by Puerto Rican newspaper *El Nuevo Día*, notable Puerto Rican scholar José Ferrer Canales recalled how Ferrer identified with the Puerto Ricans who moved to New York during the first wave of migration from the island in the 1940s; Ferrer never hesitated to greet Puerto Rican servers at restaurants, telling them that he was also Puerto Rican. He always looked forward to the time when Puerto Rico and Puerto Ricans would stop being provincial and open themselves to the world to showcase their natural talents and abilities (Ferrer Canales 1992).

Ferrer received several awards during his career. The University of Puerto Rico awarded Ferrer his first honorary doctorate in 1949. As an act of goodwill and admiration toward his homeland, he donated his Oscar to the university. Former President Ronald Reagan presented Ferrer with the National Medal of Arts in 1985; he was the first actor to receive the prestigious honor. Ferrer was also awarded an honorary Master's of Fine Arts from Princeton, as well as an honorary doctorate from Bradley University in Illinois. Ferrer died in Coral Gables, Florida, on January 26, 1992, after a brief illness. His ashes were taken to his beloved Puerto Rico shortly after his death.—S.M.M.

References and Suggested Readings

Fernández, Ronald, Serafín Méndez-Méndez, and Gail Cueto. "José Ferrer." *Puerto Rico Past and Present: An Encyclopedia.* Westport, CT: Greenwood Press, 1998. 134–135.

Ferrer Canales, José. "Recordando a José Ferrer." *El Nuevo Día* (San Juan, PR), February 16, 1992, n.p.

"Ferrer y las acusasiones que casi le cuestan el Oscar." *El Nuevo Día* (San Juan, PR), January 31, 1992, n.p.

Marias, Julián. "Adios a José Ferrer." *El Nuevo Día* (San Juan, PR), March 15, 1992, n.p.

Meier, Matt S. "Jose Ferrer." *Notable Latino Americans.* Westport, CT: Greenwood Press, 1997. 148–151.

Thompson, David. "José Ferrer." *Biographical Dictionary of Film.* New York: Alfred A. Knopf, 1998. 21–23.

CARLOS J. FINLAY
(1833–1915)

Cuban Physician and Scientist

Cuban scientist and physician Carlos J. Finlay is credited with having been the first to discover that yellow fever was spread by the mosquito *Stegomyia fasciata,* today known as *Aedes aegypti.* Even though recognition evaded this distinguished scientist for many years, he is internationally referred to as the Cuban Pasteur and increasingly has been credited with having made a significant contribution to humanity. The date of his birthday, December 3, was chosen in 1933 to celebrate "The Day of American Medicine."

Carlos Juan Finlay y de Barres, one of eight siblings, was born in Puerto Príncipe, (now Camagüey), on December 3, 1833, to Scottish physician Edward Finlay Wilson and French national Isabel de Barres. While he was still a very young boy his family moved to Havana where he lived until the age of 11, when he was sent to Edinburgh, Scotland, to study at a school run by his aunt. In 1846, after a severe attack of cholera, he returned to Cuba. It is believed this bout with cholera left him with a slight speech problem and an obvious case of absentmindedness. He returned to Europe in 1848 to continue his education in France, but the revolutionary uprising at the time forced him to flee to London. In 1851, once more afflicted with a serious disease, typhoid fever, he returned to Cuba. After recovering from this illness, he left for Philadelphia, where he completed his medical studies at Jefferson Medical College in 1855. Between the years 1857 and 1864 Finlay established medical practices in ophthalmic surgery in Lima, Peru; Paris, France; and finally Matanzas, Cuba.

Even though he had been positing the link between mosquitoes and yellow fever for quite some time, it wasn't until the period between 1875 and 1881 that Finlay's scientific work on contagious diseases and epidemics bore fruit and led to the discovery of the biological vector of yellow fever. Yellow fever is an acute viral infectious tropical disease passed to humans by the bite of an infected female mosquito; once it enters the body, the virus locates the nearest lymph node and spreads. During the 1800s yellow fever mortality rates climbed to 80 percent in Europe, the United States, and the Caribbean.

The year 1881 was pivotal for Finlay and one where he achieved numerous milestones in his quest to eradicate yellow fever. On February 18, before a scientific gathering in Washington, D.C., Finlay presented his groundbreaking thesis on the vector of yellow fever—the first time anyone had posited the mosquito as the insect carrier of a disease-producing virus. On June 28, 1881, at the Garcini Clinic in Havana, Finlay accomplished the first experimental inoculation against yellow fever on a human being. Finally, in August, at Havana's Academy of

Medical, Physical and Natural Sciences he formally presented his thesis in its final form, which included his conceptual framework hypothesizing the mosquito as the contaminating agent in the transmission of the disease.

Over the years there was some controversy over Finlay's accomplishment, and there has been a lack of proper recognition for his work. In 1900 Major Walter Reed was appointed head of a U.S. Army Medical Commission to study infectious diseases in Cuba, yellow fever in particular. Finlay welcomed the commission; shared his notes, records, and experiments; and offered to personally assist the researchers in their work. The work produced by the commission substantiated Finlay's claims of the past 20 years.

Walter Reed's biography credits Finlay with proving without a doubt that the *Aedes* mosquito was the carrier and transmitter of yellow fever. W.H. Welch, a pathologist and founder of John Hopkins University's Institute of the History of Medicine, attributed the discovery of the biological vector of yellow fever to Walter Reed and thus began the long controversy over credit for this scientific milestone. An added component to this controversy was the fact that this period coincided with the Spanish-American War and the years 1898–1902, during the first American occupation of Cuba. There was much clamoring by Cuban scientists during those years, arguing that Finlay was the legitimate discoverer of the yellow fever vector and that recognition for this accomplishment should be given exclusively to him and not to the rival claims of the Americans. Finlay did not actively refute these statements, but they never dissipated.

His work, medical publications, and contributions as a scientist have been recognized throughout the world. In 1904, 1906, and 1907 Finlay was nominated to receive the Nobel Prize in Medicine for his advancements in the medical field. The Mary Kingsley Medal, sponsored by the Liverpool School of Tropical Medicine, was bestowed on Finlay in 1907. In 1908, the French government recognized his work and gave him their highest military accolade, making him an officer of the Legion d'Honneur, and later naming a Paris street in his honor. The UN Educational, Scientific, and Cultural Organization (UNESCO) confers a coveted research microbiology prize named after him, and an entity dedicated to researching and developing vaccines, the Finlay Institute, was created in Havana, Cuba, in 1928.

His obituary in the *Journal of the American Medical Association* on August 28, 1915, noted his humility: "He lacked the genius for self-exploitation and having established his doctrine modestly lived on with no thought of further recognition" (Mortimer 1999, 618). Finlay has finally received the recognition he deserved and is referred to as the "epidemiologist who discovered that yellow fever is transmitted from infected to healthy humans by a mosquito" ("Carlos J. Finlay" 2002).—G.C.

References and Suggested Readings

"Carlos J. Finlay." *Encyclopædia Britannica*, Vol. 4. Chicago: Encyclopaedia Britannica, 2002. 783–784.

Guiteras, Dr. Juan. "Dr. Carlos Finlay, Biographical Notes." The Official Web Site of the Finlay Medical Society. *http://www.finlay-online.com/welcome/whowasdrfinlay.htm*.

López Sánchez, José. *Carlos J. Finlay: His Life and His Work.* Havana, Cuba: Editorial José Martí, 1999.

Mortimer, P.P. "The Other Dr. Finlay." *British Medical Journal* 7210 (September 4, 1999): 618.

Marcus Garvey
(1887–1940)
Jamaican Activist and Militant

Marcus Mosiah Garvey was one of the first Jamaican and international leaders to advocate for black militancy and self-reliance. A man of innovative, radical, and controversial ideas, Garvey is considered to be the first national hero of Jamaica.

Garvey was born on August 17, 1887, in St. Ann's Bay in the northern part of Jamaica. His father Marcus was a stonemason, and his mother Sarah was a religious woman considered to have high moral values. He was the youngest of 11 children, 9 of whom died during childhood. His educational background has been questioned by many of his biographers, who tend to be highly skeptical of any information reported by Garvey himself. They agree on the fact that he may have attended the local elementary and grammar schools at St. Ann's Bay, but his claims that he attended universities in England and was privately tutored remain unsubstantiated (Cronon 1969, 7–8).

Because of his family's the strained financial conditions, Garvey left school at age of 14 and became an apprentice printer at his godfather's printing shop. Garvey, always an avid reader, had the opportunity to use the print shop library and became acquainted with many of the social and political issues of the time. Three years later he left for Kingston, where he eventually became a master printer and worked for P.A. Benjamin Limited, one of the biggest printing houses in Jamaica. He also was involved in publishing the newspapers *Our View* and *Garvey's Watchman,* a tabloid. When the Typographical Union launched a labor strike to protest working conditions and wages, Garvey joined the strike. When the dispute was settled, he was blacklisted and fired from his job.

In the following years, Garvey lived and traveled throughout Latin America and England. These travels exposed him to the inhuman conditions faced by black people and West Indian migratory workers. As a result of those experiences, he became interested in finding ways to empower blacks so that they could overcome the poor working conditions and lifestyles that they had to endure. Strongly influenced by the views of Egyptian and black scholar Duse Mohammed Ali, Garvey started to refine his own views of what he saw as the perpetual exploitation of the black race by white industrial powers. For insight, he turned to Pan-Africanism, a philosophy that embraces the view that black people must empower themselves to achieve equality and freedom.

On his return to Jamaica in 1914, Garvey founded the Universal Negro Improvement Association (UNIA). Following the motto "One God! One Aim! One Country!" Garvey sought to have all black people unite and to eventually return to Africa, in a program he called "Back to Africa." He wanted to instill a sense of economic self-sufficiency and racial pride in blacks. The objectives of UNIA were:

1) to establish a universal confraternity among the races; 2) to prompt the spirit of pride and love; 3) to reclaim the fallen; 4) to administer and assist the needy; 5) to assist in civilizing the backward tribes of Africa; 6) to assist in the development of independent Negro nations and communities; 7) to establish commissionaires or agencies in the principals countries and cities of the world for the representation and protection of all Negroes irrespective of nationality; 8) to promote a conscientious spiritual workshop among the native tribes of Africa; 9) to establish universities, colleges, academies and schools for the racial education and culture of the people; 10) to conduct a world-wide commercial and industrial intercourse for the good of the people; and 11) to work for better conditions in all Negro communities. (Hill 1987, 206–210)

The headquarters of UNIA was initially located in Kingston but Garvey believed that the insular politics of Jamaica and its regional location would make it difficult for the association to grow and develop an international following. Because he had become an admirer and follower of the notable black educator Booker T. Washington, former slave and founder of the Tuskegee Institute, he decided to move UNIA to the United States to broaden the impact of his message and to gain the support of American blacks. Like Washington, Garvey believed that if blacks were to improve their lives, they needed to be educated, to succeed financially, and to gain economic freedom.

When Garvey arrived in New York City in 1916, he settled in Harlem, which at that time was undergoing the Harlem Renaissance and was the center of cultural, economic, and social activity for the city's black community. Garvey started to promote his organization successfully and created the newspaper *Negro World* in 1918, in addition to many other commercial and business ventures.

By 1919, Garvey had incorporated UNIA in the United States and launched a broad range of entrepreneurial activities. Although he boasted that the organization had as many as 30 branches and a membership of more than 2 million members, it has been impossible to corroborate the validity of these statistics (Cronon 1969, 205). At the heart of UNIA and Garvey's efforts was the foundation of the shipping company Black Star Lines. Its goal was to create a transportation network that would link and bring together black people throughout the world. The existence of this company and presence of the ships gave credibility to his organization and allowed it to grow and to increase its membership.

Garvey was an imposing character, filled with pride and determination. He toured the United States giving speeches in which he advocated pride and self-respect for the black race, and he motivated blacks to work toward self-sufficiency and independence. Dressed in imposing uniforms festooned with gold and glitter, Garvey held elaborate and ornate parades where he proclaimed himself the provisional president of Africa and awarded his members and friends nobility ranks and titles such as "Commander of the Sublime Order of the Nile," and "Distinguished Service Order of Ethiopia."

In 1920, his association held a major convention attended by more than 25,000 delegates from the United States, the Caribbean, and Latin America. The delegates approved the Declaration of Rights of the Negro Peoples of the World, which consisted of a preamble listing 15 grievances faced by blacks around the world and made 54 demands or calls for action advocating for self-determination for blacks (Clarke 1974, 445).

In 1922, after little more than three years of existence, the badly mismanaged Black Star Line began to confront economic problems and was forced into bankruptcy. Apparently, some of the organization's administrators continued to sell stock for the line through the U.S. mail despite its insolvency. J. Edgar Hoover persuaded the government to prosecute Garvey on charges of mail fraud (Muhammad 1987). In 1923, acting as his own attorney, Garvey went to trial and was found guilty on one count of mail fraud; he was sentenced to five years in prison at the federal penitentiary in Atlanta, Georgia. Faced with political pressure from Garvey's followers, President Calvin Coolidge granted him an executive pardon after he had served three years of his sentence. After Garvey left jail in 1927, he was quickly deported to Jamaica. It is important to note that in 1987, during the 100th anniversary of Garvey's birth, the House Judiciary Committee of the U.S. Congress held hearings on the validity of the mail fraud charges leveled against Garvey more than 50 years earlier. The committee resolved that the charges "were not substantiated and that his conviction on those charges was unjust and unwarranted" (*Congressional Record* 1987).

On his arrival in Jamaica, the ever-restless Garvey continued advocating for his ideas and in 1928 created the People's Political Party. He also published the newspapers *Black Man* and *New Jamaican*. During the electoral campaign, Garvey ran on a platform advocating changes in the judiciary system and fighting judicial corruption. He was quickly charged with judicial contempt and was sent to jail for three months (Alexander 1988). His party lost the elections by a large margin and Garvey, disillusioned with the system, decided to leave Jamaica and go to London. He left for London and eventually died there on June 10, 1940, poor and virtually unknown. In 1968, Garvey's body was flown back to Jamaica. He was buried with military honors and was proclaimed a national hero.—S.M.M.

References and Suggested Readings

Alexander, Robert. *Biographical Dictionary of Latin American and Caribbean Political Leaders.* Westport: Greenwood, 1988. 180–182.

Clarke, John Henrik. *Marcus Garvey and the Vision of Africa.* New York: Random House, 1974.

Congressional Record—Daily Digest. Tuesday, July 28, 1987. 100th Cong. 1st Sess. 133 Cong Rec D 1046.

Cronon, E. David. *Black Moses. The Story of Marcus Garvey and the Universal Negro Improvement Association.* Madison: The University of Wisconsin Press, 1969.

Garvey, Amy Jaques. *The Philosophy and Opinion of Marcus Garvey.* New York: Athenaeum 1980.

Hill, Robert A., ed. *Marcus Garvey: Life and Lessons.* Berkeley: The University of California Press, 1987.

Muhammad, Askia. "A Mistreated Black Pioneer; His Centennial Year, Its Time to Pardon Marcus Garvey." *The Washington Post,* August 16, 1987, n.p.

Sewell, Tony. *The Legacy of Marcus Garvey.* New York: African World Press, 1990.

Mariana Grajales
(1815–1893)

Cuban Revolutionary Patriot

Cuban patriot Mariana Grajales, mother of another Cuban patriot, **Antonio Maceo**, and a fighter in her own right, serves as a symbol of women in the fight against slavery and for national liberation. In the struggle for Cuban independence, she lost her husband and 9 of her 13 children; the most well known of all of her children was Maceo, who died in 1896. Grajales herself has acquired iconic proportions akin to **Nanny of the Maroons**, one of Jamaica's revolutionary heroes. She spent ten years running an encampment that provided soldiers with provisions and first aid for the wounded. In addition to epitomizing the mother figure, she symbolizes Afro-Cuban resistance to slavery and oppression even though she was not a slave.

Mariana Grajales Cuello was born on July 12, 1815, in Santiago de Cuba, then the capital of the eastern province of Oriente. Her parents, free mulattoes Teresa Cuello Zayas and José Grajales Matos, had fled the Dominican Republic due to the violence that had spread there during the Haitian revolution. Even though her family was free, as a child she witnessed the arrival and parading of naked slaves through the streets of the port city of Santiago. She also witnessed Spanish military troops marching to battle the maroons (escaped slaves) in the mountains north of the city.

Probably because of poverty, Grajales received very little formal schooling. Even though free blacks were allowed an education, they were required to pay tuition, which very few could afford. Her education was the learning she acquired from her parents and the experiences she had such as her visits to jailed maroons—an activity she engaged in to make sure she remebered the horrors of slavery.

Although free, she was never too removed from the discrimination of the slave society she was born and raised in, which in itself was an education for her. In 1831, she married Fructuoso Regüeyferos, who died in 1840, leaving her with four children. Described as an attractive and respectable widow, Grajales met Marcos Maceo, himself a widower with children. Maceo had been born in Venezuela and had fought with the Spanish against Simón Bolívar, who was struggling for Venezuela's independence. When he met Grajales, he already owned a farm called Las Delicias, where the couple settled.

In 1845, Maceo and Grajales' first child, Antonio de la Caridad Maceo, was born. Over the next nine years they had five more children. During the 1840s, there was great turmoil in Cuban society, particularly concerning blacks: conspiracies of slaves and free blacks were discovered, hundreds of blacks were publicly executed, and strict surveillance of free blacks and fines for those who showed "disrespect" were enacted. Blacks who were emancipated after May 1844 as well as all blacks not native to the island were to be expelled from Cuba. Somehow, Maceo was able to secure an affidavit declaring him a native of Santiago de Cuba.

Grajales and her family were moderately prosperous. They also had connections among both the white and free black middle-class communities. They were able to purchase a second farm in Majaguabo, also near Santiago de Cuba, and named it La Esperanza (which translated means "hope"). Except for when she was ready to have a child, Grajales spent all of her time at the farm. In 1851, after living together for eight years and having three children, Maceo and Grajales legalized their union through marriage.

During the rest of the 1850s, as she raised her 13 children, epidemics killed off 70,000 slaves. As the call for the abolition of slavery began to take hold, the sugar plantation owners overtly or covertly found ways to thwart the movement.

Grajales was a middle-aged woman by the 1860s and a member of one of the more prosperous black families in the Majaguabo district. The abolitionist movement in Cuba was on the upswing and beginning to take hold, particularly on the part of the island around Santiago de Cuba. Marcos Maceo had joined an underground group, and when the time came and the revolution was imminent he worried about how his wife would react. Her response was swift and determined. She had no qualms about losing everything they had for the cause: "Swear," Grajales said, "by the blood of the crucified Christ, that you will fight to liberate your country, fight tirelessly, until you see her independent, or until you die achieving it" (Henderson 1978, 140). She became a participant and actively helped them recruit people to fight the revolution. She converted Las Delicias into a military depot and encampment to supply and treat the combatants. In 1868 the Spanish captured Las Delicias and burned the farmhouse. Undaunted, Grajales settled at Las Esperanza. That year, she received the sad news that her oldest son, Justo Regüeyferos, had been killed, and later that her husband had been fatally wounded while fighting under his son Antonio's command. Realizing that staying on the farm was too dangerous, Grajales and her daughters and daughters-in-law joined the insurgency, settling at an encampment where they assisted wounded soldiers. Her skill in healing the wounded and her knowledge of herbs and plants were legendary.

In 1878, after a series of battles that resulted in a cease-fire and an end to the Ten Years' War, Antonio Maceo sent his mother and other family members into exile in Kingston, Jamaica. While her son and others plotted a renewal of the revolution, she helped care for the wives and children of the fighters. By now, she and her family had become notorious to the Spanish, labeled the "terrible Maceos." Grajales never again returned to Cuba, nor did she live long enough to see Cuba gain its independence in 1902. However, she died with the hope and knowledge that Cuba's autonomy was just a matter of struggle and time. Cuban independence leader and patriot **José Martí** visited her in 1891, two years before her death, and wrote about their meeting. He describes how Grajales, an old woman by that time, reminisced about the action on the battlefields. His narrative illustrates the sense of power that Grajales—the mother and the revolutionary—had over people. He captures her essence thus: "And if one trembled when he came face to face with the enemy of his country, he saw the mother of Maceo, white kerchief on her head, and he ceased trembling!" (Martí 1975, 617).—G.C.

References and Suggested Readings

Henderson, James. "Mariana Grajales: Black Progenitress of Cuban Independence." *Journal of Negro History* 63.2 (April 1978): 135–148.

Martí, José. *Obras Completas.* Havana: Editorial de ciencias socials, 1975.

Sanabria, Nidya. *Historia de una familia mambisa: Mariana Grajales.* Havana: Editorial Orbe, Instituto del libro, 1975.

Shepherd, Verene, Bridget Brereton, and Barbara Bailey, eds. *Engendering History: Caribbean Women in Historical Perspective.* New York: St. Martin's Press, 1995.

Nicolás Guillén
(1902–1989)

Cuban Poet

Nicolás Guillén is considered to be Cuba's "poet laureate" and its "national poet." His extensive poetic work not only helped to establish the literary genre of Afro-Cuban and Afro-Antillean poetry, but also set forth poetry with a deep social and political conscience that addressed issues of racism, political inequities, oppression, and imperialism in Cuban society and the Caribbean. His poetry transcended Cuba and his literary legacy is considered as much Caribbean as Cuban.

Guillén was born in Camagüey, a province located in the eastern part of Cuba, on July 10, 1902. He was one of six children of Nicolás Guillen, a senator for the Liberal Party, and Argelia Batista. Guillén attended the local schools in Camagüey and started to write poetry as an adolescent. On graduation from high school in 1920, he went to the University of Havana, where he intended to receive a law degree. However, with the death of his father in 1917 (as part of a politically motivated assassination) the family fell on hard times and Guillén lacked the resources to pay for his expenses as a student. He left the university to work and to pursue his interests as a poet and journalist.

When he returned to Camagüey, he took a job as a printer; one of his first literary endeavors was the publication of *Lis* (Lily), a literary magazine. He also worked as a newspaper editor for *El Camagüeyano* (The Camagüeyan), and edited the literary magazine *Las Dos Repúblicas* (The Two Republics). His first printed poetry appeared in the magazine *Camagüey Gráfico* (Camagüey Graphic) in 1919. From 1920 to 1921, his poetry also appeared in literary and general-interest Cuban publications such as *Catalia, Diario de la Marina, Orbe, Revista de la Habana, Grafos,* and *Bohemia* (Peraza Sarausa 1964).

Guillén's poetry has generally been divided in two parts. The first part is formed by his Afro-Cuban of Afro-Antillean poetry; the second group comprises socially and politically conscious poetry.

At the time of Guillén's emergence as a poet, Cuban society was strictly stratified according to race and class. Wealthy people from Spanish origins dominated the upper classes of society and there was a large underclass of poor peasants who worked in agriculture and hard labor who lived at the social and economic margins of society. They were poor and came from African ancestry. More importantly, their culture and cultural products had been ignored by generations who judged them as not having any redeeming aesthetic qualities and being "low class."

As a mulatto, Guillén had blended racial features that were the result of his Spanish and African heritages. After the death of his father, he found he had more in common with poor blacks than with the upper classes, so it is not surprising that he sought his early poetic inspiration in the *son,* a traditional musical form that originally came from the lower classes and is now part of mainstream Latin sound.

Guillén first published a collection of eight poems titled *Motivos del Son* in 1930. Using the metaphor of the *son,* Guillén was able to capture in his poetry the linguistic peculiarities of black Cubans. His poetry was significant because it not only brought forward elements of their cultures, but also reaffirmed the importance of these members of Cuban society whose cultural products and idiosyncrasies had been ignored for so long.

These poems were followed in 1931 by another book of poetry, *Songoro Cosongo.* This groundbreaking book represents the first appearance of Afro-Cuban poetry in the Caribbean. Similar to Puerto Rican **Luis Palés Matos'** *Tuntún de Pasa y Grifería, Songoro Cosongo* represents a masterful attempt to capture the contribution of the African heritage to Cuban and Caribbean cultures. In his poetry, he used an onomatopoetic technique that reproduced sounds, cadences, rhythms, idioms, and expressions of lower-class Cuban blacks. Once again, Guillén emulated the rhythmic patterns of the *son* and brought to the forefront of his readers' minds the lifestyles and unique cultural contributions and products of people of African ancestry living in Cuba.

Like Palés Matos, Guillén had some critics who accused him of stereotyping the lifestyles and expressions of this segment of society. As poets and cultural commentators, both men have been criticized for focusing on lower-class cultural expressions that may lead to generalizations and misconstructions. Nevertheless, when critics evaluate his works from a historical perspective they recognize Guillén as a groundbreaking poet who recognized the positive cultural manifestations of these groups.

The second body of Guillén's poetry addressed the political and social concerns of the author in light of the contemporary circumstances then prevalent in Cuba and the Caribbean. His book *West Indies, LTD* (1934) centered on the social, economic, and political conditions of Caribbean societies that at the time were the victims of slavery in the hands of Western imperialist nations. Guillén used the metaphor of a factory to illustrate ways in which the people of Cuba and the Caribbean had suffered exploitation at the hands of wealthy people who only cared for becoming rich from the labor of the people. This same trend was expanded in the book *Cuba Libre* (1947), published in English and co-edited by Langston Hughes. As a poet, Guillén was one of the first writers in the Caribbean to deal with social and economic concerns by writing about the oppression of Caribbean peoples by Western industrial nations.

In 1937 Guillén traveled to Spain to cover the Spanish Civil War for the Cuban publication *Mediodía*; while there he fought against Franco's Republican troops. When he returned to Cuba he became a vocal communist and started to publish articles and poetry challenging the dominant political ideology and oppressive regime of Carlos Prío Socarrás.

Throughout the 1940s and 1950s, Guillén traveled extensively throughout Cuba and Latin America. In 1942, for instance, he visited Haiti as the guest of **Jacques Roumain**, whose literary work expressed similar concerns and themes. This experience inspired him to write the book *Elegía a Jacques Roumain en el cielo de Haití* (Eulogy to Jacques Roumain and the Haitian Sky) in 1948.

As a result of his radical political views Guillén was forced to leave Cuba in 1953 after Cuban dictator Fulgencio Batista came to power. He spent six years in political exile, during which he lived and traveled throughout Europe and Latin America and continued to publish poetry that vividly depicted the pain of his experiences in exile. Among his works of this period were *La paloma de vuelo popular* (The Dove of Popular Fly) and *Elegias* (Eulogy), both published in 1958.

Guillén returned to Cuba in 1959 after **Fidel Castro** seized power in a popular revolution. He was considered a hero and became Cuba's poet laureate. He published many poetry books that pay homage to Fidel Castro and the social accomplishments of his regime, among which are *Buenos días, Fidel* (Good Day, Fidel; 1959), *Tengo* (1964), and *Ché Comandante* (Commander Ché; 1967).

Guillén, who was nominated for a Nobel Prize, continued to lecture and publish throughout his life. In 1961 Fidel Casto officially named him National Poet of Cuba. In addition, he won a large number of awards and distinctions during his life such as the Casa de las Américas Award. He was the first president of the Cuba's Union of Writers and Artists (UNEAC) and directed the organization for 25 years. Guillén has been credited for using that position to showcase Cuban cultural products to the rest world in the years following the American military embargo (Stubbs 1989). Without a doubt, Guillén is one of the more important Caribbean writers of the twentieth century. His poetry transcended Cuba and sang to the whole Caribbean. He died in Havana on July 16, 1989.—S.M.M.

References and Suggested Readings

Ellis, Keith. *Cuba's Nicolás Guillén: Poetry and Ideology.* Toronto: University of Toronto Press, 1983.

Espindola, Roberto. "Obituary, Nicolás Guillén." *The Independent* (London), July 20, 1989, 15.

Flores, Angel, ed. "Nicolás Guillén." *Spanish American Authors: The Twentieth Century.* New York: H.W. Wilson, 1992. 393–397.

Folkart, Burt A. "Nicolás Guillén, 87; Known as Cuba's National Poet." *Los Angeles Times*, July 18, 1989, 22.

Peraza Sarausa, Fermín. "Nicolás Guillén." *Personalidades Cubanas.* Gainsville, FL: Published by the Author, 1964. 68–69.

Smart, Ian Isidore. *Nicolás Guillén: Popular Poet of the Caribbean.* St. Louis: University of Missouri Press, 1990.

Stubbs, Jean. "Obituary of Nicolás Guillén." *The Guardian* (London), July 18, 1989, n.p.

Tomás Gutiérrez Alea (Titón)
(1928–1996)

Cuban Filmmaker, Director, and Writer

As a screenwriter and director, Tomás Gutiérrez Alea is the most acclaimed and best-known cinematographer in Cuba. He directed the first Cuban film ever to be nominated for an Oscar. Titón, as he was popularly known, was born and died in Havana, Cuba. While in law school in the mid-1940s, he made two short films *Un fakir* (A Fakir), and *La caperucita roja* (Little Red Riding Hood). He found his calling and went on to study film, beginning his career as a documentary filmmaker. Throughout his life he believed criticism was his obligation. Most of his films depict life in contemporary revolutionary Cuba.

Born on December 11, 1928, in Havana, Cuba, Gutiérrez Alea grew up in a well-to-do family, embraced Marxism during his teenage years, and later became a supporter of **Fidel Castro**'s revolution. In the early 1950s he attended the Italian film school Centro Sperimentale de Cinematografia de Roma, where he was influenced by the wave of neorealism in European films, which depicted lower-class life in a stark, realistic manner. Gutiérrez Alea's use of Cuban historical and contemporary fables taken to absurd heights show the influence of that period's filmmakers Luis Buñuel and Federico Fellini, icons among the neorealists. His films aim to represent incidents and problems from the everyday lives of ordinary Cubans, often with sentimental and humorous undertones. Many of the story lines in his films were taken directly from the pages of *Granma*, the official government newspaper, known for its strict adherence to the Cuban Communist Party line.

In 1959, on the heels of the new cultural laws of revolutionary Cuba, Gutiérrez Alea co-founded (with Santiago Alvarez) the Cuban Institute of Art and Cinematographic Industry (ICAIC). That same year he directed the documentary *Esta Tierra Nuestra* (This Land of Ours), an optimistic portrayal of the new government's agrarian reform initiative. The innovative years between 1966 and 1979 are considered the golden years of Cuban cinema. Much of the credit is given to Gutiérrez Alea's leadership in the area of film and his commitment to the Cuban revolution. His political commitment, however, did not deter him from criticizing and satirizing what he characterized as the incongruent and absurd realities of contemporary Cuba.

A number of his films received critical acclaim and awards during this period. In his 1966 film, *Death of a Bureaucrat*, a metaphor for the inflexibility of the revolution, Gutiérrez Alea examines and critiques the flaws of revolutionary Cuban society, mocking the political system that seems to pursue its citizens even after death. It received the Karlovy Vary Film Festival Special Jury Prize. *Memories of Underdevelopment*, filmed in 1968, firmly established his reputation as a filmmaker, and is regarded as his masterpiece. The story deals with an intellectual trying to find his place in post-revolutionary Cuba and examines the ambivalences and the sense of alienation that accompanied the transitional period. Former *New York Times* film critic Vincent Canby called it a superb film, "complete in the way that very few movies are" (qtd. in Gussow 1996, 23). Although the film was awarded the U.S. National Society of Film Critics Rosenthal Award in 1973, Gutiérrez Alea was denied a visa to attend the ceremony. When the film eventually opened commercially in New York, the *New York Times* selected it as one of 1974's ten best movies. Among the other awards it received were the New York Film Festival Chaplin and the Karlovy Vary Film Festival FIPRESCI prizes.

His films began to attract a wider audience outside Cuba and are now available in American video rental establishments. *Up to a Point* (1984) exposes and challenges the concept of male superiority, or "machismo," and the sexual double standard that is very much a fact of life in contemporary Cuba. *Strawberry and Chocolate* (1995), the first Cuban film to go into general release in the United States and to be nominated for an Oscar, marked an important opening in Cuban social mores. Through the friendship between an idealist and naive Marxist student and the gay man who is out to seduce him, the film presents a humorous plot that highlights Cuba's repressive measures against homosexuals. In his own words, Gutiérrez Alea sought to represent an even more universal theme when he told the *New York Times* that in reality this was a film "about intolerance and incomprehension of those who are different, and that applies not only to homosexuals, but to everyone who is discriminated against" (Gussow 1996, 23). On finishing his Oscar-nominated film and already afflicted with the cancer that would soon end his life, Gutiérrez Alea immediately began his work on what would be his last film.

Gutiérrez Alea died before he could complete *Guantanamera* (1997), a humorous social comment on contemporary Cuba. Longtime collaborator Juan Carlos Tabío and Mirtha Ibarra, Gutiérrez Alea's widow and protagonist in many of his films, worked to complete this project. Based on a story that had appeared in the news, and interspersed with observations and verbatim dialogue heard on Havana streets, this film takes Gutiérrez Alea's satire on the Cuban bureaucracy and its crumbling infrastructure to new heights. An old aunt of one of the protagonists, while visiting her hometown after many years, becomes romantically aroused and dies during a tryst with the lover of her youth. The film centers on the efforts to transfer her remains from one end of Cuba to another in the face of gasoline shortages and bureaucratic mix-ups. It is interesting to note that his final work combined the themes of love and death.

The exile Cuban community, particularly in the United States, criticized him for not being harsher in his depiction of hardship in Castro's Cuba. The international community, however, seems to admire this filmmaker's work and agrees with the National Society of Critics 1974 citation quoted in his obituary, praising his work as a "very personal and very courageous confrontation of the artist's doubts and ambivalences regarding the Cuban Revolution" (Oliver 1996, 24).—G.C.

References and Suggested Readings

Baseline II, Inc. "Gutiérrez Alea, Tomás." *Celebrity Biographies*. Electronically published by Lexis-Nexis.

Davies, Catherine. "Recent Cuban Fiction Films: Identification, Interpretation, Disorder." *Bulletin of Latin American Research* 15.2 (1996): 177–192.

Gussow, Mel. "Tomás Gutiérrez Alea, Cuban Film Maker, 69." *New York Times*, April 17, 1996, 23–24.

Minna, Jaskarin. "Tomás Gutiérrez Alea and the Post-Revolutionary Cuba." *Revista Xaman* (Finland). *http://www.helsinki.fi/hum/ibero/xaman/articulos/9711/9711_mj.html*.

Oliver, Myrna. "Tomas Guitierrez Alea; Cuban Film Director." *Los Angeles Times*, April 19, 1996, 24.

Rohter, Larry. "A Final Journey Into the Heart of Cuba [Biography]." *New York Times*, July 20, 1997, 11.

West, Dennis "'Strawberry and Chocolate,' Ice Cream and Tolerance: Interview With Tomás Gutiérrez Alea." *Cineaste* 21.1–2 (1995): 16–19.

STUART HALL
(1932–)

Jamaican Sociologist, Scholar, Cultural Critic and Theorist, and Media Commentator

Stuart Hall is considered one of the intellectual leaders behind the cultural studies movement that has emerged in the field of social sciences and literature in the last 20 years. His theories on the relationship between the development of cultural identity and social practice have facilitated the understanding of the role of race, ethnicity, and identity as it relates to cultural development. He is an insightful cultural critic and commentator who has been credited with coining the word "Thatcherism" and who has kept a watchful eye on the way that Margaret Thatcher's administration "exploited" racial politics. Hall is considered one of the pillars of the "New Left" movement in England.

Hall was born in Kingston, Jamaica, in 1932 and was the youngest of three children. His father, Herman, was the chief accountant for the United Fruit Company in Jamaica. His mother, Jessie, was a homemaker from white British ancestry, who had been born in a poor household but was raised by an uncle who was a prominent lawyer.

According to recent profiles in the British newspaper *The Guardian*, Hall's interests in race and class relationships may have been motivated by his early life experiences. He was the darkest-skinned child in the family and, as a result, was considered a "coolie." In addition, family relations were always strained by his mother's feeling that she deserved more than what his father could give to her and the family. His mother venerated British cultural traditions and practices and rejected native Jamaican ones. Another factor was his oldest sister's nervous breakdown, which occurred when the family forbade her to date a young, middle-class Barbadian medical student attending school in Jamaica because of race and class prejudices ("Prophet at the Margins," 2000).

After graduating from Jamaica College, Hall was awarded a Rhodes Scholarship to study at Merton College in Oxford in 1951. Hall was impressed by the flourishing class of West Indians living in England. They gave him a sense of belonging and reaffirmed for the first time his West Indian cultural identity. There he explored his cultural roots and even played piano in a jazz group made up of two West Indian bus drivers. As a student, Hall got involved with the BBC's World Service Radio program in the late 1950s and broadcast with Caribbean writers **George Lamming** and **V. S. Naipaul**.

Hall's arrival in England coincided with the emergence of a strong anti-colonial ferment among the Caribbean students and immigrants living in the country. He became involved with the many groups protesting the British colonial

Stuart Hall. Courtesy of Sut Jhally Media Education Foundation.

presence in the Caribbean. It was this awareness and involvement that led to his study of political theory and the works of Karl Marx, Antonio Gramsci, and Michel Foucault. In 1956 he became the first editor of the *New Left Review,* a publication that departed from some of the postulates of the classic left and tried to reclaim the importance of culture within economic and political constructs. It also looked at the process of cultural production as it relates to popular culture and asserted that the Soviet Union was just another imperial power trying to take over the world. Hall went on to receive a doctoral degree in American literature at Oxford.

Hall started teaching film and allied media at Chelsea College in London in 1964. He was one of the first scholars to introduce and legitimize the study of popular culture texts within academic settings. His emphasis on the culture that develops and emerges from texts such as radio, television, advertising, and film served as the basis for the later development of the fields of cultural and communication studies in Great Britain. His book *Popular Arts* (1964) is considered one of the classics in the early analysis of popular culture and cultural studies.

The next step in Hall's career was his appointment as a research fellow at Birmingham's Centre for Contemporary Cultural Studies in 1968. Along with Richard Hoggart, director of the center, Hall continued setting ground for the development of cultural studies. After Hoggart stepped down, Hall became the center's director from 1968 to 1979. His emphasis on including race, ethnicity, colonialism, and migration as key realms of cultural studies added a significant depth and breadth to the discipline. In 1979, after a period of confrontation with scholars who wanted to introduce a feminist viewpoint into the mission and the research being conducted at the center, Hall left the directorship and took a position as professor of sociology with the Open University.

The Open University is Britain's institution for nontraditional students. Hall was ready to adapt and broaden the theoretical constructs and research that he had developed at Birmingham and make it available to the older nontraditional students who attended the institution. He wanted to use his skills as a lecturer and speaker to positively impact these students. Around this time, Hall became interested in the possible election of a conservative government in Great Britain and the potential negative effects that it could have on the poor and ethnic minorities. In his book *Policing the Crisis* (1978), Hall warned about the potential dangers of electing a government that wanted to gain support on the basis of a false appeal to Britain's traditions and patriotism. He voiced his concerns that Thatcher and her followers were selling the idea that England needed to be rebuilt. They crafted an appeal to British traditional society that excluded the poor, ethnic minorities, and anyone who fell beyond the white mainstream, and they failed to acknowledge changes in the racial and class landscape of Great Britain. Hall warned early on about the potential of electing a government that would cast the blame of Britain's ills on the poor and the disenfranchised.

After Thatcher's election, Hall was proven correct as the new prime minister sought to appeal to the masses by blaming the poor for Britain's problems and by trying to push the underclasses and the underprivileged out of Great Britain's mainstream society. Hall developed the word "Thatcherism" to characterize the prime minister's racial policies and ideologies. He was a vocal critic of her work and became a central commentator in the British media. During these years he gained a great deal of visibility and credibility among the general public who watched him do his commentaries on British television.

Hall's work has had a significant implication for the understanding of the social and psychological processes that evolve from the relationship between culture and society. His theories are based on the assumption that cultures are constantly dynamic and changing. He has demonstrated that the economic forces of any society are key in shaping its culture. Hall has provided strong arguments to demonstrate that people with access to the means of production are likely to play a key, and often oppressive, role in shaping cultures by influencing the nature of the messages constructed through the media. Mainstream media messages often exclude, misconstrue, or fail to acknowledge people with different ethnicities and races. They are designed to protect and promote the interests of the power elite. His work in the area of media representation is one of the most important paradigms in the study and understanding of media representation today (Jhally 1997).

Hall retired from active teaching at the Open University in 1997 and is now a professor emeritus. He lectures often in the United States and throughout Europe. He is co-editor of *Soundings,* a new publication that comments on culture and the arts.—S.M.M.

References and Suggested Readings

Hall, Stuart. "Cultural Studies and Its Theoretical Legacies." In Lawrence Grossberg, Cary Nelson, and Paula Treichler, eds., *Cultural Studies.* New York: Routledge, 1992. 277–285.

———. "Influences" (Interview). *New Statesman and Society,* February 9, 1996, 25.

———. *Representations: Cultural Representations and Signifying Practices.* London: Sage, 1997.

Hall, Stuart, and Paddy Whannel. *The Popular Arts.* London: Beacon, 1968.

Jhally, Sut. *Stuart Hall: Representations and the Media* (video). Media Education Foundation, 1997.

Karpf, Anne. "Desert Island Storm." *The Guardian* (London), February 19, 2000, 4.

Kingston, Peter. "Higher Education: Celebrity Scholars." *The Guardian* (London), April 30, 1996, 2.

"Prophet at the Margins." *The Guardian* (London), July 8, 2000, 8.

The Hart Sisters
Elizabeth Hart Thwaites
(1772–1833)
Anne Hart Gilbert
(1773–1834)

Antiguan Writers and Religious Leaders

Antigua natives Elizabeth and Anne Hart were among the first African Caribbean women writers and educators of slaves and free blacks. Converts to Methodism on an island where the white ruling class was mostly Anglican, they used the church as a way to challenge the ideology and practice of slavery as well as to make a case for the empowerment of women. Together Elizabeth and Anne compiled a written history of Methodism in Antigua and established the first Sunday school in the West Indies. Even though they had different personalities, they were driven by a sense of racial solidarity against the injustices perpetrated by the colonial powers of the time. Working within the Methodist Church and through the formation of various educational organizations, the Hart sisters managed to open the way for self-determination for Africans in Antigua and set an example for the rest of the Caribbean.

Elizabeth and Anne, born a year apart to Barry Conyers Hart and Anne Clearkley, were members of a small but relatively privileged class of blacks in Antigua. Their mother was a religious woman and their father was a black plantation and slave owner, poet, and occasional writer for the local newspaper. The family lived on an estate in Popeshead, near the town of St. Johns. A biographer of the Hart sisters has described their father's conflict over owning slaves: "[A]s a man who agonized over punishments and tried to act humanely toward his slaves[,] Hart helped slaves execute their affairs by preparing their manumission papers without charge and by offering general advice" (Ferguson 1993, 5). Because of their social class and privilege, and the father's own level of schooling, the sisters were able to receive an education.

In 1785 their mother died and 12-year-old Anne became surrogate mother to her siblings until she married in 1798, when Elizabeth took over those duties. Both sisters, however, acted as tutors to their brothers and sisters and their slaves, teaching them how to read and write as well as providing them with religious instruction. A turning point in the sisters' lives occurred in 1786 during the visit to Antigua of one of the principal founders of the Methodist foreign missions, Dr. Thomas Coke, when the sisters were baptized into the Methodist faith. Following their conversion to Methodism, their dress became plain and modest and they renounced things they considered worldly, including the piano—which Elizabeth had previously enjoyed playing.

In the Methodist community, the Hart sisters had found an institutional base where they could legitimately advocate against an oppressive colonial system. In their roles as preachers, writers, and teachers the sisters carried out their goals within the white ruling-class establishment, but "boldly asserted their independent existence and status as free black women working for the social betterment and spiritual uplift of free and enslaved Africans in a slave colony" (Paquet 1995, 517). Through the vehicles of religious preaching and marriage, the sisters managed to challenge the practice of slave ownership. In 1798, in a move that immediately increased her social status, Anne married John Gilbert, a white man, and the cousin of Methodist Church elder and leader Nathaniel Gilbert. As a result, community members shunned Gilbert and his notary public commission was rescinded. A few years later, Elizabeth's marriage to white evangelical educator and abolitionist Charles Thwaites, along with her abolitionist views, served to clinch the white community's displeasure with the Harts.

In their marriages to white men and in their roles as educators, the Hart sisters occupied an unusual position within Antiguan society. Methodist missionary Richard Pattison asked each of them to write the island's Methodist history, which they both completed in 1804. Anne's version stresses black women's contributions, highlighting the names of particular women who had significant effects on Antiguan Methodism, an important historical and social position. Elizabeth's approach to the topic was very similar, but she laid more emphasis on the emancipation of slaves. In a very bold way, considering the time and place of black women in 1804, in a letter to an unidentified male friend, Elizabeth Hart addressed the oppression of blacks and clearly indicted Europeans and white islanders: "I agree with you, that there might be some clue to [the existence of slavery] quite unknown to us; but this does not strike me as being the sins of the Africans; for, from all I can learn of them, according to their light, though barbarous and uncivilized, they are not so depraved as the generality of the Europeans, but more especially the West Indians" (Ferguson 1993, 109).

By 1807, the Methodist Church's membership in Antigua totaled 22 whites and 3,516 black and colored members. Given the overwhelming numbers of black members, they were easily able to choose their own leaders, shape the agenda, and become a powerful lobby for change in the status quo. Having married men who were influential in the Methodist Church greatly fueled the Hart sisters' cause. They pressed on with their mission of empowering Africans, particularly women, with literacy skills and preaching the word of God in the face of the strong opposition from the Anglican ruling elite.

In 1809 they established the first Caribbean Sunday School in the West Indies, which welcomed whites and blacks regardless of social class. Elizabeth and her husband organized Sunday school classes among Antiguan plantation slaves in 1813. In 1815 the sisters established the Female Refuge Society of Antigua, an organization created to offset established stereotypes created by slavery that perpetuated the image of black female depravity and sexual excess. This organization would eventually begin to change the racist mainstream views of the time. The unprecedented and defiant commitment of two free black sisters to equality and education of slaves is especially notable given the fact that Antigua was a plantation and slave-owning society in the early nineteenth century.

The Hart sisters died a year apart. The legacy of their work and the institutions they created had a powerful impact on Antiguan life and society. The entirety of their work and their challenge to the oppressive status provided the country with a framework to confront and subvert the morally indefensible system of slavery and validated the quest for blacks' self-determination. Unfortunately, very little has been written about the life and work of these notable Caribbean women.—G.C.

References and Suggested Readings

Ferguson, Moira, ed. *The Hart Sisters: Early African Caribbean Writers, Evangelicals, and Radicals.* Lincoln: University of Nebraska Press, 1993.
Paquet, Sandra Pouchet. "Reviews." *African American Review* 29:3 (Fall 1995): 517–519.

THE HENRÍQUEZ UREÑA FAMILY

Dominican Cultural and Political Leaders

Members of the Henríquez Ureña family played important roles in the political, social, and cultural life of the Dominican Republic during the late nineteenth century and the early twentieth century. Their individual and collective legacies span the fields of politics, education, diplomacy, and literature. They are regarded as key agents in the intellectual development of the Dominican Republic during the nineteenth and twentieth centuries, whose contributions helped to shape politics and culture on the island.

FRANCISCO HENRÍQUEZ Y CARVAJAL
(1859–1935)

Physician, Lawyer, and President of the Republic

Born in the Dominican Republic to a distinguished family of lawyers and politicians, Henríquez y Carvajal was considered one of the leading intellectuals of his island during his lifetime. In addition to being a writer and a politician, Henríquez y Carvajal was also a French-educated physician. He married **Salome Ureña** in 1880 and became the father of Fran, **Pedro**, **Max**, and **Camila**.

Henríquez y Carvajal was a noted intellectual who had a visible presence in the cultural life of his island. From 1870 to 1900 he was a key figure in political circles, and his voice was always present in Dominican newspapers and public life. He was a close friend and associate of Puerto Rican intellectual **Eugenio Maria de Hostos**. By 1902 he had become disillusioned by the political affairs of his island and went to Cuba, where he spent 14 years in exile practicing medicine and trying to escape the repression and the political instability of the Dominican Republic.

In 1916, immediately following the American invasion of the Dominican Republic, Henríquez y Carvajal was asked by the Dominican Congress to return to the island and become president of the republic as a compromise candidate between the Congress and the U.S. armed forces. He took office on July 31, 1916. His mandate was characterized by his strong opposition to the American forces and by his resistance to their presence in the island. Even though he was a politically weak president, he tried his best to oppose the reactionary and fascist policies pushed by the Americans. During his administration, he tried to convey to the world that the government of the United States had violated the island's sovereignty. He was also a staunch opponent of what he perceived was the U.S. attempt to fuse Haiti and the Dominican Republic into a single government. His opposition to the Americans was so vigorous that Captain Harry S. Knapp, head of the U.S. forces occupying the island, deposed him in December 1916. Henríquez y Carvajal was forced to leave the country and launched an international crusade to bring attention to the American occupation of his island.

This crusade, however, failed; American forces occupied the island until 1924. By the time they left, Henríquez y Carvajal had lost his position of power in the island and had settled in Cuba with his family.

SALOMÉ UREÑA DE HENRÍQUEZ
(1850–1897)

National Poet and Educator

Salomé Ureña de Henríquez is often described within the Dominican Republic as the "Muse of the Country." This notable woman of letters was a poet and an educator. Her intense love and commitment to the well-being of her country made her the object of intense love and admiration by the people of the Dominican Republic during her lifetime.

María Salomé Ureña, born in Santo Domingo on October 21, 1850, was the daughter of Nicolas Ureña de Mendoza, a prominent journalist, lawyer, diplomat, and poet whose work is considered to be one of the foremost examples of customs-based poetry during the nineteenth century. Her mother, Gregoria Díaz y León, came from a land-owning Dominican family.

In order to understand Ureña's contributions to the Dominican Republic both as a poet and as an educator, it is necessary to examine her education. Ureña was tutored by her mother, who taught her to read when she was four years old. Dominican women had no opportunity to pursue a secondary or a higher education when she was growing up. After she completed elementary school, her father decided to teach her with an individualized educational curriculum that provided her with a solid education in the liberal arts, languages, and classics, disciplines that she learned to love. This education was further expanded by one of her tutors, and eventual husband, **Francisco Hernández y Carvajal**. Ureña's legacy is generally found in her dual roles as a notable poet and educator.

Ureña started writing poetry when she was 15 years old. Because it was uncommon for young Dominican women to publish poetry and to attract unnecessary attention, she disguised her real identity by using the pen name of "Herminia," a common custom at the time. Her poems were acclaimed by the public, who identified with the feelings and imagery of her verses. Critics have divided her literary work in two general categories: romantic and patriotic/political poetry. Her work seems to have been influenced by modernism and romanticism, two literary movements popular in Latin America at the time, but also by the scientific positivism she acquired from **Eugenio María de Hostos** (Castro Ventura 1998). Ureña was also influenced by the unstable and sometimes hostile political climate that permeated the Dominican Republic during her lifetime. Because she spent a substantial part of her adult life battling the deadly disease of tuberculosis, her literary production was limited. While many of her poems appeared frequently in newspapers and other literary anthologies, she published only one major book of poetry, titled *Poesias*, in 1880. Among her best-known poems are "Sombras" (Shadows), "Ruinas" (Ruins), "Anacaona," and "Tristezas" (Sadness), many of which are considered classics of Dominican literature.

One of Ureña's most lasting intellectual contributions was in the field of education. This talented woman started to work with Puerto Rican patriot Eugenio María de Hostos in 1879 to develop a progressive educational facility aimed at educating the people of the Dominican Republic. Opportunities for higher education were very limited at the time. After Hostos' establishment of Escuela Normal de Santo Domingo (Santo Domingo Normal School) in 1880, he and Ureña worked to create the Instituto de Señoritas (Young Ladies Institute). Its primary objective was to prepare women for a teaching career. Ureña became a pillar in the operation of the school, and her work as a teacher and as an administrator are thought to have set permanent marks in the future of higher education for women in her homeland (Rodríguez Demorizi 1960).

Ureña died of tuberculosis on March 6, 1897. After her death, the institute was renamed Instituto de Señoritas Salomé Ureña. She is still remembered today as one of the Dominican Republic's most important poets.

Maximiliano "Max" Henríquez Ureña
(1885–1968)
Writer, Literary Critic, and Diplomat

Writer and diplomat Maximiliano "Max" Henríquez Ureña, born November 16, 1885, was exposed to an environment of cultural and intellectual ferment as a young child. He was educated at the Dominican Lyceum in Santo Domingo and started to write at an early age. At 15, he became the drama critic for *La Lucha* (The Struggle), one of the leading newspapers in the Dominican Republic. He left the Dominican Republic during in his twenties and moved to Cuba where he obtained a law degree in 1913. While in Cuba, he became the director of La Escuela Normal de Oriente (Oriente Normal School), a teachers' college, and presided over the Ateneo de la Habana (Havana Athenaeum).

Henríquez is recognized as a leading educator, journalist, literary scholar, essayist, historian, and diplomat. He founded the Dominican Academy of History and was one of the early modernist poets in the Dominican Republic. As a journalist, he was the social and literary commentator for the *Listin Diario,* one of the island's most important newspapers. His major scholarly interests were in the fields of Cuban and Dominican history, politics, and literature. During his lifetime he published dozens of books in a wide variety of literary and scholarly genres, among them: *Estados Unidos y la Repúbica Dominicana* (United States and the Dominican Republic; 1919), *La Independencia efímera* (Ephemeral Independence; 1938), *Cuentos Insulares* (Island Stories; 1949), *Anforas* (1914), *Whistler y Rodin* (Whistler and Rodin; 1906), *Panorama histórico de la literatura dominicana* (Historical Panorama of Dominican Literature; 1945), and *Panorama historico de la literatura cubana* (Historical Panorama of Cuban Literature; 1963). Henríquez also served as a career government official and diplomat. He was secretary of the presidency and secretary of education in the Dominican Republic. As a diplomat, he represented his country in the United Nations, France, Belgium and Cuba. He died in 1968.

Pedro Henríquez Ureña
(1884–1946)
Educator, Writer, and Scholar

Pedro Henríquez Ureña was the most prominent member of the Henríquez Ureña family during the twentieth century. He was a literary critic and historian, a playwright, a teacher, and a scholar. He is considered a key figure in the recognition and establishment of the field of Latin American literary criticism and the eventual recognition of Latin American studies.

Henríquez Ureña was a gifted child with a prodigious memory and capacity to learn; he published his first book of poetry *Aquí Abajo* (Down Here) in 1898, when he was just 14 years old. He completed his early education in the Dominican Republic but left in 1901 owing to the hostile political climate that permeated the island. Most of his life was spent abroad in voluntary exile. He went to New York, where he attended Columbia University and pursued studies in languages and literature.

In 1904 Henríquez Ureña moved to Cuba, where he began his early work in Latin American literary criticism. His book *Ensayos Críticos Literarios* (Essays on Literary Criticism; 1905) presented some of the first truly literary criticism of the works of Latin American writers Rubén Darío and **Eugenio María de Hostos** (Anderson 1989). In 1906 he went to Mexico, where he immediately became involved with the most promising intellectuals of the time. In 1909, he was one of the founders of a literary and intellectual society known as Ateneo de la Juventud (Youth Athenaeum) and he also was a frequent contributor to *Revista Moderna de Mexico* (Modern Review of Mexico), a literary journal. In 1914, while still in Mexico, he also obtained a law degree.

In 1915 Henríquez Ureña left Mexico and went to the United States, where he taught in the Romance Language Department of the University of Minnesota, and where he completed a Ph.D. in 1918. His doctoral dissertation, "La versificación irregular en la poesia española" (Irregular Versification in Spanish Poetry), is still considered by many a seminal work in the field of Spanish poetry. In 1923 Henríquez Ureña moved permanently to Argentina, where he occupied a chair in Latin American literature at the University of Buenos Aires and helped to organize the university's Philology Institute. While in Argentina Henríquez Ureña made very important contributions to the field of philology.

A man of universal interests, Henríquez Ureña was one of the most prolific Latin American writers, critics, and scholars. His early validation of Latin American literature by submitting Latin American authors to accepted canons of literary criticism have led to his recognition as one of the creators of the field of Latin American studies. Among his most important works are: *Ensayos Críticos Literarios* (Critical and Literary Essays; 1905), *Horas de estudio* (Study Hours; 1910), *El Nacimiento de Dionisios*, a tragedy (The Birth of Dionysus; 1916), *El libro del idioma* (The Book of Language; 1927), *Gramática Castellana* (Castilian Grammar; 1938–1939), and *Historia de la Cultura en la America Hispánica* (History of Spanish American Culture; 1947, posthumous). He died in Buenos Aires in 1946 but his books remain classics in the field of Latin American literary criticism, and his *Gramática Castellana* continues to be a standard grammar book in many Latin American countries.

Camila Henríquez Ureña
(1892–1973)
Educator, Writer, and Scholar

Camila Henríquez Ureña was the younger daughter of the Henríquez Ureña family. She was born in 1892 in Santo Domingo, just three years before the death of her mother, **Salomé**, and was raised by her father and her stepmother. When she was a child, the family moved to Cuba to avoid the political instability of the Dominican Republic. Henríquez Ureña received most of her education in Cuba, where she graduated from college. Following in the steps of her brother **Pedro**, she went on to the University of Minnesota, where in 1920 she received a master's degree in romance languages. She returned to the University of Havana, where she finished a Ph.D. in literature in 1926; in 1927 she completed a doctorate in education. She later took graduate courses at Columbia University in New York and at the University of Paris.

After graduation, Henríquez Ureña became a professor of Spanish language and Hispanic American literature at Oriente University in Cuba, Oriente's Normal School, Matanzas Normal School, La Vívora Institute, and the University of Havana. During the 1940s she started to teach in the United States at Vassar College and Middlebury College, and was a guest lecturer in the Dominican Republic, Mexico, and Argentina.

In 1942 Henríquez Ureña accepted a full-time teaching position at Vassar College in Poughkeepsie, New York, where she eventually became full professor and chair of the Spanish Department. At Vassar, she was instrumental in bringing Chilean poet and Nobel Prize–winner Gabriela Mistral to teach for a semester. In 1947 she took a one-year leave to act as advisory editor to the publishing firm Fondo de Cultura Económica (Economic Culture Fund) in Mexico City. Two years later, in 1949, she was appointed as a member of the prestigious Cuban National Commission of UNESCO (United Nations Educational, Scientific, and Cultural Organization).

After her retirement in 1959, Henríquez Ureña, a Cuban citizen, returned to Cuba

Camila Henríquez Ureña.
Photo by Joseph T. Murphy.
Special Collections, Vassar College Libraries.

205

where she devoted the rest of her life to lending her educational expertise to the **Castro** revolution. She taught at the University of Havana and participated in a number of educational initiatives. At the time of her death in 1973, she was honored in her native Santo Domingo for her contributions to the fields of literature and education. A prolific writer and scholar, Henríquez-Ureña authored four books and scores of scholarly articles. As a scholar, she was an expert on the role of women writers during the Spanish colonial period in Latin America and wrote texts as well on the works of **Eugenio María de Hostos** and on education. —S.M.M.

References and Suggested Readings

Anderson Imbert, Enrique. "Pedro Henríquez Ureña." In Carlos A. Solé, ed., *Latin American Writers*. New York: Charles Scribner's Sons, 1989. 597–601.

Carilla, Emilio. "Pedro Henríquez-Ureña: Biografía Comentada." *Revista Interamericana de Bibliografía* 27 (1966): 227–239.

Castro Ventura, Santiago. *Salomé Ureña: Jornada Fecunda*. Santo Domingo, DR: Editora de Colores, S.A., 1998.

De Lara, Juan Jacobo. *Pedro Henríquez-Ureña: Su vida y su obra*. Santo Domingo, DR: Universidad Nacional Pedro Henríquez Ureña, 1975.

González, Maritza, ed. *Camila Henríquez Ureña: Estudios y Conferencias*. Havana, Cuba: Editorial Letras Cubanas, 1982.

Henríquez-Ureña, Salome. *Poesias Completas*. Santo Domingo, DR: Publicaciones ONAP, 1985.

Herdeck, Donald, ed. "Max Henríquez Ureña" and "Pedro Henríquez Ureña." *Caribbean Writers: A Bio-Biographical Critical Encyclopedia*. Washington, DC: Three Continents Press, 1990. 746–747.

Marting, Diane E. "Salome Ureña de Henríquez." *Spanish American Women Writers: A Bio-Bibliographical Source Book*. Westport, CT: Greenwood Press, 1990. 522–531.

Moya Pons, Frank. *The Dominican Republic: A National History*. New Rochelle, NY: Hispaniola Books Corporation, 1995.

Rodríguez Demorizi, Emilio. *Salomé Ureña y el Instituto de Señoritas*. Ciudad Trujillo, DR: Impresora Dominicana, 1960.

Vassar College's File on Camila Henríquez Ureña, Vassar College Library Archive, Poughkeepisie, New York, 2000.

Rafael Hernández
(1892–1965)

Puerto Rican Composer and Bandleader

Rafael Hernández was considered the composer laureate of Puerto Rico. In his musical compositions he captured the ethos of the Puerto Rican character and society like few other composers have been able to do. Puerto Ricans consider many of his compositions alternate national anthems. Although the bulk of his work was of a romantic nature, Hernández, also known as "El Jibarito," not only expressed the wide array of emotions that characterized Puerto Rican society during his lifetime but also commented on those unique cultural traits that differentiate Puerto Ricans from other Caribbean islanders and Latin Americans.

Hernández was born on October 24, 1892, in the Tamarindo sector of Aguadilla, a coastal city located on the northwestern tip of the island. Several of the members of his mother's family were well-known musicians. In a recent documentary about his life, his sister Victoria recalls that Hernández disliked music as a young boy. When their grandmother forced him to take music classes to learn the trombone, he cut his gums so that they would bleed and told her that he had been infected with tuberculosis, a common disease of the time, so she would allow him to stop taking classes. Instead, when he was 12, she sent him to live at the house of José "Pepé" Lequerica, a music teacher. There he was forced to sleep in a small cot and share his room with a parrot that would not allow him to sleep at night (Reyes 1999). However, he learned to play the valve trombone and moved on to take violin and piano classes with Jesús Figueroa, father of the now famous Figueroa musical family of Puerto Rico. Eventually Hernández learned to play many instruments and was particularly proficient in violin, piano, clarinet and the valve trombone.

Hernández obtained his elementary education in his native Aguadilla. A man without much formal instruction, he left school during his adolescence and started to work as a cigarmaker and as a private music teacher. An adventurous soul, Hernández left Aguadilla and joined a traveling circus visiting different cities in Puerto Rico, playing the trombone for the circus orchestra. On reaching San Juan, the circus disbanded and Hernández found himself without a job. He approached several orchestras and found a job as first violin for the San Juan Symphonic Orchestra. He then moved to the San Juan Municipal Orchestra, housed at the Tapia Theater, where he played first trombone under the direction of Puerto Rican music master Juan Tizol. During this period of his professional career, Hernández often faceed the racist attitudes of his fellow Puerto Ricans, who questioned why a black Puerto Rican was playing first trombone and violin with these groups.

At the outbreak of Word War I, James Rhys, a famous African American bandleader and composer, went to Puerto Rico to recruit musicians for the U.S. military band. Hernández joined the band and traveled throughout Europe and the United States entertaining American troops. At the end of the war, Hernández returned to the United States, where he played with many different orchestras but eventually settled in New York and he started working in a screw-manufacturing plant. While working at the plant he lost a finger operating one of the machines and was awarded $500.00 as disability compensation. During this period in his career, he interacted with many Puerto Rican literary, artistic, and political personalities living in New York at the time, among them **Luis Muñoz Marín** and poet **Luis Palés Matos**. Ethnomusicologist Lise Waxer has identified Hernández's time in New York as having a profound influence on his political and social outlook. Many of the songs that he composed during the period were filled with politically suggestive lyrics that underscored the racial and music divide that the first wave of Puerto Rican immigrants were experiencing at the time (Waxer 1997).

In 1920, Hernández left New York and accepted a position in Cuba and as music director of the Fausto Theater Orchestra. He spent five years in Cuba but returned to New York and started several music groups. He organized the Trio Borínquen, recorded with Columbia Records, and eventually, along with his sister Victoria, who acted as their manager, organized the famous Conjunto Victoria. The group popularized many of Hernández's early compositions and made many important recordings while traveling throughout the United States, Latin America, and Puerto Rico.

By the mid 1930s Hernández moved to Mexico, where he lived for more than 15 years. He was initially hired to be a music director of XED, one of Mexico City's most important radio stations. He took advantage of his position at the station to organize duets of Mexican musicians that recorded, interpreted, and popularized his songs. He also used the flourishing Mexican movie industry to showcase his compositions, and even appeared in many of the popular movies of the time.

Hernández married María Pérez, a Mexican, and attended the National Conservatory of Music, where he obtained advanced training in harmony, music direction, and composition. During his stay in Mexico, he wrote scores of songs, including "Que Chula es Puebla" (The Cute Puebla), a Mexican *corrido* (a festive and upbeat type of folk music) that became the hymn of that Mexican state. He also acted as an unofficial ambassador between Mexico and the island of Puerto Rico, welcoming many Puerto Rican students, political leaders, and artists who came to Mexico. His most significant achievements in Mexico were the writing of some of his best-known important compositions and the popularization of his music throughout Latin America, the United States, and the rest of the world.

Hernández returned to Puerto Rico to a hero's welcome on June 21, 1947. Puerto Ricans recognized him as one of their most important composers and constantly honored him. He soon started work as a consultant for the government of Puerto Rico, helping to develop WIPR, the government educational broadcasting station. Hernández used his experience in the music field to plan and implement a solid music and entertainment programming schedule for the station.

It has been estimated that this notable composer wrote more than 2,000 melodies during his lifetime. His sister Victoria, a piano teacher and a well-known musician in her own right, recalls that for Hernández, the process of producing his compositions was intense. He became pensive and anxious and used to say that he had to take the song "out of his head." He sat at the piano and did not relax until he was able to interpret and record the lyrics and music (Reyes 1999).

Among Hernández's most popular compositions are "Lamento Borincano" (Borincan Lament), "Venus," "Ausencia" (Absence), "Preciosa" (Most Beautiful), "Silencio" (Silence), Campanitas de Cristal" (Crystal Bells), "Los Carreteros" (Wagoneers), "Cachita," and "Buchipluma Na'ma." His song "Lamento Boricano" is considered almost as a second Puerto Rican national anthem. It depicts the tribulations of a farmer and peasant from the poor countryside who comes to the city filled with dreams of selling his produce to buy much-needed things for his family. Failing to sell what he had brought, he returns home empty-handed and broken-hearted. This song typifies and captures, more than any other cultural text, Puerto Rico's terrible economic conditions during the Depression and before the island's commonwealth status in 1952 (Fernández, Méndez-Méndez, and Cueto 1998). Because the song deals with the plight of Puerto Rican Jíbaros (peasants), Hernández became known as "El Jibarito" for the remainder of his artistic life.

One of Hernández's most important talents was his ability to express the popular elements of Puerto Rican society, such as political orientations and cultural expectations. He was an extraordinary recorder of Puerto Rican popular culture. His song "Cuchifritos" pokes fun at the cultural differences between Puerto Ricans, Americans, and other Latin American neighbors while underscoring Puerto Rican nationalism and their love for their culture and traditions. Hernández's compositions also documented the cultural mores of Puerto Ricans during the first part of the twentieth century. Puerto Rican social cultural patterns such as "machismo" and "familismo" emerge clearly through the lyrics of his songs "Cachita" and "Buchipluma Na' Ma."

Hernández died of cancer on December 11, 1965. His death was felt across all segments of Puerto Rican society. His music has become a symbol of Puerto Rico in the United States.—S.M.M.

References and Suggested Readings

Banco Popular de Puerto Rico. "Homenaje a Rafael Hernández" (recording). San Juan, PR, December 1965.

Fernández, Ronald, Serafín Méndez-Méndez, and Gail Cueto. "Rafael Hernández." *Puerto Rico Past and Present: An Encyclopedia.* Westport, CT: Greenwood Press, 1998. 164–165.

Hernández, Rafael. *Hasta siempre.* Río Piedras: Yarav, 1981.

Mabunda, L. Mpho, and Joseph C. Tardiff, eds. "Rafael Hernández." *Dictionary of Hispanic Biography.* Detroit: Gale, 1996. 143–144.

Reyes, Edwin. *Rafael Hernández: Jibarito del Mundo* (video documentary). San Juan: Corporación Puertorriquena para la Radiodifusión, 1999.

Waxer, Lise. "Puerto Rican Musicians in New York during the Decade of the 1930s." A presentation given at Guakia, Hartford, Connecticut, July 1997.

OSCAR HIJUELOS
(1951–)

Cuban American Writer

Oscar Hijuelos, of Cuban heritage, was the first Hispanic American novelist to win a Pulitzer Prize for fiction. His award-winning novel *The Mambo Kings Play*

Songs of Love (1989) depicts the Latin music scene in the United States during the 1940s and 50s, as well as many of the aspects of Hispanic culture that surrounded and influenced him. Hijuelos has been considered one of the top U.S. writers since the early 1990s. His stories and novels explore the world of Cuban and other immigrants in the United States and often contain autobiographical passages.

He was born in New York City on August 24, 1951, to Pascual Hijuelos and Magdalena Torrens, who emigrated to the United States from Cuba in the early 1940s. He grew up in an urban environment surrounded by Latino music and culture, where family and neighbors frequently engaged in nostalgic conversations and constant references to the country left behind, which later reappeared in his work. In the 1950s, watching Cuban musician and actor Desi Arnaz in *I Love Lucy* was a weekly ritual and a source of pride for the entire family.

Hijuelos attended public schools in his upper-west-side Manhattan neighborhood and graduated from high school in 1969. He considered becoming a cartoonist, played guitar in various Latino music bands, and for a short time worked on an insect farm in Wisconsin before he enrolled in the City College of New York, where in 1975 he graduated with a degree in English literature. In 1976 he earned a master's degree in creative writing from the City University of New York. While holding a variety of jobs, which included an eight-year stint as an ad writer, he wrote and published short stories. Some of his first published work appeared in *Best of Pushcart Press III* (1978), with the short story "Columbus Discovering America" receiving a special citation from Pushcart Press. A series of awards that included a 1980 Breadloaf Writers Conference Scholarship and grants from the Creative Artists Programs Service (1982) and from the Ingram Merrill Foundation (1983) afforded him the time and financial support to write.

His first novel, *Our House in the Last World* (1983), an autobiographical portrayal of a Cuban family's experiences in the United States in the 1940s, was unusual because it looked at the life of the immigrant family rather than Cuban politics or life in exile. In addition to good reviews, he was awarded both a National Endowment for the Arts fellowship and the American Academy in Rome fellowship for Literature. The Rome award provided him with a one-year stipend and living arrangements in Italy, where he began work on *Mambo Kings*.

In 1989 he published his second novel, *The Mambo Kings Play Songs of Love*, described by a critic as a story "imbued with the rhythms of spirited and soulful musical styles" (Shirley 1995, 70). The story is told from the perspective of its male narrator, who depicts the lives of sibling musicians Cesar and Nestor Castillo who come to the United States from Havana, have a brief moment of fame and success with a cameo appearance on *I Love Lucy*, and very quickly return to obscurity. It became a bestseller and was nominated for the National Book Award and the National Book Critics Circle Award. In 1990 it was awarded the Pulitzer Prize for fiction, and in 1992 the novel was made into a feature film with the same title starring then-newcomer Spanish actor Antonio Banderas.

Hijuelos' third novel, *The Fourteen Sisters of Emilio Montez O'Brien* (1993), examines the role of women in a Cuban American family. Unlike his previous work, it is told from various female points of view and presents a setting in which women are very powerful. Although reviews were mixed, it established him as a leading Latino writer. His 1995 novel, *Mr. Ives' Christmas,* narrates the story of a man torn by the senseless murder of his son and his personal journey through his anger and grief. This novel has been heralded as one of Hijuelos' most poignant works.

His fourth novel, *Empress of the Splendid Season,* was published in 1999. It tells the story of Cuban immigrant Lydia España, a onetime debutante–turned–cleaning lady of New York apartments. Hijuelos contrasts her life with that of her employers, whose stories she uncovers as she cleans their apartments. It is a detailed look at the struggles of working-class life described by one critic as "a testament to getting through" (Caldwell 1999, H1).

In 1998 Hijuelos briefly returned to his early love of music and guitar playing. He played lead guitar and vocals on the song "I Want to Eat," which was included in a double-CD recording *Stranger Than Fiction,* a collection of 32 songs released to benefit the PEN writers' Special Fund.

Hijuelos, who says that his goal as a writer "is going back in the time and looking at our sources and where we come from" (MacNeil/Lehrer 2002), published *A Simple Habana Melody: From When the World Was Good*, a fictionalized biography of Israel Lewis, composer of the classic tune "El Manicero" (The Peanut Vendor). The book is described by reviewer Allan Turner as "Hijuelos' most focused effort since the stunning *Mambo Kings*" (Turner 2002).

On September 7, 2000, at the John F. Kennedy Center for the Performing Arts in Washington, D.C., the Latino community awarded Hijuelos with a Hispanic Heritage Award in recognition of his literary contributions.—G.C.

References and Suggested Readings

Caldwell, Gail. "A Woman in Full; Oscar Hijuelos Gives His Heroine on the 'Upper Lower Class' All the Dignity of an Empress." *Boston Globe*, February 7, 1999, H1.

Chavez, Lydia. "Cuban Riffs & Songs of Love." *Los Angeles Times,* April 18, 1993, 22.

Haygood, Wil. "Beat Author; With the Shooting of the Film Version of The Mambo Kings Play Songs of Love Starting this Winter, Pulitzer Prize-Winning Author Oscar Hijuelos Is Singing His Own Song of Success." *Boston Globe*, November 18, 1990, 18.

Hijuelos, Oscar. *The Mambo Kings Plays Songs of Love.* New York: Farrar, Straus & Giroux, 1989.

Kakutani, Michiko. "A Test of Faith for a Father Who Longs for Grace." *New York Times Book Review,* November 28, 1995, C17.

MacNeil/Lehrer Productions "The NewsHour with Jim Lehrer." August 29, 2002, Thursday. Transcript #7406.

Turner, Allen. "Hijuelos Sings Fresh Tune." *The Houston Chronicle,* June 21, 2002. *http://www.HoustonChronicle.com*. Accessed February 26, 2003.

Shirley, Paula W. "Reading Desi Arnaz in *The Mambo Kings Play Songs of Love.*" *Melus* 20:3 (Fall 1995): 69–78.

MERLE HODGE
(1944–)

Trinidadian Novelist, Essayist, Short Story Writer, and Educator

Trinidadian writer and essayist Merle Hodge has spent most of her life exploring the Caribbean cultural identity from the perspective of a post-colonial writer. In its most generic characterization, "post-colonial" is that which has been preceded by colonization. In Hodge's case, her writing portrays the influence of colonial education, language, and culture on the colonized. She uses the post-colonial encounter to reflect on gender, race, and class function as well as cultural identities of the Caribbean. Her first novel, *Crick Crack, Monkey* (1970), is considered a literary achievement. As in her later work *For the Life of Laetitia* (1993), she writes from the point of view of a child from early youth to the moment when the young adult leaves the Caribbean.

Hodge was born in Curepe, Trinidad, in 1944. She was one of four daughters and for many years lived in an extended family setting where her grandmother served as caretaker while both parents worked. She completed her primary and secondary schooling in Trinidad. In 1962, when she graduated from Bishop Antsey High School, she was awarded a Trinidad and Tobago Girls Island Scholarship that enabled her to study abroad. That same year, she left Trinidad just a few days before it achieved independence from Britain to study at London's University College. Completing her studies in French, she received a Baccalaureate in Arts with honors in 1965 and later a Master of Philosophy in 1967, writing her thesis on writer Léon Damas and the Negritude movement. (The Negritude movement seeks to recover and define the richness of black cultural values in reaction to the dominant values of European colonialism. Negritude implies the total acceptance of African heritage.)

It was during her graduate studies that Hodge began to write *Crick Crack, Monkey*, a fictional autobiographical study of the effects of colonial social and cultural values on the Trinidadian female. It is narrated from the voice of a child (Tee) who, according to Hodges, represents Caribbean culture in its infancy. In the novel we experience Tee's development from child to young woman. It presents the bittersweet experiences of a little girl growing up in Trinidad—the cultural ambivalences, the alienation and isolation she feels being torn between two worlds. During the late 1960s, while working on this novel, Hodges traveled around eastern and western Europe, supporting herself by typing and babysitting.

In the early 1970s she returned to Trinidad and taught French, English, and West Indian literature in a school in Port-of-Spain. Shortly thereafter, she was appointed lecturer in French at the Mona Campus of the University of the West Indies (UWI) in Jamaica, where she began work on her doctorate and completed the translation of *Pigments,* a collection of poetry by Damas. She left UWI in 1979 for the neighboring island of Grenada, where Prime Minister **Maurice Bishop** appointed her to a curriculum development post with the responsibility of developing a socialist education program for the island. However, Hodge was forced to flee Grenada in 1983 during the turmoil resulting from the assassination of Prime Minister Bishop and the resulting invasion of the U.S. military forces.

On her return, she worked as a freelance writer and lecturer until her appointment to the Women and Development Studies program at the University of the West Indies in Trinidad. In 1993 she published her second novel, *The Life of Laetitia,* a story about a young Caribbean girl's first year in a school away from home. This novel has been described as "at once a magical coming-of-age story and a nightmarish tale of a young girl's psychological disintegration" (Cohen 1993, 24). She provides insights into the problems faced by women who are raised in a colonialist educational system. Most critics agree that Hodge's literary impact is based on her ability to articulate through fiction and essays critical perspectives on the impact of colonialism in the Caribbean.

Hodge presently is a lecturer at the Department of Language and Linguistics at the University of West Indies, St. Augustine Campus. In addition to her novels and short stories, Hodge has written essays and articles on the Caribbean family. In her essays she argues against the imposition of Western values and social constructs to define the concept of family in the Caribbean. In her view, current sociological posits about "broken" or "fragmented" families are culturally loaded and tied to issues of social class: "The Caribbean is not a big mental asylum. What these studies are forgetting is the business of economics. Usually the people who are to be found in nuclear families are people who are economically better off" (Balutansky 1989, 656). Overall, whether through fiction or essay, Merle Hodge's writing is concerned with social justice for everyone; as she puts it: ". . . so as a society we shall have attained to a rare degree of civilization when the rich diversity of our racial and cultural characteristics implies no conflict with the fact of our being people" (Hodge 1975, n.p.).—G.C.

References and Suggested Readings

Balutansky, Kathleen. "We Are All Activists: An Interview With Merle Hodge." *Callaloo* 41 (Autumn 1989): 651–662.

Bauermeister, Jesse, Jessie Larsen, and Holly Smith. *500 Great Books by Women: A Reader's Guide.* New York: Penguin, 1994.

Campbell, Elaine, and Pierrette Fricky, eds. *The Whistling Bird.* Kingston, Jamaica: Ian Randle Publishers, 1998.

Cohen, Elizabeth. "Children's Books." *The New York Times,* May 9, 1993, 24.

Dickison, Swift Stiles. "Transnational Carnival and Creolized Garden: Caribbean Cultural Identity and Rooting in the Narratives of Sam Selvon and Merle Hodge." Doctoral Dissertation DAI, 56.6A, Washington State University, 1994.

Hodge, Merle. *Crick Crack, Monkey.* Portsmouth, NH: Heinemann, 1981.

———. "The Peoples of Trinidad & Tobago." In Michael Anthony and Andre Carr, eds., *David Frost Introduces Trinidad & Tobago.* London: André Deutsch Limited, 1975. Available online at: *http://users.rcn.com/alana.interport/hodge.html.*

Lawrence, Leota S. "Merle Hodge." In Daryl Cumber Dance, ed., *Fifty Caribbean Writers.* Westport, CT: Greenwood Press, 1986. 225–228.

Mordecai, Pamela, and Betty Wilson, eds. *Her True-True Name.* London: Heinemann International, 1990.

Simon, Gikandi. *Writing in Limbo.* Ithaca, NY: Cornell University Press, 1992.

THE HOLDER BROTHERS

Trinidadian Artists and Performers

The Holder brothers of Trinidad have been important figures in the worlds of twentieth-century art and entertainment. They have contributed to the arts through their work as painters, sculptors, musicians, dancers, and actors.

They were born to Arthur and Louis Holder and share African, French, and Irish heritages. As they grew up, they were surrounded by art at their Richmond Street house in Port-of-Spain. The Holder household was also a meeting point for art connoisseurs and artists. Their grandfather was a prominent Trinidadian artist, and their mother was an elite seamstress.

BOSCOE HOLDER
(1920–)

Trinidadian Painter, Dancer, and Pianist

Artist Boscoe Holder holds an important place in Trinidadian contemporary cultural history because of the quality of his paintings, the legacy of his dance company, and his role in showcasing the arts and culture of Trinidad and the West Indies throughout the rest of the Caribbean, the United States, and Europe.

Holder was born in Trinidad in 1920. He credits his parents as instrumental in nurturing his artistic inclinations at a time where it was uncommon for a Trinidadian child to pursue such aspirations. Holder started painting when he was in his teens. His first exhibition, at one of the fish markets in Woodbrock, Trinidad, took place in 1937.

Part of the significance of his work is not only its superb technical quality but also the fact that Holder was one of the first Caribbean painters to use and recognize the beauty and cultural elements of his native Trinidad and incorporate them into his paintings. He has devoted a lifelong career to painting that focuses on the Caribbean and Trinidadian native cultural elements and in the black women and forms that inhabit these islands. He has said: "I love painting Caribbean people, especially the women, because they are so decorative. I capture all of the Caribbean in my work, the poverty, the strong black theme, the nature, and the beauty" (Jarrette 1999, 1). He is also a noted sculptor who has sculpted since the beginning of his career. One of his first sculptures, which he still owns, is a bust of Barbadian author **George Lamming** when he was young and still living in Trinidad. Holder's work is seen as one of the prime examples of Caribbean painters and artists using the symbols and cultural products of their African ancestors to inspire their artistic production and at the same time to validate their cultures and physical landscape (Poupeye 1998).

During his adolescence, Holder made a successful incursion into the world of musical entertainment. A talented artist who played the piano at selected parties to raise money to buy art supplies, he founded the Boscoe Holder's Dance O'Trinidad company during the 1930s. His troupe played an important role in the early history of Trinidad's music because he recognized the value of the popular cultural art forms generated by the Trinidadian people and used them as part of his dance routines. For instance, he took elements of an African funeral ritual called the Limbo and created a new popular dance with it. Most people know the Limbo as a dance where people dance backwards and go underneath a stick of wood while accompanied by lively percussion beats. In the same way, his dance company recognized the value of the steel pan and calypso music and used it to orchestrate their artistic performances and to develop choreographies specially tailored around its music. His company, in fact, was the first to bring the steel pan to New York.

Like many other Trinidadian and Caribbean artists, Holder left Trinidad during the early 1950s in an attempt to expand his career and seek new horizons. He first traveled to New York and then went on to Europe, where he was credited with helping introduce both calypso music and the steel pan. He performed as a dancer at the most prestigious clubs in London and France, and also performed alongside many other famous dancers, including African American singer and dancer Josephine Baker.

Although Holder continued painting during his stay in Europe, his music was his priority there. He launched his painting career again on his return to Trinidad in the late 1960s, and his art continues to center on the native elements and surroundings of his unique West Indian landscape. He still works every day in his Woodsford Street studio, surrounded by hundreds of paintings that re-create the development and history of a long and successful career. Although many of his paintings have been sold to very important collectors from around the world and two are part of the collection of the National Museum in Washington, Holder has a tendency to keep many of them. They now decorate a recently inaugurated gallery and studio in Trinidad. His attachment to his works of art is such that Holder has told one source that he still remembers themes and circumstances that mediated the creation of each one; he considers his paintings "old friends" (Jarred 1999, 1).

Holder played a significant role as a mentor to his brother **Geoffrey**, who has stated that Boscoe was his first and the biggest artistic influence of his artistic life (Personal communication with Geoffrey Holder, November 11, 2000).

GEOFFREY HOLDER
(1930–)

Painter, Photographer, Dancer, Actor, Theatrical Director, Choreographer, and Costume Designer

Trinidadian Geoffrey Holder has been a popular personality in the American entertainment industry for the past 30 years. Although he is often recognized for his appearance in one of the popular James Bond movies and for television advertisements as the Seven-Up Uncola Man, this multitalented artist has been recognized as a high-caliber painter and photographer who has produced multiple pictorial works in a wide array of artistic media. Holder's talents have also been showcased through many artistic venues, and many people have referred to him as a true Renaissance man.

Holder was born in Port of Spain, Trinidad, in 1930. One of the defining moments in his life took place at age 15 in an episode that he calls the "grand theft" and is repeated often in his biographies. While recovering at home from a minor illness, he borrowed some of his brother **Boscoe**'s paints and artistic tools and decided to do some painting of his own. His paintings were so good that his brother called the director of the Trinidad Public Library and they decided to hold an exhibit of his newly created art. During his very first exhibit he sold his first three paintings to a physician vacationing from the United States (Holder 1995). To this day, Holder credits his brother with opening up the doors of art.

Holder attended Queens Royal College in his native Trinidad but left when he finished the fourth form to take a job as a clerk to save money to buy art supplies. Holder also started dancing at an early age with his brother's dancing company, Boscoe Holder's Dance O'Trinidad. When Boscoe left Trinidad and went to Europe, Holder was left in charge of the company and traveled with them around the West Indies and Puerto Rico between 1951 and 1952. In 1952 he attended the First Caribbean Arts Festival held in San Juan, where he was praised for his artistic abilities. Around the same time, he also participated in experimental film in Puerto Rico with Puerto Rican artists Amilcar Tirado and **Rafael Tufiño**.

In 1953, following the encouragement of artists Agnes de Mille and Walter White, and seeking to expand his artistic horizons, Holder moved to the United States and settled in New York. He quickly landed a role as a dancer in the musical adaptation of Truman Capote's *House of Flowers*, which premiered in 1954. He also had his first very successful painting exhibit at the Barone Gallery on Madison Avenue. He received a Guggenheim fellowship that allowed him to stay in the United States and study painting between 1956 and 1957. From then on, he exhibited his work at the Barone Gallery almost every year until 1969.

Holder has credited Boscoe and the many painters who visited the family home with influencing his art. He also credits the work of Haitian primitive painters such as **Hector Hyppolite**, and Mexicans Diego Rivera, Frida Khalo, and Miguel Covarrubias as being important models in his development as an artist (Holder 1995). His paintings depict Caribbean themes such as carnivals, the water, and the beaches of his native Trinidad. He also paints portraits and has done many works depicting the beauty of the black body as represented by West Indian men and women. He has painted

Geoffrey Holder.

the faces of many prominent African American entertainment figures and artists. He uses vivid and warm colors inspired by the Caribbean landscape and environment. It has been said that "for Holder, color is the voice of the voice of the universe" (Mazo and Lawrenson 1995, 10). As a painter, he has worked in a variety of artistic media; he prefers oils, but has done extensive experimentation with media such as wax to provide more depth and texture to his work. He has painted two murals; one at the Trinidad Hilton and another at the University of the West Indies in Trinidad. In recent years he has also done photographic work, exploring the uniqueness and beauty of the black human body.

During the late 1950s and 1960s, while actively painting, Holder acted at both the Metropolitan Opera and on Broadway. He participated in the musical *Showboat* and organized his own dancing company, choreographing many works, such as *Bele, Dance for Two,* and *African Suite.* He has also traveled throughout the world. In 1964, he went to France to perform with famous African American dancer Josephine Baker. He calls Paris his second home; it was there, he has stated, that his "artistic senses exploded": he had a rush of inspiration that forced him to paint day and night (Holder 1995, 54).

Holder has been involved in other aspects of the performing arts. In 1975, his work as a costume designer and as a director of the musical *The Wiz* earned him two Tony Awards. Holder's work in television commercials earned him several Clio awards, the highest distinction that the advertising industry bestows. In 1973, he played the villain Baron Samedi, a role that he played many times before in the popular James Bond movie *To Live and Let Die.* His impressive dancing routines, his costume and makeup, his portrayals of Caribbean Voodoo traditions, and

217

his deep baritone and guttural laugh delighted audiences. He has also appeared in the films *The Gold Bug, Swashbuckler, Annie, Dance Black America,* and Eddie Murphy's *Boomerang.* He is an accomplished singer and sang the song "The Beachmaster" for the film *The Pebble and the Penguin.*

Holder is as active today as he was 30 years ago. He no longer dances much because of arthritis in his hands but continues to paint and work in costume design, his favorite medium of expression, almost every day. He believes that North America has yet to appreciate the richness of the Caribbean's artistic geniuses. He believes that Haiti has the richest artistic production of any Caribbean island, but laments that American foreign policy has truly hindered artistic exports from the Caribbean and Haiti to the United States (Personal communication with Geoffrey Holder, November 11, 2001).

Holder's artistic ability has brought him many awards in addition to his Tonys, such as the United Caribbean Youth Award (1962), a Drama Desk Award (1975), a National Council of Culture and Art Award (1982), and the Harold Jackman Memorial Award (1982).—S.M.M.

References and Suggested Readings

Berman, Avis. "Architectural Digest Visits: Geoffrey Holder and Carmen de Lavallade." *Architectural Digest* (November 1985): 150–56.

"Geoffrey Holder." *American Artist* 53 (November 1989): 38–43.

Holder, Geoffrey. "Statement by the Artist." In State University of New York at Albany, *Geoffrey Holder: The Painter* (exhibition catalogue). Utica: Brodock Press, 1995. 9–30.

Jarrette, Dionne. "Boscoe Holder's Old Friends." *Trinidad Express*, August 18, 1999, Section 2, 1.

Mazo, Joseph H. "Renaissance Man." *Horizon* (June 1984): 16–25.

Mazo, Joseph H., and Helen Lawrenson. "Geoffrey Holder: Reflections on the Artist." In State University of New York at Albany, *Geoffrey Holder: The Painter* (exhibiton catalogue). Utica: Brodock Press, 1995. 31–62.

Poupeye, Veerle. *Caribbean Art.* London: Thames and Hudson, 1998.

ERIC HOLDER
(1951–)

Barbadian American Attorney and Government Administrator

In his capacity as an attorney, Barbadian American Eric H. Holder Jr. has spent most of his professional career in public service working for the U.S. Justice Department and has accomplished a series of historical firsts. From 1976 to 1988 Holder worked as a district attorney in the Public Integrity Unit of the Justice Department, where he distinguished himself as a lawyer prosecuting corruption cases. In 1988 President Ronald Reagan appointed him to a judgeship in the

Superior Court of the District of Columbia. In 1993 he became the first black U.S. attorney for the District of Columbia, and in 1997 he was appointed to the post of deputy U.S. attorney general and became the highest-ranking black person in U.S. law enforcement history. A longtime resident of Washington, D.C., he is a very active and visible presence in community affairs, and it is speculated that he may run for public office some day. In his exemplary career as a judge, U.S. attorney, and deputy attorney general, Holder has been instrumental in leading initiatives involving new technology crimes, health care fraud, racial profiling, and Internet pornography and children, as well as efforts to increase diversity in the Department of Justice and the profession as a whole.

Holder was born on January 21, 1951, in New York City to Barbadian immigrants Eric "Sonny" Holder Sr. and Miriam Holder. He was raised in a working-class section of Queens, New York, where his father, after a series of jobs, went into real estate, and his mother worked as a church secretary in order to keep a close eye on her two sons, Eric and William. In the fourth grade, Holder was identified as a gifted student and was transferred from his mostly black elementary school to a mostly white one. Describing his first day at that school he has said: "Everybody knew everybody, and nobody was a Negro. I was feeling awkward when this kid, Frank Sardelis, walked to me and put out his hand" (Locy 1996, A01). That experience impacted the rest of his life and helped him to deal with a society where racial dynamics are still dismaying and complex. "This issue of race can, if you let it, permeate your life in a way that can be crippling. But I don't let it do that to me" (Locy 1996, A01). Holder graduated from Stuyvesant High School, an academically elite and competitive public school in Manhattan, where his high scores earned a Regents Scholarship, allowing him to attend first-rate institutions of higher education.

He received his undergraduate degree from Columbia College in 1973 and completed his legal education at Columbia University School of Law. His active involvement in the African American community began at Columbia, where he majored in American history and earned top grades. During that time he began mentoring young blacks at a Harlem youth center and joined the Concerned Black Men, a national organization that focuses on improving the lives of minority youngsters. Later, in law school he clerked at the National Association for the Advancement of Colored People (NAACP) and at the U.S. Department of Justice's Criminal Division.

After completing his law degree in 1976 he began working with the Department of Justice in Washington, D.C., as part of the attorney general's Honors Program. Holder was assigned to its newest division, the Public Integrity Unit, where he was charged with prosecuting high-level corruption cases, at times involving well-known political figures. His participation in local, state, and federal corruption cases included prosecutions of top officials such as the treasurer of the state of Florida, the ambassador to the Dominican Republic, a Philadelphia judge, agents of the Federal Bureau of Investigation, and a high-level member, or "capo," of an organized crime family.

In October 1988, President Ronald Reagan nominated him to become associate judge of the Superior Court of the District of Columbia, a nomination that was approved by the legislature and one that involved him in a wide range of cases that included homicides and crimes of violence. Saundra Torry of the *Washington Post* summarized his tenure as a superior court judge: "Holder has spent more than five years on the Superior Court bench, where he has gained the respect of prosecutors and defense attorneys as a bright, capable judge who never allowed his prosecution roots to affect his decisions on the bench" (1993, B1).

In 1993, President Bill Clinton appointed Holder U.S. attorney for the District of Columbia, the first African American to hold a position presiding over the only U.S. attorney's office in the nation that prosecutes both federal and local crimes. Although a Democrat, Holder's integrity and commitment to the law above partisan politics was proven six months after his appointment, when, in a very publicized case, he sought and secured a 17-count indictment against House Ways and Means Committee chairman Democrat Dan Rostenkowski in June 1994. With the goal of more effectively handling family violence cases, he created a new Domestic Violence Unit, implementing a community prosecution program that worked hand-in-hand with members of the community and municipal government. His efforts helped community and local governments focus on improving neighborhood safety and developed strategies to improve the way child abuse cases were handled. He launched a new community outreach program that better connected the people of the community with the U.S. attorney's office; his program has been used as a model for other cities in the country.

In 1997, Holder's place in American history was sealed when he was appointed the first African American deputy attorney general of the United States. He was confirmed by a 100 to 0 vote in the Senate and was sworn in by Attorney General Janet Reno on July 18. In his position as deputy attorney general, Holder was responsible for the supervision and day-to-day operation of the Department of Justice. One of his first projects was the establishment of the department's Children Exposed to Violence Initiative. He also emphasized enforcement efforts in health care fraud and computer crimes. As was the case in his earlier roles in the department, Holder continued to advocate for the concept of community prosecution, allowing prosecutors to connect more directly with the citizenry.

Holder has also been active in community groups, particularly Concerned Black Men, the organization he had come to know well while a law student in New York. He is concerned with youth issues, including teenage pregnancy and low educational achievement. As a historian, Holder advocates studying history in order to grasp the present and understands the importance he plays as a role model to minority youth. "History can be used as a tool to understand a present that at times seems frightening and illogical," he remarked in a keynote speech for African American Month Celebration in 1997, where he also cited the names of Frederick Douglas, Marian Anderson, and Rosa Parks as other African Americans who have achieved notable and significant accomplishments (Tell 1997).

The end of his tenure as the second-in-command at the Justice Department was marred by his connection to President Bill Clinton's last-day-in-office pardon of Marc Rich, a wealthy commodities dealer who had fled the United States 17 years earlier just before federal prosecutors brought charges against him for alleged tax fraud, racketeering, and trading with enemy countries. Holder was implicated in this last-minute pardon for his response to the White House inquiry regarding the Rich matter. There is much speculation regarding the effect this may have on Holder's prospects for a future in public life. Unable to remain at the Justice Department as acting attorney general until John Ashcroft's confirmation, he went into private law practice as a partner in the law firm Covington and Burling, where he is a litigant in white-collar crime and trial practice, and occasionally appears on talk shows addressing current affairs.—G.C.

References and Suggested Readings

Johnson, Anne Janette. "Eric H. Holder, Jr." In L. Mpho Mabunda, ed., *Contemporary Black Biography: Profiles form the International Black Community.* Vol. 9. New York: Gale, 1995. 118–120.

Locy, Toni. "D.C. Politics Beacons, Repels Holder; Racial Tensions Have Chilling Effect on Prosecutor's Ambitions." *Washington Post,* December 21, 1996, A01.

Slevin, Peter. "A Rush to Judgment; Eric Holder's Future, Once Assured, Is Marred by the Case of Marc Rich." *Washington Post,* March 1, 2001, C01.

Tell, Bernice. "U.S. Attorney Urges Responsible Behavior, Eric Holder Delivers African American Keynote." *Library of Congress Information Bulletin* 56.4 (February 24, 1997): n.p. *http://www.loc.gov/loc/lcib/970224/web/contents.html.*

Torry, Saundra. "Black Judge Nominated as U.S. Attorney; Confirmation of Holder Would Be First for D.C." *Washington Post,* July 30, 1993, B1.

LORENZO HOMAR
(1913–)

Puerto Rican Painter and Graphic Artist

Lorenzo Homar is one of the central figures of mid-twentieth-century Puerto Rican visual arts. Although Homar has produced a large number of works in a diverse array of artistic media, his greatest contribution to the Puerto Rican arts has been through his posters and printed engravings. In fact, he is considered to be the leading figure in the internationalization of the genre of Puerto Rican posters. His role as graphic artist has been complemented by his role as a teacher and mentor for other Puerto Rican artists. As the leading figure behind the artistic movement known as "Generación del Cincuenta" (Generation of the Fifties), Homar helped to define the nature and character of Puerto Rican graphic arts during the twentieth century.

Homar was born on September 10, 1913, in San Juan to Lorenzo Homar and Margarita Gelabert, who had emigrated to Puerto Rico from Spain. His family valued art and had artistic inclinations. His father was a film distributor in Puerto Rico and his mother was a pianist

As a young child Homar attended schools in Spain, where his parents relocated briefly during his childhood, and also attended local schools in his native San Juan. When he was 15 years old, his family moved to New York. Their arrival in New York coincided with the Great Depression and Homar was forced to leave school and go to work in order to help support his family (Vázquez Zapata 2001). Meanwhile, he continued pursuing his interests in the arts and received athletic training as a gymnast and acrobat at the YMCA. While he would have liked to become a musician, the lack of economic resources hindered him from receiving musical training at an early age.

In 1931, Homar enrolled in New York's Art Student's League. He was taught by the noted artist George Bridgeman, who encouraged Homar to expose himself to as many artistic influences as possible in order to develop an artistic style of his own (García Cuevas 2001). While continuing with his athletic interests, Homar focused on the development of his artistic abilities. By 1937 he had become an apprentice at the internationally known jewelry company Cartier. Working with one of their master designers, Ernest Loth, Homar acquired key engraving skills that he used later in the development of his own art. After he finished his training he continued to work for Cartier and took some courses at Pratt Institute in New York.

World War II interrupted his career. Homar volunteered for the war effort and joined the U.S. armed forces. He traveled the Orient, earning a Purple Heart after being wounded in conflict. On returning from the war, he resumed his career at Cartier and attended art classes offered at of the Brooklyn Museum of Art. While there, Homar was taught by some of the most accomplished artists of the time, such as Mexican muralist Rufino Tamayo, Ben Shahn, Arthur Osver, and Gabor Peterdi.

In 1950 Homar returned to Puerto Rico, where his career as an artist quickly developed and flourished. From the moment of his arrival, Homar and his art have been a constant in the artistic circles of Puerto Rico. In that year he had his first successful art exhibit at the Puerto Rican Athenaeum, one of the leading artistic and intellectual organizations on the island. That same year, he helped to establish the Center for Puerto Rican Arts, an organization that provided opportunities for Puerto Rican artists.

One of Homar's first and most important experiences in Puerto Rico was his work within the Community Education Division of the Puerto Rico Department of Education (DIVEDCO). Former governor **Luis Muñoz Marín** had established this department in 1949 to aid community development for poor Puerto Ricans. Through distribution of educational materials such as films, booklets, and posters, DIVEDCO launched broad initiatives to assist and educate poor Puerto Ricans. When Homar first joined the DIVEDCO in 1951, he worked as a poster-maker and illustrator for many of the projects in development. Some of his co-workers were talented artists who were beginning their artistic careers and who later became some of the most notable Puerto Rican artists and intellectuals of the time. Among them were filmmaker and photographer Jack Delano, writers José Luis González and Pedro Juan Soto, and fellow graphic artists **Rafael Tufiño** and Isabel Bernal. Homar was promoted to head of the graphic arts department in 1952.

Throughout the 1950s, Homar continued a process of rich artistic production. His engravings of native Puerto Rican images were widely acclaimed by art critics and collectors. The posters that he created to promote films, books, and projects at DIVEDCO have become unique historic testimonials to the legacy of this organization. His colorful posters are filled with rich images blended with fine engravings and calligraphy. Homar's ability to capture Puerto Rican realities through his work and to beautifully represent Puerto Rican history, culture, and social realities have made him the leader and one of the most important figure in the development of the poster as a medium of artistic, educational, and political expression. Equally important, as head of DIVEDCO, Homar encouraged and helped to launch a unique artistic ferment in the Puerto Rican arts establishment. Through his work and through his support of other artists he assisted in recreating and reclaiming the richness and uniqueness of Puerto Rican heritage and culture.

In 1957 Homar received a Guggenheim Fellowship and was asked by the government to organize the Graphic Arts Workshop at the Institute of Puerto Rican Culture. Once again, Homar helped to build another venue to teach art and promote and encourage the talents of scores of Puerto Rican artists. He served as the workshop's director until he retired in 1973.

After his retirement, Homar continued a period of prolific artistic production, exhibiting his work in art exhibitions around Latin America, the Caribbean, the United States, and Europe. His work is in the collections of the Metropolitan Museum of Art and the Library of Congress. In 1978 the Ponce Museum of Art had the first full retrospective exhibit of his art. In 1987 the University of Puerto Rico awarded him with an honorary doctorate in arts. In September 2001, the Museum of Art at the University of Puerto Rico opened the exhibit "Abra Palabra ... La Letra Mágica: Carteles de Lorenzo Homar 1951–1990," which displayed 150 of Homar's posters. A biographic sketch of the author issued in the catalogue of the recently opened Museum of Puerto Rico in San Juan best captures Homar's significance within Puerto Rican arts when it says: "Homar is one of the most important figures of the Generation of the '50s and is recognized as the innovator and towering figure of the significant graphic arts tradition" (Ruiz de Fischler and Trelles 2000, 378–379).—S.M.M.

References and Suggested Readings

García Cuevas, Eugenio. "Itinerario del Maestro: Homar, mago del cartel." *El Nuevo Día* (San Juan), September 9, 2001, n.p.

Gaya-Nuño, Juan Antonio. *La pintura puertorriqueña.* Soria, Spain: Centro de Estudios Sorianos, 1984.

Roylance, Dale. "The Art of Lorenzo Homar." *Caligraphy Review* 11 (1994): 34–37.

Ruiz de Fischler, Carmen Teresa, and Mercedes Trelles. "Lorenzo Homar." *Treasures of Puerto Rican Paintings* (Catalogue to an Arts Exhibit). San Juan: Museo de Arte de Puerto Rico, 2000. 378–379.

Vázquez Zapata, Larissa. "Lorenzo Homar: Amante de la Letra." *El Nuevo Día* (Puerto Rico), "Revista del Domingo," September 16, 2001, 10–12.

EUGENIO MARÍA DE HOSTOS
(1839–1903)

Puerto Rican Patriot, Educator, Philosopher, and Humanist

Eugenio María de Hostos is known to many as the "Citizen of the Americas." His life was a long pilgrimage throughout Europe, the United States, and Latin America advocating liberty for the Greater Antilles and spreading a message of civility, pluralism, and social justice for their people. He was a prolific author who wrote some of the most significant nineteenth-century philosophical, sociological, and educational works from Latin America. Hostos devoted his life to promote the unity of Latin American people and to endorsing a set of ideals that would enhance their lives and encourage the uniqueness of their culture and spirit. His work in the area of pedagogy helped to shape educational institutions in several Latin American countries. Hostos was one of the first Latino intellectuals to support the rights of women to receive a quality education. He criticized the inhumane treatment of Chinese immigrants in Peru at a time when no one else was reflecting on the evils of labor exploitation. A visionary man, he promoted the idea of a Trans-Andean rail line long before it was built. As a jurist, he wrote innovative treatises on constitutional law. His critical essay on *Hamlet* is still considered to be one of the most complete critiques of Shakespearean literature.

Eugenio María de Hostos was born on January 11, 1839, in the Las Cañas precinct of Mayagüez, Puerto Rico. His father, Eugenio de Hostos y Rodríguez, had been appointed by the Spanish Queen as a scribe, a sort of notary, who also had investments in agriculture. His mother was María Hilaria Bonilla. She raised eight children and provided for their early education.

Hostos attended the small schools of Doña Rafaela and Domingo Pratts for his elementary education. In 1847 he was sent to San Juan, where he studied at a lyceum headed by Jerónimo Gómez de Sotomayor, where he obtained some of his elementary education. His family later sent him to Spain to live with relatives so he could study at the Instituto de Segunda Enseñanza in Bilbao. He graduated in 1856 and the following year began law studies at Madrid's Central University.

While studying law, Hostos surrounded himself with many Puerto Rican friends who were also studying in Spain. They shared a common concern: the 400-year colonial status of Puerto Rico. The economic condition of the island was precarious, and independence from Spain was seen as the main way to improve the quality of life. Hostos worked on behalf of the independence of Puerto Rico and Cuba. At the same time, he became frustrated by the conservative mentality of his professors and by the crudeness of their educational methods. Not wanting to obtain a law degree from a colonial power, he abandoned his law studies and worked full-time on the liberation of the islands.

Hostos wrote in favor of Puerto Rico's and Cuba's independence both in Madrid and in Barcelona. In 1863 he published his epic novel *La peregrinación de Bayoán* (Bayoán's Pilgrimage), in which he condemned the colonial situation of the Greater Antilles and stressed the importance of political self-determination for the Spanish colonies in the Caribbean. Although Hostos showed his love and admiration for Spain, the issue of colonialism was not negotiable. Like the West Indian Federation advocated by Great Brit-

Eugenio María de Hostos.
Courtesy of Raúl Medina Collection.

ain and the British West Indies later in the twentieth century, Hostos believed in the viability of an Antillean Federation that would group islands of the Spanish Antilles. He thought that with a federation, Cuba, the Dominican Republic, and Puerto Rico could develop autonomous governments but maintain a positive relationship with Spain.

In 1869 Hostos went to New York to work on behalf of Cuban independence. He believed that the independence of Cuba was the first strategic step in obtaining independence for other Antilles. He corresponded with Cuban patriot **José Martí** and they exchanged ideas about the liberation of Cuba. He directed *La Revolución*, a publication advocating the independence of Cuba. Disenchanted with many Cuban leaders in New York who shifted their ideological position and wanted to join the United States, Hostos traveled through Latin America to raise awareness and gain support for the independence of the Greater Antilles. His travels lasted four years and took him to Panama, Colombia, Peru, Chile, Argentina, and Brazil. Hostos supported himself by working as a newspaper editor and continued publishing many essays and books. In building alliances with political leaders and intellectuals through Latin America, he gathered backing for his cause and advocated for specific concerns in the countries that he visited. He finally returned to New York in 1874.

Between 1875 and 1878 Hostos participated in a number of failed revolutionary campaigns aimed at gaining independence for Cuba and Puerto Rico. After spending time in the Dominican Republic and Venezuela, where he married and worked as an educator, he returned to New York but abandoned his efforts on behalf of Cuban independence. Cuban revolutionary leaders had signed the Pacto del Zanjón (Pact of Zanjón), in which they capitulated after the Ten Years War against Spanish forces. Disillusioned by their "betrayal" of the Cuban revolution, he abandoned his efforts and went to the Dominican capital, where he undertook some of the most important educational work of his lifetime.

In 1890 Hostos and **Salomé Ureña de Henríquez** co-founded La Escuela Normal de Santo Domingo. This school was the first institution of higher education exclusively for women in the Caribbean and one of the first in Latin America. A strong believer in educational equality, Hostos contributed to the formation of a strong curriculum based on the sciences, mathematics, and liberal arts. His teaching methods opposed the rote learning prevalent at the time and stressed the development of critical thinking skills among school-age children and university students. He also believed in enhancing students' lives through extracurricular activities and athletics and believed in using inductive and deductive thinking methods to educate well-rounded students. Hostos was also a professor of law at the National University of Santo Domingo, where he taught and published *Lecciones de Derecho Constitucional* (Lessons in Constitutional Law) in 1887. The award-winning book was recommended by many legal organizations and became the text of choice in many law schools throughout Latin America. He also published *Moral Social* (1888), which is considered one of the premier sociological treatises on the social problems of Latin America.

After a change of governments in the Dominican Republic in 1888, Hostos was forced to leave the island. He sought refuge in Chile for ten years, where he taught law and replicated much of the educational work that he had done in the Dominican Republic.

Hostos' political career resurged during the Spanish-American War. After Spain and the United States signed the Treaty of Paris and Puerto Rico was transferred as a war bounty to the United States, Hostos became active in New York with groups seeking Puerto Rican independence. He organized La Liga de Patriotas (League of Patriots) to stand against further colonial oppression of Puerto Rico by the United States. He wanted Puerto Ricans to have the option of a plebiscite to determine their own political future. Hostos was selected as one of a three-member commission to go before President William McKinley in 1899 to advocate self-determination for Puerto Rico. The president and Congress ignored them. Hostos then went to Puerto Rico and gave a series of lectures on independence for the island. As a jurist, he saw the issue as one of both constitutional and international law. There was ample legal precedent for the idea that a people of a country do not have to submit to colonial domination against their will. He published *The Puerto Rican Case* (1899), a compilation of essays setting forth his arguments against the colonial status of Puerto Rico.

Frustrated by Puerto Rico's status, Hostos left in 1900 and once again went to the Dominican Republic. He was asked to reorganize and strengthen the educational system of the island in line with his educational philosophy. During this stay he worked to restructure the general public educational system and founded several institutions of higher learning and graduate programs. He died there on August 11, 1903.

Hostos' legacy goes far beyond his political advocacy on behalf of the independence of Spanish colonies in America. A brilliant thinker and writer, he produced an extensive body of literature that expresses a philosophy, sociology, and psychology uniquely Latin American, which has been labeled "El Pensamiento Hostoniano" (Hostonian thought). His extensive body of scholarly works, comprising 20 volumes, was collected by Dominican poet **Juan Bosch** as part of the 100th anniversary of Hostos' birth in 1939. His teachings inform Puerto Rican and Latin American thinking to this day. During the 1990s, a group of Puerto Rican jurists from his native town of Mayagüez established a law school that uniquely incorporates Hostos' teachings, bringing his philosophy to the education of modern legal scholars.—S.M.M.

References and Suggested Readings

Bosch, Juan. *Hostos, el sembrador.* 3rd ed. Santo Domingo, DR: Editora Alfa y Omega, 1979.

Figueroa, Loida. *Hostos, el angustiado.* Río Piedras, PR: Comité del Sesquicentenario de Eugenio María de Hostos, 1988.

Hostos, Eugenio María de. *Complete Works.* Río Piedras, PR: Gordon Press. 1979.

———. *La peregrinación de Bayoán.* Reprint. Río Piedras, PR: Editorial de la Universidad de Puerto Rico, 1988.

Lautaro de Hostos, Bayoán. *Eugenio María de Hostos Intimo.* Reprint. Santo Domingo, DR: Ediciones Librería La Trinitaria, 2000.

Maldonado Denis, Manuel. *América, la lucha por la libertad: Eugenio María de Hostos; Estudio preliminar.* San Juan, PR: Ediciones Compromiso, 1988.

Pedreira, Antonio S. *Hostos: Ciudadano de América.* San Juan, PR: Instituto de Cultura Puertorriqueña, 1964.

HECTOR HYPPOLITE
(1894–1948)

Haitian Painter

Hector Hyppolite is the painter most responsible for the introduction of exuberant colors, vivid primitive images, oversized figures and religious iconography into modern Haitian painting. He is considered to be the most influential Haitian painter of the first part of the twentieth century. His work, a precursor of the primitive art movement, marked an important stage in the development of Haitian art.

Hector Hyppolite was born on September 16, 1894, in the town of Saint Marc in Haiti. He was a self-made artist with little or no education who worked most of his life as an apprentice cobbler, an innkeeper, and a house painter. His roots were firmly entrenched in the traditions of the voodoo religion where, like most of his male forebears, he was a voodoo priest. Some art historians have mentioned the possibility that he may have traveled to Africa at some point in his early life. If so, this may explain how he may have been exposed to African art, traces of which can be found in his paintings. Nevertheless, most of his biographers and critics assert that his alleged trips to Africa were invented by the painter to add validity to the religious imagery that distinguishes his work (Roberts 1997). What appears true, however, is that for most of his adult life he worked as an itinerant house painter and as a decorative painter of house doors. This was his closest connection to art.

Hyppolite's presence in Haitian arts can be traced back to painting postcards for American marines stationed in Haiti during the U.S. invasion of the island. Around 1945, Phillip Toby Marcelin, a famous Haitian writer, saw a series of paintings that Hyppolite had done to decorate a bar. Amazed by his talents Marcelin persuaded him to move to Port-au-Prince and become involved with Haiti's Centre d'Art (Art Center), which was responsible for the development of primitive painting in Haiti. Hyppolite started working at the center, where he quickly became one of its most popular artists. His art was promoted and he became the central artist behind Haiti's emerging primitive and naturalistic art movements. From the moment that Hyppolite joined the center until his death three years later, he produced a formidable number of paintings; estimates range between 250 and 600 paintings, but only about 80 of those remain today (Roberts 1997).

His art was primitive and simple in style. He has been commended for the "sophistication of his thinking and his outstanding ability to translate a complex message into visual terms" (Stebich 1978, 73). His paintings, created with bright, strong, and forceful colors, are well balanced. His art is rudimentary and has the simplicity of school drawings, with thick lines and overblown features and traits. There are no smooth transitions or demarcations between areas within the paintings. Mistakes and lack of precision are evident in his work. These imperfections quickly become invisible due to the brilliance and impressionistic traits of the overall work.

Although Hyppolite also painted secular works of an excellent quality, his most important work had religious connotations. During his process of creation, Hyppolite claimed to be in a state of hypnotic trance, possessed by the spirit of John the Baptist (Poupeye 1998). Whether this is true, the fact is that religion is central, if not inherently fundamental, to his artistic expression. As a voodoo priest, he depicted deities central to his religion; his pictures, regardless of their primitive quality, reflect the mysticism with which the painter paid homage to voodoo spirits and saints. His pictures, which often have a surreal character, evoke contemplation or fear in the viewer. The sheer simplicity of his images makes them extremely powerful.

In 1947, one year before his death, Hyppolite's work was exhibited at the headquarters of UNESCO (United Nations Educational, Scientific and Cultural Organization) in Paris. Although he only lived for a short period after his artistic abilities unfolded, Hyppolite enjoyed his success and the homage his fellow countrymen paid him. He traveled to Cuba, New York, and Africa to exhibit his work. His paintings, considered priceless, now belong to some of the most prestigious collections in the world including the Metropolitan Museum of Art in New York. This extraordinary artist has inspired, and continues to inspire, generation after generation of Haitian artists who copied his technique, emulated his style, and followed his path. He died of a heart attack on June 9, 1948.—S.M.M.

References and Suggested Readings

Hoffman, L.G. "Hector Hyppolite." *Haitian Art: The Legend and Legacy of the Naïve Tradition.* Davenport, IA: Beaux Arts Fund Committee, 1985. 237.

Lewis, Samella. *Caribbean Visions: Contemporary Painting and Sculpture.* Alexandria, VA: Art Services International, 1995.

Poupeye, Veerle. *Caribbean Art.* London: Thames and Hudson. 1998.

Roberts, Brady. "Hector Hyppolite." In Thomas Riggs, ed., *St. James Press Guide to Black Artists.* Detroit: St. James Press, 1997. 262–263.

Stebich, Ute, ed. "Hector Hyppolite." *Haitian Art.* New York: Harry N. Abrams, 1978.

Yonkers, Dolores. "Hector Hyppolite." In Jane Turner, ed., *Encyclopedia of Latin American and Caribbean Art.* New York: Grove's Dictionaries, 1999. 354–355.

C.L.R. JAMES
(1901–1989)

Trinidadian Writer, Political Activist, Political Philosopher, and Social, Cultural, and Political Commentator

Cyril Lionel Robinson James has been recognized as one of the leading Caribbean writers and ideologists of the twentieth century. His literary work provided some of the most insightful interpretations of the social and political dynamics shaping Caribbean life, culture, and society. As a Marxist philosopher, James discussed the importance of class struggles and class exploitation in the political and social development of the Caribbean. Although he spent most of his adult life in Great Britain, a number of his writings and works are concerned with the Caribbean. He was a productive writer who wrote critical essays, short stories, journalistic pieces, and plays.

James was born on January 4, 1901, in Caroni, Trinidad, to Robert Alexander James, a schoolteacher and principal, and Ida Elizabeth James. Although the family depended solely on the father's salary and lacked economic resources, the father's job did give them professional standing in the community. James, one of three children, was raised in an extended family that included his grandmother, aunts, and cousins. His parents were strict disciplinarians who instilled in him the values of learning and respect and made clear to James that they expected that he would succeed in life.

James, known as Nello to his family and friends, was tutored by his father when he was a child and attended the local school in the neighboring town of North Trace, where his dad was one of his teachers. His mother was a voracious reader who encouraged James to read and introduced him to such classic writers as William Shakespeare, Charles Dickens, Rudyard Kipling, and the Brontë sisters during his childhood (Worcester 1996). By the age of eight, James' father recognized his son's superb intellectual skills. He tutored him for one of the prestigious "Island Scholarships" offered by the government to attend the elite Queens Royal College in Trinidad. James passed the required examinations and entered Queens Royal College in 1911. While there, he developed an interest in writing and in sports developing a lifelong passion for cricket; he later became a historian and critic of the sport. James also studied language and was proficient in French, Latin, and classical Greek. The school emphasized European values and minimized or ignored Caribbean history and life.

After graduating in 1918, James worked as a schoolteacher in Trinidad. He worked at many schools including Queens Royal College. He also tutored private students in his spare time. One of these students was **Eric Williams**, future prime minister of Trinidad and Tobago. During this period, James continued his interest in literature and decided to become a writer. His parents opposed the idea on the grounds that it did not allow for a prosperous life. Nevertheless, he began publishing short stories and essays in the literary journals of the time such as *The Beacon*. One of his first significant literary works was the short story "La Divina Pastora" (The Divine Pastor), published in *The Saturday Evening Review* in 1927. Much of his early work focused on the lives and problems of the poor and on the local Trinidadian landscape but lacked the political focus that he developed later in life.

James wrote the novel *Minty Alley* in 1928, which was published in London in 1936 and was considered somewhat superficial. His first substantive political work was *The Life of Captain Cipriani: An Account of the British Government in the West Indies* in 1932. It profiled the life of Arthur Andrew Cipriani, a soldier, labor leader, and politician who was a defender of the rights of the poor and the working class in Trinidad. The book made a serious attempt to discuss issues affecting poor workers in Trinidad, criticizing the British colonial government and holding it accountable for the oppression of poor people in the West Indies.

Despite the fact that James' literary career was growing and he was being recognized as a promising writer in Trinidad, James moved to Great Britain in 1932. James was fascinated with the popular philosophy of Marxism and began to study it. He saw a link between the philosophical postulates of Marxism, historical determinism, and the different social phenomena that he had observed in the Caribbean. He secured a job as a cricket correspondent for the *Manchester Guardian* where he worked from 1932 to 1938 while continuing his studying of Marxism. He joined the Independent Political Party and edited the journal *Fight!* He also wrote about the political philosophy of Russian leader Leon Trotsky.

During his years in England, James met many prominent African intellectuals and learned about a political movement known as Pan-Africanism, which advocated the return of blacks to Africa. Promoters of this philosophy believed that Western civilization had originated in Africa, but that through a process of oppression and exploitation Greece and Rome had gained control of Western thought. Pan-Africanists believed that if blacks were to gain equality, they needed to develop social, political, and economic institutions of their own, and so encouraged people to move to Africa. James empathized with Pan-Africanists and saw a link between their message and his Marxist doctrines. He worked with them and edited the journal *International African Opinion*, which was produced by the International African Service Bureau. The organization included a large number of vocal speakers who wrote against British imperialist policies in Africa and the Caribbean. The journal was used as a platform to spread the message of Pan-Africanism and the message of independence for Africa and for the West Indies.

James became a central fixture of radical political circles and impressed people with his deep knowledge of Marxism and the dynamics of oppressed people in Africa, America, and the West Indies. While he was extremely busy publishing political pieces in journals and newspapers of the time, he also remained committed to literature. His most important publications of the times were the play *Toussaint L'Overture* (1936), *World Revolution, 1917–1936: The Rise and Fall of the Communist International* (1937), and *The Black Jacobins: Toussant L'Overture and the San Domingo Revolution* (1938). In these works he tried to demonstrate that Marxist philosophies and precepts could be applied to the circumstances of Africa and Caribbean societies. Class struggles, imperialism, and exploitation are common elements in his works of the time, and by 1938 James had become a central figure in British literary and political circles.

In 1938, James visited the United States to spread the doctrines of Leon Trotsky. His trip was partially sponsored by the Socialist Workers Party (SWP), which intended to have James lecture throughout the United States. In the American south, he witnessed the terrible racial inequities then prevalent. While class and labor exploitation continued to be important issues, the painful exploitation of black Americans and racial inequalities also became an important issue for him. After the lectures concluded, James stayed in New York, where he wrote for the journals *New International* and *Socialist Appeal.* He was against World War II and was a constant speaker on behalf of class reforms. He thought that the inequities in the world, which led to wars and to racial oppression, could be solved if the masses took control of governments and the means of production.

Instead of returning to Great Britain, James stayed in the United States, where he became involved with labor unions and wrote a manuscript titled *American Civilization,* which presented a cultural critique of America from a socialist viewpoint. James slowly moved away from Trotsky's views on socialism and moved closer to a more mainstream Marxist view.

Throughout the late 1940s and early 1950s James faced problems with American immigration authorities, who accused him of staying illegally in the country.

The real reasons for pursuing James were his political views; he was seen as a communist. In 1953, he was arrested and imprisoned at Ellis Island and was later deported to England. His book *Mariners, Renegades, and Castaways: The Story of Herman Melville and The World We Live In* (1953) was written during this period. The book provides an interesting interpretation and analysis of Melville's *Moby-Dick* within the context of socialist ideology and Marxist theoretical constructs.

The British political landscape had changed considerably since the end of the war. The general appeal of Marxism and Trotsky's ideas had diminished and true socialism had vanished. Instead, James found himself attracted to the political fervor of his fellow West Indians who were advocating for the independence of the Caribbean.

In 1956, Eric Williams, James's former student, established the People's National Movement (PNM) in Trinidad. His party won the elections that same year and Williams became chief minister of the island. Trinidad joined the Federation of the West Indies in 1958. Williams invited James to return to Trinidad in 1958, and he accepted. After his arrival, he joined the PNM and began to write political commentaries supporting the new government in the printed media. He also represented Trinidad in the Federal Labor Party at the Federation of the West Indies.

As a committed socialist, James tried to influence the political agenda of the party and became an advocate for a major restructuring of Trinidad's social orders. The island's power elite and the British colonial authorities were not ready for his radicalism. Williams disagreed with James and saw him as a potential dissenter. He was forced to leave Trinidad in 1962 under threats of imprisonment by the Williams government.

Although James later returned to Trinidad, his relationship with Williams never recovered; he spent most of the remainder of his life in Great Britain. He maintained a visible profile in academic circles and continued to produce provocative writings in many different fields. He wrote more than ten other books in the remaining years of his life. Among them were *Beyond a Boundary* (1963), *Nkrumah and the Ghana Revolution* (1977), *Black Nationalism and Socialism* (1979), and *Cricket* (1986). James died in England on May 31, 1989. At the time of his death, fellow Trinidadian writer **George Lamming** referred to him as an evangelist (Lamming 1992). His book *American Civilization*, based on a manuscript that he had developed during the 1950s in the United States, was published posthumously in 1993. He remains one of the most important West Indian writers and intellectuals of the twentieth century.—S.M.M.

References and Suggested Readings

Buhl, Paul. *C.L.R. James: The Artist as Revolutionary.* London: Verso, 1988.

Folkcart, Burt A. "C.L.R. James; Marxist Philosopher, Author Expelled from the United States in 1953." *Los Angeles Times*, June 3 1989, 30.

Grimshaw, Anna. "C.L.R. James: A Revolutionary Vision for the 20th Century." New York: C.L.R. James Institute and Cultural Correspondence and Smyrna Press, 1991.

Henry, Paget and Paul Buhle. *C.L.R. James's Caribbean.* Durham, N.C.: Duke University Press, 1992.

Lamming, George. "C.L.R. James, Evangelist." *Conversations*. London: Karia Press, 1992. 105–110.

Worcester, Ken. *C.L.R. James: A Political Biography*. Albany: State University of New York Press, 1996.

Young, James D. *The World of C.L.R. James: His Unfragmented Vision*. Glasgow, Scotland: Clydeside Press, 2000.

GRACE JONES
(1952–)

Jamaican Model, Singer, Songwriter, and Actress

Jamaican native Grace Jones has made a lasting impact on the world of music, art, and film. With her tall, muscular frame, this Jamaican-born artist began her career as a model on the catwalks of the Parisian fashion world. Her cropped military-style hair, complemented by erotic fashionable garb, imparts her signature androgynous demeanor and has become a trademark in her performance art appearances and concerts, beginning with her first performances in New York City in the 1970s. This combination of music and visuals, coined by her as the "Grace Jones way," has made her a worldwide star and icon.

She was born Grace Mendoza on May 19, 1952, in Spanish Town, Jamaica, where her grandfather and father were Pentecostal ministers and influential in local politics. The stern upbringing she described in an interview perhaps influenced her defiant nature: "It was a very strict religious upbringing. I couldn't even listen to the radio" (Shelley 1989). However, her home was also the first source of her athleticism and musicality. Like her mother, who had been a track and field Olympic contender, Grace's participation in sports included 100-meter races, high jump, and hurdles. The family was also musical: her mother sang, two uncles played and taught piano, and one of her grandfathers had a jazz band. Her musical talent, mutilingualism, and striking looks made her stand out among the other children in her school in Syracuse, New York, where her family moved when she was 12.

In the early 1970s, after graduating high school and studying theater at Syracuse University, she became a successful model working out of Paris and appeared on the covers of fashion magazines such as *Vogue, Elle,* and *Der Stern*. Her strolls on the Parisian catwalks were spectacles and marked the beginning of her move toward music and performance art. Seemingly an objet d'art, Grace's look made her one of the most sought-after, jet-setting models in the fashion world. This visibility and recognition led to an offer by a record company to make her first album in 1977, aptly titled *Portfolio.*

Portfolio included the smash hit, "I Need a Man," a song she at times performed wearing a wedding dress with suspenders. "La Vie en Rose," another big hit on

Grace Jones. Courtesy of Photofest.

that album, is considered a disco classic. She built an underground following as a cult figure and singer in New York City's gay dance clubs of the 1970s. There she developed a reputation for her roguish stylish look and the dominatrix, sexually suggestive, gender-bending theatricalities that were characteristic of her performances, such as entering the stage on a motorcycle dressed in leather with bodybuilders and/or male strippers dancing at her side, and sharing the stage with wild animals. Once, at the Savoy Club in New York, a man handcuffed himself to her ankle, and without missing a beat, she bent him over for a spanking while the audience danced in syncopation and cheered. Even though her music was widely known and played in the major U.S. discos, most of her albums regularly reached no higher than the lower end of the Billboard's Top 100, unlike in Britain and the rest of Europe, where her recordings were among the top-ten hits.

During the 1980s, disco's popularity waned and Jones moved toward rhythm and blues (R&B), soul, and rock music. Her *Warm Leatherette* recording was the beginning of her more rock-oriented music. In 1981, in collaboration with rock musicians David Bowie and Iggy Pop, she released *Night Clubbing,* an album that included her biggest R&B single, "Pull Up to the Bumper," marking her highest achievement in American R&B. The recording was also voted album of the year by England's New Musical Express. However, she is probably best known for her 1985 song "Slave to the Rhythm," and for her 1986 single "I'm Not Perfect (But I'm Perfect For You)." Both were commercial successes and dance-club classics. Critics have described her music as having foreshadowed and helped to define the "new music," which combined different genres such as rock, jazz, blues, and reggae, into the innovative music sounds that followed. Her *Private Life: The Compass Point Sessions,* which compiles music from three earlier albums, is a good example of this. A *Spin Magazine* review noted that "Jones bore her status as Diaspora artist proudly, putting across white rock songs and cabaret tunes with few of the emotional signifiers of either Rasta or Pop" (1998, 124–125).

Her film career also began during this time. Among her most memorable film appearances was her 1984 role alongside Arnold Schwarzenegger as "Zula" the warrior woman in *Conan the Destroyer* and as the man-eating villain in the James Bond film *A View to Kill* in 1986. Cast in a leading role in the little-known movie *Vamp,* she dominated the screen without uttering a single word. In 1988 she penned a song for, and made an appearance in, comedian Eddie Murphy's film *Boomerang.* It was during this time, the height of her career, that she lost many fans, friends, and collaborators in the music business to the AIDS epidemic. Increasingly, from the late 1980s to the early 1990s, the difficulties in her life escalated to the point where she found herself battling personal problems and did not record much music.

Today, her disco days behind, Jones still retains a timeless appeal and following, particularly among the world's gay community. Feeling total acceptance from the community that embraced her music early on, she describes them as her "best audience," and her performance schedule includes gay clubs. In 1993 her dance/techno single "Sex Drive" reached the number-one spot on the USA Billboard Chart. More recently she has recorded a number of soundtracks, among the more successful are "Evilmania" for the film *Freddy the Frog* and "Let Joy and Innocence Prevail" for *Toys*. In addition, in 1997, she played the character Evilene in the national tour of the Broadway show *The Wiz*.

Grace Jones resides in Paris and continues her gender-bending performances throughout the world. In 1999, VH1 named her one of the 100 Greatest Women of Rock 'n' Roll. *Hurricane*, billed as her "comeback" recording, was released in late 2000. She completed a film in Romania and was featured in the BBC's documentary *Legends of Dance*, and a newly recorded version of "Pull Up to the Bumper" made the Top-10 Billboard Dance Chart.—G.C.

References and Suggested Readings

Kershaw, Miriam. "Postcolonialism and Androgyny: The Performance Art of Grace Jones." *Art Journal* 56.4 (Winter 1997): 19–25.
Laermer, Richard. "Grace Jones Unzipped." *The Advocate* 585 (September 10, 1991): 72.
Shelley, Jim. "The Return of Grace Jones." *Blitz* (November 1989): n.p.
Usborne, David. "Grace in favour." *The Independent* (London), September 4, 2000, 1.

RAÚL JULIÁ
(1940–1994)

Puerto Rican Stage and Movie Actor

Although the island of Puerto Rico is known for having a large number of accomplished actors who have contributed to theater and film both in Puerto Rico and in the United States, very few of these actors and actresses have been able to bring the glory and recognition to the island that Raúl Juliá brought to his beloved Puerto Rico. In his relatively short but remarkable life this talented actor participated in a number of significant productions both on Broadway and in Hollywood.

Raúl Rafael Carlos Juliá y Arcelay was born on March 9, 1940, in San Juan to an affluent family of accomplished professionals. His father, Raul, was a Puerto Rican engineer and his mother was Olga Arcelay. His family valued education and

Raúl Juliá. Courtesy of Photofest.

from an early age Juliá attended the prestigious Colegio San Ignacio de Loyola, where he received an elite liberal arts education. Later in life, arts critics and the public were to compliment him on the quality of his spoken English. His mastery of the language was largely due to the fact that he had been educated at an institution where classes were taught in English, and the strict priests and nuns who ran the college underscored the importance of teaching their Puerto Rican students good command of the language.

Juliá acquired a taste for the arts at an early age. When he was five, he played the Devil in a theatrical production at his school. The family, who until then had believed that Juliá was a shy and introverted child, was astounded by his extroverted and stellar performance; both his mother and the Catholic nuns who ran the college were impressed by his acting ability. He continued appearing in theatrical productions in the school and throughout San Juan during his youth and adolescent years; however, he was never considered a serious actor there. On graduation from high school, he enrolled at the University of Puerto Rico in Río Piedras. His family wanted him to become a lawyer, but he opted for theater instead.

In 1964 Juliá moved to New York to become an actor. On his arrival, Juliá found a job in the stage production of Pedro Calderón de la Barca's *La vida es sueño* (Life Is a Dream) at the Astor Play House. His participation in this production enabled him to get an Actors Equity card, which made it possible for him to work as a professional actor. For three years he struggled working in diverse theatrical productions of minor relevance and working at odd jobs to support himself financially.

In 1967 he found backstage work with Joseph Papp's New York Shakespeare Festival. Papp eventually became his lifelong mentor, but for a time Juliá worked as on lighting and sets and finally as a house manager. After his work backstage, Juliá transitioned to an understudy and was finally given the chance to act by himself. His first production for the company was in the low-end mobile stage unit, where he played *Macbeth* in Spanish. He participated in scores of productions produced by Papp throughout the years. Some of them were *Othello, The Taming of the Shrew,* and *King Lear.* He also started to appear in some more mainstream productions such as *The Cuban Thing.*

Juliá's professional career escalated during the early 1970s. In 1971 he landed a role in the very successful television series *Sesame Street*, where he played the character of Raphael—one of the first Latinos on the program. This character was his introduction to American television, where he eventually appeared on the *Bob Newhart Show,* the soap opera *Love of Life,* and the television movie *Death Scream.* Throughout his career he underestimated television and disregarded its importance or artistic significance. While working in television he continued appearing in theater. Some of his more important theatrical credits of the time were in *The Threepenny Opera, As You Like It, The Emperor of Late Night Radio, Hamlet,* and *Dracula.* Established by then as a serious and talented actor, he received three Tony nominations during the 1970s.

During the 1980s Juliá was actively involved in both Broadway and Hollywood. He received his first Tony for his lead role as film producer Guido Contini in the musical *Nine* in 1981. He started to secure bigger and better roles in Hollywood. He participated in productions such as *Tempest* (1982), Francis Ford Coppola's *One from the Heart* (1983*), Kiss of the Spider Woman* (1985), *Tequila Sunrise* (1988), and *Romero* (1985). His brilliant performances in both *Kiss of the Spider Woman* and *Romero* brought him wide recognition by American movie critics, who were impressed by his acting and by his magnificent vocal control. A man who always kept in touch with his island, Juliá also participated in several movies produced in Puerto Rico. The most important of which was *La Gran Fiesta* (1988) produced in the island by Zaga Films. He also maintained an active involvement with human rights and political causes during this period.

Juliá was known for his capacity for hard work. In 1990 he acted in three movies: *Presumed Innocent* (1990), *Havana* (1990), and *The Rookie* (1990). It was, without a doubt, his role as Gomez in *The Addams Family* (1991), and its sequel *Addams Family Values* (1993), that brought him not only stardom but also recognition as a popular face on the silver screen. His role as Don Quixote in the revival of the popular musical *Man of La Mancha* (1992) earned him great reviews for his singing voice. Together with pop singer Sheena Easton he displayed a formidable singing capacity and a voice that very few of his followers knew he had.

Juliá suffered a major stroke and died on October 24, 1994. At the time, the popular media attributed his stroke to exhaustion and dehydration as a result of food poisoning while filming a movie in Mexico. What very few people knew was that the actor had cancer for some time and the stroke was a result of cancer complications. His widow, Merel Poloway, returned his body to Puerto Rico, where it was received at the Institute of Puerto Rican Culture. Juliá was given a state funeral and received national honors from the people of his beloved island.—S.M.M.

References and Suggested Readings

Gussow, Mel. "Raúl Juliá, Broadway and Hollywood Actor, Is Dead at 54." *The New York Times,* October 25, 1994, 23.

Meir, Matt, ed. "Raúl Juliá." *Notable Latino Americans: A Biographical Dictionary.* Westport, CT: Greenwood Press, 1997. 216–219.

Pace, Eric. "Raúl Juliá Is Remembered, With All His Panache." *The New York Times,* November 7, 1994, 12.

Tran, Mark, and Bergan, Ronald. "Actor With An Activist Spirit." *The Guardian* (London), October 26, 1994, T17.

JAMAICA KINCAID
(1949–)

Antiguan American Short Story Writer, Novelist, and Educator

Jamaica Kincaid is one of the best-known and most respected writers from the Caribbean, very possibly the first Antiguan female writer to achieve literary success and recognition worldwide. Her strong, lyrical language captures many of the realities of Caribbean culture and of her own childhood experiences rooted in the island of Antigua. Coming of age, race, class and colonialism, and the complex bond between mother and daughter are some of the issues explored in her writing. Her work has also been characterized as a metaphor for the experience of the African Diaspora. In the tradition of Caribbean post-colonialism, Kincaid's writing examines the ways in which colonialism affects society even after political independence. She is considered one of the most innovative contemporary writers.

Born on May 25, 1949, in the West Indies on the then-British-ruled island of Antigua, Elaine Cynthia Potter Richardson, was the eldest of four children and the only girl. Her family was poor; their home had no electricity, no indoor bathroom, and no running water. She was in charge of the paperwork required by the Public Works Department that assured weekly replacement of the outhouse "tub" and was required to go and get the required daily four or more buckets of water for the house. In addition, she made sure the lamps in the house were clean and filled with kerosene. She did not meet her biological father until adulthood. For the first nine years of her life she was an only child and had a deep connection to her mother, Annie Richardson. When she was nine, her mother remarried and the first of her three brothers was born. From that moment on, her mother increasingly shifted her attention to the younger siblings and the family's privation increased. The resulting conflict and isolation Kincaid experienced from her mother's emotional distancing during that time is a central feature in much of her writing.

She was educated in public schools following the British educational system and was considered bright but troublesome by her teachers. Attending an institution of higher education was impossible. Her family was very poor, and in the society in which she lived, such opportunities were provided overwhelmingly to gifted boys.

She left Antigua in 1966, at the age of 17, when her mother sent her to Scarsdale, New York, to work as an au pair. Her "servant" work, as she describes it, was short-lived. She moved to New York City, and between 1966 and 1973, went on to obtain her high school diploma. Kincaid also studied at various institutions including Westchester Community College and at the New School for Social Research, where she studied photography. She also briefly worked as an au pair for

Michael Arlen, a writer who would eventually work with her at *The New Yorker* magazine. In 1973 she began to write interviews for a magazine catering to teenage girls. It was during this time that, as a way of disguising herself, she changed her birth name from Elaine Potter Richardson to Jamaica Kincaid.

Her first pieces were published in *The Village Voice* and *Ingenue* magazine. Her big break in the world of publishing came when her work was brought to the attention of William Shawn, editor of *The New Yorker*, by Kincaid's friend and mentor at the time, George Trow, a contributor to the "Talk of the Town" section of the magazine. In 1976 she became a staff writer for the magazine, a job she would hold for the next 20 years. In the early 1980s she married William Shawn's son, composer Allen Shawn.

Jamaica Kincaid. AP Photo/François Mori.

Her first piece was in the "Talk of the Town" column and was titled "Girl," a page-long litany of rules of conduct as told by a mother to a daughter. "Girl," along with a selection of other short stories previously published in *The New Yorker*, made up the volume of stories in her first book, *At the Bottom of the River* (1983). Even though her previous writing had received very little critical attention, this work made her an instant celebrity. *The New York Times* described this work as "an enraged essay about racism and corruption in Antigua" (Garis 1990, 42). In 1983 Kincaid received the Morton Dauwen Zabel Award from the American Academy and Institute of Arts and Letters for *At the Bottom of the River*. This work, along with her first novel *Annie John* (1985), reflects her Antiguan childhood and adolescence.

Outstanding in these writings are significant elements of Antigua's post-colonialism, particularly racial and sexual discrimination and white European cultural domination. Both publications were critical successes. In 1985, *Annie John*, considered Kincaid's most autobiographical work, was a finalist for the prestigious International Ritz Paris Hemingway Award.

In contrast to the many travel books written by Europeans about the Caribbean, Kincaid's 1988 *A Small Place* is a powerful rebuttal that presents the natural beauty of Antigua while depicting the social and economic inequalities, the inadequate infrastructures, and the corruption and greed that have resulted as a consequence of British colonialism. It is an indictment of Antigua's aftermath of colonialism and exposes the island's poverty and quality-of-life issues. Consequently, the publication of this book resulted in Kincaid and her writings being banned from the island of Antigua until 1992, when the government lifted the sanction.

Her most recent books continue to expand on the experience of colonization, immigration, and human relationships. *Lucy*, published in 1990, is a continuation of Kincaid's personal history. Lucy, her main character, flees Antigua and her mother to become an au pair in New York. It is Kincaid's first piece of work set outside the Caribbean. In *The Autobiography of My Mother* (1996) the death during childbirth of the protagonist's mother serves as a metaphor for the separation from one's homeland. Considered one of her best works, it was a finalist for the National Book Critics Circle Ward and the PEN Faulkner Award in 1997. Her 1997 *My Brother*, nominated for a National Book Award was a departure from her fiction writing, and is a biographical account of her youngest brother, Devon Drew, who died of acquired immuno-deficiency syndrome (AIDS) at 33. In 2000 she was awarded the prestigious Prix Fémina Étranger for *My Brother*. Critics agree that Kincaid's collection of work places her among the outstanding writers in today's English-writing literary landscape (Bloom 1998; Paravisini-Gebert 1999; Simmons 1994).

Among those who recognize the significance of Kincaid's work is Nobel laureate **Derek Walcott**, whose work also explores the deep meanings of Caribbean life in light of the historical and social changes that have fashioned the West Indies we know today. He lauded Kincaid's writing style to *New York Times* journalist Leslie Garis, describing as "profound" and "courageous" the way she identifies and presents ordinary themes of everyday life and relationships. Writer Susan Sontag also praised this quality of her writing for its "emotional truthfulness" (Garis 1990, 42).

When she is not writing, she spends significant time tending to her garden, a hobby she wrote about while at *The New Yorker:* in fact, the title of her recent publication is *My Garden Book* (1999). It is a musing on gardening interwoven with reflections on history and life in the Caribbean. In December 2000 she published a collection of short stories, *Talk Stories*, a compilation of pieces she wrote for *The New Yorker* from 1974 to 1983. *Mr. Potter*, published in 2002, takes place in her native Antigua and is narrated by the fictional Elaine Cynthia, who describes the life of her father. Kincaid again draws from her own life to create this novel, including, as before, characters based on her mother and brother.

In 2003 the documentary *Life and Debt* was released. This documentary, narrated by Kincaid, is based on her book *A Small Place* and is an examination of the harmful effects that globalization has had on the economy of Jamaica.

A recipient of many awards, Kincaid received honorary degrees from Williams College and Long Island College in 1991, and similar recognition from Colgate University, Amherst College and Bard College in 1992. She is currently a visiting lecturer on Afro-American studies and English and American literature and language at Harvard University. Kincaid and her husband Allen Shawn, who teaches at Bennington College, live in Vermont with their two children, Annie and Harold.—G.C.

References and Suggested Readings

Andrade, Susan. "Jamaica Kincaid." In Bernth Lindfors and Reinhard Sander, eds., *Twentieth-Century Caribbean and Black African Writers*. Third Series. Detroit: Gale, 1996. 131–139.

Bloom, Harold, ed. *Jamaica Kincaid* (Modern Critical Views). Philadelphia: Chelsea House Publishers, 1998.

Curran, Beverly. "Kincaid digs up the dirt on gardening and colonialism." *The Daily Yomiuri*, August 6, 2000, 15.

Ferguson, Moira. " 'A lot of memory': An Interview with Jamaica Kincaid." *Kenyon Review* 16:1 (Winter 1994): 163.

Garis, Leslie. "Through West Indian Eyes." *The New York Times*, October 7, 1990, 42.

Jones, D., and J.D. Jorgenson. *Contemporary Authors, New Revision Series*. Vol. 59. Detroit: Gale, 1998.

Kincaid, Jamaica. *At the Bottom of the River*. New York: Farrar, Straus, Giroux, 1983.

———. *The Autobiography of My Mother*. Farrar, Straus, Giroux, 1996.

———. "Islander once, now voyager." *The New York Times*, September 22, 2000, E29, E40.

———. *A Small Place*. New York: Farrar, Straus, Giroux, 1988.

Paravisini-Gebert, Lizabeth. *Jamaica Kincaid: A Critical Companion*. Westport, CT: Greenwood Press, 1999.

Simmons, Diane. *Jamaica Kincaid*. New York: Twayne Publishers, 1994.

Weathers, Diane. "Jamaica Kincaid: her small place." *Essence* 26 (March 1996): 98.

WILFREDO LAM
(1902–1982)

Cuban Painter

Referred to as the Picasso of Cuba, artist Wilfredo Lam's paintings, sculpture, and graphics express the social conditions of blacks in his native country, making him the first Caribbean artist to achieve world-wide recognition in the field of modern art. He is considered one of the masters of Latin American art, an innovator who expanded the European scope of modern art by incorporating components from his diverse Afro-Cuban and Chinese heritage. One of the first artists to aesthetically articulate the African aspect of Caribbean culture, Lam's work has influenced many Latin American artists of the region. His works have been exhibited throughout the world and in the United States. American artist Romare Bearden, who knew Lam, considers him "one of the 20th century masters, along with Leger, Braque, Matisse, and Picasso" (Fraser 1982, 14).

This tall, skinny man, whose full name was Wilfredo Oscar de la Concepción Lam y Castilla, was better known as "El Chino." He was born in the town of Sagua la Grande in Las Villas Province on December 8, 1902. Both his biological heritage and his life and art were a paradigm of cross-cultural interface. His mother was mulatto (the offspring of Caucasian and black parents) and his father was Chinese. He was reared in a household where the practice of the African-derived religion of Santería and Roman Catholicism coexisted, a not uncommon occurrence in Caribbean cultures. His Catholic godmother was an important "santera," or high priest, of the Santería religion, and she was the person who inspired him to paint. His early education was in the working-class public schools of his town, where his desire to become a teacher gave way to his creative impulses and he began to study art.

As a young man in his mid-twenties he studied at the Academy of Fine Arts San Alejandro in Havana, and held his first solo exhibition in his native town before being awarded a scholarship to study abroad. He set sail for Madrid, Spain, in 1923, where he lived for 14 years pursuing art studies at the Escuela de Bellas Artes de Madrid. A Spanish functionary in Madrid inadvertently dropped the "l" from "Wilfredo," making Wifredo his artistic signature. While in Spain he went through a series of painful experiences. In 1931 both his Spanish wife and his only child died. From 1936 to 1939 he fought on the side of the Republicans in their unsuccessful fight against fascism during the Spanish Civil War. Both the mood of the times and his own pain surface in his paintings of desolate victims of war, which included mothers and children. One of his best-known works of that time, "Mother and Child" (1939), is now in the permanent collection of New York's Museum of Modern Art (MOMA). Somewhat broken in spirit, he left Spain.

He moved to Paris in 1938 and met fellow artist Pablo Picasso, who at the time was receiving praise for the work "Demoiselles d'Avignon," one of the first modern paintings with African influence, which greatly influenced Lam. Through Picasso, Lam was exposed to African sculpture and surrealism. He developed a lifelong friendship with Picasso and joined his circle of avant-garde artists whose interest and integration of non-European cultural aspects into their art struck a responsive chord in Lam. His paintings of that period exhibit a calligraphic style that displays the Chinese influence on Lam's art.

Lam operated on the stage of international art for most of his life and is considered the first "crossover" artist. In addition to having lived and worked in the Caribbean, Spain, and France, the United States was also briefly his home. In 1940 Lam and his friends fled to Marseilles when the Nazi forces invaded Paris. During his short time there he worked on a series of ink drawings *Interlude Marseilles* (1941), which were the illustrations for Francophile Andre Breton's poem *Fata Morgana*. In an effort to escape war-torn Europe, he joined hundreds of intellectuals aboard the *Capitaine Paul Merle* en route to Martinique, where he met the poet **Aimé Césaire**. Lam identified with and was influenced by Césaire's exploration and affirmation of Afro-Caribbean culture. Césaire would later write a tribute to Lam.

Shortly thereafter he was repatriated to Cuba as a result of World War II. Unlike in Europe, the sources of "Africanness" that surrounded him in Cuba were real and not representations on canvas. In Cuba he immersed himself in his Afro-Cuban culture—particularly the Yoruba-derived religious practice of Santería. It was during this time—starting with a 1943 painting titled "The Jungle," where his mask-like faces reflect Picasso's influence—that he established the iconographical and stylistic approach that would make him one of the "New World modernists." These were artists who changed the European radical avant-garde aesthetic and infused it with artistic elements of their cultures within the American continent. He created what is considered one of his masterpieces during this time: "The Murmur" (1943). In this work "a female figure is set against striped palm fronds that vaguely suggest Matisse's lively patterns . . . and bring Picasso to mind, but the details of her face are taken straight from West African sculpture" (Cotter 1992, 33). It was during this period, the 1940s, that Lam's art began to attract national and international recognition with numerous exhibits in Cuba, Europe, and the United States.

Lam left Cuba on April 8, 1958, right before the general strike that proclaimed **Fidel Castro**'s 1959 victory and entry into Havana. It was during this time that he painted "Exodus" as a representation of his second departure from Cuba. In 1962, Lam declined Castro's offer of an appointment as minister of culture. Even though Lam's political beliefs drew him to the left, he always characterized himself as an artist first and avoided actively involving himself in politics. However, he did consider himself a patriot and was sympathetic to the Cuban Revolution.

In the early 1960s, Lam made his home in Albisola, Italy, where he continued his work, this time as a well-known and successful artist. By the end of his life, this success had allowed him to establish homes in Italy, Sweden, and France.

The Wilfredo Lam Center, established in Cuba after his death in 1982, launched Cuban art into the international art arena.—G.C.

References and Suggested Readings

Cotter, Holland. "Review/Art; A Mulatto-Chinese Cuban With a Gift for Fusion." *The New York Times*, September 25, 1992, 33.

Fletcher, Valerie. *Crosscurrents of Modernism: Four Latin American Pioneers: Diego Rivera, Joaquín Torres-García, Wilfredo Lam, Matta.* Washington, DC: Hirshhorn Museum & Sculpture Garden/Smithsonian Press, 1985.

Fraser, Gerald. "Wilfredo Lam, 80, A Painter, Is Dead." *The New York Times*, September 13, 1982, 14.

Hughes, Robert. "Taking Back His Own Gods." *Time*, February 22, 1993, 68.

Hunter, Mark. "The Cuban Counterfeits." *ARTnews* 97.10 (November 1998): 148–155.

Ortíz, Fernando. *Wilfredo Lam y su obra.* Havana, Cuba: Publicigraf, 1993.

GEORGE LAMMING
(1927–)

Barbadian Writer

George Lamming has been called the "Caribbean Literary Giant" (McCallister 2000, 24). Although he has written poetry, essays, and speeches, he is best known for his novels. As a writer, Lamming has an extraordinary ability not only to capture the wide array of Caribbean realities, but also to explore and unravel the uniqueness of Caribbean people. As a writer and as a scholar, Lamming has tried to validate the Caribbean cultural identity through works that explore the complexities of the West Indies and the uniqueness of the Caribbean soul, mind, and land. **Rex Nettleford**, Vice Chancellor of the University of the West Indies has called him "one the Caribbean's finest intellects and foremost literary artists" (Nettleford 2000, ix).

Lamming was born on June 8, 1927, in Carrington Village, Barbados, a small community just outside the capital. Born to a poor single mother who married later during his childhood, Lamming still managed to develop a sense of security, reliance, and privilege, largely passed on by his stern mother.

As a child, Lamming went to the Roebuck Boys School at Carrington Village. He obtained a special scholarship to attend the Combermere School, an elite college preparatory school, where he was educated under a British system where most of his classmates came from affluence and privilege. In his book *Conversations,* Lamming explains that while at Combermere he was mentored by **Frank Collymore**, his English teacher. Collymore was the editor of *BIM,* a literary journal for Caribbean writers, which published Lamming's early poems. Collymore guided and encouraged his creative process and was a guide for many other writers of Lamming's generation. After graduation from high school, by at age 18, Lamming moved to Trinidad and started teaching at Colegio de Venezuela, a boys' school in Port-of-Spain established by the Venezuelan Ministry of Education for the children of Venezuelans living in Trinidad. During this time, he continued writing poetry and worked on his short stories. He also continued recruiting writers for *BIM* (Dryaton and Adaiye, 1992). Among his early works were the poems "The Rock" and "The Boy and the Sea" (1951) and the short stories "David's Walk" (1948) and "Birthday Weather" (1951).

In 1950, anxious to explore new horizons and take advantage of opportunities, work on his writing, and distance himself from the colonial oppression and the perceived cultural staleness that permeated the West Indies, Lamming emigrated to Great Britain and started a new life. Arriving in post-war London, Lamming worked as in a factory worker until he was able to secure a position as a broadcaster with the BBC Colonial Service in 1951. His work there is regarded as some of the best broadcasting being done by West Indians in London at the time. He shared the airwaves with many other young Caribbean writers such as **V. S. Naipaul** and **Stuart Hall**.

Lamming's literary production flourished in England. His first novel, *In the Castle of My Skin,* was widely acclaimed in literary circles and received the Somerset Maugham Award for literature in 1957 and is considered one of the classics of West Indian fiction. Lamming has stated that one of the reasons for the book's success is that it is an account of childhood and adolescence in his native Barbados. Because everyone has undergone this stage, people tend to identify well with the book (Dryaton and Adaiye, 1992). The book's importance lies in the fact that it explores the identity conflicts created by black and white cultures that were so typical of West Indian people growing up at that time.

Lamming has been thought of as an existentialist writer (Saakana 1988). The early literary production of Lamming explores the themes of decolonization, poverty, lack of cultural identity, identity crisis, racial conflicts, migration, oppression, and exploitation. These themes are contextualized within the very real dynamics witnessed by the author as a black man growing up in Barbados who had to co-exist with the white powers of the British colonial government. All of the work from this early period is to a large extent autobiographical and focuses on the colonial realities that the West Indies and the Caribbean experienced as a result of British and French colonialism and political exploitation by Great Britain and France. His works present beautiful but troubled landscapes of peoples and islands trying to come to terms with the realities of economic, social, and political subjugation.

One of Lamming's greatest assets as a writer is his masterful use of language. For Lamming:

> Language is at the heart and horizon of every human consciousness. It is the process which enables us to conceive of continuity on human experience; the verbal memory which reconstructs our past and offers it back as the only spiritual possession which allows us to reflect on who we are and what it may become. It is not inherited. Every child, in every culture, has to learn it as his or her necessary initiation into society. It is, perhaps, the most sacred of all human creations. (Lamming 2000, 30)

It is his ability to re-create the West Indian experience through language that has brought such levels of acclaim to his work.

In the early 1970s, Lamming published *Water with Berries* (1971) and *Natives of My Person* (1972). These novels further explored the themes of colonial identity, this time with a focus on the more modern Caribbean realities of the 1970s such as gender relations, violence, and political dissatisfaction with the post-colonial period. Other important works by Lamming are *The Emigrants* (1954), *Of Age and Innocence* (1958), and *A Season of Adventure* (1960), and *George Lamming: Conversations: Essays, Addresses and Interviews 1953–1990.*

Lamming is considered one of the most representative Caribbean writers of his period. His storytelling draws more on the individual and collective realities of the islands than on the fiction. In her recent book, *Caliban's Curse* (1996), critic Supriya Nair has undertaken an in depth analysis of Lamming's work. She suggests that he has been a leader in the integration and revisionism of Caribbean history into his work and has been instrumental in the diffusion of knowledge and history about the Caribbean through his prose (Nair 1996).

Lamming has lectured and held teaching positions at prestigious universities. He was a writer-in-residence and at the University of the West Indies in Jamaica in 1967 and 1968. He has also taught and lectured at the University of Texas, the

University of Pennsylvania, the University of Connecticut, Cornell University, the University of Dar-es-Salaam in Tanzania, and the University of Nairobi in Kenya. He has traveled to India, Australia, West Africa, and several other countries. At the request of the Barbadian government, Lamming organized the first Labor college in Barbados.

Lamming, a self-made intellectual, is identified with **Aimé Césaire**, **Derek Walcott**, **Nicolas Guillén**, and **Luis Palés Matos**—writers and thinkers who have given character and presence to the Caribbean face and spirit.—S.M.M.

References and Suggested Readings

Cumberd Dance, Daryl, ed. "George Lamming." *Fifty Caribbean Writers*. Westport, CT: Greenwood Press, 1986. 264–273.

Dryaton, Richard and Adaiye, eds. *George Lamming: Conversations: Essays, Addresses and Interviews 1953–1990*. London: Karia Press, 1992.

Lamming, George. *Coming Home: Conversations II*. St. Martin, West Indies: House of Nehesi, 2000.

———. *In the Castle of My Skin*. New York: Schocken, 1953.

McCallister, Jared. "Honors for Lamming at CCNY Graduation." *Daily News* (New York), May 28, 2000, 24.

Nair, Supriya. *Caliban's Curse*. Ann Arbor: University of Michigan Press, 1996.

Nettleford, Rex. "Introduction." In George Lamming, *Coming Home: Conversations II*. St. Martin, West Indies: House of Nehesi, 2000. ix–xiii.

Saakana, Amon. "Out of the Colonial Cocoon." *Washington Post*, July 3, 1988, 15.

Paquet, Sandra Pouchet. *Dictionary of Literary Biography, Volume 125: Twentieth Century Caribbean and Black African Writers*. Detroit, MI: Gale, 1993.

Woodworks, Manitou. "George Lamming." *Modern Black Writers*. Detroit, MI: Saint St. James Press, 2000.

ELIZABETH CLOVIS LANGE
(1784–1882)

Haitian Founder of the Oblate Sisters of Providence and Educator

A Haitian native and pioneer educator, Mother Elizabeth Clovis Lange founded and organized the nation's first African American Roman Catholic order, the Oblate Sisters of Providence, which is recognized as the first of its kind in the world. The order's first school opened in 1828 in Baltimore, Maryland. By the time of her death, the Oblate order had expanded to other cities in the United States, the Caribbean, and Central America. During the 1990s an effort was launched to have her canonized as the first African American saint of the Roman Catholic Church.

Very little is known about Lange's childhood. It is thought that she was born in 1784 in St. Domingue (renamed Haiti after the revolution) to Clovis and Annette Lange, who fled to Cuba sometime before the Haitian Revolution led by **Toussaint L'Ouverture**. Annette later left Cuba with her daughter Elizabeth, but Clovis did not accompany them. They went to the United States, where they spent a short period of time in Charleston, South Carolina, before settling in Baltimore in 1817. For unknown reasons, soon after their arrival, Annette returned to the West Indies, and Lange, already in her thirties, remained in Baltimore.

During the late 1700s and early 1800s, large waves of French political refugees fleeing the French Revolution and Haitians fleeing the slave uprising that led to the Haitian Revolution arrived on the shores of Baltimore, Maryland, a slave-holding state. This large French-speaking population included a sizable educated and wealthy community of free blacks, also referred to at the time as "colored" émigrés. When Lange arrived she joined this overwhelmingly Catholic community in the Fells Point area of the city at St. Mary's Seminary Chapel, the nucleus of religious activity for black and white Haitians. However, the African or black congregants were relegated to worshipping in the basement of the church—what they referred to as the "chapelle basse."

Finding that public education for blacks, and girls in particular, was strongly discouraged in Maryland, Lange, in collaboration with her friend Marie Magdalene Balas, opened a school for girls in her home around 1820. However, in 1827 she was forced to close the school for lack of funds. A strong and deeply religious woman, she did not waver in her desire to establish a school for black children, and soon found a supporter in Father James Hector Joubert, a member of the Sulpician order. Joubert had been encountering difficulties in teaching black children the catechism because they could not read. Lange's familiarity with the ethnicity and language of the refugees and her teaching ability were important to Joubert's goals. He actively supported not only her educational aspirations but also her religious vocation at a time when only white women were admitted to religious orders. In defiance of the existing order, Lange, a black woman in a slave-holding state in a male-dominated society, a Catholic at a time when this was unpopular, and a Francophile in an English-speaking community, established a school for neglected black children and a religious order for black women who were not welcomed in the existing Catholic religious orders.

In June 1828, with the approval of the archbishop of Baltimore, she established the religious order of the Oblate Sisters of Providence and its first school. Reflecting the male-dominated society of that time, sponsor Father Joubert was named director and administrator of the institution. The first group of Oblate Sisters of Providence took their vows on July 2, 1829, and began teaching the previously neglected black children in their new school, St. Frances Academy, which also served as one of the earliest teacher-training institutes for black women in Baltimore. Lange's vision of what real learning should encompass encouraged her students to strive for excellence. She developed a curriculum that went beyond the three R's to include music, classics, and fine arts. Central to the young ladies' education was religious instruction and vocational training in domestic arts and embroidery.

In addition to their work as educators, the order also became involved in the community and cared for the sick and the poor. During the city's cholera epidemics the sisters worked in the almshouses, caring for the black inmates. They faced very difficult times after Father Joubert's death in 1843, when the Catholic Church authorities abandoned their support of the Oblate Sisters. The archbishop, whose family were slave owners, ordered them to disband. It was a shock to the white community when Lange refused to follow his orders and continued to work for the advancement and freedom of the black community. Notwithstanding the hardship, for four years the Oblates survived by sewing and taking in other people's washing.

In addition to St. Frances Academy, Lange and her religious community established an orphanage and a widows home and conducted a night school that provided literacy training to black adults. In 1857 they started St. Joseph's School in South Baltimore and St. Michael's School in Fells Point. Very little, if any, public recognition was given to them, and for years the Oblate Sisters had to tolerate racist Catholics who thought it was disgraceful that black women should wear a "holy habit." There was even a time when an angry mob broke down their front door. Nevertheless, by the time of Lange's death in 1882 the Oblate Sisters had established schools and orphanages beyond the boundaries of Maryland in Philadelphia, New Orleans, and in 1880 began their westward movement, opening the St. Louis Missions.

It wasn't until the 1980s, long after the beginning of the civil rights movement, and 100 years after Lange's death, that her memory resurfaced. In light of this resurgence, it is important to recognize that Lange's establishment of a religious order was a first for black women in the history of the Catholic Church and that her religious fervor and devotion to God did not stand in the way of her advocating for social justice. Her devotees now await a miracle that can have no possible human or scientific explanation, which will allow her route to sainthood to unfold.—G.C.

References and Suggested Readings

Biography of Mother Mary Elizabeth Lange, O.S.P.: *http://www.louisdiggs.com/oblates/ Biography.html*.

Breslaw, Elaine, and Joan Andersen. *Notable Maryland Women*. New York: Cambridge University Press, 1977.

Clark Hine, Darlene, Rosalyn Terborg-Penn, and Elsa Brown, eds. "Elizabeth Clovis Lange." *Black Women in America: An Historical Encyclopedia*. Brooklyn, NY: Carlson Publishing, 1993. 695.

McWilliams, R. "We the People: African Americans." *Maryland Magazine* 22 (Spring 1990): 26–35.

Morrow, Diane Batts. "The Oblate Sisters of Providence: Issues of Black and Female Agency in Their Antebellum Experience, 1828–1860." *Dissertation Abstracts International* 579A (1996). University of Georgia.

Posey, Thaddeus John. "An Unwanted Commitment: The Spirituality of the Early Oblate Sisters of Providence, 1829–1890." *Dissertation Abstracts International* 54.7A (1993). St. Louis University.

Ernesto Lecuona
(1895–1963)

Cuban Composer and Pianist

Cuban composer Ernesto Lecuona was one of the most important musicians of the twentieth century. A prolific musician and composer who achieved critical and commercial success in classical as well as popular music, Lecuona also led some of the first major Latin groups to perform in Europe and the United States. In the 1920s and 1930s he had many radio and film hits. Considered the "Cuban George Gershwin"—whom he happened to be acquainted with—Lecuona also was very active composing for musical theaters in Cuba, Spain, and Latin America. Notwithstanding the fact that he achieved worldwide recognition and that his songs are easily recognized classics, very little information is available on him in major musical history texts.

Lecuona was born in Guanabacoa, Cuba, on August 6, 1895, into a family where all his siblings played a musical instrument. His father, a newspaper editor, supported his children's musical training, and at a very young age, Lecuona began training in music with piano lessons from his sister Ernestina. By the age of 5 he was recognized as a child prodigy and performed his first public piano concert. By the age of 11 he had published his first composition, and was the piano player for the silent films shown at the Fedora Theater in Havana. At 14 he entered the National Conservatory of Havana and in 1913 graduated with highest honors in piano performance. He first traveled outside Cuba in 1916 when he went to New York City to begin his professional concert career.

Even though Lecuona was a classically trained musician, his musical compositions, from the very beginning, were imbued with Afro-Cuban rhythms. After leaving Cuba, his first professional success came in the early 1920s when he brought major Latin groups to perform in the United States and Europe. While in Paris he met and briefly studied with composer Maurice Ravel and shortly thereafter wrote one of his best-known compositions, "Malagueña." He first played this composition to the public at the Roxy Theatre in New York City in 1927. In 1930 this hit was followed by "Andalucía," another major success, which became much more popular in the United States in its English translation in 1940: "The Breeze and I." During the late 1920s and 1930s Lecuona was at the peak of his musical career and was a leading composer in early sound films, writing music scores for

American and Latin American movies. He wrote the music for a number of MGM films—among them *Under Cuban Skies* (1931), *Free Soul* (1931)—and in 1942 received an Oscar nomination for the song "Always in My Heart" for the Warner Brothers film of the same name. Two classical Latin American films that carry some of his signature songs are *María la O* (1947) and *Adios, Buenos Aires*, made in Argentina in the 1940s. His song "Siboney" has been heard in at least three movies, including Italian director Federico Fellini's *Amarcord* (1973).

In 1932, Lecuona arrived in Spain with his group Lecuona's Cuban Boys. They appeared in theaters, dance halls, and nightclubs of major European cities and won over the public with their lineup of rumbas, congas, and Afro-Cuban tunes enhanced by percussion instruments that were still unknown in most of Europe. Lecuona's Cuban Boys had one of the longest durations of any orchestra. Even after Lecuona's death they continued performing until the bandleaders at that time, the Bruguera brothers, died in 1975.

Lecuona was also a well-known interpreter of Gershwin's *Rhapsody in Blue,* which inspired him to write *Rapsodia negra* (1937) for piano and orchestra. This included his signature use of percussion and called for the orchestra to use a *quijada*, or donkey's jawbone, as one of the musical instruments. Like Gershwin, he was a prolific composer whose body of work includes zarzuelas (Spanish operas), cantatas, and operettas. Lecuona's catalog includes 406 songs, 176 piano pieces, 53 theater works, 31 orchestral scores, and 11 film scores, as well as ballets, violin works, and numerous compositions for piano and orchestra totaling over 800 works. His most memorable works are his songs: "The Breeze and I," "Dust Over the Moon," "Say Si Si," "Always in My Heart," "Siboney," "La Comparsa," "María My Own (María la O)," and "Malagueña." In 1997 Lecuona was posthumously inducted into the Songwriters' Hall of Fame.

A lifelong bachelor, Lecuona lived in Cuba until 1960, when he became an exile due to the **Castro** regime. He lived the last few years of his life in New York and Florida. In addition to his musical compositions, he was one of the founders of the Havana Orchestra and is considered to have been instrumental in the development of classical performance in Cuba. His works are considered standard components of any pianist's repertoire. He died on November 29, 1963, while vacationing in the Canary Islands.—G.C.

References and Suggested Readings

Bauman, Carl. "60 Piano Pieces." *American Record Guide* 60.40 (July–August 1997): 239.

Falstaff, John. "Cuban Overture, the George Gershwin of Havana," *Atlanta Weekly,* March 7, 1998, n.p.

Henderson, Richard. "And the Winners Are . . ." *Billboard* 109.24 (June 14, 1997): 35.

Holston, Mark. "Ernesto Lecuona: The Chopin of the Tropics." *Americas* 48.6 (November–December 1996): 56.

Jacobson, Gloria Castiel. "The Life and Music of Ernesto Lecuona (Cuba)." *Dissertation Abstracts International* 43.09A (1982). University of Florida.

Salzman, Eric. "Rediscovering Ernesto Lecuona, A Cuban Master." *Stereo Review* 62.2 (February 1997): 129.

Vega, Aurelio de la. "Lecuona, A Century Later." *Latin American Music Review* 19.1 (1998): 106.

MOSES LEVEROCK
(1814–1875)
Pioneer Reformer from Saba

Saba native and reformer Moses Leverock is best remembered for his idiosyncratic sense of justice. Appointed by the Dutch government as lieutenant governor in 1863, his legacy on this small island in the Netherlands Antilles was underscored when he granted freedom to all slaves within his first week in office. He also undertook one of the Caribbean's earliest redevelopment projects.

Leverock's leadership exemplified the paternalistic role that characterized men's positions in leadership at that time. Initially, he received no salary; his income was based on his ability to collect taxes. For seven years, he fought for a change and was finally successful in 1875, the year of his death. His town, The Bottom, was quite behind the times even for the standards of those days. Streets were unpaved, and the construction of houses followed no established pattern. When it rained, the village would turn into a giant mud pool; when it was dry, the dust was overwhelming. There was no such thing as sanitation or garbage removal and refuse was just thrown outside. As the rocky remains of an extinct volcano, Saba is characterized by its abundance of rocks strewn about the island. Leverock is remembered for the changes he helped to bring about on the island as well as his sense of justice.

Describing how Leverock handled issues of justice gives us insight into what life was like on Saba at that time. Typical problems were boisterousness and quarreling for which the lieutenant governor imposed fines and sometimes short prison sentences. Cases involving quarrels, disturbances of the peace, robberies, and the like were considered too minor for the court of law (which was based on Dutch jurisprudence) and were handled by Leverock.

Leverock used prison labor as a means of cleaning up The Bottom. Lazy youngsters were imprisoned, then released a few hours a day and made to pick up stones, thus making public roads more accessible and clean. With immediate consequences for unlawful behavior, the jail that had been built in 1837 soon became too small to hold all the prisoners.

During his years as leader of Saba, Moses Leverock's efforts in establishing order on the island made him a respected and loved figure. In 1868 the citizens of the island honored him by officially changing the name of the capital from The Bottom to the Town of Leverock. He stepped down from his official duties that year and continued to live as a citizen of Saba until his death in 1875.—G.C.

Reference and Suggested Reading

Hartog, J. *History of Saba.* Saba, Netherland AA: Van Guilder N.V., 1975.

ARTHUR LEWIS
(1915–1991)

St. Lucian Nobel Laureate in Economics

Sir W. Arthur Lewis was a native of St. Lucia and co-winner of the 1979 Nobel Prize for economics. His work explains the economic planning and histories of emerging countries and why some prospered and others did not. He was the first black person to receive the Nobel Prize in economics and was an outspoken critic of industrialized nations' disregard for the needs of developing nations. Lewis was the author of 12 books, including his seminal work, *The Theory of Economic Growth.* He is also credited with publishing over 80 technical works in what is referred to as developmental economics. An advisor to several nations, Lewis was an authority in the study of economic development and political and social change in developing countries, as well as one of the first scholars to study the role of women in developing economies. A Princeton faculty member for 20 years, Lewis also served as adviser to many world government leaders and institutions and held a number of international positions.

Born Arthur Lewis at Castries on the Island of St. Lucia on January 23, 1915, he was the fourth of five sons of schoolteachers George Ferdinand and Ida Lewis. At the age of seven, Lewis became ill and was forced to stay home for many weeks. During this time his father, who died later that year, tutored him so he would not fall behind in his studies. His father did such a thorough job that when Lewis returned to school he was skipped from fourth to sixth grade, where he found himself physically smaller and younger than his peers. In his biography for the Nobel Museum Lewis describes how this affected his life until he was 18: "This gave me a terrible sense of physical inferiority, as well as an understanding, which has remained with me ever since, that high marks are not everything" ("Sir Arthur Lewis" 1979). He credits his mother, a widow by the time he was seven, with encouraging him to succeed. By age 14 he had completed the equivalent of secondary education but was considered too young to apply for or take the government scholarship exam to study in Great Britain. For the next three years he worked as a civil service clerk for the St. Lucia government, an experience he credits with developing his skills in writing, typing, and organization. Then he went to the London School of Economics (LSE), where he completed a Bachelor of Commerce degree with first honors in 1937. On graduation the LSE offered him a scholarship to pursue a Ph.D. in industrial economics, which he completed in 1940.

He began his career as an academician and scholar at LSE, where he worked until 1948, when he was appointed full professor at the University of Manchester. At the University of Manchester he was also appointed to the Stanley Jevons Chair in Political Economy, making him, at 33, the youngest person in Britain or the British Commonwealth to hold a chair in economics. His visits to Africa and Asia during the 1950s and the large number of Asian and African undergraduate students at Manchester were pivotal influences that "set me lecturing systematically on development economics from about 1950" ("Sir Arthur Lewis"). A strong believer in learning through teaching led to his best-known work, *The Theory of Economic Growth* (1955), in which he provides a framework for studying economic development. His views, dubbed the "Lewis model," describe "how traditional societies make the economic transition to modern nations" (Jones 1979, A1).

Lewis' life work in his capacity as an economist combined administration and international consulting work as well as academic scholarship. In 1957 he was tapped by the Mona campus in Jamaica (what was then called the University College of the West Indies) to serve as principal and later vice-chancellor. Over the next five years he transformed and expanded the institution's academic offerings and increased the student body to 2,000 from 690. Under his leadership it was recast into an independent and prestigious Caribbean institution renamed University of the West Indies (UWI). In addition to his work as vice chancellor of UWI from 1957 to 1963 he was also a United Nations (UN) economic adviser to the prime minister of Ghana and deputy managing director of the UN Special Fund. In 1963, the year he was knighted by Queen Elizabeth for his pioneering work at UWI, he was also appointed professor of public and international affairs at Princeton University's Woodrow Wilson School of Public and International Affairs. He worked at Princeton from 1963 to 1968 and also served as Distinguished University Professor of Economics and International Affairs from 1982 to 1983. In the late 1960s he served as director of Jamaica's Industrial Development Corporation, and from 1970 to 1974 he established the Caribbean Development Bank (CDB) and served as its president. His administrative and intellectual leadership of the CDB is believed to have provided for the first time a "viable and internationally recognized development institution culturally attuned, sensitive and responsive to its quest for social and economic development" ("Sir Arthur Lewis Nobel Laureate" 1979). He shared the 1979 Nobel Prize with Theodore Schultz who, like Lewis, was a scholar in the field of economics applied to the problems of developing countries.

Among his many publications are *Economic Survey* (1939), *Racial Conflict and Economic Development* (1985), and an edited compendium, *Selected Economic Writings of W. Arthur Lewis* (1983). The Institute of Social and Economic Research at UWI was named after him in 1963. Lewis died in Barbados in June 1991. He was laid to rest on the grounds of the Sir Arthur Lewis Community College in St. Lucia.—G.C.

References and Suggested Readings

Bhajan, Lisa. *Sir Arthur Lewis.* San Juan, Trinidad: Imprint Caribbean, 1987.

"Caribbean Visions: A Tribute to Sir Arthur Lewis." Caribbean Studies Association XIV Annual Conference, May 23–26, 1989, Dover Convention Centre, Barbados.

Jones, William H. "Development Theorists Citied; Development Economists Win Nobel; American, W. Indian Share Nobel Prize." *Washington Post,* October 17, 1979, A1.

Lalljie, Robert. *Sir Arthur Lewis, Nobel Laureate: A Biographical Profile.* Castries, St. Lucia: R.Ferdinand-Lalljie, 1996.

Lewis, Arthur. *The Theory of Economic Growth.* Homewood, IL: Richard D. Irwin, 1955.

Premdas, Ralph R., and Eric St. Cyr. *Sir Arthur Lewis: An Economic and Political Portrait.* Mona, Jamaica: Regional Programme of Monetary Studies, Institute of Social and Economic Research, University of the West Indies, 1991.

"Sir Arthur Lewis." Nobel E-Museum–The Official Web Site of the Nobel Foundation: *http://www.nobel.se/economics/laureates/1979/lewis-autobio.html.*

"Sir Arthur Lewis Nobel Laureate in Economics 1979." United Nations. *http://www.un.int/stlucia/Sir%20Arthur%20Lewis.htm.*

Wilkinson, Audine. *Sir Arthur Lewis: A Bibliographical Portrait.* Cave Hill, Barbados: Library Institute of Social and Economic Research, University of the West Indies, 1999.

MARIA LIBERIA-PETERS
(1942–)

Politician and Prime Minister of the Netherland Antilles

Maria Liberia-Peters is the first woman to serve as prime minister of the Netherlands Antilles, five Caribbean islands colonized by the Dutch and now self-governing (Curaçao, Bonaire, St. Maarten, Saba, and St. Eustatius). Notwithstanding comparisons with Margaret Thatcher, this former kindergarten teacher and leader of the National People's Party considers former congresswoman **Shirley Chisholm** and the late Indira Gandhi as her role models.

Liberia-Peters was born on May 20, 1941, in Willemstad, Curaçao. She was educated in Curaçao and later completed her teaching degree in Holland. A polyglot who speaks four languages, Liberia-Peters began working as an early childhood teacher in 1962, then returned to college to complete a degree in education.

Her teaching experience opened her eyes to societal needs and the importance of organizing communities for political and social action. Her years as a teacher also made her realize the importance of the early years in the development of human beings, and she became involved in children's issues from the beginning of her political career. Liberia-Peters believes that her political rise came about as a result of her interest in improving the quality of life for children and families: "There comes a moment when you realize that if you really want to make a difference, the only way is through politics, and then you walk right into it" (Gewertz 1997). It was this awareness that made her "walk" and join the National People's Party in the early 1970s. In 1975 she won a seat on the Curaçao island council and was selected to an executive council, whose duties included regular meetings with the representative of The Netherlands' Queen Beatrix. This experience gave her exposure and access to power.

In 1982 Liberia-Peters won another elective office, this time to the Staten (legislature), and also became minister of economic affairs in a coalition government. Unfortunately, the coalition collapsed by 1984. However, her political star began to rise when she was asked to form a new coalition government, and she was inaugurated as prime minister that month. This was a first in Netherlands Antilles politics, and she is one of only three women who have ever held the highest elected office of their country in the Caribbean. Dame **Mary Eugenia Charles** of Dominica achieved that distinction in 1980, and Governor of Puerto Rico **Sila María Calderón** in 2000.

One of the most memorable moments of her leadership, and one that revealed her exultant personality, was during the 1985 annual carnival parade on the island of Curaçao. Instead of taking the prime minister's traditional place in the reviewing stand, Liberia-Peters danced in the parade as she had done every year in the past, this time, though, with the populace cheering her on. She feels strongly that leaders should be close to the people: "I don't like situations where, let's say, security officers keep me at distance from the people, and that's why I participate" (Liswood 1995, 102).

During her first tenure as the leader of her country she faced a blow to the territory's economy when one of the major employers of the island, the Shell Oil refinery, closed and reduced the economy's income by 50 percent instantly. Liberia-Peters' challenge was to find a way to keep other refineries from closing. In a territory that is composed of so many islands, Liberia-Peters, more than any other prime minister before her, managed to galvanize the population through use of the radio and television. Her first tenure as head of state lasted until 1986, when the government again was dissolved, and she became leader of the opposition for two years.

In 1988 she again was elected prime minister. Only one of the two oil refineries that the country was so dependent on was left. This resulted in a very high unemployment rate and forced the government to begin exploring ways to diversify the economy. One of her approaches was to experiment with different types of specialized tourism. Bonaire, for example billed itself as a scuba diver's paradise.

Throughout both her terms as prime minister, she relied on a group of advisers that she called her think tank, but many of her supporters and critics believe that she has a mind of her own and was the one who actually called the shots.

Her supporters believe that among her strengths was the ability to reach consensus from the governing Council of Ministers and other groups with which she had to work. As she herself has said: "One advantage of consensus is that you can get a broader participation. But you have to know when the moment has been reached to say, well, OK, now I have to assume my responsibility" (Liswood 1995, 126).

Married and the mother of two children, Liberia-Peters moved back into her role as leader of the opposition after losing the 1994 elections.—G.C.

References and Suggested Readings

Gewertz, Ken. "Women Who Lead: New Organization Supports Female World Leaders." *The Harvard University Gazette,* September 25, 1997, n.p. *http://www.hno.harvard.edu/gazette/1997/09.25/WomenWhoLead.html.*

Liswood, Laura A. *Women World Leaders: Fifteen Great Politicians Tell Their Stories.* London: HarperCollins, 1995.

Treaster, Joseph B. "In the Caribbean, A Popular New Leader." *The New York Times,* August 19, 1985, 12.

JENNIFER LÓPEZ
(1970–)

Puerto Rican American Actress, Singer, and Dancer

Jennifer López, a Bronx native of Puerto Rican descent, has emerged from acting in a series of minor television and movie roles to become a leading lady in major Hollywood feature films. She began her career as a dancer in musicals and got her first break in 1991 when she was hired as a "fly girl"—one of the dancers in the Fox television variety series *In Living Color.* She has co-starred with some of Hollywood's leading actors and has played the title role in a number of major films, including her breakthrough film, *Selena.* She is also a successful singer, receiving Grammy nominations in 2000 and 2001, and has been given some of the top awards in the entertainment business. Her $10 million salary for the film *Enough* (2002) made her the highest-paid Latina actress in Hollywood today.

López was born on July 24, 1970, in the Bronx, New York, to David and Guadalupe López, a computer specialist and a kindergarten teacher. The second of three sisters, she began dance classes at the age of five and later continued with the New York City–based Ballet Hispánico, where she practiced flamenco, ballet, and jazz dancing. Her first stage was her living room, where as children, she and her sisters would entertain family members. Her early academic education took place at the Holy Family School, and in 1986 she graduated from Preston High School in the Bronx. After high school she moved to Manhattan, where in 1986 she landed a dancing part in the European tour of *Golden Musicals of Broadway* and danced in the chorus in the Japanese tour of the theater production *Synchronicity*. That same year she made her feature film debut with a small part in *My Little Girl*.

In what many consider to be a meteoric ascension to celebrity, López auditioned for and landed a spot as a dancer, or "fly girl," on the television show *In Living Color* (1991), a role that is considered as her big break because, apart from being on a weekly national television show, it required her to relocate to Los Angeles. In 1993, after two seasons on *In Living Color*, she was cast as Lucy in the short-lived television series *South Central*. She appeared in her first made-for-television movie, *Nurses on the Line: The Crash of Flight 7*, and a few other television series, and then landed her first supporting role in a feature film in Gregory Navas' 1995 *My Family/Mi familia*, a chronicle of three generations of a Mexican immigrant family in the United States. That same year, she had her first leading role in the film *Money Train* with actors Woody Harrelson and Wesley Snipes. Her acting caught the eye of director Francis Ford Coppola, who cast her in a supporting role in the 1996 film *Jack*, where she co-starred with Robin Williams.

In 1997 she played a Cuban-exile, opposite Jack Nicholson and Michael Caine in *Blood and Wine*. López then landed a role in the film that is considered her breakthrough—*Selena*. Playing the title role of Tejano musical star Selena Quintanilla, López emerged as one of Hollywood's leading actresses. *Selena* won López the American Latino Media Arts Award (ALMA) for Outstanding Actress, and gained her attention from critics. That same year, she also appeared in the hit film *Anaconda*, where she was cast as a documentary film director. Grossing over $100 million in the United States alone, *Anaconda* became 1997's highest-ranking film featuring a Latino in a starring role. One of her first non-ethnic roles was in director Oliver Stone's critically acclaimed film noir *U-Turn* (1997), where she played opposite actors Nick Nolte and Sean Penn. From 1998 through 2000 López continued appearing in a broad range of roles. She starred with George Clooney in the crime thriller *Out of Sight* (1998) and was the voice of Azteca, a worker ant in the animated film *Antz* (1998). In 1999 she appeared in *Thieves* and *Pluto Nash*, and in 2000 played a psychologist in the psychological thriller *The Cell*. In her multitude of roles López has avoided being typecast as a Latina actress.

In 1999 she recorded her first album, *On the 6*; the title is a tribute to the subway that she took from the Bronx to Manhattan for dance lessons. A single from that album, "If You Had My Love," became a major hit. Singles from this album received two Latin Grammy Award nominations in 2000 for Best Dance Recording and Best Pop Performance, and another in 2001 again for Best Dance Recording. In addition, it was nominated in three categories for the Billboard 2000 Latin Music Awards. The simultaneous release of her 2001 film *The Wedding Planner* and her second music CD, *J.Lo*, and their concurrent rise to the top of the charts in their respective categories made her the third woman, after singers Barbra Streisand and Whitney Houston, to achieve such level of success. In September 2001 López's first two concert performances were held in **Roberto Clemente** Stadium in San Juan, Puerto Rico. The concert was released in as the album *Let's Get Loud*.

López has become almost as famous for her clothes as for her acting, making headlines worldwide when she appeared at the 1999 Grammy awards ceremony with a Versace dress that plunged down to her navel. She won VH1/Vogue Fashion Awards' Most Fashionable Female Artist in 2000 and was awarded the Most Influential Artist of the Year prize at the VH1/Vogue Fashion Awards in 2002. She was also named in *People* magazine's 2001 "best dressed" list and received the MTV Movie Award for best dressed in the film *The Cell* (2001). However, the recognition she has received for her performances outnumber those for fashion. Among them are the 1998 Image Foundation and Lone Star Film and Television awards for best actress for her portrayal of Selena. In 1999 she was awarded the Outstanding Actress/Crossover Role for her role in *Out of Sight* from the American Latino Media Arts, who also selected her as Female Entertainer of the Year in 2001. Lopez's 2002 music video "Love Don't Cost a Thing" was awarded the People's Choice Award for Outstanding Video at the ALMA Awards, and at MTV's Music Awards she won Best Hip Hop Video for the remix of "I'm Real." López starred in *Angel Eyes* (2001) and *Maid in Manhattan* (2002). Also in 2002 she released the album *This Is Me . . . Then*, which was certified Double Platinum worldwide by early 2003.— G.C.

References and Suggested Readings

Baker, Trevor. *Jennifer Lopez*. London: Carlton, 2001.

Carr, Jay. "Actors Rise Above Stilted Script for 'Selena.'" *The Boston Globe*, March 27, 1997, C5.

———. "Stone Takes a Fresh 'U-Turn.'" *The Boston Globe*, October 3, 1997, D1.

Colón, Suzan. "You Go J. Lo." *Latina* (June 2001): 81.

Duncan, Patricia. *Jennifer López: An Unauthorized Biography*. New York: St. Martin's Press, 1999.

Jennifer López Homepage: *www.jenniferlopez.com*.

Johns, Michael-Anne. *Jennifer Lopez*. Kansas City, MO: Andrews McMeel Publishers, 1999.

Murray, Steve. "Selena" (movie review). *The Atlanta Constitution*, March 21, 1997, 12P.

Tracy, Kathleen. *Jennifer Lopez*. Toronto: ECW Press, 2000.

LORD KITCHENER (ALDWYN ROBERTS)
(1922–2000)

Trinidadian Calypso Singer and Composer

Aldwyn Roberts, known as "Lord Kitchener" in the world of calypso music, was one of Trinidad's most famous calypso singers and composers. His music is characterized by a spicy and daring style that makes funny yet important political and social commentaries of contemporary events in his native Trinidad and abroad. Roberts had a highly refined poetic sense filled with wit and sarcasm. He was a defender of steel bands and calypso traditions throughout his life, and was credited with writing more than 1,000 calypsos during his lifetime. He was one of the first musicians to incorporate the use of the steel pan (made of a 55-gallon oil drum modified as a pan) in the playing of calypso music in Trinidad (Mason 1998). Along with calypso singer **Mighty Sparrow**, he represented the voice and soul of Trinidad's calypso scene and became a formidable cultural icon for the people of this Caribbean island.

Roberts was born in the town of Arima in eastern Trinidad on April 18, 1922. He was one of six children of a well-known blacksmith. There are two explanations commonly given for his early involvement with music. Some of his biographers trace his interests in music to his father's blacksmith shop—in addition to his blacksmithing his father was also a musician and many other fellow musicians went to his smithy to play and listen to each other's tunes. Kitchener acquired a taste for music and learned music and guitar from his dad (Pareles 2000, 9). Other biographers reasoned that Kitchener developed an interest in singing as a way to counteract stammering, a speech problem that afflicted him throughout his life (Waley 2000, 6).

As a composer and musician, Roberts is generally considered to be self-taught and self-made. He started composing calypsos when he was 10. Although he attended the Arima Boys Government School as a child, he had to abandon his education after his father's death, when he needed to work in order to help support his family. He took a job as a musician in 1936, singing and entertaining the employees of the Water Works Department in Trinidad for 12 cents a day. Known during the beginnings of his career by the artistic sobriquet of the "Arima Champion," Roberts was a tall and lanky youngster whose sisters teased and called him "string bean."

Roberts started his professional career as a calypso singer and composer when he was 15. He changed his artistic name to "Lord Kitchener," inspired by the British field marshall, and by 1938 was a popular singer in the town of Arima. That year he won the first local calypso competition with the song "Shops Close Too Early." During his early years as a singer, Roberts worked as a musician in Arima, where he was able to successfully popularize many songs and win several local competitions. In 1942 he moved to Port of Spain, where calypso was more popular than in Arima and he was able to reach much larger audiences during the yearly carnival season.

On his arrival in Port of Spain, Roberts immediately affiliated himself with some of the important performers of the time and joined several singing troupes and calypso nightclubs. Eventually he formed his own calypso troupe known as the Young Brigade and worked with the most important groups of the time. "Green Fig Man," his first major song, was released during the carnival season in 1944. This song was the first in a string of successes.

Like many other Trinidadians of his generation, Roberts decided to leave the island in search of new horizons. After touring the Caribbean, he emigrated to London in 1948. He was the first person to import Trinidadian calypso and steel pan music to Europe. He lived both in London and in Manchester, England, where he experienced considerable success and was able to make substantial amounts of money with his recordings. He also opened a nightclub that helped to build his name not only as a composer and singer but also as an entrepreneur and businessman. For the British, the often caustic and witty lyrics of Lord Kitchener represented a dramatic new style of music. In fact, it is said that the late Princess Margaret of England was a fan of his shows (Mason 2000, 24). Even when he was in England, he kept abreast of calypso trends in Trinidad and continued to write and enter his calypsos in the yearly festival competitions.

In 1962, after 14 years abroad, Roberts returned to Trinidad, where he received a hero's welcome and was able to pick up his career where he had left it. He started winning the Road March competitions, awarded to the performer whose songs are interpreted most often in the streets during Carnival. Winning ten road marches competitions between 1963 and 1976, Roberts and calypso singer Mighty Sparrow decided to stop competing in 1976 to give an opportunity to other younger competitors. He also won 19 Panorama awards, a prize given to the best composer of steel pan tunes.

Lord Kitchener's importance lies not only in his extraordinary talent as a composer and performer but in his powerful defense of the steel pan. For instance, he was one of the first composers to write exclusively for steel band orchestras. Historically, steel drum musicians and their calypsos were seen as a lower cultural product and were kept at the margins of Trinidadian society. Roberts was a powerful advocate for calypsos and made a strong effort to ensure that the calypso traditions were kept alive. He brought respect to the genre and contributed to its acceptance by mainstream society. Like the songs of his fellow Trinidadian, Mighty Sparrow, Roberts' interpretations often had powerful social messages and direct criticism of situations that affected the people of Trinidad. Among his most important compositions were "Give Me the Ting," "Pan in Harmony," "Green Fig Man," "Flag Woman," and "Nora."

Despite his resounding successes in Trinidad and abroad, the government of Trinidad shunned Roberts' talents by denying him the Trinity Cross, the island's highest decoration. Instead, they offered him the Chaconia medal, a less-valued distinction, which he refused. His fans were enraged by this gesture, collected money, and built a statue in his honor that was placed in the outskirts of Port of Spain. Although the government of Trinidad issued a commemorative stamp in his honor in 1994, their earlier attempts to ignore his legacy left him frustrated and upset. When he died on February 11, 2000, his family refused the government's offer of a state funeral and instead decided to give him a people's funeral, where his beloved masses were able to bid him farewell. Despite his resounding popularity and success, he died a relatively poor man.—S.M.M.

References and Suggested Readings

Anthony, Michael. "Lord Kitchener (1922–2000): Kitchener, A Man Destined for Greatness." *The Express* (Port of Spain), February 23, 2000, 4–5.

"Legendary Calypso Artist Lord Kitchener Dies at 77." Reuters, February 11, 2000.

Mason, Peter. *Bacchanal! The Carnival Culture of Trinidad.* Philadelphia, PA: Temple University Press, 1998.

———. "Master of Trinidadian Music Who Introduced Calypso to Britain." *The Guardian* (London), February 12, 2000, 24.

Mora, Anthony. "How Lord Kitchener Got His Sobriquet." *Newsday* (Port of Spain), May 2, 2000, 11.

Pareles, Jon. "Obituary: Lord Kitchener, 77 Calypso Songwriter." *The New York Times*, February 11, 2000, 9.

Waley, Paul. "Obituary of Lord Kitchener." *The Independent* (London), February 23, 2000, 6.

AUDRE LORDE
(1934–1992)

Grenadian American Poet, Essayist, and Activist

Audre Lorde, daughter of Grenadian immigrants, was an American poet, essayist, and feminist, known for works that weave personal and political themes and that make a point of challenging racial and sexual stereotypes. For Lorde, activism and writing were one: "The question of social protest and art is inseparable for me" (Homans 1991, 274). Her personal identity was a very important part of her literary persona. She characterized herself as a "black lesbian mother warrior poet" (Graham 1992, 33). Her writing is distinguished by her ability to bring together her worlds and the worlds of her ancestry—Africa, the Caribbean, and New York. Her writing, carved out of the complexity of her race and sexual preference, challenged female stereotypes. Beginning with the publication of her first book, *The First Cities*, in 1968, Lorde's works reflected her abhorrence of racial and sexual prejudice. The body of literary work produced by Lorde consists of 17 volumes of poetry, essays, and autobiography that chronicle racism, sexism, and homophobia; the overarching tone is urgency and sense of purpose.

Audrey Geraldine Lorde was born on February 18, 1934, in Harlem, New York, the youngest daughter of Grenadian immigrants Frederic Byron and Linda Bellmar Lorde. Her parents never considered New York their home and had planned to return to Grenada, but the economic depression and the advent of a world war in 1939 shattered that hope. Witnessing her parents' yearning for their country and the racism they faced fueled in young Lorde a sense of displacement as well as the sense of social justice that is characteristic of much of her work. A brilliant and eloquent writer and orator, Lorde did not begin to speak until the age of five. By the time she was six and beginning to write poetry, she demonstrated the self-determination that would characterize her work and her life by dropping "y" from her name, changing it to Audre.

Lorde graduated from high school in 1951 and attended Hunter College, receiving her B.A. in 1959. While at Hunter, she spent a year as a student at the National University in Mexico and became cognizant of her lesbianism. On her return to New York she became involved with the Harlem Writer's Guild, a predominantly male, and in Lorde's experience homophobic, group. At the same time, she was active in the mostly white "gay-girl" culture of Greenwich Village. She worked as a librarian and continued to study and write poetry during this time. In 1960 she received her Master's in Library Science from Columbia University in New York.

Lorde came of age as a poet in the 1960s, a time of political protests and assassinations, which instilled in her work a sense of gravity and resolve. Very little is known about this time of her life, except that for eight years during the 1960s she was married to Edward Ashley Rollins. Together they had two children, Elizabeth and Jonathan. In 1968 he was invited to serve as poet-in-residence at Tougaloo College in Mississippi, a historically black institution. Lorde credits this six-month period as the defining moment in her career. In Tougaloo she found a black community that embraced her and her work, discovered her love of teaching, and fell in love with a woman. It was during her time at Tougaloo that Lorde's first book of poetry, *The First Cities,* was published. Tougaloo also provided her with the time and inspiration to write the poems that would make up the next volume of her poetry, *Cables to Rage,* published in 1970.

Lorde returned to New York and continued writing and teaching. She taught at various colleges in the City University of New York system. In 1973 her third book of poetry, *From a Land Where Other People Live,* was nominated for a National Book Award. The fame brought by this nomination broadened her readership. Starting with the publication of *Coal* in 1976, she began a long association with the publisher W.W. Norton and poet Adrienne Rich, who wrote the jacket copy for all of Lorde's Norton publications.

The Black Unicorn, written in 1978, is considered her masterpiece. In this work she thoroughly explores mythologies of African goddesses and the experiences of the black Diaspora. The positive reviews of *Zami: A New Spelling of My Name,* her 1982 "biomythography" (a fictionalized chronicle of her childhood and early adulthood), brought her wider recognition and established her as a poet who also wrote prose.

Sister Outsider (1984), a book considered a feminist classic, established Lorde as an important feminist theorist. It exposes and challenges the issue of racism within the women's movement in the United States. Specifically, the phrase "sister outsider" refers to Lorde's relation to the mostly white lesbian community she interacted with in the 1950s, and expands to the other groups in her life. During this period, and through the stroke of her pen, Lorde also confronted the racist and homophobic rhetoric of political leaders like Senator Jesse Helms; and in sad and angry prose exposed the 1984 killing of Eleanor Bumpers, an elderly black woman who was shot to death in her apartment by overzealous New York City police officers.

Her work is characterized by social criticism intertwined with personal revelation. In 1978 Lorde was diagnosed with breast cancer and underwent a radical mastectomy. *The Cancer Journals* (1980) document the first years of diagnosis, hospitalizations, and treatments, as well as her feelings of hopelessness and despair in the face of death. It depicts her struggle with a medical establishment that was at times insensitive to cultural differences and women's health issues and helped put the issue of women's health care at the forefront of the feminist movement. Her hospital caretakers were shocked when Lorde, in her characteristic way, refused to wear a prosthesis to hide her "disfigurement," challenging the conventional wisdom that dictates women must have, or at least appear to have, two breasts. Her second bout with cancer and her decision to forego further invasive treatment in 1984 is documented in *A Burst of Light*. On November 17, 1992, Lorde lost her 14-year battle with cancer and died on the U.S. Virgin Island of St. Croix, the country of origin of her partner Gloria I. Joseph and the place they had called home during the last seven years of her life.

Lorde's contributions to society went beyond the written word. Her activism led her to co-found the first woman-of-color publishing house in the United States, Kitchen Table: Women of Color Press (1981), the St. Croix Women's Coalition, and the Sisterhood in Support of Sisters in South Africa (1985). In 1991 Lorde was honored with the Walt Whitman Citation of Merit, which conferred on her the title of New York State's poet laureate. She also received honorary doctorates from Hunter, Oberlin, and Haverford Colleges, and scores of literary awards and citations.

Lorde was also known by her African name, Gamba Adisa, meaning "Warrior: She Who Makes Meaning Clear"—a name that truly characterized her life and work.—G.C.

References and Suggested Readings

Black Women Writers at Work. "Audre Lorde." Voices from the Gaps: Women Writers of Color. Biography. *http://voices.cla.umn.edu/authors/AudreLorde.html.*

Brooks, Jerome. "In the Name of the Father: The Poetry of Audre Lorde." In Mari Evans, ed., *Black Women Writers (1950–1980): A Critical Evaluation.* Garden City, NY: Doubleday, 1984. 269–276.

Gómez, Jewel. "Passing of a Sister Warrior." *Essence* 24.1 (May 1993): 89.

Graham. Renee. "The Spirited Resolve of Audre Lorde." *The Boston Globe,* November 20, 1992, 33.

Griffin, Ada, and Michelle Parkerson. *A Litany for Survival: The Life and Work of Audre Lorde* (film). Third World Newsreel, 1995.

Hammond, Karla. "Audre Lorde: Interview." *Denver Quarterly* 16 (Spring 1981): 10–27.

Homans, Margaret. "Audre Lorde." In Lea Baechler and A. Walton Litz, eds., *African American Writers.* New York: Charles Scribner's Sons, 1991. 273–287.

Lorde, Audre. *The Audre Lorde Compendium: Essays, Speeches, and Journals.* Introduction by Alice Walker. London: Pandora, 1996.

———. *A Burst of Light*. Milford, CT: Firebrand Books, 1988.

———. *The Cancer Journals*. Argyle, NY: Spinsters, 1980.

———. *The Collected Poems of Audre Lorde*. New York: W.W. Norton, 2000.

———. *Zami: A New Spelling of My Name*. Trumansburg, NY: Crossing Press, 1982.

McDowell, Margaret. "The Black Woman as Artist and Critic: Four Versions." *Kentucky Review* 7 (1987): 19–41.

Winter, Nina. "On Audre Lorde" and "Audre Lorde." *Interview with the Muse: Remarkable Women Speak on Creativity and Power*. Berkley, CA: Moon Books, 1978. 72–81.

DULCE MARÍA LOYNAZ
(1902–1997)

Cuban Poet and Novelist

Dulce María Loynaz was one of Cuba's best-known poets. A lifelong writer, Loynaz finally achieved recognition during the last decades of her life, including the Spanish-speaking world's highest literary award, the Miguel de Cervantes Award. Her late recognition was in many ways the result of her own desire to stay out of the limelight. Postmodern writer Loynaz has been described as having a sensibility that "reveals itself through the themes of lost time, loneliness, yearning, and love in an intimate and emotional atmosphere rarely encountered in these times" (Martin 1994, 62). While she is best remembered for her mastery of poetry, perhaps Loynaz's greatest contribution to literature was her pioneering novel *Jardín* (Garden; 1951), a story that depicts the position of women in the modern world and is considered the precursor to the magic realism genre in today's Latin American literature. Magic realism, the incorporation of fantastic or mythical elements in realistic fiction, sometimes blurring the distinction between fantasy and reality, has come to dominate the contemporary Latin American fiction of such well-known authors as **Alejo Carpentier**, Gabriel García Márquez, and Isabel Allende.

Loynaz was born in Havana on December 10, 1902, into a well-to-do family who lived in a colonial-style mansion overlooking the sea with art, antiques, and all the trappings of affluence. Her father, Enrique Loynaz, a war hero, had fought in the Spanish-American War and was the author of the "Himno Invasor," the national song of Cuba's rebel troops. Loynaz and her younger siblings, a sister and two brothers, were tutored at home. Loynaz's mother, an able artist and musician, encouraged her children to write, paint, and learn several languages. The Loynaz family home was frequently a calling place for writers visiting Cuba, such as Spain's Federico García Lorca and Chile's Gabriela Mistral, who became Loynaz's lifetime friend. So comprehensive was her home schooling that she was admitted to the University of Havana, where she completed her law degree in 1927.

Although she had been publishing some of her poetry in the Havana newspaper *La Nación* since 1919, it wasn't until 1938 that *Versos*, her first three-volume collection of poetry, was formally published .

Loynaz traveled extensively, and some of her work was published well after she wrote it. She visited the United States during the early 1920s and the Middle East in 1929. After seeing the Egyptian tombs she wrote the acclaimed *Love Letter to King Tut-Ank-Amen*, which was published in 1953. It was also during this time, between 1928 and 1935, that she wrote her only novel, the seminal work *Jardín*, which was published in Spain many years later and was described in her obituary as "a fine, difficult novel about the position of women in the modern world—although it had been written 20 years earlier" ("Obituary of Dulce María Loynaz" 1997, 23).

While still in her early twenties, and against her parents' wishes, Loynaz fell in love with Canary Islander Pablo Alvarez de Canas, whom she was forced to leave to enter into a loveless marriage with her first cousin Enrique in 1937. Except for the 1938 publication of *Versos*, that six-year period of her first marriage was uneventful. It wasn't until her divorce and her 1946 return and marriage to de Canas that she began to travel and write, publishing most of her subsequent works in Spain. During the 1940s and 1950s, she published several collections of poems, including *Juegos de Agua* (Fountains; 1946), *Poemas sin nombre* (Poems Without a Name; 1953), and *Obra lírica* (Lyrical Work; 1955). "Poema CXXIV," which appeared in her 1953 volume of poetry *Poemas náufragos* (Shipwreck Poems), is considered one of the most eloquent poems written about Cuba. *Tenerife*, a travel book based on her visits to the Canary Islands, was published in 1958. Throughout these years, she had also continued to practice law when in Cuba.

Although she always insisted that she was not a feminist, some of her best poems fall into this category. Her poems "Song to a Barren Woman" (1937) and "The Last Days of a House" (1958) are considered aesthetic denunciations of patriarchal society and a brilliant uplifting statement on women's inherent worth in the world.

The Cuban revolution of 1959 and the period following brought an end to Loynaz's creative activity. Although she did not consider herself a political activist, she considered herself a self-exile in her own country, and vowed never to publish her work in Cuba again. She abandoned her legal practice and stopped writing poetry, unwilling to include communist themes in her work. However, that year she became a member and later served as president of Academia Cubana de la lengua (Cuban Academy of Language). She also wrote for journals, translated the works of Walt Whitman, a poet she greatly admired, and continued to write essays devoted to Spanish American women poets. In 1968, she was appointed a member of Spain's prestigious Real Academia Española de la lengua (Spanish Royal Academy of Language), guardian of the Spanish language in the world. Throughout her life, even when she ceased her creative activity, her house was a meeting place for other Cubans artists and writers like Alejo Carpentier Valmont and **Nicolas Guillén**, both of whom she considered great friends.

A compilation of Loynaz's best poetry was published in 1984 as *Poesías escogidas* (Selected Poems). After this publication, the Cuban public took notice of her once more. She received most of the recognition and accolades during the last decade of her life, beginning in 1987 when she was awarded the Cuban National Prize for Literature. In 1991 *Dulce María Loynaz: Valoración múltiple* (Multiple Appraisal), a volume of critical essays by and about Loynaz, was published. In 1992 Spain conferred on her its highest literary award, the Miguel de Cervantes Award, making her only the second Cuban, after Alejo Carpentier Valmont, to be honored with this prestigious award. Loynaz died in her native city of Havana in 1997 at the age of 94.—G.C.

References and Suggested Readings

Behar, R. "Dulce María Loynaz. A Woman Who No Longer Exists." *Michigan Quarterly Review* 36.4 (Fall 1997): 529–538.

Davies, Catherine. *A Place in the Sun? Women Writers in Twentieth-century Cuba.* Atlantic Highlands, NJ: Zed Books, 1997.

Fernández, Pablo Armando, and David Frye. "Bridges of the Heart." *Michigan Quarterly Review* 33.4 (Fall 1994): 821–827.

Loynaz, Dulce María. *Jardín.* Barcelona, Spain: Seix Barre, 1993.

———. *Poesías completas.* Havana, Cuba: Editorial letras Cubanas, 1993.

Martin, Jorge Hernández. "Cuban Muses." *Americas* 46:1 (January–February 1994): 61–63.

"Obituary of Dulce María Loynaz Cuban Poet Who Fell Silent Under the Castro Regime." *Daily Telegraph,* May 19, 1997, 23.

JON LUCIEN
(1942–)

Singer/Songwriter from the Virgin Islands

Jazz singer and songwriter Jon Marcus Lucien has been described as having the musical ability to capture the essence of romance. His love songs have been hailed as musical experiences of spirituality and harmony. His music seamlessly bonds jazz, R&B, Caribbean rhythms, and Brazilian music and is considered an outstanding expression of the twin musical formats popular on jazz radio stations: "quiet storm" and "smooth jazz." His deep baritone voice and his commanding presence have made him extremely popular on the cabaret/supper-club circuit.

The eldest of eight children, Lucien Leopold Harrigan was born into the musical family of Elouise Turnbull-Harrigan and Eric Lucien Harrigan on the island of Tortola, British Virgin Islands, on January 8, 1942. Jon Lucien spent his childhood on the island of St. Thomas in the American Virgin Islands and learned music from his father, a musician who played a stringed instrument called the tre in his Latin jazz band, Rico and the Rhythmeres.

To keep him away from trouble when he was nine years old, Lucien was sent away to school and by the time he returned home at 17 he was a self-taught musician who could play bass, guitar and piano. While in St. Thomas he played bass with English musician Marty Clark, whose musical repertoire included many jazz standards. Through this experience he met and jammed with established jazz musicians such as Cy Coleman and Bobby Short who vacationed on the island.

Jon Lucien.

Lucien left St. Thomas at the age of 19 and arrived in New York City, where he tried to establish himself in jazz circles, and played in the Catskills music scene. For many years he honed his musical skills playing weddings, bar mitzvahs, and in the Broadway musical *Don't Bother Me I Can't Cope.* It was a period of his life where he found himself playing with musicians from all over the world and was exposed to musical rhythms and tempos that differed vastly from his own repertoire. As he began to establish his own sound, he also did away with the Leopold Harrigan part of his name—a name he had never identified with—and legally changed his name to Jon Marcus Lucien (Jon Lucien, personal communication, March 5, 2003).

His 1970 RCA debut, *I Am Now,* began to reveal what would become his trademark style as a romantic crooner with a powerful baritone voice. The album included Brazilian songwriter Carlos Jobin's classic "Dindi," characterized by Brazilian bandleader Sergio Mendez as one of the best renditions of the song he has ever heard.

His second album, 1973's Grammy-nominated *Rashida,* was critically acclaimed as innovative in its infusion of bossa nova rhythms. From the early days of their airplay on New York City's R&B radio stations, the songs "Would You Believe in Me" and "Lady Love" were hailed as classics and are still heard today. His music is so eclectic and difficult to pinhole into a particular style that it has been difficult to market him to mainstream audiences. Frustration over this and the surge of the disco genre during the 1970s and 1980s led him to drop out of the recording business for almost a decade. However, after the 1991 release of the CD *Listen Love* he has recorded and performed steadily.

In 1993 he released *Mother Nature's Son,* an album that has begun to reward him with a new generation of fans. His 1996 CD, *Endless Love,* is perhaps the most powerful and profound of all his albums. He began recording it about the same time his 17-year-old daughter Dalila perished on TWA Flight 800, which was destined to land in Paris but exploded in mid-air, killing all passengers aboard.

Lucien's most requested songs were re-recorded and released in 1999 in an album titled *By Request*. A compilation of his classics was also released under the title *Sweet Control: The Best of Jon Lucien*. Adding to these successes is the inclusion of cuts from his songs into hip-hop and acid jams music recordings. Original copies of his earlier albums such as *Rashida* and *Mind's Eye* are considered collector's items and command very high prices, prompting the recent release in the UK of a double CD anthology containing *I Am Now, Rashida,* and *Mind's Eye.*

In 2001 Lucien's established a high-tech production company, Sugar Apple Music Group, Ltd., and released *Lucien Romantico*. His 2002 album, *Man From Paradise*, showcases his Caribbean roots and heritage.—G.C.

References and Suggested Readings

Amen, Sunyatta. "The Sultry Soulful Sound of Jon Lucien." *Unfold* (Summer 1999): 70–71.

Francis, Naila. "You Can't Put Your Finger on Him." *The Intelligencer Record,* August 18, 2000, 19.

Harrington, Richard. "Jon Lucien: In His Own Voice." *The Washington Post,* February 28, 2003, T08.

Jon Lucien Homepage: *http://www.jonlucien.com/.*

"Jon Lucien Survives on His Own Terms." *Jazziz* 14.12 (December 1, 1997): 94.

Mattingly, Rick. "Jon Lucien, Singer's 'Quiet Storm' warms cold night." *The Courier-Journal* (Louisville, KY), January 30, 2000, n.p.

Puckett, Jeffrey Lee. "Quiet Storm Rolls into Town for Midnite Ramble." *The Courier-Journal* (Louisville, KY), January 23, 2000, n.p.

ANTONIO MACEO
(1845–1896)

Cuban Patriot and Military Leader

Freedom fighter Antonio Maceo is one of Cuba's national heroes and a principal figure in the history of Cuba's struggle for independence. Referred to as "Titán de Bronce" (Bronze Titan) because of his heroics on the battlefield, he fought in both the Ten Years' War (1868–1878) and the War of Independence (1895). As a black man, racial equality was an integral part of his struggle. In addition to being a great military commander, he also became an entrepreneur and successful businessman. Revolutionary zeal extended to other members of his family; his father and brothers all participated in the struggle for independence, and **José Martí**, another Cuban national hero, immortalized Maceo's mother, **Mariana Grajales**, in his writings.

Baptized Antonio de la Caridad Maceo y Grajales, he was born on June 14, 1845, in Santiago de Cuba, in the eastern province of Oriente. His father Marcos had emigrated from Venezuela after fighting with the Spanish against Simón Bolívar. He purchased a small farm and eventually married Mariana Grajales, a widow with four sons. Grajales, a black woman of Dominican background who lost her husband and several children to the Cuban cause, was a strong supporter of independence. Four sons and a daughter were born of Marcos and Mariana's union; Antonio Maceo was the eldest.

Even though they were not slaves, blacks at that time were not allowed to study beyond a primary education. However, the family instilled in their children a love for their country. Before he was 20 years old, Antonio Maceo had married María Magdalena Cabrales y Fernández.

On October 12, 1868, a group of mostly liberated slaves led by Carlos Manuel de Céspedes, ate supper at the Maceo house in Majaguabo. After dinner, Marcos Maceo and four of his sons joined the revolutionary army and began the Cuban revolt against Spain—or, as it is historically known, the Grito de Yara (Cry of Yara). Antonio, who saw his father killed that year, moved up the ranks very quickly. He was a brilliant tactician who did a great deal of damage to the enemy with his small army of poorly trained soldiers. In May of that year he received the first of 26 bullet wounds he suffered during the war. His wife and mother, who had joined the insurgency and were aiding wounded soldiers in one of the camps, nursed him back to health.

Dominican Máximo Gómez, who had come to Cuba to direct some of the war campaigns against the Spaniards, was the general and chief of the First Corps under which Maceo fought. In 1870, Maceo led the now famous attack on Barigua, considered one of the most brilliant military feats of the century. With a relatively small number of men armed with machetes, they fought back the Spaniards. The rebels' knowledge of the terrain, their guerrilla tactics, and their higher level of immunity to tropical diseases, coupled with their patriotic fervor, helped them overcome the vastly superior Spanish forces.

Slavery continued to exist on the island during the Ten Years' War. Maceo's popularity and approval as a hero was becoming a threat. One of the issues Maceo had to confront during that time was his race, since the enemy and the white ruling class in Cuba used the "race card" as a strategy. They maintained that allowing Maceo to lead would result in a takeover by the black race, leading Cuba to become another Haiti, a prospect that greatly distressed all whites on the island. Undeterred, Maceo continued his struggle throughout the Ten Years' War, and by 1878 a small group of insurgent leaders, Máximo Gómez among them, had signed an agreement known as the Pact of Zanjon. In essence, the articles of the pact granted Spain continued governance of the island and granted freedom to indentured Asians and slaves who had taken part in the war. Interestingly, slaves who had remained loyal to their masters were not to be freed. Maceo was unwilling to go along with this agreement—for him it represented a defeat he was reluctant to accept. Instead, with other Cuban freedom fighters, he carried out the Baraguá Protest, an open demonstration where they announced their disagreement with the Pact of Zanjon. Nevertheless, the war ended with the approval of the Pact of Zanjón, and 17 years (1878–1895) of unease followed.

With a sense of personal defeat, Maceo spent many of those years in exile in different countries, dodging assassination attempts on his life. He knew that the plan to have him leave Cuba was in part a scheme to deter him from continuing the fight for independence. In 1879 he spent time traveling to Haiti, Grand Turk Island, the Bahamas, Jamaica, the Dominican Republic, and other islands trying to garner funds and support for his revolutionary ideals, but to no avail.

Still in exile 1880 to 1892 were his entrepreneurial years and perhaps the only time he was not totally focused on the cause for independence. Known throughout his life as an avid reader, he now had ample time to engage in this pursuit. In 1882, he received a letter from another Cuban exile José Martí that probed Maceo's feelings and interest in perhaps joining preparations for a plan of revolt being planned in New York, then the center of Cuban revolutionary activity. Maceo, who was currently living in Honduras, responded affirmatively. For a few years they continued to exchange letters discussing the possibility of a military invasion of Cuba.

In 1886 Maceo moved to Panama, where he earned a living building houses for the workers during the Panama Canal construction. He sent money back home to his wife and returned to Cuba in 1888 for a brief visit. However, it wasn't until 1894 that he became completely involved in José Martí's elaborate preparations for an incursion into Cuba.

On March 30, 1895, Antonio and José Maceo landed in eastern Cuba and were joined there by José Martí and Máximo Gómez from Santo Domingo, Dominican Republic. The leaders of the final insurrection for Cuba's independence were José Martí, Máximo Gómez, and Antonio Maceo. Martí died in one of the first skirmishes and leadership of the rebel forces passed on to General-in-Chief Gómez and Lieutenant-General Maceo. Poor blacks and whites joined the forces and boats brought arms from North America. Tens of thousands of peasants provided food and supplies and helped them by spying on the Spanish Army. Maceo and Máximo Gómez led the invasion to the west, and Maceo's troops arrived in Mantua, the westernmost town of Cuba, on June 22, 1896. The fighting was intense and Maceo, who had started with 6,000 well-armed men and plenty of artillery, was left with 200 men by October 1. On December 7, 1896, he was killed in combat. He was 51 years old and had spent 27 years fighting for Cuba's independence, losing his father and several brothers to the war. In death, Antonio Maceo, the Bronze Titan, became a symbol for Cuba's independence.—G.C.

References and Suggested Readings

Foner, Philip S. *Antonio Maceo: The "Bronze Titan" of Cuba's Struggle for Independence.* New York: Monthly Review Press, 1977.

History of Cuba Web Site: *http://www.historyofcuba.com*.

Marmol, José. *Antonio Maceo Grajales: El Titán de Bronce*. Miami, FL: Ediciones Universales, 1999.

Pando, Magdalen M. *Cuba's Freedom Fighter, Antonio Maceo: 1845–1896*. Gainesville, FL: Felicity, 1980. *http://198.62.75.1/www2/fcf/antonio.maceo.ff.html*.

Smith, Joseph. "Heroes of the Cuban Revolution, Martí, Maceo and Gómez." *Historian* 44 (1994): 3–8.

Weiss Fagan, Patricia. "Antonio Maceo: Heroes, History and Historiography." *Latin American Research Review* 11:3 (1976): 69–94.

MACHITO (FRANK GRILLO)
(1909–1984)

Cuban American Singer, Musician, and Humanitarian

Frank Raúl Grillo, alias Machito, made important contributions to Cuban and American music during the twentieth century. Grillo was mainly responsible for integrating the musical elements that constitute the roots of what we know today as Latin jazz. His unique technique and style influenced the music of big bands, jazz and blues, and bebop. Grillo was also a pioneer in the development of Afro-Cuban jazz and played an important role during the mambo craze of the 1950s. His musical style influenced the development of salsa music.

Grillo was born in Tampa, Florida, on February 16, 1909, one of six children of Rogelio and Marta Grillo. His parents returned to Cuba when Machito was an infant and settled in Havana. In an interview conducted by Larry Birnbaum for the magazine *Down Beat*, Machito stated that he did not have a lot of formal education, something that he regretted later in life (Birnbaum 1980). His father wanted for him to go into the food distribution business but he chose a music career instead.

The documentary *Machito: A Latin Jazz Legacy* reconstructs his formative years and describes the path that led him to music. When he returned to Cuba, his father operated several businesses in the hospitality industry. At different times he had a cigar warehouse, a grocery store, a restaurant, and a food distribution business. As part of the food distribution business, Grillo traveled extensively with his father through the different provinces of Cuba delivering food to small grocery stores that served the laborers working in sugarcane plantations and sugar mills. Many of these workers were musicians with impressive skills and a command of Afro-Cuban musical rhythms. His father often bartered food with them in exchange for their participation at small musical gatherings held in his grocery store. Musical groups made up of "rumberos" and "conjuntos" visited the Grillos and performed for them. Musicians and groups such as Taganito, Malanga,

Descoyuntado, and Andrea Baroa participated in these performances, which profoundly impressed young Grillo (Ortiz 1987).

As an adolescent during the late 1920s, Grillo was exposed to American jazz music and started a collection of jazz records that included musicians such as Duke Ellington and Fletcher Henderson (Moritz 1983). He also started attended music rehearsals of a group known as the Jóvenes de la Rendición. While at these practices, a maraca player named Champitos performed powerful and complex pieces. Grillo decided that he wanted to learn the maracas and through long hours of practice at home, he learned to play them on his own. After a fellow musician heard him play, Machito was invited to play and sing with some local music groups. Eventually he started to perform professionally with the Sexteto Nacional and the Orquesta de María Teresa, two important Cuban groups of the time.

In 1937 Grillo was persuaded by Mario Bauzá, his brother-in-law, to go to New York and work as a musician. Bauzá, who was married to Grillo's younger sister Graciela, had been a prominent classical musician in Cuba and had already moved to New York, where he was working as a music director for both the Chick Webb and Cab Calloway bands. In New York Grillo found himself surrounded by the huge music boom of America's big band movement and the great interest in jazz created by the Harlem Renaissance. Grillo visited the ballroom of the Hotel Savoy and The Palladium, two of the important musical nightclubs of the time. His first music job in New York was with the Happy Boys Orchestra. This engagement led to his playing and recording with the orchestras of Alberto Soldarrás, Xavier Cugat, Noro Morales, Estrellas Habaneras, and the prominent Orquesta Siboney. He also came in contact for the first time with the work of legendary jazz performers Louis Armstrong and Count Basie, who were regular performers at the most popular nightclubs in Harlem.

Grillo formed his own band, Machito and the Afro-Cubans, in 1940. According to music historian John Storm Roberts, the formation of the Afro-Cubans constituted "the single most important event of the decade for Latin music's development as an autonomous U.S. sub style" (Roberts 1999, 101). Bauzá joined the band as its musical director and they developed musical arrangements blending their Afro-Cuban music with jazz. Their style was characterized by the use of strong multi-tempo percussion arrangements with jazz wind instruments. This fusion became known as bebop and replaced the sound of swing and the big bands. Grillo's band signed a four-year contract with La Conga Club in New York, but had to abandon the band for a brief period of time when he was drafted into the army. His sister Graciela took his place as singer and maraca player. Machito also signed a contract with Decca Records and released the songs "Sopa de Pichón," and "Tanga." The song "Tanga," written by Bauzá and sung by Machito, became very popular. It was Machito's theme song for the remainder of his musical life. The band was very successful and was featured on many of the popular radio shows of the time.

Bauzá, who had an excellent knowledge of the African American jazz musical establishment and who knew the American musical markets, paired the band with a number of jazz arrangers and performers such as Cuban **"Chico" O' Farrill**, and Dizzy Gillespie. These collaborations started an exchange of musical forms that evolved into a new style of music. They also wanted to capture the interest of a new wave of Puerto Rican immigrants who were arriving in New York and longed to listen and dance to Latin music. During the early years of the band, they collaborated and recorded with Charlie Parker, Herbie Mann, Joe Phillips, Buddy Rich, Johnnie Griffin, and Stan Kenton.

In 1948 producer Norman Grantz brought together Charlie Parker, Joe "Flip" Phillips, and Machito for a recording. The final product was a unique distinct music style known as Latin jazz. These successful collaborations continued throughout the 1950s with other African American musicians such as Buddy Rich, Howard McGhee, Brew Moore, Johnny Griffin, and Cannonball Aderley. These musicians influenced Machito, who in turn was a strong influence on the American jazz establishment as it moved toward the Latin style.

During the 1950s and early 1960s, American music went through the mambo craze. Triggered by the hits and popularity of **Damaso Pérez Prado** and **Cachao**, Grillo and his band produced several mambo hits. Performing at the Palladium, the home of mambo music in New York, he lent a hand to younger musicians such as **Tito Puente** and helped them establish themselves in New York.

As the mambo mania came to an end in the early 1960s, Grillo was once again left to perform Latin jazz. During the 1970s he toured with his band throughout the world. He collaborated with new musicians, establishing the genre of salsa. In 1982, as Latin jazz started to resurface, he was awarded a Grammy for the record *Machito and His Salsa Band*. During his career, Grillo worked and performed with almost every famous artist working in jazz, mambo, and salsa. He recorded more than 75 albums in a span of 50 years.

There is a significant dimension of Grillo's life that has not been stressed enough by either his biographers or music historians. From the time his band reached success, he became a humanitarian with deep concerns for the well being of Latino youth and the under-privileged people of New York. During the 1940s and 1950s he played an important role in preventing gang violence among Latino youth. He also was a strong supporter of the rehabilitation of drug addicts, and for many years helped Project Return by providing free concerts in New York's parks. Toward the end of his life, he worked closely with Project SCOUT (Senior Citizens Outreach Unit Team).

Grillo died in 1984 from a stroke while on tour in London. His son Mario continues to lead his band and his daughter Paula now sings with it. Although he has been gone from the musical scene for more that 15 years, he is now perhaps at the top of his popularity among the followers of Latin jazz. Commenting on a series of concerts sponsored by the Smithsonian in Washington that featured Machito's work, the *Washington Post* noted: "There are two distinct eras in 20th-century popular Latin music: 'before Machito,' and 'after Machito'" (Byers 1999, C5).—S.M.M.

References and Suggested Readings

Birnbaum, Larry. "Machito: 1908–1984 [*sic*]." *Down Beat* 51 (July 1984): 14.
———. "Original Macho Man." *Down Beat* 47 (December 1980): 25–27.
Byers, Mim. "The More Machito, the Better, Latin Series Gets Off to a Sizzling Start." *The Washington Post*, March 1, 1999, C5.
Loza, Steven. *Tito Puente and the Making of Latin Music.* Urbana: University of Illinois Press, 1999.
Moritz, Charles, ed. "Machito." *Current Biography Year Book.* New York: The H.W. Wilson Company, 1983. 241–244.
Ortiz, Carlos. *Machito: A Latin Jazz Legacy.* New York: First Run/Icarus Films, 1987.
Roberts, John Storm. *The Latin Tinge: The Impact of Latin American Music on the United States.* 2nd ed. New York: Oxford University Press, 1999.

THE MANLEY FAMILY

Jamaican Artists and Political Leaders

The Manley family of Jamaica permeated the political and cultural ferment of Jamaica for almost a century. As politicians, artists and sports enthusiasts, they are considered pillars of twentieth-century Jamaican society.

EDNA MANLEY
(1900–1987)

Sculptor, Painter, Writer, and Mother of Jamaican Art

Internationally acclaimed artist Edna Manley is considered the leader of Jamaica's modern artistic movement. Her legacy touched not only the art world, but the political scene as well. She was the widow of **Norman Washington Manley**, one of Jamaica's national heroes, and the mother of former prime minister **Michael Manley**. As an artist, her work reflected her deep social consciousness rooted in the collective realities of a struggling Jamaica. Manley's depictions of Jamaicans in the midst of their struggle for independence from England buoyed the country's sense of worth, and her encouragement of other artists led to a movement that eventually became institutionalized in the 1950s as the Jamaica School of Art. She also wrote stories, poems, plays, and essays and helped found a publication that served as a vehicle for new artists. Her artistic accomplishments and leadership were instrumental in launching Jamaica's artistic legacy, and for this she is recognized as the mother of Jamaican art.

Edna Swithenbank, the fifth of nine children was born at Bournemouth, England on February 29, 1900, to Harvey Swithenbank, an English Methodist missionary, and Jamaican native Ellie Swithenbank. She grew up in rural Cornwall, where her father had his ministry. Her love for animals, particularly horses (which later appeared in her art), developed during this time. Manley's father died when she was nine; after his death her family settled in Penzance, where her interests turned to art and she attended West Cornwall College. Even while growing up in England, she considered Jamaica her true home. In 1914 she met her "handsome" first cousin, 22-year-old Norman Manley, a Jamaican national and Rhodes Scholar who was studying at Oxford University. A short time later, World War I broke out and he went to war as part of the British Royal Field Artillery, and she, an excellent horsewoman, worked at the Army Remount Department at Wembley, breaking in Canadian horses. In 1918, against her mother's wishes, she left home for London to study art.

While in London she worked during the day and studied at the Regent Street Polytechnic, the Royal Academy Schools, and the St. Martin's School of Art. That same year marked the end of the war and Norman Manley's return to England to finish his studies, and while there rekindled his relationship with Edna. In 1921 he obtained his degree and they married. They returned to Jamaica in 1922 in the midst of the anti-colonialist movement that culminated in independence from Britain in 1962. At that time there was little, if any, native art tradition save that representing the colonial establishment. Thus with the strong support of Norman, she began 65 years of stirring and inspiring generations of Jamaicans in the development of a national aesthetic identity.

From the very beginning of her life in Jamaica, Manley's art reflected a strong identification with Jamaica and its people. Her first son, Douglas, was born in 1922 and they returned to Jamaica. *Beadseller* (1923) was her first Jamaican sculpture completed just months after her arrival. After the birth of her second son, Michael, in 1924, Manley spent much of her time working on her art, and in 1929 had the first exhibition of her work in London at the Goupil Gallery. Her work continued to be exhibited in England, with a life-size hardwood-carved sculpture titled *Eve* receiving much critical acclaim. Its originality attracted critical acclaim due to its "vigorous treatment of form, with a sculptural simplification that owed nothing to modernistic theories" ("Obituary of Mrs. Edna Manley" 1987). She was awarded a silver medal and earned the distinction of being elected a member of the British artists' London Group. As the Jamaican independence movement increased, particularly toward the late 1950s, she stopped exhibiting her work in England.

In Jamaica, the Manleys' home was a hub of political activity. While Norman Manley's political involvement was centered on the development of the framework for independence from Britain, Edna Manley's art became increasingly political, reflecting the social turmoil. In particular, her 1935 wood carving "Negro Aroused," a torso of a man seated with his head straining upward in suppressed anger, clearly reflected her solidarity with the struggles of Jamaica's working class. "Negro Aroused," together with "The Prophet" (1936), "Pocomania" (1936), and "Tomorrow" (1939) are considered icons of the pro-independence struggle period in Jamaican history. During the 1940s she also carved the well-known "Horse of the Morning" and "Moon." During this time of riots and pro-independence demonstrations, Manley supported the cause and her husband's founding and leadership of the People's National Party.

Along with other artists in the 1940s, in order to foster interests in the arts Manley started free art classes for adults at the Junior Centre of the Institute of Jamaica. The goal of the artwork was the establishment of a national art identity. Many beginning or unknown artists of that time who have since become internationally known found a venue for their work in *Public Opinion* (1937) and *Focus* (1943), cultural journals Manley founded for the work of up-and-coming young Jamaican and Caribbean artists. In 1950 this venture developed into the establishment of the Jamaica School of Art.

Norman Manley became chief minister of the country in 1955 and served until 1962. During this time, Edna Manley was commissioned by the Sheraton Hotel in Kingston to carve "He Cometh Forth" (1962), an allegorical representation celebrating Jamaican independence. Her last series of carvings was produced after her husband's death in 1969 and was her way of dealing with the sorrow of her loss. During this period of grief she produced a series of wood carvings "The Angel," "Adios," "The Phoenix," "The Faun," "Journey," and "Mountain Woman," described in Betty LaDuke's 1991 essay as Manley's expression of "grief, despair, and finally the acceptance of her loss" (LaDuke 1991, 136). Perhaps the most dramatic of these works was "Journey," a life-sized rising figure of Norman Manley, produced in 1973. She briefly experimented with fiberglass, but found it was damaging to her lungs. In 1985 she stopped sculpting and turned to painting.

Some of Manley's work strongly reflects the matriarchal structure of the Jamaican family, particularly "Mountain Woman" (1970), "The Ancestor" (1974), and "The Message" (1977), a sculpture of two women she observed in the market and drew in the back of her checkbook: "They were probably sharing some earthy secret. I never knew what it was, but it was a secret an older woman tells a younger woman" (E. Manley 1989, 36).

She received many awards during her lifetime and was the first recipient of the country's highest honor, The Gold Musgrave Medal, for her contribution to Jamaican arts, including the establishment of the Jamaican School of Art and Craft. She also received an honorary doctoral degree from the University of the West Indies in 1977. In 1980, a year in which she had major exhibitions in Jamaica and London, she received the Order of Merit and was voted a Fellow of the Institute of Jamaica, known today as Jamaica's National Gallery. The City University of New York honored her in 1984 and the Jamaican Bureau of Women's Affairs conferred on her their Woman of Distinction Award in 1985.

It has been said that her art was a visual representation of Jamaica's transformations. The 1987 London *Times* obituary of Edna Manley described her as a "tall, elegant, and slender lady, with darting eyes and a determined will. She adored horses; signed her work ME; and called her home 'Regardless.'" Edna Manley, who died in 1987, was given an official funeral by the Jamaican government and was buried beside her husband in National Heroes Park. That same year, the Jamaica School of Art was renamed the Edna Manley School for the Visual Arts.—G.C.

MICHAEL MANLEY
(1924–1997)

Prime Minister of Jamaica, Labor Leader, Member of the Jamaican Parliament, and Jamaican Statesman

---

Michael Norman Manley was one of the most important Caribbean politicians and leaders of the second half of the twentieth century. A visionary leader, popularly known as "Joshua" (like the biblical prophet), he was instrumental in defining the political, social, and economic landscape of Jamaica after it gained independence from Great Britain in 1962.

Manley was born in St. Andrews, Jamaica, on December 10, 1924, to an affluent, upper-middle-class Jamaican family. He was one of two children of **Norman Washington Manley** and **Edna Manley**. His father was a politician and lawyer and his British-born mother was a noted artist and sculptor.

Manley finished his primary schooling in Jamaica and attended the prestigious Jamaica College for his secondary education, where he excelled as a student leader and as an athlete. While at Jamaica College he challenged the headmaster over a change in policy. Abandoning the school after a confrontation with the headmaster, he triggered a massive student protest over his departure. After graduating from high school, Manley enrolled at McGill University in Montreal but only attended for a year before joining the Canadian Air Force in 1942. When he completed his military service, Manley moved to London and enrolled in the prestigious London School of Economics in late 1945. While there, he was influenced by the economic and political doctrines of Harold Laski, the leading thinker behind the social democratic ideas that Manley later adopted in Jamaica (Levi 1989). During his years in London, Manley was involved with the West Indian Student Union and co-founded the Caribbean Labor Congress of London. He led these organizations in their efforts for Jamaica's independence from Great Britain.

Michael Manley.

After graduating from the London School of Economics in 1949, Manley worked briefly as a book reviewer and freelance journalist for the BBC and for the *London Observer*. In 1951 he returned to Jamaica, where he immediately became involved in public affairs. He was an editor for the Jamaica weekly *Public Opinion* and joined the People's National Party (PNP), founded by his father, and became a member of its National Executive Council. Nevertheless, his most important work on his return to Jamaica was as a labor leader. He became a negotiator and a leader of the of the National Worker's Union, and in 1959 led a major strike against the sugar companies in Jamaica. The strike and Manley's criticism of the sugar barons triggered discoveries of fraud and brought major reforms to the sugar industry.

Because of his involvement in both the PNP and the labor movement, Manley gained substantial recognition from the Jamaican people island-wide, paving the way for his incursion into politics when he entered the Jamaican Senate in 1962 and became a member of the Parliament in 1967. Manley was a vocal and articulate spokesperson on behalf of his party. He developed a platform to press for more liberal social and economic reforms that could benefit those Jamaicans who were disenfranchised from society. After his father's death in 1969, he succeeded him as the leader of the PNP and was elected prime minister of the island in 1972.

Throughout the campaign to become prime minister, Manley compared himself to the biblical prophet Joshua. Trying to win the vote of the Rastafarians, he appeared wearing native African costumes and carried an ivory and ebony baton, given to him by Ethiopian emperor Haile Selassie during a visit to Jamaica in 1966. Baptized by Manley as Joshua's Rod of Correction, the baton symbolized his promise to break the yoke of capitalism that had oppressed the Jamaican people for so long (Rother 1997, 52). Manley was elected by an overwhelming majority and immediately instituted a series of radical social and economic reforms that were consistent with his socio-democratic ideals.

During his first two terms as prime minister of Jamaica Manley imposed strong regulation over businesses and positioned the government, rather than the private sector, as the key agent to promote economic growth. He forced private businesses to partner with government in different enterprises and nationalized many of them. His sponsorship of agrarian reform led to a major exodus of the British and American economic elite from Jamaica. Following his socialist ideologies, Manley also promoted a major redistribution of wealth in Jamaica, raised taxes for the wealthy, and instituted progressive social programs to help the poor. At the same time, he became close friends with **Fidel Castro** of Cuba and was perceived by the U.S. government and by other capitalist and industrial powers as a major threat to the economic stability of Jamaica and the Caribbean. Manley worked hard forging partnerships with socialist regimes and became a leader of the organization of Non-Aligned Nations and the Group 77. From his position of leadership as prime minister and as a leader of these groups, Manley launched strong attacks against the International Monetary Fund, whose policies he thought were strangling the economic and social well being of developing nations. Moreover, he advocated for a new world economic order that would benefit the underdeveloped nations of the Third World. Manley's economic policies and changes threw the country into desperation and chaos. The rich power elite perceived him as a socialist who was crippling the island's economy by attacking industries and business owners. However, his popularity among the poor and underclass, who were positively impacted by his policies, was so great that he managed to be reelected in 1976. He was successful in building strong alliances with the Rastafarian movement in Jamaica, whose members revered him as a humane reformer who wanted to empower blacks and poor people. Although his policies were well intentioned, the island's economy deteriorated and the island turned to violence and chaos.

By 1980 the economic situation and the political pressure from the International Monetary Fund and the United States was so great that when Edward Seaga, leader of the Jamaican Labor Party, challenged him in the elections, Manley lost. Manley spent nine years in retirement rethinking his political ideas and writing books. A passionate follower of boxing and cricket, he wrote *A History of West Indies Cricket* (1988) and a political and economic interpretation of Jamaica's society, *Jamaica: Struggle in the Periphery* (1982). During this time, he reconsidered his political and economic philosophies and transformed himself into a social liberal, believing that working with industries and the private sector would better lead to economic growth. The London *Independent* said that during this time: "Manley rebuilt his strength, and his nerve and took stock of changing ideas about economic development" (Payne 1997, 18). In 1988, he ran again for prime minister with a new platform and won by landslide.

During his second term as prime minister, Manley sponsored private investing and basically shifted his socialist economic views to give power to business. He followed the principles of trickle-down economics and sought to assist businesses that, in turn, would help the lower classes. As a result of his new policies, there was a quick increase in the economic vitality and prosperity for Jamaica's society. Unfortunately, in 1992 he was diagnosed with prostate cancer and was forced to resign. He died on March 6, 1997.

A review of the obituaries that were published after his death reveals that he was thought of as the quintessential statesman. He was commended for his superb oratory, political presence, negotiating skills, and for his unbending love for Jamaican arts and culture. He was one of the key architects of modern Jamaican society and became one of the national heroes of Jamaica after his death. **Rex Nettleford**, chancellor of the University of the West Indies, described him in an obituary as "Jamaica's Passionate Populist" (Nettleford 1997, 21).

NORMAN WASHINGTON MANLEY
(1893–1969)

Jamaican Lawyer, Athlete, Labor Activist, Politician, and National Hero

In his many roles Norman Manley created some of the most important institutions of modern Jamaica, empowering the Jamaican people and leading them toward independence and democracy.

Norman Washington Manley was born on July 4, 1893, in the city of Roxbury, Jamaica, one of four children of Thomas and Margaret Manley. His parents had both Irish and African heritages. The family was relatively poor but his parents instilled in their son a strong work ethic. They relocated to Belmont, Jamaica, when Manley was six years old, where he received his primary education. Manley attended Womer's College, a secondary school, and later Jamaica College, an eighteenth-century high school that offered a solid academic curriculum with a strong emphasis on athletics as a means to build character.

During his school years, Manley excelled as a student athlete. He won three track and field championships between 1911 and 1913. He established an all-time collegiate record in track and field by winning the 100-meter race in 10 seconds in 1911, which stood unbroken until 1952. His accomplishments and records as a student athlete sometimes surpassed existing world records of the time. He also served as captain of the cricket team at Jamaica College, was an excellent bowler, and practiced boxing. An avid sportsman throughout his life, he helped to create the Jamaica Boxing Board of Control and the Jamaican Olympic Association (Carnegie 1993).

Norman Manley also was also a brilliant student who had superb oratorical skills. On his graduation from Jamaica College in 1913 he was offered a position there as an instructor. In 1914 he received a Rhodes Scholarship to Oxford University. He studied law at Oxford but suspended his studies in 1915 to fight in World War I. He was assigned to an artillery regiment of the British Army and was deployed to France. He received the British Military Medal for his performance during the war. In 1919, Manley resumed his studies at Oxford and graduated with honors in 1921. The following year he was admitted to the bar at Gray's Inn. During his years in Great Britain, Manley married his cousin **Edna** Swithenbank, an artist and sculptor who became a central figure in Caribbean art.

He returned to Jamaica in 1922 and established a law practice. He excelled as both a trial and corporate attorney and became known for being a very persuasive orator and a strong litigator. A man of great empathy for the less privileged, he was a champion of the poor and disenfranchised and used the legal system to empower people. Manley's legal expertise was also sought by the sugar and agricultural corporations of Jamaica.

Manley's political involvement in Jamaica started during the 1930s. The economic supremacy and human right abuses of Jamaican corporations controlled by British interests had led to economic oppression and exploitation of Jamaican workers. British control of industry had resulted in a lack of sound social and economic development on the island. Although Manley was initially retained by the West Indian Sugar Company to represent them in their labor disputes, he slowly shifted positions and became one of the leading legal defenders.

By 1938, the social and political climate of Jamaica had deteriorated and Jamaican workers were staging violent strikes to obtain universal adult suffrage. There were many human right abuses. For instance, **Alexander Bustamante**, Manley's cousin, was one of the labor leaders and was imprisoned for his role in the riots. Manley eventually became a labor leader.

Following his successful attempts to free Bustamante, the cousins joined forces and founded the People's National Party (PNP) on September 19, 1938. The PNP adopted a socialist platform to champion the rights of Jamaican laborers. According to one source, it became a model for other socialist parties that emerged in the West Indies (Hintzen and Hill 1988). A member of Socialist International, the party advocated better working conditions and social development for Jamaica. At the heart of the success and popularity of the party was the support given by the Bustamante Industrial Trade Union.

By 1942, Manley had developed disagreements with Bustamante, who moved away from the PNP and created the Jamaica National Party. The two cousins were political adversaries for the rest of their lives. In preparation for the 1944 elections Jamaica created a two-party system and granted universal adult suffrage. Manley and Bustamante ran against each other. Manley lost the elections and became the leader of the opposition in the House of Representatives.

Manley appealed to the Jamaican people on a strong nationalistic platform. As an effective and charismatic leader, he won support from Jamaican professionals. He lost the elections again in 1949 but started to change the socialist discourse of his party to appeal to a broader constituency. He also expelled party members who identified themselves as communists. In 1953, Jamaica changed to a ministerial system of government and when Manley won the 1955 elections he became a chief minister.

As chief minister of Jamaica, he gave more power to the labor unions and at the same time transformed the social, political, and economic structure of the country. He created organizations and institutions that allowed Jamaica's society and government to operate effectively. He won his second term of office in 1959.

One of Manley's more passionate goals was to integrate Jamaica into the West Indies Federation, an organization planned since 1947 to maximize the power of the West Indies. Great Britain sponsored and favored the creation of a federation that grouped West Indian colonies into a unified political federation that would bring together resources and facilitate faster development. Jamaica joined the federation in 1958 but the opposition party strongly criticized it for being an ill-conceived political experiment that was going to deprive Jamaica of its chances to develop more fully as an independent nation. The opposition was so staunch that Manley agreed to hold a referendum in 1961 to decide whether to secede from the federation. The referendum was held in 1961 and the people voted to separate.

It was then clear that Jamaica needed to move toward independence. Manley and Bustamante joined forces in 1961 and asked Great Britain for Jamaica's independence. Elections were held soon after and Manley lost to Bustamante. Jamaica was granted independence in August of 1962.

Despite his defeat in the elections, Manley played an instrumental role in negotiating the terms of the transition to independence. He maintained his position of leadership within the PNP for most of the next decade and continued as a member of the House of Representatives.

Norman Washington Manley has been credited with creating some of the most important and enduring social and economic institutions of Jamaica. Manley is mostly remembered, however, for the support that he gave to Jamaican workers. He was seen as a daring and humane leader who led Jamaica's move into a successful and independent Caribbean island. He died on September 2, 1969. His unique contributions to the island were recognized when he was designated as one of Jamaica's National Heroes.—S.M.M.

References and Suggested Readings

Brown, Wayne. *Edna Manley: The Private Years*. London: Deutsch, 1976.

Carnegie, Jimmy. "Norman Manley: Sporting Hero and More." *Jamaica Journal* 25.1 (1993): 38–43.

Hintzen, Percy C., and W. Marvin Hill. "Norman Washington Manley." In Robert Alexander, ed., *Biographic Dictionary of Latin American and Caribbean Political Leaders*. Westport, CT: Greenwood Press, 1988. 281–282.

LaDuke, Betty. "Edna Manley, The Mother of Modern Jamaican Art." *Africa Through the Eyes of Women Artists*. Trenton, NJ: African World Press, 1991.

Levi, Darrell E. *Michael Manley: The Making of a Leader*. Athens: The University of Georgia Press, 1989.

Manley, Edna. *Edna Manley: The Diaries*. Kingston, Jamaica: Heinemann Publishers (Caribbean), 1989.

Manley, Michael. *The Politics of Change: A Jamaican Testament*. Washington, DC: Howard University Press, 1990.

Manley, Norman Washington, and Rex M. Nettleford, eds. *Norman Washington Manley and the New Jamaica: Selected Speeches and Writings, 1938–68*. Kingston, NY: Africana Publishing Company, 1971.

Merriam, Dena. "A Merging of Cultures in the Sculpture of Edna Manley." *Sculpture Review* 44.3 (Winter 1996): 20–26.

Miller, Anthony. *Norman Manley: National Hero.* Kingston, Jamaica: JAMAL Foundation, 1986.

Nettleford, Rex. "Michael Manley: Jamaica's Passionate Populist." *The Guardian* (London), March 8, 1997, 21.

"Obituary of Michael Manley." *The Daily Telegraph* (London), May 8, 1997, 17.

"Obituary of Mrs. Edna Manley." *The Times* (London), February 25, 1987, n.p.

Payne, Anthony. "Obituary: Michael Manley." *The Independent* (London), March 8, 1997, Gazzette, 18.

Rogozinski, Jan. *A Brief History of the Caribbean: From the Arawak and Carib to the Present.* New York: Facts on File, 1999.

Rother, Larry. "Michael Manley, Ex-Premier of Jamaica, Is Dead at 71." *The New York Times,* March 8, 1997, 52.

Whitehead, Lenox. *Two Great Heroes: Norman Manley and Alexander Bustamante of Jamaica.* Toronto, ON: Front Line Publications, 1985.

JUAN ANTONIO MARICHAL
(1937–)

Dominican Baseball Player

Juan Antonio Marichal was the first Latin American baseball player to be inducted into the Baseball Hall of Fame. This notable Dominican was also one of the pioneers who left the Caribbean islands to play baseball in the American major leagues. As a pitcher, he developed a unusual style in which he pushed his body backward and powerfully kicked his left leg upward to where it was almost parallel with his body, thereby blocking the early departure of the ball from the view of the batter. During his 16 seasons in the major leagues, mostly with the San Francisco Giants, Marichal developed a unique collection of more than 13 pitches that confused and devastated thousands of batters. For his achievements on the mound, he was considered one of the best major league pitchers of the 1960s. By the time he retired from the major leagues, he had a winning record of 243–142, a 2.89 earned-run average (ERA), 2,303 strikeouts, and was chosen for the All-Star Game eight times.

Juan Antonio Sánchez Marichal was born in the town of Laguna Verde in the Dominican Republic on October 30, 1937, one of four children born to an impoverished family dedicated to agriculture and farming. His father died when he was just three years old, leaving his mother alone with few resources to take care of her family. As a result, her children, including Juan, worked from an early age to support the family. As a child, Marichal worked in the sugarcane fields and trapped lobsters to bring food to the family's table.

Juan Marichal. AP Photo.

The story of Juan Marichal is similar to the stories of other Caribbean payers such as Orlando Cepeda, **Roberto Clemente**, and **Sammy Sosa**. Like many other Dominican boys, Juan grew up playing baseball during his childhood. And like them, he used materials such as discarded golf balls, tree branches, and pieces of carton to improvise and create rudimentary baseball equipment (Libby 1971). One wonders if the fact that these players started their life in baseball with such low-end materials helped to enhance their playing capacity and ability.

During his youth Juan was mentored by his brother Garrido, who was a semi-professional baseball player, and by his brother-in-law Prospero Villalona. Both of them saw a future in Juan's game and encouraged him to practice and to play. Juan left school after the eleventh grade and was hired by the United Fruit Company as a pitcher on their team for $18 a week (Stump 1967, 68). He also played for Monti Christi, a local team. During a game between the United Fruit team and a team from the Dominican Air Forces, regarded as the "best team in the country" (Marichal and Einstein 1967, 24). Juan's pitching led his team to a 1–0 victory. The next morning he received a visit from one of Dominican dictator Rafael Leonidas Trujillo's lieutenants, asking him to enroll in the forces so that he could play in the team. The telegram was succinct: "REPORT TO AIR FORCE RIGHT AWAY" (Marichal and Einstein 1967, 25). After receiving his mother's approval, he spent 14 months with the Air Force team, playing baseball the entire time.

By the time that Marichal was 19, he was being heavily recruited by American baseball scouts. In 1958, Marichal was signed by two scouts from the San Francisco Giants who gave him a $500.00 bonus. As is the custom of American teams, he was first placed in their minor league system. He was assigned to Michigan City, Indiana, where he established a 21–8 winning record during his first season. After stints with two other minor league clubs (18–13) and (11–5), Marichal was finally called up to the San Francisco Giants.

Sporting the number 27, Marichal had success with the Giants since his very first day with the team. In a recent book titled *The Game I'll Never Forget* (Vass 1999), Marichal recounted how he pitched a one-hitter during his first game with the Giants. He won the game 2–0 and struck out ten men. During his first season he established a 6–2 record and a 2.62 ERA.

Juan Marichal was known in the United States as the "Dominican Daddy." He built an impressive record in the major leagues: during the 1960s: he won more games (191) than any other pitcher in the majors; had ten shutouts in 1965; led the National League in victories in 1963 and 1968; was an All-Star player from 1962 to 1969 and again in 1971; was the winning pitcher in All-Star games in 1962 and 1965; and in 1965, was selected as the most valuable player of the All-Star Game.

During the 1965 baseball season, Marichal was embroiled in a major controversy. While batting in a game between the Los Angeles Dodgers and the Giants, Marichal lost his temper and hit Dodgers pitcher John Roseboro on the head with the bat because he pitched a ball that came too close to his ears. At the time when there was more civility in the game of baseball than today, there was national outcry over Marichal's "uncivilized" behavior. He received large amounts of hate mail and was eventually fined $1,750 and suspended for nine games. Because of his suspension, Marichal missed several games of the season and was blamed for the Giants losing the season to the Dodgers (Pietrusza 2000).

Marichal, like many of his predecessors in baseball, blamed negative publicity and criticism on racism throughout his career. In a 1967 profile of Marichal in *The Saturday Evening Post*, Al Stump wrote:

> Inequality seems to be an obsession with Marichal. He believes that he and the rest of the major league Latins—Cepeda, Clemente, Mota, Versalles, Cardenas, Aparicio, Oliva, Rojas, Pascual, Davilillo, González, Javier, Pizarro, Santiago, Pérez and the Alou brothers, among others— are victims of a subtly functioning prejudice. It is, he thinks, a prejudice that goes beyond the evident limitations of the American Negro player. "Our skins may be lighter," he has said, "but the breaks we get from base- ball and on the outside are much less than the Negro player gets." (68)

Marichal spent 16 years in the major leagues and did not experience a losing season until 1972. In 1973, the Giants traded him to the Boston Red Sox, and in 1975, the final year of his career, he played with the L.A. Dodgers. By the end of his career, he had pitched 50 shutouts, completed 235 games, and struck out more than 200 batters.

He retired in 1975 to his native Dominican Republic. A savvy man with good financial vision, Marichal invested the money that he had made during his career wisely. He retired to a 1,000-acre farm, where he supervises the farming of sugar- cane, bananas, green plantains, and coffee. In 1983 he became the first Domini- can and the 180th player to be inducted in the U.S. National Baseball Hall of Fame. In 1996 Leonel Fernández, president of the Dominican Republic, appointed Marichal to the post of minister of sports, physical education, and recreation. This position placed him in charge of supervising all amateur sports and the building and management of sport facilities and events.—S.M.M.

References and Suggested Readings

Gutierez, Paul. "Catching Up With. . . ." *Sports Illustrated* 87.11 (September 15, 1997): 8.
Libby, Bill. *Star Pitchers of the Major Leagues.* New York: Random House, 1971.
Marichal, Juan, and Charles Einstein. *A Pitcher's Story.* New York: Doubleday, 1967.
Pietrusza, David, ed. *Baseball: The Biographical Encyclopedia.* Kingston, NY: Total Sports, 2000. 709–710.

Stump, Al. "Always They Want More, More, More." *The Saturday Evening Post*, July 29, 1967, 68–71.

Vass, George. *The Game I'll Never Forget*. Chicago: Bonus Book, 1999.

BOB MARLEY
(1945–1981)

Jamaican Singer, Songwriter, and Pacifist

Bob Marley is considered the father of modern reggae, a popular Jamaican musical rhythm. Although his life was short and his career was brief, this singer and songwriter was an artistic figure of iconic proportions in Jamaica. His musical legacy is politically charged and filled with the values of love, hope, togetherness and redemption. Although he has been dead for over two decades, his musical legacy lives on throughout the world.

Robert Nesta Marley was born in the rural town of Nine Miles, a suburb of the St. Ann Parish in Jamaica on February 5, 1945. His mother, a black peasant by the name of Cedelia Booker, had married Norval Marley, a captain of the Jamaican army who was on duty in their town. Although Captain Manley, an older man, loved his wife, he eventually left her because his family did not approve of his marriage to a poor woman who they perceived as from an uncultured descent. He continued providing his son with financial support but died when Marley was just ten years old, never having gotten to know him well.

During his infancy, Bob lived with his maternal family in the countryside. In one of the most comprehensive documentaries about Marley's life, his mother states that her son had a passion for music since he was small, and demonstrated great sensibility and mystic powers. According to her, he started composing music early in his life (Blackwell and Yentob 1986). During his adolescence, Marley was sent to live with his maternal aunt in Trenchtown, a suburb of Kingston, to learn music and pursue his musical inclinations. Trenchtown was a poor neighborhood made up of cramped housing projects with a history of violence and hostility. His new surroundings represented a marked contrast from the peaceful rural settings that Marley had known. Eventually, he would use his early experiences in Trenchtown as the background for many of his songs.

The move to the big city gave Marley an opportunity to explore his musical inclinations. He was exposed to several musical influences such as calypso and American rhythm and blues. He also had the opportunity to take music classes with Joe Higgs, a famous Rastafarian Jamaican singer who would later become a member of his band. It was also there that he met and became friends with Bunny "Wailer" Livingston and Peter Tosh Mackintosh, who were to be his lifelong music partners.

Following his musical inclinations, Marley cut his first single, "Judge Not," in 1962. The recording had little success. In 1963, he formed a group called the Teenagers with Mackintosh, Livingston, and three other friends, a group that underwent several names, eventually becoming the Wailers. During their first artistic period, the Wailing Wailers were signed by producer Coxsone Dodd under the label Studio One. They became very popular in Jamaica and recorded more than 70 singles that rose through the Jamaican music charts before the group disbanded in 1966.

In 1966 Marley married a young Jamaican singer by the name of Rita Anderson, a member of the group the Soutlettes, and later one of the backup singers in the I-Threes. Shortly after marrying, Marley left for Wilmington, Delaware, where his mother had moved. He worked briefly in a factory and in a hotel. He planned

Bob Marley. Courtesy of Photofest.

to save some money and return to Jamaica, where he could invest the money in his music career. However, he missed his wife and his island so much that he rejoined her in Jamaica after living eight months in the United States (Marley 1995, 114).

On his return Marley solidified his spiritual bond with the Rastafarian movement. The religious doctrines of this movement influenced him for the rest of his life. The Rastafarian movement has its roots in **Marcus Garvey**'s ideas that oppressed blacks should return to Africa. Eventually the members became followers of Ethiopian emperor Haile Selassie. In fact, the Rastafarian name comes from Selassie's birth name, Ras Tafari Maknonnen. The members of this religious sect were based in the neighborhood of Bulls Bay in St. Andrews, Jamaica. They saw Selassie as one of God's prophets, who had been entrusted with the mission of bringing blacks to Africa, as Garvey had wished (White 2000). Rastafarians are extremely peaceful people who seek to gain an understanding of the world by exploring spirituality, faith, community life, and love. The movement embodies a series of spiritual beliefs centered on peace and togetherness, a spiritual counterpart to the hostile and violent life prevalent in many cities and suburbs of Jamaica at the time. The followers of Rastafarianism are easily identified by the green, red, and yellow clothing and head caps that they wear along with their long, braided hair. They have been maligned for their use of marijuana, which they claim enhances their spirituality and their contact with God. The principles and values of this faith were reflected in the themes and lyrics of many of Marley's songs.

When Marley returned to Jamaica, he reconstituted the Wailers, but this time only with Livingston and Tosh. This started the most important period in Marley's career. The group changed from ska, a traditional and lively Jamaican rhythm popular at the time, to a new rhythm that eventually became known as reggae, filled with bass and acoustics. The band created their own recording label named Wail 'N' Soul. Since the label was not very successful in promoting their music, Marley founded the label Tuff Gong, after one of his nicknames. The band was immensely popular in Jamaica and in the Caribbean but not known in the rest of the world. There was a perception, in part motivated by the look of its members, that the musicians were rebels and troublemakers who were not likely to conform to the demands of the music industry at large.

While on tour in London in 1972, the Wailers ran out of money and sought the help of Island Records' chair Chris Blackwell. Blackwell had a great deal of expertise with Jamaican music and liked the lyrics and the sound of Marley and his band. He liked their style, advanced them £8,000, and signed them to his company's label. Using the same marketing and promotion strategies that had been successful in promoting rock bands in Europe and the United States, Blackwell was able to make them a huge success. Their two records with the company, *Catch Fire* (1973) and *Burning* (1973), were immediate international hits and were seen as one of the first reggae albums ever to be released to an international market. Marley and his group had access to the best recording studios and booking and touring arrangements that put them in the forefront of the recording and entertainment industry.

From 1973 to 1976 Marley toured extensively in the United States, where many of his songs became hits. Makintosh and Livingston eventually left the band and Marley became the central figure. The successes of the band escalated and in 1976 they released *Rastaman Vibration,* which was seen as the best reggae album of the time. Marley and the Wailers were awarded the Band of the Year Award by *Rolling Stone* magazine. Marley established his own recording studios and manufacturing plant in Jamaica to record and distribute his own work.

The lyrics of Marley's songs were filled with his political convictions for love and peace. His anti-violence message was of particular significance and relevance to the social and political environment permeating Jamaica. In 1976 he planned Smile Jamaica Concert, an attempt to create unity among Jamaicans who were divided along political party lines. Unfortunately, it was perceived by some political sectors as Marley's attempt to boost the popularity of the Labor Party in the upcoming elections. Two days before the concert, Marley suffered an assassination attempt while he was rehearsing in his house in Kingston. Even after being injured, he performed at the concert, which was attended by more than 80,000 people (White 2000). However, he was so traumatized by the event that he decided to leave Jamaica for two years. He returned in 1978 and gave the One Love Peace Concert at Kingston National Stadium. There he succeeded in bringing together **Michael Manley** and Edward Seaga, leaders of the opposition parties in Jamaica, to promote peace. Because of his efforts toward peace, he was awarded the United Nations' Peace Medal of the Third World in 1978.

In 1977 Marley discovered that he had skin melanoma. Following the precepts of his religious faith, he refused to have an operation that would have removed the malignancy. He continued touring extensively in Africa and throughout the world between 1978 and 1980. By late 1980 his had cancer spread to the rest of his body, forcing him to seek aggressive medical treatments both in the United States and in Europe. Unfortunately, the treatments proved ineffective and he died at a Miami hospital on May 11, 1981.

Marley was given a state funeral in Jamaica, characterized by a festive environment filled with celebrations and songs. He was buried in a humble crypt in his place of birth. In 1981 he was awarded the Jamaica Order of Merit and in 1984 he was inducted into the American Rock 'n' Roll Hall of Fame. Some of his hit songs are "Scratch," "No Woman No Cry," "Talking Blues," "Slave Driver," "I Shot the Sheriff," and "Trenchtown Rock." His family still operates his multi-million-dollar music enterprise and a museum in his honor. He is remembered as a talented performer who brought international recognition to reggae through a message of peace and love.—S.M.M.

References and Suggested Readings

Blackwell, Chris, and Alan Yentob. *Bob Marley and the Wailers: The Bob Marley Story*. New York: Island Visual Arts, 1986.

Frickle, D., and J. Collier. "Talkin' Blues: Bob Marley Wails On." *Rolling Stone*, March 7, 1991, 79–80.

Marley Rita. "Remembering Bob Marley." *Essence* (February 1995): 114.

Palmer, Robert. "One Love." *Rolling Stone*, February 24, 1994, 38.

White, Timothy. *Catch a Fire: The Life of Bob Marley*. New York: Henry Holt, 2000.

JOSÉ MARTÍ
(1853–1895)

Cuban Patriot, Writer, Lawyer, and Diplomat

Cuban-born José Martí is considered one of the Western Hemisphere's most important thinkers and the architect of Cuban independence. Martí's politics were linked to the defense and vindication of the poor, thus his compelling vision for Cuba's independence was grounded in the eradication of racial and social inequalities. The name José Martí is tantamount to liberty throughout Latin American independence movements. In exile for long periods of his life, he articulated revolution as a journalist, poet, and orator. A prolific writer, in his short life Martí's literary and political writings totaled close to 30 volumes, and this extensive body of work has transformed him into one of the most outstanding literary figures in the Spanish language. As a patriot, he was the organizer and unifier of the Cuban independence movement and died on the battlefield in the Cuban War of Independence against Spain. Verses from his seminal 1881 work, *Versos Sencillos* (Simple Verses), were incorporated into Joseito Fernández's well-known song "Guantanamera" popularized in the United States by Pete Seeger in 1966.

His father, Mariano Martí y Navarro, a Spaniard, a policeman, and sometimes a tailor of uniforms, had arrived in Cuba in the mid-1800s as part of a Spanish battalion. He married Leonor Pérez y Cabrera, who came from the Canary Islands; they settled in Havana and less than a year later started their family of one boy and seven girls with the birth of José Julián Martí y Pérez on January 28, 1853.

Martí attended the private elementary school Santa Anacleta, and during this time Martí's sense of social justice was engendered. He was only nine, when he witnessed the whipping and lynching of a slave, which became a subject in his *Versos Sencillos*.

Between 1866 and 1869, while at the Secondary Institute of Havana, he also worked on and founded the underground newspaper *La Patria Libre* (The Free Fatherland), championing the cause of Cuban independence from Spain. In 1869 Martí published *Abdala*, considered an autobiographical work, a theatrical patriotic essay written in verse that glorified dying for one's country. The very public articulation of his political views and the discovery by the Spanish authorities of a letter written by Martí and friend Fermín Valdés Domínguez accusing a classmate of treason for enlisting in the Spanish army led to his arrest and a six-year prison sentence. Although he served only four months in prison, the experience led to a leg injury caused by a blow from a chain that forced him to use a walking cane for the rest of his life. Through the intercession of his mother, his sentence was commuted to banishment to Spain.

Thus Martí began the exile that characterized the better part of the rest of his life. In Madrid, he completed a law degree at the University of Madrid (1874) and at the University of Zaragoza, a degree in philosophy and letters. During his years in Spain he also published *El presidio politico en Cuba* (Political Prison in Cuba), an exposé of the horrors of political imprisonment in Cuba.

In 1875 he moved to Mexico and worked as a journalist for *Revista Universal* (Universal Magazine), where his writings continued to criticize Spanish colonialism in Cuba, particularly the slave colonies. However, in 1876, with the change to a more conservative government in Mexico, Martí was looked on with suspicion and was no longer free to write about Cuba from a radical perspective. It was suggested he would be welcomed in Guatemala and before he left Mexico he proposed to Carmen Zayas-Bazán, the daughter of a wealthy Cuban exile.

Well known for his literary and political writings, Martí's reputation covered other arenas. In 1877 he established himself in Guatemala, where he taught literature and philosophy at the University of Guatemala, and where he met María García Granados, the subject of one of his best known poems, "La Niña de Guatemala" (The Girl From Guatemala), the story of a young Guatemalan woman who languished and in 1877 died of a broken heart when she learned Martí was engaged.

In 1878 Carmen gave birth to their only child and they returned to Cuba in hope that the signing of the treaty ending the Ten Years' War providing amnesty to political exiles would bring about a more lenient government. Their hopes proved short-lived: in 1880, after spending two years in Cuba, Martí, who had continued his activism, was once more deported. He moved with his family to the United States where he spent most of his exile years (1880–1895) in New York City, but also traveled extensively to Santo Domingo, Haiti, Jamaica, Florida, Costa Rica, Panama, and Mexico.

During his exile years, Martí embarked on a period of intensive revolutionary activity through speeches, published articles, travel throughout Latin America, and constant correspondence with his counterparts in Cuba. In his capacity as journalist he reported on life in the United States for many Latin American newspapers including *Opinión Nacional* (Venezuela) and *La Nación* (Argentina). His writings also reflected his admiration for the founding fathers and framers of the U.S. Constitution. In his poetry and prose he described his admiration for his country of exile, particularly the energy and work production of the industrial economy. The bulk of his writings about the United States, referred to as *The American Chronicles of José Martí*, included portraits and commentaries on writers and thinkers such as Ralph Waldo Emerson, Walt Whitman, Helen Hunt Jackson, and Louisa May Alcott; inventors such as Thomas Alva Edison; and the bandit Jesse James. These essays, which are considered "his greatest contribution to Spanish-American letters," were innovative in their prose and instrumental in promoting "better understanding among the American nations" ("Martí, José Julián" 2003). He chronicled major events like the inaugurations of the Brooklyn Bridge and the Statue of Liberty, the centennial celebration of the American Constitution, snowstorms in New York, a lynching in New Orleans, workers' strikes, elections campaigns, and many other everyday affairs that gave Latin Americans a glimpse into the life and culture of their northern neighbor. He began the publication of *La edad de oro* (The Age of Gold), a literary magazine for children that only published four issues from July to October 1889. It included essays, poetry, and short stories on science, literature, history, and all facets of American life past and present. It has since been published in book form.

His political life was also flourishing; while residing in New York City, he was consul of Uruguay, Argentina, and Paraguay. He was celebrated as a representative to the International Monetary Conference, where he was able to avert policies that would have been damaging to Latin American countries. His struggle for Cuba's autonomy led to new alliances with black Cuban exiles and the founding of La Liga, an organization committed to promoting the rights of Cuban and Puerto Rican blacks. In 1892 he embarked on a period of intensive revolutionary activity that culminated in the establishment of the Cuban Revolutionary Party. Between 1892 and 1895 Martí devoted himself almost exclusively to the cause of Cuban independence. Using his newspaper *La Patria* as the vehicle for speaking about the war against Spain, he gained fame as a dedicated Cuban nationalist. Perhaps recognizing that Martí's destiny transcended the political context, he was hailed as "el apóstol" or apostle by his followers. By 1894 Martí had become impatient and believed it was time to launch the "crusade" for independence against Spain.

He left for the Dominican Republic and on February 24, 1895, in the town of Montecristi, began to draw up plans for an uprising in Cuba. The resulting document, the seminal Manifesto de Montecristi, set down the goals of Cuba's war of independence, and was signed on March 25, by Martí and Mexican freedom fighter Máximo Gómez, who was involved in Cuba's struggle. On April 11, 1895 both men landed in Cuba, incorporating themselves with the Liberation Army to set in motion once more, the armed struggle for Cuba's independence. By this time, Martí had also become disillusioned with the United States' expansionist intentions in Latin American and on the day before his death wrote of his hope "of preventing in time, with Cuba's independence, the United States from spreading through the Antilles, and with that increased strength, overpowering our lands of America" (Rotker 2000). Martí's death on May 19,1895, in battle on the plains of Dos Ríos, Oriente province, came only seven years before his lifelong goal of Cuban independence was achieved.

The literary movement known as modernism is believed to have begun with his work. Most critics and literature experts consider his essays a great contribution to Spanish American literature and important in bringing about innovations in Spanish prose. José Martí, whom Chilean Nobel Prize–winner Gabriela Mistral called "the race's purest man," was honored all over Latin America one hundred years after his death in 1995 (Fernández Retamar 1995, X08). In memory of this centennial, UNESCO described Martí's vision of Cuba's independence as "absolute democracy, without privilege based on race or class, grounded on a fair distribution of wealth and culture, and on the demands of the productive masses" (Fernández Retamar 1995, X08).—G.C.

References and Suggested Readings

Belnap, J. and R. Fernández, eds. *José Martí's 'Our America': From National to Hemispheric Cultural Studies (New Americanists)*. Durham, NC: Duke University Press, 1999.

Fernández Retamar, R. "José Martí: A Cuban for all seasons." *The Washington Post*, May 15, 1995, X08.

Lizaso, F. *Marti, Martyr of Cuban Independence*. Westport, CT: Greenwood Press, 1974.

Martí, J. *Latin American Integration*. Havana, Cuba: Editorial José Martí, 1998.

———. *Versos sencillos/Simple Verses*. Translated by Manuel A. Teillechea. Houston: Arte Público Press, 1997.

"Martí, José Julián." Encyclopædia Britannica Online. *http://0-search.eb.com.csulib.ctstateu.edu:80/eb/article?eu=52402*. Accessed March 6, 2003.

Rodríguez-Luis, Julio, ed. *Re-reading José Martí: One Hundred Years Later*. Albany: State University of New York Press, 1999.

Rotker, Susana. *The American Chronicles of José Martí*. Hanover, NH: University Press of New England, 2000.

Smith, Joseph. "Heroes of the Cuban Revolution, Martí, Maceo and Gómez." *Historian* 44 (1994): 3–8.

RICKY MARTIN
(1971–)

Puerto Rican Singer and Dancer

Puerto Rican performer Ricky Martin, who made his stage debut at age 12 as a member of the all-boy group Menudo, is today an international superstar who has put Latin pop music on the map. Dubbed the "Puerto Rican Elvis" by talk show host Rosie O'Donnell, Martin has won wide acclaim for his singing and sensual hip swinging that was seen in 1999 by more than one billion television viewers in 187 countries during the Grammy awards ceremony, where his performance made him a crossover success, and where he also won his first Grammy. Martin, who has appeared on many television shows and on the cover of *Time* and *TV Guide* has become an international superstar with record sales surpassing the 40-million mark.

Enrique José Martín Morales IV was born in San Juan, Puerto Rico, on Christmas Eve, 1971, to psychologist Enrique José Martín III and accountant Nereida Morales. By the time he was two years old, his parents separated and eventually divorced. At age six, already appearing in television commercials, Martin told his father he wanted to become an entertainer. His parents enrolled him in acting and singing lessons with the understanding that his grades not suffer while attending Catholic parochial school. At one point, his mother took him to a concert by salsa music "queen" **Celia Cruz**—an experience that influenced Martin's eventual embrace of Latin pop.

By 1977, the all-boy group Menudo was becoming a global phenomenon, cited in the *Guinness Book of World Records* for the largest audience ever assembled—150,000 at Mexico's Azteca Stadium—and breaking sales records worldwide. The group consisted of five boys between the ages of 12 and 16. Once a member turned 17, he had to leave the group, and was replaced by a new boy. Martin had set his goal on becoming a member of Menudo from the first time he saw the group, and after his third audition finally landed a spot in the group. A year after joining Menudo, he legally changed his name to Ricky and recorded and toured the world with the group until 1989.

On leaving Menudo he completed his high school education and lived in New York City for a brief time before moving to Mexico, where he was offered a leading role in the musical *Mamá Ama al Rock* (Mom Loves Rock). Impressed by his performance, a television producer signed him on to play the role of musician Pablo in the soap opera *Alcanzar una estrella II* (To Reach for a Star II), and the soap's ratings soared. In 1992, a spin-off of the show, the film *Mas que alcanzar una estrella* (More than Reaching for a Star) earned Martin a Heraldo Award, the Mexican version of an Oscar.

Ricky Martin. AP Photo/Andrew Medichini.

By 1992, Martin had a singing as well as an acting career in Latin America. That year he won two of Mexico's top awards for recording artists with his first solo Spanish album, *Ricky Martin* (1991), which produced four hit singles and remained in the Latin Pop charts for 41 weeks. This was followed with his successful *Me amarás* (Will You Love Me) album that sold more than 700,000 copies and earned him Billboard's Best New Latin Artist Award in 1993, the year he moved to Los Angeles.

Martin debuted on American television in a few episodes of the short-lived sitcom *Getting By.* That was followed by a two-year stint as the character Miguel in the soap opera *General Hospital,* where his role as a musician afforded him the opportunity to sing on the show on a regular basis. In 1996, his last year on this soap, he released his third album, *A medio vivir* (Halfway Across the Bridge of Life), which produced the international hit "María," Billboard's top-selling international single of 1997. By this point, Martin had landed a three-month engagement in the role of Marius in the Broadway musical hit *Les Misérables,* where he made his theater debut on June 24, 1996, with most of his entire family present. He received good reviews for his acting on Broadway, and the following year he was the voice of Hercules in the Spanish version of the Disney animated film and also recorded the film's theme song "No importa la distancia" (Go the Distance).

His other big project in 1997 was working on the recording of *Vuelve* (Come Back to Me), the 1998 album that would make him one of the most successful crossover artists of all time. Very soon the album was number one on Billboard's Latin top 50 recordings. A big fan of soccer, Martin was chosen to perform the hit song from this album, "La copa de la vida" (The Cup of Life)—also the official song of the World Soccer match—during the July closing ceremonies for an international audience estimated at over two billion people. That fall he embarked on an international tour that took him to most of Asia, where he began to study Buddhism and engage in meditation in order to reduce the stress of touring.

Martin decided he was ready to record an all-English album "where he could tell the American people about his country's ideals and cultural pride" (Zymet 2001, 50). He began to work on *Ricky Martin,* his 1999 crossover recording, early that year. In addition, he was invited to perform during the February 1999 nationally televised annual Grammy Awards ceremonies. Martin's performance of "La copa de la vida" made television history and was the highlight of an otherwise-uneventful show. His show-stealing carnival-style performance, "joyous, hip-swiveling, eye-catchingly over-the-top" and his Grammy for Best Latin Pop Performance that evening helped popularize Latin pop music and made him a superstar (Farley 1999, 84).

That success was followed by the hit single "Livin' La Vida Loca," a song that combined Latin salsa and American pop music with infectious rhythmic melody. In April 1999 it became number one on Billboard's Hot 100, the biggest selling single in Columbia Records history. It was the number-one single in five international markets, including the United States, Britain, Canada, New Zealand, and Ireland. The recording won MTV's Best Dance Video and Best Pop Video and resulted in one of the most successful concert tours in history, with over 250 sold-out concerts in 25 countries. This success was followed by the May release of his first English-language album, *Ricky Martin*, which also made history with the highest first-week sales in Columbia Records history. It became a number-one album in ten international markets, certified platinum or better in over 30 countries selling over 15 million copies. In 1999 he also released *The Ricky Martin Video Collection* and *Ricky Martin One Night Only*, his first network television special filmed at Liberty Park in New York City. Both video releases went platinum shortly after their release. *Sound Loaded*, released in 2002 is one of the best representations of the up tempo and danceable tunes that are so characteristic of his music.

1999 was one of Martin's best years. He won three international MTV awards including MTV's Russia Viewer's Choice Award. At the World Music Awards, Martin was named the World's Best Selling Pop Male Artist, and World's Best Latin Artist. He won Favorite Male Artist at the Teen Choice Awards. During Billboard's 10th Annual Music Awards he was recognized as Male Artist of the Year and Male Hot 100 Singles Artist of the Year. In 2000 he received the People's Choice Award for Favorite Male Musical Performer, and the Blockbuster Award for Favorite Male Pop Artist.

Time magazine described Martin's success as being "in the center of something bigger than himself," referring to the phenomenon in the popularity of what is now referred to as Latin pop music (Farley, Thigpen et al. 1999, 74). Martin has been at the forefront, offering this music to a worldwide audience. No matter how long his stardom lasts, his record-breaking sell-out performances and the sheer number of recordings sold have already broken records and made history. In 2000 Martin began what was to become a year and a half of rest and was out of the public eye. During that time he honed his skills as a composer and expects to release an album that will contain many original compositions. In 2002 he received the Hispanic Heritage Award in Art for his contribution to music.

Martin's success and visibility have led him to support many worthy causes, including the Pediatric AIDS Foundation, and has joined rock star Sting in supporting the Rainforest Foundation. In 2002 he donated a million dollars in musical instruments in his native Puerto Rico in order to foster the musical talents of young people.—G.C.

References and Suggested Readings

Bergquist, Kathie. *Ricky Martin*. Paris: Hors Collection, 2000.

Farley, Christopher. "Get Ready for Ricky." *Time* 153:18 (May 10, 1999): 84.

Farley, Christopher John, David E. Thigpen et al. "Latin Music Pops." *Time* 153:20 (May 24, 1999): 74+.

Furman, Elina. *Ricky Martin*. New York: St. Martin's Press, 1999.

Johns, Michael-Anne. *Ricky Martin*. Kansas City, MO: Andrews McMeel, 1999.

Krulik, Nancy E. *Ricky Martin: Rockin' the House!* New York: Pocket Books, 1999.

Marrero Letisha. *Ricky Martin: Livin' La Vida Loca*. New York: HarperCollins, 1999.

Raso, Anne M. *Ricky Martin: A Scrapbook in Words and Pictures*. London: Ebury, 1999.

Ricky Martin Homepage. *http://www.rickymartin.com*.

Sparks, Kristin. *Ricky Martin: Livin' the Crazy Life*. New York: Berkley Boulevard Books, 1999.

Tracy, Kathleen, and Ricardo de Izaguirre. *Ricky Martin: The Unofficial Book*. New York: Billboard Books, 1999.

Zymet, Kathy Alter. *Ricky Martin*. Philadelphia: Chelsea House Publishers, 2001.

ANTONIO MARTORELL
(1939–)
Puerto Rican Graphic Artist, Writer, and Scholar

Antonio Martorell has helped to define Puerto Rican arts from the 1960s to today. He is a talented graphic artist who has produced works in a variety of media such as oils, xylographs, and serigraphs. He has used his art to comment on the social and political realities of Puerto Rico with a great deal of inquisitiveness, wit, sarcasm, and imagination. In addition to his work as a graphic artist, Martorell has also been involved in Puerto Rican theater and television. He is an artist-in-residence at the University of Puerto Rico in Cayey, where he directs the Pío López Martínez Museum.

Martorell was born in 1939 in the Santurce suburb of San Juan. He attended the local public schools and on graduation moved to Washington, D.C., where he obtained an undergraduate degree in diplomacy from Georgetown University. Although Martorell has always maintained a strong interest in world politics and human rights, he did not pursue a career as a diplomat. Instead, he decided to exploit his artistic abilities and went to Spain to study drawing, painting, and arts.

His return to Puerto Rico coincided with one of the most significant artistic periods in Puerto Rican arts. A group of talented artists known as the Generation of the 50s had started a new type of artistic production that not only drew on the local traditions and folklore of Puerto Rico but also made strong cultural, social, and political comments on contemporary Puerto Rican life. Artists such as **Lorenzo Homar**, **Myrna Báez**, Isabel Bernal, and **Rafael Tufiño** were creating art that was entirely Puerto Rican. Martorell worked under the tutelage of Lorenzo Homar at the Graphics Arts Workshop of the Institute of Puerto Rican culture.

Martorell's early work creating posters drawing on the Puerto Rican experience was important in the development of the poster as one of the leading media of artistic expression with a social commentary during the 1960s and 1970s. His serigraphs of former Puerto Rican governor **Luis Muñoz Marín** and former San Juan mayor and "Woman of the Americas" **Felisa Rincón de Gautier** present a highly stylized but sarcastic depictions of these controversial political leaders. As part of the series *Barajas* (1968), Martorell presented Muñoz Marín as the central image of an ace in a card deck wearing the Puerto Rican *pava* (a hat), which was the emblem of his political party. Martorell filled Muñoz Marín's head with a series of images and symbols of the Puerto Rican *jíbaros* (peasants) and the many illnesses affecting them. His depiction of Felisa Rincón de Gautier was far more shocking and revealing. Doña Fela, as she was commonly known, was shown as the Queen of Aces, wearing a Carmen Miranda–like hat and surrounded by small icons of her robust figure wearing a bikini.

In 1968 Martorell established Taller Alacrán (Scorpion Workshop) to produce his work and to mentor other Puerto Rican and Caribbean artists. He worked in book illustration and textiles. According to art historians and critics, the work that emerged from Alacrán is some of Martorell's best. Among his work of that time is "Los Salmos" (1971), a graphic representation of the works of Nicaraguan poet Ernesto Cardenal. (Hermandad de Artistas Gráficos 1998). In 1968 he exhibited his work at Galeria Colibrí and in 1972 at the Latin American Museum of Engraving, both in San Juan.

Martorell worked as an instructor of serigraphy in both Argentina and Colombia. In 1978 he went to Mexico and taught drawing and engraving at the National School of the Arts and lived there until 1984. Of his experiences there he has said: "Mexico attracted me as a daily education. Mexicans are incapable of doing anything with their hands that is not beautiful. They have a marvelous sense of aesthetics" (Hernández 1998). Martorell took a position as artist-in-residence at the University of Puerto Rico in Cayey after his return from Mexico, which he holds today. As part of his academic responsibilities, he helped establish and currently directs the Pío López Martínez Museum.

Martorell has been described as a humanist who is deeply concerned about the effects of violence in society as well as war and political repression in the world. His work on the exhibit "El bosque de papel; el papel del bosque" (A Forest of Paper, a Paper from the Forest) manifested his concerns on deforestation and the environment. His art reflects, if it does not protest, the colonial status of Puerto Rico.

In addition to his work as a teacher and artist, Martorell has worked as a theater designer. He has also collaborated on several books. Among them are: *ABC de Puerto Rico* (ABC of Puerto Rico; 1968), *El libro dibujado, el libro hablado* (The Drawn Book and the Spoken Book; 1995), *Brincos y saltos: el juego como disciplina teatral* (Jump and Leaps: Play as a Theatrical Discipline; 1995), and *Allá donde florecen los flamboyanes* (Where the Flame Trees Bloom; 2000).

Martorell has exhibited work at Museo de Bellas Arte de Chile (1978), Institute of Puerto Rican Culture (1978), Mexican Museum of Modern Arts (1981), and Museo de Arte de Ponce (1992). In 1998 he held three simultaneous exhibits in Puerto Rico: "Blanca Snow in Puerto Rico," "Como-unión," and "El bosque de papel; el papel del bosque." Among his many awards are the Children's Book Award (1968), III Bienal de Grabado, San Juan (1974), and Bienal del Grabado, Florence, Italy (1986).

Although he maintains a visible presence in Puerto Rican and Caribbean arts he has protested the traditionalism of many arts organizations in Puerto Rico and Latin America, which he believes are not open to consider new artistic forms of expression, have failed to evolve, and maintain very formal canons in the arts. He has stopped participating in many exhibits because the organizers constrain his art.

Martorell's works are part of many important collections both in Puerto Rico and abroad. His majestic painting "Visiones de Proteo" occupies a central place in the Puerto Rican contemporary collection in the Ponce Museum of Modern Art. His work has been shown at the Museum of Modern Art and El Museo del Barrio in New York, La Casa de Las Américas in Cuba, and the Mexican Museum of Modern Art. Antonio Martorell feels equally comfortable painting, writing, and working in theater and in television. In 2001 he started *En la punta de la lengua* (On the Tip of the Tongue), a well received television program on Puerto Rican public television.—S.M.M.

References and Suggested Readings

Hermandad de Artistas Gráficos 1998. *Puerto Rico: Arte e identidad.* San Juan: Editorial de la Universidad de Puerto Rico, 1998.

Hernández, Carmen Dolores. "Antonio Martorell: un hombre que ve." *El Nuevo Día* (San Juan), October 5, 1998, n.p.

Rivas Nina, Myrna. "Sabiduría del alma compartida." *El Nuevo Día* (San Juan), October 28, 2001, n.p.

Rivera, Nelson. *Visual Artists and the Puerto Rican Performing Arts, 1950–1990: The Works of Jack and Irene Delano, Antonio Martorell, Jaíme Suarez and Oscar Mestey-Villamil.* New York: P. Lang, 1991.

MIGHTY SPARROW (SLINGER FRANCISCO)
(1935–)

Trinidadian Calypso Composer and Singer

Calypso singer Mighty Sparrow, born Slinger Francisco, is considered to be Trinidad's king of calypso. Francisco has been a revolutionary and important force in the world of calypso owing to his talent as a singer and performer, his prolific compositions, and the substantive and formal changes that he introduced to calypso music. His contributions to calypso are so important that music critics have said that Francisco "is to calypso what **Bob Marley** is to reggae" (Mascoll 1996, B16).

Francisco was born in Gran Roi, Grenada, on July 9, 1935. His parents, Clarissa and Francisco, moved to the neighboring island of Trinidad when he was an infant. The family settled in the province of St. James, in a town that neighbors Port of Spain. Although Francisco owns houses around the world, he has spent most of his adult life in Port of Spain.

As a child, Francisco attended the Newtown Boy's Roman Catholic School in Port of Spain. His teachers identified his singing abilities early on and asked him to participate in school concerts. He also joined the choir at St. Patrick Church, where he sang both baritone and tenor. Since most school concerts were formal affairs where popular music was not played, Francisco generally refrained from singing the calypso tunes that attracted him. However, at one such concert he surprised the audience by singing "The Yankees Invade Trinidad," one of the popular calypso hits of the time.

Francisco abandoned his education after finishing elementary school, but he has said that he became an avid reader after leaving school (English 1995, A53). This interest in reading exposed him to the cultural, social, and political issues that he has consistently incorporated into his song lyrics.

Francisco tried several career paths and worked in several odd jobs before pursuing a musical career. He learned music and took guitar classes, which he knew would prove useful if he was ever to undertake a career as a professional calypso singer. Although his mother encouraged him to pursue a career in music, his father vehemently opposed it due to the seasonal nature of the career in Trinidad. Festivals take place in February of each year and singers can only earn income during the season. Thus, the economic well being of calypso singers tends to be highly insecure and unstable.

Francisco made his professional debut during the 1954 carnival season. In Trinidad, calypso singers establish themselves with performers who operate from tents set throughout Port of Spain through the carnival season. He performed at the Old Brigade Tent under the name "Little Sparrow" and opened with his composition "The Parrot and the Monkey." His performance was well received (Baksh 2000). In 1955, he performed again, this time adding four new compositions.

The year 1956 was especially significant for Francisco because he introduced five new calypsos, adopted the name "Mighty Sparrow," and won the Calypso King Competition with his hit "Jeane and Dinah." He also changed his affiliation and moved to the Young Brigade Tent. It was there that he started the now-famous calypso competitions, or duels, with Lord Melody, another calypso star.

In 1956 Francisco established a record by winning the largest number of the competitions held during the annual carnivals. Twenty years later, he and **Lord Kitchener** agreed to stop participating in the Calypso Monarch competition to give opportunities to new participants. At the time, both men were tied, having each won the contest 10 times. In 1992, however, Francisco staged a comeback and won the contest again, establishing a record of 11 victories. He has also won the Road March contest eight times (Feist 1993, E11).

In a society where calypsos are important cultural and artistic products, there is no doubt that Francisco, who is fondly called "The Bird," is one of its leading exponents. In the process, he has been credited with introducing many important changes in the art of calypso singing and calypso making. For instance, he has lengthened the lyrics and lines of calypso songs. He also introduced the use of the electric guitar, promoted more intense lyrics for calypsos, and was influential in the development of the steel pan as another addition to the steel bands. He has been a leading force behind the development of soca, which is a calypso form with lighter lyrics that resembles American jazz and soul. Many of his songs, written with profound social and political messages, are catalysts for social change. His themes range from exhortations for people to pay their taxes, anger about the breakup of the Federation of the West Indies, and cries for calypso singers to get better prizes than beauty queens to admonishments against teens drug use. He also produced hilarious songs about the marital problems of Prince Charles and Princess Diana of Great Britain and the trial of O.J. Simpson. Francisco has made it clear that calypso is more than musical entertainment—it is social commentary and political criticism. He states:

> We calypsonians have educated and energized our audiences. Many of the things that newspapers and radio and TV refuse to elaborate on. We come out and tell it like it is. We do it with rhyme and melodies and sometimes wonderful lyrics, and of course with humor, and it lasts forever. The world has become a smaller place for now in that calypso is more popular, more recognized and accepted and more in demand. (English 1995, A53)

Francisco was the first calypso singer to establish his own recording company. He has recorded more than 70 albums. Although he acknowledges the influence of artists such as Nat King Cole, Billy Eckstein, and Frank Sinatra in his music, he also credits fellow calypso singers and composers such as Lord Melody, Lord Kitchener, and Lord Invader as major sources of inspiration in his work (Baksh 2000). Although he has been credited with writing hundreds of calypsos, questions have been raised about the authorship of his music. Many critics have argued that he is not the sole author of his songs, Nevertheless, they praise him for his capacity to capture contemporary themes with unique incisiveness and incorporate them into his songs (Herdeck 1979).

Another important dimension of Francisco's work is his effort to protect the rights of calypso singers. He has boycotted many calypso festivals to protest unsuitable conditions. In fact, the Trinidad Carnival Development Committee, a planning body that oversees carnivals to ensure safety and fairness for the performers, was created after one such protest (Caribbean Festival Organization).

Francisco has traveled the world showcasing Trinidadian calypso. Among his most important compositions are "Federation," "Obeah Wedding," "Mr. Walker," "Only a Fool Breaks His Own Hearty," "Sparrow Dead," and "Melda."

His art and his music have been honored with many distinctions throughout his career, including the Humming Bird Silver Medal from the government of Trinidad and Tobago in 1969 and the Chaconia Gold Medal in 1993. In 1984, Edward Koch, then mayor of New York declared May 18 "Mighty Sparrow" day. One of the biggest honors bestowed on him was the award of an honorary doctorate in letters in 1987 by the University of the West Indies, where he is fondly known as Dr. Bird.—S.M.M.

References and Suggested Readings

Baksh, Vaneisa. "Calypsonian of the Century: The Mighty Sparrow." *The Express* (Trinidad), January 1, 2000, 15.

Caribbean Festival Organization: The Mighty Sparrow. *http://www.caribbeanfestival.org/mighty_sparrow.htm*.

English, Merle. "A Sparrow Has Flown for 60 Years." *Newsday* (New York), July 9, 1995, A53.

Feist, Daniel. "Calypso Star Mighty Sparrow Plays at Caribbean Jam Thursday. "*The Gazette* (Montreal, Canada), June 19, 1993, E11.

Herdeck, Donald, ed. "Slinger, Francisco." *Caribbean Writers: A Bio-Bibliographical-Critical Encyclopedia*. Washington, DC: Three Continents Press, 1979. 202.

Mascoll, Phillip. "Sparrow Wings in for Calypso New Year, His Fame Spans Three Generations of Caribbean Music." *The Toronto Star*, December 26, 1996, B16.

Mason, Peter. *Bacchanal! The Carnival Culture of Trinidad*. Philadelphia: Temple University Press, 1998.

PABLO MILANÉS
(1943–)

Cuban Composer, Singer, and Guitarist

Pablo Milanés, the troubadour of the Cuban revolution, has become one of the most visible and well-known contemporary Cuban singers. He is one of the leading creative geniuses behind the Cuban and Latin American musical movement known as La Nueva Trova. His musical creations, as well as his recordings and interpretations, have traveled the world and constitute an example of Cuba's musical production during the post-revolutionary period.

Milanés was born in the Cuban city of Bayamo on February 24, 1943. His mother recognized his musical talents early in his childhood and encouraged him to sing

Pablo Milanés. AP Photo/Marco Ugarte.

at gatherings of family and friends. A testimonial to his mother's encouragement is revealed by the fact that he dedicated his first album to her because she was the one "who forced me to sing" (Díaz 1994, 16). He has said that he is an atheist since his childhood. Nevertheless, he characterizes himself as being highly spiritual. His God, he has says, is the human race ("Pablo Milanés" 2001).

Like many other Cuban performers, such as **Celia Cruz**, he had an active amateur career during his childhood and adolescent years, participating in the television and radio musical contests that were very popular in Cuba at the time. Although he studied at the Havana Municipal Conservatory, he generally is considered to be self-taught.

Milanés professional musical career began at the age of 16, when he joined the group Cuarteto del Rey (King's Quarter) as a guitarist and lead singer. He also started his serious work as a composer during this period. During these early years, he explored various musical genres focusing primarily on romantic lyrics that led to the Cuban musical genre known as "feeling." This rhythm relied on Cuban boleros for its platform but incorporated Cuban spirituals, *güajiras, son,* and even American jazz. His involvement with this genre is significant because it allowed him to introduce new elements into the Cuban *balad* by speeding its tempo and making it more festive. Critics have said that his work has been characterized by "musical syncretism," in which he integrated stylistic features from many styles and genres (Díaz 1994). Some of his early musical compositions include "Tú, mi desengaño" (You Disappoint Me), "El Manantial" (The Spring), "Ya ves" (See Now), and "Estás Lejos" (You Are Far Away). From 1962 to 1964 he was a solo performer, and in 1964 he joined the musical group Los Bucaneros (The Buccaneers) as a guitarist and singer. From this group, he launched some of the most important changes in Cuban music during the 1960s and 1970s.

The year 1965 marked a crucial point in Milanés' career. That year he composed the song "Mis Veintidós Años" (My Twenty-two Years), where he pioneered a new musical style. Along with **Silvio Rodríguez** and Noel Nicola, Milanés became one of the leading forces in the creation of "La Nueva Trova Cubana o La Nueva Canción" (The New Song). Similar to North American protest songs, "La Nueva Canción" is characterized by intense lyrics that explore political and social problems that Cuba and Latin America were experiencing during the turbulent 1960s. Many of the themes developed by Milanés and the Nueva Trova singers were seen as responsible for creating a renewed sense of awareness and optimism toward the unique challenges faced by Caribbean societies, such as economic exploitation, racism, imperialism, and armed conflict. One of the unique characteristics of Milanés' musical style was his tendency to incorporate poetry and romance into his song lyrics. *New York Times* music critic John Pareles has said that Milanés started a movement that combined "a reclamation of rural traditions, a sense of political commitment (often obliquely expressed) and a tone of longing for love, purpose and for better times" (Pareles 1997, C17).

In 1967 Milanés participated in the First Encounter of the Protest Song held in Havana. This event included individual performers and groups from Latin America and the United States. His appearance at the first festival gave him the perennial title of being one fathers of the *Nueva Canción*. That same year he joined the Center for the Protest Song at Cuba's prestigious Casa de las Americas, a cultural center that promotes Cuba's cultural endeavors. In 1969 he began working with the Grupo de Experimentacion Sonora del ICAIC (Group of Sound Experimentation at the Havana Film Institute). Since then, he has participated in more than 90 tours throughout the world. Milanés has gained the love of his audiences and has entertained them with the beauty of his songs.

Cliff Davis is one of many music critics who has compared Milanés' work to the music of singers Bob Dylan and Curtis Mayfield (Davis 1999). Milanés, however, perceives himself as a troubadour. Although the lyrics of his songs are intensely social and political, they are framed within a flavor of hopeless romanticism. One of the characteristics of his music is the heavy use of symbols and metaphors in their lyrics. Davis has said that in his music "words always count as much as the music" (1999).

Milanés' vocal style is melodious, which makes his audiences perceive him more as a romantic than as a political singer or a social activist. His tenor voice is soft and uniquely suited to convey the complex feelings that he explores. He says that he has been influenced by a wide array of other Latin American poets such as César Vallejo, **Nicolás Guillén**, and **José Martí**. He admits to musical influences from Brazilian singers and composers such as Caetano Veloso and Chico Buarque.

In his three decades as a performer, Milanés has produced dozens of compositions and recordings. Some of the his best known songs are "La vida no vale nada" (Life Is Worth Nothing), "El breve espacio en que no estás" (The Brief Space Where You Are Not), "Para vivir" (To Live), "Yo me quedo" (I Stay), "No me pidas" (Do Not Ask), "Años" (Years), and "Canción de cuna para una niña grande" (Lullaby for a Grown-up Girl). His signature song, however, is "Yolanda." Although many of his recordings have not been released in the United States, his songs have become hits among Latino and Caribbean audiences here. Some of his most recent albums are *Plegarias* (Prayers; 1996), *Despertar* (Awakening; 1997), *Proposiciones* (Propositions; 1998), *Orígenes* (Origins; 1999), and *Días de Gloria* (Glory Days; 2000). His albums and compositions have won many awards.

Although Milanés generally supports the Cuban revolution, he is also an independent voice who has found his ideological positions at odds with **Fidel Castro**'s regime. In 1999 he criticized Castro sharply by saying that the people of Cuba had sacrificed enough for the revolution and that it was time for them to be rewarded. In 1994 he opened the Milanés Foundation to sponsor the music and cultural work of young Cubans only to have it closed by the Castro government in 1995. Many of Castro's supporters linked his remarks to the failure of his initiative. He has been an independent member of the National Assembly (the Cuban parliament), and recently organized a group of Latin American and Spanish musicians to issue a recording to raise funds for music organizations in Cuba. Despite the fact that he had hip replacement surgery in 1998, he resumed his career in 1999 and continues to actively record and tour the world. In the summer of 2001 he announced the joint recording of an album with famous Jamaican American singer **Harry Belafonte**. To date he has recorded 36 albums—S.M.M.

References and Suggested Readings

"Cuba no es un Paraíso, dice Pablo Milanés en México." Associated Press Wire Services, February 11, 1999.

Davis, Cliff. "The voice of Cuba's torment." *The Times* (London), June 8, 1999, n.p.

Díaz, Clara. *La Nueva Trova*. Havana: Editorial Letras Cubanas, 1994.

Llewelyn, Howell, and Nigel Williamson. "Cuban music industry is showing signs of life." *Billboard*, May 3, 1997, 1.

Muñoz, Nefer. "Musica: Cuba mantuvo la dignidad, asegura Pablo Milanés." *Semana* (Madrid), April 5, 2001, n.p.

"Pablo Milanés afirma que su Dios es el ser humano." EFE (Spanish Newswire Agency), April 5, 2001.

Pareles, Jon. "Private Longings, Not Politics From Cuba." *The New York Times*, August 28, 1997, C17.

MINNIE MINOSO
(ORESTES SATURNINO ARRIETA ARMAS)
(1925–)

Cuban Baseball Player

There are some baseball players who become famous for their abilities and accomplishments in the game, while others are known for their historic roles in the sport. Minnie Minoso fits both categories and holds the unique distinction of having been active in the American major leagues for six consecutive decades. The man known as the "Cuban Comet" was one of the first successful Cuban players to make it to the American major leagues. Puerto Rican baseball player **Orlando "Peruchín" Cepeda** has said: "Minnie Minoso is to Latin ballplayers what Jackie Robinson is to black ballplayers" (Minoso 1994, xi).

Orestes Saturnino Arrieta Armas was born in the town of El Perico, part of Cuba's Camagüey Province, on November 29, 1925. His father, Carlos Arrieta, was a worker in a sugarcane plantation. His mother, Cecilia Armas, had been married before and had four older children of her own. Although Minoso was born to a poor family who had to work extremely hard to make ends meet and who lacked basic amenities, he has acknowledged a very happy childhood. His two older brothers were accomplished baseball players and his childhood activities were defined by the sport.

Minoso was active in baseball since childhood and organized baseball teams with the local boys of La Lonja, the farm where he had been born. Because his mother and his father separated when he was eight, Minoso moved to Havana with his mother. After she died when he was 10, he returned to La Lonja and continued playing baseball with the local teams organized by the farm workers. By the age of 14, Minoso was shuttling between the houses of friends and relatives. Because baseball was the only consistent element in his life, he decided to become a professional baseball player. In order to obtain his father's permission to leave the farm and to return to Havana, Minoso asked a friend to write a letter inviting him to join a semi-professional baseball team in the capital. Impressed by the fake invitation, the family not only granted him permission but also gave him money to go.

On his arrival in Havana in 1941, Minoso went to live with his older sisters and took a job in a cigar factory so he could play with their team. At the time, most big businesses on the island had their own baseball teams. Since professional clubs in Havana were restricted to white Cubans, Minoso had no choice but to look for jobs playing semi-professionally with teams established and sponsored by these businesses. He played semi-professionally with the Partagás Cigar Factory team and later moved to play third base with the Ambrosia Candy Factory team. Although only 16 years old, Minoso was a very strong player and accumulated impressive statistics.

During the 1943 and 1944 baseball seasons Minoso moved out of Havana and joined the Cuban Miners, based in the Oriente Province. Although the Miners were semi-professional, they were considered one of the best teams in Cuba. Minoso excelled on the team and his skills landed him a place on the Marianao Tigers, a professional team, in 1944. During his first year with the Tigers he hit a .301 average and was selected Rookie of the Year.

His performance with this club attracted the attention of coach José Fernández, who recommended Minoso to Alex Pompez, owner of the New York Cubans, a Negro League team. At the time, teams from the Negro League recruited heavily in Cuba. Minoso, whose lifelong dream had been to play professional baseball in the United States, signed a contract to play with the Cubans for $150.00 per month. This figure was eventually raised to $300.00.

Minoso reported for training with the New York Cubans in New Orleans during the spring of 1945. Although he noticed the racial segregation of the South he was not strongly affected by it. After finishing training, he moved to New York, where he was well received by his fellow team members and enjoyed the city's atmosphere. He quickly developed a taste for fancy clothes and expensive cars. Minoso started to play with the Cubans during the 1945 season and stayed with the team until 1948. Although he was a well-rounded player, he didn't accumulate impressive statistics during his years with the Cubans. He has said, however, that the Cubans gave him an excellent opportunity to play with some of the best talent available in the Negro League and to learn the American playing style (Minoso 1994).

With the signing of Jackie Robinson to play with the Brooklyn Dodgers in 1947, doors were opened for other talented black and Latino players who wanted to play professionally in the United States. After Minoso played in the Negro League's 1948 All-Star Game, he was recruited to play professionally with the Cleveland Indians. As is often the custom with new talent, the Indians sent him to play with their Class-A team located in Dayton, Ohio, to refine his playing skills. Meanwhile, he continued to play with the Marianao Tigers in Cuba during the winter months. He did well during his first season in Dayton and the following year was allowed to play seven games with the Indians before being traded to the San Diego Padres, then a member of the Pacific Coast League. Although disappointed with the trade, which had been motivated by poor performance, Minoso continued to play with San Diego during both the 1949 and 1950 seasons, accumulating good statistics and scores.

There is no doubt that the most important moment in Minoso's career came when he signed with the Chicago White Sox in 1951. This was his best opportunity to shine as a baseball player in the major leagues. If the White Sox had any doubts about signing Minoso, their doubts were dissipated when he batted a home run during the first inning of his first game with the team. During his first season at Comiskey Park, he won 14 straight games and was named American League Rookie of the Year. Minoso, known as the Cuban Comet, scored an impressive array of statistics, leading the league with 31 stolen bases. He had four seasons where he scored more than 20 home runs, led the league in triples three times, and participated in eight All-Star Games (González Echevarría 1999). During his first years in the major leagues, he was often the object of racist jokes and insults by fellow players and fans of the sport. A player with an extremely positive mindset, Minoso ignored racism to concentrate on the game.

Minnie Minoso played with the White Sox from 1951 to 1957. In 1957 he was traded back to the Cleveland Indians but returned to the White Sox in 1959. His participation on the team was instrumental in the Sox's winning their first championship in 40 years during the 1959 season.

During the 1960s Minoso played with the St. Louis Cardinals and the Washington Senators before being released from the majors in 1964 by the White Sox. In the mid-1960s and 1970s Minoso continued his baseball career in Mexico, where he coached and played with several teams in the Mexican leagues. He coached for the Sox during the 1970s and was allowed to play with the team in both 1976 and 1980 so he could claim to be the longest-playing sportsman in the major leagues.

When in the summer of 1993, Minoso donned the uniform of the St. Paul Saints, a team in the Northern Baseball League, and played a game against the Thunder Bay Whiskey Jacks, he became the first baseball player to have played for six decades in American professional baseball. During his career, he accumulated an impressive .298 batting average, 1023 runs batted in (RBIs), 1,963 hits, and 186 home runs (Pietruzsa 2000, 786). Many sports critics have argued for his inclusion in the Baseball Hall of Fame.—S.M.M.

References and Suggested Readings

González Echevarría, Roberto. *The Pride of Havana: A History of Cuban Baseball.* New York: Oxford University Press, 1999.

Minoso, Minnie, and Herb Fagen. *Just Call Me Minnie: My Six Decades in Baseball.* Champaign, IL: Sagamore Publishing, 1994.

Pietruzsa, David, ed. "Minnie Minoso." In *Baseball: The Biographical Encyclopedia.* New York: Total Sport, 2000. 786.

PEDRO MIR
(1913–2000)

Poet Laureate of the Dominican Republic, Novelist, Essayist, Historian, and Scholar

---

Don Pedro Mir, as he was known in his beloved Dominican Republic, is considered to be the leading poet and one of the most important twentieth-century literary figures of the Dominican Republic. His poetry, characterized by an unlimited love and admiration for his country and a thoughtful and critical social and political commentary, served as a catalyst for political mobilization and awareness for scores of people from the Dominican Republic during the years of Rafael Leonidas Trujillo's dictatorship.

Pedro Mir was born in the town of San Pedro de Macoris in the Dominican Republic on June 3, 1913. His Cuban-born father was a mechanical engineer who worked in the sugarcane processing plants of the island. His mother was from Puerto Rico. An understanding of his formative years in San Pedro de Macoris is essential to explain the later literary production of this distinguished writer. The city of San Pedro de Macoris is located in the eastern region of the Dominican Republic. During the earlier part of the twentieth century, the city boasted some of the biggest and most productive sugarcane plantations in the Caribbean. As was often the case in other Caribbean islands, these plantations were owned by members of the Spanish power elite who had stayed after the independence of the island and by other wealthy European foreigners who exploited the agricultural resources of the island. Local peasants who worked as agricultural laborers were forced to cultivate the crops under a harsh working environment, where they were often exploited and abused. Because of his father's work, Mir was exposed as a child to the many hardships suffered by sugarcane laborers working in the plantations around the city. These experiences strongly influenced the development of Mir's social and political conscience and eventually shaped his socialist philosophy, calling for social justice and equality for all Dominicans.

Mir was an inquisitive and sensitive child. In an extensive critical profile of the author's life and work published after his death, reporter Daryelin Torres, from the Santo Domingo *Listín Diario*, told a story that revealed the extraordinary sensitivity of the poet. Mir used to say that his first disillusion with the world occurred when he was six years old. One night, he felt alone in the darkness of his house at night, and he called his mother, hoping and praying to God that she would answer. When she didn't answer, he became disenchanted, and from then on, he felt deceived by her, by God, and by the world (Torres 2000, n.p.).

Mir studied journalism and law at the National Autonomous University of Santo Domingo. At the age of 24 he started to publish his poetry to great acclaim. By the 1930s, he was already well known in literary circles for the controversial critical political and social tones that his poetry conveyed against the dictatorship of Rafael Leonidas Trujillo. He sought political asylum in Cuba in 1947. While there he published what is perhaps his best-known poem "Hay un País en el Mundo" (There Is a Country in the World) in 1949. Tortured by his exile, he expressed his longing for the beauty of his island, spoke against its political and social illnesses, and spoke to the need to for political change.

Mir took advantage of his exile in Cuba to organize opposition against Trujillo's regime. He also lived in Mexico and traveled throughout Latin America and Europe raising awareness of the precarious political situation faced by the Dominican Republic. In 1962, after 15 years in exile, and shortly after Trujillo's 1961 assassination, Mir returned to the Dominican Republic. He immediately became involved with the Popular Socialist Party, which proposed a political platform to bring substantial changes to the economic and social orders of the island. Unfortunately, after the American invasion of 1965 and the tumultuous events that followed, Mir had to go into exile once again. This time he sought refuge in New York.

Once democracy was re-established in 1968, he returned to the island and accepted a teaching position at the National Autonomous University of Santo Domingo, where he became a professor of aesthetics and journalism. Once again, he resumed his powerful critical and literary work. Mir, who was also a pianist, also chaired the Dominican Arts Critics Association. During the late 1960s and 1970s, Mir became a fixture of Dominican intellectual and literary circles, which were always delighted to hear his poetry and his often-sardonic views of Dominican society.

Mir's work was influenced by poets such as Federico García Lorca, Ruben Darió, Pablo Neruda, and Walt Whitman (Torres 2000). His work has also been associated with the work of **Juan Bosch**, another Dominican writer with a reformist ideology. In fact, Bosch gave Mir an opportunity to publish his work when Bosch was an editor of *La Nación* newspaper. Mir's work was often concerned with many Dominican and Caribbean realities such colonialism, militarism, poverty, economic slavery, political repression, and corruption. Much of the relevance of and acclaim for his poetry comes from the fact that he had an uncanny ability to generate strong social and political commentaries about the terrible realities of the Dominican Republic while still praising its beauties and reaffirming his endless love for his island.

A multi-talented man, Mir wrote more than a dozen books in the genres of poetry and fiction, as well as essays. Among his most important poetry works are *Hay un País en el Mundo* (There Is a Country in the World), *Amén de las Mariposas* (Amen to the Butterflies), *Viaje a la Muchedumbre* (Trip to the Multitude), *Huracán Neruda* (Neruda Hurricane), and *Contracanto a Walt Witman* (Walt Whitman's Countersong). Other non-fiction books are *Fundamentos de la teoría y crítica del arte* (Fundamentals of Art Theory and Criticism), *Orígenes del hambre en la República Dominicana* (Origins of Hunger in the Dominican Republic), and *Cuando Amaban las Tierras Comuneras* (When the Communal Lands Were Loved).

Toward the end of his life, Mir started voicing his displeasure with what he perceived as a decadence that characterized these times: "The 20th century has fallen in the deepest disgrace, its ideas have been exhausted, and the chaos is a sign of these times" (Almanzanar 2000, A59). He encouraged the next generation to make their voices heard in the same way he had done. He was awarded the National Prize for History in 1975, and the National Prize in Literature for his life work in 1993. Mir was also appointed Poet Laureate of the Dominican Republic in 1982 by congressional decree. Hunter College of the City University of New York awarded him an honorary doctorate in literature in 1991.

At the time of his death on July 11, 2000, Ylonka Nacids-Perdomo, Director of the Center for Literary Research at the National Library in the Dominican Republic said: "Pedro Mir was, without doubt, the vital voice of Dominican poetry of the 20th Century, and a universal poet: meditative, and purifying" (Almanzanar 2000, A59).—S.M.M.

References and Suggested Readings

Almanzanar, Ramón. "Dominican Poet Mir Dies." Associated Press. *Newsday* (New York), July 11, 2000, A59.

Guerrero Marínez, Donald. "La Opinión: Homenaje and Don Pedro Meir." *Listín Diario* (Santo Domingo, DR), July 14, 2000, n.p.

Mir, Pedro. *Poesías (casi) completas.* Mexico, D.F.: Siglo Veintinuno Editores, 1994.

Pace, Eric. "Pedro Mir, Whose Poems Spoke to Latin Workers Dies at 87." *The New York Times.* July 14, 2000, B10.

Torres, Daryelin. "La Vida." *Listin Diario* (Santo Domingo, DR), July 14, 2000, n.p.

The Mirabal Sisters
Patria Mercedes Mirabal
(1924–1960)
Minerva Argentina Mirabal
(1927–1960)
María Teresa Mirabal
(1935–1960)

Dominican Political Activists and Martyrs

The Mirabal sisters were political activists and martyrs from the province of Salcedo in the Dominican Republic. They were also known as the "Butterflies," the code name used by one of them during their underground political activities against the dictatorship of Rafael Leonidas Trujillo in the 1950s. During their lives, the sisters were incarcerated several times and finally ambushed and brutally assassinated on November 25, 1960, by the secret police. The murder of the Mirabal sisters outraged the majority of the population and is considered one of the events that helped propel the anti-Trujillo sentiment that led to his assassination six months later. A fourth sister, Bélgica Adela Mirabal Reyes, affectionately known as Dedé, is the sole survivor of the four siblings and the caretaker of the family's legacy.

Patria (February 24, 1924), Minerva Argentina (March 1, 1925), and María Teresa (October 15, 1935) Mirabal Reyes were born in Ojo de Agua, a village in the province of Salcedo to Enrique Mirabal Fernández and Mercedes Reyes. They were business owners whose holdings included a coffee plantation, a warehouse, a processing plant for coffee and rice, cattle, and a butcher shop. The couple had only one son, who died shortly after birth. All four sisters completed their primary and secondary education in one of the most prestigious private boarding school in the Dominican Republic, El Colegio de la Imaculada, a Catholic school in the town of La Vega.

Patria, the oldest, married Pedro A. González at age 16, and although she was politically inquisitive, she sought out news from foreign magazines such as *American Home, Selecciones del Reader's Digest,* and other publications that reported on the dictatorship, and included tips on how to improve and beautify the home and garden—something she thoroughly enjoyed.

From very early on, Minerva displayed the strongest patriotic passion, beliefs, and leadership. She was a voracious reader who verified the validity of news published in the local papers by listening to radio stations from Cuba and Venezuela, which she felt provided a better perspective on politics. In 1946 she competed the equivalent of a bachelor's degree specializing in social studies. Although the Mirabals' were very proud of their daughter Minerva's political commitment and integrity, her outspokenness made them apprehensive due to Trujillo's very repressive dictatorship, and they did not allow her to immediately proceed to law school. Minerva stayed at home and continued her political activity, familiarizing herself with all the sources of politics and poetry.

Gregarious, good-looking, and politically active Minerva frequently visited the capital Santo Domingo to spend time with friends who shared her anti-Trujillo sentiments. In her native Salcedo, both her political fervor and her beauty attracted attention. The Mirabal family was well regarded and was invited to high-level social functions and activities, even one hosted by Trujillo. The family was keenly aware that invitations of that sort came with strings attached. In this case, it was the dictator's interest in the very attractive Minerva, who in 1949 boldly rejected his overtures. The entire Mirabal family was in attendance and became aware of the situation. Taking advantage of the sudden rain that began to fall during the outdoor celebration, Enrique Mirabal gathered his family and left.

Trujillo's particular rules of etiquette did not allow for anyone to leave his activities without his authorization or before his own departure. The following day, in an act that was repeated many times, Enrique Mirabal was jailed and his wife and Minerva were kept in a local hotel under house arrest. One of the conditions for Minerva's release was that she write a letter of apology to the dictator, which she never did. Two years later the family was re-arrested after Enrique Mirabal refused to buy a book praising Trujillo and his government. While jailed, Enrique Mirabal developed a cardiac condition that is believed to have precipitated his early death in 1953.

In 1952, a year before her father's death, Minerva finally began to pursue a law degree, but the government revoked her registration the following year. Under pressure of government authorities, she wrote a paper praising Trujillo just three days before her father's death. Although she felt that this would compromise her ideas, she also felt that education would be the key in her struggle against the regime. As a result, she was able to resume her law studies and in 1955, while still in law school, she married Manuel Tavárez Justo, a law school classmate and an activist in the movement against the dictatorship.

By this time, her oldest sister Patria Mercedes was living in nearby Conuco. Dedé, who had married Jaime Fernández Camilo in 1948, lived nearby in San Francisco de Macorí. María Teresa had completed her degree in land surveying at the University of Santo Domingo in 1957. María Teresa had carried on a clandestine romantic relationship with Leandro Guzmán since the age of 14. They were married in 1958. The Mirabal sisters each had met and married men who not only became their husbands but also their partners in organizing the leadership activities of the anti-Trujillo movement.

Realizing that creating a resistance movement required recruitment and organization of other like-minded citizens, Minerva and her husband organized El

Movimiento 14 de Junio, a name derived from a group of Dominican exiles whose invasion to overthrow the government was set for June 14, 1959. The initial group numbered 13 and very quickly grew to include some of the most prominent members of the community. With the expansion of the movement, secrecy became more vulnerable, and soon the secret military police uncovered the movement's activities, and arrested many of its leaders, including Minerva and María Teresa and their husbands, Manuel and Leandro, in early January 1960. Patria's husband, Pedro González, escaped arrest by going into hiding.

The men were placed in solitary confinement in a prison called "la 40," which was notorious for extreme torture, including electric shock and pulling off prisoners' fingernails. Minerva and María Teresa, on the other hand, were released relatively unharmed on February 7. Once free, they continued their underground political work, albeit more discreetly. However, in May they were rearrested, taken to "la 40" and sentenced to 30 years. Again, the sisters were released. Their husbands Manuel and Leandro were transferred to a prison in Puerto Plata, a location much closer to their homes, which made visiting them frequently possible. Unbeknownst to them, this was all under orders of Trujillo.

With rumors rampant that an order for their death had been issued, the sisters traveled with an entourage that included children and elderly people, even though Minerva questioned whether the dictator would indeed dare to kill them. On November 25, 1960, Minerva, María Teresa, Patria (who had decided to accompany them out of solidarity), and their driver, a young anti-Trujilloist named Rufiño de la Cruz, set off by jeep to visit their husbands in Puerto Plata. Under orders from Trujillo, a group of six specially selected members of the secret military police ambushed the sisters and their driver and ordered them out of the car. They were taken to separate locations in a ravine so that the victims could not see each other's execution. All four were handcuffed, strangled, and clubbed to death. To make it seem as if it were an accident, the bodies were returned to the car and pushed down the ravine. The regime's cover story of an "accident" backfired. No one believed the government's account. People all over the country were outraged that Trujillo would go so far as to kill women. Many believe that this incident was the beginning of the end of the Trujillo era, which culminated in his own assassination six months later.

The Mirabal sisters' memory was commemorated for years in a very restrained manner, and the government treated the question of how and why they died guardedly. The main reason for this attitude was **Joaquín Balaguer**, the Dominican Republic's figurehead president during Trujillo's dictatorship, who remained in power until 1996 (Aquino García 1999). **Julia Álvarez** wrote a novel *In the Time of Butterflies* (1994), a fictionalized account of the lives of the Mirabal sisters that deals with this issue.

Today the Mirabal sisters are considered symbols of feminism in Latin America. November 25, the anniversary of their death, is commemorated, as the International Day Against Violence Against Women. In the Dominican Republic, a monument that Trujillo had built to himself has been changed and now the 137-foot obelisk is a mural with the image of the three murdered sisters and the surviving sister Dedé. Dedé, who made the decision not to actively participating in the insurgency, has dedicated her life to keeping the spirit of her sisters alive. One of the Mirabal homes in Salcedo, whose construction was overseen by Minerva in 1954, has been converted into the Mirabal Sisters Museum.—G.C.

References and Suggested Readings

Alvarez, Julia. *In the Time of Butterflies*. Chapel Hill, NC: Algonquin Books, 1994.

Aquino García, Miguel. *Tres heroínas y un tirano: la historia veridical de las hermanas Mirabal y su asesinato por Rafael Leonidas Trujillo*. Santo Domingo, DR: Departamento de Cutura y Publicaciones/Universidad Interamericana (UNICA), 1999.

Diederich, Bernard. *Trujillo: The Death of the Goat*. Maplewood, NJ: Waterfront Press, 1990.

Mirabal Sisters Foundation: *http://www.conectados.net/mirabal/biographies.html*.

Rohter, Larry. "The Three Sisters Avenged: A Dominican Drama." *The New York Times*, February 15, 1997, 4.

RITA MORENO
(1931–)

Puerto Rican American Actress, Singer, and Dancer

Rita Moreno is a pioneering actress, singer, and dancer who broke ground in every branch of the American entertainment industry. As a film actress, she was awarded an Oscar in 1961 for best supporting actresss as Anita in *West Side Story*. In 1975 she won a Tony for the role of Googie Gómez in Terrence McNally's *The Ritz*—a character and comedic routine she developed. Her singing brought her a Grammy for her work in a soundtrack album for *The Electric Company* in 1972. Her work on *The Muppet Show* and *The Rockford Files* earned her two Emmys in 1977 and 1978. This Puerto Rican actress has gained fame and glory because of her unique talent, her ability to cross over between different genres in the world of entertainment, and her tenacity and artistic qualities.

Rosa Dolores Alverio was born in the small town of Humacao, Puerto Rico, in the southeastern region of the island. Her father was Paco Alverio and her mother was Rosa María Marcano. Her mother moved to the United States when Rita was just 5 years old and worked as a seamstress until she saved enough money to go back to the island and bring her daughter with her. A child of bright disposition, she expressed interest in dancing early on in her life. "I was the kid who danced on tables at age 5 for Grandpa or anybody who would watch" (Stack 1998, 58). As a child, she took dancing lessons with Paco Cansino. To supplement her

Rita Moreno. Courtesy of Rita Moreno.

family's income, she acted in children's theater productions, such as those in the toy department of Macy's in New York (Moritz 1995).

Despite the fact that she attended public schools and lived in the poor immigrant district of Washington Heights in New York, she pursued a career in entertainment and by the age of 13 debuted on Broadway in *Skydrift* as a flamenco dancer. Although the play lasted only a few performances, it introduced Rita to the world of entertainment which she never again left. During her teens, she danced and worked in different nightclubs throughout the United States. When she was 17, a talent agent who had contacts with MGM, scouted her and introduced her to the legendary Louis B. Mayer who signed her as an actress with his studio. MGM asked her to change her name, so she shortened from Rosita to Rita and adopted her stepfather's last name.

During the 1950s, the 5'3" Puerto Rican actress was typecast by Hollywood in many B-rated movies that lacked importance or artistic significance. Since Hollywood producers limited anyone who had a different ethnic background to tight ethnic roles, she was recruited to play Latino roles but also a wide array of other "ethnic" roles. She had very little chances to showcase her talents or to be perceived as something other than an ethnic actress. One of Moreno's best acting opportunities of that period came in 1956, when she appeared with Yul Bryner as the Burmese slave girl Tuptim in the film the *King and I*. Moreno has said that Bryner was a wonderful mentor who paid for her acting lessons because he wanted her to be as good as he was (Lipton and Arias 1998). During the 1950s, while still working in films, she acted on the stage and worked with summer repertoire companies in California and throughout the United States. Ironically, she was offered the opportunity to audition for the stage version of *West Side Story* but refused because she was too involved in her film and acting careers on the West Coast.

Even when she had a steady professional career during the 1950s, Moreno lived through a series of turbulent events and difficult love affairs in Hollywood that gave her a reputation as a hot and difficult Latina. After breaking a long and tumultuous relationship with actor Marlon Brando that had lasted almost ten years, she tried to commit suicide by overdosing on sleeping pills. Of that period she has said: "It was a turning point in my life, though. Life is really very precious and, I was reminded of that" (Lipton and Arias 1998, 168). She emerged from that situation with a renewed sense of direction and motivation, and with an energy that allowed her to build the stellar career for which she is known today.

Moreno's significant career break occurred when she was selected to play the rebellious and rambunctious Anita in the film adaptation of *West Side Story*. Interestingly, she was to duplicate on film the role that brought such great accolades on Broadway to fellow Puerto Rican actress **Chita Rivera**. Directed by Robert Wise and choreographed by Jerome Robbins, the role gave Moreno an opportunity to display her vocal and dancing talents. *West Side Story* is an adaptation of Shakespeare's *Romeo and Juliet*, modernized and contextualized within the gang rivalries that permeated New York during the 1950s. Her energetic dancing as the girlfriend of Bernardo, one of the gang leaders, undisputedly made her one of the central performers in the movie. She has said that its heavily orchestrated choreography "damn near killed me, I was the old lady of that group" (Lipton and Arias 1998, 168). Even though today *West Side Story* is seen by many as politically incorrect, damaging, and stereotypical of Puerto Ricans, her singing and dancing routines—particularly the one for the song "America"—have become historic milestones, as one of the first times a Puerto Rican woman occupied such a relevant role in a mainstream American film.

During the 1960s and early 1970s, Moreno continued to garner great reviews in both film and theater projects. In an interesting career move, she joined the cast of the Children's Television Workshop's *Electric Company*, along with entertainer Bill Cosby. Her participation in the show's soundtrack earned a Grammy in 1972 as the best recording for children. In 1975 she appeared in Terrence McNally's *The Ritz* as Googie Gómez. The role had been created by Moreno herself as a diversion while filming *West Side Story*. Her performance at the Longacres Theater in Broadway brought her a Tony Award in 1975. To some extent, this role, where she plays a Puerto Rican singer with a strong Spanish accent, has been seen as her way of getting back at Hollywood and Broadway for her earlier typecasting in ethnic roles. *The Ritz* was made into a film, but although she got great reviews, it had little success at the box office. Later in the 1970s, she appeared on *The Muppet Show* (1977) and *The Rockford Files* (1978), for which she earned two Emmys.

This restless performer continues to work with relentless zeal and energy. She recently acted in HBO's dramatic series *Oz* as Sister Peter Marie Reimondo, a witty and no-nonsense nun. She has become active in educational campaigns to promote language competency among Americans, and has also written to support the pro-choice movement in the United States, describing her own difficult choice to have an abortion earlier in her career (Bonavoglia 1991). In 1998, the Latino film festival Cine Acción in San Francisco was dedicated to her. She was also awarded an honorary doctorate by Trinity College in Hartford, Connecticut, in 1999. She has been recognized in the *Guinness Book of Records* as the only entertainer to win all of the four most prestigious awards in the American entertainment industry. In addition to the abovementioned awards, she has also received a Golden Globe Award, the Golden Apple Award, the Joseph Jefferson

Award, and the Sarah Siddons Award, among others. In 1995 she received a star on the Hollywood Walk of Fame. She has served on the National Foundation of the Arts, as a commissioner on the President's White House Fellowships and is presently a member of the President's Committee on the Arts and Humanities. She is regarded as one of the best role models for Puerto Rican actors in the United States. Moreno takes advantage of every opportunity that appears to empower Puerto Rican and Latino children in American society.—S.M.M.

References and Suggested Readings

Bonavoglia, Angela. *The Choices We Made: 25 Women and Men Speak Out About Abortion.* New York: Random House, 1991.

Lipton, Michael, and Ron Arias. "Entertaining Rita." *People,* September 21, 1998, 167–168.

Moritz, Charles, ed. "Rita Moreno." *Current Biography Yearbook, 1995.* New York: H.W. Wilson, 1995. 299–302.

Stack, Peter. "Rita Is on a Roll." *The San Francisco Chronicle,* September 12, 1998, 58.

Luis Muñoz Marín
(1898–1980)

Puerto Rican Patriot, Journalist, and Writer

Luis Muñoz Marín was the leading political figure of Puerto Rican history during the twentieth century. Between 1932 and 1964 he occupied a central role in Puerto Rican politics. As founder of the Popular Democratic Party, Muñoz Marín guided an economic and social transformation in the island of Puerto Rico after 1952 and was the leading architect of its current Commonwealth status. His vision of Puerto Rico as a "free associated state" of the United States formalized the relationship between Puerto Rico and the United States but also perpetuated the colonial status of the island.

Luis Muñoz Marín was born in San Juan on February 18, 1898. His father, Luis Muñoz Rivera, a journalist and a patriot, fought actively to end colonial domination of Puerto Rico. Through his journalistic work in the newspaper *La Democracia,* Muñoz Rivera played a role in the approval of the autonomic charter that gave more political autonomy to the people of Puerto Rico. Muñoz Marín's mother was Amalia Marín, who also came from a family of journalists and political activists.

Muñoz Marín received his early education in the local public schools of Santurce, Puerto Rico. His father became Puerto Rican Resident Commissioner in Washington, and the family moved to New York City, where Muñoz Marín attended public school for a year before going to Georgetown University Preparatory School. He studied there until 1914.

Muñoz Marín became an administrative assistant in his father's office in Washington. These years were significant because his father was working on the process that led to the approval of the Jones Act of 1917, which granted American citizenship to Puerto Ricans. It gave more autonomy to the island but kept most political decision making in the hands of the United States and its appointed governors. The act was contradictory for Muñoz Rivera. As a promoter of independence for the island, he had concerns over forcing American citizenship on Puerto Ricans. Despite the intense and interesting nature of the ongoing legislative process, Muñoz Marín has stated in his memoirs that at the time he lacked any serious ideological position on these issues (Muñoz Marín 1982).

Luis Muñoz Marín.
Courtesy of Raúl Medina Collection.

After his father's death in 1916, Muñoz Marín traveled frequently between Puerto Rico and the United States and studied for a short time at Columbia University. He wrote a short story book titled *Borrones* (1917) in New York and wrote for *La Democracia* in Puerto Rico. He returned to Puerto Rico toward the end of 1917 and developed an interest in Puerto Rican affairs, interacting with some of the most important intellectuals of his time. One of them was the poet **Luis Palés Matos**. His friendship with Palés Matos brought him to the interior of the island, where he became acquainted with many of the social problems of the time and saw the importance of the political process in the resolution of social and economic problems. He developed an understanding of Puerto Rican *jíbaros*, the poor peasants who worked in agriculture in the countryside. In 1918 he once again returned to New York, where he published a literary journal known as *Revista de Indias* (Indies' Journal), worked as a journalist, and continued meeting with notable American and Puerto Rican intellectuals. He also wrote poetry.

Muñoz Marín's first incursion into Puerto Rican politics took place in 1920 when he joined the Socialist Party of labor leader Santiago Iglesias Pantín. His decision to work with Iglesias Pantín was problematic, as Iglesias favored Puerto Rican annexation to the United States and Muñoz Marín supported independence. However, Muñoz Marín was attracted to the party not because of the political status issue, but because of Iglesias Pantín's desire to improve the working conditions of Puerto Rican laborers. He toured the island with Iglesias Pantín and noted poverty and exploitation endured by *jíbaros*, who were employed by sugar and coffee plantation owners who were not concerned with the well being of their workers.

Muñoz Marín's association with Iglesias Pantín lasted only a short time. He spent the next ten years traveling between Puerto Rico and New York. He continued writing against the United States and met with many important socialist leaders of the time who were visiting New York City. He accepted the editorial directoship of *La Democracia* in 1926. The paper had strong ties with the Liberal Party of Antonio R. Barceló. While the party advocated Puerto Rican independence, Muñoz Marín's primary concern was restructuring the government to create social and economic changes to benefit the poor working class.

On his definite return to Puerto Rico in 1931, Muñoz Marín joined the Liberal Party. He was elected to the Puerto Rican senate in 1932. Although he still believed in independence, he became attracted to the potential positive impact that Roosevelt's New Deal policies could have on Puerto Rico. Because Muñoz Marín attributed the underdevelopment of Puerto Rico to the former economic and political policies of the United States, he saw the New Deal as a way for the United States to help Puerto Rico. He slowly drifted away from his pro-independence stance and saw the importance of having a better relationship with the United States. He lobbied officials in Roosevelt's government to include Puerto Rico in the New Deal projects. The introduction of federal programs that provided free food for poor Puerto Ricans and the availability of American technical assistance for farmers gave him hope.

At this time, Barceló and Muñoz Marín grew apart ideologically. Their differences were exacerbated when Muñoz Marín supported an American legislation known as the Tydings Bill. The legislation was a response to the nationalist violence that had occurred in Puerto Rico in 1936. The legislation provided for independence of Puerto Rico over a four-year period. Members of the Liberal Party saw the bill as an opportunity to obtain independence for Puerto Rico. Muñoz Marín did not support the bill and tried to gain control of the party. With this, his relationship with Barceló soured and Muñoz Marín was expelled from the party in 1937. He was considered responsible for the Liberal Party's overwhelming defeat in the 1936 elections.

Muñoz Marín founded the Popular Democratic Party on July 22, 1938, in an attempt to distance himself from the contentious issue of Puerto Rican political status. Instead, he developed a political platform based solely on an effort to build Puerto Rican society and provide economic equality for all Puerto Ricans. At the time, more than one third of Puerto Rican families had a yearly income below $200 (Rivera and Alvarez 1998). Sugar processing companies were the island's largest landowners, and the island's economy was in ruins. Puerto Rican *jíbaros* lived in deplorable conditions, and illnesses such as anemia, malaria and tuberculosis were rampant. Muñoz Marín wanted to build an economic infrastructure that would allow the government to improve the quality of life for its people. He hoped to receive assistance from the United States in order to accomplish his goals.

In 1938, Muñoz Marín started a fierce island-wide political campaign that promised poor Puerto Ricans that voting for him could offer a democratic process of change that would lead to a better society. He wished to put an end to a corrupt political system in which poor peasants were often forced to sell their votes without receiving any useful support from the government. Using powerful rhetoric, Muñoz Marín traveled to every town on the island and met with thousands of poor Puerto Ricans. He could relate to the Puerto Rican *jíbaros* like no other politician had done before.

The Popular Democratic Party won the elections, capturing almost 38 percent of the vote (Bayrón Toro 2000) and taking control of the Puerto Rican house and senate. Muñoz Marín became president of the senate.

In a recent documentary on his life, Muñoz Marín said that immediately after the elections, he started to push for a series of political reforms that included: the creation of a land authority; the approval of a minimum wage law and a law that restricted the work day to eight hours; improvement of the educational system, including better salaries for teachers; price controls on basic needs; the approval of laws that allow for collective bargaining between workers and employers; a more equitable tax system; and improvement of health services (Rivera and Alvarez 1998). Muñoz Marín was able to accomplish these changes because New Deal federal money became available.

In 1946 President Truman appointed Jesus T. Piñeiro as governor. He became the first Puerto Rican governor in the island's 450-year history. The following year, the U.S. Congress modified the Jones Act to allow Puerto Ricans to elect their own governor. Muñoz Marín ran for governor and became the first Puerto Rican governor democratically elected by its people.

His first term as governor was influenced by the approval of Public Law 600 in the U.S. Congress. It gave Puerto Rico the right to its own internal government under the general terms of a Commonwealth, or a "Free Associated State." It asked that Puerto Ricans develop and approve their own constitution subject to the ratification of the U.S. Congress. This law led to formation of a Constitutional Assembly that wrote a constitution that was later ratified by Puerto Ricans. The document received congressional approval in 1952. By accepting this legislation and accepting Commonwealth status for Puerto Rico, Muñoz Marín perpetuated the colonial relationship between the United States and Puerto Rico. While Puerto Rico has the right to develop and enact its own laws, they have to be consistent with the American constitution. Puerto Ricans are subject to all federal laws yet have no representation in the U.S. Congress and do not vote in presidential elections. The adoption of the new status continued the controversy that exists to this day.

Muñoz Marín was reelected governor in 1952, 1954, 1956, and 1960. One of his major initiatives during the 1950s was Operación Manos a la Obra (Operation Bootsraps). This initiative created an economic infrastructure to promote the development of Puerto Rico as an industrial society, rather than as an agrarian one. The government gave priority to developing and strengthening more efficient systems of education, transportation, health maintenance, communication, and public utilities. It gave industrial incentives that made it attractive for American corporations to move to Puerto Rico. It also encouraged the migration of Puerto Ricans to the United States as a way to reduce unemployment. Muñoz Marín's government led a vigorous campaign to sterilize women of childbearing age as a means of controlling population growth.

Many of the elements of Muñoz Marín's vision for Puerto Rico finally materialized as Puerto Rico became highly industrialized. These changes had profound implications for Puerto Rican society and life. Muñoz Marín made significant advances in health and education. The quality of life of all Puerto Ricans generally improved. There was substantial parity among the social classes, and the exploitation of the poor *jíbaros* at the hands of wealthy landowners virtually disappeared. The sugar and coffee industries suffered, as people preferred to seek jobs in the industrial sector rather than in the agriculture. Muñoz Marín's policies were largely responsible for the migration of hundreds of thousands of Puerto Ricans. He was the social engineer that created a huge Puerto Rican Diaspora in the United States.

After constant refusals from the U.S. Congress to increase autonomy, Muñoz Marín decided not to run for governor in the general elections of 1964, believing that Puerto Rico needed a change. He became a senator-at-large until 1968, when he retired from politics and made only sporadic appearances on behalf of his party.

In 1984 Puerto Rican writer Edgardo Rodríguez Juliá, published a book titled *Las Tribulaciones de Jonás* (Jonah's Tribulations). He used two meetings and interviews he had with Muñoz Marín as the basis for creating a series of fictional conversations where the leader addressed some of the most important issues of his administration and political career. The book had a profound effect among readers and critics because it was the first time that someone established a parallelism between the biblical prophet Jonah and Muñoz Marín. Jonah, a prophet of God, had refused to obey God's mandate to preach redemption to the people of Nineveh because he considered them corrupt and hopeless. He ran away in a boat to escape his mandate. When the boat was struck by a huge storm, he jumped overboard to save other travelers from the ire of God. He knew that the boat was being stricken because of his failure to obey God's orders. While at sea, he was swallowed by a whale and endured three days of malady and horror inside the whale.

While the parallelisms do not seem evident, there is a great deal of correlation between this biblical story and Muñoz Marín's life. A firm believer in Puerto Rican independence during his youth, Muñoz Marín sold out his beliefs to take advantage of the economic resources available to Puerto Rico from the United States. He used American assistance to launch one of the most important social and economic transformations of any country in the Americas. Jonah eventually accepted the will of God and preached his prescribed message to the people of Nineveh and saved himself. Muñoz Marín lived to see the transformation of Puerto Rico created by his government but came to regret many of the changes that he had provided. His real troubles came as a result of the perpetuation of the island's colonial status and from the many social problems that were created as a result of the transformation.

Luis Muñoz Marín died on April 30, 1980. Thousands of Puerto Ricans took to the streets to bid a final farewell to the man considered to be the architect of modern Puerto Rican society.—S.M.M.

References and Suggested Readings

Bayrón Toro, Fernando. *Elecciones y Partidos Políticos de Puerto Rico: 1809–2000.* Mayagüez, PR: Editorial Isla, 2000.

Benítez, Rexach. *Vida y Obra de Luis Muñoz Marín.* San Juan, PR: Editorial Edil, 1989.

Bernier, R. Elfren. *Luis Muñoz Marín: Anecdotario Mumarino II.* San Juan, PR: Fundación Luis Muñoz Marín, 1999.

Fundación Luis Muñoz Marín. *El Archivo Luis Muñoz Marín: una ventana para el estudio de la historia puertorriqueña.* San Juan, PR: Fundación Luis Muñoz Marín, 2000.

Muñoz Marín, Luis. *Memorias: 1898–1940.* San Juan, PR: Interamerican University Press, 1982.

———. *Memorias: 1940–1952.* San Juan, PR: Interamerican University Press, 1992.

Picó, Fernando. *Luis Muñoz Marín: Discursos: 1934–1948, Volumen I.* San Juan, PR: Fundación Luis Muñoz Marín, 1999.

———. *Luis Muñoz Marín: Ensayos del Centenario.* San Juan, PR: Fundación Luis Muñoz Marín, 1999.

Rivera, Franklin, and Eric Alvarez, producers. *Luis Muñoz Marín, 1898–1980* (video). San Juan, PR: Producciones Siglo XXI, 1998.

Rivera, José A. *El Pensamiento Político de Luis Muñoz Marín.* San Juan, PR: Fundación Luis Muñoz Marín, 1996.

Rodríguez Juliá, Edgardo. *Las tribulaciones de Jonás.* Río Piedras: Ediciones Huracán, 1984.

Rosario Natal, Carmelo. *Luis Muñoz Marín: Servidor Público y Humaista (Cartas).* San Juan, PR: Producciones Históricas, 1998.

V. S. NAIPAUL
(1932–)

Trinidadian Writer

When the Swedish Academy awarded the 2001 Nobel Prize in Literature to Trinidadian writer V. S. Naipaul, it recognized his "united perceptive narrative and incorruptible scrutiny in works that compel us to see the presence of suppressed histories" (Nobel Academy 2001). The Nobel is one of the highest distinctions that can be given to a writer, and celebrates Naipaul's literary accomplishments in a career that spans more than four decades. Naipaul's literary merits cannot be challenged. His narratives reflect his inquisitive eye as a social and cultural commentator with a flawless style that meets the highest standards of British literary canons. They also reflect, however, many inconsistencies in the life of this notable

V. S. Naipaul. AP Photo/Alastair Grant.

author. Although he has showcased Trinidad and the Caribbean to the rest of the world, he has minimized the influence of the Caribbean in his life and in the development of his own individual identity.

Vidiadhar Surajprasad Naipaul was born on August 17, 1932, in Chaguanas, Trinidad. He was one of six children of Seepersad Naipaul, a journalist, and Bropatie Capildeo Naipaul, a homemaker. Although a journalist, his father aspired to become a serious writer but was never able to launch a successful career. He died from a heart attack in his forties. His mother came from a family that emigrated from India to Trinidad at the end of the nineteenth century looking for work in agriculture. In 1832, after the independence of African slaves in Trinidad, the British government found itself with a shortage of workers. As a result, they were forced to implement a system of imported labor where they brought immigrants from several countries in Asia and Africa, especially India. As a result, Trinidad, one of the Britain's Caribbean colonies, became a diverse mixture of cultures. This cultural variety became a source of inspiration for Naipaul's work.

Naipaul grew in Port of Spain, the capital of Trinidad. Naipaul attended the Chaguanas Government School, Tranquility Boys School in Trinidad, and Queen's Royal College, where he graduated in 1949; from there went on to study at University College in Oxford after winning a scholarship. Although missing his family during his first months at Oxford, he embraced the intellectual ferment of University College and the world of opportunities that it opened for him. As an individual, and as a writer, Naipaul maintained a strong allegiance to European intellectual traditions and to British literature and writers. He took advantage of his stay at Oxford to learn about these writers and to write as an Englishman. In addition, he became involved as a writer in the BBC's Caribbean Voices program, for which he worked as an editor after his graduation from Oxford in 1953. He also worked as a fiction reviewer for the *New Statesman* from 1957 to 1961. Naipaul tried to return to live in Trinidad in 1956, but he found the intellectual landscape of the island dry and decided to go back to London. His rejection of Trinidad's colonial and post-colonial realities has led critics to call him "a man without a country" (Singh 1998, 54).

Naipaul's first novel was *The Mystic Masseur,* which he published in 1957. It was well received by the critics but it was not recognized as either very original or as a masterpiece. It was his 1961 novel, *A House for Mr. Biswas*, that first brought Naipaul both recognition and praise. The autobiographical novel explores the cultural and colonial experiences of a Trinidadian family of Indian ancestry, fairly similar to his, that tries to find freedom and independence on the island. The book reflects not only the effects of British colonial influence on these individuals but also details the dynamics and conflicts created by the multiplicity of races, cultures, and traditions that came together in Trinidad.

To date, Naipaul has written 26 books, including *Miguel Street* (1959*), El Dorado* (1969), *India: A Wounded Civilization* (1977), *A Bend in the River* (1979), *Among Believers: An Islamic Journey* (1981), *The Enigma of Arrival* (1987), and *Half a Life* (2001). The Caribbean theme and setting has slowly faded from his stories, and he has broadened his work to encompass fiction, social commentary, and travel writing. Some of his recent work reflects his quest for understanding India, in some ways his motherland, and also the traditions of Islam.

Most of his writings reveal the influences of colonial experiences on his life. His work has explicit moral values and virtues ascribed to the themes, storylines, and plots that he advocates. Some of Naipaul's themes include the cultural and psychological displacement caused by immigration, the impact of colonial rule in the process of individual and collective identity; the cultural alienation created by colonial rule; the evil effects of imperialism, the inability of post-colonial societies to thrive and flourish; and the inherent political instability and chaos that typifies post-colonial societies so that even when they have gained independence from foreign powers, their people remain politically, socially, and economically marginalized, and what is worse, enslaved.

Many of his critics consider him extremely pessimistic. In a recent conversation with one of Naipaul's relatives, he expressed to the author that he felt Naipaul's experiences in Great Britain had "colonialized" him. Although Naipaul calls himself a liberal, many critics and writers have criticized him for writing from a position of privilege that adversely affects his point of view. A review of biographical material available about Naipaul and a book of the letters that he exchanged with his father during his first years at Oxford suggests a more complex reality. The letters bring forth an image of Naipaul as someone who had to struggle to overcome the obstacles of colonial life. Poverty, suffering, and fear of failure were a constant presence early in his life. These elements undoubtedly led him to blame the victim rather than attacking the roots of the problems that affect colonial societies.

In the recent book *Sir Vidia's Shadow,* author Paul Theroux depicts Naipaul as having an intense and enigmatic personality filled with contradictions. While he had the great gift of expressing himself through beautifully crafted prose, he was depicted as a manipulative friend and husband who always wished to be recognized and to have control. He criticized British colonial authority in the world but accepted a knightship from the queen (Theroux 1999).

One of Naipaul's greatest accomplishments is the heightened recognition of Caribbean literature and his role as a facilitator for those Caribbean writers who followed him, such as **George Lamming** and **Derek Walcott**. He has been seen as the first truly Caribbean writer to gain recognition and success in the very elitist British literary establishment. More importantly, he has been seen as someone who has tried to objectively depict social and political relations in the world by bringing those "suppressed histories" that sometimes are ignored under the disguise of "political correctness."

Naipaul's work has been recognized throughout the world. In 1971, he won a Booker prize for his book *In a Free State* and in 1990 was knighted by the Queen of England. There is no doubt that the Nobel Prize in Literature is his biggest recognition of all. Regardless of our individual opinions about his work, there is little controversy about his status as a formidable writer. He does not make it easy for those seeking individual explanations about him—in his Nobel address he said: "I will say I am the sum of my books" (Naipaul 2001).—S.M.M.

References and Suggested Readings

Hamner, Robert D. *V. S. Naipaul.* New York: Twain Publishers, 1973.

Herdeck, Donald, ed. *Caribbean Writers: A Bio-Biographical Encyclopedia.* Washington, DC: Three Continent Press, 1979. 155–162.

Naipaul. V. S. *Between Father and Son: Family Letters.* London: Little, Brown, and Co., 1999.

———. *A House for Mr. Biswas.* London: Deutch, 1961.

———. "Two Worlds: Nobel Address." December 7, 2001. *http://www.nobel.se/literature/laureates/2001/naipaul-lecture-e.html.*

Nobel Academy. "The Nobel Prize in Literature 2001." Press Release. October 11, 2001.

Singh, Rahul. "Telling It as He Sees It." *Newsweek,* March 16, 1998, 54.

Swain, Stella. "V. S. Naipaul." In Meritt Moseley, ed., *Dictionary of Literary Biography.* Detroit: Gale, 1999. 202–212.

Theroux, Paul. *Sir Vidia's Shadow.* Boston: Houghton Mifflin, 1999.

NANNY OF THE MAROONS
(1680?–1750?)

Jamaican National and Folk Hero

The Jamaican national hero also known as Grandy Nanny was one of the spiritual and military leaders of the Windward Jamaican Maroons, escaped Jamaican slaves who became famous for fighting off repeated incursions from the British army and the Jamaican government for three centuries, defiantly keeping their own culture and traditions to this day. Queen Nanny of the Maroons, as she is also known, is revered as the most noble and valiant of the maroon warriors. She united all the maroons in Jamaica and preserved the traditional African culture and knowledge. The only woman among Jamaica's seven national heroes, she is properly referred to as the "Right Excellent Nanny."

It is believed Nanny was born in Ghana in Africa in the second half of the seventeenth century during the 1680s. Historians have concluded that she voyaged to

Jamaica as a free person who owned slaves herself. An Akan ethnic, Nanny's name derived from "nana," a title of respect given to chiefs, spiritual leaders, and elderly women ("ni" meaning first mother). Based on information garnered from written land grants and treaties of that time, Nanny was middle-aged when she led the Windward Maroons.

Under Spanish rule, African slaves in Jamaica were sent out to the countryside to herd wild cattle and to hunt boar. As a result, they developed knowledge of the country's terrain, data that would serve them well during the war. In 1655 Britain invaded and successfully took control of Jamaica, making it a British colony. During this time of upheaval, many slaves equipped with knowledge of the terrain escaped to the eastern part of the country and organized into what would later be known as the Windward Maroons. It is believed that the word "maroon" came from the Spanish *cimarrón* meaning wild or fugitive; thus, escaped animals or slaves were referred to in Spanish Jamaica as *cimarrones*, which eventually gave way to the anglicized "maroons" when the island became a British colony.

The years 1728 to 1740 represent Queen Nanny's reign as leader of the maroons. The roles this revolutionary woman played in the struggle against the British included warrior, general, and spiritual leader. As a priestess, or obeah woman, she was considered to have spiritual and supernatural powers and the capacity to perform miracles. As a military strategist she was one of the greatest planners of successful maroon raids, ambushes and counterattacks. Under her leadership, the maroons used the abeng to create an effective system of communication over vast areas of the terrain. The African term *abeng* means conch shell, but for the maroons, abeng was a cow horn with a hole drilled on one end allowing it to produce many sounds. The use of the abeng horn put the British at a great disadvantage because they had no way to communicate over long distances. The maroons had very few guns, and the weapons they did manage to obtain were from dead soldiers. Fighting from the maroon perspective depended very much on guerrilla tactics. As an obeah priestess, Queen Nanny led the maroons in the practice of traditional African religion that believed that spiritual or supernatural abilities are powers inherited from one's ancestors. The practice, itself known as "obi," includes rituals and magic. As "cheftainess" she encouraged the maintenance of customs, music, songs, and legends that had come with the people from Africa, believing that this strengthened and instilled their pride and confidence.

Even though the maroons were at times outnumbered ten to one by the better-armed British, Queen Nanny was able to lead them to victory from their base in the rugged Blue Mountains area of Jamaica. Eventually, the maroons were able to hold off countless British incursions, swooping down on plantations and freeing slaves to continue inciting rebellion. The Maroon Wars that started in 1663 finally ended under a 1739 treaty and land grant that included Nanny's name but not her signature and guaranteed autonomy and freedom for the maroons, including the Leeward Maroons who settled in the west naming their area Accompong. Nanny was skeptical about Britain's ability to keep its side of the agreement and after the treaty did not actively participate in maroon political affairs. It is said that she was killed by a "quashee," a slave faithful to his white master, but this is not corroborated by evidence.

The land given the maroons, originally called Nanny Town, is known today as Moore Town. The area is regarded as sacred and few outsiders are allowed to visit it. It comprises 2,000 acres and is considered an autonomous territory where Nanny's final resting place, Bump Grave, is located.—G.C.

References and Suggested Readings

Brathwaite, Edward Kamau. *Wars of Respect: Nanny and Sam Sharpe.* Kingston, Jamaica: Agency for Public Information, National Heritage Week Committee, 1977.

Campbell, Mavis C. *The Maroons of Jamaica 1655–1796: A History of Resistance, Collaboration & Betrayal.* Granby, MA: Bergin & Garvey, 1990.

Deramus, Betty. "Some of Us Are Brave." *Essence* 28:10 (February 1998): 84.

Gottlieb, Karla. *The Mother of Us All: A History of Queen Nanny, Leader of the Windward Jamaican Maroons.* Trenton, NJ: Africa World Press, 2000.

REX NETTLEFORD
(1933–)

Jamaican Artist, Writer, and Scholar

Whether witnessing one of his performances as a member of the National Dance Theater of Jamaica, watching one of his choreographies for the company, reading one of his articles on Caribbean cultural studies, listening to one of his lectures on Jamaican arts and culture, or visiting the University of the West Indies, one is bound to be impressed by the unique intellectual and artistic talents of Rex Nettleford. He has been at the center of the cultural production process in his native Jamaica and the West Indies since the 1950s and maintains a strong influenve even today. As an artist he has showcased the arts and culture of Jamaica for the whole world to see, enjoy, and appreciate. As a cultural critic he has documented, commented on, and helped to preserve the artistic and cultural legacy of Jamaica as no other Caribbean critic has done before. As a scholar he has been one of the intellectual dynamos who has helped to shape the University of the West Indies into the premier Caribbean university that it is today.

Rex Milton Nettleford was born in Falmouth, Jamaica, on February 3, 1933, the child of Lebertha Palmer and Charles Nettleford. He has traced his exposure and involvement in the arts to his days as a choirboy at church, where he sang Handel, Hayden, and Mendelssohn. When he was in sixth grade he participated in an adaptation of Shakespeare's *Winter's Tale* into Jamaican dialect, and also played Bassanio in *The Merchant of Venice* (Edgecombe 1997). Complementing his early artistic exploits, Nettleford received a traditional Jamaican education at the

Falmouth and Unity Government Schools in Jamaica, the Montego Bay Boys School, and Cornwall College. After graduation from high school he attended the University of the West Indies, where he received a bachelor's degree in 1956.

Rex Nettleford.

To understand Nettleford's genius, talent, and appreciation for Jamaican arts and culture, it is important to understand the political and cultural environment of Jamaica during his formative years. Nettleford was profoundly affected by the strong cultural ferment prevalent in Jamaica at the time. Struggling to become an independent nation, the leaders of Jamaica emphasized the native cultural forms of the island as an attempt to differentiate themselves from the British motherland. Jamaica's graphic arts, music, literature, and theater were brought to the forefront of the public mind as an attempt not only to underscore their native values, but also as an effort to collect their unique Caribbean identity and present it to the world. Since 1941, Nettleford had been involved with the production of pantomimes and other theatrical works that served as the basis for his foundation of the National Dance Theater Company of Jamaica in 1961. In 1948 the British government established the University of the West Indies (UWI), which served as another forum to channel the creative talents of Jamaican artists, labor leaders, and intellectuals of the island who longed to have a school of their own (Nettleford 1990). During his studies at UWI, Nettleford not only acquired an interest in the national politics of the island, but he also continued his involvement in a wide array of artistic endeavors that furthered his passion for Jamaican arts.

After his graduation from UWI in 1956, Nettleford moved to England to attend Oriel College of Oxford University as a Rhodes Scholar. While there, he finished another degree and conducted post-graduate work in political science. From his stay at Oxford Nettleford has said: "Oxford gave me the opportunity to do a lot because, although I was the choreographer, I was virtually co-director of lots of productions. I remember Dudley Moore, a fellow called Stan Daniels, and I did Aristophanes' *The Birds* to rock music. It was fantastic! I did the choreography and Dudley did the music. That was the last production I did in Oxford itself" (Edgecombe 1997, 3). His Oxford experience not only gave Nettleford further academic training, but it also provided him with a wealth of artistic practice and experience that he brought back to his native Jamaica.

On his return to Jamaica, Nettleford resumed his involvement in a variety of artistic and academic pursuits. He used the National Dance Theater Company as a platform for establishing the Jamaica School of Dance, which later became part of the **Edna Manley** College for the Visual and Performing Arts. He also resumed his association with the University of the West Indies where he continued his work as a resident tutor in continuing education.

Throughout the years, Nettleford has served in a wide array of positions at UWI ranging from resident tutor, lecturer, professor, director of Extra Mural Studies and of the School of Continuing Studies, deputy vice chancellor, and since 1998, vice chancellor of the University. He has developed academic expertise in the areas of labor, Caribbean history, Caribbean politics and social development, creative arts, culture and development, and Caribbean dance theater. He has authored seven books, including *Roots and Rhythms: The Story of the Jamaican Dance Theater* (1969), *Manley and the New Jamaica: Selected Speeches and Writings, 1938–1968* (1971), *Caribbean Cultural Identity: The Case of Jamaica, an Essay in Cultural Dynamics* (1979), and *Inward Stretch Outward Reach: A Voice from the Caribbean* (1992). He has also written dozens of articles and book chapters in his areas of expertise. Since 1967, he has been the editor of the journal *Caribbean Quarterly*.

Nettleford has been described as a Renaissance man. He is equally comfortable delivering and writing an academic paper or dancing a lively Caribbean beat with his dance company. His artistic and academic endeavors are vast and cover many areas of the process of cultural production within Jamaica and the Caribbean. He has been a relentless advocate for Caribbean arts and culture. As an artistic producer, a recorder, and a cultural critic, Nettleford has been a leading figure working to preserve, promote, and value Jamaican and Caribbean cultural forms. His sense of vision and his erudition have garnered worldwide respect for his work and for the arts and cultures he supports. His dynamic understanding of culture moves him away from the binary and Afro-centric canons perpetuated by other cultural critics. He sees the Caribbean as being generative and inclusive. His writings, teaching, and artistic legacy reflect an open voice and a plurality that is seldom found among Caribbean cultural critics and producers.

Nettleford's work has been widely recognized and rewarded in Jamaica, the Caribbean, and the United States. He has received the Jamaican Order of Merit (1975), and nine honorary doctorates from American and European universities.—S.M.M.

References and Suggested Readings

Edgecombe, David. "Nurturing the Yeast that Makes the Dough Rise: Caribbean Theatre and Dance in a Cultural Context: An interview with Rex Nettleford." *Caribbean Writer* 11 (1997): 1–8.

Kinsman, Clare D., and Mary Ann Tennenhouse, eds. "Rex Nettleford." *Contemporary Authors*. Detroit: Gale, 1973. Volumes 37–40, 374–375.

Nettleford, Rex. "Curriculum Vitae." Provided by Nettleford to the Author. 2000.

———. *Inward Stretch, Outward Reach: A Voice from the Caribbean*. New York: Longman, 1992.

Nettleford, Rex, and Sir Phillip M. Sherlock. *The University of the West Indies: A Caribbean Response to the Challenge of Change*. New York: Macmillian, 1990.

Phelps, Shivelle, ed. "Rex Nettleford." *Who Is Who Among African Americans*. Detroit: Gale, 1998. 966.

"CHICO" O'FARRILL
(1921–2001)

Cuban Musician, Composer, and Arranger

For over 50 years, Chico O'Farrill was at the forefront of infusing Afro-Cuban music into jazz. Often called the Duke Ellington of Latin jazz, he was among the greatest composers, arrangers, and bandleaders of the Afro-Cuban jazz genre. Over his long career, he wrote and arranged material for musicians Dizzy Gillespie, Charlie Parker, **Machito**, Benny Goodman, Mario Bauzá, and even rock star David Bowie. Along with Dizzy Gillespie and Machito, he is considered one of the architects of what we now call "Latin jazz." Although overlooked for years, he was "rediscovered" when his 1995 album *Pure Emotion* was nominated for a Grammy. That was followed by two other Grammy nominations for *Heart of a Legend* (1999) and *Carambola* (2000).

Chico was born Arturo O'Farrill in Havana, Cuba, on October 28, 1921, into a middle-class family with Irish, German, and Cuban roots. Early on, his German father expected that Arturo would study law and eventually join his law firm. His truant behavior in school, however, resulted in his father sending him to the Riverside Academy in Gainsville, Georgia, in hopes that a military environment would provide structure and discipline. As O'Farrill himself described it "That's where I heard the great big bands: Benny Goodman, Artie Shaw . . . that's when my career as a lawyer actually died" (González 2000, 5). It was also when he fell in love with bebop. He joined the school's band as a trumpet player, and after graduation returned to Cuba and enrolled in the University of Havana to study law, as his family had wanted. However, he quickly dropped out of college in the late 1940s and began to study music with Cuban composer Felix Guerrero. At the same time, O'Farrill, drawn by Havana's musical nightclub scene, began playing trumpet for some of the local jazz bands. He was also a trumpet player for several popular dance bands at the time such as Orquesta Bellemar, Lecuona Cuban Boys, and the Newyorkers.

With a solid foundation in classical and Cuban music he left Havana for New York City in 1948. He was soon working with Dizzy Gillespie, Stan Kenton, and other big band musicians who were very interested in the way his musical arrangements linked jazz with Latin music. While working for Benny Goodman, who hired him in 1949, the diminutive O'Farrill acquired the name Chico. According to legend, Goodman, finding it very difficult to pronounce "Arturo" and observing that Cubans tended to call each other "chico," addressed him one day as "hey, chico," and it stuck. Goodman's popular hit "Undercurrent Blues" was one of O'Farrill's first major compositions. That same year, Cuban band leader Machito recorded two of O'Farrill's most influential and classical works,

"Manteca Suite" (originally written for Dizzy Gillespie), and the ground break-ing "Afro-Cuban Jazz Suite." The latter is considered his first masterpiece and has been described as "a dazzling 17-minute, six-movement composition seamlessly joining Afro-Cuban drumming, modern jazz, and classical styles" with saxophone solos by acclaimed jazz musician Charlie "Bird" Parker (Weinstein 1996, 15).

Throughout the 1950s, O'Farrill led his own orchestra and wrote the hit tune "Chico's Cha-Cha-Chá." His work integrating Latin songs and big-band Ameri-can music was instrumental in the evolution of the mambo craze of the 1950s and the salsa explosion of the 1970s. During the mid-1950s, O'Farrill relocated to Mexico, where he met and married Lupe O'Farrill. While living in Mexico, he wrote and arranged music and led bands for other musicians.

He accepted an invitation from **Fidel Castro** in 1965 to conduct in Havana, where he "had a grand time and never went back" (Sachs 1998, 1). That same year, he returned to the United States, and for the next 25 years worked with top musicians in the business including Count Basie, Dizzy Gillespie, and Gato Barbieri. For Count Basie alone, he was responsible for over 80 musical arrange-ments. A versatile musician, his work during this time was not limited to big bands and jazz—he also composed music for commercials, jingles for TV, sym-phonic orchestras, and chamber music. In 1993 he orchestrated several numbers for David Bowie's *Black Tie White Noise* album. Even though he was making a good living, he was not well known or acknowledged within the mainstream music scene until the release of his 1995 album *Pure Emotion,* his first in 30 years, which earned him his first Grammy nomination.

Chico O'Farrill recorded *Pure Emotion* with his group, the Afro-Cuban Jazz Or-chestra, which he assembled in collaboration with his son Arturo Jr. in the early 1990s. One of his most important final compositions was "Trumpet Fantasy," written for and premiered by trumpeter Wynton Marsalis at a 1996 tribute to O'Farrill at Lincoln Center. One of his last recordings, *Heart of a Legend* (1999), a musical retrospective of his career that includes some of his classic mambos and ballads, has been highly acclaimed and includes well-known musicians Gato Barbieri, **Israel Cachao López**, Freddy Cole, and **Paquito D'Rivera**.

A few years before his death, O'Farrill was commissioned to write the music for a Broadway musical version of *The Mambo Kings,* and his Afro-Cuban Jazz Big Band was a Sunday regular at New York City's legendary Birdland Jazz Club. **Oscar Hijuelos**, author of the novel *Mambo Kings* wrote the liner notes to O'Farrill's album *Cuban Blues* (1996), a compilation of his sessions recorded be-tween 1951 and 1954, a time, according to some critics, when he wrote his best work. In June 2000, O'Farrill, together with Cuban Israel Cachao López were pre-sented with the International Latin Music Hall of Fame's Lifetime Achievement Award; their presence together on stage made music history. O'Farrill was one of the featured artists in Spanish director Fernando Tuba's 2001 jazz documentary *Calle 54*. O'Farrill died in New York City on June 27, 2001.

In August 2001, the film *Cómo se forma una rumba* (How to Create a Rumba) premiered in New York City to a sold-out audience. The premiere was dedicated to Chico O'Farrill, who also appears in the film discussing the evolution of Cuban music.—G.C.

References and Suggested Readings

Acosta, Ivan (director). *How to Create a Rumba*. Released by Hargrove Entertainment, 2002.

Cobol, Leila. "Blue Note Soundtrack 'Calle 54' Ups the Ante for Latin Jazz." *Billboard* 113:13 (March 31, 2001): 11.

Cuban Blues: The Chico O'Farrill Sessions (recordings). Unit/Verve, 1996.

González, Fernando. "Sweet Refrain for a Big-Band Jazzman." *The Washington Post*, September 23, 2000, 5.

Gordon, Diane. "Chico O'Farrill." *Jazz Times* 25:10 (December 1, 1995): 46.

Heckman, Don. "At the heart of a legend." *Los Angeles Times*, January 9, 2000, 7.

Holston, Mark. "Oye Chico: Arturo O'Farrill's sound is back on the bandstand." *Hispanic Online* 13.6 (June 1, 2000): 70. *http://www.hispaniconline.com/a&e/ltn_grmy/grammy2k_sptlight/ofarril_b.html*.

Martha, R.S. "Brilliant Intro to Afro-Cuban Big Band Jazz." *New Straits Times* (Malaysia), May 24, 2000, 5.

Navarro, Miry. "A Master of Latin Jazz Is Rediscovered at 79." *The New York Times*, December 30, 2000.

Ovellette, Dan. "Chico O'Farrill's Afro-Cuban Passions." *Down Beat* 67:9 (September 8, 2000): 40.

Sachs, Lloyd. "Chico Hits Scene." *Chicago Sun-Times*, August 30, 1998, Show section, 1.

Trueba, Fernando (director). *Calle 54* (film). Distributed by Miramax Pictures, 2001.

Weinstein, Norman. "Master of Latin Jazz Brings Crowd to Its Feet at San Francisco Festival." *The Christian Science Monitor*, December 13, 1996, 15.

JOHNNY PACHECO
(1935–)

Dominican American Musician, Composer, Arranger, and Bandleader

At a time when salsa and Latino music have become major forces within the American entertainment industry, the influence and legacy of Johnny Pacheco has become of crucial importance to understanding this sudden explosion of Latino music products. Composer, flutist, music entrepreneur, and bandleader Johnny Pacheco is a musical genius who has worked relentlessly to bring the visibility and recognition to Latino and salsa music. During the 1960s he co-founded Fania Records, a recording company and music label that was to define the form and character of salsa music for the remainder of the century. He has received a place

Johnny Pacheco.

in Latino music history in the United States and in Latin America as one of the fathers of salsa music.

Pacheco, one of five children of Rafael and Octavia Pacheco, was born in 1935 in Santiago de los Caballeros in the Dominican Republic. His father was a professional musician who played the clarinet and worked as a music conductor with the Orquesta de Santa Cecilia. Some sources credit his mother's love for radio as a central force in exposing him to many Cuban music styles as he was growing up (Kent 1993). He showed his love for music early on and as a child mastered the harmonica and the bass drum.

In 1946, when he was 11 years old, Pacheco's family moved to New York City during the first wave of Dominican migration. He attended a vocational school in the Bronx but continued to play music on the side and learned to play many different instruments. However, it was his talent for percussion, saxophone, flute, and clarinet that were to make him famous. After graduating from high school, he went on to pursue formal music training at the Julliard School of Music.

The professional music career of Johnny Pacheco started in the 1950s and was boosted by the popularity of Latino music at the time. His early successes are associated with the emergence of the musical styles of mambo, pachanga, charanga, and the cha-cha-chá. He played in many local bands and also formed his own music group, known as Los Chuculecos Boys. While his biographers tend to underscore the importance of his early work with musicians such as **Tito Puente**, **Dámaso Pérez Prado**, and Xavier Cugat, his first significant and lasting professional experience was through his association with pianist Eddie Palmieri and joining the band Charanga Duboney in 1959 (Larkin 1998). His first major recording, "Let's Dance the Charanga," was released in 1960 with this group.

After having disagreements with Palmieri, Pacheco abandoned the group and moved on to create his own ensemble known as Pacheco y su Charanga in 1960. The recording *Johnny Pacheco y su Charanga*, released under the label Alegre, became a great mega hit and sold more than 100,000 copies. It was the top selling Latin record in the United States at the time (Kent 1993). One of his most popular hits was the song "El Güiro de Macorina." This recording opened multiple opportunities for Pacheco. He suddenly became a famous star and toured the world. He was one of the first Latino performers to appear at the Apollo Theater in 1961 and on mainstream television programs such as the *Tonight Show*. In 1963, he broke his association with Alegre Records, in part because he resented their profiting from his hit recording but also because they signed Charlie Palmieri as their lead artist. His rupture with Alegre Records was a turning point in Pacheco's life. Two events were to change his career forever: the creation of a new recording label and the transition to a new music style.

When Pacheco met with Jerry Massuci, his divorce attorney, Massuci was impressed with his musical talents and proposed the formation of a partnership to launch their own music label. They created Fania Records in 1964 with the meager investment of $5,000.

Simultaneously with the development of Fania, Pacheco started to create an entirely new style of music influenced by the music being imported to New York by musicians who were leaving Cuba after **Castro**'s revolution. Ernesto Lechner has best explained the origins of this new style:

> The key to the Fania aesthetic was mixing venerable Cuban dances such as the guaracha, the guaguanco or the son montuno with the textures of American jazz and even some R&B. This was Afro-Cuban music as experienced mostly by Puerto Rican immigrants in the heart of New York. It was a sassy, street-smart sound, daring as it was seductive, representing the essence of salsa, which ironically, would return to Cuba and end up influencing a generation of local musicians. (Lechner 1999, F16)

Around this same time, Pacheco formed a new and smaller group named Pacheco y su Nuevo Tumbao. Along with Eddie Palmieri, Charlie's brother, he produced a rhythm that caught the attention of Latino audiences in New York. In 1964 they released the recording, "Cañonazo," his first recording under Fania. Although the music was heavily Afro-Cuban in nature, Pacheco began to market it under the rubric of salsa music. There was a growing interest among Latino youth in New York for a music style that would capture the realities of their lives as immigrants to the big city. Through his introduction of salsa music, he was able to cater to these needs and develop a new genre.

Initially, Fania was a small operation where Pacheco and Massuci handled both the talent and the business side of the industry. However, Pacheco was able to recruit some famous Latino entertainers to record and perform concerts with him, thereby increasing Fania's penetration of the Latino music market. During the late 1960s and early 1970s, Pacheco and Massuci attracted many well-known and famous Latino performers to the Fania label. Fania eventually became Fania All Stars label. They were also able to organize the some of the most successful music concerts of the time. By 1971, Pacheco and the Fania All Stars were able to bring together artists of the stature of Larry Harlow, **Willie Colón**, **Celia Cruz**, **Tito Puente**, Papo Luca, Joe Batán, Mongo Santamaria, Hector Lavoe, Ray Barreto, and Ruben Blades. They produced concerts that changed the music history of Latino performers in New York. They also established partnerships with some mainstream American music labels such as Columbia Records and Atlantic Music and secured the distribution for their recordings. Salsa music quickly became the established music genre of Latino audiences in the United States and Latin America.

During the 1980s, Fania ran into financial difficulties as the boom of salsa music started to lose popularity. The company was sold to an Argentinean music conglomerate. Despite the ups and downs of this label and the music business, Pacheco has been able to stay in the forefront of the Latino musical scene consistently through the years. Pacheco is credited with the composition of more than 150 songs and the release of more than 40 records. He writes for himself as well as for other performers. Some of his best-known songs are: "Mi Gente"(My People), "Quitate Tú Pa' Ponerme Yo," "La Dicha Mía"(My Luck), "Quimbara," and "Coro Miraye." He has been nominated for nine Grammys.

Pacheco is still a prominent figure in Latino music. He actively tours the United States and Latin America and he regularly records and collaborates with some of the biggest Latino performers of today, such as Celia Cruz. His talent has been recognized both in the United States and in Latin America. In 1996, he was awarded the Presidential Medal of Honor by Dominican Republic President **Joaquín Balaguer**. He was inducted into the Latin Music Hall of Fame in 1998. Pacheco has collaborated with several philanthropic organizations and in 1994 established the Johnny Pacheco Scholarship Fund.—S.M.M.

References and Suggested Readings

Kent, Mary. "Johnny Pacheco y Su Tumbao." *Descarga* (1993), n.p.

Larkin, Colin, ed. "Johnny Pacheco." *The Encyclopedia of Popular Music*. London: Muze, 1998. 4097–4098.

Lechner, Ernesto. "Return of a Salsa Hero; Johnny Pacheco Is Back with His Blend of Cuban Dance Music, Jazz, and R&B." *Los Angeles Times*, February 18, 1999, F16.

Mangual, Rudy. "Pacheco y las Estrellas." *Latin Beat Magazine* (September 1999): 38.

Roberts, John Storm. "Johnny Pacheco." In *Penguin Encyclopedia of Popular Music*. London: Penguin, 1989. 458.

EUZHAN PALCY
(1958–)

Martinican Filmmaker, Writer, Director, and Producer

A Martinique native, Euzhan Palcy has won international recognition as a filmmaker, and was the first black woman to direct a Hollywood feature film. Palcy's cinematographic productions center on social change and cultural issues. Her concern for social justice and the belief in the strength of the human spirit extends to all areas of her cinematic work including dramas, thrillers, animation, science fiction, and action genres.

Born on January 13, 1958, in Martinique, Euzhan Palcy's experiences growing up in that French colony provoked the themes of inequality and race that would later appear in her films. Romuald, a member of one of the most prominent and wealthy families in Martinique married Leon Palcy, a chief mechanic, eventually the head of personnel in a pineapple factory. Leon Palcy, who Euzhan describes as the "first feminist" she ever knew, was adamant about education and managed to send all six of his children to France to finish their schooling (Acker 1997).

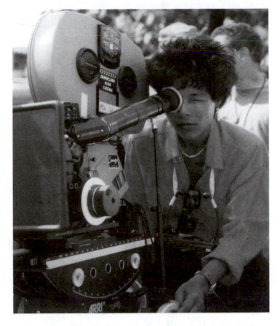

Euzhan Palcy. Courtesy of Euzhan Palcy.

As a child, she cast shadow-plays on her bedroom wall—her first experiences in filmmaking. She was exposed to much cinematography that had no relation to her life or culture, and by the age of 14 she was familiar with such filmmakers as Fritz Lang, Alfred Hitchcock, and Orson Welles. While attracted by the workings of film, she was also disturbed by the invisibility of people of color and the distorted way they were presented when included. Confident she could make a difference and entertain at the same time, she decided to become a filmmaker. In 1974, at the age of 16, she wrote and directed a critically acclaimed drama for French television in Martinique titled *La Messagère* (The Messenger). A year later she left for Paris to continue her formal education at the Sorbonne and received a master's degree in French literature, a master's degree in theater, and a doctoral degree in art and archeology. Later she earned a film degree as director of photography from Louis Lumiere School of Cinema.

On completing film school, she spent some time working as an assistant editor on films with young African filmmakers in France and revising a script she had begun to write when she was 17 for what would become her first feature film, *Sugar Cane Alley* (1983). Recognizing her talent, director François Truffaut, her French "godfather," and director Constantin Costas-Gavras provided support for this film, which was a hit at New York City's 1984 New Directors/New Films Festival. The film was hailed internationally and Palcy was described as "a new writer-director of exceptional abilities" (Canby 1984, 17). The response in Martinique was unprecedented. During the first week alone, almost half of the country's population of 400,000 saw the film. Based on the book of the same title by Joseph Zobel, it relates the struggle of blacks in the 1930s working on a white man's plantation in Martinique, and one child's successful journey out of the exploitative sugarcane fields. At age 22, Palcy was on her way to becoming a famous filmmaker. The film received over 17 international prizes, including the Silver Lion and Best Lead Actress Award at the Venice Film Festival, the Cèsar Award for Best First Feature Film, and the First Prize Critics Award at the Houston Film Festival.

Her 1989 *A Dry White Season*, considered her masterpiece, is an exposé on the struggle against apartheid in South Africa during the 1970s. It was heralded for putting the politics of apartheid into meaningful human terms. She convinced actor Marlon Brando to end a nine-year seclusion period to play the role of a well-known South African lawyer, for which he received a Best Actor Academy Award nomination. At the international level, Brando received the Best Actor award for this film at the Tokyo Film Festival, and Palcy received the Orson Welles Prize for Special Cinematic Achievement.

In 1992, Palcy again chose Martinique as the subject of her work, but this time it was in the form of a Caribbean musical fairy tale. Critically acclaimed, the film *Simeon* won awards at the Milan, and Montreal, and Brussels film festivals in 1993. Her 1994 portrait of the Martinique poet, playwright, and philosopher, *Aimé Césaire, A Voice for History,* which also garnered international critical acclaim, followed this success. Palcy's representation of **Aimé Césaire** has been critically lauded: "by means of an immense, live documentation, covering more than a half century of histories, [the film] inscribes the entire Antillean destiny through one of the most determining figures of human liberation of the twentieth century" (Kemedijo 1998, 198).

Palcy has been the recipient of awards at home and abroad. In 1994 she was honored by French President François Miterrand with the Chevalier Dans L'Ordre National Du Merite (Knight in the National Order of Merit), and in 1997 the city of Amiens, France, named its movie theater after her. Perhaps the honor she holds closest to her heart came from her compatriots—the first high school dedicated to film study in Martinique has been named after her. At the 2001 Cannes Film Festival she was awarded the Sojourner Truth Award by Agora, an organization that specializes in presenting African films at Cannes. More recently, in 2003, French president Jacques Chirac named her Chevalier de la Legion d'Honneur.

President Bill Clinton introduced her 1998 television film *The Ruby Bridges Story* when it was aired on ABC Television. *The Ruby Bridges Story* is a movie that presents a chapter of the history of school desegregation through the stirring true-life story of Ruby Bridges, the little black girl who braved racist mobs to successfully integrate an all-white school in New Orleans.

Among her most recent work is *The Killing Yard* (2001), a drama based on the true events surrounding the 1971 Attica prison uprising in New York State. She is also working on a World War II love story set in Martinique and a thriller set in Paris and New York. She is currently co-writing and will be executive producer of an animated feature for Fox Studios.—G.C.

References and Suggested Readings

Acker, Ally, and Judith Crist. *Reel Women: Pioneers of the Cinema 1896 to the Present*. New York: Continuum, 1993.

Canby, Vincent. "Third World Truths From 'Sugar Cane Alley." *The New York Times*, April 22, 1984, Section 2, 17.

Collins, Glen. "A Black Director Views Apartheid." *The New York Times*, September 25, 1989, 15.

Ebert, Roger. "Pages From a Cannes Diary." *Chicago Sun-Times*, May 21, 2001, 41.

Karani, Marcia Leslie. "Filmmaker Euzhan Palcy—A Palette of Passion." *American Visions* (August/September 2000): 40–43.

Kemedijo, Cilas. "When the Detour Leads Home: The Urgency of Memory and the Liberation Imperative from Aimé Césaire to Frantz Fanon." *Research in African American Literatures* 29.3 (Fall 1998): 191–202.

McKenna, Kristine. "Tough, Passionate, Persuasive." *American Film* 14 (September 1989): 32–37.

Thomas, Kevin. "'Dry Season' a Potent Look at South Africa." *Los Angeles Times*, September 22, 1989, Part 6, p. 1.

Whitfield, Lynn, and Euzhan Palcy. "An Interview with Filmmaker Euzhan Palcy." November 26, 1999. *http://www.tbwt.com/views/specialrpt/special%20report-3_11–26–99.asp.*

LUIS PALÉS MATOS
(1898–1959)

Puerto Rican Poet

Luis Palés Matos was one of the premier lyric poets of Puerto Rico and one of the originators of the Afro-Antillean genre of Negroid poetry. This genre draws its inspiration from the lives, experiences, and culture of Caribbean islanders of African ancestry. Although these people have been an integral component of the fabric of Puerto Rican and Caribbean societies for centuries, racism and criticism have kept their culture, mores, and traditions far from the mainstream. It was Luis Palés Matos, through his masterful poetic production, who was largely responsible for recognizing the importance of the Afro-Antillean element within Puerto Rican culture and society and who brought it to the forefront of Puerto Rican cultural and literary circles.

Palés Matos was born in Guayama, a town located in the southeastern corner of Puerto Rico, on March 20, 1898. His father, Vicente Palés Anés, was a schoolteacher; his mother was Consuelo Matos Vácil. The town of Guayama has historically had one of the largest enclaves of people of African ancestry in the island. This town is still called La Ciudad de los Brujos (The City of Witches) because many of its inhabitants still follow religious rituals and practices brought to Puerto Rico by African slaves. Although critics have downplayed Guayama's role in Palés Matos' life, his exposure to people holding these traditions undoubtedly influenced his later work on Afro-Antillean poetry.

Both of his parents were poets, who shared with their son their love for poetry. Palés Matos started to write during his adolescence. His father died when Palés Matos was a sophomore in high school and Palés Matos was forced to abandon his studies and go to work to help support his family. Throughout his life he held a variety of clerical positions and worked as a postmaster. His writing skills eventually allowed him to become secretary to the president of the Puerto Rican senate (López-Baralt 1992). He was considered to be self-educated.

Palés Matos' literary works are fairly limited; he published only two major books during his life. The first of these was *Azaleas,* which he wrote when he was 17. Literary critics assert that his poems in *Azaleas* reflect the influence of modernism, as the author tries to bring in influences from other countries, as well as postmodernism. In addition, as with many other writers of his time, his early poetry reflects his concerns with the political situation of Puerto Rico after the transfer of sovereignty from Spain to the United States and conveys his negative reaction to the colonial status of the island (Marzán 1999).

His other major book was *Tuntún de pasa y grifería* (1937), which first introduced Palés Matos' work in the Negroid poetry genre. His poems are inspired by the cultural characteristics, lives, and rich heritages of black Puerto Ricans. His writing technique was rich and complex. Along with José de Diego Padró, he set forth a style known as *diepalismo,* a unique onomatopoeic technique where his verses imitate the archetypal accents and the sounds of people, animals, and the environment. His verses, filled with short syllables resembling accents and sounds, were structured with a highly rhythmic cadence that duplicates the essence of Afro-Antillean speech patterns and musical beats. Verses such as "ritma una conga bomba que bamba," illustrate the sound of the conga, one of the most important instruments used by Afro-Antilleans (Palés Matos 1937). Like Cuba's **Nicolás Guillén**, Palés Matos has been identified by critics and cultural historians as one of the first Caribbean writers to use the lifestyles and cultural products of people of African American ancestry as a source of literary inspiration. Puerto Ricans of all races and social groups value Palés Matos' poetry as perhaps one of the most unique literary works to emerge from the island during the early part of the twentieth century.

Palés Matos' Afro-Antillean poetry has a comedic, ironic and satiric tone that undoubtedly poses questions about the marginalization and racism of the African element in Puerto Rican society and in the Caribbean. Palés Matos dealt with the black element in terms of its cultural contributions rather than as social phenomenon of Caribbean and Puerto Rican society. He valued the presence of blacks within Puerto Rican and Caribbean culture and brought their legacy to the mainstream cultural establishment. Critics have questioned whether Palés Matos' poetry is authentic in terms of his depiction of black Caribbeans, but his work should be valued for its artistic and creative merits, if not for its sociological ones. Palés Matos used the cultural products of blacks as a source of aesthetic inspiration and contemplation, rather than as a sociological artifact to be studied.

In 1944, Jaime Benítez, a literary critic and the legendary chancellor of the University of Puerto Rico in Río Piedras for more than 25 years, appointed Palés Matos as the university's poet-in-residence. This appointment marked a third stage in Palés Matos' literary production. He wrote a series of romantic odes in which he depicted his platonic love and attraction for a mulatto woman known only as Filí

Mele. While most of his critics never determined the identity of Palés Matos' muse, it was no secret that Filí Mele was one of his students at the university. In fact, until the 1980s, when this author was a student at the university, it was almost a tradition for students taking the basic Spanish literature courses at the University of Puerto Rico to receive a challenge from the professor asking them to identify Filí Mele. The alleged source of Palés Matos' inspiration eventually came to light when one of the most distinguished literature professors on the faculty wrote a book revealing her identity (Arrillaga 1999).

In 1949, Palés Matos published the novel *Litoral: reseña de una vida inútil* (The Coast: Review of a Useless Life). The novel, considered by many to be autobiographical in nature, draws on Palés Matos' early life experiences in the countryside and expresses his sense of fatalism as a youngster. He died of a heart attack on February 23, 1959.—S.M.M.

References and Suggested Readings

Arce de Vázquez, Margot, ed. *Luis Palés Matos: Poesía completa y prosa selecta.* Caracas, Venezuela: Biblioteca Ayaucho, 1978.

Arrilaga, María. *Yo soy Filí Mele.* Río Piedras: University of Puerto Rico Press, 1999.

López-Baralt, Mercedes. "Luis Palés Matos." In Angel Flores, ed., *Spanish American Authors: The Twentieth Century.* Bronx, NY: H.W. Wilson, 1992. 641–643.

Marzán, Julio. "Luis Palés Matos." In Susan Salas, ed., *Hispanic Literature Criticism Supplement.* Detroit: Gale, 1999. 779–784.

———. *The Numinous Site: The Poetry of Luis Palés Matos.* Madison, NJ: Fairleigh Dickinson University Press, 1995.

Palés Matos, Luis. *Tuntun de Pasa y Grifería.* Ed. Mercedes López-Baralt. Río Piedras, PR: University of Puerto Rico Press, 1994.

ANTONIA PANTOJA
(1921–2002)
Puerto Rican Educator, Activist, and Community Organizer

As an educator, activist, and community organizer for the past 50 years, Antonia Pantoja established herself as one of the most well known and visible advocates against injustice and as a unique Puerto Rican voice committed to her people and her country. She was greatly influenced by her family's activism and by the racial injustices she witnessed both growing up and when she emigrated to the United States. Driven by her commitment to the struggle to eliminate social, political, and economic inequities, Antonia Pantoja was known for founding some of the most important and longest-lasting institutions serving the Puerto Rican community in the United States.

Pantoja, who never knew her father, was born to Alejandrina Pantoja on September 13, 1921 in Puerta de Tierra, Puerto Rico, a poor section of San Juan. Toni, as she was affectionately called, witnessed the struggles of her family and friends organizing for better wages and living conditions. Antonia Pantoja Acosta was raised by her maternal grandparents Conrado Pantoja Santos and Luisa Acosta Rivera in the working-class neighborhood of Barrio Obrero. Her grandfather, a cigar factory worker at the American Tobacco Company, was also an active union leader whose organizing efforts led to one of the first successful labor strikes in Puerto Rican history, notwithstanding the fierce and violent confrontations with the police and strikebreakers that ensued. After the workers won the strike, the company packed up and left Puerto Rico. She reported that being an eyewitness to this struggle impacted her life: "My life's work has always been influenced by the memory of this inequity" (Perry 1998, 246).

Among the early disturbing experiences that influenced her life, Pantoja described social and economic malaise, prejudice against blacks, and sexism against women. During the Great Depression she became cognizant of the marked class differences and the contrast in housing, dress, and status that existed between whites and people of color. These experiences influenced and developed in her a leadership style that encouraged people to work collectively to reach consensus, an approach that today is considered to be very effective in eliminating prejudice.

In 1941, Pantoja received a scholarship to the University of Puerto Rico and began to train as a teacher. She left the university before the required two years for a normal school diploma to replace a teacher in a rural one-room school in Cuchillas. Pantoja would spend all week in the small town, where she would arrive and leave by horse that "would move very slowly because the children would hold on to its tail" (Pantoja 2002, 44). In her autobiography she describes the experience as "most unforgettable . . . that helped me to become who I am" (44).

In 1944, Pantoja sailed on the S.S. *Florida* to New Orleans and then took the train to New York City. During her train voyage she experienced the racist Jim Crow system of the south, where as a woman of color she was refused service at "whites only" establishments. In the beginning of her time in New York, she worked 15 hours a day in a factory as a welder, building radios for submarines. However, at her next job, an assembly-line position at a lamp factory, she painted designs on lamps. The art courses she took at the university prepared her for a rapid move to a better job as a designer in a lampshade factory, which exposed her to a new circle of artistic friends; it also was the job where Pantoja began what would be her lifelong work—activism. She saw oppression and inequity being wielded against the factory workers, and with the memory of her grandfather's union struggles still fresh in her mind, she engaged in education and very successful union organizing. She refers to this time as her "years of Bohemian life" (Pantoja 2002, 64), when she lived in Greenwich Village with struggling artists and writers and described her apartment as a "school of art, politics, literature and philosophy" (Pantoja 2002, 66). By the late 1940s Pantoja began her direct work with the community, working at the 110th Street Community Center in New York City's Spanish Harlem. At the center she participated in organizing a union and later a successful union strike. These experiences motivated her to continue her education and prepare for a better job. By 1950 she had enrolled at Hunter College to complete her baccalaureate. It was at Hunter that Pantoja began to network with other Puerto Ricans and Latinos, who were disturbed by the poverty and isolation of the Hispanic community and were interested in improving conditions for this sector of the population. The meetings of this group eventually spawned the Hispanic Young Adult Association (HYAA), which would later be changed to the Puerto Rican Association for Community Affairs (PRACA).

In 1952 she received a fellowship to Columbia University's School of Social Work, and as part of her student practice she organized a group of students to research the causes of poverty and to volunteer to improve Puerto Rican neighborhoods. This experience informed Pantoja on the living conditions of Latinos and helped her make a case with the city's Housing Authority and the mayor for policy changes in housing that would help her community. With her social work degree in hand, she continued to work in the area of community affairs and in 1958 she helped establish the National Puerto Rican Forum (NPRF) to help promote career development and business ventures in the community. The NPRF also served as a source of information about the scope of issues surrounding the Puerto Rican and Latino community and as a means of interpreting that information to generate constructive solutions.

Pantoja was alarmed by the dropout rate among Puerto Rican students and by the poor images that so many students had about themselves and their community. In 1961, as a response to what she observed to be a lack of education and leadership among Puerto Rican youth in New York City, she established a non-profit organization and named it ASPIRA, from the Spanish verb "to aspire." ASPIRA is perhaps the organization for which Pantoja is best known. It is a non-profit educational organization whose purpose is to increase the number of minority students who graduate high school and go on to higher education. There are now eight chapters of ASPIRA around the country.

Pantoja left ASPIRA in 1966 and returned to her alma mater, Columbia University, as a faculty member in its School of Social Work. Despite the demands of her position 1967 saw the beginning of her years of contributions to the education and leadership development of Puerto Ricans in the United States and on the island. That same year she was chosen as a delegate-at-large to the New York State Constitutional Convention and helped to write a new constitution for the state. After the work was completed, she was named by New York Mayor Lindsay to be a member of the Bundy Blue Ribbon Panel that designed a legal process for decentralizing the New York City Board of Education. In 1970 she was awarded a grant to establish the Universidad Boricua and the Puerto Rican Research and Resource Center in Washington, D.C. In 1973 Pantoja became the chancellor and that university's first president. In the mid-1970s she also established the Graduate School for Community Development in San Diego, California.

In 1984 Pantoja returned to her native Puerto Rico to retire in the village of Cubuy. However, she remained active in the community and in 1985 Pantoja helped establish PRODUCIR (literally, "to produce"), a non-profit economic development corporation that promotes economic independence and leadership development in a low-income rural community. Homesick for New York City, Pantoja left PRODUCIR and Puerto Rico and returned to New York in 1998.

Pantoja's work has not gone unrecognized. In the early 1990s, Independent Sector, the national association of non-profit organizations, honored her with its John W. Gardner Leadership Award for her skill in grassroots organizing and creating community organizations.

In 1996 President Bill Clinton included Pantoja's trademark expression, "dare to dream," in his introduction when honoring her with the Presidential Medal of Freedom, the highest award bestowed civilians in the United States. She was the first Puerto Rican woman to receive this award. In addition, she was the recipient of an honorary doctoral degree from the University of Connecticut in 1997, and the Points of Light Foundation presented her with its Lenore and George W. Romney Citizen Volunteer Award in 1999.

One of her last acts of social and political activism was her testimony before an international tribunal advocating for Puerto Rican autonomy and the termination of U.S. Navy military maneuvers on the Puerto Rican island of Vieques in 2000. The woman that *The New York Times* called "The Champion of Bilingualism" died on May 24, 2002. She had just published *Memories of a Visionary*.—G.C.

References and Suggested Readings

A Guide to Celebrate Puerto Rican Heritage and Culture (manual). New York: Hunter College, November 1991. 12–25.

Lavietes, Stuart. "Antonia Pantoja, Champion of Bilingualism, Dies at 80." *The New York Times*, May 28, 2002, B6.

Maldonado, Adal. *Portraits of the Puerto Rican Experience*. IPRUS, 1984.

Pantoja, Antonia. *Memoir of a Visionary: Antonia Pantoja*. Houston, TX: Arte Publico Press, 2002.

Perry, Wilhemina. "Memories of a life of work: An interview with Antonia Pantoja." *Harvard Educational Review* 68:2 (Summer 1998): 244–258.

Rosenberg, Robert, María Peralta, and Moe Foner. *Women of Hope*. Princeton, NJ: Films for the Humanities, 1996.

Tardiff, Joseph C., and L. Mpho Mabunda, eds. "Antonia Pantojas." *Dictionary of Hispanic Biography*. New York: Gale, 1996.

MARIE-JOSÉ PÉREC
(1968–)

Guadeloupean Sports Figure and Olympic Gold Medallist

In 1996 Guadeloupe native Marie-José Pérec slipped past her Jamaican competitor in the Olympic 200 meters race to win the gold medal. Three days earlier, she had become the first athlete, male or female, to win consecutive Olympic 400-meter gold medals, making her time the third fastest ever for a woman in Olympic history. Discovered at a high school track meet in 1983, she was given a full scholarship and moved to Paris in 1984. Ten years later she became France's most successful athlete in track and field history. A graceful sprinter with a long-legged physique, when not racing, she modeled in the Parisian catwalks for some of the top world designers. Dubbed the "Greta Garbo" of sports because of her reclusive and mysterious nature, she left her hotel in Sydney during the 2000 Olympic Games, thereby eradicating any hope of winning an unprecedented third straight 400-meter Olympic gold medal.

Marie-José Pérec. AP Photo/Michael Probst.

Marie-José Juliana Pérec was born on May 5, 1968, in Basse-Terre on the face of the Soufrière volcano, one of two islands in the West Indies that make up the French territory of Guadeloupe. Her parents Josette Distin and José Pérec separated when she was eight years old. Pérec and her two siblings were raised in a household full of children by their paternal grandmother.

By the age of 13 Pérec was 5'9" tall and was still growing. Notwithstanding the mocking she received at school being called "La canne a sucre" (sugarcane) because of her long, lanky body, she found support from her uncle George, a former basketball player who persuaded her into trying out the sport, and she eventually became the center player of her team. Her coaches noticed the speed and grace with which she moved and invited her to compete in her school's track and field meets. Marie José was skeptical about running and worried about injuries. With her coach standing outside her house and her grandmother coaxing her out of a closet, Pérec did make it to her first race and ran the 200 meters in under 26 seconds, impressing visiting coaches from France who immediately signed her on for the French junior national championships in Paris. Thus began her spectacular career.

The following year, having just turned 16, she moved to France to continue her education and to train in track and field. With a full French government scholarship she enrolled in France's national training center for promising athletes and joined the renowned Paris sports club, Stade Français.

By 1987 Marie-José Pérec had lowered her 200-meter running time from 24.52 seconds to 22.72—a world-class time and one that qualified her for the 1988 Seoul Olympics. In her Olympic debut, she advanced to the quarterfinals of the 200 meters. She also ran her first 400-meter event in 51.35 seconds, a French national record for that year. In 1989 she demonstrated her potential when she won the World Cup 400 meters but was disqualified for running outside her line.

In the early 1990s Pérec won her first two 400-meter races. Her first was a gold medal at the world championships in Tokyo, and her second was a gold medal at the 1992 Barcelona Summer Olympics. She became the first Frenchwoman in 24 years to win a gold medal in track and field. That summer, because of her graceful running stride, she earned the title "la Gazelle" from an adoring French and Caribbean public. In 1993 Pérec, escaping the pressures of her celebrity in France, began to train with new American coach John Smith in California. With Smith's training system she picked up two gold medals at the 1994 European championships and the 400-meter world championship title in August 1995 in Gothenburg, Sweden.

In the 1996 Atlanta Olympic Games she was crowned one of the all-time great women's champions after her performance in both the 200- and 400-meter races, where she won two gold medals. She raced against six runners who completed the 400-meter race in 50 seconds or less, itself a record, and set her own Olympic record that day of 48.25 seconds. She had become the first athlete to win consecutive Olympic 400-meter gold medals, and the third-fastest woman in the history of the sport.

In the last few years, Pérec has been plagued by Epstein Barr syndrome, a virus that causes chronic fatigue. She was forced to drop out of a number of races, and when she arrived in Australia for the 2000 Sydney Olympic Games, she had not raced in a major 400-meter race since 1996. For reasons that have not been made clear, she did not stay with her French team in the Olympic Village and even refused to train or march with them during the opening ceremonies. On September 20, a few days before she was scheduled to begin her 200- and 400-meter races, she abruptly disappeared from her hotel room and left the country.

Her Olympic and World Championship gold medals have brought her fame beyond the running track. She has made the cover of such major fashion magazines as *Elle* and earned over $1 million a year from her endorsements with sports shoes, soda, and tire companies. For a period of time after the Olympics in Sydney, Marie-José Pérec's wherabouts remained unknown. In an interview with a French newspaper in 2003, Pérec said she was in training preparing to return to racing and would comeback at the World Championships to be held in Paris, her hometown.—G.C.

References and Suggested Readings

Associated Press. "Former Olympic Champion Perec Aims for Comback at Worlds." February 5, 2003.

"'I cracked': French team says track champion is out of Games." *CNNSI.COM Sports Illustrated*, September 21, 2000. *http://sportsillustrated.cnn.com/olympics/2000/track_and_field/news/2000/09/28/perec_interview_ap/*.

Khouri-Dagher, Nadia. "Having a ball." *UNESCO Sources* 97 (January 1998): 22.

Laushway, Ester. "Marie-Jose Perec." *Europe* (June 1996): 38.

Roden, William C. "Perec Takes on Double Mission." *The New York Times*, August 1, 1996, B12.

DÁMASO PÉREZ PRADO
(1916–1989)
Cuban Pianist and Bandleader

Dámaso Pérez Prado was a legendary figure on the world musical stage during the 1940s and 1950s. The man who called himself "The King of Mambo" brought music and entertainment to scores of music fans throughout the world. His music has recently seen resurgence with the filming of the 1992 movie *The Mambo Kings Play Songs of Love*. His orchestra, now led by his son, keeps his the musical compositions alive.

Pérez Prado was born in the province of Matanzas in Cuba on December 11, 1916. His mother was a schoolteacher and his father was a print journalist working for Cuban newspapers. As a child, he learned to play the piano and the organ. He developed a love for music and a series of musical skills that led to a musical career that lasted a lifetime. His brother, Pantaleón Pérez Prado, was also a prominent musician and bandleader who has a successful musical career in Europe.

The origins of Pérez Prado's music career can be traced back to the early 1940s, when he moved from Matanzas to Havana. During his early years in Havana, Pérez Prado played the piano and the organ, worked as a musical arranger, and directed several important Cuban orchestras. Among them were the Orquesta Playa de Mauricio, Orquesta Cubaney, and Paulina Alvárez's Orchestra. Yet it was his with work with Havana's Orquesta Casino de la Playa that opened the doors for his development as a music master and for his work with the mambo.

There have been many debates among music scholars about Pérez Prado's role in the invention of the mambo. Music historian John Storm Roberts has identified two schools in the development of mambo: the "Cuban School" and the "New York School." While Pérez Prado liked to take credit for its invention and was very fond of his "King of Mambo" moniker, there were many other important musicians who worked simultaneously on mambo's development. People such as Cuban musicians **Israel Cachao López** and his brother Oreste, Arsenio Rodríguez, and Oreste Ramos worked together with Pérez Prado in the development of the genre and were interpreting similar music with their respective orchestras. While Pérez Prado was developing this rhythm in Cuba, musicians Xavier Cugat and **Tito Puente** were also playing a similar style of music during the 1940s and 1950s in New York. It is acknowledged, however, that Pérez Prado was ultimately responsible for the popularization of the genre throughout Latin America, the United States, and the rest of the world.

Mambo, as interpreted by Pérez Prado, is a combination of Afro-Cuban rhythms such as the rumba and the cha-cha-chá, underscored by the use of wind, brass, and percussion instruments. Roberts characterizes Pérez Prado's mambo as: "a bright octave sound with ingenious and fairly rhythmic sections based on such fine percussionist as Mongo Santa Maria, though even the best of Peréz Prado's work lacks the richness of the New York school" (1999, 128). According to one source, Pérez Prado's work was also influenced by American swing and jazz, especially the music of Stan Kenton (Loza 1999a). Pérez Prado's mambo incorporates a series of cries or grunts such as "Dilo," "Uh," "Vaya," and "Ahí." While critics have called these distinctive internal features of his mambo style, in reality Pérez Prado used these calls as musical commands to cue and hype the musicians in his orchestra.

During the 1940s Pérez Prado left Cuba and traveled to Puerto Rico and the rest of Latin America. In 1948 he finally settled in Mexico, where he formed an orchestra with the late Benny Moré, another famous musician of the time. Their collaboration brought a refinement to the mambo, which led to its wide acceptance and success in Mexico and Latin America. The Latin division of RCA records, based in Mexico, signed him up in 1949. Working with RCA and Moré, Pérez Prado released many successful records and songs. One of his most popular creations of the time was "Mambo #5." He continued traveling to Latin America where he played to sold-out dance houses and appeared in scores of Mexican films.

The 1950s represented one of the most fertile and popular periods for Latino music and musicians in the United States. Scores of innovative Latino performers were emerging, creating, and influencing the music and dancing styles of the times. In 1951 Pérez Prado made his first visit to the United States to tour with his band. He initially targeted mostly Latino audiences in New York, as he thought that his music would only appeal to Latino audiences. Although he was successful in New York, he found that Cugat and Puente already dominated the music market in the city. Moreover, non-Latino audiences who frequently attended the ballrooms at the big hotels in New York preferred the more stylized big band adaptations of Latin music and mambo than the ones generally played by Pérez Prado. During his stay in the United States, music unions threatened to stop Pérez Prado from appearing unless he accepted American musicians in his band. Thus, he had to open the band to American performers who eventually influenced his music with their own unique playing style.

Pérez Prado and his orchestra eventually went to California, where they played in concerts attended by thousands of people in Los Angeles and in San Francisco. Latino radio stations started to play his records vigorously. As a result, American audiences began to listen to the music and were caught in the frenzy that led to what was known as Mambo Fever. Since the majority of mambo interpreters marketed the genre as dance music, the vocals eventually disappeared from the songs interpreted by Pérez Prado and his band.

Throughout the decade of the 1950s Pérez Prado was an important Latino performer in the United States and catered mostly to the American market. His band released the hit "Cerezo Rosa" (Pink and Apple Blossom White) in 1955. This song was number one in the Top 40 charts for ten consecutive weeks and was used as a soundtrack for Jane Russell's movie *Underwater*. He also scored other hits with the songs "Voodoo," "Suite Havana 3:00 A.M.," and "Exotic Suite of the Americas." Peréz Prado's recording of the mambo "Patricia" in 1958 also reached number one in the charts and was his last major hit. The song became so popular that Italian filmmaker Federico Fellini used it in his 1960 movie *La Dolce Vita*.

Toward the end of the 1950s, the popularity of Pérez Prado's band started to decline as the nation's music styles and tastes began to change and audiences favored other rhythms. Pérez Prado returned to Mexico and continued to tour the world until the end of his life. In 1981 he had a successful musical titled *Sun* in Mexico City. Although he never reached the level of success and popularity that he had attained during the 1950s, he was perceived as a world-class bandleader and arranger. Pérez Prado died on September 14, 1989, of a stroke in Mexico City. Although he has been dead for more than a decade, his son, Dámaso Pérez Prado Jr., keeps the band alive. One of the authors recently witnessed a performance of the band in Tokyo, Japan, that was extremely well received. The band, which tours the world every year, not only retains the quality established by Pérez Prado but it also manages to attract scores of fans to their performances. Some of Pérez Prado's other hits were "Que Rico el Mambo," "Mambo Universitario," "El Ruletero," "Mambo en Sax," "La Niña Popof," "Mambo del Taconazo," and "Caballo Negro."— S.M.M.

References and Suggested Readings

Bradshaw, Paul. "Obituary: Dámaso Pérez Prado." *The Independent Gazzette* (London), September 19, 1989, 15.

Hijuelos, Oscar. *The Mambo Kings Play Songs of Love*. New York: Farrar, Straus, Giroux, 1989.

Loza, Steven. "Dámaso Pérez Prado." In John Garraty and Mark C. Carnes, eds., *American National Biography*, Vol. 17. New York: Oxford University Press, 1999a. 330–331.

———. *Tito Puente and the Making of Latin Music*. Urbana: University of Illinois Press, 1999b.

Roberts, John Storm. *The Latin Tinge: The Impact of Latin American Music on the United States*. New York: Oxford University Press, 1999.

ALEXANDRE SABÈS PÉTION
(1770–1818)

Haitian Liberator and Politician

Remembered as one of the liberators of Haiti, Alexandre Pétion is also known for establishing a land distribution policy. This policy resulted in the division of large plantations as a way of paying soldiers, giving officers larger portions than enlisted men. This practice, characterized by some historians as socialist, was instrumental in determining the social and economic structures that are still central in Haitian life today. Some see this system as having provided benefits to the mass of Haitian peasants at the time; others see it as a calamity that destroyed the economic base of the sugar plantation, resulting in terrible social and economic consequences for the country. Many believe that Pétion's rule was one of the most important in the history of Haiti.

Alexandre Sabès Pétion, born April 2, 1770, is considered one of the best educated of Haiti's early revolutionary leaders. The son of a wealthy white French colonist and a mulatto mother, his father refused to recognize him or give him his name—the surname "Pétion" was chosen by Alexandre himself. At he 18 joined the militia troops of **Toussaint L'Ouverture**, and later joined the opposing forces of André Rigaud. He fled to Paris when Toussaint L'Ouverture defeated Rigaud, and while there, studied at the School for Colonials and at the Military College, specializing in military tactics and munitions. At 18 he returned to Port-au-Prince and became a member of the mounted militia, and later joined Toussaint L'Ouverture's revolutionary forces, fighting for the freedom of mulattos and blacks. Later, believing that Toussaint L'Ouverture would impose an autocratic dictatorship, he again allied himself with the opposing forces of André Rigaud in the civil war of 1800. However, when he learned that the French intended to restore slavery and reduce mulatto ascendancy, he deserted the French cause and again joined the revolutionary cause with another Haitian revolutionary leader, Jean-Jacques Dessalines.

After proclaiming Haiti's independence on New Year's Day of 1804, Dessalines became Emperor Jacques I. He was assassinated two years later in 1806. Pétion's rival, Henri Christophe, then became ruler of the northern part of the island, where monarchism and black supremacy was favored, and Pétion became president of the mostly mulatto south. Pétion's 12-year administration set many precedents.

His decision to distribute land was a response to Haiti's situation during the early years of independence from France. A vast majority of the now-free population had been enslaved and the major landowners were either dead or had fled the country. The population of former slaves had worked on plantations and had farming and other agricultural skills. The land reform policy of dividing the large plantations into small parcels and giving them to his soldiers was also a response to Christophe's attempt to enforce a serf-like system called *fermage*, which was too similar to slavery and the discipline and hardship that had accompanied the previous oppressive structure. Pétion's policy created a society of peasants living on their own plots of land, with little if any involvement with the government or the cities. Sugar was replaced by coffee, which was easier to harvest and grow on the smaller plots. Thus, while he gave financial stability to his administration by the land distribution policy and established a rural democracy, the new landowners were no longer forced to produce surplus amounts for the master and turned out only enough crops for their own needs, which resulted in a devastated economy and a very high economic inflation problem.

Pétion established a free educational system for younger children and secondary education for boys. In addition, he established one of the first girls' schools in Latin America. In the spirit of revolutionary solidarity with other countries in the region, he provided sanctuary and later money, arms, and men to Simón Bolivar, who was fighting the Spanish colonists in South America. His quest to find a balance between personal freedom and public authority was not met successfuly. Quarrels were avoided to the point where he was inaccessible to the public. One historian summarized his presidency: "By the end of his career, however, republicanism seemed a failure in this land not yet ready for unrestrained freedom, and the people had shown themselves quick to take advantage of gentle government" (Baur 1947, 310). In total, he served from 1806 until his death from yellow fever on March 29, 1818.

He is described as "well-meaning" and "cautious beyond reason; he conformed too easily to others' views" (Baur 1947, 310). There is much of debate among historians and scholars about Pétion's rule.—G.C.

References and Suggested Readings

Baur, John Edward. "Mulatto Machiavelli, Jean Pierre Boyer, and the Haiti of His Day." *Journal of Negro History* 32.2 (July 1947): 307–353.

Burton Sellers, W.F. *Heroes of Haiti. http://www.windowsonhaiti.com/heroes.htm.*

Nicholls, David. *From Dessalines to Duvalier: Race, Colour, and National Independence in Haiti.* New Brunswick, NJ: Rutgers University Press, 1996.

Nuñez, Benjamin. "Alexandre Sabrès Pétion." *Dictionary of Afro-Latin American Civilization.* Westport, CT: Greenwood Press, 1980. 380.

CAMILLE PISSARRO
(1830–1903)

Impressionist Painter and Printmaker from St. Thomas

Camille Pissarro is one of St. Thomas' most famous sons. His paintings are some of the finest examples of the impressionist movement and can be found in most of the major museums around the world. Pissarro's art was greatly influenced by his Caribbean roots and his travels to Central America. He was a key figure in organizing the famous impressionist exhibitions between 1874 and 1886 and was the only artist to exhibit his work in all eight shows.

Jacob Camille Pissarro was born on July 10, 1830, in the port town of Charlotte Amalie, capital of St. Thomas, Danish Virgin Islands, and today part of the U.S. Virgin Islands. His father, Fédéric Pissarro, was of Portuguese and Sephardic Jewish ancestry and had moved to St. Thomas from France to take care of his dead uncle's affairs. In the process, he married his uncle's widow, a Dominican by the name of Rachel Petit, with whom he had four boys. The Pissarro marriage caused a negative reaction in St. Thomas' Jewish society. The children were excluded from the Jewish schools and were forced to attend the all-black primary school, an experience that influenced Pissarro's early work.

In 1842 he was sent to Passy on the outskirts of Paris to continue his secondary education, where his artistic talent became apparent. In 1847 he returned to St. Thomas, where he was expected to take over his family's business. However, he was befriended by Danish artist Fritz Melbye, who encouraged him to paint and served as one of his first teachers. Together, they traveled to Caracas, Venezuela, where they set up a studio and painted for over a year. His first depictions of blacks were unusual for a white artist. The experience of living in St. Thomas and Caracas later appeared in his work, particularly the light of tropical settings and his observations of peasant life, as in his 1856 work, "Two Women Chatting by the Sea." However, later in his career he produced paintings of rural and urban landscapes and river scenes, as well as Paris street scenes.

In 1855 he moved to Paris and never returned to America. During his first years there he was befriended by established painters of the day such as Ludovic Piette and the Puerto Rican Francisco Oller. Pissarro attended the well-known École des Beaux-Arts in 1856 and the Académie Suisse in 1859, where he first met and painted with other emerging impressionists such as Edouard Manet and Pierre Auguste Renoir. It was also during this time that he became Claude Monet's close friend and collaborator. Some of the paintings he created during this early period of his career were "Banks of the Marne in Winter" (1866) and "Coast of Jallais (Pointoise)" (1867). During the 1860s he met painter Edgar Degas, described as "the artist with whom he most shared his passionate technical audacity" with whom he worked in partnership in the late 1870s (Pissarro 1993). He moved to England in 1870 to escape the Franco-Prussian War. During his year in London he established with Monet the Anonymous Society of Artists, Painters, Sculptors, and Engravers, which organized and held the eight art shows between 1874 and 1886 that eventually came to be known as the Impressionist Exhibitions.

When he returned to France after the war, his artwork bore all the trademarks of impressionist art: people, sites, and scenes of that era, and in Pissarro's case, the depiction of rural and river landscapes as well as Paris' urban streets. They were part of the first impressionist exhibit in Paris in 1874. The term impressionism came from the title of one of Monet's works at the 1874 exhibit, "Impression, Sunrise." Pissarro was a mentor who had a great influence on Cézanne, whom he guided and collaborated with for many years. Paintings such as "Quarry (Pontoise)" (1875) and "Climbing Path (l'Hermitage, Pontoise)" (1875) are said to provide an understanding "of the evolution of modern art" that was later developed by the younger Cézanne (Turner 1996, 879).

In 1885, after meeting painters Paul Signac and Georges Seurat, he adopted their pointillist style. However, the work produced using this technique proved unpopular in the art market and he returned to painting in the impressionist style during the latter years of his life. In spite of an eye condition that eventually blinded him, Pissarro produced a large number of works after 1884, when he moved to the French village of Eragny. During the last few years of his life he gained recognition and earned high prices for his work, something that had eluded him earlier in his life. He died in 1903 and was buried in the Père Lachaise Cemetery in Paris.

From December 1996 to March 1997, as part of the bicentennial observance of the Hebrew Congregation of St. Thomas, Virgin Islands, Pissarro's work was exhibited in his hometown's synagogue and a two-and-a-half-hour film documentary was produced by the island's public broadcast station. It was the first exhibition of Pissarro's work in his homeland.—G.C.

References and Suggested Readings

Becker, Christoph, Wolf Eiermann, Ralph Melcher et al. *Camille Pissarro*. New York: Hatje Cantz, 1999.

Denvir, Bernard. *The Thames and Hudson Encyclopaedia of Impressionism*. New York: Thames and Hudson, 1990.

Doeser, Linda. *The Life and Works of Pissarro*. Bristol, England: Parragon, 1994.

"Pissarro, Camille Jacob." *Microsoft Encarta Online Encyclopedia 2001. www.encarta.msn.com.*

Pissarro, Joachim. *Camille Pissarro*. New York: Harry N. Abrahms, 1993.

Richardson, John. "Camille Pissarro." *Impressionist and Post Impressionist Paintings from the U.S.S.R.* New York: M. Knoedler and Co., 1973. 97.

Stone, Irving. *Depths of Glory: A Biographical Novel of Camille Pissarro*. New York: Plume, 1995.

Turner, Jane, ed. "Camille Pissarro." *The Dictionary of Art*, Vol. 24. New York: Macmillan, 1996. 878–884.

Williams, Robert. *Camille Pissarro and His Descendants: Impressionism to the Present*. Fort Lauderdale, FL: Museum of Art, 2000.

TITO PUENTE
(1923–2000)

Puerto Rican Bandleader and Percussionist

Tito Puente was known in the world of entertainment as the "King of Latin Jazz." A legendary performer of Puerto Rican descent, he was also referred to as "The King of Mambo" and "The King of the Timbales." When looking at the emergence and popularity of Latino music in the United States, one finds that Tito Puente was usually found at the center of many of the Latino musical innovations such as the mambo, salsa, and eventually Latin jazz. When he died on May 31, 2000, *The New York Times* referred to him as "the most important Latin musician of the last half century and key figure in the fusion on Latin music with jazz" (Walder 2000, 1).

Tito Puente. Photo by Ricardo Betancourt.

Ernest Anthony Puente Jr. was born in New York on April 20, 1923, one of three children of Ernest Puente, a foreman at a razor blade plant, and Ercilia Ortiz, both Puerto Rican immigrants in New York. He grew up in the neighborhood that eventually became known as Spanish Harlem. Puente attended elementary school at Public Schools 43 and 184, Cooper Junior High School, Galvani High School, and Central Commercial High.

Puente's interest in music dated back to his early childhood and the times when he participated in dancing contests with his sister. He later accompanied radio tunes with percussion beats using his mother's cooking utensils; his talent was so evident that his mother enrolled him in music classes so that he could learn how to play. In an interview with *The New York Times* in 1996, Puente said: "My mother, God rest her soul—she got drum lessons for me. It was 25 cents a lesson. She stole the quarters for my lessons from my father's pockets. He was a gambler and didn't believe in music" (Eichenberger 1996, 11). One of his first piano teachers was Victoria Hernández, a member of the Victoria Quartet, and the sister of Puerto Rican music composer **Rafael Hernández**. He eventually enrolled in the New York School of Music, where he expanded his training to other instruments and eventually became proficient in many different instruments such as piano, xylophone, clarinet, and saxophone. However, he achieved his major accomplishments playing the drums, particularly timbales, which are very popular in salsa music.

As an adolescent Puente participated in several youth music groups including the Stars of the Future. His first professional engagement took place when he was just 11 years old with the band the Happy Boys, playing at the ballroom of the Park Palace Hotel in New York. He also played the drums for Cuban musician **Machito** and his Afro-Cubans. Shortly after, Puente joined an orchestra led by José Curbelo and Noro Morales and went on a national tour; he was 13 years old. By the age of 16, Puente dropped out of Commercial High School knowing that he wanted to pursue a career in music and continued playing with some of the popular Latin bands of the time.

Puente was drafted into the navy in 1942. Unlike many other musicians of the time, who were assigned to fulfill entertainment duties while in the service, he was placed on an aircraft carrier and participated in active combat during the war. He eventually received a medal for his role during World War II. One of his fellow soldiers on the carrier was jazz musician Charlie Spivak, who has been credited with exposing Puente to jazz and with teaching him jazz arrangement and instrumentation (Walder 2000).

One of the lesser-known facts about Puente's musical formation was that he also had substantial training in classical music, theory, orchestration, and conducting, having attended the prestigious Julliard School of Music between 1945 and 1948. However, as someone with clear preferences for the sounds of popular Latino music, he left to form his own band; by 1948, Puente already had his own successful band, which became known as Tito Puente and His Orchestra. The launching of his band coincided with the boom of Latin music in New York. At the time, scores of Puerto Rican immigrants in New York longed to have entertainment that catered to their interest for Latino music.

During the 1950s Puente performed regularly at New York's famous Palladium nightclub and took advantage of the popularization of the mambo, a music style created in Cuba and popularized by Cuban performers **Dámaso Pérez Prado**, Xavier Cugat, and **Machito** in New York. His recordings in the genre were extremely popular among New York's Latino radio stations. A review of his discography reveals that he released 13 mambo recordings during this part of his career. He also recorded swing, pachanga, and cha-cha-chá music. After winning a competition with Pérez Prado's orchestrain New York, his visibility on the New York and the Latin American musical scene was so huge that he was baptized as the "King of Latin Music" and the "King of the Timbales."

One of Puente's most significant talents was his ability to integrate Latino beats such as mambo, swing, jazz, and cha-cha-chá and to blend Latino musical styles with North American musical styles, helping to create the distinctly unique musical genre known as Latin jazz. As a musician, Puente evolved as a musician and adapted his music to new styles. His composition "Oye Como Va" (1963), a jazzy ballad recorded by Mexican American Carlos Santana years later, became a huge hit. As the mambo craze faded from the dance halls, Puente started collaborating and recording with scores of other musicians such as Tito Rodríguez, Woody Herman, Rolando La'Serie, Buddy Morrow, La Lupe, Los Hispanos, **Celia Cruz**, **Johnny Pacheco**, Sophie Hernández, and members of the Fania All Stars. Many of these collaborations lasted for the rest of his musical career. He joined the bandwagon of performers working in the new music style known as salsa. During the 1960s and 1970s, Puente continued to adapt his style to fulfill the needs of the music market and the demands of the public, even when he claimed that there were no differences between salsa music and Latin jazz.

Puente reached the peak of his popularity and career during the last two decades of his life. Between 1979 and 1999, Puente won four Grammys. His first Grammy was awarded for an album honoring the work of famous Cuban musician Benny Moré, released under the Tico label in 1979. He also won for his albums *On Broadway* (1990), *Mambo Diablo* (1990), and for his last album, *Mambo Birdland* (1999). He kept up with the pace and the growing popularity of Latin jazz in New York and the United States for the past 50 years. His popularity continued to increase and Puente became a music icon. For example, **Oscar Hijuelos'** Pulitzer Prize–winning novel *The Mambo Kings Play Songs of Love* (1989) was loosely inspired by both Puente's and Pérez Prado's careers. He also appeared in the 1992 movie *Mambo Kings* as himself.

Puente died on June 1, 2000 of complications from heart disease. Despite his age, his popularity was so great that he had continued to give as many as 300 concerts per year up until the week before he died, and that week he had been scheduled to perform in San Juan with the Puerto Rico Symphonic Orchestra. He recorded with some of the most important labels of the day such as Tropical, RCA, Tico, Tropijazz, and RMM, releasing 117 records throughout his music career.

With his passing, a major chapter in the history of Latin music in the United States came to an end. Puente had a major role in the fusion of jazz and Latin music in the United States and was also a leader in the popularization of Latin music on the American continent. He was a major role model for Latinos in the United States, having won the National Medal of the Arts, awarded to him by President Clinton in 1997, two honorary doctorates, countless other honors and distinctions, and had a star in Hollywood's Walk of Fame. Consistent with his interest in helping young musicians, Puente left a foundation that runs the Tito Puente Scholarship Fund for Young Latinos who want to study music. Puente left behind two daughters and two sons. Tito Puente Jr., one of his sons, is an accomplished musician who in March 2001 released the song "Here's to You," a tribute to his father. The music of this notable performer continues to enchant fans of Latin music everywhere. In February 2003, Puente was posthumously awarded a Lifetime Achievement Grammy Award by the Academy of Recording Arts and Sciences. *The New York Times* noted in Puente's obituary that "[h]e came to be as much of a symbol of New York City as the Yankee Stadium . . . the last of the real, true band leaders, in the line of Duke Ellington and Count Basie" (Walder 2000, 1).—S.M.M.

References and Suggested Readings

Agencia EFE. "Tito Puente Jr. rinde tributo a su padre." *El Nuevo Día* (Puerto Rico), July, 21, 2001, 103.

Eichenberger, Bill. "Tito Puente Taps Life's Steady Upbeat." *The New York Times*, March 17, 1996, 11.

Hijuelos, Oscar. *The Mambo Kings Play Songs of Love.* New York: Farrar, Straus, Giroux, 1989.

Loza, Steven. *Tito Puente and the Making of Latin Music.* Urbana: University of Illinois Press, 1999.

Moreno-Velázques, Juan. A. "Se apaga el timbal." *Diario La Prensa* (New York), June 2, 2000, 1.

Roberts, John Storm. *The Latin Tinge: The Impact of Latin American Music on the United States.* 2nd ed. New York: Oxford University Press, 1999.

Walder, Joyce. "Tito Puente, Famed Master of Latin Music, Is Dead at 77." *The New York Times*, June 2, 2000, 1.

JEAN RHYS
(1890–1979)

Novelist from Dominica

Jean Rhys' native island of Dominica and her Creole heritage were strong influences on the writer's work. Her complicated and difficult life was very much connected to and revealed in the stories she wrote. Her female protagonists are often Creole women in socially subordinate positions, beholden to men; they are women who live on the margins of life. Race, gender, and class all surface in Rhys' novels. She is credited for the depth of her characters, particularly the expounding of female experience and anxiety in a male-dominated society. A woman who perhaps was ahead of her time, Rhys' writing brought to life a disturbing picture of victimized women, their lives, and the resulting construction of female self-identity. She published what is considered her best work, *Wide Sargasso Sea* (1966), when she was in her 70s.

Ella Gwendolen Rhys Williams was born in Roseau, Dominica, on August 24, 1890. Her father, Rhys Williams, was a London-educated Welsh doctor, and her mother, Minna Lockhard, was a third-generation Dominican Creole from an established slave-owning family. Even though her family was Anglican, she was educated in a convent school and found the rituals and the non-segregated seating within the Catholic Church remarkable. These experiences, later found in her work, were enhanced by her exposure to the language of Patois (a blend of the regional dialect and English), and to the African religious rituals gained through her interaction with servants and the black women who raised her. Her biographers describe her deep attraction to Dominica's black culture and to the contrasts she observed between her Creole life and that of the island's black natives, all of which made her feel uncertain about her identity.

In 1907 Rhys went to live with her aunt Clarice Williams in England and continued her education at the Perse School, where her Creole background caused clashes with intolerant classmates. However, even at that time, she was already exhibiting an uncanny ability in writing. In 1909, interested in pursuing an acting career, she transferred to the Academy of Dramatic Art. Shortly thereafter, her father died and she dropped out of school and worked as a chorus girl for two years under the names of Emma or Ella Gray. During this period she began her lifelong habit of drinking and took numerous odd jobs to make ends meet. She worked as an artist's model and posed for advertisements. Her experiences and relationships during this time provided material that she would write about later: "During this period Rhys lived with women who eventually served as prototypes for characters in her books: disenfranchised women who depended financially on men, fatalistic and satiric . . . whose slang drew Rhys to them" (Gale Literary

Databases 1999). Her first writing came from the notes she kept describing her feelings when her affair with upper-class Englishman Lancelot Hug Smith ended. Even though she stored these notes for many years, they eventually provided the material for *Voyage in the Dark* (1934).

In 1917, and for the next ten years, she embarked on a characteristically unsettled life, traveling throughout cities in Europe. In London she met and soon thereafter married (1919) Jean Lenglet, a man of French and Dutch descent. Lenglet wrote under the name of Edouard de Neve and delved into painting and singing as well. After living in Holland for two years, Rhys and Lenglet moved to Paris, where their son was born. He died a few weeks later. Even though Rhys was still not a recognized author, she continued writing diaries, and accounts of her son's life and death would later appear in her autobiographical novels *After Leaving Mr. Mackenzie* (1930) and *Good Morning, Midnight* (1939). Unbeknownst to Rhys, her husband, who had left for Vienna, had become involved in clandestine espionage activities. She worked as an English tutor and later, after joining her husband in Vienna, worked as an interpreter dealing in black-market currency exchange, a job that for a short time provided the couple with a very good income. From there, the couple traveled to Budapest, but left after Lenglet's espionage activities were uncovered. In 1922 a daughter was born in Brussels, and with her they returned to Paris, where Lenglet, who by now was involved in the buying and selling of improperly obtained art, was arrested and imprisoned. "Vienne," published as part of a series of stories that were inspired by her experiences during these years, captures the restlessness of the time she traveled throughout Europe.

In 1924, in serious financial difficulty and with her husband still in prison, Jean Rhys met British author Ford Madox Ford, editor of the *Transatlantic Review*. As Ford's protégé, Rhys became acquainted with other expatriate writers in Europe, including Gertrude Stein and Ernest Hemingway. What had started out as a mentoring relationship—where Ford introduced Rhys to other writers, published some of her stories and helped her in her writing—turned into a short-lived, abusive ménage á trois with him and his live-in mistress. It was a devastating time in Rhys' life, compounded by the breakup of her marriage to Lenglet, who had discovered the nature of her relationship with Ford. During this time Rhys worked on the translation of a novel and completed her own first novel, *Quartet* (1929). This novel marks the first appearance of the characteristic heroine who returns in other works, a sensitive and vulnerable, sexually attractive, and eventually, self-defeated woman. The story line of the novel came from the devastating relationship she had with Ford and the earlier breakup with Lancelot Smith. It is interesting to note that there was not much critical acclaim for this work, and a recent biographical essay suggests her isolation "from the intellectual and literary sources of modernism, along with her position as an economically and culturally disenfranchised woman, may partially explain the longtime critical neglect of her work" (Gale Literary Databases 1999).

In 1934 Rhys married Leslie Tilden Smith and published her most autobio-graphical novel, *Voyage in the Dark.* In 1939 she published *Good Morning, Midnight.* Smith died in 1945, and she married his cousin Max Hamer. Her personal and professional life began to decline at that time due to severe depression and prob-lems with alcohol. Interest in Rhys' work surfaced in 1957 when the BBC radio aired an adaptation of her novel *Good Morning, Midnight.* A contract from a pub-lishing company followed and for the next six years she worked on *Wide Sargasso Sea* (1966), considered her masterpiece. She died in 1979 while still working on the story of her life, which was eventually published as *Smile Please: An Unfin-ished Autobiography* in 1979.—G.C.

References and Suggested Readings

Angier, Carole. *Jean Rhys.* Lives of Modern Women Series. Harmondsworth: Penguin, 1985.

Gale Literary Databases. "Jean Rhys." *Contemporary Authors Online.* Accessed March 3, 1999.Harrison, Nancy R. *Jean Rhys and the Novel as Women's Text.* Chapel Hill: University of North Carolina Press, 1988.

Howells, Coral Ann. *Jean Rhys.* New York: St. Martin's Press, 1991.

Mellown, Elgin W. *Jean Rhys: A Descriptive and Annotated Bibliography of Works and Criti-cism.* New York: Garland, 1984.

Miles, Rosalind. *In The Female Form: Women Writers and the Conquest of the Novel.* Boston: Routledge and Kegan Paul, 1987.

Rhys, Jean. *Jean Rhys, the Complete Novels.* New York: Norton, 1985.

———. *Smile Please: An Unfinished Autobiography.* New York: Harper & Row, 1979.

FELISA RINCÓN DE GAUTIER
(1897–1995)
Puerto Rican Politician

One of the first female political leaders on the island, Felisa Rincón de Gautier—"Doña Fela," as she was affectionately known—became an important political fig-ure in Puerto Rico, and the first woman to be elected mayor of San Juan, the largest city and the capital of Puerto Rico. Rincón de Gautier was one of the founders of the Popular Democratic Party (PDP), which led Puerto Rico's move from an agri-cultural to an industrial economy under its current U.S. commonwealth status.

Felisa Rincón Marrero was born on January 9, 1897, in the town of Ceiba, the year before Puerto Rico was ceded to the United States after the Spanish-Ameri-can War. In 1907, her father, Enrique Rincón Plumey, an attorney, and her mother, Rita Marrero Rivera de Rincón, a teacher, moved with their seven children to San Juan. A year later, her mother died in childbirth. With her father in a state of deep depression, the children were each sent to live with different relatives. Rincón was sent to the town of San Lorenzo with her aunt and activist uncle, where her political schooling began in their local drug store.

Following the small-town tradition of the time, her uncle's pharmacy served as a central meeting place where townspeople, mostly men, debated local politics, particularly the new relationship between Puerto Rico and the United States. It was through these discussions that she learned about "machismo"—the superiority of men over women—a prevailing double standard for women on the island. She attended public schools in Fajardo, Humacao, and Santurce, where she completed her junior year of high school. By 1909 her father had recovered from his depression and Rincón returned to San Juan to take care of her siblings. Don Enrique remarried, but his philandering drove his wife away after a few years and Rincón was forced to drop out of school and again take charge of the household.

Don Enrique settled his large family on a farm in the coastal town of Vega Baja, an experience that awoke Rincón to the extreme poverty and malnutrition of Puerto Rico's impoverished *jíbaros*, or country people. Welfare or social services were unknown on the island at the time. The level of need she witnessed among her neighbors in Vega Alta would stay with her.

In 1917 Puerto Rican women were beginning to organize and demand suffrage like their U.S. counterparts. By this time, Rincón was living in San Juan with her father and making a living as a seamstress, enjoying and learning from the *tertulias* (political discussions) around the dinner table. In 1932 Puerto Rican women won the right to vote and Rincón was fifth in line to register.

Rincón realized that real success lay in the business side of sewing and emigrated to New York's garment district in 1935 to learn all the aspects of fashion design. A short time later, after working in an exclusive Fifth Avenue shop, she returned to Puerto Rico and set up Felisa's Style Shop in San Juan. Rincón became a successful businesswoman in Old San Juan, and was involved in local politics. At the same time, she was eagerly helping **Luis Muñoz Marín** form the Popular Democratic Party in preparation for the upcoming elections in 1940. In 1938, at the behest of Muñoz Marín and other political friends, she sold her business to work full-time on the Popular Party's campaign. It was during this time that she met her future husband, Jenaro Gautier, a source of support and one who believed that Felisa had more important things to do than cook. He advised her to "use your talents to help the party and the poor. Others can do the cooking" (Gruber 1972, 103). She used her talent as the newly appointed president of the San Juan Committee of the Popular Democratic Party, a position she would occupy for the next 30 years.

In 1940 the Popular Democratic Party lost the city of San Juan, but won the Senate, with Muñoz Marín presiding, and 18 of 39 seats in the House. Now married and known as Felisa Rincón de Gautier, she continued working tirelessly for the party and helped the citizenry improve their quality of life through housing, health, and education projects, a practice she continued throughout her political career.

During the party convention for the 1944 elections, the delegates declared Rincón de Gautier as their candidate for mayor of San Juan, but her husband objected. Rincón de Gautier, in many ways a traditional woman, acquiesced and did not run for office. As she continued her work within the party, she began to encounter and become aware of the existent sexism in the system.

In 1946, the mayor of San Juan, Roberto Sánchez Vilella, resigned to accept another political appointment. When Rincón de Gautier was approached with the offer to take his place, she accepted, thus becoming the first woman mayor of San Juan and the first Puerto Rican woman to hold such a high political post. From that time on, and with her trademark upswept hairstyle, she became known as "Doña Fela." She made city hall the "house of the people." Every Wednesday she would open the doors of city hall to droves of people who came to tell her their problems and ask for help.

One of Doña Fela's major concerns was cleaning up the city of San Juan, and she had no qualms about personally calling up the sanitation department informing them that they had not cleaned a certain street. She was a tireless crusader for San Juan's quality of life improvements everywhere she went, particularly Washington, D.C., where she lobbied for initiatives such as Operation Bootstrap and commonwealth status.

A recipient of hundreds of awards, Doña Fela served five terms and retired from city hall in 1968 at the age of 71. By the time she retired, San Juan had grown from a city with a population of 180,000 to 600,000 residents. During her mayoralty, her administration provided the growing city with new and well-equipped medical dispensaries, new schools, and housing projects. She was an advocate for and increased the number of day-care centers and senior-citizen housing and provided legal aid for the poor.

Rincón de Gautier received hundreds of awards during her lifetime. In 1954 she was named Woman of the Americas by the United Women of America, and during her career was recognized internationally with the French Joan of Arc Medal, the Israeli Order of Merit, and the Vatican's Pope Pius XII Medal. She was given honorary degrees from Marymount College, Temple University, and the University of Puerto Rico.

She remained politically active throughout her retirement, participating in elections and serving as delegate to the U.S. Democratic Party throughout all of its conventions until 1992, where at the age of 95 she made her last political appearance as the oldest delegate to the National Democratic Party's Convention. She died in her beloved city of San Juan in 1994, after a short illness.—G.C.

References and Suggested Readings

Fernández, Ronald, Serafín Méndez-Méndez, and Gail Cueto. *Puerto Rico Past and Present: An Encyclopedia.* Westport, CT: Greenwood Press, 1998. 278–281.

Gruber, Ruth. *Felisa Rincón de Gautier: The Mayor of San Juan.* New York: Thomas Y. Crowell, 1972.

Meier, Matt S. "Felisa Rincón de Gautier." *Notable Latino Americans.* Westport, CT: Greenwood Press, 1997. 308–311.

Navarro, Mireya. "Three Candidates Wage Tough Campaign in Drive to Become San Juan's Second Female Mayor." *The New York Times,* September 29, 1996, 16.

Pace, Eric. "Felisa Rincón de Gautier, 97, Mayor of San Juan." *The New York Times,* September 19, 1994, D9.

CHITA RIVERA
(1933–)

Puerto Rican American Dancer, Actress, and Singer

The career of legendary Broadway performer Chita Rivera has spanned almost 50 years. Endowed with great talent, dramatic flair, energy, and motivation, Rivera has found herself at the center of some of Broadway's most significant productions, bringing her artistic skills to support and enlighten many of them. Her experiences on Broadway can serve as an outline to the history of the most important theatrical productions of the second part of the twentieth century.

Conchita Figueroa del Rivero was born in Washington, D.C., on January 23, 1933. Her Puerto Rican father, Pedro Julio Figueroa, was a professional musician who played saxophone and clarinet. He died when Rivera was seven years old. Her mother, Katherine Anderson del Rivero, worked for the federal government as a clerk. Rivera, who has four other siblings, demonstrated an early interest in arts and as a child complemented her piano and dancing classes by staging her own shows at home.

Her dancing abilities were so great that her dancing teacher encouraged Rivera to apply for a ballet scholarship at the Balanchine School of American Ballet in New York City when she was 15. She had a stellar audition and received the scholarship. She moved from Washington to New York and lived with an uncle in the Bronx, where she studied at Taft High School. On graduation in 1952, she attended Balanchine's School of American Ballet full-time.

The woman who has been described by *Newsweek* as "a one-woman dance marathon" started her Broadway career shortly after finishing high school and immediately became one of Broadways best-regarded dancers during the 1950s (Peyser 1993). Rivera, who changed her artistic name from Conchita to Chita at the beginning of her career, has never been typecast as a Latina. Even though she is a woman of Puerto Rican ancestry, Rivera has played a wide range of roles since her first Broadway performances. Her first professional dancing job was in Irving Berlin's musical *Call Me Madam*, choreographed by Jerome Robbins. The show opened in 1952 and her dancing received excellent reviews. From there Rivera was chosen to be the lead dancer in *Guys and Dolls* and then was one the chorus girls in *Can-Can* (1953). Her roles were challenging and diverse and she ranged from Marilyn Monroe, in *Shoestring Review* (1955) to a prostitute in *Seventh Heaven* (1957).

One of her biggest roles of all time was as Puerto Rican Anita in *West Side Story* (1957). The musical, written by Arthur Laurents, was a modernized take on Shakespeare's *Romeo and Juliet.* Staged by Jerome Robbins, scored by Leonard Bernstein, and with lyrics by Stephen Sondheim, *West Side Story* was about an impossible love story amid the violent realities of gang fights in New York. Rivera appeared as the girlfriend of Bernardo, one of the gang leaders. She considers this her signature role (Horsfall 1996). Her dynamic dancing and powerful singing, as revealed in the song "America," made of Rivera

Chita Rivera.

one of the best and most powerful supporting actresses and dancers in the musical. This role brought her first nomination for a Tony Award. During her participation in *West Side Story*, she married Anthony Mordente, another cast member, became pregnant, had a baby girl, Lisa, and rejoined the cast during the show's London tour. The English producers delayed the London opening until Lisa was born.

One of the interesting aspects of Rivera's career is her ability to work across different genres and media within the artistic realm. Throughout the 1970s, and in most of her artistic life, Chita was very active on the Broadway scene, alternating musical roles as actress, singer, and dancer. She also worked in television and developed her own cabaret acts. Her most important of works of the period were *Wonderful* (1956), *Bye Bye Birdie* (1960–1961), *Zenda* (1963), *Bajour* (1964), *Threepenny Opera* (1966), and *Sweet Charity* (1969). Her work on *Bye Bye Birdie* earned her another Tony nomination and she toured the United States with many of these productions. She also appeared as a guest on many classic television programs such as the *Ed Sullivan Show* and *Sid Caesar's Show.* In 1964, she appeared with the Beatles at a fundraiser in London. She played the role of Nikki in the film version of her Broadway hit *Sweet Charity* in 1969. Although the film was not well received by critics, she received stellar reviews for her role. America's television audiences also got an opportunity to watch Rivera in the role of Connie Richardson, a nosy neighbor, in the *Dick Van Dyke Show* during the 1973–1974 television season.

Rivera has always been interested in transforming her Broadway performances and adapting them into cabarets acts. She has a warm artistic demeanor that charms the typically smaller cabaret audiences. In 1966 she toured the United States with a highly successful cabaret show. This show served as the basis for *Chita Plus 2*, a cabaret act created for her by Fred Ebb and Ron Field that opened to rave reviews in 1975. It was very successful in Las Vegas, London, and other cities.

Rivera's participation in the musical *Chicago* (1975) was her most important work during the 1970s. The show, which ran for more than two years on Broadway, depicts crime and debauchery in 1920s Chicago. Her role as Velma Kelly, her first as a criminal and villain, earned her another Tony nomination. The show was revived in 1998 but was cancelled after a short season; however, it became a successful film in 2003.

Despite Rivera's long list of accomplishments and successes, she did not receive a Tony Award until 1984. Her participation in the musical *The Rink*, with Liza Minelli, finally persuaded the critics that she was not only an accomplished singer and dancer but that she also had significant dramatic skills.

One of Rivera's most important roles to date was that of Aurora in the adaptation of Manuel Puig's novel *Kiss of the Spider Woman*, which opened in 1993. She earned her second Tony for her role as a 1950s movie idol idealized by an Argentinean prisoner who has visions of her in his jail cell. Rivera gave a breathtaking performance characterized not only by her powerful dancing but also by her dramatic flair. Her most recent work, *Chita and All That Jazz* (1996) was a retrospective work that included hits and numbers from her 40-year musical career. The production, which showcased the multiple dimensions of her artistic talent, toured the United States and was extremely well received by the public and critics alike.

Despite having a serious car accident in 1986 that required the insertion of 12 screws on her leg, Rivera, a woman of incredible energy, recovered and has continued working with the same level of energy and enthusiasm. In 1985 she was inducted into the Television Hall of Fame and the School of American Ballet gave her a Lifetime Achievement Award in 1992.

Rivera, an ardent liberal, has been involved in many Democratic causes. She is a highly professional woman who doesn't know when or where to stop. And as she said to the publication *In Theater*: "Of course: the best is yet to come" (Horsfall 1996, 25).—S.M.M.

References and Suggested Readings

Frimark, Merle. Personal Communication with Ms. Rivera's publicist. November 2000.
Horsfall, George. "Chita A Go-Go." *In Theatre*, December 26, 1996, 24–25.
Moritz, Charles, ed. "Chita Rivera." *Current Biography Yearbook*. New York: H.W. Wilson, 1984. 351–355.
Peyser, Marc N. "The Dancing Diva of Broadway." *Newsweek*, May 24, 1993, 63.
Telgen, Diane, and Jim Kamp, eds. "Chita Rivera." *Notable Hispanic Women*. Detroit, MI: Gale, 1993. 341–343.

GERALDO RIVERA
(1943–)
Puerto Rican Television Reporter, Journalist, and Lawyer

Geraldo Rivera is the most recognizable Puerto Rican face in mainstream American television. As a maverick reporter, investigative journalist, talk show host, and news commentator, Rivera has had a continuous presence in American television for more than three decades. His provocative reports, kamikaze reporting techniques and practices, and aggressive demeanor have made him one of the most controversial news personalities in the United States. He was kicked out of Iraq during the Gulf War of 2003 for disclosing the location of American forces in the Persian Gulf.

Gerald Rivera was born on July 4, 1943, at Beth Israel Hospital in Manhattan, New York. He is one of four children of the late Cruz Rivera and Lilly Friedman. Throughout his life, Rivera has explained often his Puerto Rican heritage. According to Rivera's autobiography, his father was born in Puerto Rico and was one of thousands of Puerto Ricans who migrated to the United States seeking work and better living opportunities during the 1930s. When he married Rivera's mother, Lilly Friedman, he changed his first name to Allen to avoid offending her Jewish family; the name Cruz means cross in Spanish. At the time of their marriage, cross-cultural marriages and families were not well accepted in U.S. society. Thus, when Rivera was born, his mother named him Gerald and changed the spelling of his name to Riviera to give it a more generic European connotation (Rivera 1991).

Rivera was raised in the town of Babylon in Suffolk County, Long Island. His father worked as a cook at the cafeteria of the Republic Aviation Company and his mother stayed at home to take care of the children. He attended the local public schools and has described his childhood as being filled with constant internal conflicts over his dual ethnic heritage. While he was exposed to the Spanish language, his Puerto Rican relatives, and Puerto Rican customs and traditions as a child, he was raised within the Jewish faith and was not fully accepted by either ethnic group. An average student during most of his academic career, Rivera graduated from West Babylon High. After being encouraged by his high school principal to attend college, Rivera gained admission to the New York State Maritime College. He attended but became disenchanted with the idea of becoming a professional merchant marine. He left the school after his freshman year and, with one of his best friends, headed west and enrolled at the University of Arizona in Tucson. After graduation in 1965, he married and moved to California, working briefly as a salesperson in a clothing store. He then came back to New York and attended Brooklyn Law School. He did an internship at the Manhattan District attorney's office, where he gained some experience in criminal law and became exposed to the many complex social problems affecting American society at the time. Rivera's law school experience is significant not only because

Geraldo Rivera. AP Photo/Mark Lennihan.

it influenced his later journalistic work, but also because for the first time he started to accept and seek understanding of his Puerto Rican ethnicity.

On graduation from law school in 1969 as one of the top students in his class, Rivera was admitted to the University of Pennsylvania, where for a summer he took part in the Reginald Heber Smith Fellowship in Poverty Law. After completing the fellowship and passing the New York State Bar, Rivera took a job as an attorney working for the Community Action for Legal Services (CALS) in lower Manhattan, where he became involved with the Young Lords, a group of Puerto Rican activists fighting for social and economic equity for the city's poor Puerto Ricans. Rivera joined the Young Lords as their attorney and became one of its most outspoken members. Wearing their trademark purple beret, he assisted members of the organization in fighting diverse social causes. He eventually left his work on CALS and opened a small law practice.

Rivera's assertiveness and combativeness had made him a fixture on local New York television stations, which covered many of the activities of the Young Lords. Al Primo, news director for WABC, the New York ABC affiliate, asked him to leave his legal work to work as a television reporter for them. Rivera accepted the offer in the spring of 1970. Because he lacked journalistic training, he was given a scholarship to attend a summer journalism fellowship at Columbia Journalism School. The program was geared toward preparing members of minority groups for careers in the news media.

During his first months at WABC (Channel 7), Rivera went through the process of learning his new trade. His most important story of the period was his exposé of the inhumane treatment faced by mentally retarded patients at the Willowbrook State Hospital School on Staten Island. At the time, Willowbrook was one the largest facilities for the mentally retarded in the United States, providing services for more than 6,000 patients. Because of Rivera's popularity, the station gave him the coveted position of cultural reporter to cover cultural activities and celebrities in New York. He reported on celebrities such as John Lennon and Yoko Ono, Bianca Jagger, and Johnny Mathis, and fairly quickly was recognized as a celebrity on his own. This gave him the opportunity for a career with television networks.

In 1973 Rivera founded Maravilla Productions, his own production company, and started producing a series of news programs following the *60-Minutes* style for ABC's *Good Night America*. The program aired between 1974 and 1976 but he continued working as a reporter for WABC until 1975. That year he moved to *Good Morning America* and continued doing his late night show. In 1977 he was hired by the news division of ABC and also reported on special stories for them. Rivera joined ABC's news magazine *20/20* in 1978 as a chief reporter and immediately launched a series of investigative reports that gave credibility and prestige to the program. His coverage of the death of singer Elvis Presley and his eventual uncovering of Presley's addiction to prescription drugs helped establish *20/20* as a serious news show. He continued with ABC until 1985, when he was fired for criticizing the network's refusal to air a report about the alleged links between the Kennedy family and the death of movie star Marilyn Monroe.

In 1987 Rivera began producing *Geraldo*, a talk show that was characterized by controversial, sexually charged, and violent topics. His nose was broken during one episode while trying to break up a brawl between a group of neo-Nazis appearing. Despite much criticism, the show aired until 1998.

During the 1990s, Rivera made a remarkable comeback as a serious television reporter. In 1994 he began airing *Rivera Live* for the cable network CNBC. Capitalizing on the trial of O.J. Simpson, Rivera brought a wide array of news commentators and lawyers to offer their views on the Simpson case. He signed a $30 million six-year contract with NBC. In 1998 he was a news reporter on the NBC *Today* show and also began *Upfront Tonight*, a news commentary program, on CNBC. In 2001 he left CNBC to join the Fox News Network. Despite his professional mistakes during the 1980s and 1990s, one source has said: "Geraldo Rivera, wearing a look of contentment that comes with the feeling that one's sins have been redeemed, is unabashed—as he has so often been in his 25 year career in television—pronouncing himself born again" (Carter 1997, D1).

Rivera has been credited with being the first and most prominent Puerto Rican reporter in the United States. He has earned a number of awards and distinctions such as the Emmy, the Columbia University Dupont Award, the Associated Press Broadcasters Award for Excellence in Individual Journalism, and the George Foster Peabody Award.—S.M.M.

References and Suggested Readings

Carter, Bill. "The $30 Million Man; With a New Deal, Rivera Seeks Respect." *The New York Times,* December 15, 1997, D1.

Marin, Rick. "Geraldo Pulls a Punch." *Newsweek,* August 17, 1998, 56.

Miller, John. "Geraldo Jive." *National Review,* September 1, 1998, n.p.

Rivera, Geraldo, with Daniel Paisner. *Exposing Myself: Geraldo Rivera.* New York: Bantam Books, 1991.

Graciela Rivera
(1921–)

Puerto Rican Opera Singer

The artistic career and musical gifts of this beloved Puerto Rican singer broke ground in Puerto Rico, the United States, Europe, and Latin America during the

1940s and 1950s. Graciela Rivera opened doors of opportunity to many other Puerto Rican and African American classical singers who followed her as the first Puerto Rican woman to succeed in the elite world of classical opera in New York City. During her career she performed in the most prestigious music halls of the United States and the world.

Rivera was born in Ponce, Puerto Rico, on April 17, 1921. Her father, Gonzálo Salvador Rivera, was an evangelical minister, and her mother was Enriqueta Padilla. She was one of eight children born to a family of limited resources and modest economic means. Due to the nature of her father's job, they were forced to move often around the island, and went from Ponce to the town of Cataño when Rivera was two years old. She received her education at the public schools in Cataño, and attended the Escuela Superior Central (Central High School) in Santurce, in the metropolitan San Juan area. The school was well regarded both for its educational programs and for its solid music and arts training.

Graciela began to sing when she was a young child. She attended her father's religious services and sang religious hymns accompanied by a foot-pedal organ. It was not until she was in high school, however, that her musical talents were discovered. One day, music teacher Dwight W. Hiestand was testing the students' voices to classify their vocal registers. He asked Rivera to sing and discovered that she had a superb coloratura soprano voice. He took her under his wing and taught her the foundations of music. Soon she started to appear in the school's music productions, where she received great accolades. She was cast as the lead in the school productions of Donizetti's *Lucia de Lammermoor* and Verdi's *Rigoletto* where the audience was charged a 25- or 50-cent admission.

Her talent was so great that her teachers encouraged her to pursue a professional career in music. After graduation from high school, Rivera was admitted to Julliard. She had to work and offer summer recitals to support herself and pay for her school expenses. After her second year at Julliard, she received a scholarship that covered her tuition. In 1940 she met Joseph Zumchak, a U.S. military officer stationed in San Juan. After the Japanese attack on Pearl Harbor, his ship was ordered to travel to New York. Taking advantage of Rivera's Christmas break from Julliard, they married in 1941. Acting often as her professional manager, he was one of her greatest supporters throughout her career.

Rivera graduated from Julliard in 1943 and immediately started a professional career in opera. She was so well received by the public that her career received an immediate boost. During the war, Rivera toured the world with the USO, singing for the American troops, appearing on the U.S.S. *Missouri* and the U.S.S. *Philippine Sea*. In 1950 she appeared in Rossini's *Barber of Seville* in the Royal Theater in Rome. After the performance, His Holiness Pope Pius XII welcomed her to the Vatican, praised her talents, and blessed her voice.

On February 4, 1952, Rivera became the source of national pride for her fellow Puerto Ricans when she became the first Puerto Rican to perform at the Metropolitan Opera House in New York, appearing as Lucia in *Lucia di Lammermoor*. *The New York Times* noted that:

[h]er tones were pure, clear, and beautifully modulated from the start, and there were real indications that she was going to be a real hit when the applause after her legend of the fountain area caused a pause in the show. But it was after the mad scene that that the cheers and the applause really broke loose. They continued until she had answered seven curtain calls. (February 5, 1952, 15)

After her performance at the Met, Rivera continued appearing on all the most important stages of New York such as Carnegie Hall, Madison Square Garden, and Radio City Music Hall.

In 1952, Rivera was invited by Archbishop of Mexico Luis María Martínez to sing with the chorus of Mexico's Cathedral of the Virgin of Guadaloupe in a special television program broadcast to the Mexican nation. She became the first woman invited to sing with the chorus since its founding in 1553. Her quick chain of artistic successes positioned her as one of best coloratura sopranos of the time. She sang with the most important opera companies in the all the important theaters of United States and Europe. She has said that the only theater in Europe where she never performed was La Scala in Milan—and that was because Maria Callas, the theater's resident star, felt threatened by Rivera's talents and blocked her from appearing (Personal communication with Graciela Rivera August 4, 2001).

Rivera was also active making appearances with radio and television in the United States throughout the 1950s. She participated in radio through the *CBS Concerts* and had her own radio show on WHOM in New York titled *Graciela Rivera Sings*. When television emerged, she appeared on shows such as CBS' *Name that Tune, Your Show of Shows,* and NBC's *The Jack Paar Show.*

One of Rivera's most important attributes was her devotion to new talent. She felt a sense of duty and obligation to help fellow Puerto Rican performers to succeed. She was one of the founding members of the Puerto Rico Opera Company and sponsored a music contest to offer scholarships for underprivileged children. After her retirement from professional music she started a new career in education. For 15 years she worked as a professor of music at the Hostos Community College in New York and held the Graciela Rivera Opera Workshops.

After many years living in the United States, Rivera retired to Puerto Rico in 1987. She makes sporadic appearances in the Puerto Rican electronic media, and her audiences still remember and admire her. Her husband published a biography of this notable Puerto Rican diva in 1990, where he tells the story of her path to fame and success. Because of her incredible accomplishments as an opera singer, the newly renovated theater of the Central High School, her alma mater, will carry her name.—S.M.M.

References and Suggested Readings

Alejandro Moreira, Rubén. "Memorias de una Voz." *El Mundo* (San Juan, PR), May 6, 1990, 6–8.

"Graciela Rivera Wins 7 Calls before Curtain as Lucia in Her 'Met' Debut." *The New York Times*, February 5, 1952, n.p.

"Herald Tribune Publica trabajo sobre la Diva Graciela Rivera." *El Mundo*, January 31, 1952, n.p.

Rivera, Graciela. Personal Documents from Her Collection. Interamerican University, San Germán, Puerto Rico. November 10, 1989.

Zumchak, Joseph. *Graciela Rivera: la diva puertorriqueña*. San Juan, PR: Joseph Zumchak, 1990.

CARLOS MANUEL RODRÍGUEZ ("EL BEATO CHARLIE")
(1918–1963)

Puerto Rican Religious Figure

On April 29, 2001, Pope John Paul II beatified Carlos Manuel Rodríguez. This constitutes the first step in the canonization process followed by the Catholic faith to recognize someone as a saint. The beatification of Rodríguez marks the first time that a Puerto Rican and Caribbean layman has received such recognition from the Catholic Church. Rodríguez was a humble and devout Catholic who touched the lives of hundreds of Puerto Ricans through his pastoral work at the University of Puerto Rico at Río Piedras and in his local parish in Caguas. Rodríguez has become one of the most significant Puerto Rican religious figures, and his religious principles are now followed by scores of Puerto Ricans.

Carlos Manuel Rodríguez Santiago was born on November 22, 1918, to Herminia Santiago and Manuel Baudilio Rodríguez, a small business merchant. He was one of five children of a deeply religious Catholic family. One of his brothers became the first Benedictine abbot on the island and one of his sisters is a Catholic nun. Rodríguez was an altar boy at his local parish in Caguas, a city near San Juan. Many of Rodríguez's biographers have traced his religious vocation to the faith of his grandmother Alejandrina Esteras, a deeply devout woman.

As a child, Rodríguez attended the local parochial school in Caguas and Our Lady of Perpetual Help Catholic School in Miramar. He eventually graduated from the José Gautier Benítez High School in Caguas. In school, Rodríguez was a bright student who excelled in religious courses and in classes related to the humanities. An enthusiast of sacred and religious music, Rodríguez taught himself to play the piano and organ, and organized and participated in several choirs in his local parish.

On his graduation from high school in 1939, Rodríguez worked in several clerical positions in both Caguas and San Juan. In 1946 he enrolled at the University of Puerto Rico in Río Piedras, where he studied humanities for a year. Even though he excelled at his studies, he had to leave the university because of illness.

Rodríguez's stay at the university is significant because it marks the beginning of a strong association with the institution and the launching of his most significant ministry. Noticing the lack of religious activities and spiritual counseling at the university, Rodríguez became a leader within the Catholic Student Center. His friendliness, accessibility, and love of God made him a popular religious leader with the students.

One of Rodríguez's religious interests was liturgy, the way in which God is exalted at religious services. He organized a liturgical circle in his Caguas parish and became an ardent proponent of the reinstatement of the Easter vigil ceremonies. During the Inquisition and the Crusades, some factions within the European Catholic church had taken shelter in caves and catacombs to avoid persecution. As part of the Easter services, they held an Easter vigil where they conducted services and offered baptism to people seeking refuge in the church. These liturgical ceremonies were banned by the Catholic Church at the beginning of the twentieth century. Rodríguez became an ardent supporter of the restoration of the services on the island. After his death, the Second Vatican Council recognized the importance of his claim and ordered churches from around the world to restore these services, which are generally held on the eve of Easter Sunday.

Carlos Manuel Rodríguez.

Despite constant bouts of colitis, Rodríguez continued to spread the Christian faith vigorously among scores of students and professors at the university and among parishioners in Caguas. By 1962 Rodríguez's health had deteriorated significantly and he underwent major gastric surgery to alleviate his colitis, which had evolved into an aggressive and terminal cancer. While recovering from a painful surgery, he told his priest brother that he had developed cracks in his faith and that he was not ready to die. According to many theologians, this sudden doubt is a common behavior found in among many other saints. In fact, they have used that statement to help validate his sainthood. After a long period of meditation, his faith was restored and he declared himself ready to die. (In fact, many people have affirmed that he predicted the day of his death.) He died on July 13, 1963.

The process of being declared a saint by the Catholic Church is complex. The church requires that the person not only live a glorious or sanctified life but that a verifiable miracle be attributed to the candidate. While studying Rodríguez's life, Father Mario Maza from San Juan's San Juan Marco parish, discovered that there was a significant miracle attributed to Rodríguez. In 1981 Rodríguez's friend Deli Santana de Aguiló was diagnosed with a lethal form of cancer known as non-Hodgkins lymphoma. The disease had spread to her lungs and her head. Her doctors advised her that the cancer had metastasized and that there was nothing that they could do for her. She prayed to Rodríguez to intercede with God and her cancer suddenly vanished, she fully recovered, and is still alive today. Her medical records were submitted to a panel of notable medical scholars that included Dr. Norman Maldonado, former president of the University of Puerto Rico and a cancer specialist and hematologist. The panel concluded that there was no scientific reason to explain her recovery.

After seeking permission from the San Juan Catholic Archdiocese, father Meza presented a comprehensive case to the Vatican for the Rodríguez's beatification. (A beatification allows Catholic followers to venerate Rodríguez and ask for his intercession before God.) In 1997 the All Saints Commission from the Vatican met and certified the validity of the miracle attributed to Rodríguez. In 1999 it was recommended to the Pope that Rodríguez be blessed or beatified. His body was exhumed from its original burial place and taken to Rome for examination. The Pope declared Rodríguez to be blessed in a ceremony at St. Peter's Square in Rome attended by more than 2,000 Puerto Rican Catholics. His remains were returned to Puerto Rico, where they now rest at a place of honor in Caugas' Sweet Jesus Cathedral. To elevate Rodríguez to the status of saint, another major miracle must be attributable to him.—S.M.M.

References and Suggested Readings

Hernández Beltán, Ruth. "Peregrinaje latino por el beato boricua." *El Nuevo Día* (San Juan, PR), March 29, 2001. *http://www.adendi.com.*

Parés Arroyo, Marga. "Los restos de Charlie en su morada en Caguas." *El Nuevo Día* (San Juan, PR), May 24, 2001. *http://www.adendi.com.*

———. "Se preparan los criollos para recibir los restos de Charlie." *El Nuevo Día* (San Juan, PR), May 24, 2001. *http://www.adendi.com.*

Rivera Marrero, Miria. "Celebran el 38.vo aniversario de la muerte de Charlie." *El Nuevo Día* (San Juan, PR), July 29, 2001. *http://www.adendi.com.*

Roldán Soto, Camile. "Un ejemplo a seguir el beato." *El Nuevo Día* (San Juan, PR), July 14, 2001. *http://www.adendi.com.*

Valdivia, Yadira. "Elevado Carlos Manuel al honor de los altares." *El Nuevo Día* (San Juan, PR), May 28, 2001. *http://www.adendi.com.*

———. "Emotivo final en la Catedral." *El Nuevo Día* (San Juan, PR), May 28, 2001. *http://www.adendi.com.*

———. "Primera recordación litúrgica en el día official del beato." *El Nuevo Día* (San Juan, PR), July 12, 2001. *http://www.adendi.com.*

CHI CHI RODRÍGUEZ
(1935–)

Puerto Rican Golfer and Philanthropist

In a sport generally reserved for the financially affluent or socially privileged, Juan A. "Chi Chi" Rodríguez was the first Puerto Rican to break golf's color and class barriers and score major victories in professional tournaments throughout the United States. With talent, vision, and endurance, Rodríguez, a professional golf star, has won some of the country's more prestigious tournaments and has made an effort to help the poor and disenfranchised with his earnings.

Chi Chi was born in Río Piedras, a suburb of San Juan, on October 23, 1935, one of six children of Juan Rodríguez, a worker in sugarcane farms, and Modesta Vilá. His family was extremely poor and his boyhood and adolescence were filled with hardships. He suffered many debilitating illnesses as a result of his poor diet and living conditions (Berkow 1987). By the time he was seven years old, he was working under the scorching sun on a sugarcane plantation.

Chi Chi Rodríguez.

When he was nine, he became a caddy, making 35 cents for 18 holes. Of his early days as a caddy he has said: "[Y]ou didn't dare lose a ball for the man whose bag you were toting. If you did, though, they kicked your butt off the course. It was tempting though. It was in the Depression and you could get 75 cents for any good ball you found. That was enough to feed our family" (Hafner 1992, C7).

His work as a caddy gave him a liking for the sport and he dreamed that one day he could become a golf star. However, his beginnings in the game were not easy. Rodríguez often reminisces about those early attempts at playing the game:

> The irony of me learning to play this great game of golf—initially with a guava stick for a club and a crushed tin can for a ball, and later with a "real" ball, but only a five iron, is that that was an advantage, not a disadvantage, as one might naturally perceive to be. Both of these rather rustic types of apprenticeship sharpened my hand-eye coordination and heightened my sense of touch or "feel" for hitting a particular distance. (Rodríguez and Andrisani 1990, xv–xvi)

In 1955 Rodríguez played his first professional golf tournament, the Puerto Rico Open. Even though he placed second, it was clear that he had a great future as a golf player. However, because of his family's financial hardships, Rodríguez was forced to enter the armed forces in 1955 to make some money. He continued to play while in the military.

When Rodríguez left the army in 1957 he decided to return to Puerto Rico with the goal of becoming a professional golfer. A man with a charming personality and temperament, Rodríguez has been fortunate to have good mentors throughout his career. One of these was Ed Dudley, then head professional at the Dorado Beach Hotel in Dorado, who gave him a job as a caddy master and tutored him. His steady coaching and practice, along with his ability for the sport, allowed him to quickly join the professional golfing circuit and to turn professional in 1960. While he was able to earn some money, it was not until 1963 that he won the Denver Open, his first victory in a professional tournament.

From 1963 to 1979 he became one of the hottest performers on the professional golf circuit and won eight regular tour victories, earning $1,037,105. Some of his early victories were the Denver Open (1963), the Lucky International Western Open (1964), the Texas Open (1967), the Sahara Invitational (1968), the Byron Nelson Classic (1972), and the Greater Greensboro Open (1973).

Rodríguez is considered a master of short games. His book *101 Supershots: Every Golfer's Guide to Lower Scores* (1990) outlines some of his most successful techniques in the golf game. In 1985, at the age of 55, Rodríguez entered the senior golf tournament circuit, where he has had many resounding successes, with 22 victories and earned $6,524,472. From 1986 to 1993 he often ranked within the first five positions of the senior tour and has won such important tournaments as the Digital Seniors Classic (1986), the Doug Sanders Classic, (1988), the Las Vegas Senior Classic (1990), and the Senior PGA Tour Burner Classic (1993). He was asked by Jack Nicklaus to be endorser of MacGregor clubs and signed a lifetime promotional and endorsement contract with the Toyota Motor Company and with Choice Hotels International. His winnings on the golf course, as well as his commercial endorsements, have brought him considerable wealth.

One of the most significant dimensions of Rodríguez's career has been his philanthropic work. A man who was undoubtedly scarred by the illnesses of poverty, Rodríguez has made a strong effort to use his wealth and visibility to help the poor and disenfranchised. During the late 1960s Rodríguez opened a golf school for underprivileged kids in Florida. Many of his former students have pursued both professional golf and college educations. In 1979, he established the Chi Chi Rodríguez Youth Foundation to serve inner city youths who are at risk of dropping out of school. His foundation supports a series of scholarship programs and inner city initiatives to guarantee that underprivileged children get access to educational opportunities.

Rodríguez has become an admired and beloved figure both on the golf circuit and on the national scene. Fellow golfer Jack Nicklaus has called him "the game's finest ambassador of goodwill" (Rodríguez and Andrisani 1990, xiii). He has served on the President's Council on Health and Physical Fitness and is a relentless advocate for children's educational opportunities. He has also won several important awards for his charitable undertakings. He was inducted into the PGA World Golf Hall of Fame (1992), received the American Education Award from the American Association of School Administrators (1993), and was given the Ford Achievement Award (1998).

Rodríguez is a knowledgeable investor who has become very wealthy. He has multiple business interests and divides his time between Florida and Puerto Rico. In 1998 he had a heart attack that required multiple bypass surgery. Despite this, he has seen a recent resurgence in his game.—S.M.M.

References and Suggested Readings

Berkow, Ira. "Golf; at the head of the Senior Class." *The New York Times*, July 5, 1987, Section 5, p. 2.

Bonk, Thomas. "Win by Revitalized Chi Chi Would be Victory for Youth." *The Los Angeles Times*, October 26, 2000, D14.

Díaz, Jaime. Golf: "Errol Flynn? No, It's a Swashbucking Rodríguez in Lead." *The New York Times*, July 10, 1993, 29.

Hafner, Dan. "Rodríguez Recalls Good Days of Caddying." *The Los Angeles Times*, January 25, 1992, C7.

Meier, Matt S. "Chi Chi Rodríguez." *Notable Latino Americans*. Westport, CT: Greenwood Press, 1997. 323–326.

Moritz, Charles. *Current Biography Yearbook*. New York: H.W. Wilson, 1969.

Pucin, Diane. "Rodríguez Has Heart of Champion." *The Los Angeles Times*, March 15, 1999, 12.

Rodríguez, Chi Chi, with John Andrisani. *101 Supershots: Every Golfer's Guide to Lower Scores*. New York: Harper and Row, 1990.

Yannis, Alex. "Golf: Chi Chi Putts-Putts Into the Picture." *The New York Times*, June 5, 1993, 34.

Silvio Rodríguez
(1946–)

Cuban Singer, Composer, and Guitarist

If there were a singer laureate from Cuba during the years immediately after the Revolution, Silvio Rodríguez would hold that distinction. Together with **Pablo Milanés**, Rodríguez was one of the key members of Cuba's Nueva Canción or Nueva Trova movement. He does not call himself a singer but rather refers to himself as a troubadour—someone who finds music from the world and delivers it to the world. Rodríguez is even more than this. He is a songwriter and a poet, a singer and a humanist. The beauty of his many compositions have earned him a unique place in the modern musical history of Cuba and Latin America. The romantic tone of his songs has led critics in the United States to compare him to Bob Dylan; a label that he dislikes and is prone to disregard.

Rodríguez was born on November 26, 1946, in the city of San Antonio de los Baños in central Cuba. His parents, Dagoberto Rodríguez and Argelia Domínguez,

Silvio Rodríguez. AP Photo/Daniel Muzio.

were tobacco workers. He inherited love of music and his musical abilities from his mother, who had been a singer in her youth and would have continued had it not been considered an unbecoming activity for a woman.

Rodríguez is mostly a self-taught musician, as he received only limited musical training in piano during his youth. Nonetheless, he started to show his general artistic inclinations by the age of seven when he started to write poetry and to draw. As a schoolboy, he was often distracted in his classes and filled his notebook with cartoons. In fact, one of his first jobs was as a cartoonist. His family and relatives have characterized him as a child with deep sensitivities and imagination, and he has been labeled an idealist with a deep love for nature and for the humanities.

One of the defining events in Rodríguez's life was the Cuban Revolution of 1959. As someone who grew up in a working class family, he witnessed the hardships faced by poor Cubans before **Fidel Castro**'s rise to power. He saw the revolution as a catalyst for change and as a way to improve the lives of people in his country. By the age of 15, he was working as a youth volunteer in literacy and education projects sponsored by the government. He eventually joined the Cuban Armed Forces. In 1964 when he was in the Cuban army, he started to play the guitar and to write songs. On leaving the military, Rodríguez started a friendship with a group of young writers publishing their work in a newspaper known as *El Caiman Barbudo* (The Bearded Alligator). A group of idealists filled with talent, they all shared similar views and concerns for Cuba during the turbulent 1960s.

Rodríguez debuted professionally in 1967 at the First Encounter of the Protest Song held in the Palace of Fine Arts in Cuba. This event is of major significance in modern Latin American music history, as it opened the door for the emergence of the Nueva Trova music movement in Cuba and eventually throughout Latin America. The singers and songwriters affiliated with this movement explored the traditional musical forms of their lands but built a message of social conscience into the lyrics of their songs. Their music acts as social and political commentary, and quite often as poignant criticism too. To a large extent, this genre has many similarities with the "protest songs" music being sung by Joan Báez and Peter, Paul, and Mary in the United States. However, it has many more poetic and metaphorical qualities.

Rodríguez received artistic mentorship and support from La Casa de las Americas—an organization that promoted Cuban culture and arts. It was at La Casa that on February 19, 1968, Rodríguez, along with Noel Nicola and **Pablo Milanés**, gave a concert that established him as the leader of La Nueva Trova. During this period, he worked on the Cuban television program *Música y Estrellas* (Music and Stars) and received mentoring from many Cuban literary and artistic figures. With his friend and colleague Pablo Milánes, he became one of the members of the Grupo de Experimentacion Sonora del ICAIC (Group of Sound Experimentation at the Havana Film Institute) in 1972. His first solo album, titled *Días y Flores,* was released in 1975. By that time, he was already touring the world with his music.

In many interviews, Rodríguez has acknowledged the influences of other Cuban and Latin American musicians such as Lucho Gatica, Barbarito Diez, Sindo Garay, Benny Moré, María Teresa Vera, Vicentico Valdés, and Violeta Parra. He also acknowledges his early admiration of Tchaikosky, who had a great influence on him. He even credits American musicians such Paul Anka, **Harry Belafonte**, and Johnny Mathis with shaping his music (Correa 1997). He has also been heavily influenced by many of Cuba's native rhythms such as the *son.*

His music can best be understood by looking at it as poetry accompanied by music, beautifully crafted into songs. His lyrics reveal his poetic and idealist soul. These lyrics are highly symbolic and perhaps can be better understood as a chain of metaphors. Songs such as "Como esperando a abril" (Like Waiting for April) reveal his technique of linking a series of symbols into a unified poetic narrative. He is a master at creating surrealist metaphors that link such dissimilar elements as the morning clouds, a flower born from a train, and an old man's cape to create the thrilling feeling of new love. None of the many symbols that he uses makes much sense when looked at in isolation. However, when they are seen in totality, one marvels at his ability to select isolated images and blend them into a unified messages that are not only capable of delivering a powerful message, but more importantly, are extremely effective in eliciting an emotional response.

Rodríguez writes relevant and practical songs that reflect a sense of urgency and immediacy. One critic has said that he uses "pop songs as revolutionary anthems and catalysts for personal exploration" (Lechner 1998, 62). They are often framed within a poetic surrealism that appeals to the listeners' sense of social and political responsibility and, at the same time, to their common sense. His song "Unicornio" (Unicorn), for example, was written in 1982 for the people of San Salvador during the Salvadorian civil war. He uses the myth of the unicorn as a metaphor for pain and loss. The song tells the story of how his blue unicorn has been lost and how he is longing for the friendship, trust, and love they shared. After its release, the song became a huge success in Latin America. Other songs, such as "Canción Urgente para Nicaragua" (Urgent Song for Nicaragua; 1982) and "Maza" (1982), are more heavily laden with political messages and social commentaries. Rodríguez's instrumentation, accompanied by his high tenor voice, is lively and vibrant.

Rodríguez has written more than 500 songs and has recorded more than 100 of them. He says that he can write anywhere—hotel rooms, ships, in the middle of wars, and in his bathroom. In fact, one of his most famous songs, titled "Playa Girón," was written on a fishing boat during a creative trip he took during the

1970s. He has recorded more than 13 albums throughout his career. Among them are *Días y Flores* (Days and Flowers; 1975), *Mujeres* (Women; 1978), *Unicornio* (Unicorn; 1982), *Tríptico* (Triptic; dedicated in 1984 to the twenty-fifth anniversary of the Cuban revolution), and *Descartes* (1998).

In 1998, he built Abdala, a state-of-the-art music studio in the Miramar sector of Havana, as an outlet for his artistic production and the production of scores of other young Cuban musicians. Although many members of the Cuban exile community see him as an ardent communist and protest his music wherever he goes, he tours regularly throughout the world and has even been to the United States. Although he has criticized certain events during the Castro regime, he is a fervent supporter of the Cuban revolution. He has said: "[I]f the revolution falls, I will fall too" (Vázquez-Díaz 1992, 37). He currently sits as a representative in the National Assembly of Cuba.—S.M.M.

References and Suggested Readings

Correa, Armando. "Entrevista para el Nuevo Herald" Unpublished interview. Havana, Cuba, April 13 and 14, 1997. *http://www.komunika.net/silvio/entrevistas/entrevista20.html.*

Daley, Dan. "Havana Gets World-Class Studio." *Billboard*, January 30, 1999, 40.

Domínguez, Daniel. "Silvio, el eterno trovador." *La Prensa* (Panama), December 7, 1996, n.p.

Lechner, Ernesto. "Pop Music, Latin Pulse: From Exhilarating Highs to Whiny Lows, from Cuba." *The Los Angeles Times*, January 4, 1998, 62.

Rodríguez, Maria de los Angeles. "Silvio Rodríguez: Un arquero con expresión legendaria." *Revista Catálogo* 5, EGREM (Empresa de Grabaciones y Ediciones Musicales), n.p.

Rother, Larry. "Troubadours of the Cuban Revolution." *The New York Times*, August 9, 1987, 22.

Vázquez Díaz, René. "Silvio Rodríguez: Si cae la revolución, caigo yo." *Este País* (Mexico City), August 1, 1992, 32, 37.

ILEANA ROS-LEHTINEN
(1952–)

Cuban American Politician and Educator

Cuban-born Ileana Ros-Lehtinen is a politician of many firsts. In 1982 she was the first Latina elected to the Florida State House, where she served four years as a representative and three years as a state senator. After the death of long-time Congressman Claude Pepper in 1989, Ros-Lehtinen won his seat in a special election and became the first Latina and first Cuban-American elected to the U.S. Congress. In addition, she was the first Latin American woman to chair a congressional subcommittee and the first Hispanic member of the House's Republican Caucus, as well as the first woman to be elected its secretary-treasurer. A staunch Republican, she enjoys the support of an unwaveringly anti-Castro and anti-communist constituency made up of mostly Cubans living in Miami. She commutes to Washington and continues to remain a Miami resident, where she has run unopposed for her last five congressional elections.

Ileana Ros Adato was born in Havana, Cuba, on July, 15, 1952, to Armanda Adato and Enrique Emilio Ros, respected members of the education establishment. She attended primary school in Cuba. In 1959, during the initial wave of emigrants who fled **Fidel Castro**'s regime, Ros' family sought refuge in Miami, Florida. In Miami, Ros completed primary and secondary school and entered Miami-Dade Community College, where she completed her associate's degree in arts in 1972. In 1975 she received her bachelor's degree in education, with a concentration in English and later completed a master's in education from Florida International University. After a short stint as a teacher at Miami Killian Senior High School, she was certified as an elementary-level teacher and taught in a few local schools until she decided to establish a private elementary school, Eastern Academy, where she was also a teacher and an administrator.

Her interest in politics began nine years after launching her school, when she volunteered to work on a friend's political campaign. In 1982, after a redistricting of the Miami area, Ros ran and was elected the first Latina to a newly created seat in the Florida House of Representatives. There she met and married another representative, Dexter Lehtinen. The mid-1980s was a time when Cubans in Florida increased in number and were becoming a significant political force, particularly in south Florida. Four years later, she won a seat in the state senate, and became the first Latina to hold that political post. She is remembered for her focus on the welfare and interests of women, children, and education—issues to which she is still committed. Two key pieces of legislation championed by Ros included the creation of a Victim's Bill of Rights and the Florida Pre-Paid College Tuition Program, a financial assistance program for Florida higher education students.

In 1989, following the death of long-time Congressman Claude Pepper, Ros won a special congressional election, beating ten opponents to represent the Miami–Dade County District. The history-making election marked the first time a Latino woman had been elected to the U.S. House of Representatives. Very early on, she became involved in committees that made her a leading figure in shaping foreign policy. She held membership in the Government Operations and Foreign Affairs Committee and more recently has sat on both the House International Relations Committee and on the Government and Oversight Committee. Her seat on the Foreign Affairs Committee led her to play key roles in supporting the passage of the Cuban Liberty and Democratic Solidarity Act of 1996, better known as the Helms-Burton Act, tightening the 38-year-old embargo against Cuba. The act, which penalizes countries and companies doing business with Cuba with assets seized by Castro from Cuban-Americans, is seen as a step for the eventual ouster of Castro and democratization of the island. A tireless crusader of human rights, she chairs the House Subcommittee on International Operations and Human Rights.

More recently, Ros-Lehtinen, whose Florida District 18 is over 75 percent Hispanic (and mostly Cuban), found herself intensely involved in the 1999–2000 uproar over Elián González and the ensuing debate over whether he should be given political asylum in the United States or be allowed to return to Cuba with his father. Ros-Lehtinen, whose district of Cuban-Americans overwhelmingly supported preventing immigration officials from sending him back home, found herself vilified on Cuban television and in the press. This touched a chord in Ros-Lehtinen, a steadfast anti-Castro Cuban national, for whom the struggle against Castro is personal as well as political. Pleased that she was able to provoke the Castro regime to the point where she was denounced in a headline—"Loba feroz disfrazada de mujer" (The ferocious wolf disguised as a woman)—she ordered a "ferocious wolf" vanity license plate: LOBA FRZ.

Unlike many of her Congressional colleagues, Ros-Lehtinen maintains her primary residence in Miami. She credits the active role both of her parents have taken in supporting her political career. Not only do they take care of her two daughters when she is in Washington, D.C., but they are integral to her political campaigns: her father as campaign manager, and her mother as the organizer for volunteers, mapping out the door to door election operations. Her congressional aides speak very highly of the support and encouragement they receive from their boss: "She encourages us to get our degrees, and she even gives us flex-time to attend classes" (Stuart 2000). Ros-Lehtinen was named Youth Crime Watch of America's Elected Official of the Year 2000. Since 1994, she has run unopposed in her district's congressional elections. Considering her relatively short time in politics, Ros-Lehtinen wants to stay in Congress for as long as possible.—G.C.

References and Suggested Readings

Alvarez, Lizette. "Fight Over Boy Is Latest in Lawmaker's War With Castro." *The New York Times,* January 10, 2000, 12.

Bonillo-Santiago, Gloria. *Breaking Ground and Barriers: Hispanic Women Developing Effective Leadership.* San Diego, CA: Marin Publications, 1992.

Fernandez, Mayra. *Ileana Ros-Lehtinen, Lawmaker.* Parsippany, NJ: Modern Curriculum Press, 1994.

Martínez, Al. "Ileana Ros-Lehtinen." In *Rising Voices: Profiles in Leadership.* Glendale, CA: Nestle USA, 1993. 64–65.

Meier, Matt S. *Notable Latino Americans: A Biographical Dictionary.* Westport, CT: Greenwood Press, 1997.

Office of Congresswoman Ileana Ros-Lehtinen: *http://www.house.gov/ros-lehtinen.*

"Rep. Ileana Ros-Lehtinen (FL-R)." *Congressional Digest* 78:3 (March 1, 1999): 81.

Stuart, Victoria. "Alumna Ileana Ros-Lehtinen: Opening Doors in Congress and the Community." *FIU Magazine* (Spring 2000): n.p. *http://www.fiu.edu/orgs/fiumag.*

JACQUES ROUMAIN
(1907–1944)

Haitian Writer, Ethnologist, Political Leader, and Diplomat

Jacques Roumain has been identified by many as one of the leading Haitian intellectuals and politicians of the twentieth century. He was a passionate nationalist who advocated for the rights of the poor in his native land. As a political leader, he founded the Haitian Communist Party and was one of the early proponents of socialism and communism in the Caribbean. As an ethnologist, he was a pioneer who recognized the value of indigenous cultural forms in Haiti and in the rest of the black Caribbean. He was also a prolific writer who used his literary talents to spread his nationalist ideas as an advocate for the underprivileged, and to bring attention to the plight of Haiti and other Caribbean countries. Although he died young, his multiple contributions influenced the political philosophies of major literary and political figures in Haiti and the Caribbean.

Jean Baptiste Roumain, known mostly by the name of Jacques Roumain, was born in Port-au-Prince on June 4, 1907. Roumain grew up in Port-au-Prince's suburb of Bois Verna, known for its affluence and prestige, as a member of a distinguished Haitian family who had been active in Haitian politics and who owned substantial agricultural land. His maternal grandfather, Tancrede Auguste, was president of Haiti from 1912 to 1913. Roumain, who was considered to be part of Haiti's "mulatto elite," received his primary education at the Institution St. Louis the Gonzague in Port-au-Prince, a school run by French priests and friars. After completing primary school around 1920, his family sent him to Switzerland to provide him with a sophisticated education that was not available in Haiti at the time. During his stay in Switzerland he studied in Berne at the Institut Grünau, and after completing his secondary education there, he traveled through Europe and expanded his education by attending schools in France, Germany, and Spain. In Europe he was exposed to the leading European intellectuals, political philosophers, and literary figures of the time such as Karl Marx, Friederich Nietzsche, Arthur Schopenhauer, and Charles Darwin (Fowler 1980).

Roumain returned to Haiti in 1927 when he was 20 years old to find the island in a state of social, political, and economic turmoil that had been fermenting since the American occupation of the island in 1915. The oppressive economic and social policies imposed by the American government had led to great resentment among the populace. This, in turn, led to the emergence of a nationalist movement among Haitian intellectuals and local political leaders who wanted to liberate the island. Roumain immediately identified with the fight for Haitian liberation and became one of the most vocal spokespersons against the occupation. One of his first accomplishments was the foundation of the Haitian Youth Patriotic League, which organized Haitian youth against military intervention. With the assistance of many other intellectuals, he helped to establish *La Trouée,* and *La Revue Indigène* (Indigenous Review), two publications that provided a platform for criticizing the American occupation forces. In addition to using these publications for political activism, he also used them as literary journals to showcase and value Haitian native forms of popular culture and expression. His writings were also seen as a way to empower Haitian people and to reduce the inferiority complex fostered by the occupation forces and by the economic power elites (Nicholls 1996).

Throughout the occupation of Haiti, French elements within Haiti's Catholic church and some members of the Haitian power elite had been extremely supportive of American policies and their armed intervention. Roumain resented what he thought were reactionary and submissive postures among the power elite. After he published an article criticizing their position and the political stance of the Catholic Church, he was arrested held in prison for seven months.

When the Americans left Haiti in 1930 and a new government was chosen, Roumain was appointed minister of the interior. Because he was a revolutionary at heart, he realized that to accomplish change the existing economic order in Haiti had to be transformed radically. Growing frustrated with his position and with the status quo, he resigned and founded the Haitian Communist Party in 1934. His party, like many others established around the world at the time, was based on Karl Marx's economic and political theories. Historian David Nicholls has explained that Roumain:

> put emphasis upon the economic basis of Haiti's problems, seeing the history of the country in terms of class conflict based upon the ownership of wealth rather than as a conflict between colour groups. . . . The nationalism of the occupation period was, he claimed, a valid protest as far as it went; but its true foundations lay in the poverty and suffering of the masses. (1996, 173)

Unfortunately, the Catholic Church and the political regime at the time saw Roumain's ideals as a threat to their interests. He was charged with conspiracy to overthrow the government and sentenced to three years in prison. By the time he left prison in 1936, the government had forbidden the existence of the Communist Party. Because Roumain was still deeply committed to his communist ideals, he left the island and went into an extended exile that took him back to Europe and eventually to the United States, where he pursued studies in sociology and anthropology.

Roumain was finally allowed back to Haiti in 1941. Using his newly acquired knowledge of anthropology and his interest in Haiti's indigenous cultural forms, he established the Bureau of Ethnology of Haiti in 1941. The bureau was mostly concerned with researching, recording, and protecting the culture of the indigenous people of Haiti. As a member of the bureau, Roumain valued the native cultural forms of Haitians such as their voodoo religion, their music, their painting, and their uniquely Haitian Creole language. The bureau was entrusted with preserving any archeological sites or artifacts that would help to explain the relationships between, race, culture, class, and the development of Haitian civilization. At the time of its foundation, it was considered to be one of the Caribbean's premier archeology institutions in the Caribbean.

While Roumain's political and anthropological legacies are certainly significant, his literary works are undoubtedly his most important contribution to Haitian and Caribbean literature and arts. He wrote essays, poetry, short stories, and novels and was also a journalist. Among his most important works are *La proie et L'ombre* (The Prey and the Darkness), a collection of short stories published in 1930; *Les Fantoches* (The Puppets) and *La Montagne Ensorcelé* (The Enchanted Mountain), two novels published in 1931; and *Gouverneurs de la Rosée* (Masters of the Dew), a novel published in 1947.

Although he started to write poetry during his stay in Switzerland, most literary critics focus on his literary production once he returned to Haiti in 1927. As a writer, he was a master at translating those issues and concerns that also characterized the political and scholarly dimensions of his life. His works are filled with themes such as class differences and inequities, appreciation for life in the countryside, the values of Haitian peasants, the fatalism of the poor, the inhumanity of labor exploitation, colonialism, andracial oppression (Popkin 1999). He constructed these themes within fictional narratives created with sensitivity, eloquence, and beauty.

Another important dimension of Roumain's work is his contributions to the literary movement known as Afro-Caribbean literature or Negritude (see **Luis Palés Matos** and **Nicolás Guillén**). Perhaps better than any other writer representing this literary movement, and most likely because of his knowledge and understanding of anthropology, Roumain knew and valued the importance of the cultural manifestations of the lower classes in Haitian society. From their religious practices to their speech patterns, he masterfully integrated the cultural products of poor Haitians into his narratives and into his writing style. He also understood that there was a common bond between the social and political realities of all blacks across the Caribbean and the United States. He forged long-lasting friendships with Cuban writer Nicolás Guillén and American poet Langston Hughes. Hughes, for instance, translated his novel *Masters of the Dew* into English. His writings and ideas were so powerful that many other Caribbean thinkers and political ideologists, such as **Aimé Césaire**, **Jean-Bertrand Aristide**, and **Frantz Fanon** credit him as a source of inspiration in their work.

Toward the end of his life, and almost in a forced exile, Roumain took a position as Haiti's charge d'affaires in Mexico. He died at the age of 37 on August 18, 1944, in Port-au-Prince.—S.M.M.

References and Suggested Readings

Draper, James P., ed. "Jacques Roumain." In *Black Literature Criticism.* Detroit, MI: Gale 1992. 1627–1646.

Fowler, Carolyn. *A Knot in the Thread: The Life and Work of Jacques Roumain.* Washington, DC: Howard University Press, 1980.

Nicholls, David. *From Dessalines to Duvalier: Race, Colour and National Independence in Haiti.* New Brunswick, NJ: Rutgers University Press, 1996.

Pear, Nancy. "Jacques Roumain." In Hal May and Susan M. Trosky, eds., *Contemporary Authors.* Detroit, MI: Gale, 1989. Vol. 125: 391–393.

Popkin, Debra. "Jacques Roumain." In Steven R. Serafin, ed., *Encyclopedia of World Literature in the 20th Century.* Farmington Hills, MI: St. James Press, 1999. 713.

LUIS RAFAEL SÁNCHEZ
(1936–)

Puerto Rican Playwright, Essayist, Novelist, and Scholar

Luis Rafael Sánchez is one of today's most prominent and significant Puerto Rican writers. His ability to make social commentaries about Puerto Rican society and its people is unique. As a playwright, short story writer, essayist, novelist, literary critic, and scholar, Sánchez has made important contributions to Puerto Rican literature.

Sánchez, known to his family and friends as Wico, was born in Humacao, Puerto Rico, to a working class family on November 17, 1936. He completed his elementary school in Humacao, a coastal town located in the southeastern part of the island. His family relocated to San Juan when he was 12 years old, where he attended the Román Baldorioty Castro High School.

Sánchez's interest in drama can be traced to his days as a high school student. After moving to San Juan, he came in contact with Victoria Espinoza, now a professor of drama at the University of Puerto Rico, an accomplished scholar and theatrical director. As his teacher, Espinoza was one of the first to cultivate and nurture his interests in theater and drama. While still a young teenager, he founded an experimental theater group and acted in theatrical productions at the school (Meier 1997).

Sánchez went on to study drama at the University of Puerto Rico because he wanted to become an actor. While attending the drama department at the University of Puerto Rico (UPR), he won a prestigious competition to participate in a play sponsored by the National Mexican Youth Institute. His role in the play *El Boticario,* staged in Mexico, won him an award for best actor of the year in 1955. During his university years, Sánchez was a member of Tablado del Coquí, a theater company producing plays at the university, and also became a member of Comedieta Universitaria, a theater troupe that brought drama to students in Puerto Rican schools. He also began to write during his years as a college student. He entered a theatrical competition in 1958 with his play *La Espera* (The Waiting), which he wrote for a drama class. His next play, *Farsa del Amor Compradito* (Farce of Purchased Love), opened in 1960 and is considered his first serious theatrical composition. This play is now a Puerto Rican literature classic and has been staged in recent years by theatrical companies in Puerto Rico. He graduated from UPR in 1959 with a degree in drama.

After graduating, Sánchez began teaching at the University of Puerto Rico High School and also worked as an actor in the very popular soap operas broadcast on Puerto Rican radio. He obtained a master's degree in creative writing from Columbia University in 1963, and a doctoral degree in Spanish literature from the Complutence University in Madrid in 1973.

Sánchez wrote prolifically in the 1960s. Among his early plays were: *O casi el alma* (1964), *La hiel nuestra de cada día* (Our Daily Bile; 1961), and *La Pasión según Antigona Pérez* (Passion According to Antigone Pérez; 1968). He also published short stories such as "Sol 13, interior" (Sol 13, Inside; 1962) and "En cuerpo de camisa" (Wearing a Plain Shirt; 1966). These works illustrate the early development of his literary style and also reflect his first attempts at writing works with social and political commentaries about Puerto Rico.

Sánchez's masterpiece, however, is his novel *La guaracha del Macho Camacho* (Macho Camacho's Beat), which was first published in 1976 and has been translated into English. The novel, which takes place in a traffic jam in Puerto Rico, is an intense and somewhat bitter commentary on Puerto Rican society. The plot revolves around the metaphorical dimensions of a fictitious song that he entitles "La vida es una cosa fenomenal" (Life is a Phenomenal Thing). It does not rely on a linear or structural narrative leading to the development of a plot. Instead, the author uses a technique that presents a series of snapshots depicting a wide cast of characters and their behaviors. He illustrates the mindsets of Puerto Rican struggling with their chaotic lives. In the novel he uses what he has termed "la poética de lo soez" (the poetics of the uncultured), and "hablar en puertorriqueño" (speaking in Puerto Rican) to illustrate the complex social processes that transformed and characterized Puerto Rico during the past century (Barradas 1981, 1992). His writing style is characterized by his use of everyday Puerto Rican speech often relying on common or dirty expressions to elicit a reaction from the reader. In addition, it incorporates the blending of Spanish and English among Puerto Rican speakers.

"La guagua aérea" (The Air Bus; 1994) is one of Sánchez most popular and provocative short stories. As a gifted writer, Sánchez has been uniquely able to capture the experience of Puerto Rican migration to the United States. Anyone who has traveled between **Luis Muñoz Marín** International airport in San Juan, Puerto Rico, and John F. Kennedy Airport in New York is often likely to be amazed by the variety of peoples, behaviors, and experiences commonly witnessed during the flight. Picture a son carrying a huge cake for his mother living in Puerto Rico, which cannot be accommodated in any of the bulkhead compartments of the plane. Imagine a father bringing a live rooster to a relative who lives in New York, a rooster that eventually decides to start singing during the flight. Many passengers taking this journey often witness amazing human episodes that are hard to explain without knowing the sociological basis of the process of migration between the Puerto Rico and the United States. If you have taken that flight and read this story, you quickly realize the reasons why Sánchez has become one of the most important literary forces in the island of Puerto Rico and in Latin America. Among his important themes are the cultural inconsistencies of modern-day Puerto Rico, the existential tragicomedy of Puerto Ricans, and the complexities of Puerto Rican emigration to the United States. His writing conveys the fragmentation of Puerto Rican identity as a result of its colonial relationship with the United States (Figueroa 1994).

Sánchez often combines texts from Puerto Rican media and popular culture within his works. In fact, his use of the media suggests not only a criticism of mass media as a system that he sees as turning out an inferior cultural product, but it also underscores the ways in which radio, television, and the recording industry have been misused by the power elite in the United States and Puerto Rico.

His novel *La Importancia de Llamarse Daniel Santos* (The Importance of Having the Name Daniel Santos; 1988) uses the character of Daniel Santos, a popular Puerto Rican singer during the 1940s and 1950s, to comment on the relationship between Puerto Ricans and Latin Americans and on their popular culture. Sánchez implies that Latin American and Puerto Ricans channel and express their personal and collective chaos and frustrations into identification with popular culture and singers.

His latest book, *No llores por nosotros Puerto Rico* (Don't Cry for Us Puerto Rico) was published in 1997. Here he presents 17 essays dealing with a broad array of subjects and issues ranging from contemporary problems of Puerto Rican writers, his motivation for writing, Puerto Rican politics, and issues of race and prejudice on the island.

Sánchez currently has a joint teaching appointment at the University of Puerto Rico and at New York University. Many of his literary works are now mandatory reading for Puerto Rican students who wish to learn about the island's social and political problems. He has taught at many other prestigious universities in the United States and in Europe and has been awarded many prizes for his works. In 1992, Guakia, the Puerto Rican Culture and Arts Organization in Hartford, Connecticut, named their children's theater after him.—S.M.M.

References and Suggested Readings

Barradas Efraín. "Luis Rafael Sánchez." In Angel Flores, ed., *Spanish American Authors: The Twentieth Century*. New York: The H.W. Wilson Company, 1992. 795–798.

———. *Para leer en puertorriqueño: Acercamiento a la obra de Luis Rafael Sánchez*. Río Piedras, PR: Editorial Cultural, 1981.

Figueroa, Alvin Joaquín. "Luis Rafael Sánchez." In Willliam Luis and Anne González, eds., *Dictionary of Literary Biography*. Detroit, MI: Gale, 1994. 285–290.

Gunton, Susan, and Jean C. Stine, eds. "Luis Rafael Sánchez." *Contemporary Authors*. Vol. 23. Detroit, MI: Gale, 1983. 360.

Meier, Matt S. "Luis Rafael Sánchez." *Notable Latino Americans*. Westport, CT: Greenwood Press, 1997. 351–355.

Menton, Seymour. "*La impotancia de llamarse Daniel santos*: book review." *World Literature Today* 64.2 (Spring 1990): 281.

Sánchez, Luis Rafael. *La guaracha del Macho Camacho*. Buenos Aires: Ediciones del Norte, 1976.

———. *No llores por nosotros, Puerto Rico*. Hanover, NH: Ediciones del Norte, 1997.

Tardiff, Joseph, and L. Mpho Mabunda, eds. "Luis Rafael Sánchez." *Dictionary of Spanish Biography*. Detroit, MI: Gale, 1996. 801–802.

Watson-Espener, Maida. "Luis Rafael Sánchez." In Nicholas Kanellos, ed., *Biographical Dictionary of Hispanic Literature in the United States*. Wesport, CT: Greenwood Press, 1989. 267–274.

ARTURO SANDOVAL
(1949–)

Cuban Musician, Trumpet Player, Composer, and Arranger

Cuban trumpet player Arturo Sandoval is one of the most prominent figures in the jazz world and "may be the greatest trumpet player in the world" (Schudel 1993). Originally trained as a classical musician, Sandoval turned to jazz during the 1970s and attracted worldwide attention. He was a founding member of the renowned Grammy-winning musical group Irakere. In 1981 he began a career as a soloist, appearing in major venues around the world. His musical range and depth is evident in his extensive recording catalogue, which includes music for the Disney feature *Pocahontas*, rhythmic Cuban jam sessions or *descargas*, Latin jazz, and renditions of Mozart, Hummel, and other classical trumpet concertos. The turning point in his musical career came in 1977, when jazz great Dizzy Gillespie attended a Havana nightclub where Sandoval was performing. Neither one spoke the other's language, but they clicked musically and Sandoval became Gillespie's protégé and a featured member of his United Nations Orchestra. In 1990, while on tour in Europe, and with Gillespie at his side, he asked for political asylum at the American embassy in Rome. In the United States, his career went into full swing.

Arturo Sandoval was born in Artemisa, a small town on the outskirts of Havana, on November 6, 1949. Unlike many great musicians who come from musical families, nothing in his upbringing suggested that he would become a world-renowned musician. His father was a mechanic and his mother worked at home. He remembers wearing his first pair of shoes when he was 12 years old. Growing up in Artemisa, Sandoval was exposed almost exclusively to traditional and rhythmic Afro-Cuban music and played congas and cymbals in his high school band. He reminisced how "one day, I started to look at the trumpet with the corner of the eyes, I said, 'I think it is trumpet I want to play'" (Shudel 1993).

At 12 he began to play an old battered pocket cornet, a miniature version of the trumpet, and on the streets of his hometown participated in jam sessions of *son* and other traditional forms of Cuban music with much older and experienced musicians. Although his family's expected that he would study to become a doctor or lawyer, he was focused on the trumpet, and for a while learned what he could from borrowed methods books he painstakingly copied by hand as well as from the other musicians in Artemisa. He continued gaining experience in Cuban music as a member of a band until right before his 15th birthday, when he earned a scholarship to begin three years of serious classical trumpet studies at the School of Music and Arts in Havana. By the time he was 16, he was a member of Cuba's all-star national band. In 1971 he interrupted his trumpet studies to serve his three years of compulsory service in the Cuban armed forces. He played with the Cuban Orchestra of Modern Music and quickly became lead trumpet player. While in the military, he covertly listened to jazz on the Voice of the America radio station and received a punishment of four months in prison when he was caught listening to this music.

At 23, he became one of the founders of the legendary and exuberant Irakere band, known for its fusion of jazz, rock, and classical music with traditional Cuban rhythms. It was also then that he began to garner critical global recognition and reputation as an accomplished trumpet player. During Sandoval's tenure with Irakere, the group won many international awards, including a Grammy, and Sandoval's musical reputation was solidified.

The first jazz that Sandoval ever encountered was a bootleg copy of a Dizzy Gillespie record that he heard while learning to play trumpet. In 1977, when Dizzy Gillespie was visiting Cuba, young Sandoval was more than eager to acquiesce to Gillespie's desire to visit black Cuban neighborhoods where musicians customarily played Afro-Cuban rhythms on the streets. In his dilapidated Opel, Sandoval shepherded his idol through Havana to hear "real" Cuban music. That evening, Gillespie was amazed to see and hear his driver playing incredible jazz on his trumpet. Sandoval laughs when he remembers this experience, "Somehow, it never got across to him that I played trumpet, too. He thought I was a driver assigned to him. His jaw dropped!" (Gudbaur 1997). He quickly became a worldwide sensation after performing at the 1978 Newport Jazz Festival in New York City and was offered a recording contract with Columbia Records.

In 1981 he organized his own band and from 1982 to 1984 was voted Cuba's best instrumentalist. He continued his musical career playing Latin music and jazz, and on occasions traveled abroad as a guest artist with the BBC Symphony Orchestra in London and the Leningrad Symphony in Russia.

A jazz lover, Sandoval's artistic freedom became increasingly curtailed by the government, which disregarded jazz and monitored performances and recordings.

By the late 1980s, Sandoval had signed on as a member of Dizzy Gillespie's United Nations Orchestra, and was traveling to all parts of the world, except the United States, which was prohibited to him by the Cuban government. Although he was familiar with jazz by the time he met Gillespie, he credits "Diz," "his spiritual father," with teaching him the American jazz tradition and sharing stories of his experiences in the United States as a black musician in the Jim Crow days of the South.

In 1990 Sandoval was on a six-month tour of Europe with Gillespie's band and had persuaded the Cuban government to allow his wife and son to visit him there. Aware that his wife and son were given political asylum in the American embassy in London, Sandoval was escorted by Gillespie and armed Italian police to the American Embassy in Rome, where he defected. In Cuba, his music disappeared from shelves, and could not be played on the radio. Three years later, in 1993, his parents escaped the island on an overcrowded fishing boat and joined him in Miami.

After his defection he made his American debut album, *Flight to Freedom*. Since 1990, he has recorded an average of one CD per year. His *Danzon* CD won him a Grammy in 1994. Over the years, Arturo Sandoval has had 12 Grammy nominations and has been awarded four Grammys. He has also written and performed on several feature film soundtracks including *Havana* (1990), *The Mambo Kings* (1992), and *The Pérez Family* (1995). In 2001 he was the subject of the HBO film *For Love of Country: The Arturo Sandoval Story*, produced by actor Andy García, winner of an American Latino Media Award (ALMA), and nominated for four Emmys. He also won an Emmy for Outstanding Musical Composition for the film's score. On May 10, 2001, Sandoval was honored with an award from the American Society of Composers, Authors and Publishers (ASCAP) for his contributions to Latin music. His piano-playing debut, *My Passion for the Piano*, was released in 2002.

As a professor, he conducts music clinics for students and has lectured at the Conservatoire de Paris, the Tchaikovsky Conservatory in Russia, the University of California and at many institutions all over the world. Presently, he holds the rank of full professor at Florida International University, and offers over 50 performances and lectures per year in institutions of higher education across the United States.—G.C.

References and Suggested Readings

Gudbaur, Michael. "Arturo Sandoval's Flight to Freedom Has Led to the Trumpet He Calls, 'Perfect.'" Zumpano Studios, Inc., 1997. *http://www.gleblanc.com/gleblanc/bell97-2/bell97b2.html.*

Mandel, Howard. "Comes Out Swinging." *Downbeat Magazine* (October 1996): n.p. *http://www.arturosandoval.com/ComesOut1.asp.*

Schudel, Matt. "Song of Freedom." *Sunshine: The Magazine of South Florida*, November 7, 1993, n.p. *http://www.arturosandoval.com/Freedom2.asp.*

CRISTINA SARALEGUI
(1948–)

Cuban American Journalist, Talk Show Hostess, and Publisher

In a little over a decade, Cristina Saralegui has become one of the most recognized faces on Latino television. As hostess of the *Cristina Show*, and publisher of her own magazine, she is a powerful force in the Latino media and entertainment industries.

Cristina Saralegui was born in Havana, Cuba, on January 29, 1948, to Francisco and Cristina Saralegui. One of five children, she was raised among the wealthy Saralegui publishing family in the Miramar suburb of Havana. In most of her biographical interviews and profiles, she credits her paternal grandfather, Francisco "Pancho" Saralegui, for instilling in her an early love for journalism. He was one of Cuba's most influential figures in print journalism and owned the publications *Carteles, Vanidades,* and *Bohemia,* three of the most important Latin American magazines of the time. He was also known as "The King of Paper" in his native Cuba because he owned the largest paper-distribution conglomerate on the island.

In 1960, when Cristina was 12, the family fled Cuba to escape the new regime of **Fidel Castro**. Castro was in the process of nationalizing all the private businesses in Cuba and the family eventually lost all of its properties on the island. The Saraleguis settled in Miami, where her grandfather was able to continue printing some of his publications but eventually had to sell them to a Venezuelan media conglomerate. Through bad business decisions, Saralegui's father lost the family fortune and they became poor and resourceless.

The process of adapting to immigrant life in Miami was not easy for Saralegui, who had been born to great wealth and privilege. She has commented that shortly after her arrival she experienced racism from her classmates and had to learn to cope with American children calling her hateful names such as "spic" and telling her that she should go back to Cuba ("Cristina Saralegui" 1998).

Saralagui knew that she wanted to pursue a career in journalism, so she enrolled at the University of Miami and majored in communication and creative writing. As part of the undergraduate curriculum, she was required to complete a media internship. Using her family's connections, she interned at *Vanidades,* the magazine formerly owned by her family. After graduating from college, Saralegui was offered a job at the magazine and worked as a features editor from 1970 to 1973. This job allowed her to develop the basic journalistic skills that she would use throughout the rest of her professional life. She became a staff writer for *Cosmopolitan en Español* in 1973 and three years later, in 1976, she moved to the *Miami Herald*, where she became the entertainment editor.

After a brief interlude when she married, had a child, and stopped working, Cristina returned to *Cosmopolitan,* once again as a staff writer. At the same time,

to make ends meet, she also took on the responsibility of co-editing a small publication called
Intimidades. This was one of the first magazines
that offered mainstream sexual information,
education, and counseling to Latin American
women. Even though Saralegui tends to dis-
count the importance of that job, there is no
doubt that her experience editing a magazine
that broke new ground with sexually explicit
articles served her well in her eventual television career.

In 1979, Saralegui became the editor of *Cosmopolitan en Español,* which, like its English
counterpart, caters to the image of the Cosmo
girl. As editor of this popular magazine,
Cristina was able to effectively adapt and
translate this image for Latina women. She also
was seen as responsible for increasing the sales
and visibility of the magazine among the
Latino market and audience. Around the same

Cristina Saralegui. Photo by Sixto Nolasco.

time, Saralegui, who was in the process of divorcing her husband, met Marcos
Avila, the bassist of the pop music Miami Sound Machine. They fell in love and
married in 1984. Happy with her marriage and family, Saralegui continued with
her job at *Cosmopolitan* until 1989, when her husband quit the Miami Sound
Machine and persuaded his wife to leave *Cosmopolitan* and enter the television
business.

In 1989 Saralegui became the hostess of the *Cristina Show,* broadcast through the
Latino network Univision at a time when the talk show genre had become very
popular in the United States. Saralegui became the first person to capitalize on
the huge vacuum that existed in the Latino market for such programs. In the beginning of her show's run she followed a format similar to the ones successfully
established by the likes of Oprah Winfrey and Sally Jessy Raphael. Acting as a
hostess—but more importantly, as an agent provocateur—Saralegui brought scores
of controversial, spicy, daring, and provocative stories to the television sets of
million of Latino households in Latin America and the United States.

During the first seasons, Saralegui, like Puerto Rican American journalist
Geraldo Rivera, came across as a very blunt, coarse, and direct moderator who
would exploit any issue, no matter how delicate or painful, to keep her audiences
tuned in. Some audiences and media critics complained about the risqué nature
of her program's content. Despite these protests, it was that same controversial
nature of the shows that generated high ratings and huge viewing audiences. It
quickly became one of the top programs on Latino television and today is watched
by more than 100 million viewers daily. Saralegui herself takes credit for the fact
that she was able to popularize such a controversial genre in Latin American and,

above all, to challenge the common misconception that Latino guests will never talk about sensitive topics or their personal and family affairs.

With the passing of time, Saralegui has somewhat mellowed in her ways and has created a more mainstream television persona. While still direct and assertive, she has modified her themes and topics to better appeal to a more general audience. Her show is now perceived as being in the mainstream and her audiences continue to grow. The show won an Emmy in 1991 and has consistently been the number-one favorite of Latin American audiences. In 1992 she attempted to cross over to North American audiences and to present an English version of her show. While the program scored fairly well in the ratings, Saralegui didn't agree to CBS' proposed salary and eventually the show was cancelled.

Saralegui often comments that her early years as an immigrant in Miami when she struggled to make ends meet, left deep scars. She is in constant motion creating new business ventures and new work. It has been noted that

> [a]n old sense of having everything as a child, losing it, and then having to rebuild your life in a new country is what pushes Cuban Americans like Cristina to work so much and so hard. She calls herself "Miss 10 Jobs" because she hates the idea of earning all her income from one source. Too limiting, too dependent. She is always looking to expand, hence the professional juggling. (Anders 1996, C01)

In addition to her programs, since 1991 Saralegui has published *Cristina: La Revista,* a human interest and entertainment magazine with a circulation of 150,000 issues monthly (mostly in the Latino market). She also has a daily radio program with commentaries on the ABC International and Radio Unica radio networks. She is now a millionaire, and *The New York Times* has called her business "a multi media empire" (Navarro 1999, E1).

With the passing of the years, and despite the controversial topics that she often highlights in her shows, Cristina has managed to become one of the most influential figures in Spanish-speaking television markets both in the United States and in Latin America. Like Oprah Winfrey, Cristina is slowly shifting into programming carrying a more humane agenda.

A woman of direct demeanor but with a soft humane side, Cristina had the highest viewing audiences in the Latino world when she had her daily show. The show airs only weekly now. She has become involved in many charitable causes such as HIV/AIDS and has become a spokesperson for the American Foundation for AIDS Research, which has honored her for her work. In fact, she has become the leading HIV/AIDS activist within the Latino entertainment industry. She appeared on the cover of the first edition of the Spanish language version of *People* magazine, has been co-chair of the National Association of Hispanic Journalists, and in 1996 received a Golden Eagle Excellence Award. She is a restless media mogul who constantly ventures into new business deals in the Latino media. She has said: "I define myself as an adult woman who has struggled very hard to be able to determine the destiny of her own life. I think that one can achieve everything she sets out to, although not always at once. That is the secret" ("Cristina Saralegui" 1998, L9).—S.M.M.

References and Suggested Readings

Anders, Gigi. "She's Speaking their Language: Millions of Hispanics Are Tuning in to Talk Show Cristina." *The Washington Post*, January 18, 1996, C1.

"Cristina Saralegui: The Hispanic Oprah." *The Ottawa Citizen* (Ottawa, Canada), September 5, 1998, L9.

Navarro, Mireya. "Arts in America—With Latin Flair (and Flare); Diverse Audiences Present a Balancing Act for Talk Show Host." *The New York Times*, June 23, 1999, E1.

Perez Feria, Richard. "Talk Show Star Cristina Signs for Three More Years." *Chicago Sun Times*, June 19, 1996, 56.

ARTURO SCHOMBURG
(1874–1938)

Puerto Rican American Bibliophile, Curator, and Historian

Arturo Schomburg, a renowned bibliophile and scholar of African culture, was born in Puerto Rico. Early in his youth his interest in the history and heritage of blacks led him to assemble a collection of over 10,000 books and artifacts, ranging in time from the sixteenth to the twentieth century, documenting the African Diaspora. The collection, the Schomburg Center for Research in Black Culture, is housed in Harlem in the 135th Street branch of the New York City Public Library and is now considered the foremost collection in its field.

Arturo Alfonso Schomburg was born on January 24, 1874, to Mary Joseph from St. Croix, Virgin Islands, and Carlos Féderico Schomburg, a German-born businessman. Schomburg and his sister were raised in San Juan. He attended the Jesuit-run Escuela de Párvulos but dropped out before completing his studies. His lifelong preoccupation with the heritage of black people began at a very early age. He experienced racist attitudes in elementary school and in a mostly white literary club, where the common belief among the membership was that black people had no history. Schomburg spent some of his childhood years in the Virgin Islands with his grandparents. During a visit by Puerto Rican independence activist **Ramón Emeterio Betances** to St. Thomas, young Schomburg became aware of the revolutionary fight for independence occurring in Cuba and Puerto Rico. He left the Virgin Islands with the purpose of continuing his education in New York City, where he arrived in 1891 after a short time in San Juan working in a printing shop.

Arturo Schomburg. Courtesy of Raúl Medina Collection.

New York City in the 1890s was a center for Puerto Rican and Cuban immigrant workers and revolutionaries who founded social, cultural, and revolutionary organizations that raised money and published newspapers supporting the independence movement in both islands. Cuban revolutionary icon **José Martí** and Puerto Rican Emeterio Betances were among the speakers who influenced Schomburg during this time. In New York he attended Manhattan Central High School while holding a series of odd jobs that included elevator operator, bellhop, printer, and porter. He was a militant activist in the Puerto Rican and Cuban liberation movements and in 1892 he became a founding member of a political club Las Dos Antillas (The Two Islands). The club's activities included sending weapons and medical supplies to revolutionary groups in the Caribbean. By the time this group disbanded, his interest had shifted to focus on universal freedom for people of color.

His 1892 visit to New Orleans was a pivotal moment in his life: his "first significant contact with black Americans" (Sinette 1989, 22). By 1898, with the end of the Spanish-American War and the official disbanding of the Puerto Rican section from the Cuban Revolutionary Party, Schomburg concentrated almost exclusively on the struggle for the liberation of people of color in the United States and across the world.

By 1907 Schomburg was twice a widower and a father of five boys. Three sons from his first marriage were being reared in Virginia, and the youngest two in New Jersey. Traveling to visit his sons had further and more realistically revealed the country's system of segregation and oppression of American blacks. Moreover, his involvement in freemasonry with the El Sol de Cuba Lodge No. 38 was also an important factor in his involvement with the black community. He translated documents into English to encourage English-speaking blacks to join the lodge. His work in preserving the lodge's history by organizing their documents and photographs, as well as his rise to important leadership positions over 40 years, led to his election as master in 1911 and grand secretary of the Grand Lodge of the State of New York from 1918 to 1926. His bilingual skills in contacting other Masons in the Caribbean helped him become the first chairman of the lodge's Committee on Foreign Relations. By 1925 he had become a thirty-third-degree Mason.

During the early 1900s Schomburg met fellow Mason and outspoken journalist John Edward Bruce and joined his Men's Sunday Club, an organization that discussed world issues in the context of their relationship to black people. This group had established a library that focused on black history. In 1911 he and Bruce founded the Negro Society for Historical Research, an archival institute that compiled books and the study of African American history, as well publishing several works on black history. In addition to collecting books and artifacts by and about African people, Schomburg wrote essays promoting the study and research of black themes. In 1913 his essay "Racial Integrity: A Plea for the Establishment of a Chair of Negro History in Our Schools, Colleges, etc." was included in Nancy Cunard's book *Negro*. He became a documentarian of the accomplishments of blacks and Afro-Latinos such as Haitian liberator **Toussaint L'Ouverture** and Cuban general **Antonio Maceo**. In 1914 he was inducted into the American Negro Academy, which supported black history and was against the discriminatory Jim Crow laws and other forms of racism. He traveled widely around the United States searching out publications and materials that dealt with black culture and began to amass a collection of literature about the historical accomplishments of black people. In 1926, after his only trip to Europe, he returned with many contacts and sources that later help him augment his collection to include works from England, France, Spain, and other countries. In 1916 he published *A Bibliographical Checklist of American Negro Poetry* and "Economic Contribution by the Negro to America," published as an occasional paper by the American Negro Academy.

Self-described as an *Afroborinqueño* (Black Puerto Rican), Schomburg lived in Harlem for many years and was involved in the social and literary movement known as the Harlem Renaissance that later spread to other African-American communities in the United States. During his lifetime he corresponded and had friendships with a number of prominent individuals such as Henrietta Buckmaster and Langston Hughes. Educator and writer W.E.B. Du Bois edited many of Schomburg's writings. In May 1925 the New York Public Library established the Division of Negro History, Literature and Prints in its 135th Street Branch. Exactly one year later, the library purchased Schomburg's personal collection for $10,000, totaling over 10,000 books, manuscripts, artworks, photographs, and other memorabilia, and added it to this division. From 1932 until his death in 1938, Schomburg served as curator of the collection he had created. Today the center houses over 5 million items and provides international services and programs. A superb Web site makes many or their resources available to the public.—G.C.

References and Suggested Readings

Allen, James Egert. *The Legend of Arthur A. Schomburg.* Cambridge, MA: Danterr, 1975.

Kaiser, Ernest. "Arthur Schomburg." In Raymond W. Logan and Michael R. Winston, eds., *Dictionary of American Negro Biography.* New York: Norton, 1982. 546–548.

Knight, Robert. *Arthur 'Afroborinqueño' Schomburg.* Washington, DC: U.S. Commission on Civil Rights, 1995.

Mabunda Mabundo, M. "Arthur Schomburg." *Contemporary Black Biography.* Detroit, MI: Gale, 1995. Vol. 9: 208–212.

Schomburg, Arthur Alonso, and Nanette Dobrosky. *A Guide to the Microfilm Edition of the Arthur A. Schomburg Papers.* Bethesda, MD: University Publications of America, 1991.

Schomburg, Arthur Alonso, and Flor Piñeiro de Rivera. *Arthur Schomburg: A Puerto Rican's Quest for His Black Heritage.* San Juan, PR: Centro de Estudios Avanzados de Puerto Rico y el Caribe, 1989.

The Schomburg Center for Research in Black Culture. *http://www.nypl.org/research/sc/sc.html.*

Sinette, Elinor Des Verney. *Arthur Alonso Schomburg, Black Bibliophile and Collector.* Detroit, MI: Wayne State University Press, 1989.

SIMONE SCHWARZ-BART
(1938–)

Guadelopean Novelist and Playwright

Simone Schwarz-Bart is a French-language feminist writer who has been greatly influenced by the Negritude movement. Her writing celebrates and seeks to define the collective black experience and black cultural values in reaction to the dominant values of European colonialism. The women in her stories struggle with racism, superstition, poverty, and the violence of their male partners. Her work, which includes references to the history of Guadeloupe, has been heralded for depicting a strong image of women and for its use of the technique of magical realism.

Schwarz-Bart was born on January 8, 1938, in Charent-Maritime, France, and moved to Guadeloupe with her mother when she was three. In 1958, having completed her primary studies in Pointe-a-Pitre, Guadeloupe, Schwarz-Bart returned to France for her baccalaureate and studied at the University of Paris. In addition, she spent time traveling in Africa and Europe and studied at the universities of Dakar in Senegal and Lausanne in Switzerland. In France she met and married writer Andre Schwarz-Bart, with whom she has published two novels, *Un Plat de porc aux bananas vertes* (A Dish of Pork with Green Bananas; 1967) and *La Mulatresse Solitude,* translated in 1973 as *A Woman Named Solitude.* Both novels exemplify the suffering and spiritual struggle of black and mulatto peasant women in Guadeloupe.

Among her most recognized works is the first novel she wrote without the collaboration of her husband. The 1972 novel *Pluie et vent sur Télumée Miracle* has been translated to English as *The Bridge Beyond* and depicts its Guadeloupean women protagonists as courageous and self-reliant, surviving in the most extreme poverty and deprivation. It is believed that this work is a fictionalized biography commemorating Stéphanie Priccin, a woman who had fascinated Schwarz-Bart during her childhood in Guadeloupe. One critic touched on Schwartz-Bart's skill with French when he described the protagonist Télumée as speaking "a French that feels like the Creole of an illiterate but intelligent woman" (Murphy 1996, 922). Other reviews have hailed the work for the way it uplifts the human spirit and have credited her use of magical realism for giving the narrative a dream-like structure. The magazine *Elle* awarded *Pluie et vent sur Télumée Miracle* its literary prize, Gran Prix 1973 de Lectrices.

Another of her well-known novels, *Ti-Jean l'Horizon* (1971), translated in 1981 as *Between Two Worlds,* is considered one of Schwarz-Bart's best examples of magical realism, with its narrative based on a popular oral story passed down over generations. Its main character, Ti-Jean, can change at will from one gender to the other in this account that weaves the history of Guadeloupe with the island's myths.

In 1987 she published the play *Ton Beau Capitaine* (Your Handsome Captain), taken from a real-life situation of Haitian men who leave their country looking for work. Its protagonist, Wilnor Baptiste, goes to Guadeloupe as an agricultural worker while his wife remains in Haiti. It has been hailed as analogous to the condition of migrant workers as well as a representation of the forced removal of African natives who were brought to the Caribbean and the American continent as slaves.

Between 2001 and 2003 she published three volumes of a four-part series, *In Praise of Black Women.* In the first volume, *Ancient African Queens,* she presents historical accounts of black women from the African Diaspora—from prehistory to the nineteenth century—whose contributions have not been acknowledged in written history. The second book, *Heroines of the Slavery Era,* covers historical data from the fifteenth to the nineteenth century, and the third volume, *Modern African Women,* covers the nineteenth century to the present.—G.C.

References and Suggested Readings

Emory University English Department. "Simone Schwarz-Bart." December 21, 2000. *http://www.emory.edu/ENGLISH/Bahri/Schwarz.html.*

Garane, Jeanne. "A Politics of Location in Simone Schwarz-Bart's 'Bridge of Beyond.'" *College Literature* 22:1 (February 1995): 21–37.

Jones, Bridget. *Introduction to Simone Schwarz-Bart. The Bridge of Beyond.* London: Heinemann, 1982

Larrier, Renée. "Schwarz-Bart, Simone." In Steven Serafin, ed., *Encyclopedia of World Literature in the 20th Century.* Detriot, MI: St. James Press, 1999. 55–56.

Miller, Judity. "Caribbean Women Playwrights: Madness, Memory, But Not Melancholia." *Theatre Research International* 23:3 (Autumn 1998): 225–232.

Murphy, Bruce, ed. *Benét's Reader's Encyclopedia.* New York: HarperCollins, 1996.

Robinson, Lillian S., ed. "Simone Schwarz-Bart." *Modern Women Writers.* New York: Continuum, 1996. 85–90.

MARY JANE SEACOLE
(1805–1881)

Jamaican Nurse and Writer

Jamaican Mary Jane Seacole was a famous nurse who cared for the sick and wounded in the Caribbean, Central America, and Europe. She was one of two women who are considered heroes of the Crimean War (1854–1856) for their nursing work. Although the other nurse, Florence Nightingale, has been much acclaimed, Seacole has been relegated to obscurity, probably because she was black.

She was born Mary Jane Grant in Kingston, Jamaica, in May 1805 to a white Scottish army officer and a mulatto mother, a legal classification given by the British colonists to persons of mixed race. By standards of that time, her family was considered well off. Her mother was the daughter of freed slaves and was a well-known doctress and sutler. Seacole's education was twofold: she learned from formal schooling and from observing her doctress mother, who was particularly skilled in diagnosing tropical diseases and treating them with herbology. The knowledge derived from African herbal medicine combined with the practice of treating ailments and injuries, known as "Creole medical art," was born from the need for blacks in the plantations to look after each other because conventional medical training and care was denied them at the time. In her autobiography, Seacole wrote about watching her mother attend the soldiers who stayed in the boarding house she ran for military personnel and how this kindled her ambition to follow in her mother's footsteps. By the age of 12, when not practicing medicine on her dolls and pets, she assisted her mother in the treatment of patients.

Seacole traveled throughout her life and was confronted with issues of race many times. During the 1820s, she traveled twice to England and also visited the Bahamas, Haiti, and Cuba. In 1836 she met and married Edwin Horatio Seacole, with whom she traveled throughout Central America and the Caribbean. The brevity of the marriage and the trauma of Horatio's death made Seacole pledge she would never marry again.

In 1843, while living in London, she received news of her mother's death and returned to Jamaica to manage the boarding house. That same year, the property was burned to the ground in the great fire of Kingston. Seacole was able to rebuild an improved version and, following in her mother's steps, became nurse and doctress to the military personnel who stayed at her hotel. When a severe cholera epidemic hit Kingston in 1850, Mary Seacole treated hundreds of victims. A year later, she followed her bother to Panama, where a gold rush was underway. There she found herself in the midst of another cholera epidemic, and wanting to better understand the disease, she performed her first autopsy. Although it was an illegal procedure, she used it to teach herself much-needed surgical skills.

Seacole followed her brother Edward in his travels through Colombia and other Latin American countries, where she continued to treat victims of cholera, yellow fever, and other diseases. In 1853 she returned to Jamaica when professional medical personnel there recruited her during an outbreak of yellow fever. She continued to perform the medical skills that would make her famous, but her next challenge would occur thousands of miles away from home.

In 1854 Turkey, France, and Britain were waging war against Russia in Crimea. Soldiers were dying at a fast rate and nursing help was needed. Florence Nightingale was heading a group of nurses to assist in this effort. Seacole, who had traveled to London, applied, but the authorities refused to interview her or grant her permission to go. Undaunted by this rejection, she bankrolled her own mission and just as her mother had done, she established and opened the British Hotel, two miles from Balaclava, where she attended the wounded and served as sutler, selling provisions to the soldiers.

Unlike Nightingale's nurses, whose work was limited to attending the wounded in the hospital wards, Seacole worked out of improvised hospitals on the battlefields. She displayed courage on the frontline and "carefully picked her way through the mutilated bodies of men hit by round shot and shell, seeking out the wounded and dying whether enemy or ally" (Alexander and Dewjee 1984, 28).

After the Crimean War, Seacole found herself with a sizeable quantity of unusable and unsellable provisions. Back in London she was bankrupt, but by 1857 British soldiers and citizens had raised enough money to pay off her debts. That same year in London, 40,000 people joined a four-day celebration honoring Seacole, who by then was known as "The Crimean Heroine" and "The Mother of the Regiment."

Also in 1857, Seacole's autobiography became a best-seller. Although her writing is seemingly optimistic, the reader understands the difficulties she experienced as a black woman confronted by the racism of the times. On her return from the United States to Jamaica she was intimidated by white passengers who were unwilling to tolerate a black woman passenger. When she called the captain, he characterized the harassment as being "the custom of the country" and arranged for her fare to be refunded so that she could get off and take a British ship. The identity problems caused by the "mulatto" racial classification are reflected in some of the narrative in Seacole's autobiography.

Even though Seacole lived in a slave society for the first 30 years of her life, her writing seems to let the status quo of the time go unchallenged: "In her and in her writing are combined the conflicting elements of pride in her African ancestry and unquestioning acceptance of British culture and attitudes, which sometimes manifested itself in her use of pejorative European terminology" (Alexander and Dewjee 1984).

Between 1857 and 1881 Seacole spent her time traveling and working between London and Kingston. During that time she was honored with the Crimean Medal, the French Legion of Honour, and a medal from Turkey. She died in 1881 and was buried in the Kensal Rise General Cemetery in West London.—G.C.

References and Suggested Readings

Alexander, Ziggi, and Audrey Dewjee, eds. *Wonderful Adventures of Mrs. Seacole in Mand Lands*. Reprint. Bristol, England: Falling Wall Press, 1984.

Brooke, Elizabeth. *Women Healers: Portraits of Herbalists, Physicians, and Midwives*. Rochester, VT: Healing Arts Press, 1995.

Franck, Irene M., and David M. Brownstone. *Women's World: A Timeline of Women in History*. New York: HarperCollins, 1995.

SAMMY SOSA
(1968–)

Dominican Baseball Player and Philanthropist

Baseball great Sammy Sosa has broken many records and has used his fame and fortune to help the needy in his native Dominican Republic and the United States. In the world of professional baseball, Caribbean baseball players have been characterized by their extraordinary abilities. Quite often these players are also recognized because their path to success is filled with emotional tales of hardship and sacrifice. This is the case of Sammy Sosa. As a young Dominican teenager, he believed that a career in baseball was the only possible road to success. With determination and self-discipline, he undertook a long voyage that led him to his performance in the 1998 World Series, which equaled him with that of some of the biggest sport figures of all times. During the 1998 season, he scored 66 home runs, surpassing the records of Babe Ruth and Roger Maris. However, his accomplishments go beyond the baseball diamond and the ballpark. Having earned more than $60 million during his career, Sosa has selflessly helped his fellow Dominicans by establishing the Sammy Sosa Foundation.

Samuel Montero was born in the city of San Pedro de Macoris on November 12, 1968. His father, Juan Bautista Montero, was an agricultural worker, and his mother, Lucrecia, cooked and delivered meals for other agricultural workers in town. Sosa was one of seven children. His parents worked very hard to make ends meet and to provide for all of them. His father died of a brain aneurysm when Sosa was seven years old. His death created a major disruption for the family, which although poor had until then been able to sustain a stable life.

After his father's death, the family moved into a spare two-room apartment located in a building that once had been a hospital. His mother worked as a housemaid for a wealthy family to support her children. Sosa and his older brother had to go and find odd jobs to help the family. He washed cars and sold fruit and agricultural produce to help, but like many other children of San Pedro, he worked primarily as a shoeshine boy.

When Sosa was in eighth grade, he left school to work full-time as a shoeshine boy. Around that time, he became interested in baseball and started to play with local teams and friends in his neighborhood. Since he was not able to buy sports equipment, he used whatever household materials he could find, such as milk cartons and tree branches, to manufacture his "equipment." In the beginning, Sosa was not very good but worked hard to get better at the game. His older brother Luis, who had played baseball in a local league, watched him play and thought that he might have a natural ability for the game. Luis visited Hector Pesquera, a baseball trainer who had a small baseball league in San Pedro, and asked him to take his brother under his wing. He paid the coach 67 cents per week to give Sosa extra lessons. Around the same time, Sosa met Bill Chase, an American businessman in the city who was very impressed by Sosa's work ethic as a shoeshine boy. Sosa followed him everywhere and asked to shine his shoes. When he saw that the boy was responsible and was taking baseball seriously, he brought Sammy a baseball glove during one of his trips to the United States. This kind act started a friendship that has lasted a lifetime.

By the time Sammy was 16, he changed his last name to Sosa, the family surname of the man his mother had married. He practiced constantly to improve his batting and pitching skills. His game steadily improved and, like many other Dominican boys, he dreamed of being "discovered" by one of the American scouts who visited the island searching for tal-

Sammy Sosa. © MLB Photos.

ent. This finally happened in 1985 when Amado Dinzey, a scout for the Texas Rangers Organization, saw Sosa play. He called Omar Minaya, a coach for the Ranger's farm league system, and asked him to fly to the Dominican Republic to observe and interview Sosa. Because there were several other scouts already aware of Sosa's ability, Minaya arranged for Sosa to travel to Puerto Plata for a tryout because Minaya didn't want to jeopardize losing Sosa to other scouts. After playing ball with him for more than three hours, Minaya offered to sign Sosa and give him a $3,000 bonus, a standard sum for entry-level players at the time. Sammy asked him for $4,000 and they agreed on $3,500. When he received the money, he gave most of it to his mother and kept a small amount to buy himself a bicycle.

After his signing, and with little English, Sosa went to the United States in 1986, where the Texas Rangers Organization assigned him to several of their teams. From 1986 to 1988 Sammy played with several teams within the farm system and was consistently promoted from team to team. He played in Sarasota for the Gulf Coast Rookie League, in Gastonia, South Carolina, with the Atlantic League, and in Port Charlotte, Florida, with the South Atlantic League. Although he generally batted well, he was an impulsive, over-ambitious, and self-centered player who made too many errors. Coaches saw him as a player full of promise but as someone who was having a difficult time conforming to the order and structure of U.S. baseball. During the 1989 season Sosa was transferred to Tulsa, where he played with the Rangers' Double-A team. He had such a good record during the beginning of the season that they transferred him to their major league team, the Texas Rangers.

Sosa played his first professional major league game on June 16, 1989. He played for 25 games, had 85 batting opportunities, and averaged .238. The owners, including future president George W. Bush, returned him to the minor leagues after deciding that he wasn't ready to be in the major leagues. Sosa was extremely disappointed at the transfer but had no choice other than to go back to the Triple-A league. By the end of the season the Rangers Organization traded him to the Chicago White Sox. The White Sox decided not to incorporate him to their major league team, and sent him instead to their Triple-A team in Vancouver. The manager promised him that if he performed well, he would promote him to the majors the next year. His performance in Vancouver during the first 13 games of the season was so outstanding that the White Sox sent him to the major leagues immediately.

In 1990 Sosa became a right fielder for the Chicago White Sox. Unfortunately, his performance was just average. His batting average at the end of the season was. 233. Sosa hit 15 home runs and 26 doubles, but also struck out 150 times and made 13 errors. He was unfocused and seemed to lack self-control. His supporters grew concerned that he was not learning the American playing style fast enough, and again he was seen as an immature player who lacked discipline. During the 1991 season Sosa retained his position in the lineup but his performance was so mediocre that he was returned him to Vancouver to play with the Triple-A team. He became depressed and continued to play poorly.

In spring 1992 the Sox traded Sosa to their neighbors, the Chicago Cubs. The trade proved to be advantageous for Sosa, as he was given the position of starting right fielder in the lineup. Although he had some health problems and injuries during his first season with the Cubs, his game improved. The Cubs coached him and he started to mature and acquired patience. They taught him to pace and time his hits. Sosa became more analytical and helped the Cubs substantially during the season. He had an excellent season in 1993 and was the first player in the Cubs' history to hit more than 30 home runs and steal more than 30 bases in a single season (Duncan 1998). In 1994 he also had an excellent season and by the end of the season the Cubs signed him up for $4 million for one year. He was equally successful in 1995 and was twice named the National League Player of the Week, won his first Silver Slugger Award, and attended the All-Star Game. During the 1996 and 1997 seasons, he became the Cubs' star outfielder and continued breaking records and receiving awards.

However, Sosa's claim to fame came during the 1998 baseball season. The entire nation turned its attention to a sports duel between Sammy Sosa and Mark McGuire of the St. Louis Cardinals. The two had performed so well during the season that both were close to breaking the record of 61 home runs in one season established by Roger Maris in 1961. Although McGuire was eventually the first to break the record, his triumph only lasted 116 hours because Sosa matched him. They ended the season with Sammy scoring 66 home runs and McGuire 70. In 1998 he was selected as National League's Most Valued Player; received the **Roberto Clemente** Award, one of the most significant distinctions of the major leagues; and his performance during the season helped the Cubs reach the playoffs.

To date, he has earned more than $60 million. Nevertheless, he still says that playing and helping his people are the most important things that the game allows him to do. He established the Sammy Sosa Foundation, which gives money to needy people in the Dominican Republic and to youth around the Chicago area. The foundation, headed by his long-time friend and American mentor Bill Chase, is responsible for undertaking major charitable projects in his native San Pedro de Macorí (Duncan 1998, 95).—S.M.M.

References and Suggested Readings

Christopher, Matt. *At the Plate with Sammy Sosa.* Boston: Little, Brown, and Company, 1998.
Duncan, P.J. *Sosa! Baseball's Home Run Hero.* New York: Simon and Schuster, 1998.
Gutman, Bill. *Sammy Sosa: Home Run Hero!* New York: Pocket Books, 1998.
Pietruzsa, David, ed. "Sammy Sosa." *The Encyclopedia of American Baseball.* Kingston, NY: Total Sports Illustrated, 2001. 1060.

TEÓFILO STEVENSON
(1952–)

Cuban Boxer

Cuban boxer Teófilo Stevenson is one of post-revolutionary Cuba's greatest sports figures and is considered by many to be the greatest amateur heavyweight boxer of all time. A three-time Olympic gold medal winner and two-time world heavyweight boxing champion, Stevenson dominated world amateur heavyweight boxing for over a decade and attained demi-god status among Cuban fans. Many times during his career he was offered millions of dollars to defect and have a professional career that would have guaranteed him millions in purses and endorsements. There was almost unanimous consensus among boxing professionals that Stevenson was the most impressive Olympic boxer since Muhammed Ali. Stevenson has always said that leaving Cuba was inconceivable to him: "I owe everything to the revolution" (O'Connor 1995, 7H). A supporter of **Fidel Castro** and the Cuban revolution, in his twenties Stevenson was president of Havana's Communist Youth Group, and for over a decade represented his district of Las Tunas in Cuba's National Assembly.

Teófilo Stevenson Lawrens was born on March 29, 1952, in Delicias–Puerto Madre, Cuba, and spent his early years on the island of Jamaica. His parents, who were agricultural workers, moved to Cuba in the late 1950s and settled in the southern community of Antonio Guiteras, where they worked for the Central Delicias sugar mill. His father, who had been raised in St. Vincent, and his Jamaican mother spoke English at home and their five children learned their first words of Spanish outside the home, interacting with neighborhood children. Stevenson was always tall for his age and once in Cuba, participated in government-run school sports programs. However, it was a Soviet track coach who discovered the tall, lanky Stevenson playing basketball in the mid-1960s. Observing his long, strong arms, he suggested to the Cubans that Stevenson be placed in the school's boxing program. By the time Stevenson was 14, he was participating in his first boxing tournament. Although he was still a few inches short of his adult 6′5″ frame, he was very skinny, weighing 137 pounds. However, from the very beginning he seemed to move around the ring with great ease. During his late teens, he developed his trademark right-hand punch, which he used very successfully against all of his opponents in his first Olympics in 1972, where he won his first gold medal.

In 1976 Stevenson arrived at the Montreal Olympics with the Amateur World Heavyweight and the Pan American Games boxing titles under his belt. At Montreal, he defeated his first three opponents. For those first three bouts, he had spent a total of 7 minutes and 22 seconds in the ring. Towering over most of his opponents, he would wait until they tired of evading his punches and then brought out his trademark right-hand punch, knocking them out in the third and final round of the bouts to take home his second Olympic gold medal. In 1980 he laced up his gloves once again for the Moscow Olympics and in the final round defeated his Russian opponent and became the first boxer to win three Olympic golds in one division. He was expected to box in the 1984 Olympics in Los Angeles, but Cuba was one of the many countries to boycott the games that year. By 1987, at 35 years old and with a 1983 defeat to an American boxer at the North American Championships, many had dismissed him. However, that year at the World Championships held in Reno, Nevada, Stevenson won all four initial bouts and made it to the finals, where his punch—described by a sportswriter as a "shotgun right hand"—knocked out his opponent twice and on two occasions sent him staggering to the ropes until the referee finally stopped the fight. At 35, Stevenson had once again won the World Championship Heavyweight amateur boxing title and declared "the king of amateur boxing" (Gustkey 1987, 7).

In socialist Cuba, Stevenson has been well rewarded for the glory he has brought to the island. On retiring in 1986 Stevenson became an advisor to Cuba's National Institute for Sports, Physical Education and Recreation, and has served as vice-president of Cuba's boxing federation. Stevenson enjoys legendary status on the island, as well as a personal relationship with Fidel Castro, at whose side he is often found trading mock punches for spectators at sports matches and awards ceremonies.—G.C.

References and Suggested Readings

Gustkey, Earl. "The Year of the Old Sport." *The Times Mirror,* January 1, 1987, Part 3A, p. 7.
Iezzi, B. "Teófilo Stevenson: The Best Interview 50 Bucks and a Bottle of Rum Could Buy." *Ring* 77:12 (December 1998): 22–65, 60–62.

O'Connor, Anne-Marie. "The World Comes to Atlanta: The Fighters; Cuba's Best Boxers Remain Loyal, Forgo Riches." *The Atlanta Constitution*, October 29, 1995, 7H.

Robinson, Eugene. "The Cuban Ali; Boxing Legend Teófilo Stevenson Spurned Millions for the Island He Loves." *The Washington Post,* June 10, 2001, W30.

Talese, Gay. "Boxing Fidel." *Esquire* 126:3 (September 1996): 138.

PIERRE TOUSSAINT
(1766–1853)

Former Haitian Slave and Entrepreneur

Pierre Toussaint, a Haitian slave who migrated to New York City with his slave owners toward the late 1700s, overcame incredible odds and became the most sought-after hairdresser of his time by the social elite of the city. A devout Catholic, his work helping to free Haitian slaves, supporting orphans, and assisting the poor earned him a tomb in St. Patrick's Cathedral, one of the most prestigious places of worship in America. In 1996 Pope John Paul, in the first step toward sainthood in the Roman Catholic Church, proclaimed him "venerable." He might be the first black American and businessman ever to be declared a saint.

Pierre Toussaint was born on June 27, 1766, to slaves who were devout Catholics. The Toussaints belonged to the owners of a sugar plantation in Haiti, then a French colony known as St. Domingue. During the late 1700s the French Revolution touched off the beginning of slave insurrections that made Haiti the first independent black nation in the Western world. Toussaint's master, Jean Jacques Bérard, accompanied by his wife and five of his slaves—including Toussaint and his sister Rosalie—fled to New York City. Described as a "kind and sensitive" master, Bérard, on the advice of his wife Marie, apprenticed Toussaint to a hairdresser with the intention of giving him a way to make a living.

Because French was popular in New York at the time, the young hairdresser became an immediate success among the city's elite. In 1790 New York was the nation's capital and the site for George Washington's first inaugural ball. "Monsieur Pierre," then in his early twenties, was sought after by many of the women attending the festivities, who wanted Toussaint to be the one to fashion their hair in the stylish bouffant of the time. It has been speculated that Martha Washington herself was one of Toussaint's clients.

Meanwhile, Bérard had fallen on hard times and returned to Haiti with the hope of rescuing the remains of his investments. Toussaint, still legally a slave, was left with the responsibility of guarding Marie during her husband's absence. Bérard died of pleurisy while in Haiti, shortly after learning that all the family's assets had been lost during the insurrection. Although he had financial prosperity and independence, Toussaint refused to abandon the widow Bérard, and remained legally a slave for the next 20 years. By this time he was earning enough money to be able to secretly support her socialite lifestyle. He took over the responsibilities of the home, paying bills as well as sending invitations for and sponsoring invitations to her parties. Routinely, Toussaint rescued black orphan boys from the city streets and gave them a place to stay until he found them employment, usually with one of the wealthy women whose hair he styled. His greatest wishes came true when he was able to buy freedom for his sister Rosalie and for Juliette, the woman he eventually married. On her deathbed in 1807, Marie Bérard made all the legal arrangements for Toussaint's freedom.

In 1811, at the age of 45, Pierre married Juliette. They did not have any children, but adopted their niece Euphémie after Rosalie died from tuberculosis. With Juliette, he embarked on a life of charity to friends, strangers, the poor, and the sick. He founded one of New York's first orphanages and raised money for the original St. Patrick's Cathedral in the Wall Street area of Manhattan. Interestingly, he and his wife were once refused admittance to the cathedral because of the color of their skin. His biographers note that he never lost his temper and simply walked away thanking God "that Euphémie would never know his humiliation" (Tarry 1971). Euphémie died in 1829 of the same disease that had killed her mother. He grieved this loss for a long time and sought comfort by intensifying his charitable works in the community. By the time of his death in 1853, he was a known personality within the community and his leadership and generosity were celebrated in obituaries in much of the New York press.

Pierre Toussaint overcame incredible odds to become one of America's first rich, black professionals. In 1996, the Catholic Church declared him "venerable"—the first step in the realization of sainthood. Church biographies describe him an "ordinary man doing extraordinary things through the grace of God" and recount how he used the money he earned to buy freedom for many Haitian slaves. They tell how he risked his life during various plagues in New York City, where he went through barricades to nurse people afflicted with yellow fever, cholera, and other infectious diseases.

For some, his life is not without controversy. There are black Catholics who see him as having been too servile—"a Catholic Uncle Tom"—for not rebelling against slavery and for his devotion to Bérard at the expense of his own freedom. His advocates, however, see him as decent, pious, and extraordinarily magnanimous. His business achievements and personal piety are an interesting combination of traits, and are uncommon in the Catholic tradition of saint canonization. In the 1950s Cardinal Terence Cooke formed the Pierre Toussaint Guild to champion Toussaint's canonization.

After Cardinal Cooke's death, the late Cardinal John O'Connor, who was entombed in St. Patrick's Cathedral near Pierre Toussaint in May 2000, was one of the main advocates for Toussaint's sainthood. The next step toward being declared a saint is "beatification," which requires the verification of a miracle. Presently, the Vatican is considering the case of a 5-year-old boy whose scoliosis (curvature of the spine) improved significantly after his family prayed to Toussaint. Strengthening the case was the surgeon's declaration that the improvement could not be medically explained. It will take years of documentation to satisfy the Catholic Church's Congregation for the Causes of Saints of the validity of this case, but many believe that this is not a question of if, but of when Pierre Toussaint will become the first African-American saint.—G.C.

References and Suggested Readings

Broadway, Bill. "Family Takes Boy's Healing on Faith; Declaration of Miracle Might Hasten Canonization of Haitian Immigrant." *The Washington Post*, May 27, 2000, B09.
———. "Shades of Sainthood: Americans Near Canonization; Black Catholics Hope for One of Their Own." *The Washington Post*, February 12, 2000, B09.
Jones, Arthur. "Pierre Toussaint, a Slave, Society Hairdresser, Philanthropist, May Become Nation's First Black Saint." *National Catholic Reporter*, August 25, 2000. *http://www.nchr.org/resources/pierre_toussaint.htm*.
Renner, Gerald. "The Slave Who Could Be Saint." *The Hartford Courant*, February 19, 2000, D1.
Sheehan, Arthur. *Pierre Toussaint: A Catholic Gentleman of Old New York, 1766–1853*. New York: The Candle Press, 1953.
Tarry, Ellen. *The Other Toussaint: A Modern Biography of Pierre Toussaint, a Post-Revolutionary Black*. Boston: Daughters of St. Paul, 1971.

TOUSSAINT L'OUVERTURE
(1743–1803)

Haitian Patriot and Military Leader

Haitian general François Dominique Toussaint L'Ouverture led the only successful slave revolution in history. Inspired by the French Revolution, he led his troops to victory over British and Spanish armies and over the French political establishment in what was then St. Domingue, known today as Haiti. An awe-inspiring leader, he emancipated all slaves and led Haiti to become the first independent black nation in the new world.

Toussaint L'Ouverture was a slave during the first three decades of his life. Very little is known about his childhood. His father, Gaou-Guinou, had been captured in West Africa and brought to the American continent as a slave to the Count de Breda, who was considered somewhat more humane than other slave-owners. Gaou-Guinou was an educated slave and a member of the Catholic Church who married and had eight children, the eldest of whom was François Dominique Toussaint. Toussaint received a rudimentary education from a Jesuit missionary, but continued to speak in his father's native African tongue within the family. He read the works of Julius Caesar and other military leaders, and is believed to have developed his skill in strategic and tactical military planning at this time. As a slave, he worked his way from shepherd to coachman and later steward. During these early years he witnessed all the misery of slavery, including the beating and separation of families. As he grew older he became more distressed about the incompatibility that existed between Catholic teaching and the institution of slavery. Legally freed by his owner in 1777, he began his quest to liberate Haiti's slaves.

The first slave revolt in 1791 was the beginning of the Haitian Revolution, and Touissant joined the black forces that were rebelling against the plantation owners. Rising rapidly in power, in 1793 he added L'Ouverture, the French word for "the opening," to his name. That year he also organized his own group of slaves and trained them in guerrilla warfare tactics. Touissant and his army were victorious against the French and their Spanish allies. He pledged his support to France, which had pledged to end slavery, and in 1794, with the "Declaration of the Rights of Man" as its foundation, France abolished slavery in its colonies, declaring Toussaint commander-in-chief of St. Domingue.

His next move was to assure that St. Domingue would continue to be an autonomous state. However, racial animosity with mulattoes from the south led by André Rigaud resulted in violent clashes between these two groups. Toussaint wrote to American president John Adams requesting assistance. In return, Touissant pledged that he would deny the French use of the island as a base for their operations in North America. Adams sent off arms and ships to aid the black forces, which in late 1800 succeeded in defeating Rigaud's forces. In 1801 Toussaint abolished slavery and appointed himself governor general of the entire island of Hispaniola, which included what is now the Dominican Republic as well as St. Domingue.

In 1802 General Charles Leclerc was sent to the island by his brother-in-law, Napoléon Bonaparte, to restore French rule and slavery to St. Domingue. Due to the aid sent by President Adams, Leclerc's army was unable to succeed, but Toussaint was betrayed by two of his generals and taken prisoner. He died in Fort-de-Joux, a prison in the French Alps in 1803. His legacy, however, was established. He is considered a Haitian patriot, martyr, and a symbol of freedom, whose life is celebrated in William Wordsworth's sonnet "To Toussaint L'Ouverture."

Toussaint's dream and his legacy became a reality in 1804, when St. Domingue's name was changed to Haiti—meaning "higher place"—and achieved its independence.—G.C.

References and Suggested Readings

Beard, Rev. John R. *The Life of Toussaint L'Ouverture: The Negro Patriot of Haiti.* Westport, CT: Greenwood Press, 1970.

Bell, Madison Smartt. *Master of the Cross Roads.* New York: Pantheon Books, 2000.

Hannon, James Jess. *The Black Napoleon: Toussaint L'Ouverture Liberator of Haiti.* First Books Library, 2000.

James, Cyril Lionel Robert. *The Black Jacobins: Toussaint L'Ouverture and the San Domingo Revolution*. New York: Vintage Books, 1989.

"Toussaint-Louverture." *Encyclopædia Britannica*. Chicago: Encyclopedia Britannica, 2002. Vol. 11: 874.

RAFAEL TUFIÑO
(1922–)

Puerto Rican Artist

Rafael Tufiño is considered one of Puerto Rico's greatest living artists. One of the leading members of the Puerto Rican artistic school known as the "Generation of the Fifties," his work includes paintings, printmaking, posters, drawings and illustrations that capture the essence of the island's culture and landscape. Tufiño has exhibited worldwide and his work can be found in the permanent collections of major institutions such as the Museum of Modern Art, the Metropolitan Museum of Art, the Library of Congress, and the most important cultural institutions on the island such as the Institute of Puerto Rican Culture and the renowned Ponce Museum of Art.

Rafael Tufiño Figueroa was born in Brooklyn, New York, on October 30, 1922, in a household with strong Puerto Rican ties. References to the island taken from magazines and newspapers could be found clipped to walls at home and would later become the themes of his art. Tufiño lived and played within proximity of the Brooklyn Bridge, which he immortalized in one of his paintings. He first visited Puerto Rico at the age of five when he and his mother, Gregoria "Goyita" Figueroa, spent a year with his maternal grandmother who lived in one of San Juan's poorest neighborhoods, La Perla. In 1932 his family permanently returned to Puerto Rico, where he completed his elementary education at the Brumbaugh School. In junior high school he distinguished himself by his artistic ability.

In 1937 he worked at the Art Sign Shop in the Puerta de Tierra neighborhood, where he was a sign maker and letter painter, and where part of his work included creating allegorical floats for carnival celebrations. Spanish painter Alejandro Sánchez Felipe who visited the sign shop was impressed with his sketches and invited him to art class. This led to his first series of paintings and prints that included *Sevillana* (1939), a number of prints that depicted urban life in San Juan *Desde mi estudio* (From My Studio; 1940) and a painting named after his neighborhood, *Puerta de Tierra* (1940). By the time he was 20, he had his first solo exhibit at the Puerto Rican Athenaeum. During that time he also produced an ink painting, *La Perla*, the neighborhood where he first lived with his mother and grandmother, a theme that was repeated in other works during the 1940s and 1950s.

In 1943 Tufiño was drafted by the U.S. Army and sent to Panama. During the war years, his drawings depicted daily life in the military: *Soldado I* and *Soldado II* (Soldier I and II; 1944) and *De vez en cuando* (Once in a While). After the war, he benefited from the G. I. Bill and enrolled in the Academia de San Carlos in Mexico City, where he stayed until 1949. Tufiño painted in oil a series of Indian women—*Lucha, Concha* and *La indiecita*—that characterize his sense of realism, intensity, and sobriety in the characters of his portraits. During this time he also produced his first etchings and linographs.

By 1950 he had returned to Puerto Rico and to his sign shop, the Art Sign. While making signs for the Department of Instruction's Division for the Community he was invited to illustrate a series of books that were being published by that division. From 1951 to 1963 he worked as a poster designer and book illustrator for programs targeted at the rural adult population of the island. This experience nurtured his ability to define and present Puerto Rican culture and everyday life through his art.

By the 1950s Tufiño's art was beginning to get recognized. He won awards for various works of art, and in 1954 the Library of Congress purchased his linograph *Goyita y su nieto,* a depiction of his mother with her grandson. His mother was a subject in a number of his paintings and was immortalized in what is considered his masterpiece *Goyita* (1953), described as one of the most extraordinary paintings in Puerto Rican art; the painting is now in the permanent collection of the Puerto Rican Institute of Culture. In addition, he produced his first individual portfolio, *El café* (1953–1954), made up of seven linographs on the theme of rural life.

After 13 years at the Division for the Community, six of them as its director, Tufiño joined the Institute of Puerto Rican Culture, where he produced a great number of posters for plays, exhibition, fairs, contests, concerts, and many of the institute's other activities. During this time he continued to exhibit on and off of the island. In 1964 he reached a milestone when the Metropolitan Museum of Art purchased the print *La ceiba centenaria* (1963), a depiction of the island's oldest tree. That same year, the Museum of Modern Art acquired one of his many self-portraits, *Tefo* (1963).

In a competition sponsored by the Puerto Rico Chess Federation in 1969, Tufiño designed chess pieces depicting characters and aspects of the island's culture. The figure of the king is represented by one of the three Magi; the queen is represented by Puerto Rico's patron saint, the Virgin of Monserrate; and the pawns were carvings of the Mystical Lamb that appears in the official seal of the island.

In 1970 Tufiño returned to New York City, where he resided until 1974. During this time, he was a founding member of the Taller Boricua, a visual arts organization in Spanish Harlem that offers studio space to artists and art classes to area youth. When he returned to Puerto Rico in 1974, he was greeted with a tribute in his honor—the third Bienal de San Juan del Grabado Latinoamericano y del Caribe—an exhibition of over 150 posters, etchings, woodcuts, and Christmas cards from Latin American. That year began a 17-year period when Tufiño did not hold individual exhibitions. For two years he was unable to paint because of deteriorating eyesight. Although he continued to produce art, he had lost some of his visual skills. He now continues to produce works of art, although medical conditions and age have slowed him down somewhat.

In 1986 filmmaker Ramón Almodóvar made a documentary film about his life titled *Rafael Tufiño: pintor del pueblo* (Rafael Tufiño: Painter of the People). He was elected Resident Artist of San Juan for the year 1990, and in 1993 his masterwork, *Goyita*, was exhibited in the Puerto Rican pavilion of the Expo in Seville, Spain. The National Puerto Rican Coalition of New York honored him with its Life Achievement Award in 1996 and New York Mayor Rudolph Giuliani presented him with the Crystal Apple Award in 1999.

In 2001 the Museum of Puerto Rican Art held a retrospective of Tufiño's work. Heralded as perhaps the best and broadest representation of his work, it included illustrations, posters, etchings, and paintings.—G.C.

References and Suggested Readings

Corretjer, Juan Antonio. *Yerba bruja: Portada de Rafael Tufiño.* Guaynabo, PR: N.p., 1957.

Fernández, Ronald, Serafin Méndez-Méndez, and Gail Cueto. *Puerto Rico Past and Present: An Encyclopedia.* Westport, CT: Greenwood Press, 1998. 327.

Gaya-Nuño, Juan Antonio. *La pintura puertorriqueña.* Soria, PR: Centro de estudios sorianos, 1984.

Rafael Tufiño: Pintor del Pueblo (exhibit catalogue). San Juan: Museo de Arte de Puerto Rico, 2001.

Reyes, Edwin. *Tufiño: una vida para el arte, un arte para la vida* (VHS documentary). San Juan, PR: Creativos Associados, 1996.

CICELY TYSON
(1933–)

Nevian Actress and Activist

Cicely Tyson, an actress of Nevian heritage with a career extending over 40 years, has been recognized with numerous awards in her field. She is committed to portraying strong women and was nominated for an Oscar in 1972 for her performance in *Sounder.* Her more notable performances include roles in *The Heart Is a Lonely Hunter* (1968), *Bustin' Loose* (1981), *The River Niger* (1976), and *Fried Green Tomatoes* (1991), in a catalogue of over 50 films. On television, she has starred a wide range of starring roles such as *The Autobiography of Miss Jane Pittman* (1974), *Roots* (1977), *The Women of Brewster Place* (1989), *Blessed Assurance* (1997), and *The Rosa Parks Story* (2002). She is a civil rights advocate admired for her dedication to her community as well as to her craft. In 1976, along with Arthur Mitchel, she founded the internationally acclaimed Dance Theater of Harlem.

Tyson is the daughter of devoutly religious parents who emigrated from the island of Nevis. Her father, William, a carpenter and painter, periodically sold fruits and vegetables from a stand in order to make ends meet. The youngest of three children, Cicely Tyson was born on December 19, 1933, and grew up in Harlem in the 1950s, where she attended New York City public schools and graduated from Charles Evans High School in Manhattan. She came from a poor background, but was certain that she would succeed in life, a self-confidence that carried over into her acting career. One critic alluded to this in a review: "Cicely Tyson's considerable reputation as an actress on television and movies is primarily based on her ability to personify conviction under siege, as exemplified by her performances as such pioneering women as Miss Jane Pittman, Harriet Tubman, and Marva Collins" (Gussow 1983, 13).

Her parents separated when she was ten years old, and her mother, Theodosia, dedicated her life to her children, more so after the 1962 death of their father. Tyson and her siblings had a religious and strict upbringing, and were not allowed to watch films except when they were shown at Sunday school, where she sang in the choir and played the piano and organ.

In the 1950s she was discovered working as a secretary at *Ebony* magazine and rapidly became a successful model, and then an actress. She studied at the Actor's Workshop, Actor's Studio, and New York University, and went on to small roles in many film and television productions including *Twelve Angry Men* (1957) and *Odds Against Tomorrow* (1959). During this time she received a Vernon Rice Award her performance in *The Dark of the Moon*. In 1961 she joined a groundbreaking group of black actors that included James Earl Jones, Maya Angelou, and Roscoe Brown, who appeared together in Jean Genet's *The Blacks,* a play that marked the beginning of avant-garde theatre. Her first real break was in 1963, playing George C. Scott's secretary on the TV series *East Side/West Side*; she became the first black actress to appear in a recurring role in a television series. In 1966 she signed on with the daytime soap opera *The Guiding Light.* In 1968, after having played small roles in a series of films, she was given her first major role, Portia, in *The Heart Is a Lonely Hunter.* However, it was her acclaimed 1972 Oscar-nominated performance in *Sounder* that made her a star.

In 1974 she earned two Emmy Awards for her convincing portrayal of a 110-year-old woman who was born in slavery and lives to see the beginning of the civil rights movements in *The Autobiography of Miss Jane Pittman.* Among her most memorable roles was Binta, the mother of slave Kunta Kinte, in the 1977 *Roots* miniseries. "Giving birth to Kunta Kinte was a forceful point in my career," said Tyson, who will only portray dignified, positive images of black women, while acknowledging the dearth of meaningful film roles that fulfill these requirement (Stoynoff 1998, 31). Alex Haley, author of *Roots* and a close friend of Tyson until his death in 1992, also wrote the script for *Mama Flora,* a two-part miniseries where Tyson played the title role and won an Image Award for her acting. In a 1997 interview with M. S. Mason she refers to the fact that since the beginning of her career her role as an advocate for civil rights was connected to her work. When confronted by what she perceived was racism toward blacks, particularly black women, she said, "There is something going on in this society that I need to address, and I will find a way in my career to address it" (Mason 1997, 13).

Another of her great performances was that of Sipsey in the 1992 film *Fried Green Tomatoes*, which addresses such issues as battered wives, female friendship, the roles of women, and racism in the south. In 1994 she was the only black performer to win an Emmy Primetime Award, a year in which out of a field of 350 nominations, only 3 blacks were nominated. She won outstanding supporting actress for her role as Castalia in the miniseries *Oldest Living Confederate Widow Tells All*. The decrease in the numbers of awards given to black actors is a vital issue for Tyson. "There aren't any choices," she said in 1999. "In my time, I have been optimistic that we would be hired simply because of our ability. But we have to understand the fact that we're . . . constantly proving ourselves over and over. I live for the day when that will become obsolete" (Waxman 1999, 1F). In 2002 she co-starred in the highly acclaimed drama *The Rosa Parks Story*.

Over the years, she has received many awards and recognition from many sources. Very early in her career, her positive portrayal of strong black women in *Moon on a Rainbow Shawl* (1962) and *The Blacks* (1962) earned her two prestigious Vernon Rice Awards. She was inducted into the Black Filmmakers Hall of Fame in 1977. In 1979 she received an honorary Doctor of Fine Arts degree from Marymount College, and has received additional degrees from Atlanta, Fisk, Loyola, and Lincoln universities. She has also received citations from numerous civil rights groups such as the NAACP, the National Council of Negro Woman, and Urban Gateways. As co-founder of the Dance Theater of Harlem, she serves on its board and shares the responsibility of tapping and fostering new talent. Tyson was the first actor to be recognized by Harvard University Faculty Club with a day in her honor.—G.C.

References and Suggested Readings

Gussow, Mel. "Theater: *The Corn Is Green*." *The New York Times*, August 23, 1983, 13.

Mason, M.S. "Cicely Tyson's 'Ms. Scrooge' Adds New Layers to Tale." *Christian Science Monitor* 90:7 (December 4, 1997): 13.

Sanders, Charles L. "Cicely Tyson: She Can Smile Again After a Three-Year Ordeal." *Ebony* 34 (January 1979): 27–36.

Smith, Jessie Carney. "Cicely Tyson." *Notable Black American Women*. Detroit, MI: Gale, 1991. 1160–1164.

Stoynoff, Natasha. "Talking with . . . Cicely Tyson." *People* 50:17 (November 9, 1998): 31. *http://people.aol.com/people/981109/picksnpans/tube/tube2.html*.

Waxman, Sharon. "Why Can't More Blacks Get a Chance at an Oscar?" *The Buffalo News*, February 21, 1999, 1F.

LORETA JANETA VELÁZQUEZ
(LIEUTENANT HARRY BUFORD)
(1842–1897)
Cuban Military Officer and Writer

Cuban-born Loreta Janeta Velázquez is said to have broken through the traditional barriers of Victorian womanhood in disguise. Under an alias she took up arms and fought in the American Civil War disguised as the Confederate soldier, Lt. Harry T. Buford. *The Woman in Battle,* an autobiographical account of her adventures, was published in 1876. In it she recounts her fervent support for the Confederacy and how she fought in various Civil War battles. Although there are some contradictions in her narrative, scholars claim that there is enough evidence to assert that she did exist and that there is some truth to her account.

According to her autobiography, Velázquez was born in 1842 into a Cuban plantation-owning family. Her mother was the daughter of a French naval officer. She writes about being sent to New Orleans for her education and about her fixation with the idea of being a man. In an early display of the independence that would characterize her life, she ran away from home at age 14 to marry William, a U.S. Army officer. In her book we learn that they had three children, who by 1860 had died of unknown causes.

Velázquez's adventures as a soldier started in 1861, the first year of the American Civil War. At the time it was common for wives to accompany their husbands into battle to care for them. Veláquez's husband, who had resigned his commission and joined the Confederate Army, however, would not go along with her scheme of infiltrating the armed forces disguised as a man. Once he left for the war, Velázquez's wealth allowed her to hire a Memphis, Tennessee, tailor who made her two Confederate uniforms that concealed her female characteristics.

For women, joining the army during the Civil War was not a difficult feat. It is believed that over 750 women served during the war. There were no standardized medical exams, and most recruiters looked for visible disabilities such as deafness or poor eyesight. In addition, this was the Victorian era; men were modest by today's standards. Soldiers slept in their uniforms, and many refused to use the odorous and revolting open-trenched latrines of the camps. It was not unusual for soldiers to saunter into the woods to relieve themselves or leave camp before dawn to bathe privately in a nearby stream. Velázquez, wearing her specially tailored uniform and a false mustache, and with a well-developed masculine gait, successfully managed to enlist under the name of Lt. Harry T. Buford. Her uniform was padded to make her look more muscular, and she had become skilled at smoking cigars.

In her book she states that she recruited over 200 men and dispatched them to Pensacola, Florida, her husband's military post. She presented him with the recruits for his command, but while training them in the use of arms he was accidentally shot and killed. Free from her husband's restraining concern, she was now able to fulfill her desire to display her military talents. Her career as commander of the grays in the front lines began at the First Battle of Bull Run. She also served in battles in Tennessee during the surrender of Fort Donelson and in Kentucky.

After being wounded twice, she joined another activity in which an elite group of southern women participated: espionage. During this time she was a drug smuggler, a blockade-runner, and a double agent. She traveled to Richmond, Virginia, where she worked as a spy in the secret service, traveling freely between the North and South. During this time she met Captain Thomas DeCaulp, whom she married and whose widow she became a short time later. From spying she moved on to travel. She visited Canada and Europe and returned to New York City the day after General Lee's surrender. Her post-war narrative claims that she again traveled to Europe. On her return she lived in Salt Lake City, where she had a baby, and a shortly thereafter married an unnamed gentleman, left him, and took off with her baby. *The Woman in Battle* ends with the hope that the public will buy the book so that she can provide for her child.

The veracity of Velázquez's narrative remains to be determined. However, there are historians who have found evidence to support some of her claims, although there are data that cannot be corroborated. In some cases she is historically accurate in her placement of people in certain events, but in other cases, the names and activities are very vague. Nevertheless, some say that the importance of Velázquez's narrative lies in how her accounts shed light on gender roles and relations of that time.—G.C.

References and Suggested Readings

Blanton, DeAnne. "Women Soldiers of the Civil War." *Prologue: Quarterly of the National Archives* 25.1 (Spring 1993): 27.

De Grave, Kathleen. *Swindler, Spy, Rebel: The Confidence Woman in Nineteenth-Century America.* Columbia: University of Missouri Press, 1995.

Hoffert, Sylvia D. "Heroine or Hoaxer?" *Civil War Times* 38.4 (August 1999).

Leonard, Elizabeth. *All the Daring of the Soldier: Women of the Civil War Armies.* New York: W.W. Norton, 1999.

Velázquez, Loreta Janeta. *The Woman in Battle: A Narrative of the Exploits, Adventures, and Travels of Madame Loreta Janeta Velázquez, Otherwise Known as Lieutenant Harry T. Buford, Confederate States Army.* Richmond, VA: Dustin Gilman & Co., 1876. *http://www.ibiblio.org/docsouth/velazquez/menu.html.*

Nydia Velázquez
(1953–)

Puerto Rican American Politician, Educator, and Journalist

In 1992, nine years after having become active in local New York City politics, Nydia Velázquez became the first Puerto Rican woman to be elected to the U.S. House of Representatives. She has spent most of her political career as a progressive, focusing on improving the quality of life for people in inner-city districts such as her own 12th Congressional District in New York City, composed of predominately Hispanic neighborhoods in Brooklyn, Manhattan, and Queens. She has sponsored legislation to improve housing and education, as well as job and economic development. She is known as an ardent advocate for the rights of Latinos, women, and the poor.

A twin and one nine children of Benito and Carmen Luisa Velázquez, Nydia Margarita Velázquez was born March 28, 1953, in Yabucoa, Puerto Rico, where her father was a sugarcane cutter who eventually owned a legal cockfighting business. It was, however, his work as a local political leader and founder of a political party in Yabucoa that had a profound influence on his daughter Nydia. She credits her father and the family's dinner table discussions of workers' rights and current political issues as having influenced her political views. Her mother's home-based business making and selling *pasteles*, a traditional Puerto Rican dish, to sugarcane field workers, also influenced her in her role as ranking Democrat of the Small Business Committee.

Velázquez distinguished herself as an exemplary student and was the first member of her family to complete high school and obtain a university degree. In 1974 she graduated magna cum laude from the University of Puerto Rico with a bachelor's degree in political science and shortly thereafter enrolled at New York University, where in 1976 she completed a master's degree. She returned to Puerto Rico and was professor of political science at the University of Puerto Rico's Humacao campus until 1981, when she returned to the United States. Her reasons for leaving Puerto Rico were political: She supported Puerto Rican autonomy, which was contrary to the policies of the conservative pro-statehood faction in power at the time. She was labeled a leftist radical and a Communist. On her return to New York she became an adjunct professor of Puerto Rican studies at Hunter College and began her entry into the political arena.

In 1983 she was a special assistant to New York Congressman Edolphous Towns. She was appointed the first Hispanic woman to the New York City Council in early 1984, when the incumbent was convicted of a felony and was forced to resign. Virtually unknown at the time, Velázquez served in the interim, but ran and lost the election to the council later that year. Also in 1984 she was appointed national director of the Migration Division Office of the Department of Labor and Human Resources of Puerto Rico by then-governor Rafael Hernández Colón. Shortly thereafter, she became head of the newly created Department of Puerto Rican Community Affairs in the United States. In this cabinet-level position under Governor Hernández Colón, Velázquez oversaw regional offices in five U.S. cities from headquarters in New York. Her work in this position eventually brought her to the forefront of New York City politics.

In her function as a major liaison between Puerto Rico and the U.S. government, Velázquez was able to exercise her political influence. First during Hurricane Hugo in 1989, through a personal call and request to General Colin Powell, head of the Joint Chiefs of Staff, she was able to secure federal assistance to help rebuild the devastation left by the storm. Perhaps her greatest accomplishment, and one that garnered her local name recognition and visibility, was a voter registration drive—Atrévete (Dare to Go for It)—financed by the Department of Puerto Rican Community Affairs. This effort targeted Hispanic communities in the northeast and registered more than 200,000 new voters between 1989 and 1992. The increase of minority voters is believed to have been key in the 1989 election of New York City's first black mayor, David Dinkins. Shortly after the election, Velázquez made her bid for Congress.

In 1992, in order to increase minority-voting power under the Voting Rights Act, the 12th Congressional District was created. The representative whose district was dissolved as a result of the redistricting process, popular nine-term Congressman Stephen Solarz was left without a district. With name recognition and a campaign fund of $2 million, he decided to run for the newly created district against Velázquez. Velázquez's connection to the community and lack of funds forced her to run a grass-roots campaign against Solarz and four other Hispanic challengers. Instrumental to her primary victory was the support from many labor unions, the Rev. Jesse Jackson and a thank-you in the form of a political endorsement from Mayor David Dinkins.

With polls indicating Velázquez's victory by wide margins, her campaign hit a snag when the *New York Post* published her medical records, which disclosed treatment for mental depression and an attempted suicide. In a press conference, surrounded by family and friends, Velázquez acknowledged this "troublesome" period in her life, and also expressed her outrage that confidential medical records had been released to the public in violation of hospital confidentiality regulations. Major Democratic and Republican political figures in New York State repudiated the incident as underhanded and unfair. Velázquez overcame this adversity, and at age 39 defeated her Republican opponent and became the first Puerto Rican woman elected to Congress.

Since 1992 she has been re-elected four times, even after a 1998 court-ordered redistricting reduced the Hispanic population in her district from 58 percent to 49 percent. Both 1998 and 2000 election results netted her 85 percent of the total vote. In 1998 Velázquez was named Ranking Democrat on the House Small Business Committee; she was the first Hispanic woman to serve in this capacity. Her tenure in the House has been characterized by her role in community empowerment, promotion of business development in economically depressed areas, and her contribution to streamlining tax codes to allow small businesses to run more efficiently. She has also served on the Banking, Finance, and Urban Affairs Committee, and has supported unpaid family and medical leave legislation.

In May 2000 Velázquez joined other Latino members of Congress and scores of Hispanic politicians and other protesters to oppose the U.S. Navy's use of Vieques as a bombing range.—G.C.

References and Suggested Readings

Biography of Nydia M. Velázquez: *http://www.house.gov/velazquez/bio.htm.*
"Career Paths: How They Got Where They Are." *Campaigns and Elections.* 21.3 (April 2000): 18.
Creamer, Matthew. "Velázquez, Nydia, M." *Current Biography* 60.7 (July 1999): 54–57.
Domínguez, Robert. "No-nonsense Nydia." *Hispanic* (October 1995): 16–18.
González, Juan, and Candace Lyle Hogan. "Nydia Draws the Line." *Latina* (April 1998): 34.
Hicks, Jonathan P. "With Redistricting in Vogue, Velazquez Takes a Spot in Line." *The New York Times*, September 8, 1996, 45.
Meier, Matt, Conchita Franco, and Richard García. *Notable Latino Americans: A Biographical Dictionary.* Westport, CT: Greenwood Press, 1997. 395–399.
Representative Nydia M. Velázquez Homepage: *http://www.house.gov/velazquez/.*
Telgen, Diane, and Jim Kamp, eds. "Nydia M. Velázquez." *Notable Hispanic American Women.* Detroit, MI: Gale, 1993. 406–408.

DEREK WALCOTT
(1930–)

Winner of the Nobel Prize in Literature, Poet, Painter, and Playwright from St. Lucia

Derek Walcott is one of the great poets of the English language. His seductive uses of the written word, his capacity to capture the dilemmas and realities of Caribbean cultures, the passionate and lyrical nature of his verses, and his command of the poetic technique have made him the most important contemporary writer to emerge from the West Indies. When the Swedish Academy awarded him the Nobel Prize in Literature in 1992, the work of this distinguished poet and playwright was further legitimized and immediately transcended the boundaries of Caribbean American literature for him to become a poet of the world.

Walcott was born in Castries, the capital of St. Lucia, one of the Windward Islands, on February 23, 1930. His father was an artist who died when Walcott was a little boy. His mother, Warwick Walcott, raised Derek, his twin brother, Roderick (also a poet and playwright), and an older sister. As a schoolteacher, she instilled in Walcott her love for books and words. From early on, she encouraged him to write and helped him pay to publish his early work. Walcott credits his mother and his teachers for his career choice because they encouraged him to continue writing (Styron 1997).

He received his early education at St. Mary's College in Castries and obtained a scholarship to attend the University of the West Indies in Kingston, Jamaica, where he majored in French, English, and Spanish, graduating in 1950. He published his first literary work, *25 Poems*, in 1948 while he was still an undergraduate. Walcott also wrote art and literary criticism for

Derek Walcott.
Courtesy of Boston University Photo Services.

Trinidad's *Guardian* and for Jamaica's *Public Opinion*. After graduation, he worked as a teacher on several Caribbean islands and also started writing plays. One of his first dramatic creations was *Henri Christophe: A Chronicle*, which he wrote and staged in Trinidad in 1950. He was awarded a scholarship by the Rockefeller Foundation to study theatrical directing from 1957 to 1958. In 1959, when he returned to Trinidad, he founded the Carib Theater, which later became the Trinidad Theater Workshop.

Walcott's first major poetic work was *In a Green Night: Poems: 1948–60*. It was published in 1962 and brought him major recognition as a poet. It was followed by, among others, *Selected Poems* (1964), *The Castaway and Other Poems* (1965), *The Gulf and Other Poems* (1969), *Another Life* (1973), *Sea Grapes* (1976), *The Fortunate Traveler* (1982), *Midsummer* (1984), *The Arkansas Testament* (1987), *Omeros* (1990), and *The Bounty* (1997). *Omeros* is an epic poem inspired by *The Odyssey* but adapted to the Caribbean.

The themes of Walcott's works are varied. One critic summarized them as: "his choice of vocation as a poet, his dilemma as perennial outsider . . . his affection for that island [St. Lucia and Trinidad], his desire to give a voice to a voiceless society colliding with his knowledge that he must leave his country to survive as a poet" (Taylor 1999, 32). Like the works of most of the Caribbean writers profiled in this book, Walcott's poetry explores the inherent realities and contradictions of a Caribbean writer who writes in English and is influenced by European cultures and styles, but who was raised and educated in a completely different cultural world. The critics who review his work almost always point to the ever-present conflicts that exist between those "classic" European forces that influenced him during his upbringing and the images of the Caribbean that he has depicted.

His work explores, and tries to unravel, the inner significance and meanings of Caribbean cultures in light of the historical and social background and changes that have shaped the West Indies. Another critic has written that "Walcott's plays and poems are distinguished by the tensions between the European and African Caribbean Cultures and by the resolution of those tensions" (Presson and Mclees 1996). Walcott, like Caribbean writers **Austin C. Clarke** and **Nicolás Guillén**, has been praised for translating into his poetry the linguistic nuances and speech patterns of West Indian people.

Although commended most often for his poetry, Walcott is also a talented painter and playwright. His colorful and stylized paintings frequently illustrate the covers of his books. He has written and staged dozens of plays. Most of his dramatic works follow the same thematic and ideological lines as his poetry. Among the most important are *Ti-Jean and His Brothers* (1957), *Dream on Monkey Mountain* (1967), and *The Capeman* (1998). *The Capeman*, a musical written with Paul Simon, is based on the events surrounding a 1959 gang murder in New York City. Because the main character is Puerto Rican, Walcott explored the island's culture. However, critics panned the show and Puerto Ricans in New York City thought it romanticized violence and crime and perpetuated negative ethnic stereotypes.

In 1992 Walcott was awarded the Nobel Prize in literature. He became the first black Caribbean writer from the West Indies to receive that distinction. In the citation, the Swedish Academy stated that "with Walcott the West Indian culture has found its great poet. He is commended for his talent in speaking with a wide array of voices with lustre and force" (Swedish Academy, October 8, 1992).

Walcott is a university professor and holds a chair in English at Boston University, where he teaches literature and creative writing. Actively involved in his theatrical productions, he divides his time between Boston University and Trinidad, his adopted home.—S.M.M.

References and Suggested Readings

"Introducing Derek Walcott: 1992 Nobel Laureate." *Ebony*, February 1993, 46.

Presson, Rebekah, and David Mclees. *In Their Own Voices: A Century of Recorded Poetry.* Los Angeles: Rhino/Word Beat, 1996.

Taylor, Robert. "Derek Walcott." *Crisis* (May/June 1999): 31–33.

Styron, Rose. "Derek Walcott: An Interview." *American Poetry Review* (May/June 1997): 41–46.

Swedish Academy: The Permanent Secretariat. "Press Release: The Nobel Prize for Literature 1992." October 8, 1992. *www.nobel.se/literature/laureates/1992/press.html.*

"Verse and Better: Sentiment without Sentimentality." *The Economist*, September 6, 1997, n.p.

BERNIE WILLIAMS
(1968–)

Puerto Rican Baseball Player and Musician

Bernie Williams, the successful center fielder and designated hitter for the New York Yankees, is considered among the best contemporary batters and fielders of this century, but his humility and caring demeanor have led sports writers to refer to him as the "Quiet Superstar" (Kernan 1998).

He was born Bernabe Williams in San Juan, Puerto Rico, on September 13, 1968, one of two children of Bernabe Williams, a sailor working with the Merchant Marine, and Rufina Willams, a dedicated schoolteacher who sacrificed and eventually became a high school principal. The family lived in the Bronx but moved to Puerto Rico when Williams was one year old.

From an early age, Williams' father used to take him to the gym and to sporting competitions. Bernie Sr. encouraged his son to play baseball with him and often threw him more than a 150 balls in a single practice (Fine 1998). His father also used to take him to sport clinics held by famous Puerto Rican baseball stars who taught the sport to Puerto Rican children. Baseball became Williams' sport of choice and he played for the Puerto Rican minor leagues.

Music was also an important activity in the Williams household. Bernie Sr. was an amateur guitar player and Williams started to play on his own at a young age. He developed a love for classical music and for American jazz. His musical skills were so promising that on finishing junior high, he auditioned and gained admission to the elite Escuela Libre de Música in Hato Rey, a specialized music school for Puerto Rican children who intend to pursue professional music careers. Because of his musical talents, his teachers firmly believed that he could have become a professional musician and gone on to receive training at a music conservatory.

By the time that Williams was 15, he was already making his mark as an amateur musician, as a baseball player, and as an athlete. His mother wanted him to pursue an academic career and encouraged Williams to take pre-med classes at the University of Puerto Rico. At the same time, Williams became one of Puerto Rico's best 400-meter runners and won four medals in international track and field events (Pietrusza 2001). Williams decided to pursue a sports career and was confident that he was going to be signed by an American baseball team to play in the United States.

The New York Yankees signed Williams in 1985 and the team sent him to the minor leagues, where he had a chance to learn the professional game and polish his skills. Between 1986 and 1992 Williams played with several teams in the minor league system. He played in Sarasota, Florida, in Columbus, Ohio, and in Albany, New York. Although he performed well enough during his seven-year apprenticeship, it was clear that he needed to perfect his skills. He was seen as a player with speed and potential power but whose shyness and calmness might handicap the development of the competitive edge necessary for success (Kernan 1998). After the first few years in the minor leagues, Bernie became frustrated waiting to make the transition to the majors. At one point, he told his mother that he wanted to quit and go back to Puerto Rico to study music and go to college. While supportive of him, his mother told him in no uncertain terms that he had to stick to sports and finish what he had begun.

On July 7, 1991, Bernie made his major league debut with the Yankees, playing against the Baltimore Orioles. The next year he divided the season between playing with the Triple-A Columbus Team and playing in 62 games with the Yankees. His first full season in the majors was 1993. During this season he improved his batting considerably. In 1994 he tied a major league record by hitting two doubles in the same inning. The next year, he scored his 100th career double, and led the Yankees in games (144), runs (93), hits (173), and total bases. Williams, who had once been called Bambi for his soft playing demeanor, became one of the strongest and most forceful players in the major leagues. In 1996 he was designated Most Valuable Player of the World Series. His role during the season was pivotal in carrying the Yankees to their first title national title since 1978.

Williams has managed to maintain an excellent performance throughout the years. During the 2000 season his batting average was .307, with a career average of .304. The Yankees organization signed him to a seven-year contract in 1998 for $87.5 million.

While Williams has dedicated his professional life to baseball, he is still interested in playing his guitar and has not hesitated to entertain his fellow players. He has appeared and played on *Late Night with David Letterman* as well as other major television programs. He has also made several amateur performances with well-known musicians, appearing on David Letterman's show and playing with Paul Simon and Ruben Blades in New York. He has said that while he needs to stay focused on his baseball, he plays his music every day and looks forward to the day when he retires and can finally enroll in a music conservatory to expand his music training (Fine 1998).

Williams is married and lives in Puerto Rico in the off season. He is considered by many to be to be one of the kindest and most decent players in American baseball.—S.M.M.

References and Suggested Readings

Fine, Josh. "Bernie Williams." *Biography* 2.4 (April 1998): 86.
Kernan, Kevin. *Bernie Williams: Quiet Superstar.* Champaign, IL: Sports Publishing, 1998.
"#51 Bernie Williams." ESPN. *http://baseball.espn.go.com/mlb/players/profile?statsId=4695.*
Pietruzsa, David, ed. "Bernie Williams." *The Encyclopedia of American Baseball.* Kingston, NY: Total Sports Illustrated, 2001. 1227–1228.
Verducci, Tom. "Legend of the fall." *Sports Illustrated*, October 21, 1996, 28.

ERIC WILLIAMS
(1911–1981)

Trinidadian Scholar, Politician, Prime Minister, and Statesman

Eric Williams is considered by many to be the "Father of the Nation" for the two former British colonies of Trinidad and Tobago in the West Indies. An Oxford-educated historian, Williams had a unique understanding of the racial and economic processes that affected the development of the West Indies and the Caribbean. He authored some of the most important texts on the history of the area. As politician and prime minister of Trinidad and Tobago, Williams used his broad knowledge of the region to build a social and economic infrastructure that lent itself to the development of the islands and the region. Although he ruled the islands in an autocratic fashion, Williams remained true to democratic principles and respected the individual and collective freedoms of the people and institutions of Trinidad and Tobago.

Eric Eustace Williams was born on September 25, 1911, in the Trinidadian capital of Port-of-Spain to Thomas Henry Williams, a civil servant who worked for the postal service, and Elisa Bossiere Williams. Williams attended the Tranquility Boy's School before winning a scholarship to attend the elite Queen's Royal College, where he excelled in his studies and as a soccer player. Because of his scholastic achievements, Williams obtained a prestigious "Island Scholarship" to attend Oxford University in England, where he studied history and obtained a first-class honors bachelor's degree. He received a doctorate in history from Oxford with a concentration in the social history of the Caribbean in 1938. His doctoral dissertation, "Economic Aspects of the Abolition of Slavery in the British West Indies," argued that Britain gave freedom to the slaves in their colonies not for humanitarian reasons but because slavery no longer served Britain's economic interests. The dissertation was the basis of his book *Capitalism and Slavery* and is considered a classic in the field of Caribbean studies.

After finishing his studies, Williams moved to the United States, where he taught social and political science at Howard University. By 1945 he had attained the rank of full professor at the institution.

Because of his considerable expertise in Caribbean history and politics, Williams was hired in 1947 to serve as a consultant to the Anglo-American Commission, which later became the Caribbean Commission. This organization was established by Great Britain to examine the social and economic problems of the Caribbean and to serve as a resource for development in the region. Williams left Howard in 1948 and accepted a full-time position with the Commission as deputy chairman in charge of research. He worked for them until 1955, when he left because he thought that the commission supported the continued colonial status in the Caribbean.

After leaving his post at the commission, Williams became interested in politics and gave a series of lectures and speeches at Woodford Square in Port-of-Spain about the problems faced by Trinidad and Tobago and other Caribbean nations. He presented ideas for solving their problems and strengthening their social and economic development. In 1956 he founded the People's National Movement (PNM), a new political party on the island. Like **Norman Manley** from Jamaica, Williams fostered nationalistic and patriotic fervor on the island and was a strong advocate of independence for West Indian colonies. One of the most serious problems hindering the social and economic development of Trinidad and Tobago was the lack of unity due to the ethnic diversity on the two islands. Williams called for the unity among the Trinidadians, an important strategy toward development. His new party won the elections and obtained a majority in the Legislative Council and Williams became the chief minister of Trinidad and Tobago.

In 1959, largely because of Williams' efforts, the island achieved its first comprehensive cabinet government, and by 1960 achieved full internal self-government as well as its own constitution. Like many other Caribbean political leaders, Williams worked hard to integrate Trinidad and Tobago into the West Indian Federation. The federation had been planned by the British West Indian colonies since 1947 with the support of Great Britain. It was intended to unify the different islands under a federal political apparatus that would facilitate their social and economic development. Finally established in 1958, the federation was short-lived because there was a great deal of dissent among its different members, who preferred to focus their energies on obtaining independence from Great Britain rather than in developing a regional unity. When Jamaica left the federation in 1962, Williams pulled Trinidad and Tobago out of the federation and petitioned Great Britain for independence.

Trinidad and Tobago became independent on August 31, 1962, and established a parliamentary form of government. Williams became prime minister and stayed in control of its government for the next two decades. Using his profound knowledge of economics and development, Williams focused his efforts on attaining self-sufficiency for his island. One of his achievements was free mandatory education for all Trinidadian children. Under his governance, school enrollment increased by eleven-fold and literacy rate increased to 78 percent (Thomas 1981). He developed an economic strategy by which the government was able to control significant assets such as the oil industry, traditionally controlled by transnational companies. He also worked with the private sector by assuring them of the stability of his government.

Eric Williams recognized the importance of creating an organization that could facilitate economic exchanges between Trinidad and Tobago and other Caribbean nations. He was instrumental in establishing the Caribbean Free Trade Organization in 1966 and the Caribbean Community and Common Market (CARICOM) in 1973.

In 1970 Trinidad and Tobago faced serious social problems when its population rebelled and demanded more power. Following the precepts of the popular Black

Power movement and inspired by American leaders such as Trinidadian **Stokeley Carmichael**, Trinidadian blacks complained of many inequities in their treatment. They felt other island minority groups such as Hindus and Muslims discriminated against blacks. This period was difficult for Williams and he decided to resign as prime minister in 1971, but later withdrew his resignation.

Like neighboring Venezuela, Trinidad and Tobago have significant oil reserves. After Arab nations and OPEC (Organization of Petroleum Exporting Countries) decided to control the production and export of oil in 1973, world markets saw a significant increase in the cost of oil. Williams maneuvered carefully to take control of the production of oil in Trinidad and Tobago. Williams used the funds from oil investments for businesses and industries. This surplus income led to a strengthening of the economic and social infrastructure of the island and to an increase in the quality of life of most Trinidadians.

Despite his successes, Williams has been criticized for his autocratic and totalitarian governing style. Williams exercised almost absolute control over the most important agencies and organization of his government. One scholar points out that Williams stayed in power by controlling opposition attempts to raise awareness about the problems with his administration or government (Parris 1983).

Even with his autocratic traits, Eric Williams has been one of the most diligent and capable Caribbean leaders of the twentieth century. Using his knowledge of the history of the Caribbean he was able to strategically maneuver Trinidad and Tobago into one of the most prosperous and stable islands of the Caribbean. He made some of the most significant contributions to the social, political, and economic development of these Caribbean islands. Together with the PNM, Williams kept control of the government until his death on March 29, 1981. He remembered not only for his political achievements but also by the superb scholarly legacy that he left through books such as *The Negro in the Caribbean* (1942), *Capitalism and Slavery* (1944), *The Historic Background of Race Relations in the Caribbean* (1955), *Constitution Reform in Trinidad Tobago* (1955), *Britain and the West Indies* (1969), and *From Capitalism to Castro: the History of the Caribbean* (1969).—S.M.M.

References and Suggested Readings

Caribbean Community Secretariat: *http;//www.caricom.org*.

Devries, Hilary. "Eric Williams, Caribbean Premier." *The Christian Science Monitor*, March 31, 1981, 2.

Fraser, C. Gerald. "Eric Wiliams, Leader of Trinidad and Tobago Is Dead." *The New York Times*, March 31, 1981, D22.

Hintzen, Percy C., and W. Marvin Hill. "Eric Williams." In Robert Alexander, ed., *Biographic Dictionary of Latin American and Caribbean Political Leaders*. Westport, CT: Greenwood Press, 1988. 450–460.

Kiernan, James Patrick. "Eric Williams: Trinidad's Man for All Seasons." *Américas* 51.4 (July/August 1999): 56–57.

Parris, Carl D. "Personalization of Power in an Elected Government: Eric Williams and Trinidad and Tobago, 1973–1981." *Journal of Inter-American Studies and World Affairs* 25 (May 1993): 171–191.

Rogozinski, Jan. *A Brief History of the Caribbean: From the Arawak and Carib to the Present.* New York: Facts on File, 1999.

Thomas, Jo. "Shadow of Dead Leader Lies Over Trinidad Vote." *The New York Times,* November 5, 1981, A2.

Williams, Eric. *Capitalism and Slavery.* Rev. ed. Chapel Hill: University of North Carolina Press, 1994.

———. *From Columbus to Castro: The History of the Caribbean 1492–1969.* Rev. ed. New York: Vintage Books, 1984.

Appendix A:
Fields of Professional Activity

The fields of professional activity of the individuals profiled in the book are classified under the following headings:

Actors and Actresses
Business Leaders
Dancers and Choreographers
Diplomats
Economists
Educators and Scholars
Entertainment Personalities:
    Television and Film
Filmmakers, Producers,
    and Directors
Folklorists
Journalists
Labor Activists
Lawyers

Literary and Cultural Critics
Military Leaders
Musicians, Singers and Songwriters
National Heroes, Patriots, Ideologues,
    and Nationalists
Painters and Sculptors
Philanthropists and Humanitarians
Physicians and Health Professionals
Political Philosophers
Politicians and Government Leaders
Religious Leaders
Scientists
Sports Figures
Writers and Literary Figures

Actors and Actresses

Harry Belafonte
Miriam Colón
Benicio Del Toro
José Ferrer
Geoffrey Holder
Grace Jones
Raúl Juliá
Ricky Martin
Rita Moreno
Rex M. Nettleford
Chita Rivera

Business Leaders

Alexander Bustamante
Sila María Calderón
Oscar de la Renta
Luis A. Ferré
Cristina Saralegui

Dancers and Choreographers

Alicia Alonso
Boscoe Holder
Geoffrey Holder
Jennifer López
Ricky Martin
Rita Moreno
Rex Nettleford
Chita Rivera
Cicely Tyson

Diplomats

Nita Barrow
Minerva Bernardino
Edward Wilmot Blyden
Guillermo Cabrera Infante
Alejo Carpentier
Maximiliano (Max) Henríquez Ureña
Eugenio María de Hostos
Arthur Lewis
José Martí
Jacques Baptiste Roumain

Economists

Arthur Lewis

Educators and Scholars

Julia Álvarez
Myrna Báez

Edward Wilmot Blyden
Karl Broodhagen
Alejo Carpentier
Aimé Césaire
Shirley Chisholm
Austin C. Clarke
Michelle Cliff
Miriam Colón
Maryse Condé
Gilberto Croes (Betico)
Paquito D'Rivera
Eugenio María de Hostos
Mervyn M. Dymally
Gus Edwards
Rosario Ferré
Stuart Hall
Elizabeth Hart Thwaites
Anne Hart Gilbert
Merle Hodge
Jamaica Kincaid
George Lamming
Elizabeth Clovis Lange
Arthur Lewis
Maria Liberia-Peters
Audre Lorde
Pedro Mir
Rex M. Nettleford
Antonia Pantoja
Ileana Ros-Lehtinen
Jean Baptiste Roumain
Luis Rafael Sánchez
Arturo Sandoval
Salomé Ureña de Henríquez
Nydia Velázquez
Derek Walcott

Entertainment Personalities: Television and Film

María Celeste Arrarás
Harry Belafonte
Miriam Colón
Celia Cruz
Benicio Del Toro
Gloria Estefan
José Ferrer
Geoffrey Holder
Raúl Juliá
Rita Moreno
Euzhan Palcy
Geraldo Rivera
Cristina Saralegui

Filmmakers, Producers, and Directors

José Ferrer
Euzhan Palcy
Tomás Gutierrez Alea (Titón)

Folklorists

Jacques Roumain
Arturo Schomburg

Journalists

María Celeste Arrarás
Edward Wilmot Blyden
Guillermo Cabrera Infante
Maximiliano "Max" Henríquez Ureña
Michael Norman Manley
José Martí
Luis Muñoz Marín
Geraldo Rivera
Cristina Saralegui
Nydia Velázquez

Labor Activists

Pedro Albizu Campos
Alexander Bustamante
Robert L. Bradshaw
Nicolás Guillén
Michael Norman Manley
Antonia Pantoja

Lawyers

Grantley Adams
Pedro Albizu Campos
Herman Badillo
Joaquín Balaguer
Maurice Bishop
Fidel Castro
Mary Eugenia Charles
Francisco Henríquez y Carvajal
Eric Holder
Norman Washington Manley
José Martí
Geraldo Rivera

Literary and Cultural Critics

Guillermo Cabrera Infante
Alejo Carpentier
Frank Collymore

Maryse Condé
Rosario Ferré
Stuart Hall
Maximiliano "Max" Henríquez Ureña
Pedro Henríquez Ureña
Camila Henríquez Ureña
José Martí
V. S. Naipaul

Military Leaders

Fidel Castro
Alexander Sabès Petion
Loreta Janeta Velázquez
   (Lieutenant Harry Buford)
Toussaint L'Ouverture

Musicians, Singers, and Songwriters

Joan Armatrading
Harry Belafonte
Cachao (Israel Cachao López)
Calypso Rose (McCartha Lewis)
Michel Camillo
Willie Colón
Celia Cruz
Des'ree (Desiree Weeks)
Justino Díaz
Paquito D'Rivera
Gloria Estefan
Luis A. Ferré
Rafael Hernández
Grace Jones
Jennifer López
Ernesto Lecuona
Lord Kitchener (Aldwyn Roberts)
Jon Lucien
Machito (Frank Grillo)
Bob Marley
Ricky Martin
Mighty Sparrow (Slinger Francisco)
Pablo Milanés
Rita Moreno
"Chico" O'Farrill
Johhny Pacheco
Dámaso Pérez Prado
Tito Puente
Chita Rivera
Graciela Rivera
Silvio Rodríguez
Arturo Sandoval

Appendix A: Fields of Professional Activity

National Heroes, Patriots, Ideologists, and Nationalists

Pedro Albizu Campos
Ramón Emeterio Betances
Edward Wilmot Blyden
Stokeley Carmichael (Kwame Ture)
Fidel Castro
Eugenio María de Hostos
Juan Pablo Duarte
Marcus Garvey
Mariana Grajales
C.L.R. James
Moses Leverock
Nanny of the Maroons
Antonio Maceo
José Martí
Patria Mercedes Mirabal
María Teresa Mirabal
Minerva Argentina Mirabal
Alexandre Sabès Pétion
Toussaint L'Ouverture

Painters and Sculptors

Myrna Báez
Jean-Michel Basquiat
David Boxer
Karl Broodhagen
LeRoy Clarke
Edouard Duval-Carrié
Frank Collymore
Tomás Esson
Boscoe Holder
Geoffrey Holder
Lorenzo Homar
Wilfredo Lam
Edna Manley
Antonio Martorell
Camille Pissarro
Rafael Tufiño

Philanthropists and Humanitarians

Gigi Fernández
Luis A. Ferré
Chi Chi Rodríguez
Sammy Sosa

Physicians and Health Professionals

Nita Barrow
Ramón Emeterio Betances

Frantz Fanon
Carlos J. Finlay
Francisco Henríquez y Carvajal
Mary Jane Seacole

Political Philosophers

Edward Wilmot Blyden
Pedro Albizu Campos
Stokeley Carmichael (Kwame Ture)
Eugenio María de Hostos
Frantz Fanon
Marcus Garvey
C.L.R. James
José Martí

Politicians and Government Leaders

Grantley Adams
Jean-Bertrand Aristide
Pedro Albizu Campos
Herman Badillo
Joaquín Balaguer
Nita Barrow
Maurice Bishop
Juan Bosch
Robert L. Bradshaw
Alexander Bustamante
Sila María Calderón
Fidel Castro
Aimé Césaire
Mary Eugenia Charles
Shirley Chisholm
Gilberto Croes (Betico)
Mervyn M. Dymally
Luis A. Ferré
Francisco Henríquez y Carvajal
Moses Leverock
Maria Liberia-Peters
Michael Norman Manley
Norman Washington Manley
Luis Muñoz Marín
Felisa Rincón de Gautier
Ileana Ros-Lehtinen
Alexandre Sabès Pétion
Toussaint L'Ouverture
Nydia Velázquez
Eric Williams

Religious Leaders

Jean-Bertrand Aristide
Errol Walton Brown

Edward Wilmot Blyden
Sor Isolina Ferré
Elizabeth Clovis Lange
Carlos Manuel Rodríguez
 ("El Beato Charlie")
Pierre Toussaint
Elizabeth Hart Thwaites

Scientists

Edward Cheung
Carlos J. Finlay

Sports Figures

Roberto Alomar
Sandy Alomar Sr.
Sandy Alomar Jr.
Orlando "Peruchín" Cepeda
Roberto Clemente
Minnie Minoso
 (Orestes Saturnino Arrieta Armas)
Tim Duncan
Patrick Ewing
Gigi Fernández
Mary Joe Fernández
Norman Manley
Juan Antonio Marichal
Marie-José Pérec
Chi Chi Rodríguez
Sammy Sosa
Teófilo Stevenson
Bernie Williams

Writers and Literary Figures

Julia Álvarez
Joaquín Balaguer
Edward Wilmot Blyden
Juan Bosch
Guillermo Cabrera Infante
Alejo Carpentier
Aimé Césaire
Michelle Cliff
Frank Collymore
Maryse Condé
Austin C. Clarke
Edwidge Danticat
Frantz Fannon
Rosario Ferré
Gus Edwards
Nicolás Guillén
Oscar Hijuelos
Merle Hodge
Jamaica Kincaid
George Lamming
Audre Lorde
Dulce María Loynas
José Martí
C.LR. James
Pedro Mir
Luis Muñoz Marín
V.S. Naipul
Luis Palés Matos
Jean Rhys
Jacques Baptiste Roumain
Luis Rafael Sánchez
Simone Schwarz-Bart
Salomé Ureña de Henríquez
Derek Walcott

Appendix B:
Island of Origin or Roots

Antigua

Gus Edwards
Anne Hart Gilbert
Jamaica Kincaid
Elizabeth Hart Thwaites

Aruba

Edward Cheung

Barbados

Grantley Adams
Nita Barrow
Karl Broodhagen
Errol Walton Brown
Shirley Chisholm
Austin C. Clarke
Eric Holder
George Lamming
Des'ree (Desiree Weeks)

Cuba

Alicia Alonso
Guillermo Cabrera Infante
Alejo Carpentier
Cachao (Israel Cachao López)
Fidel Castro
Celia Cruz

Paquito D'Rivera
Tomás Esson
Gloria Estefan
Carlos J. Finlay
Mariana Grajales
Nicolás Guillén
Tomás Gutiérrez Alea (Titón)
Oscar Hijuelos
Wilfredo Lam
Ernesto Lecuona
Machito (Frank Grillo)
Dulce María Loynaz
Antonio Maceo
José Martí
Pablo Milanés
Minnie Minoso
    (Orestes Saturnino Arrieta Armas)
"Chico" O'Farrill
Dámaso Pérez Prado
Silvio Rodríguez
Ileana Ros-Lehtinen
Arturo Sandoval
Cristina Saralegui
Loreta Janeta Velázquez
    (Lieutenant Harry Buford)
Teófilo Stevenson

Curaçao

Gilberto Croes (Betico)
Maria Liberia-Peters

Appendix B: Island of Origin or Roots

Dominica

Mary Eugenia Charles
Jean Rhys

Dominican Republic

Julia Álvarez
Joaquín Balaguer
Minerva Bernardino
Juan Bosch
Oscar de la Renta
Juan Pablo Duarte
Mary Joe Fernández
Michelle Camilo
Camila Henríquez Ureña
Maximiliano "Max" Henríquez Ureña
Pedro Henríquez Ureña
Francisco Henríquez y Carvajal
Juan Antonio Marichal
Pedro Mir
Patria Mercedes Mirabal
María Teresa Mirabal
Minerva Argentina Mirabal
Johnny Pacheco
Sammy Sosa
Salomé Ureña de Henríquez

Grenada

Maurice Bishop
Audre Lorde

Guadeloupe

Maryse Condé
Simone Schwarz-Bart

Haiti

Jean-Bertrand Aristide
Jean-Michel Basquiat
Edouard Duval-Carrié
Edwidge Danticat
ector Hyppolite
Elizabeth Clovis Lange
Alexandre Sabès Pétion
Jacques Roumain
Pierre Toussaint
Toussaint L'Ouverture

Jamaica

Harry Belafonte
David Boxer
Alexander Bustamante
Michelle Cliff
Patrick Ewing
Marcus Garvey
Stuart Hall
Grace Jones
Edna Manley
Michael Norman Manley
Norman Washington Manley
Bob Marley
Nanny of the Maroons
Rex M. Nettleford
Mary Jane Seacole

Martinique

Aimé Césaire
Frantz Fanon
Euzhan Palcy
Marie-José Pérec

Puerto Rico

Pedro Albizu Campos
Roberto Alomar
Sandy Alomar Jr.
Sandy Alomar Sr.
María Celeste Arrarás
Herman Badillo
Myrna Báez
Ramón Emeterio Betances
Sila María Calderon
Orlando "Peruchín" Cepeda
Roberto Clemente
Miriam Colón
Willie Colón
Eugenio María de Hostos
Benicio Del Toro
Justino Díaz
Gigi Fernández
Luis A. Ferré
Rosario Ferré
Sor Isolina Ferré
José Ferrer
Rafael Hernández
Lorenzo Homar
Raúl Juliá
Jennifer López
Ricky Martin
Antonio Martorell
Rita Moreno
Luis Muñoz Marín
Luis Palés Matos

Antonia Pantoja
Tito Puente
Felisa Rincón de Gautier
Chita Rivera
Geraldo Rivera
Graciela Rivera
Carlos Manuel Rodríguez
("El Beato Charlie")
Chi Chi Rodríguez
Luis Rafael Sánchez
Arturo Schomburg
Rafael Tufiño
Nydia Velázquez
Bernie Williams

Saba

Moses Leverock

St. Kitts

Joan Armatrading
Robert L. Bradshaw

St. Lucia

Arthur Lewis
Derek Walcott

Trinidad and Tobago

Calypso Rose (McCartha Lewis)
Stokeley Carmichael (Kwame Ture)
LeRoy Clarke
Frank Collymore
Mervyn M. Dymally
Merle Hodge
Boscoe Holder
Geoffrey Holder
C.L.R. James
Lord Kitchener (Aldwyn Roberts)
Mighty Sparrow (Slinger Francisco)
V.S. Naipaul
Eric Williams

**St. Thomas, St. John and St. Croix
(United States Virgin Islands, Formerly
Danish Virgin Islands)**

Edward Wilmot Blyden
Tim Duncan
Jon Lucien
Camille Pissarro

Index

Page numbers in **bold** type refer to main entries in the dictionary.

About the Authors

SERAFÍN MÉNDEZ-MÉNDEZ is Associate Professor of Communication at Central Connecticut State University. A native of Puerto Rico, he is the co-author of *Puerto Rico Past and Present: An Encyclopedia* (Greenwood 1998).

GAIL A. CUETO is Associate Professor of Education at Central Connecticut State University. She is the co-author of *Puerto Rico Past and Present: An Encyclopedia* (Greenwood 1998).